The Practitioner's Guide to

INVESTMENT BANKING
MERGERS & ACQUISITIONS
CORPORATE FINANCE

Other books by the authors

The Recruiting Guide to Investment Banking

SCOOPBOOKS
THE PRACTITIONER'S GUIDE TO

INVESTMENT BANKING MERGERS & ACQUISITIONS CORPORATE FINANCE

Jerilyn J. Castillo and Peter J. McAniff

circinus Business Press

First edition 2007
Printed in the United States of America
Library of Congress Control Number: 2004097887

Castillo, Jerilyn J.

The practitioner's guide to investment banking : mergers & acquisitions, corporate finance / Jerilyn J. Castillo and Peter J. McAniff. -- 1st ed. -- Circinus Business Press, 2007.

p. ; cm.
(ScoopBooks)
Includes bibliographical references and index.
ISBN 13: 978-0-9761548-0-8
ISBN 10: 0-9761548-0-3

1. Consolidation and merger of corporations. 2. Corporations--Finance. 3. Corporate reorganizations. 4. Corporate divestiture. 5. Investment banking. 6. Securities. I. McAniff, Peter J. II. Title. III. Investment banking.

HG4028.M4 C37	2007 2004097887
338.8/3--dc22	0307

Cover and interior designed by Alejandro Paul

♾ The paper used in this publication meets the minimum requirements of the American National Standard for Information Sciences – Permanence of Paper for Printed Library Materials, ANSI Z39.48-1992

circinus Business Press
www.scoopbooks.com

To those who believe in the virtue of hard work
and just need someone to turn on the light.

Preface

One of the people who played a major role in the creation and execution of this book is a well respected corporate attorney. He served in the U.S. Navy on active duty prior to attending law school and served in the U.S. Naval Reserve for many years while practicing law. This gentleman has worked on some of the largest and most important transactions in his field of corporate law. And yet he views as one of his greatest achievements participation in the revision of a Navy manual. It turns out that the survival manual for pilots who were shot down was a hardcover book, some eight inches wide by fourteen inches long, and nearly two inches thick. Its sheer size limited its utility, except perhaps to stop bullets. This officer worked as part of a team which dramatically reduced the size of the manual for ease of carrying. The new covers were made of silk so they could be used to bind wounds if necessary. The all-encompassing contents of the previous version were discarded in favor of a limited set of critical information on topics such as first aid, drinking water, and food. The type was converted to large font because the readers of the manual might be in shock and could have difficulty reading small type. The team received a Navy Commendation Medal for its work.

Figuratively speaking, when we began in investment banking there were times when we felt as if we had been "gunned down." At such times it would have made a remarkable difference to have had some type of guide that focused on the most important day-to-day aspects of the job. Such a guide is what we have attempted to provide here.

This book is neither as important nor as worthy of attention as the survival manual described above. However, its goal is similar: to provide those who find themselves in a difficult situation with the information they need to achieve the best possible outcome under the circumstances.

The secret of success in life
is for a man to be ready
for his opportunity when it comes.

Benjamin Disraeli

Contents

Figures, Tables and Text Boxes

Commonly Used Financial Acronyms

Acronym	Meaning
ADR	American depositary receipt
AICPA	Association of Independent Certified Public Accountants
APB	Accounting Principles Board
AVP	Analysis at various prices
CA	Confidentiality Agreement
CAGR	Compound annual growth rate
CDS	Credit default swap
CF	Cash flow
CFADS	Cash flow available for debt service
CFO	Cash flow from operations
CP	Commercial paper
DCF	Discounted cash flow
DD&A	Depreciation, depletion and amortization
DEV	Discounted equity value
DPS	Dividend per share
DRD	Dividends-received deduction
EBIAT	Earnings before interest after tax
EBIT	Earnings before interest and taxes
EBITDA	Earnings before interest, taxes and DD&A
EBT	Earnings before tax
EPS	Earnings per share
EV	Enterprise value
EV	Equity value (also called market value of equity)
FASB	Financial Accounting Standards Board
FCF	Free cash flow
FMV	Fair market value
FTC	Federal Trade Commission
FV	Firm value (also called enterprise value)
g	Growth rate
GAAP	Generally Accepted Accounting Principles
HSR	Hart-Scott-Rodino Act
IPO	Initial public offering
IRC	Internal Revenue Code
IRR	Internal rate of return
IRS	Internal Revenue Service
JV	Joint venture
LBO	Leveraged buyout

Acronym	Meaning
LTD	Long-term debt
LTM	Last twelve months
M&A	Mergers and acquisitions
MAC	Material adverse change
MACRS	Modified accelerated cost recovery system
NAICS	North American Industry Classification System
MBO	Management buyout
MD&A	Management's discussion and analysis
MOE	Merger of equals
MTN	Medium term note
MV	Market value of equity
NASD	National Association of Securities Dealers
NASDAQ	National Association of Securities Dealers Automated Quotations
NDA	Non-disclosure agreement
NI	Net income
NOL	Net operating loss
NOPAT	Net operating profit after tax
NRSRO	Nationally Recognized Statistical Rating Organization
NYSE	New York Stock Exchange
OCF	Operating cash flow
PCAOB	Public Company Accounting Oversight Board
PIPE	Private investment in public equity
P&L	Profit and loss statement or income statement
PP&E	Property, plant and equipment
P/E	Price to earnings multiple
r	Discount rate used in discounting or interest rate used in compounding
R&D	Research and development
ROA	Return on assets
ROE	Return on equity
ROI	Return on investment
ROIC	Return on invested capital
SEC	Securities and Exchange Commission
SG&A	Selling, general and administrative expenses
SIC	Standard Industrial Classification
SOX	Sarbanes-Oxley Act of 2002
S&P	Standard and Poor's
STD	Short-term debt
WACC	Weighted average cost of capital
YTM	Yield to maturity

Foreword

When the authors first told me about this book project a few years ago, I thought it sounded like a noble but Herculean effort. They told me they wanted to share knowledge from the world of investment banking with a practitioner's guide that would serve as the reference manual of choice for any professional new to the worlds of M&A and corporate finance. The book would, for the first time, describe in layman's terms and in great detail most of the analyses and strategic thinking that take place within the walls of an investment bank. Figuratively speaking, they wanted to 'open the doors' so that anyone interested in becoming a banker or anyone working on an M&A deal --including bankers, corporate attorneys, and company executives-- could have access to tools of the trade that for many years had only been available to those in the inner circle.

As many practitioners will tell you, M&A and corporate finance are an art and a science. No two deals are ever the same because no two companies are identical. There is no black and white when it comes to executing strategic options for a company. Therefore, although I was supportive of the book's concept, I wondered whether, in one book, it was possible to capture the essence of what an investment banker does on a day-to-day basis in a way that was useful, succinct, engaging and, above all, explanatory.

I am delighted to report that Jerilyn and Peter have hit the proverbial ball out of the park. For anyone interested in learning how M&A transactions are executed and what types of analyses are performed, this book is the most comprehensive primer I have seen made publicly available. It should be in the personal library of any professional new to corporate finance or M&A.

I'll continue briefly with a baseball analogy. Having grown up in West Texas where football and baseball are as Texan as oil, I have come to appreciate the inner workings of the game. I sometimes think of baseball players when I think of my own career. Major league baseball players play 162 games per season. Prior to entering the major league, the typical player is in the minors for maybe three to five years and is likely to have started hitting a ball at the age of six or seven. That's a lot of baseball.

During the season, the player is either playing in a game, warming up for a game, reviewing his performance from a game, traveling to a game, or returning home from a game. Some days there are clutch plays, while on others there are only errors. Some games are mundane and, for the most successful teams, a few games a year are in the

World Series. The player does not have much time to attend birthday parties or family engagements during the season, nor does the player have much time to indulge in other hobbies since, if he is not playing, preparing, or traveling, he is usually resting. And no matter how tired the player is, or how poorly he is playing, or how much he misses his family, the player's life is shaped by getting up every day and just playing.

The life of an investment banker is not all that different.

And like baseball players, the finest investment bankers are those who just get up every day and play. In the world of banking, you must earn your stripes with experience. That means you have to be out there every day--doing, learning, winning, failing, and trying again. If you don't know how to do something, instead of becoming frustrated with yourself for not knowing how to do it, you simply must learn how to do it. Sometimes you will have a coach or mentor by your side teaching you how. Other times you will be alone and the road forward will be paved by you and you alone. This book, unlike anything that might have come before it, will go a long way in helping you during those times when you have no one to turn to.

Like baseball, you must learn to read your opponent's pitches to develop your own hitting strategy. You must know your teammates' hitting abilities and trust that they will deliver so that you know when to try a hit and run. And like baseball, every day in banking is a new game. Regardless of how much experience you have, you must walk up to the plate every day and swing as best you can. In other words, three home runs in one game do not provide you any runs in another game. For an investment bank like JPMorgan, if we do not hit the ball out of the park on one deal for a client, then a competitor may come in and take our place in that client's batting order. At the individual level, if you do not hit the ball out of the park day in and day out, then someone else who wants it more and does it better will take your place. Just as in baseball, younger, faster, more agile players are walking onto the banking field with each recruiting cycle and they are willing to do whatever it takes to succeed in the game. There is absolutely no coasting. You must perform every day.

This nonstop level of performance is not for everyone. How else to explain the fact that so many people leave the investment banking business every year? For some, the expectation to perform day in and day out wears them down. Or the competitive nature of the game is not suited to their personalities. This is a natural aspect of banking and those of us who have been around for a long time have come to expect it. This high turnover in players, however, is precisely the reason knowledge transfer and learning tools like this book are so important.

In baseball there are certain players or members of a team whom others fear. Either they fear these players when they come to the plate, or they fear them in the locker room after a bad game. I have been known to be feared by junior bankers. I have spent many nights thinking about why someone would be afraid of coming into my office to discuss business with me and I have come to the conclusion that it is not me they fear. Rather, since I am well known for asking rigorous questions, I believe what they fear is not knowing the answer to a question I might ask them. Ultimately, they are afraid of not being prepared in front of me or other colleagues.

My feelings on this are quite simple: There is nothing to fear if you are prepared. And if you are not prepared, you have no business providing advice to a client and, therefore, you should not be in a meeting with me or other colleagues. This relates to banking and most other things in your life. If you speak to the coaches of some of the finest athletes in the world (Michael Jordan, Lance Armstrong, Tiger Woods, Michael Phelps, etc.), one comment is universal. These athletes train and work harder than any other person the coach has worked with. They are always prepared. This commitment to the game and endurance is paramount in banking just as in athletics.

I have been practicing investment banking for more than twenty-five years and I currently co-head the global M&A business for JPMorgan. In spite of my many years of transaction experience, I still spend several hours preparing for each meeting with a client or board of directors. My lovely wife Patti will attest to the fact that I have not read a book for leisure in years. This is because I spend my time reading about my clients and preparing for meetings. I call it "studying." I study by reading through all of the materials provided by my team. I study the company with which I am meeting and the companies I will discuss during the meeting. I stress test my knowledge by running through mock questions in my mind and I prepare answers to these questions. If I am unclear about something then I will call a meeting with my team to discuss the issue so that I can be sure we are giving the client our collective best advice. I read, I think, I take copious notes, and I try every day to work as hard as the most junior person on the team. Not only do I owe it to our clients and the people who report to me, I owe it to myself. In other words, I am always on the field playing.

Over the years I have watched many changes take place in this business. New financial products have been created, technology and software have changed the way information is analyzed and disseminated, new industries have emerged, some investment banks have been bought and folded into larger commercial banks and new boutiques have been created in their place. What has not changed, however, is the nature of the business. At its core, investment banking is an apprenticeship business. Banking is a craft, and the skills of the trade are handed down. As such, it is critical that you find a mentor from whom you can learn the craft. I am not talking about a mentor who is formally assigned by your company's human resources department and with whom you may have occasional lunches. I am talking about one or two people with whom you can develop a long-lasting and trusted relationship in which you learn and he or she teaches. It is through this teacher/student interaction that the art of any professional skill is passed on.

For those who haven't yet found that mentor, this book can begin to teach you both the technical and strategic aspects of banking. Although no book can take the place of a seasoned practitioner, this book is comprehensive in its scope and can play the role of teacher or coach until you have found someone who can teach you the tools of the trade. Jerilyn and Peter have spent many years in investment banking and are highly competent practitioners. Also, over 50 senior bankers, attorneys and specialists at some thirty major investment banks, law firms, private equity firms, and corporations reviewed, edited and improved those sections of the book in which they have expertise. The collective knowledge and experience of these seasoned professionals has been distilled and included in this practitioner's guide. Therefore, treat this book as your access key to numerous experienced mentors. While mastering the concepts in this book is not equivalent to actual transaction experience, it is an opportunity to learn important technical and professional skills "at the side" of vice presidents and managing directors from firms all across Wall Street.

I often tell young bankers who have just joined my team that, as a junior professional, nothing is more important than attitude and aptitude. Attitude is innate and cannot be taught. Fortunately, aptitude can be developed. The opportunity to develop an aptitude for this business rests in your hands. Those who take the time to read and learn from books like this one will go far in this business. Those who walk around proudly upon receiving their first offer and expect to be taught as opposed to wanting to learn are quickly weeded out.

I have mentored many young bankers over the years. Many important people have played that role for me as well. To those men, including Joe Perella and David Coulter, I am forever grateful. For me, there is nothing more satisfying than working with a young person who is hungry and willing to learn, and watching knowledge and understanding grow in him or her. If this book helps turn on a light for you, then the authors will have succeeded in their original goal and for that I am very proud.

I leave with you a few words of advice. In all your professional endeavors, do what is right, do it right, and love what you do.

Jimmy Elliott
Head of Global M&A
JPMorgan, New York City, September 2006

Introduction

Every job is a self-portrait of the person who does it.
Autograph your work with excellence.

Unknown

How to Use This Book

The Practitioner's Guide to Investment Banking, Mergers & Acquisitions, Corporate Finance is organized into five distinct parts:

Part I: The Basics (Chapters 1-7) begins with an overview of the different functional areas within an investment bank as well as a refresher course on corporate finance and accounting fundamentals. It goes on to introduce concepts including: the nature of strategic planning and how strategic transactions are used in conjunction with internal efforts to grow a business; synergies and how they can increase value for the participants in a transaction; an introduction to types of strategic transactions as well as types of deal processes; a list of the various kinds of analyses investment bankers and financial advisors undertake on behalf of clients who are considering a strategic transaction; and an introduction on how to screen for M&A opportunities.

Part II: Valuation (Chapters 8-13) includes dedicated chapters for each of the major valuation methods used in mergers and acquisitions (M&A), including comparable company analysis, comparable transaction analysis, discounted cash flow (DCF) analysis, leveraged buyout (LBO) analysis and breakup analysis. The benefits and challenges of each of these valuation methods are described and step-by-step descriptions of how to perform each analysis are provided using numerical examples. The leveraged buyout chapter also includes a description of how financial sponsors are organized and compensated as well as a description of how to screen for leveraged buyout targets.

Part III: M&A Analysis (Chapters 14-18) begins with a multi-step description of how to perform accretion/dilution analysis and other merger consequences analyses. Part III goes on to describe a number of more intermediate topics in M&A, including but not limited to: the benefits and challenges of using stock versus cash as an acquisition currency; fixed versus floating exchange ratios in a stock-for-stock exchange; merger of equals (MOE) and considerations specific to this type of transaction; and an introduction to risk arbitrage.

Part IV: Transaction Structuring (Chapters 19-23) begins with a description of the key players most often involved in a transaction and describes the fiduciary obligations of the board of directors. The section also reviews and provides insights into important aspects of deal mechanics, including: the process and preparation for due diligence; the pros and cons of various methods of selling a company, including a comparison of tender offers and mergers; a detailed description of the legal agreement signed by parties to a transaction; and a description of the methods to restructure a company, including spin-offs, split-offs, letter stock, and sales of subsidiaries and divisions. A dedicated tax chapter describes the various tax issues that arise in transactions, including deferred taxes, inside and outside basis, capital gain tax, and tax-deferred transaction structures. The section concludes with a chapter on corporate defense which describes hostile takeovers and the most common structural defenses.

Part V: Credit and Financing (Chapters 24-25) begins with a complete chapter on credit analysis, including: descriptions of what credit ratings are; an introduction to the role played by rating agencies; assessing credit risk; and how banks make lending decisions. The section concludes with a comprehensive introduction to the sources of capital available to a company, including plain vanilla debt and equity as well as more complex forms of capital such as leveraged loans, trust preferred securities, and convertible debt.

The Glossary provides more than 50 pages of M&A and corporate finance terms and concepts, all of which are described in detail within this book.

The Appendix provides a listing of investment banks, resources and recommended reading.

Text boxes

Finally, throughout the book there are text boxes to highlight important concepts. These text boxes are set off from the surrounding text. Boxes with the (eyeglasses icon) represent reminders, frequently asked questions and/or common mistakes. Boxes with the (stopwatch icon) represent time-sensitive concepts or comments.

A Practical Note

You may have thought that what you learned in business school or in a college finance class was enough to prepare you for a job in banking, private equity, corporate development, or strategic planning. Now, upon reviewing the contents of this book, you are beginning to have second thoughts. And if that is the case for those who have studied finance, what about those who have no background in finance?

Have no fear. As a junior professional you will not be expected to know all of these concepts at the outset. Some of them you will learn in training, but most of them you will learn on the job. When you sit down to build a financial model or draft a presentation for a client, you will not be asked to do so without being able to consult old presentations, textbooks, or other reference materials. Moreover, you will have a large pool of people who will be able to help you, including people in your group, friends from training, and tax and accounting specialists. Do not be afraid, for example, to call the accounting, tax, modeling, or legal specialists, either within the firm or at an outside firm that your group uses (the company where you work is likely to have relationships with a number of outside firms specifically for these situations). Try your best to get to know these experts well. Not only are they valuable resources, but you are likely to learn a substantial amount from them. When working on a live transaction, these experts (not books) should serve as your definitive resource. Asking for help is not a sign of weakness; if anything, it is a sign of maturity and indicates a desire to do things properly.

Most importantly, if there is something you do not understand, pick up a reference book and figure it out. Taking responsibility for your own learning and development is the only way you will increase your knowledge. If you want to succeed in advisory work, you need to constantly challenge yourself and teach yourself new things. Others may help to teach you, but the desire to learn has to come from within.

This book describes most of the major quantitative and qualitative analyses performed by investment banking, corporate development and strategic planning professionals. For those who also work within the world of M&A and corporate finance, including corporate attorneys, strategic consultants, accountants, public relations professionals, regulatory experts, and business journalists, you may not need to perform all these analyses yourself. However, you may need to perform some of them, and in any case the concepts surely will come up during certain aspects of your job. It is worth highlighting that even seasoned and highly competent practitioners do not necessarily know all of the topics covered in this book. A senior banker, for example, might have forgotten how to perform some of the more technical analyses since he has not had to do it on his own for many years.

It is also important to note that this is not intended to be a finance or accounting textbook. There are a number of very fine books on corporate finance, accounting, and financial statement analysis, and the Appendix provides a list of some of those the authors find particularly useful. Instead, this book provides a practical framework for the types of analysis normally performed on an M&A or corporate finance assignment and also provides meaningful "big-picture" descriptions with respect to how to understand and think about these different concepts. Whereas most textbooks focus on the "theoretical," this book focuses on the "practical" with the intent of taking the mystery out of the analytics performed on the job.

Judgment is more important than numbers

It is important to remember that numbers alone do not tell the whole story. There are many financial professionals who undergo "analysis paralysis." That is to say, they analyze something so much that they lose sight of the big picture. Numbers are a part of the big picture. When analyzing a company, financial analysis is a tool and should be used in conjunction with other tools such as qualitative analysis (including an analysis of a company's management team), study of the industry in which a company competes, a company's competitive position within its sector, and the overall economy. Judgment, which comes with experience, is what you should use to make decisions. Everything else, including the numbers, is input to be considered in making decisions. Also, remember that numbers can be manipulated and only from experience will you learn how to determine whether numbers are representative of reality.

The authors would like this practitioner's guide to be as useful as possible. If you have suggestions, ideas or comments about the book, they would enjoy hearing from you via email at **jerilyn@scoopbooks.com** and **peter@scoopbooks.com**.

The Practitioner's Guide to

INVESTMENT BANKING
MERGERS & ACQUISITIONS
CORPORATE FINANCE

Part I

The Basics

Investment Banking

Chapter 1

I love the man that can smile in trouble,
that can gather strength from distress,
and grow brave by reflection.

Thomas Paine

An investment bank is an organization that helps clients raise and invest capital and advises clients on strategic matters, including mergers, acquisitions, financings, and restructuring transactions. Specifically, an investment bank serves as an intermediary between clients who need capital (e.g., corporations, governments, municipal agencies) and clients with capital to invest (e.g., institutional investors, funds, insurance companies, corporations, high net worth individuals). Within an investment bank there are various groups, one of which is the Investment Banking Group (often called IB or IBD for Investment Banking Division). Bankers in the Investment Banking Group advise clients who need capital or are contemplating a strategic action (such as a merger) and execute transactions on behalf of their clients.

Figure 1.1 (opposite page 5) illustrates the organization of an investment bank. Every year, each of these groups hires new analysts and associates. However, the largest pool of entry-level analysts and associates is for the Investment Banking Group (shown in the left-most column). A brief description of each group is provided in Figure 1.1. Not every investment bank operates in all of the lines of business listed under the column "Other Businesses."

Companies provide bankers in the Investment Banking Group access to confidential information which is not generally available to the public, in the same way companies provide confidential information to other advisors such as attorneys and accountants. Bankers outside of the Investment Banking Group (such as bankers in Sales and Trading or Equity Research) do not have access to a company's confidential information. These bankers do their work using public information. Whereas a banker in the Investment Banking Group generally interfaces day-to-day with corporations, a banker in Sales and Trading or Equity Research generally interfaces day-to-day with investors.

Figure 1.1 - Typical Functional Breakdown of an Investment Bank [1]

An Investment Bank serves as an intermediary between clients who need capital (e.g., corporations, governments, municipal agencies), and clients with capital to invest (e.g., institutional investors, funds, insurance companies, corporations, high net worth individuals).

Investment Banking Group[2]

Corporate Finance (Coverage Groups)
Advise clients in partnership with product groups

- Healthcare
- Energy & Power
- Chemicals
- Financial Sponsors
- Banks & Insurance
- Real Estate
- Middle Market
- Industrials
- Consumer
- Retail
- Technology
- Media
- Telecom
- Public Finance
- Governments

Corporate Finance (Product Groups)
Execute transactions for clients

- Mergers & Acquisitions
- Leveraged Finance
- Restructurings and Workouts
- Credit Advisory
- Project Finance

Capital Markets (Product Groups)
Execute capital raising transactions for clients

- Equities
- Equity Linked[3]
- High Yield
- Syndicated Finance
- Structured Finance
- Fixed Income
- Loans
- Private placements
- Municipals
- Derivatives

Trading and Principal Investments[4]

Sales & Trading
Sell and trade securities in the secondary market

- Equities
- Equity Linked[3]
- Treasuries
- Municipals
- Currencies
- Credit Derivatives
- Fixed Income
- Derivatives
- Commodities
- Asset Backed
- Mortgage Backed

Investment Research
Further subdivided by industry and company

- Equity[5]
- Credit
- Commodities
- Currencies
- Fixed Income
- High Yield
- Economic
- Global Markets

Proprietary Trading
Trade with bank's own capital

- Trading
- Risk Arbitrage

Private Equity / Merchant Banking
Acquire companies using bank and investor capital

Risk Management
Internal risk management

Other Businesses

Investment Management
Sell and manage mutual funds and other products

Private Banking
Banking for high net worth individuals and estates

Treasury and Securities Services
Clearing, trade, custody, and securities services

Commercial Banking[6]
Provide corporate credit and banking services

Consumer Banking
Accept deposits and provide consumer credit

Retail Brokerage
Sell mutual funds and products to retail investors

Mortgage Banking
Provide mortgages to retail and commercial borrowers

Insurance
Provide insurance services to clients

[1] Banks may organize and name their business units in different ways. For example, some Mergers and Acquisitions bankers work within client coverage groups.
[2] When working on a transaction on behalf of a client, bankers in the Investment Banking Group have access to confidential information.
[3] Equity Linked products include options, convertibles, and other specialized products the value of which is derived from underlying equity securities.
[4] Bankers in Trading and Principal Investments generally do not have access to confidential information; the dividing line between Investment Banking and Sales, Trading and Research is called the "Ethical Wall" or the "Chinese Wall". At some banks, all of the groups shown under the columns Investment Banking Group and Trading and Principal Investments are considered part of Investment Banking. They are separated here to show the functional delineation between the two groups.
[5] Some banks have separated equity research into its own independent group.
[6] Some "universal banks" fold their Corporate Banking function into the Investment Banking Group.

Advisory vs. Capital Raising

The Investment Banking Group can generally be divided into two major functions: (1) Corporate Finance and (2) Capital Markets.

The Corporate Finance Group is principally responsible for winning new business from clients and executing strategic transactions, such as a merger, on behalf of clients. Many bankers in the Corporate Finance Group are industry specialists (who call on clients in a particular industry such as energy, healthcare or consumer products). The largest specialty group within the Corporate Finance Group is usually the Mergers and Acquisitions Group. Other specialties within Corporate Finance include the Financial Sponsors Group (whose clients are private equity and leveraged buyout firms), the Middle Market Group (whose clients are mid-sized companies, many of which are privately owned), and the Restructuring Group (which focuses on bankruptcy-related restructurings or workouts).

While bankers in the Corporate Finance Group advise clients on strategic transactions and/or cover clients in a specific industry, bankers in the Capital Markets Group raise capital for clients, usually across all industries. Equity and Fixed Income Capital Markets raise capital directly from investors by issuing securities such as stocks and bonds on behalf of clients. The Syndicated Finance Group provides large loans and lines of credit to clients and then sells portions of the loan to banks and other investors. Other specialties within the Capital Markets Group include Equity Linked Capital Markets, which works with clients to issue specialty financial products the value of which is derived from underlying equity securities (e.g., convertible debt and preferred stock), Structured Finance, which works with clients on highly structured transactions (e.g., leveraged leases, sale leasebacks), and High Yield Capital Markets, which works with clients to issue high yield debt and preferred stock.

Bankers from the Corporate Finance Group and the Capital Markets Group often work together on a transaction on behalf of a client. For example, if a steel company wanted to acquire a competitor for cash, bankers from the M&A group might advise the company on valuation, deal structure, and deal negotiations, bankers from the Capital Markets Group and the Syndicated Finance Group might help the company raise capital to fund the acquisition, bankers from the Credit Advisory Group might help address potential rating agency and/or debt holder concerns, and bankers from the Industrials Corporate Finance Group might oversee the transaction and ensure that all of the product groups are sharing information and working together to best serve the client.

Product bankers vs. coverage bankers

Bankers who specialize in either advisory work or capital markets work are often referred to as **product bankers**. Product bankers are distinct from **coverage bankers** who, instead of focusing on a particular product such as M&A, focus on building relationships with clients. Product bankers execute transactions for clients whereas coverage bankers originate new business and maintain client relationships. Coverage bankers are also called "relationship bankers."

It is important to note that this is a general description of how an investment bank might be organized. Some banks may be organized differently from what is described here. Many banks, in fact, reorganize every few years if they believe a different organizational structure will allow them to serve their clients better. Instead of thinking of the various groups of an investment bank statically, think of them as a dynamic functional group of specialists. If a client has a problem, teams of specialists are formed to address the client's problem and then, when the client's issue has been solved, that specific team disbands and the specialists join other client teams, to solve other clients' needs.

Strategic Planning vs. Financial Management

In order to better understand the distinction between a corporate finance and a capital markets banker, it may make sense to look at it from the perspective of a financial manager within a company. Excluding the accounting function, there are two major financial responsibilities within a company: (1) strategic and financial planning, which is generally forward looking, and (2) financial and liability management, which tends to focus on the financing needs of a business, including the management of financial risk. In smaller companies, these two roles might be undertaken by the same group of people (and in the smallest of companies these roles might be the responsibility of only one or two people). However, in larger companies these two roles tend to be handled by two separate groups.

1. The **Strategic Planning Group** or **Corporate Development Group** would likely handle the strategic and/or financial planning for the company, including preparing forward-looking financial statements and projections, identifying and analyzing potential strategic transactions, and executing mergers, acquisitions and divestitures on behalf of the company. This group is often headed by a Director of Strategic Planning, who usually reports to the company's Chief Financial Officer. In general, the Strategic Planning Group works on transactions that affect the asset side of the balance sheet. Corporate De-

velopment professionals usually interface with bankers from the Corporate Finance and M&A Groups.

2. The **Treasury Group** is likely to handle functions related to financial management, financings, liability management and risk management. Whereas the Strategic Planning Group tends to work on issues related to the asset side of the balance sheet, the Treasury Group tends to work on issues related to the liability and shareholders' equity side of the balance sheet in addition to cash and marketable securities. For example, the Treasury Group generally takes the lead when a company issues new bonds or refinances an existing loan that is coming due. The Treasury Group also handles all of the issues related to short-term liquidity and financing. Because of its role in raising and managing financing for a company, the Treasury Group also tends to handle most of the responsibilities related to managing the company's credit rating. The Treasury Group is generally headed by the Treasurer, who typically reports directly to the company's Chief Financial Officer. Sometimes, the accounting and financial reporting responsibilities (headed by the company's Controller) are rolled into the Treasury Group. Many companies, large and small, have a Controller who doubles as a Treasurer. In smaller companies, the Chief Financial Officer also functions as a Treasurer. Professionals in the Treasury Group usually interface with bankers from the Capital Markets Group or Syndicated Finance Group.

Confidential Information

When bankers, lawyers, consultants, accountants, and others ("advisors") are working for a company on a transaction, their work products are generally privileged (meaning confidential) and seldom made publicly available. One of an investment bank's few work products that is disclosed is a fairness opinion provided to public companies. Since these advisors have access to confidential or "inside" information, there are many SEC governed restrictions on their actions (from insider trading, for example) that are designed to protect shareholders. All inside participants in an M&A or capital raising process for a public company are subject to these SEC rules and regulations. These advisors also may be subject to additional rules and regulations set forth by their companies, industry oversight boards or other organizations.

Those without access to inside information include investors, traders, arbitrageurs, hedge fund managers, research analysts, the general public, and others who could potentially profit from a transaction. It is a breach of confidentiality if someone with access to inside information shares it with someone without access to inside information (including spouses, relatives and friends). It is illegal if someone with access to inside information makes, participates in, or facilitates investment decisions in public companies based on that confidential information.

What is a CA or an NDA?

Advisors are required to sign a Confidentiality Agreement prior to gaining access to confidential information. A **Confidentiality Agreement** ("CA" for short) is synonymous with a **Non-Disclosure Agreement** ("NDA" for short). A CA or NDA is a legal agreement which prevents the recipient of confidential information from sharing that confidential information with anyone except under highly defined circumstances (for example, with members of the deal team). If confidential information is shared with an unauthorized person, the party that shared the information is considered to be in breach of the Confidentiality Agreement and could be legally liable to the other party for the consequences of the breach.

A few third-party participants, such as credit rating agencies and federal or state regulatory commissions, are sometimes provided confidential information before it is made publicly available. These participants are in a position of public trust and are not allowed to profit from that inside information. Outsiders who are provided confidential information are subject to the same insider trading restrictions that apply to other insiders.

The **ethical wall** or **Chinese wall** is an imaginary line drawn within an organization between those with access and those without access to confidential information. Within an investment bank, for example, there is an ethical wall between bankers in the Investment Banking Group and other bankers (Sales and Trading, Equity Research, Private Banking). Bankers in the Investment Banking Group are provided confidential information whereas others bankers utilize public information to conduct their business. Because of the ethical wall, a banker in the M&A Group, for example, is not allowed to have a company-specific conversation with an equity research analyst.

A Career in Banking

From lowest to highest level of seniority, the titles within an investment bank include analyst, associate, vice president and managing director. Some banks subdivide the vice president and managing director levels into two additional levels. College graduates are recruited for analyst positions. MBAs and JDs are recruited for associate positions. Analyst positions generally last two years, although if after the second year an analyst seems to be on track for direct promotion to associate, the analyst may be asked to stay for a third year. Typically, associates are promoted to vice president after four or five years as an associate. From first-year associate to managing director can take anywhere from eight years for those on a particularly fast track up to fifteen years.

Table 1.2 – Levels within Investment Banking

Level	Sublevel	Hiring Pool	Term
Analyst	-	• College graduates	2 to 3 years
Associate	Some banks have senior associate designations	• Third-year analysts • MBAs • JDs • Industry hires	4 to 5 years
Vice President	Some banks have senior vice president designations	• Senior associates • Senior level industry hires	4 to 10 years
Managing Director	Some banks first promote to director, then subsequently to managing director	• Vice presidents • Senior level industry hires • Senior level law hires	Indefinite

Traditionally, transactions are staffed with four bankers, one of each level. Larger or more complex deals often require more than four bankers and smaller deals might function with only two or three bankers. In general, for each project, an analyst reports to an associate, vice president and managing director; an associate reports to a vice president and managing director and manages one analyst. Below are brief descriptions of the general responsibilities of analysts, associates, vice presidents and managing directors.

Analysts: On a typical project, the analyst runs the analytical models, gathers and analyzes information, writes sections of presentations, and coordinates activities on a transaction. Analysts usually begin interacting regularly with clients in their second or third year. Most analysts only have two or three projects at a time due to the in-depth nature of their involvement with each project. Internally, analysts participate in recruiting and help organize training sessions.

Associates: The associate manages the day-to-day aspects of the project, is primarily responsible for drafting presentations and writing memos, is ultimately responsible for the analyst's financial models, runs the more complex financial models and interfaces regularly with the client. On smaller transactions, the associate runs the deal and is usually the primary contact with the client. An associate might have two to five projects at a time. Internally, associates are expected to train and mentor analysts and actively participate in recruiting.

Vice Presidents: The vice president is ultimately responsible for running the deal. He or she reviews all of the analyst's and associate's work, communicates on major issues with the client, makes critical decisions, presents conclusions to the client, mobilizes any other groups within the bank and is actively involved in negotiations on behalf of the client. Vice presidents are also expected to cultivate relationships and win business. A vice president might have five to seven projects at a time. Internally, vice presidents participate actively in recruiting, development, training and mentoring.

Managing Directors: Managing directors are generally responsible for winning business, managing relationships, making critical decisions, presenting materials to the client, negotiating the transaction agreement, and ensuring that the firm's resources are used appropriately for each deal. Managing directors might have up to ten transactions at any given time. A managing director who is also a group head could have more than ten projects at any given time. Like vice presidents, managing directors are expected to lead recruiting and development efforts. In addition, managing directors drive internal strategy, allocate resources, determine compensation levels, and make decisions whenever the firm's capital is at risk.

Corporate Finance Basics

Chapter 2

He who does not risk
will never drink champagne.

Russian proverb

Corporate finance basics are implicated regularly in investment banking. Time value of money principles and the concept of risk vs. reward are used in almost every valuation method and, therefore, bankers use these principles in daily practice. For example, traders use these principles to value stocks and bonds and M&A specialists use them to value assets and companies when advising their clients interested in either buying or selling a company. As a professional new to finance, a clear understanding of all of the core principles described in this chapter will go a long way in helping you to perform your job well. Corporate finance basics are in essence the first principles of your M&A and corporate finance tool chest upon which many more complex tools will be layered.

The goal of this chapter is to provide a layman's understanding of corporate finance principles. Numerous finance textbooks are available to describe the theories behind these concepts; therefore, this chapter will not delve too deeply into the theoretical details. Instead it will focus on describing the concepts that are used on a day-to-day basis in investment banking. For those readers who have some background in finance, hopefully this chapter will clear up any confusion you might have. If you are new to finance, you may want to supplement this chapter with some of the recommended readings in the Appendix and/or a college level class.

As a practical note, corporate finance concepts are not particularly intuitive and many first-timers struggle with them initially. For others, dexterity with these concepts may take even more practice and study. However, when the light does go on, you will realize that basic corporate finance concepts are elegant in their simplicity.

Time Value of Money

The concepts of **time value of money** and **risk vs. reward** are the most fundamental concepts in corporate finance. Simply said:

1. ***Time value of money:*** The value of $1 today is worth more than the value of $1 tomorrow because that $1 today can be invested to yield more than $1 tomorrow.

2. ***Risk vs. reward:*** An investor will lend money in exchange for a return in the future. That return must compensate the investor for the risks involved with the investment.

Consider an overly simplified investment scenario: If you have $100 today and you invest it in a savings account paying interest of 3 percent annually, one year from now you will have earned $3 interest and have a total of $103. In this example, the value of lending the bank $100 today is the receipt of $103 next year. Said another way, the value (to you) of receiving $103 from the bank in one year is $100 today. *This is the concept of time value of money.*

This simple math can be computed as follows (formulas and numerical examples will be reviewed later in the chapter):

$100 at 3% next year	=	$100 × 1.03	= $103
$103, one year ago at 3%	=	$103 / 1.03	= $100

The return of 3 percent (or $3) is coming from a bank and you are fairly certain that you will get the total of $103 one year from now because the bank is a reputable institution and unlikely to default on its debt (not to mention the fact that deposits with a U.S. chartered bank are insured by the FDIC up to $100,000). Putting money in the bank is a low risk investment and the low return is commensurate with that low level of risk. That is, the 3 percent that the bank pays you in order to induce you to "lend" them $100 is a sufficient return since you are fairly certain you will receive your $100 plus interest when you need it. Given the low risk, you receive a commensurately low return of 3 percent. *This is the concept of risk vs. reward.*

Now let's look at it from the bank's perspective. The bank has to pay you interest in order to have the use of your money. 3 percent is its cost for borrowing money from you. If the bank, however, can take that $100 and earn a return on it (which is what the bank does when it loans money out), say 8 percent, the bank will earn $8 and only have to pay you $3 interest, thereby earning $5 of net interest margin ($8-$3 = $5) in the process. *This is another example of risk vs. reward.*

This additional $5 that the bank can earn by lending out the money does not come without its own risk. The bank assumes the risk that the borrower of that $100 will repay it. Whereas you invested your money in a bank, the bank is investing the money (via a loan) with an individual who wants to use it to make a purchase, such as a car or a house, or with a company that wants to use it to build a plant or buy another company.

The risk that these borrowers do not repay the bank is higher than the risk that the bank does not repay you. The bank assumes a higher level of risk than you and, therefore, should earn a higher return. *This is another example of risk vs. reward.*

Why is Time Value of Money Important?

With most investments, you pay something up front in exchange for something in the future. That something in the future might be a stream of periodic interest payments and then a lump sum payment in the future (as is the case with a bond), or it might be a stream of irregular cash flows and an unknown value at the end of the investment period (as is the case when you buy shares in a company, an asset, or even a company). In every investment situation you receive something in the future in exchange for an investment (or a cash payment) made today. Therefore, it is important to understand how to think about valuing those streams of future cash flows in order to determine what the investment is worth today.

In addition to potentially being an investor, there will be many situations in which you will borrow capital – perhaps to buy a new car or home. If you borrow money, you need to understand the manner in which you are being charged interest to fully understand your borrowing costs. Time value of money concepts play into how the bank or your investor will charge you interest when you borrow capital.

Another reason time value of money is important is that it allows "apples-to-apples" comparisons of different types of investments. Different investments have different time horizons, and each will have a different risk profile; however, by calculating a present value, the two different investments can be compared since they are both quoted on a risk-adjusted basis and as of the same point in time.

The importance of cash flow and risk

Cash flow (the amount of cash received over time) and the risk of receiving that cash flow (numerically represented as the **discount rate**) are the two most important components of investment decisions. Risk is the likelihood or probability that you will receive the cash flow in the future. Other factors such as the length of the investment and the frequency of payments also play an important role, but it is critical to gain an appreciation for the importance of cash flow and risk up front.

What is an Investment?

An **investment** is the purchase of any **asset** (usually a physical investment such as a building or a car) or **security** (a paper investment representing an interest or claim to something in the future) for cash in exchange for a claim or right to the asset or a stream of cash payments from the security in the future.

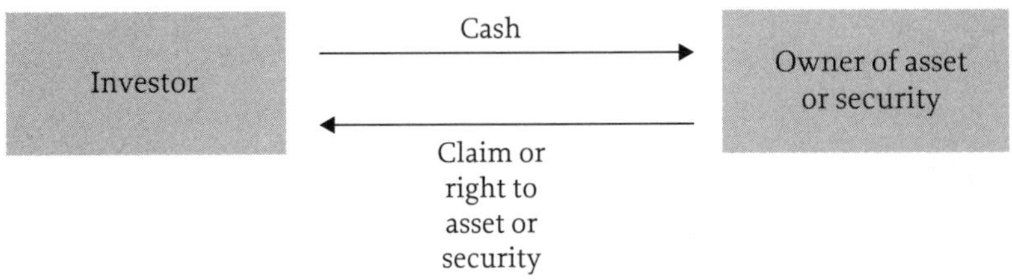

Assets can be tangible, such as a building or a manufacturing plant, or intangible, such as intellectual property rights or a patent. A security can represent the debt of a company. Debt pays a fixed stream of interest payments and the repayment of principal, or the original amount of the investment, at the end of the term. A security can also be a percentage of equity in a company. For example, one share of stock in a company with one hundred shares represents a one percent ownership interest in the company. Unlike debt, equity does not provide for interest payments or even the return of the initial investment; it may, however, provide for dividend payments and appreciation in the value of the equity. A security can also be a derivative, such as an interest rate lock or a foreign exchange forward. Each of these different securities will be discussed in more detail in later chapters.

Simply said, an investment is an asset or security you buy in exchange for rights to either the physical asset itself, a stream of cash flows generated from the asset or security, or sometimes both. For example, consider the following assets and securities and notice what you "get" in exchange for each investment.

Asset or Security	**Value to the investor**
Car	Use of the car and outright ownership (unless the car is leased)
A home you will rent out	Rental income and ownership of the home
Share in a vacation home	Right to use the home during the year
Stock in a company	Percentage ownership interest, dividends, and the right to sell the stock
Loan to a friend	Interest and principal repayment at some point in the future
Manufacturing plant	Cash flow generated from running the plant and outright ownership of the plant

Separate value from financing

How you decide to "pay" for the asset or security is not a factor in the value of the investment. This is an important concept that will resurface in later chapters. How you pay for an asset or security (how you "finance" the purchase) is independent of the intrinsic value of the asset or security. The value of the asset or security is dependent on what you get from the investment and the likelihood (the risk) that you will or will not receive those benefits. Consider a purchase at your favorite shoe store. The fact that you are considering paying cash versus paying with a credit card for a pair of shoes does not change the total cost, or "value," of those shoes. How you pay will affect the cost of your payment (if you pay with a credit card you may have to pay interest), but it will not affect the value of the shoes.

Present Value and Future Value – Conceptually

Prior to working with the numerical examples and formulas, it is worth reviewing basic concepts. First let's discuss the concepts present value and future value, which are closely interrelated.

Consider an investment with a timeline of five years. The timeline is referred to as the **investment period,** the **investment horizon,** or the **duration of the investment.**

	Today	Tomorrow				
Year	0	1	2	3	4	5

Year 0 is representative of *today.* It marks the beginning of the investment period under consideration. Generally, if making an investment, you pay *some money today* in exchange for *something of value tomorrow.*

Years 1 to 5 are representative of *tomorrow.* They represent the period of time *within* the investment period. With some investments, you will receive *periodic payments in the future* in exchange for your investment today.

Year 5 (in the timeline figure above) is representative of *the end* of the investment period. With some investments, you will receive a *lump sum payment at the end of the investment period* in exchange for your investment today.

Some investments are perpetual, meaning they go on indefinitely, or at least until you decide to sell the investment.

Now, let's name these concepts.

	Today	Tomorrow				
Year	**0**	**1**	**2**	**3**	**4**	**5**
	Present value	Future value 1	Future value 2	Future value 3	Future value 4	Future value 5

The value at Time 0 is the **present value**. This is the value today of an investment. It represents the amount of money an investor would pay at the beginning of an investment period in exchange for a right or claim to the asset or security in the future.

Anything received *after* Time 0, including periodic payments received during the investment period or a lump sum payment at the end of the investment period is a **future value,** which is the amount of cash to be received in the future. Sometimes tomorrow is a fixed date, sometimes tomorrow is indefinite.

So, the present value is the value today and the future value is the value tomorrow. Sounds simple enough. Let's move on and add some numbers to this example.

Assume that you invest $100 in a money market account and your $100 earns 5 percent per year. In the first year, you will earn $5 on your $100 [$100 × (1 + 0.05) = $105]. In the second year, you will earn $5.25 on your $105 (your initial $100 became $105 with the addition of $5 interest in the first year). In the third year, you will earn $5.51 on your $110.25 ... and so on. This concept of earning interest on interest is called **compounding** or **compounded interest** (as opposed to **simple interest** in which you do not earn interest on interest so that you would earn just $5 each year). $100 is the present value, and the future value grows each year with the addition of the interest income.

	Today	Tomorrow				
Year	0	1	2	3	4	5
	Present value	Future value 1	Future value 2	Future value 3	Future value 4	Future value 5
You pay	$100					
Value in future		= $100×1.05	= $105.00×1.05	= $110.25×1.05	= $115.76×1.05	= $121.55×1.05
		$105.00	$110.25	$115.76	$121.55	$127.63
Earned each year		$5.00	$5.25	$5.51	$5.79	$6.08
Total value earned		$5.00	$10.25	$15.76	$21.55	$27.63

The future value is nothing more than the value of your initial investment ($100 in our example) *plus* the value of what you have "earned" on your initial investment. After one year you will have earned $5. Assuming you do not withdraw your money, after three years you will have earned $15.76, and after five years you will have earned $27.63. While depositing money into a bank account is a simple example of how compounding works, it highlights the relationship between present value and future value. The future value at time x represents the amount of principal (your $100) plus the amount earned up to time x. For example, in year three, the future value of $100 earning 5 percent per year is $115.76 and in year five the future value of $100 earning 5 percent per year is $127.63.

This is the first critically important concept in the time value of money: The value of $1 today is worth more than the value of $1 tomorrow because that $1 today can be invested to yield more than $1 tomorrow.

What happens if, instead of knowing what you will deposit or contribute to an investment up front (as is the case with our savings account example), you know what you expect to receive in the future (that is, you know the future value)? How do you determine what you should pay for it today? In other words, you know the future value and you are trying to determine the present value, or what you should pay for the investment *today* (as opposed to the savings account example in which you know the present value and you want to calculate the future value).

To illustrate this point, let's look at an example. You pay $500 today for a lemonade stand (at Time 0) and in exchange the lemonade stand will generate $100 of cash each year for five years. $500 represents the present value and it is denoted as a negative number because it is a cash *outflow*. Each of the periodic payments of $100 represents a future value and is a positive number because it represents a cash *inflow*. The first cash flow of $100 is the future value in year 1. The second cash flow of $100 is the future value in year 2, and so on.

	Today	Tomorrow				
Year	**0**	**1**	**2**	**3**	**4**	**5**
	Present value	Cash flow 1	Cash flow 2	Cash flow 3	Cash flow 4	Cash flow 5
You pay	($500)					
You get		$100	$100	$100	$100	$100

Thus, for your initial investment of $500 at Time 0 you will be repaid $100 each year for five years for a total nominal stream of payments of $500. You are probably thinking *"That doesn't sound like a good business deal because I am not earning anything on my $500."* Exactly! In the real world, an investor would not make this investment because he is giving someone $500 *today* in exchange for $500 nominally in the *future* – without earning any interest on the money, or, as investors say, "without earning a return on the money."

And it gets worse because not only are you not receiving a return on this $500, but you could have taken that $500 and invested it in an alternative investment and earned a rate of return on it. You have foregone interest by putting your capital into this investment rather than somewhere else. Said another way, there is an **opportunity cost** to your capital, which is the cost of foregoing a different investment. It would be even worst if, in order to invest the $500 to buy the lemonade stand, you borrowed that $500 from your brother and had to pay him interest on the $500! You would have invested in a venture that did not offer a return but, in order to make the investment, you had to borrow money and pay interest on it. This would be a guaranteed money loser.

Knowing all of this, how much would you be willing to pay for this lemonade stand today *or*, what would you need to earn in terms of future cash flow for this same investment of $500? You can think of this investment in two ways.

1. If you are to pay $500 today for the lemonade stand, what cash flow would you need to earn each year in the future in order for the investment to be worth it to you?

or

2. What would you be willing to pay for the lemonade stand today in exchange for five periodic cash payments of $100 each year?

For both scenario 1 and scenario 2, you need to determine the rate of return you require for this investment. Would you accept a 2 percent rate of return, or would you require something greater, like 5 or 10 percent? It would depend on the likelihood, or the *risk*, that you would get your money back plus interest.

Risk vs. Reward

Risk is a relative concept. For example, how do you determine the rate of return you are willing to accept on an investment in a savings account? Is that a number you choose yourself? Perhaps, but it is more likely that you accept a 3 percent return because other banks offering similar savings accounts are also paying about 3 percent. And how about the lemonade stand? Is the likelihood of earning $100 at a lemonade stand in California in the summer equal to the likelihood of earning $100 at a lemonade stand in Boston in the winter? Why can a bank get away with paying only 3 percent when other investments might pay 5 percent or even up to 30 percent? Because you know with relative certainty that if you put your money in a savings account with an FDIC insured bank, you will get your money plus interest whenever you want to take it out. The risk that you will not receive your principal plus interest is very low. Banks do not need to offer you a higher interest rate to entice you into this type of investment because of its low risk.

And what of higher risk investments? Assume you were investing $10,000 with a friend who is starting a new yoga mat business and needs money to develop the prototype. Are you *just as likely* to get your $10,000 back from your friend as compared to your trusty bank? Probably not. Therefore you will probably require your friend to pay you *more than* 3 percent interest (since you have the opportunity to take your hard-earned $10,000 and put it in the bank for 3 percent with very little risk). There is an opportunity cost of your capital and your friend needs to compensate you in return for the higher risk you undertake by being an investor in her venture.

Here we have the second critically important concept of time value of money: An investor will lend money in exchange for a return in the future. That return must compensate the investor for the risks involved with the investment.

From a numbers perspective, what does this mean? If you were to invest $10,000 in a bank savings account that pays 3 percent per year (compounded annually), then you would have $11,593 after five years, having earned $1,593 in interest during those five years.

	Today	Tomorrow				
Year	0	1	2	3	4	5
	Present value	Future value 1	Future value 2	Future value 3	Future value 4	Future value 5
You pay	($10,000)					
Value in future		= $10,000 × 1.03	= $10,300 × 1.03	= $10,609 × 1.03	= $10,927 × 1.03	= $11,255 × 1.03
		= $10,300	$10,609	$10,927	$11,255	$11,593
Earned each year		$300	$309	$318	$328	$338
Total value earned from bank		$300	$609	$927	$1,255	$1,593

Let's now consider investing this same $10,000 with your friend instead of putting it in the bank. Let's assume she agrees to pay you 15 percent annual interest on your money and, like a savings account the interest would compound (meaning that you would reinvest the interest in the investment at the same interest rate). What would you earn from your friend?

	Today	Tomorrow				
Year	0	1	2	3	4	5
	Present value	Future value 1	Future value 2	Future value 3	Future value 4	Future value 5
You pay	($10,000)					
Value in future		= $10,000 × 1.15	= $11,500 × 1.15	= $13,225 × 1.15	= $15,209 × 1.15	= $17,490 × 1.15
		$11,500	$13,225	$15,209	$17,490	$20,114
Earned each year		$1,500	$1,725	$1,984	$2,281	$2,624
Total value earned from friend		$1,500	$3,225	$5,209	$7,490	$10,114

With the same $10,000 investment, you would earn a return of $10,114 after five years from your friend as compared to $1,593 from your trusty bank. So why wouldn't you choose to take the offer from your friend? Because you are not certain that you will get the money back from her. She has offered you a higher interest rate to compensate you for the additional risk that she might not be able to pay you back. You might determine that a 15 percent return is sufficient to compensate you for the risk. You might, however, determine that it is not enough and demand an even higher rate of return. You do not know with certainty whether she will be able to repay you the principal plus interest. All you know with certainty is that this yoga mat investment is riskier than an investment with the bank and you will need to determine what additional return you would require in order to loan money to your friend.

Discount Rate and Interest Rate

The **discount rate** (also referred to as the opportunity cost of capital) represents the annual return an investor requires in order to make a particular investment. The discount rate is what is used to "discount" future cash flows to the present value. The riskier an investment or project, the higher the required return and therefore the higher the discount rate. This means that if an investment is very risky, the investor would require a high rate of return to induce her to make the investment (even though there is a high risk that she will lose all of her investment). Conversely, the lower the risk of an investment or project, the lower the discount rate or required rate of return. Projects or investments with the same level of risk should have the same discount rate.

> **Discounting vs. compounding**
>
> Before we go any further, let's clarify the concepts of **discounting** and **compounding** cash flows, which people often confuse. Discounting is the act of bringing a future value backward to a present value number. Compounding is the act of bringing a present value forward to a future value number. When we get into the numerical formulas and examples you will see that the formula for discounting is the inverse of the formula for compounding.

Present Value and Future Value – Numerical Examples

Now let's consider the numerical formulas for present value and future value. For each:

PV or CF_0 = initial amount (cash flow at Time_0 or "today")

FV or CF_n = future amount (cash flow in the future at Time_n or "tomorrow")

r = discount rate for discounting and interest rate for compounding

g = annual growth rate

n = number of periods over which the amount is being discounted or compounded

m = number of payments per period

Notice how the present value formula is the inverse of the future value formula, and vice versa.

$$PV = \frac{CF_n}{(1 + {}^{r}/_{m})^{n\,m}} \qquad FV = CF_0 \times [(1 + {}^{r}/_{m})^{n\,m}]$$

Present value = future cash flow (CF_n) **discounted** to a present value (value *today*)
Future value = present cash flow (CF_0) **compounded** to a future value (value *tomorrow)*

Discount rate vs. interest rate

Discount rate is different from interest rate. An interest rate is the stated amount you will *earn* on an investment (such as when you put your money in a bank account or when you buy a bond with a stated interest rate or coupon rate). The discount rate, on the other hand, is a measure of the opportunity cost of capital, meaning the return you would earn on similarly risky investments (and therefore the return you require for the investment). The interest rate is *not necessarily* indicative of the risk of the cash flows (meaning the interest rate is not necessarily equal to the discount rate). If the investment is priced properly, then it will pay a level of interest commensurate with its risk. However, the market is not always efficient in the short term and therefore you cannot be sure that the security will be priced perfectly. Therefore be careful in assuming that the interest rate and the discount rate are identical because in some circumstances they are different.

Let's apply the present value formula to the periodic cash flows of $100 per year from our previous example to calculate the present value of each $100 future cash flow.

Let CF_n = $100, r = 0.05, n = the year and m = 1 (since only one payment is made each year).

	Today	Tomorrow				
Year	0	1	2	3	4	5
	Present value	Future value 1	Future value 2	Future value 3	Future value 4	Future value 5
PV_1	$= \$100 / (1.05)^1$	← \$100				
PV_2	$= \$100 / (1.05)^2$	←	\$100			
PV_3	$= \$100 / (1.05)^3$	←		\$100		
PV_4	$= \$100 / (1.05)^4$	←			\$100	
PV_5	$= \$100 / (1.05)^5$	←				\$100

Year	0	1	2	3	4	5
	Present value	Future value 1	Future value 2	Future value 3	Future value 4	Future value 5
PV_1	\$95.24	← \$100				
PV_2	\$90.70	←	\$100			
PV_3	\$86.38	←		\$100		
PV_4	\$82.27	←			\$100	
PV_5	\$78.35	←				\$100

As mentioned at the beginning of the chapter, one of the benefits of the time value of money is that you can make apples-to-apples comparisons. Now that all five of the future cash flows have been discounted and converted to present values, these numbers can be added together to determine the total present value of the five future cash flows.

> **Adding up values**
>
> You can only add values that are discounted to the same time period. For example, you can add present values together but you cannot add a present value to a future value. Also you can add the future values of different items if they represent the future value at the same time period in the future. However, you cannot add the future value in year three of one item to the future value in year six of another item since that would be an apples-to-oranges comparison.

If you add the present values for the five payments of \$100 per year for five years, the total is \$432.95.

	Today
Year	**0**
	Present value
PV_1	\$95.24
$+ PV_2$	\$90.70
$+ PV_3$	\$86.38
$+ PV_4$	\$82.27
$+ PV_5$	\$78.35
Total	\$432.95

If the discount rate is 5 percent, you should be willing to pay \$432.95 today in exchange for payments of \$100 per year for five years. Notice how \$432.95 is less than the nominal sum of the five \$100 cash flows (\$500). In other words \$500 spread out over five years is not equal to \$500 today or, the value of a dollar today is greater than the value tomorrow.

Let's now calculate the future value of \$100 in each year for five years. We will assume a 7 percent interest rate.

Let $CF_0 = \$100$, $r = 0.07$, $n =$ the year and $m = 1$ (since only one payment is made each year).

	Today	Tomorrow				
Year	**0**	**1**	**2**	**3**	**4**	**5**
	Present value	Future value 1	Future value 2	Future value 3	Future value 4	Future value 5
	= \$100 →	$= \$100 \times (1.07)^1$				
	= \$100 →	→	$= \$100 \times (1.07)^2$			
	= \$100 →	→	→	$= \$100 \times (1.07)^3$		
	= \$100 →	→	→	→	$= \$100 \times (1.07)^4$	
	= \$100 →	→	→	→	→	$= \$100 \times (1.07)^5$

Year	**0**	**1**	**2**	**3**	**4**	**5**
	Present value	Future value 1	Future value 2	Future value 3	Future value 4	Future value 5
	\$100 →	\$107.00				
	\$100 →	→	\$114.49			
	\$100 →	→	→	\$122.50		
	\$100 →	→	→	→	\$131.08	
	\$100 →	→	→	→	→	\$140.26

Since future values were calculated for different years, the future values cannot be added together.

Let's review additional examples using the present value and future value formulas.

Present Value Example 1: You will receive royalties of $500 per year for five years for music you have written. How much is this royalty worth today if the discount rate for the royalties is 8 percent?

Table 2.1 – Present Value Example 1

Year	0	1	2	3	4	5
Cash flows (CF_n)		$500	$500	$500	$500	$500
Discount rate (r)		8.0%	8.0%	8.0%	8.0%	8.0%
Present value formula		$= \frac{\$500}{(1.08)^1}$	$= \frac{\$500}{(1.08)^2}$	$= \frac{\$500}{(1.08)^3}$	$= \frac{\$500}{(1.08)^4}$	$= \frac{\$500}{(1.08)^5}$
Present value		$462.96	$428.67	$396.92	$367.51	$340.29
Total present values	$1,996.36					

Present Value Example 2: You will borrow money from the bank. You will repay the bank $100 per year for three years and $150 per year for the next two years. How much will the bank lend you today if its discount rate for you is 5 percent?

Table 2.2 – Present Value Example 2

Year	0	1	2	3	4	5
Cash flows (CF_n)		$100	$100	$100	$150	$150
Discount rate (r)		5.0%	5.0%	5.0%	5.0%	5.0%
Present value formula		$= \frac{\$100}{(1.05)^1}$	$= \frac{\$100}{(1.05)^2}$	$= \frac{\$100}{(1.05)^3}$	$= \frac{\$150}{(1.05)^4}$	$= \frac{\$150}{(1.05)^5}$
Present value		$95.24	$90.70	$86.38	$123.41	$117.53
Total present values	$513.26					

Present Value Example 3: Assume you have won $100,000 in a lottery. You can elect to receive $100,000 in a lump sum payment at the end of five years or you can elect to receive the $100,000 in equal annual installments of $20,000 for five years beginning in year one. Your discount rate is 10 percent. In the first scenario, you calculate the present value by using the present value formula on the Year 5 cash flow.

Table 2.3 – Present Value Example 3

Year	0	1	2	3	4	5
Nominal cash flows (CF_n)						$100,000
Discount rate (r)						10.0%
Present value formula						= $100,000 / (1.10)^5
Present value						$62,092
Total present values	$62,092					

For the second scenario, you simply add the present values of the cash flow streams from each year to calculate the present value of the investment. For each year, you would use the same present value calculation applied above.

Year	0	1	2	3	4	5
Cash flows (CF_n)		$20,000	$20,000	$20,000	$20,000	$20,000
Discount rate (r)		10%	10%	10%	10%	10%
Present value formula		$= \frac{\$20,000}{(1.10)^1}$	$= \frac{\$20,000}{(1.10)^2}$	$= \frac{\$20,000}{(1.10)^3}$	$= \frac{\$20,000}{(1.10)^4}$	$= \frac{\$20,000}{(1.10)^5}$
Present value		$18,182	$16,529	$15,026	$13,660	$12,418
Total present values	$75,816					

Since the value of receiving cash today is greater than the value of receiving cash tomorrow, the present value of receiving the $100,000 spread out over five years in equal installments is worth more ($75,816) than the value of receiving the $100,000 in one lump sum five years from now ($62,092).

Future Value Example: You invest $1,000 in a certificate of deposit, or CD (an investment whereby you contribute funds up front in exchange for the principal plus interest at maturity), at a rate of 6 percent. What will you receive from the bank in five years?

Table 2.4 – Future Value Example 1

Year	0	1	2	3	4	5
Cash flows (CF_0)	($1,000)					
Compound rate (r)						6.0%
Future value formula						$= \$1,000 \times (1.06)^5$
Future value at Time 5						$1,338

Net Present Value

There are times when an investor will pay an amount that is greater than the present value of the future cash flows and there are times when an investor will pay an amount that is less than the present value. The **net present value** or **NPV** of an investment is equal to the value initially paid for the investment (stated as a negative cash flow number because the money is paid out or invested at the outset) plus the present value of the investment's future cash flows.

$$NPV = CF_0 + PV_{\text{future cash flows}} \quad \text{where } CF_0 \text{ is generally a negative number}$$

If the net present value is equal to zero, then the investor is "earning his cost of capital." In other words, the investor will earn a return on his initial cash flow (i.e., his investment) that is equal to the discount rate he applied in calculating the present value of the investment. Said another way, the investor's discount rate is equal to the interest rate that his money is earning.

Let's consider a simple bond. Assume that DebtCo is issuing or selling $100 million of bonds with a five-year maturity and paying interest of 8 percent. Interest will be paid annually. This means that DebtCo will sell bonds (which are essentially interest-paying IOUs) and each year for five years DebtCo will pay investors 8 percent on their investment (or $8 million per year during the life of the bond). At the end of the fifth year, DebtCo will pay its last interest payment and return the principal to the investors. How much would this investment be worth to an investor considering buying $10,000 of these bonds at par (at the face value of the bonds)? The investor's discount rate is 8 percent.

Table 2.5 – NPV Example 1

Year	0	1	2	3	4	5
Interest rate		8.0%	8.0%	8.0%	8.0%	8.0%
Interest received		\$800	\$800	\$800	\$800	\$800
Principal received						\$10,000
Cash flows (CF_n)		\$800	\$800	\$800	\$800	\$10,800
Discount rate (r)		8.0%	8.0%	8.0%	8.0%	8.0%
Present value formula		$= \frac{\$800}{(1.08)^1}$	$= \frac{\$800}{(1.08)^2}$	$= \frac{\$800}{(1.08)^3}$	$= \frac{\$800}{(1.08)^4}$	$= \frac{\$10,800}{(1.08)^5}$
Present value at $Time_0$		\$740.74	\$685.87	\$635.07	\$588.02	\$7,350.30
Total present value (PV)	\$10,000					
Cost of investment (CF_0)	(\$10,000)					
NPV (CF_0 + PV)	\$0					

Notice that the discount rate is equal to the coupon or interest rate paid on the bond. In this situation, the present value (or investment value) of the cash flows is equal to the original investment amount. Why is that? Because, if you can earn your "cost of capital," then the present value of an investment is equal to the amount paid for the investment. This is an example of a situation in which the NPV is zero. The amount paid was \$10,000 and the present value of the cash flows earned was \$10,000 because the interest rate earned was 8 percent and the investor's discount rate was 8 percent. The investor's discount rate is 8 percent because there are similarly risky investments available in the market that are currently paying 8 percent – not because the bond is paying a coupon of 8 percent interest.

What would happen if, instead of 8 percent, the cost of capital, or discount rate, were 5 percent but the investor still paid \$10,000 for the investment? Let's see how the net present value of the investment would change.

Table 2.6 - NPV Example 2

Year	0	1	2	3	4	5
Coupon or interest rate		8.0%	8.0%	8.0%	8.0%	8.0%
Interest received		$800	$800	$800	$800	$800
Principal received						$10,000
Nominal cash flows (CF_n)		$800	$800	$800	$800	$10,800
Discount rate (r)		5.0%	5.0%	5.0%	5.0%	5.0%
Present value formula		$=\frac{\$800}{(1.05)^1}$	$=\frac{\$800}{(1.05)^2}$	$=\frac{\$800}{(1.05)^3}$	$=\frac{\$800}{(1.05)^4}$	$=\frac{\$10,800}{(1.05)^5}$
Present value at $Time_0$		$761.90	$725.62	$691.07	$658.16	$8,462.08
Total present value (PV)	$11,298.84					
Cost of investment (CF_0)	($10,000)					
NPV (CF_0 + PV)	$1,298.84					

A positive NPV, as in this example, means that you bought an investment or asset at a price that was less than the present value of its future cash flows. That is good since it means that you earned a *return* on your capital which is greater than the *cost* of your capital (the opportunity cost or your discount rate for the asset). An NPV-negative transaction, on the other hand, is not good since it means that you do not even earn enough to cover your cost of capital.

Not earning the cost of capital

People in the financial community will often say something "is not earning its cost of capital ..." They are referring to this concept of NPV-positive versus NPV-negative transactions. If an investment is NPV-positive, then it is earning a return greater than its discount rate. If an investment is NPV-negative, however, it is earning a return that is less than its discount rate. Such a transaction is "not earning its cost of capital" and, therefore it costs more to put money into this investment than what the investor will earn on it.

Internal Rate of Return

Now that we have described NPV, we can introduce the **internal rate of return** or **IRR.** IRR is simply a specialized discount rate, namely the discount rate that yields a net present value of zero.

For example, if an investment will pay \$10,000 in five years and the investor paid \$8,000 for it at time zero (t_o), then the internal rate of return IRR is equal to 4.6 percent.

$$0 = (\$8{,}000) + \frac{\$10{,}000}{(1.046)^5}$$

Since an IRR is simply a discount rate that yields a certain NPV (0), calculating an IRR involves trying many iterations until you arrive at the correct discount rate. As such, it is easier to use a financial calculator or spreadsheet software to perform the iterations required. The important point is that the IRR is simply a specified discount rate in which the present value of the investment is equal to the amount paid for the investment. Said differently, the IRR is the discount rate which causes the NPV to be equal to zero.

IRR is often used by investors to measure their return based on varying purchase prices. In our example above, if the investor paid \$5,000 instead of \$8,000, the IRR would be 14.9 percent (as compared to a return of 4.6 percent if the investor were to pay \$8,000 for it). Investors will compare the projected IRR with their opportunity cost of capital and some will choose to invest if the IRR on a project is greater than their cost of capital – which is the same as determining whether the NPV is greater than zero.

Multiple Payments in a Compounding Period

If you are paid interest semiannually, you will earn slightly more at the end of the year than if are only paid interest once a year. With interest paid semiannually, the interest earned in the first half of the year will itself earn interest for the remaining six months of the year.

Let's consider a simple example of an investment of \$1,000 that pays 6 percent annually and compare that to an investment that pays 6 percent semiannually.

Annual Interest Payments Example:

$$\begin{aligned}\text{Interest} &= \text{principal} \times 6\% \text{ interest for one year}\\ &= \$1{,}000 \times 0.06\\ &= \$60.00\end{aligned}$$

Semiannual Interest Payments Example

Interest = (principal × 3% interest for first 6 months) + (principal × 3% interest for second 6 months) + (interest from first 6 months × 3% interest for second 6 months)
= ($1,000 × 0.03 = $30) + ($1,000 × 0.03 = $30) + ($30 × 0.03)
= $60.90

Thus over the course of one year, an account earning interest semiannually with the interest rates set forth above would earn $0.90 more in the year than the same account earning interest annually. In terms of applying the present value formula to account for compounding interest within periods, let's consider the following example.

Assume you will loan $1,000 today to a local café. The café owner will pay 6 percent interest annually. However, the interest payments will be paid four times a year (in other words, the interest will be compounded quarterly). How much money will you receive after five years?

Recall the future value formula is:

$FV = CF \times [(1 + {}^{r}/_{m})^{n\,m}]$, where m is the number of payments in the period

$CF = \$1,000$

$r = 6\%$ or 0.06

$n = 5$ periods of one year each

$m = 4$ (assumes that interest is paid four times per year)

$$FV = \$1,000 \times [(1+(0.06 / 4)]^{(5)\times(4)}$$
$$= \$1,000 \times (1.015)^{20}$$
$$= \$1,000 \times (1.347)$$
$$= \$1,346.85$$

Compare this to the same investment for which interest is compounded only once per year:

$$
\begin{aligned}
FV &= \$1{,}000 \times [(1+(0.06 / 1)]^{(5)\times(1)} \\
&= \$1{,}000 \times (1.06)^{5} \\
&= \$1{,}000 \times (1.338) \\
&= \$1{,}338.23
\end{aligned}
$$

Notice how the present value is greater when the interest is compounded quarterly (\$1,346.85) than when the interest is only compounded annually (\$1,338.23).

Annuities and Perpetuities

Calculating the present values of multiple years' cash flows can become tedious, especially if you are not using a financial calculator or computing software. Fortunately, there exist a few shortcuts that can be applied in certain situations. Annuities and perpetuities are seen in a number of investment scenarios. Understanding how to apply these formulas will lead to greater efficiency in your work.

An **annuity** is a financial instrument whereby the investor will pay something today in exchange for *equal payments* paid periodically in the future for a predetermined period of time. The financial instrument will have no value at the end of the period (future value will be zero). The payments in the future will include an implied interest rate such that at the end of the period the investor will have received the initial investment plus the corresponding interest. The present value of the annuity is the amount the investor will pay today in exchange for the future payments. An example of an annuity is a mortgage. With a mortgage, the bank lends money to the homeowner and the homeowner makes equal periodic payments to the bank.

A **perpetuity** is an annuity without a term (or, said differently, with a *perpetual* term). An example of a perpetuity is a royalty with no expiration date.

The formulas to calculate the present value of a perpetuity and an annuity are as follows:

Perpetuity (perpetual or infinite term; CF is the same in each period)

$$PV = \frac{CF}{r}$$

Growing (perpetual or infinite term; CF grows at a growth rate "g")

$$PV = \frac{CF}{r - g}$$

Annuity (fixed term)

$$PV = \frac{CF}{r} - \frac{CF}{(r \times (1+r)^n)}$$

Compare the two formulas and notice that [CF/r] is the first part of the annuity equation and that from [CF/r] you subtract the quantity [CF / (r × (1+r)^n)] to arrive at the perpetuity equation. Consider if *n* (the number of periods) were 1,000, or 10,000 or even 1,000,000. Play with the numbers in your calculator and you will notice that as *n* gets larger, the second value (in the annuity calculation) becomes smaller and smaller, heading toward zero (the denominator moves toward infinity so the quotient moves toward zero). Therefore, if you are calculating the present value of a perpetuity (which technically means that you will receive the cash flows *forever*), you can see why you would not need to calculate the second part of the annuity calculation. Rather, you can assume that the value of this second part of the equation moves towards zero as *n* gets larger (i.e., toward infinity). Therefore, the value of the perpetuity is simply equal to [CF/r] since there is no need to write [CF/r] - 0.

Annuity Example: If the bank were to offer a thirty year mortgage for which the annual mortgage payment were $36,000 and the annual interest rate 7 percent, what would be the present value of the annuity, or the amount of cash the bank would provide today in exchange for the $36,000 annual payments for 30 years?

CF = $36,000

r = 7% or 0.07

n = 30

Solution:

$$\begin{aligned} PV &= (\$36{,}000 / 0.07) - [\$36{,}000 / (0.07 \times (1.07)^{30})] \\ &= \$514{,}285.71 - (\$36{,}000 / 0.533) \\ &= \$514{,}285.71 - (\$67{,}560.23) \\ &= \$446{,}725.48 \end{aligned}$$

The $446,725.48 represents the present value of the annuity or the mortgage amount, which is the amount of cash the bank would give you today in exchange for thirty annual payments to the bank of $36,000 each. If you simply multiplied $36,000 per year by 30 years you would get $1,080,000. Notice how the present value of $446,725.48 is significantly less than $1,080,000. This is because the present value to the bank of those payments spread out over 30 years is only $446,725.48. Said another way, in exchange for $446,725.48 today, you must pay your bank $1,080,000 over 30 years.

Perpetuity Example: Assume your father receives $60 each year forever from the royalties of a song he wrote many years ago, and that royalty will transfer to his heirs (therefore the royalty is perpetual). Assume a 5 percent discount rate. What is this royalty worth on a present value basis today?

CF = $60

r = 5% or 0.5

n = Perpetual

Solution:

PV = $60 / 0.05

= $1,200

If the amount received each year were to grow by a certain percentage (the "growth rate"), then the present value of a perpetuity formula would change as follows to become the present value of a growing perpetuity.

$$PV = \frac{CF}{(r - g)}$$

where g is the annual growth rate.

In our previous example, assume the royalty of $60 per year were to grow by 2 percent per year, then the calculation would change as follows:

PV = $60 / (0.05 - 0.02)

= $60 / 0.03

= $2,000

Valuing a Bond

A bond is a financial instrument whereby the investor pays an amount today in exchange for (1) a stream of interest payments (or coupon payments) during the life of the bond and (2) the repayment of the **face value** (or **principal**) of the bond at the end of the period. A bond is a form of debt for a company since the bondholders or investors only have claim to the value of the bond and do not have an ownership claim to the company (as an equity holder would). Now that you have learned the formula for an annuity and a perpetuity, you can calculate the present value of a bond using shortcuts.

You can think of a bond as two separate financial instruments. First, you receive a fixed stream of interest payments over a set period of time (this is an annuity). Second, you receive the face value, or the principal amount, at the end of the period (for this you would use a present value calculation). The present value of a bond is simply the sum of these two values: (1) the present value of the interest payments during the term of the bond plus (2) the present value of the principal payment at maturity.

For example, consider an investment in a bond that has a face value of $10,000, a semiannual coupon of 6 percent and a ten-year term. Let's assume that your discount rate is 5 percent (because there are other investments of similar risk that will allow you to earn 5 percent). How much is this bond worth to you today? Let's first divide it into two parts, valuing the interest payments or the annuity portion first.

CF_{annual} = $600 (or $10,000 principal amount × the coupon rate of 6%)

$CF_{semiannual}$ = $300

r_{annual} = 5% or 0.05

$r_{semiannual}$ = 2.5% or 0.025

n = 20 periods of six months each

Recall that the formula for an annuity is:

$$PV = \frac{CF}{r} - \frac{CF}{(r \times (1+r)^n)}$$

Value of the interest payments (the annuity):

$$\begin{aligned} PV &= (\$300 / 0.025) - [\$300 / (0.025 \times (1.025)^{20})] \\ &= \$12{,}000 - (\$300 / 0.0410) \\ &= \$12{,}000 - (\$7{,}323.25) \\ &= \$4{,}676.75 \end{aligned}$$

Now let's value the principal paid at the end of 10 years:

CF	=	\$10,000
r_{annual}	=	5%
n	=	10 years
m	=	2 (since interest compounds semiannually)

Recall that the formula for present value is:

$$PV = \frac{CF}{(1 + r/m)^{nm}}$$

Value of the principal paid at the end of 10 years is:

$$PV = \$10{,}000 / [(1+(0.05 / 2)]^{(10) \times (2)}$$
$$= \$10{,}000 / (1.025)^{20}$$
$$= \$10{,}000 / 1.639$$
$$= \$6{,}102.71$$

Now add the two portions together to get the value of the bond today:

PV of annuity	=	\$4,676.75
PV of principal	=	\$6,102.71
Total PV of bond	=	\$10,779.46

\$10,779.46 represents the combined present values of two sets of cash flow streams: the semiannual coupon payments of 6 percent per year as well as the repayment of principal at the end of ten years. Since you would receive both of these two cash flow streams, you should be willing to pay \$10,779.46 for this bond if your discount rate were 5 percent. Note that the discount rate is *less than* the coupon or interest rate, and so the investment is worth *more than* the face value of \$10,000.

Said differently, since the discount rate of 5% is *less than* the interest rate of 6%, the net present value of this investment (that is, the value after accounting for the \$10,000 face value of the bond) is greater than zero.

Net present value = value of associated cash flows - cost of purchasing the asset

$10,779.46 - $10,000 = $779.46

NPV = $779.46 when r = 5%

With a calculator try this same exercise when r = 6% and you will find that NPV = 0. Going back to the earlier discussion on IRR, the IRR of this particular bond is 6%. Since the discount rate of 6% is *equal to* the interest rate of 6%, the net present value = 0 .

NPV = 0 when r = 6%

Now try this same exercise when r = 7% and you will find the NPV = - $710.62. Since the discount rate of 7% is *greater than* the interest rate of 6%, the net present value of this investment is less than 0.

NPV = - $710.62 when r = 7%

Financial Statement Basics

Chapter 3

A good decision is based on knowledge and not numbers.

Plato

Financial statements are the (secret) language of finance. Any professional involved in making business decisions must develop a facility and ease with numbers, financial ratios and related terminology. Much can be learned by studying the financial statements of a company, but you must first learn how to read them.

Financial statements are used by many parties for different reasons (some of which are described below). This chapter will describe the financial statements, how they interrelate, and introduce financial ratios and terminology commonly used in M&A and corporate finance.

Constituent	Reasons for using financial statements
Company managers	Measure performance and make strategic, operating and financial decisions
Suppliers and vendors	Measure creditworthiness and liquidity; make credit decisions
Equity investors	Value the equity investment; determine solvency; make buy and sell decisions
Debt investors	Measure creditworthiness and bankruptcy risk; make buy and sell decisions
Regulators	Determine whether the company is operating according to regulations and law
Acquirors	Value the company; make investment decisions

Whereas *historical financial statements* represent what has happened in the past, the *financial projections* of a company attempt to predict what the financial statements will look like in the future. When preparing financial projections, companies make assumptions regarding various items, including future sales and revenues, the costs to achieve those sales, and required capital expenditures. Public companies must follow certain rules when preparing their historical financial statements (some of which will be described in the next section). Whereas historical financial statements are often used by investors, regulators, and outside parties, financial projections are generally used internally to make corporate decisions, and by financial advisors to assist companies in making strategic decisions.

Financial Accounting Basics

This book is not intended to be an accounting textbook. Instead, the goal is to provide a practical description of how the financial community uses financial statements. On the following pages a summary of major financial accounting concepts is provided. These are some of the most important and fundamental concepts in financial accounting and some of the first principles in a finance professional's technical tool chest. If you have never taken a financial accounting class, you should supplement this section with a financial accounting textbook and consider taking a college-level accounting class. A list of recommended accounting textbooks can be found in the Appendix.

Major GAAP accounting concepts

1. ***GAAP:*** Generally Accepted Accounting Principles is a set of financial reporting guidelines. The Financial Accounting Standards Board (FASB) is considered by the Securities and Exchange Comission (SEC) and the American Institute of Certified Public Accountants (AICPA) to be the authoritative governing body of GAAP. Currently, U.S. public companies must file their GAAP financial statements with the SEC, where they become public record. GAAP is not a fixed set of rules; it is a continuously evolving set of principles and there are gray areas in which management has room to use judgment. Since GAAP is not static, be sure to reference current accounting standards whenever in doubt about an accounting rule or issue. FASB's website is www.fasb.org. A list of GAAP reference books is provided in the Appendix.

2. ***Tax accounting:*** In addition to the GAAP books, companies also prepare a separate set of corporate records for tax purposes (tax books), which are used to determine the company's taxable income and tax liability for a reporting period. Material differences might exist between the GAAP books and the tax books. Tax accounting (which has different rules than GAAP accounting) is regulated by the **IRS** (Internal Revenue Service) and other taxing authorities. Whereas GAAP financial records for public companies are publicly available, tax records are not made public.

3. ***Financial statements:*** There are three basic financial statements which public companies must prepare in accordance with GAAP - the income statement, balance sheet, and cash flow statement. Companies also provide (1) a schedule that describes changes in owner's equity; (2) footnotes to the financial statements, which further describe the financial statements; and (3) management's discussion and analysis (MD&A), in which management describes key issues and changes related to the financial performance during the period. GAAP financial statements for public companies are filed quarterly and annually with the SEC based on the company's fiscal year.

4. ***Materiality:*** GAAP only applies to material economic events. The test is, if a reasonable person would make a different decision based on, or would be influenced by, an economic event, the event is material and must be accounted for according to GAAP.

5. ***Revenue recognition:*** In accrual accounting, revenues are recognized when services or goods are delivered and when cash collection certainty is *reasonable.* This means that, technically, a company can only record a sale if it reasonably believes it will be paid for its goods or services. Larger companies use accrual accounting more often than the cash-based method of accounting, which recognizes revenues when cash is actually received or paid.

6. ***Matching principle:*** Any expenses associated with obtaining related revenues should be charged as an expense during the period when the revenues were recognized. If a cost cannot be matched to revenue, it is generally expensed in the period when the cost was incurred.

7. ***Tax-deductible expenses:*** Expenses are (generally) tax deductible and are offset against revenues to calculate taxable income. Thus, a company subtracts salaries and production costs, for example, from revenues before it calculates how much tax it must pay.

8. ***Capitalizing assets:*** An asset is anything (except for employees) owned by the company and used in providing or delivering goods or services and used in the generation of future cash inflow. If the asset purchased has a useful life longer than one year, it should be **capitalized** or put on the balance sheet as a long-term asset. This means that the total cost of the asset is put on the balance sheet when it is initially purchased and each period a portion of the capitalized asset's value is depreciated (for tangible assets) or amortized (for intangible assets).

9. ***Depreciating assets:*** Depreciable assets are depreciated over their useful life. Depreciation is charged through the income statement as an offset to revenues (see matching principle above). The cost of an asset should be depreciated according to a depreciation schedule based on the useful life of the asset.

10. ***Fair market value:*** Assets and liabilities are recorded on the company's balance sheet based on fair market value (FMV) at the time the item is purchased and added to the balance sheet. Most assets and liabilities are carried on the books based on this historical cost less any corresponding depreciation or amortization plus improvements. The balance sheet is not routinely adjusted upward from this historical cost if an asset increases in value. Only when a transaction takes place to sell the asset does the asset's fair market value get captured on the balance sheet (the asset value is recalculated at that time). Conservatism,

however, does provide that if there is a material *decrease* in the fair market value of an asset or liability, that item should be written down to the lower fair market value (even in the absence of a transaction). Write-offs flow through the income statement as a charge and ultimately reduce net income.

11. ***Mark-to-market:*** Certain assets or investments (e.g., trading securities) are mark-to-market every period, meaning their carrying value on the balance sheet is adjusted up or down to reflect their current market value as opposed to being carried on the balance sheet at historical cost.

12. ***Discontinued operations:*** Income from discontinued operations and other non-recurring items should be shown separately from income from continuing operations on the income statement.

13. ***Management's intentions:*** Financial reporting should reflect management's intentions. For example, if management intends to sell an asset in the near term that would otherwise be categorized as a long-term asset (and management is fairly certain they will sell it and receive cash proceeds for it), this should be reflected in the financial statements by re-categorizing the asset as available-for-sale or even as a short-term asset.

Sarbanes-Oxley Act of 2002

Sarbanes-Oxley created the Public Company Accounting Oversight Board (PCAOB). It requires that any accounting firm that audits an SEC registrant company must by registered with the PCAOB. Other requirements of Sarbanes-Oxley include greater auditor independence, certifications from a company's CEO and CFO regarding financial reports, stricter regulations over equity analysts, and greater accountability for corporations in the event of corporate fraud and criminal action.

Financial statements for foreign issuers

In 2007, the SEC voted to approve rule amendments such that financial statements from foreign issuers selling securities in the U.S. will no longer need to reconcile their financial statements to U.S. GAAP if those statements are prepared using International Financial Reporting Standards (IFRS) as issued by the International Accounting Standards Board (IASB). As of 2007, there is active discussion/consideration around the possibility of giving U.S. public companies this same option to use either IFRS (sometimes called "international GAAP") or U.S. GAAP.

Basic Financial Statements

There are three basic financial statements: (1) the balance sheet; (2) the income statement; and (3) the cash flow statement (also referred to as the sources and uses statement). These statements are generally computed at the end of every **reporting period** (period in which a company's financial performance is measured, such as quarterly, semiannually, or annually) and are used to measure the actual financial results and financial health of a company. Financial statements are used to report actual results, whereas budgets and financial projections are used for future planning purposes.

The following descriptions are used to provide a conceptual framework for understanding the basic financial statements. The best way to learn how to read financial statements is to actually *read financial statements.* That means, after you have reviewed the basic descriptions provided here, you should spend time reading through various annual reports, specifically the financial statements, the footnotes of the financial statements, and the MD&A. The footnotes and the MD&A provide important context that will allow you to better understand the numbers in the financial statements. Financial statements for SEC registered companies can be found at www.sec.gov.

Let's first consider a timeline to understand the time frames of the three statements. Notice in the figure below how the balance sheet is taken at the beginning and end of a reporting period. The reason there are two balance sheets -opening and closing- is because a balance sheet measures assets and liabilities at a *point in time,* whereas the income statement and the cash flow statement are representative of what happens *during* a reporting period. A full set of financial statements includes: (1) an opening balance sheet, (2) an income statement, (3) a cash flow statement, and (4) a closing balance sheet. The opening and closing balance sheets are usually shown together.

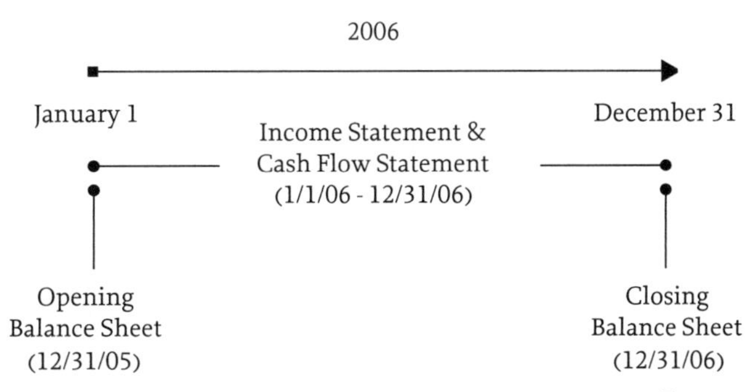

To illustrate important financial concepts we will use the financial statements of SampleCo, a fictional company. We will refer to SampleCo's financial statements throughout this chapter.

Table 3.1 – SampleCo's Balance Sheet

Balance Sheet	**2004**	**2005**
Assets		
Cash	$200	$165
Accounts receivable	125	150
Inventory	150	125
Other current assets	45	50
Total current assets	520	490
Gross PP&E	1,500	1,900
Accumulated depreciation	(300)	(450)
Net PP&E	1,200	1,450
Other long-term assets	300	300
Goodwill	250	250
Total assets	**$2,270**	**$2,490**
Liabilities & Shareholders' Equity		
Short-term debt	$125	$100
Accounts payable	100	150
Salaries payable	75	65
Taxes payable	45	40
Total current liabilities	345	355
Deferred tax liabilities	200	225
Other long-term liabilities	120	120
Long-term debt	600	700
Common equity	1,005	1,090
Total liabilities & equity	**$2,270**	**$2,490**

Table 3.2 – SampleCo's Income Statement

Income Statement - for the year ending	2005
Revenues	$1,000
Cost of goods sold	(400)
Gross profit	600
Selling, general and administrative (SG&A)	(100)
Earnings before interest, taxes, DD&A (EBITDA)	500
Depreciation, depletion & amortization (DD&A)	(150)
Earnings before interest and taxes (EBIT)	350
Interest expense	(125)
Earnings before taxes (EBT)	225
Income taxes	(90)
Net income (earnings)	$135
Shares outstanding-basic	100
Shares outstanding-diluted	105
Earnings per share (EPS) - basic	$1.35
Earnings per share (EPS) - diluted	$1.29
Dividends	$50
Dividends per share (DPS)	$0.50
Earnings to common	$85

Table 3.3 – SampleCo's Cash Flow Statement

One of the inputs for calculation of the cash flow statement is the Change in Working Capital. Generally speaking, this is the sum of all of the changes in each of the working capital accounts. Working capital includes current assets and current liabilities but does not include Cash (which is what we are solving for) and debt (which is included in a separate part of the cash flow statement, Cash Flow from Financing). If an asset increases from one period to the next it is a use of cash (and if it decreases it is a source of cash). If a liability increases from one period to the next it is a source of cash (and if it decreases it is a use of cash).

Change in Accounts receivable	(25)
Change in Inventory	25
Change in Other current assets	(5)
Change in Accounts payable	50
Change in Salaries payable	(10)
Change in Taxes payable	(5)
Changes in Working capital	30

Table 3.3 – SampleCo's Cash Flow Statement continued

Cash Flow Statement	2005
Operating	
Net income	$135
DD&A	150
Changes in deferred taxes	25
Changes in working capital	30
Cash flow from operations	340
Investing	
Capital expenditures	(400)
Other changes in assets/liabilities	0
Cash flow from investing	(400)
Financing	
Common dividends paid	(50)
Changes in short-term debt	(25)
Changes in long-term debt	100
Changes in equity	0
Cash flow from financing	25
Beginning cash	200
Total change in cash	(35)
Ending cash	$165

The balance sheet: The balance sheet is a snapshot taken at a point in time. It represents what a company owns (its **assets**) and the claims on those assets (its **liabilities** and **shareholders' equity**) on the date of the balance sheet. The balance sheet may not have the same values the day before the snapshot was taken nor the day after. In addition, the balance sheet always has to "balance," which means that its assets must equal its liabilities plus shareholders' equity.

In the figure below see how SampleCo's assets of $2,490 at the end of 2005 equal its liabilities of $1,400 plus its equity of $1,090.

Assets = Liabilities + Shareholders' Equity

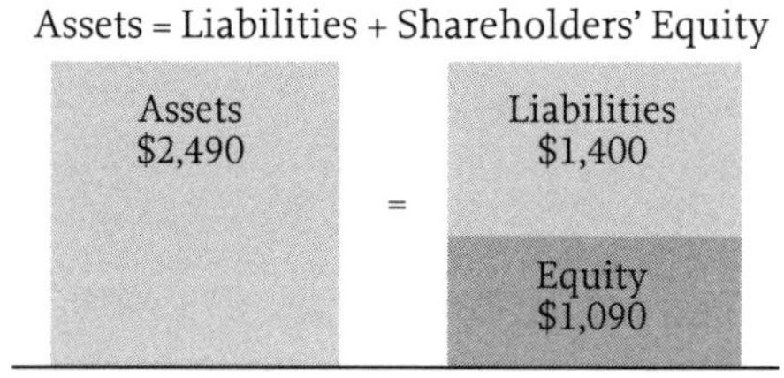

Consider your own personal balance sheet to gain a better conceptual understanding. Let's say you own a house and a car, which together cost $500,000. The value of the house and the car would be listed on the asset side of your personal balance sheet (minus depreciation, which we will touch on later). How did you pay for the house and the car? You might have a mortgage on the house with your local bank and that mortgage has a principal balance of $400,000. And you might have paid for the car with cash. Therefore, your liabilities amount to $400,000 and your shareholders' equity (the value of the owner's portion) amounts to $100,000. Your personal balance sheet would look like this:

Assets		**Liabilities and Owner's Equity**	
Car and house	$500,000	Debt (bank loan)	$400,000
		Owner's equity	100,000
Total	**$500,000**	**Total**	**$500,000**

A balance sheet can be assessed on any given day, although it is generally provided at the end of a **reporting period**, such as the end of a quarter or the end of a **fiscal year**. When a company prepares a full set of financial statements, generally both an **opening balance sheet** and a **closing balance sheet** are provided. They represent the balance sheets at the beginning of the reporting period and at the end of the reporting period, respectively.

What is fiscal year vs. calendar year?

The **fiscal year** is the annual period for a company's financial reporting. **Calendar year** is from January 1 to December 31. Companies are free to choose their own fiscal year, although many choose a fiscal year that is the same as the calendar year. Certain companies find that having a fiscal year end on December 31 is very difficult, due to the nature of their business. For example, most retail companies are very busy during the December holiday season dealing with sales and customer service-related issues. Many of these companies prefer to have their fiscal year end after the holiday season. A company's fiscal year end is listed in its financial statements.

Current assets and **current liabilities** represent those assets that the company will either receive (e.g., accounts receivable) or those liabilities that are due to a third party (e.g., accounts payable) within an operating cycle. However, if the operating cycle is less than one year, then one year is considered the cutoff between "short-term" and "long-term." Most companies have an operating cycle that is less than one year.

At the end of 2005, SampleCo has $490 of current assets, including cash of $165, and $355 of current liabilities. Current assets and liabilities are also referred to as short-term assets and liabilities.

Items on the balance sheet are listed according to **liquidity** or likeliness that the item will be converted to cash (if an asset) or cash will need to be paid (if a liability). Therefore, current assets are always listed at the top of the asset section of the balance sheet and current liabilities are always listed at the top of the liabilities and shareholders' equity section of the balance sheet. In almost every situation, cash is listed as the first current asset.

Assets: the assets of a business are used to run the business and to generate the company's revenues and other cash inflows. Examples of assets include accounts receivable, inventory, and **PP&E** (property, plant and equipment). Employees are clearly assets for many companies, but accounting rules do not recognize "people" as assets. The salaries for those employees are recognized as expenses on the income statement when they are paid, and salaries payable are listed on the balance sheet as liabilities if the employees have earned salaries but the company has not yet paid them.

PP&E is property, plant and equipment. PP&E is often quoted both on a gross basis and on a net basis after accounting for **accumulated depreciation**, which is the aggregate amount of depreciation recognized on the company's assets.

At the end of 2005, SampleCo has gross PP&E of $1,900; however, $450 of it has already been depreciated. Therefore, the net PP&E amount at the end of 2005 is $1,450.

Depreciation represents the portion of an asset that is accrued as an expense against the period's revenues.

For example, assume CarCo buys a new car for its car rental business, which costs $20,000. That car will have a depreciable life of five years (meaning it will help generate revenues for five years). Instead of listing the cost of $20,000 as an expense in the first year, the company would first list the item as an asset on the balance sheet (**capitalize** the asset), and then charge off a portion of the $20,000 every year for five years (**depreciate** the asset). If a straight-line method of depreciation were being used (such that an equal amount of depreciation is recognized each year during the useful life) and assuming the car has no value at the end of the five years, then $4,000 ($20,000/5 years=$4,000 per year) would be recognized as depreciation expense each year on the income statement. After one year ($4,000 worth of depreciation has been recognized), the net PP&E account for the car would be:

Gross PP&E (car)	$20,000
Accumulated depreciation	(4,000)
Net PP&E (car)	$16,000

Many assets that have been fully depreciated from a balance sheet perspective are still useful in terms of their productive capacity. In our example above, although the car is fully depreciated after the fifth year from an accounting perspective, it could still be useful to CarCo after five years.

Other items on the balance sheet include other long-term assets and intangible assets. Intellectual property and patents are examples of intangible assets (which are also long-term assets). Intangible assets are assets of a company that cannot be felt or touched. Goodwill is an intangible asset and represents the amount paid for a target company above the identifiable book value of assets and liabilities.

Liabilities and shareholders' equity: Together **liabilities** and **shareholders' equity** represent all of the claims on the company's assets. They are what "paid" for the assets and include any and all obligations of the company.

Equity holders have claims on the assets after all liabilities have been accounted for or paid; they have rights to the residual interest of a company, net of other obligations including debt. The relationship is similar to ownership of a home in which Alyssa is the owner, but her ownership interest (her equity interest) will not be free and clear until she pays off her entire mortgage. If she were to sell today, the sale proceeds would go first to repay the mortgage and anything left over (the residual interest) would go to Alyssa. Similarly, in a bankruptcy scenario, equity holders are only paid after all of the company's debts have been paid.

Shareholders' equity can be comprised of preferred stock and common stock. Preferred stockholders receive a preferential dividend and are higher in **liquidation preference** than common stockholders (meaning preferred stockholders are paid before common stockholders in the event of bankruptcy). Common stockholders do not receive a preferential dividend, but they do retain all of the residual interest after the debtholders and preferred equity holders are paid. Not all companies have preferred stockholders, but all companies have common stockholders. Within common stock is an account called **retained earnings**.

For example, in 2005 SampleCo had earnings of $135 and paid dividends of $50. Therefore, $85 ($135 – $50 = $85) would flow to the common equity account via retained earnings. At the end of 2005, SampleCo had $1,090 of common equity, an increase of $85 from 2004.

Debt is an obligation of a borrower to a lender or to an investor to repay borrowed funds with interest by a certain date in the future. Debt is a liability of the company and it is often listed on the balance sheet according to the type of debt. For example, some companies might list **bank debt** (money borrowed from and owed to banks) separate from bonds (debt securities sold directly to investors). Debt that must be paid within one year is considered short-term debt and debt that has a **maturity** (the date on which the money must be paid back) beyond one year is considered long-term debt. Short-term debt is listed separately in the current liabilities section, while long-term debt is usually near the bottom of the liabilities section, befitting its long-term orientation. Recall that assets and liabilities are listed in terms of liquidity, which is how quickly the asset is expected to be converted to cash or the liability is expected to be paid.

At the end of 2005, SampleCo has $100 of short-term debt and $700 of long-term debt.

The debt and equity obligations of a company constitute the company's **capital structure** or **capitalization**. Different types of investors have claims to different parts of a company's capital structure. Depending on the type of investment an investor has in a company, the investor can sell her investments or securities in a secondary market (such as the **NYSE,** or New York Stock Exchange) and the value of the investment can rise or fall relative to the balance sheet value, or **book value**. The **market value** of a company's security (which is the price an investor must pay to obtain the security in the open market) might be materially different from the book value of the investment. There are other long-term liabilities that are obligations of the company. Examples of non-debt long-term liabilities include deferred taxes, and environmental reserves.

At the end of 2005, SampleCo has $225 of deferred tax liabilities and $120 of other long-term liabilities.

The income statement: The income statement is a measure of financial performance during a period of time (e.g., quarterly, annually). It measures profitability over time as opposed to the balance sheet, which is a point in time measurement.

At the top of the income statement is the company's revenues (or sales) for the period. In 2005, SampleCo had $1,000 of revenues. From those revenues, a series of expenses are deducted to arrive at net income or earnings for the period. Expenses are any costs that were incurred in order to generate the revenues, such as cost of goods sold, salaries, and advertising expenses. Interest expense is an expense since the cost to borrow money is a cost of doing business, as are taxes paid to the government.

DD&A represents the portion of a capitalized asset that is being expensed for the period in question. Note that DD&A is not always separated in a company's financial statements. Sometimes it is included within another account on the income statement (although it will always be disclosed on the cash flow statement since it is one of the non-cash charges that will be added back to net income to calculate operating cash flow).

EBITDA is a commonly used metric and it represents *earnings before interest, taxes, and DD&A*. EBITDA is a proxy for (but not a substitute for) cash flow generated by the assets of a company before debt holders and tax authorities are paid. EBIT is another commonly used metric and it represents *earnings before interest and taxes but after DD&A*.

What is DD&A?

DD&A stands for depreciation, depletion and amortization. Depreciation relates to physical assets, depletion relates to natural resources (except for land, which value is not depleted for accounting purposes), and amortization relates to intangible assets such as intellectual property and patents. Since depletion only applies to natural resources, most companies do not have depletion. Therefore, the financial community uses "EBITDA" and not "EBITDDA."

Earnings (also known as net income) is calculated after adjusting for all of the year's revenues and expenses. Earnings is an after-interest and after-tax number. **Earnings per share** is the amount of earnings per share of equity (calculated by dividing earnings by the number of shares outstanding). The income statement must also take into account in its EPS calculation the effect of any potentially dilutive securities. For example, a convertible bond is a bond which, under certain circumstances, can be converted into shares of the company; in that event, the same numerator (earnings) will be distributed over a larger denominator (the now-increased number of shares); this convertible bond may be a dilutive security because its conversion may dilute (reduce) earnings per share. Calculating fully diluted EPS is described in more detail later in this chapter. It is important to note that "earnings" is not equal to "cash flow." Many non-cash items are included in earnings.

Dividends are a return of capital to shareholders and are paid out of retained earnings. Dividends per share represents the amount of dividends paid per share of equity. Net income less dividends for a period is called **earnings to common.** Earnings to common flows from the income statement into the common equity account on the balance sheet.

The income statement also reflects any gains or losses resulting from the sale of a company's assets. In addition, companies will generally separate any one-time or non-recurring charges on their income statements, including the effects on the company's earnings of a change in exchange rates, changes in accounting policies, and one-time costs associated with mergers or restructurings.

The cash flow statement: The cash flow statement reconciles the income statement and the balance sheets at the end of a period to determine the actual cash flow generated by the company or business. The income statement reflects the earnings of the company for a period. However, many non-cash items, such as depreciation, are deducted from revenues to calculate earnings. The cash flow statement is important since it tracks actual cash inflows and outflows. Both investors and creditors care about the health of a company's cash flow since a significant cash shortfall can have serious implications with respect to a company's ability to fund its growth or pay its obligations going forward. A cash flow statement can be created with an opening and closing balance sheet and an income statement.

The cash flow statement is a reconciliation of the opening and closing balance sheets and income statement and is divided into three sections based upon three distinct management actions or decisions.

The first section is called **cash flow from operations** and represents cash flow related to the day-to-day operations of the business. It begins with net income and adjusts for any non-cash charges found in the income statement, including DD&A. Balance sheet changes related to a company's operations, such as changes in deferred taxes and changes in working capital, are also reconciled in this section.

What are non-cash charges?

Non-cash charges are expenses on the income statement which do not in fact relate to a cash payment. Depreciation is the classic example. Going back to our car example, the car has a depreciable life of 5 years. Thus, for accounting purposes, $1/5^{th}$ of the depreciable value of the car is charged as an expense on the income statement each year for five years. However, the company paid the $20,000 in cash on Day 1. There is no additional payment of cash in each of the five years which coincides with the annual depreciation of $4,000. Therefore the $4,000 of annual DD&A is a non-cash charge. Other non-cash charges include non-cash restructuring charges related to a reorganization or non-cash charges related to changes in an accounting method.

The second section, called **cash flow from investing,** represents cash paid to acquire assets, land, or stock in other companies (except for stock held as marketable securities.) Cash received from the sale of assets or subsidiary companies is also included in the cash flow from investing section.

The third section, called **cash flow from financing,** relates to changes in how a company finances its assets. It is the section that accounts for any cash changes related to debt and equity holders, including items such as the payment of dividends, the issuance or repayment of debt, and the issuance or repurchase of equity.

What about investments financed with new debt?

GAAP requires that a company report the allocation of capital (which is an investment decision) separately from the source of the capital (which is a financing decision). For example, assume a company purchased an asset for $500 but issued debt of $500 to pay for it. The purchase of the asset would be a cash outflow of $500 in the cash flow from investing section and the $500 of new debt would be a cash inflow of $500 in the cash flow from financing section. Although this amounts to a neutral effect on cash, both transactions must be disclosed separately on the cash flow statement.

The amounts calculated from the three sections are added together to calculate the cash flow generated for the period. This cash flow for the period, also called total change in cash for the period, is then added to the cash balance from the opening balance sheet to determine the cash balance for the closing balance sheet.

The balance sheet and sources and uses of cash

An increase in an account on the asset side of the balance sheet from the previous reporting period represents a "use of cash," or a negative number in the cash flow statement. A decrease in an account on the asset side from the previous reporting period represents a "source of cash," or a positive number on the cash flow statement. Conversely, an increase in an account on the liabilities and shareholders' equity side of the balance sheet from the previous reporting period represents a "source of cash" and a decrease represents a "use of cash." If you understand this concept intuitively it will make life easier since you will not have to worry about memorizing the "rule."

An example may help clarify this important concept. Let's say you buy a car and therefore an asset account goes up by $30,000. This increase in the asset account represents a use of cash since you had to "pay" $30,000 to the dealer. The increase in an asset account represented a *use of cash* since you now have $30,000 *less cash on hand* because you used it to buy the car. Now let's say you took out a loan of $30,000 from the bank to pay for the car. The new loan would increase your debt by $30,000 and that increase would represent a *source of cash* since the cash was being provided to you by the bank. The increase in a liability represented a source of cash even though you have to pay it back. You have $30,000 *more cash on hand.* The cash flow statement only tracks flows of cash into and out of the company coffers (that is, shown on the balance sheet), it does not account for whether the cash *belongs* to the company.

Additional examples of sources and uses of cash are provided in the following table.

Sources of Cash	**Uses of Cash**
Decrease in an asset	Increase in an asset
• Sale of a manufacturing plant	• Acquisition of manufacturing plant
• Reduction in accounts receivable	• Increase in accounts receivable
Increase in a liability or equity	Decrease in a liability or equity
• Issuance of new debt	• Repayment of debt
• Issuance of common stock	• Decrease in accounts payable
• Increase in deferred taxes	• Decrease in deferred taxes
• Increase in salaries payable	• Decrease in salaries payable
• Increase in accounts payable	• Buyback of common stock

Creating the Cash Flow Statement

Let's now discuss how the financial statements are interrelated. First, let's discuss those items on the income statement that are also related to the balance sheet. The cross-references between SampleCo's balance sheet and income statement are highlighted in Table 3.4. (Note that these are common relationships between the income statement and balance sheet. However, these are not all of the relationships between the income statement and balance sheet.)

Table 3.4 – Ties Between the Income Statement and the Balance Sheet

Balance Sheet	2004	2005		Income Statement	2005	
Assets				Revenues	$1,000	
Cash	$200	$165		Cost of goods sold	(400)	
Accounts receivable	125	150		Gross margin	600	
Inventory	150	125		Selling, general and administrative	(100)	
Other current assets	45	50		EBITDA	500	
Total current assets	520	490		DD&A	(150)	[1]
Gross PP&E	1,500	1,900		EBIT	350	
Accumulated depreciation	(300)	(450)	[1]	Interest expense	(125)	
Net PP&E	1,200	1,450		Earnings before taxes	225	
Other long-term assets	300	300		Income taxes	(90)	[2]
Goodwill	250	250		Net income (earnings)	$135	
Total assets	**$2,270**	**$2,490**				
				Shares outstanding	100	
Liabilities & Shareholders' Equity				Earnings per share - basic	$1.35	
Short-term debt	$125	$100		Earnings per share - fully diluted	$1.29	
Accounts payable	100	150		Dividends	$50	
Salaries payable	75	65		Dividends per share	$0.50	
Taxes payable	45	40		Earnings to common	$85	[3]
Total current liabilities	345	355				
Deferred tax liabilities	200	225	[2]			
Other long-term liabilities	120	120				
Long-term debt	600	700				
Common equity	1,005	1,090	[3]			
Total liabilities & equity	**$2,270**	**$2,490**				

See corresponding footnotes on next page.

Notes to Table 3.4 are provided below.

1. DD&A from the income statement is added to accumulated depreciation from the previous period's balance sheet to arrive at the new accumulated depreciation.

Accumulated depreciation (2004)	$300
Add: 2005 DD&A	150
Accumulated depreciation (2005)	$450

2. Differences in cash taxes paid (the actual amount of cash paid to taxing authorities this year), as opposed to taxes on the GAAP or book income statement, result in a mismatch in cash. A deferred tax liability is created when the tax liability calculated for the GAAP books is greater than the actual taxes paid. You can think of the deferred tax liability in this circumstance as an IOU to Uncle Sam (a tax payment has been recognized in the GAAP books that will be paid to Uncle Sam in the future). For SampleCo, $25 of the $90 in taxes is deferred and deferred taxes increased by $25 from 2004 to 2005. An adjustment must be made to the cash flow statement to adjust for any cash differences based on taxes.

3. Common equity increases based on net income earned during the period and decreases based on dividends paid during the period. The amount of earnings less dividends is the amount contributed to retained earnings. Also, equity issuances during the year are an increase to the common equity account and repurchases of equity are a decrease to the common equity account. We will assume no equity issuances and no equity repurchases in 2005 for SampleCo.

Common equity (2004)	$1,005
Add: 2005 net income	135
Less: 2005 dividends paid	(50)
Add: equity issuances	0
Less: equity repurchases	0
Common equity (2005)	$1,090

Now we will describe how the cash flow statement is tied to the balance sheets and the income statement. The comments are listed after Table 3.5.

Table 3.5 – Creating the Cash Flow Statement

Cash Flow Statement	2005	
Operating		
Net income	$135	1
DD&A	150	2
Changes in deferred taxes	25	3
Changes in working capital	30	4
Cash flow from operations	340	
Investing		
Capital expenditures	(400)	5
Other changes in assets/liabilities	0	6
Cash flow from investing	(400)	
Financing		
Common dividends paid	(50)	7
Changes in short-term debt	(25)	8
Changes in long-term debt	100	8
Changes in equity	0	9
Cash flow from financing	25	
Beginning cash	200	
Total change in cash	(35)	10
Ending cash	$165	

1. The cash flow statement begins with net income from the income statement. Be careful to start with net income and not net income *after dividends.* Dividends are captured in the section Cash Flow from Financing.

2. DD&A is a non-cash charge on the income statement and therefore it is added back to net income in the cash flow statement.

3. SampleCo's deferred taxes increase by $25 from 2004 to 2005. This is a source of cash since the company is paying less in cash taxes than its tax liability on its GAAP books.

4. Changes in working capital represents the total change of both current assets and current liabilities. Neither cash nor short-term debt is included in the working capital calculation because, like dividends, short-term debt is captured in the section Cash Flow from Financing, and cash is what you are solving for. An increase in a current asset from one period to the next represents a use of cash and an increase in a current liability from one period to the next represents a source of cash. The $30 change in working capital on SampleCo's cash flow statement is calculated as follows:

Changes in working capital	**2004**	**2005**	**Source/(use)**
Current assets [1]			
Accounts receivable	$125	$150	($25)
Inventory	150	125	25
Other current assets	45	50	(5)
Sub-total	$320	$325	($5)
Current liabilities [2]			
Accounts payable	$100	$150	$50
Salaries payable	75	65	(10)
Taxes payable	45	40	(5)
Sub-total	$220	$255	$35
Total change in working capital			$30

1. An increase in an asset is a use of cash. A decrease in an asset is a source of cash.
2. An increase in a liability is a source of cash. A decrease in a liability is a use of cash.

5. Capital expenditures represents the amount spent on new assets and investments during the period. Since SampleCo did not sell or retire any assets during the year, the amount of capital expenditures is also equal to the difference in gross PP&E from 2004 to 2005.

6. There were no other changes in other assets and other liabilities for SampleCo from 2004 to 2005.

7. Dividends paid to common stockholders is a financing action; therefore, it is captured as a cash outflow in the section Cash Flow from Financing.

8. An increase in debt represents a source of cash (since the new debt is cash flow that the company can now use). A decrease in debt is a use of cash.

9. Changes in equity represents any change in the common equity account *excluding* net income or dividends. A change in equity would occur if the company issued new common stock or if it repurchased common stock.

10. Total change in cash is the sum of Cash Flow from Operations, Cash Flow from Investing, and Cash Flow from Financing.

Financial Ratios and Terminology

Like many things, financial statements can be meaningless without a method of reading or analyzing them. For example, if a company earns $50 in net income, is that good or bad? What if it earned $50 million, or $500 million? Financial ratios and financial terminology provide readers of financial statements with the ability to compare a specific company's financial performance to that of other companies using a shorthand method or language. We will discuss some of the most commonly used terms here. Many of the calculations and ratios described here are used in performing M&A analysis, including comparable company analysis and comparable transaction analysis. The rest of this chapter will refer to the financial statements of SampleCo.

Market Value of Equity

Shares in a public company can be bought and sold in a secondary market and the value of a share in the secondary market can be significantly different from its accounting book value. The market value (also known as **equity value**) represents the aggregate value of shareholders' equity based on the current stock price. It is calculated by multiplying the number of diluted shares outstanding by the current stock price.

Diluted shares outstanding × Stock price = Market value

Market value is usually quoted based on fully diluted shares outstanding. The closing stock price on a given day should be used for the calculation and the day on which the stock price is taken should be noted with the market value (since prices change from day to day).

Assuming a current stock price for SampleCo of $20, its market value would be calculated as follows:

105 diluted shares outstanding × $20 stock price = $2,100 market value

Shares Outstanding, Options and Converts

Basic shares outstanding and ***fully diluted shares outstanding***: Basic shares outstanding are the total number of shares issued and outstanding by a company. The issued and outstanding shares may be significantly fewer than the shares *authorized* in a company's charter or bylaws. **Treasury shares** (shares that have been repurchased by the company in the open market) are considered issued, but they are *not* considered outstanding and, therefore, are not included in the calculation of shares outstanding. The basic shares outstanding for a public company can be found on the first page of its most recent 10-Q (or 10-K if the first 10-Q of the year has not been filed yet).

Fully diluted shares outstanding represents a company's shares outstanding, adjusted for any stock options and/or potentially dilutive securities such as the equity component of **convertible debt** (which is debt that can be converted into equity under certain circumstances).

The **treasury stock method** of accounting is used to calculate fully diluted shares outstanding for options and the **if-converted method** is used for convertible debt or preferred stock. In the treasury method, the options are assumed to have been exercised and the proceeds from the sale of shares are used to repurchase shares in the market at the current market price, thereby partially offsetting the number of new shares issued from the options. Similarly, the if-converted method assumes that potentially dilutive securities are converted to equity. Therefore, the number of shares outstanding increases, but the amount of debt or preferred equity on the balance sheets declines, as does interest expense (in the case of convertible bonds) or dividends paid (in the case of preferred equity), reflecting the fact these securities no longer "exist" since they are assumed to have been converted into common equity.

Options: An option is a security that allows the owner to buy a share of common stock at some predetermined price. The predetermined price is called the **strike price** (also known as the **exercise price**).

Assume that SampleCo has 20 options issued with a strike price of $15. This means that the owner of one of these options could exercise her option to purchase a share at $15 from the company. If the current market price is $20, she could also take the share that she just purchased at $15 and sell it in the public market for $20, thereby making a $5 profit just by exercising the option. Options are often provided to employees as a form of compensation. Options to purchase shares that are issued with debt securities or preferred stock are called **warrants**.

For SampleCo, the fully diluted shares would be calculated by adding the basic shares to the additional shares that could be issued from the options. To calculate the additional shares from the options using the treasury method, calculate the available cash based on the difference between the strike price and the current stock price and determine the number of additional shares that could be repurchased with this cash.

20 (options exercised)	×	$15 (strike price)	=	$300 (proceeds from sale)
$300 (proceeds)	/	$20 (current price)	=	15 (repurchased shares)
20 (shares from options)	-	15 (repurchased shares)	=	5 (net shares from options)
100 (basic shares)	+	5 (additional shares)	=	105 fully diluted shares

Once you understand the theory behind the treasury stock method, you can apply a shortcut formula to calculate the additional shares. This formula is:

$$\frac{\text{Current stock price} - \text{Strike price}}{\text{Current stock price}} \times \text{Number of options} = \text{Additional shares}$$

For SampleCo, the calculation would be

$$\frac{\$20 - \$15}{20} \times 20 = 5 \text{ additional shares}$$

100 basic shares + 5 shares = 105 diluted shares

If the exercise price of an option is less than the current price, then the option is considered to be **in the money**. If the exercise price of an option is greater than the current price, then the option is considered to be **out of the money**. The SEC and FASB believe that investors are rational and that options will only be exercised if, in fact, they are in the money. If they are out of the money (strike price is greater than market price), then rational holders of the options would not exercise them and, therefore, there will be no additional shares to issue as a result of the options. If, in our example, the current stock price were $10, no rational investor would exercise his option with a $15 strike price. If he did, he would pay $15 for a security that is only worth $10 in the open market. On day one he has already lost $5 per share in value. Thus, if options are out of the money (the strike price is greater than the current price), the options are **anti-dilutive** and no adjustment would be made to the shares outstanding for a fully diluted shares outstanding calculation. Public companies disclose options outstanding in their 10-K SEC filings.

> **Expensing options**
>
> In December 2004, FASB issued a revision to FAS-123 Accounting for Stock-Based Compensation. The newly revised GAAP requirement is that companies are required to expense the value of their options on the income statement based on the fair value of the option as of the grant date. The fair value of the option must be expensed during the time that an employee is required to provide service to the company. The argument is that companies should recognize the value of the options as an expense since the options do have value when companies issue them to employees (else why would companies issue them to employees?). All companies are required to use the Fair Value Method. Historically, companies used the intrinsic valuation method which allowed them to bypass the income statement if the options were out of the money at the time that they were issued, as many were.

Convertible securities: Convertible securities (often called "converts") are debt or preferred securities that can be converted into a predetermined number of shares (either at the company's option or the investor's option). They are hybrid securities that are part debt and part equity and offer the upside of equity with the defensive characteristics (fixed income and liquidation preference over common equity) of debt. A convertible security has a maturity date and, if it is not converted prior to the maturity date, the security falls due for repayment (just like debt).

To calculate the effects of convertible securities for fully diluted shares outstanding using the if-converted method, you must determine if the convertible is in or out of the money. If it is in the money, then you would calculate the number of shares that would be issued if the convert were exercised. The steps to calculate the new shares issued for a convertible bond are as follows (note that the par value for bonds is usually $1,000, but not always, and that the conversion premium is often in the range of 20-40 percent, but not always):

1. Nominal value of bond issue / par value = number of bonds

2. Issue price × (1 + conversion premium) = conversion price

3. Par value / conversion price = conversion ratio

4. Par value / conversion ratio = conversion price

5. Number of bonds × conversion ratio = number of new shares issued

6. If conversion price < stock price then convert is "in the money"

7. If conversion price > stock price then convert is "out of the money"

8. If conversion price is close to the stock price then convert is "at the money"

Let's consider an example in which a company has $350 million 2-percent convertible bonds outstanding. The bonds have a par value of $1,000 and a conversion ratio of 33.333. The current stock price is $40. In this example we are given the conversion ratio and so we must calculate the conversion price. Other times, companies will disclose the conversion premium and you must calculate the conversion price and then the conversion ratio, as described in steps 2 and 3 above.

1. $350,000,000 / $1,000 = 350,000 bonds

2. $1,000 / 33.333 = $30.00 (conversion price)

3. Conversion price of $30 is < current price of $40, so the converts are in the money

4. 350,000 bonds × 33.333 conversion ratio = 11,666,550 new shares

In addition to calculating the new shares that would be issued if the converts were exercised, you must also calculate the after-tax interest expense that you would save if the security were converted from debt into equity (since if it were equity, the company would no longer have to pay the interest expense associated with the convertible when it was considered debt).

Assume the corporate tax rate is 35 percent.

1. $350,000,000 × 0.02 = $7,000,000 (pretax annual interest)
2. $7,000,000 × (1 – 0.35) = $4,550,000 (after-tax annual interest)

Now let's apply this understanding to SampleCo. Assume that $200 of SampleCo's $700 of long-term debt is comprised of 15 convertible bonds. The convertible bonds pay a 5 percent coupon and the conversion ratio is 1.0. We must calculate the effect on net income of eliminating the bonds and the effect on the shares outstanding of converting the bonds.

Recall that SampleCo has net income of $135:

$$\text{Basic EPS} = \frac{\$135}{100} = \$1.35$$

Diluted EPS using the if-converted method:

$$\frac{\$135 + \$6.5^{\text{(note 1)}}}{100 + 15^{\text{(note 2)}}} = \frac{\$141.5}{115} = \$1.23$$

Where:

1. After-tax interest = face value × coupon × (1-tax rate) = ($200 × 0.05 × (1 – 0.35) = $6.5)
2. New shares = convertible bonds × conversion ratio = (15 × 1.0 = 15)

Total Debt and Net Debt

Total debt represents the aggregate amount of debt (and capitalized leases) that a company has outstanding at any given point in time. Cash is subtracted from total debt to determine **net debt**. Ideally, the market value of debt would be calculated and used in performing financial analysis. However, since most companies have debt whose book value is similar to its market value, the book value is often used based on the company's most recent balance sheet. Be careful, however, in using book value of debt if you are dealing with a company whose debt is likely to have a market value significantly less than its book value (for example, this is the case with companies that are in the process of a bankruptcy restructuring).

The total debt for SampleCo for 2004 is $800 (based on $100 of short-term debt and $700 of long-term debt). The net debt for SampleCo is $635 (based on $800 of total debt and $165 of cash).

Why is net debt calculated?

Excess cash is subtracted from total debt to calculate net debt because investors assume that cash on the balance sheet could be used to pay down debt. If the cash were used to pay down debt, then the debt would be reduced by the amount of cash available. This is also why it is assumed that companies with significant levels of cash are vulnerable to a takeover - because a would-be acquiror could buy the company with debt and, once in control of the target, use the company's own cash to pay down the acquisition debt.

Enterprise Value

Enterprise value (also known as **firm value**) represents the value of both the equity (common equity and preferred equity) and the debt of a company, based on the current market value of common equity. The market value of equity is added to the book value of the preferred stock and the net debt to arrive at the enterprise value. Also, minority interest is usually included in enterprise value.

Market value + Net debt + Preferred equity + Minority interest = Enterprise value

Since the market value for SampleCo is $2,100, its net debt is $635, and SampleCo has no preferred stock and no minority interest, the firm value or enterprise value (based on diluted shares outstanding) is $2,735.

SampleCo Enterprise Value

$2,100 + $635 + $0 + $0 = $2,735

Consider SampleCo, which for 2005 has book values of $2,490 in assets, $800 in debt liabilities, $600 in other liabilities and $1,090 in shareholders' equity. The market value of equity for SampleCo is $2,100 (based on a $20 current stock price and 105 diluted shares outstanding). Could Acquiror take over the assets of SampleCo just by paying the market value of equity of $2,100?

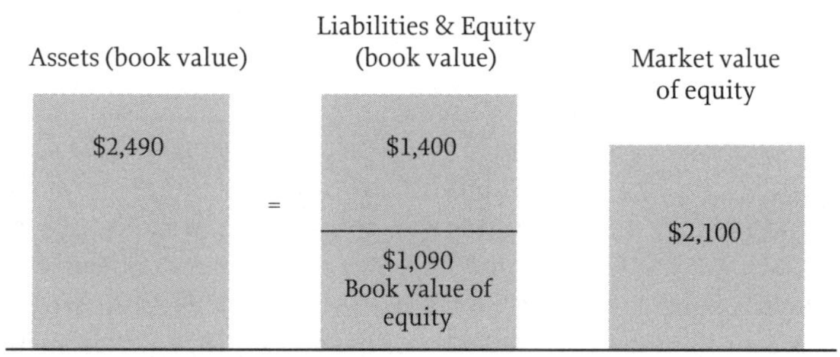

No, because that $2,100 is only enough to buy the equity in the public market. Acquiror still would have to *assume* (take responsibility for) the liabilities before it could assume control of all of the assets. In essence, Acquiror would have to pay $2,900 to acquire the assets of SampleCo (comprised of $2,100 to the equity holders and $800 in assumed debt). Acquiror would also assume $600 of other non-debt liabilities. Note that this simple example does not take into consideration control premiums, which will be covered in more detail in later chapters.

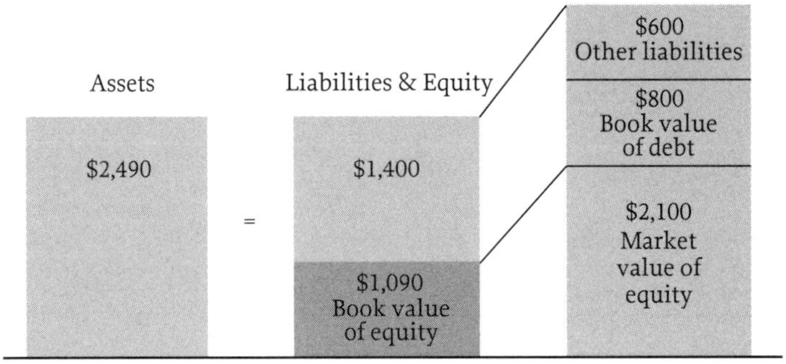

Earnings Per Share

EPS is calculated by taking the net income (also known as earnings) for a period, and dividing it by the number of basic and fully diluted shares for the same period to calculate the basic EPS and fully diluted EPS, respectively. Usually, EPS is quoted for a company's fiscal year (e.g. $1.00 for 2005), although public companies will also report quarterly EPS during the year (e.g. $0.25 for Q1 2005). FAS-128 of GAAP governs the proper accounting for basic and fully diluted EPS. Since EPS is such an important metric for investors, the rules governing the calculation of EPS are very specific. Consult FAS-128 if you have any questions regarding the calculation of EPS.

EPS is calculated based on the **weighted average shares outstanding** for the period in order to account for any shares that were issued or repurchased during the period. For example, assume a company with 200 shares outstanding issued 50 shares on June 30, 2005. Since the company had 200 shares outstanding as of January 1, 2005, then the weighted average number of shares for the year would be 225, and this number would be used to calculate the EPS for 2005.

200	×	50%	=	100 (200 shares weighted for ½ the year)
250	×	50%	=	125 (250 shares weighted for ½ the year)
100	+	125	=	225 (weighted average shares for year-end EPS)

Remember to use weighted average shares

A common error is to calculate EPS based on the shares outstanding at the end of the period, instead of calculating EPS based on the *weighted average* number of shares for the period. This is especially true when calculating the effects of various transactions. Be sure to watch out for this common error. In addition, be sure to watch out for **stock splits** when reviewing a company's shares outstanding. A stock split occurs when a company decides to literally split its shares in two (or whatever ratio it determines) such that the owner of one share becomes the owner of two shares (if there were a 2-for-1 stock split, resulting in twice as many shares outstanding after the stock split).

What is quality of earnings?

Investors are particularly interested in the **quality of earnings.** In other words, is the earnings per share sustainable (high quality of earnings) or is it based on non-recurring or one-time items (low quality of earnings)? Investors take special care to determine whether earnings include **non-recurring items** (items that are special and are not part of the company's regular course of business), which will not or cannot be replicated in future years. In general, non-recurring items would be excluded from the earnings or EPS number an investor uses to make investment decisions. Investors are also especially interested in how fast a company's EPS will grow over time. This metric is referred to as the company's growth rate and generally represents the compound annual EPS growth over a five-year period. For example, a company with Year 1 EPS of $1 and a 10 percent growth rate would be expected to have Year 2 EPS of $1.10, Year 3 EPS of $1.21, Year 4 EPS of $1.33 and Year 5 EPS of $1.46, with each year's EPS being 10 percent greater than the year before.

Public companies will generally provide investors and equity analysts some guidance as to what they believe their EPS will be for a given year. In certain cases, they might even provide guidance for the following year's earnings. Investors will factor this guidance into their investment decision making and are especially critical of situations in which a company's actual earnings are materially different from the company's previously provided guidance, since investment decisions earlier in the year were predicated on those numbers.

Key Multiples and Metrics

Price-to-earnings multiple or P/E: a P/E multiple represents the market value of a stock relative to its EPS. It is the most commonly used multiples-based valuation metric. It is calculated by dividing the current stock price by the annual earnings per share, based on diluted shares outstanding.

$$\frac{\text{Market price}}{\text{EPS}} = \text{P/E}$$

A P/E multiple is usually calculated based both on the **LTM EPS** (the EPS for the latest twelve months) and on a **forward** basis (EPS for the upcoming fiscal year) in order to capture any disparity between the last year's and the coming years' performance.

For example, if the LTM EPS for a company is $2.00 and the current year's EPS (also referred to as FY1 EPS) is projected to be $2.25 and the current stock price for the company is $40, then the LTM P/E = 20x ($40 / $2) and the FY1 P/E = 17.8x ($40 / $2.25).

For SampleCo, the P/E based on 2004 EPS would be calculated as follows:

$$\frac{\$20.00}{\$1.29} = 15.5\text{x}$$

Since the P/E multiple is calculated based on the current stock price and the current stock price represents the market's perception of the company and its future growth prospects, the P/E of a company is generally correlated to the growth prospects of the company. As such, companies with higher growth rates tend to trade at higher P/E multiples and companies with lower growth rates tend to trade at lower multiple levels.

If SampleCo has a five year growth rate of 10 percent, that would imply an EPS in FY2 (forward year 2) of $1.42 ($1.29 × (1+0.10) = $1.42) and a FY2 P/E of 14.1x ($20 / $1.42 = 14.1x).

Book value of equity: The book value of equity is the accounting value of the shareholders' equity and it is often used to establish the base level value of equity for a company. Since it is based on a company's accounting records, it is a historical-based method of considering value as opposed to other methods which are based on future earnings power. In general, the book value of equity is stated for the common equity and excludes preferred stock. The challenge with using book value of equity as a metric is that it does not take into account the market value of the equity as reflected by the stock price.

For SampleCo, the book value of equity at the end of 2005 is $1,090. As with most balance sheet-related items, it is common to refer to the most current balance sheet information.

Price-to-book ratio or price/book multiple: Price/book (also known as market/book) is another commonly used multiple. It represents the market value of equity as a multiple of the book value of equity. Most companies have a market value which is higher than their book value. The price/book multiple is calculated by dividing the market value of equity by the book value of equity.

$$\frac{\text{Market value of equity}}{\text{Book value of equity}} = \text{Price/book multiple}$$

For SampleCo, the price/book ratio would be calculated as follows:

$$\frac{\$2{,}100}{\$1{,}090} = 1.9\text{x}$$

Do you include or exclude preferred equity?

In general, the book value of equity refers to a company's common equity and, therefore, preferred equity should be excluded when calculating a price/book multiple. Be careful, however, when reviewing a company's financial statements since companies often will include preferred equity as part of their summary equity section.

Enterprise value to EBITDA: Like P/E, the EV/EBITDA multiple is commonly used to measure a company's relative valuation. Unlike P/E, however, which is related to the market value of equity of a company, an enterprise value to EBITDA multiple is related to the enterprise value (or the firm value). It is calculated by dividing the enterprise value by EBITDA.

$$\frac{\text{Enterprise value}}{\text{EBITDA}} = \text{EV/EBITDA multiple}$$

For SampleCo, the EV/EBITDA multiple would be:

$$\frac{\$2,735}{\$500} = 5.5x$$

Enterprise value vs. equity value multiples

When calculating multiples, be careful to differentiate between when to use enterprise value and when to use equity value in the numerator. In general, the numerator should match the denominator. For example, EBITDA is a pre-interest or pre-debt number, meaning it represents a value to the firm and not just to the equity holders. That is why enterprise value is used with EBITDA when calculating multiples. Net income, on the other hand, is an after interest or after debt number. It is a value that flows only to equity holders, which is why P/E is calculated using equity value and not firm value.

Return on equity (ROE): Return on equity represents the earnings power of the shareholders' equity and is calculated by dividing the earnings by the shareholders' equity. It is stated as a percentage:

$$\frac{\text{Earnings or net income}}{\text{Book value of equity}} = \text{Return on equity (ROE)}$$

ROE is often used as a measure of financial performance. Since earnings is an after-interest number, ROE is considered a metric for leveraged returns (or returns after accounting for debt). Similar calculations such as return on invested capital (ROIC) which is earnings divided by the sum of debt plus equity, and return on assets (ROA) which is earnings divided by assets, are used in conjunction with ROE. Since these other metrics relate to the assets of a company (as opposed to just the equity component), these are considered metrics for unleveraged returns.

For SampleCo, the ROE would be calculated as follows:

$$\frac{\$135}{\$1,090} = 12.4\%$$

Dividend per share (DPS): Dividends per share represent the amount of dividends paid per each share outstanding. They are calculated by dividing the total amount of dividends by the number of basic shares outstanding.

$$\frac{\text{Dividends}}{\text{Shares outstanding}} = \text{Dividends per share (DPS)}$$

The dividend per share for SampleCo would be calculated as follows:

$$\frac{\$50}{100} = \$0.50$$

To calculate the indicated DPS, take the most recently announced quarterly dividend and multiply it by four (note that this is prospective for the coming year).

Dividend yield: Dividend yield represents the amount of dividends received per share of stock owned relative to the current stock price. It is calculated by dividing the DPS by the current stock price and is stated as a percentage. Most commonly, people use the indicated DPS.

$$\frac{\text{DPS}}{\text{Current stock price}} = \text{Dividend yield}$$

Dividend yield is an important number since it provides investors with a proxy for how much cash flow they will receive each year for holding the stock relative to the investment price. Dividend yield is often considered in combination with a company's growth rate to calculate the **total return** for a company (dividend yield plus earnings growth), since earnings growth is a proxy for stock price appreciation. Generally, slower growth companies have higher dividend yields (compared to higher growth companies) in order to compensate for their slower growth and therefore slower stock price appreciation. Some companies, especially higher growth companies, do not pay dividends.

For SampleCo, its dividend yield would be calculated as follows:

$$\frac{\$0.50}{\$20.00} = 2.5\%$$

Assuming a 10% EPS growth rate, total return would be calculated as follows:

$$2.5\% \text{ (dividend yield)} + 10.0\% \text{ (EPS growth)} = 12.5\% \text{ (total return)}$$

Payout ratio: the payout ratio represents a company's dividends per share as a percentage of earnings. It is calculated by dividing DPS by EPS.

Higher growth companies tend to have lower payout ratios because they are reinvesting cash back into the business. More mature, slower growth companies tend to have higher payout ratios since – with fewer calls on the cash to grow the business – they return more of the cash to shareholders.

The payout ratio for SampleCo is calculated as follows:

Based on basic shares

$$\frac{\$0.50}{\$1.35} = 37\%$$

Based on diluted shares

$$\frac{\$0.50}{\$1.29} = 39\%$$

Strategic Transactions

CHAPTER 4

Better one safe way than a hundred on which you cannot reckon.

Aesop

Strategic Planning

Every company, big or small, should have a strategic vision or strategic plan. One of the primary goals of that strategic plan should be to:

> Improve, maintain, and/or accelerate the market leadership, profitability, and growth trajectory of a company, thereby leading to enhanced shareholder value.

A strategic plan goes beyond geographic expansion plans and new product ideas. It also goes beyond the financial projections for the company. Rather, a company's strategic plan is a roadmap addressing a fundamental question: What type of company does it aspire to be and how does the company expect to achieve that goal in the next five to ten years.

A strategic plan must balance the desires to grow shareholder value, and thereby appeal to equity investors, with a complementary financing strategy that appeals to debt investors as well. A **strategic transaction** is any action that helps implement a company's strategic plan. That action can be on a small scale (such as the sale of one manufacturing plant) or a large scale (such as a corporate merger with another company). In addition to building, buying and/or selling assets, a strategic action can be related to financing, such as the decision to implement an aggressive stock buyback program or recapitalization. The value of a strategic transaction is measured by many metrics, the most important of which is a company's stock price.

The product of any strategic planning exercise is usually a "base case" financial forecast for the next five to ten years. The base case forecast should incorporate the most likely operating and financial strategy. Alternative scenarios as well as upside and downside cases are usually prepared as sensitivities to the base case. The strategic plan is usually updated once a year after a company-wide effort to capture the most likely operating and financial scenario. Throughout the year, the base case strategic plan and financial forecast are used as planning tools.

Strategic and Financing Transactions

A company can maximize shareholder value using both strategic transactions and financing transactions. Strategic transactions are further divided into two main categories: (1) transactions to enhance or grow a business, such as a strategic acquisition, and (2) transactions to clarify a business, such as the sale of a non-core division. Financing transactions are also further divided into two main categories: (1) transactions to fund growth, such as a major equity offering and (2) recapitalization transactions, such as a share buyback program.

Figure 4.1 – Maximizing Shareholder Value

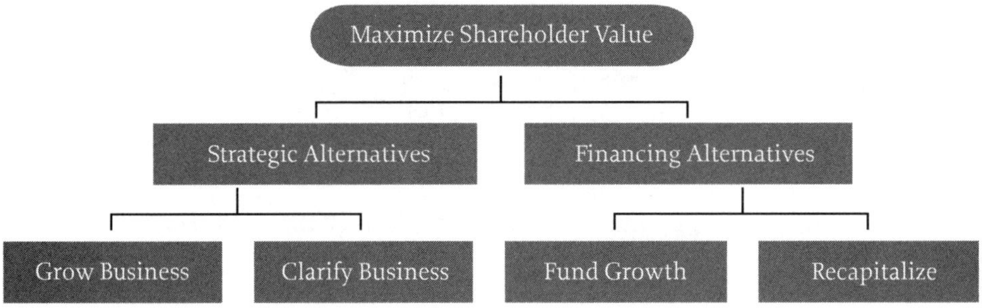

Specific examples of transactions to grow, clarify, fund and recapitalize a business are provided in Figure 4.2. To maximize flexibility, many companies consider more than one strategic option at any given time. When a company pursues a **dual path**, it prepares for two or even three options and follows each path as if it were going to be executed. This way, the company is prepared to execute a number of strategic options and can decide on one or two depending on market conditions as the time for a final decision approaches. Because many companies pursue dual path processes, it is important that advisors be well versed in all of the strategic options shown in Figure 4.2.

Figure 4.2 – Strategic Options to Maximize Shareholder Value

Strategic Alternatives	Financing Alternatives
GROW BUSINESS Organic growth Invest in research and development Strategic alliance Joint venture Acquire assets Strategic merger	FUND GROWTH Private placement Issue bank debt Issue public debt Issue public equity Issue private equity Manage liabilities
CLARIFY BUSINESS Sale of major subsidiary Spin-off or split-off of major subsidiary IPO of major subsidiary Tracking stock Sale of company for cash	RECAPITALIZE Special dividend Change dividend policy Large share repurchase Ongoing share repurchase Major recapitalization Leveraged buyout

Buy vs. Build

To grow a business, a company's management must decide between buying and building. Buying allows a company to satisfy certain strategic goals in a shorter period of time, whereas building allows a company to develop products or services exactly as it wants. Buying and building are not mutually exclusive, and many successful companies are both aggressive buyers *and* builders. Some of the advantages of building and buying are described below.

Advantages of building

- Full control over how the work is performed, how the products are made and how customers are treated
- No need to pay a control premium for another company
- Pride of ownership (e.g., Apple)
- Protection of proprietary technology (e.g., The Coca-Cola Company, Procter & Gamble)
- Maintenance of corporate culture, as desired (e.g., IBM)

Advantages of buying

- Opportunity to enter a new geographic or product market immediately (e.g., Deutsche Telekom/Voicestream to create T-Mobile USA)
- Acquisition of an irreplaceable asset (e.g., a patent or market-leading brand)
- Elimination of a competitor
- Reduction or elimination of execution risk inherent in trying to build the business from scratch
- Acquisition of an existing distribution network (e.g., Federal Express/Kinko's)

Strategic Rationale

A transaction should only be considered if it makes good strategic sense for a company. Buying a non-strategic company on the cheap (just because one can profit from the deal) is the business of leveraged buyout and private equity companies; it is not the business of a strategic player. The first litmus test of any transaction for a company should always be: What is the strategic rationale of the transaction?

Examples of strategic rationales are listed below. Either independently or in conjunction with others, each might provide a good reason for undertaking a transaction. They are organized into one of three categories: (1) revenue growth, (2) cost savings and margin improvement, and (3) technology enhancements. In addition to these strategic rationales, you may be able to think of others.

1. Revenue growth

- Gain access to a faster growing customer base or product market
- Benefit from cross-marketing opportunities among various products and/or markets
- Better manage and utilize strategic assets
- Improve penetration in core markets
- Strengthen brand portfolio with a complementary but growing business
- Elevate a business or brand to a regional, national or global scale by leveraging customer or distribution channels

2. Cost savings and margin improvement

- Improve manufacturing and operating margins (achieve economies of scale)
- Reduce risk by reducing volatility of earnings and cash flow
- Leverage purchasing power
- Leverage sales force and/or distribution infrastructure
- Reduce work force while maintaining efficiency

- Enhance sourcing capabilities
- Fill an operating gap

3. Technology Enhancements

- Gain access to proprietary intellectual property or technology
- Complement and leverage core skills and technology
- Combine technology and R&D functions and reduce operating costs
- Increase flexibility to accommodate product innovation (may also produce revenue benefits)

Increasing Shareholder Value

If a transaction makes strategic sense for a company, then the next important question is: *Does the transaction increase shareholder value?* Value creation for a public company is measured most transparently by the company's stock price. Ultimately, however, the most important consideration is whether a transaction increases the intrinsic value of a company (even if not immediately reflected in share price appreciation).

To measure whether a transaction increases shareholder value, the financial impact of a transaction must be considered. Attractive financial impact occurs if the transaction:

- Provides earnings per share accretion and/or accelerates EPS growth
- Diversifies credit risk and reduces cost of capital
- Achieves strategic objectives and financial targets more rapidly
- Increases financial return metrics such as return on equity (ROE) or return on invested capital (ROIC)
- Provides for trading multiple expansion

The main factor that drives the value of a company's stock price is growth, of both earnings per share and cash flow per share. For start-up companies, revenues or sales growth is a key indicator since many start-ups do not have earnings and may even have negative cash flows. Investors look for a return on their investment, and earnings and cash flow appreciation are proxies for shareholder return. The faster a company grows, the faster value and/or capital may be returned to shareholders in the form of stock price growth or dividends.

If a company's stock price is a measure of a company's ability (or inability) to increase shareholder value, and if stock prices are driven by an investor's expectation of growth, then how do strategic transactions play into the quest for value creation?

Two variables factor into a company's stock price (when using a multiples-based valuation method). The first is the company's earnings and/or cash flow, and the second is the valuation multiple that investors use to price the stock. Ideally, strategic transactions will affect both of these variables in the stock price equation. An important consideration in determining which strategic transaction(s) to undertake, therefore, is to identify on a per share basis which transaction(s) will increase the earnings and cash flow side of the equation and/or the company's valuation multiple.

The impact of a transaction on earnings per share and cash flow per share depends on a number of items, including: (1) the price paid for Target, (2) the consideration used (e.g., stock vs. cash), (3) the accounting treatment of the transaction and (4) any synergies generated from the transaction. **Accretion/dilution analysis** considers all of these factors to calculate a pro forma EPS for the transaction. Accretion/dilution is a fancy way of saying "Does a transaction increase (accrete) or decrease (dilute) the earnings per share (or other financial metric) of acquiror?"

Earnings and cash flow per share are just one part of the valuation calculation. If a strategic transaction causes a company to be valued in the market at a higher multiple than its current multiple, then the stock price will increase even if no incremental earnings or cash flow are generated. This in itself is value enhancing. The act of a valuation multiple increasing is called **multiple expansion** and the act of a valuation multiple decreasing is called **multiple compression**.

For example, if a company's EPS is $1.50 and its current P/E multiple is 15x, the implied stock price is $22.50.

$$\$1.50 \text{ EPS} \times 15\text{x P/E multiple} = \$22.50 \text{ stock price}$$

However, assume the company undertakes a transaction that is consistent with its strategic plan and enhances the company's future growth prospects (but does not actually increase EPS in the current year). The transaction also minimizes the company's financial risk and credit risk, and the transaction repositions the company to become the market leader in its sector. All of these things would be viewed positively by the market and the market might subsequently "re-rate" the company with a higher P/E multiple. Let's say the market re-rates the company at a 17x P/E multiple. Even with the same EPS of $1.50, the new stock price would be $25.50, or 13 percent greater than the status quo stock price of $22.50.

$$\$1.50 \text{ EPS} \times 17\text{x P/E multiple} = \$25.50 \text{ stock price}$$

$$(\$25.50 / \$22.50) - 1 = 13.3\% \text{ increase}$$

It should be noted that price to earnings is not the only valuation multiple that investors care about. Enterprise value to EBITDA (EV/EBITDA) and price to cash flow (P/CF) are also important, among others. Valuation multiples are described in Comparable Company Analysis and Comparable Transaction Analysis. (Ch.9,10)

It is never easy to determine with certainty the multiple at which a company will trade in the future. A company's trading multiple will be driven not only by its own performance but also by the performance of its peers, the state of the overall market and interest rates, and the market liquidity of the stock, among other factors. However, certain transactions will be viewed positively by investors if the transaction is consistent with the company's strategic plan and will be viewed even more positively if the transaction also provides an attractive financial impact. Conversely, a transaction that is not consistent with a company's strategic plan, even if the transaction provides an attractive financial impact, is likely to be viewed negatively by the financial community and investors. This might result in the company's trading multiple being re-rated down (multiple compression), so that even with a higher EPS from the proposed transaction, the Acquiror's stock price might be lower.

$$\$2.00 \text{ EPS} \times 10\text{x P/E multiple} = \$20.00 \text{ stock price}$$
$$(\$20.00 / \$22.50) - 1 = 11.1\% \text{ decrease}$$

As Table 4.3 shows, a benefit to *either* Acquiror's EPS *or* its P/E multiple leads to an increase in stock price (or shareholder value) at a percentage rate equal to the change in *either* EPS or P/E. Accretion/dilution analysis should be performed for any contemplated transaction because, as shown in Table 4.3, it is a proxy for share price accretion or dilution on a pro forma basis (post-transaction).

Table 4.3 – EPS and P/E Multiple Impact on Stock Price

Scenario: Status quo

Earnings per share (EPS)	$1.50
P/E multiple	12.0x
Status quo stock price [1]	$18.00

Scenario: Earnings change

Note what happens to the implied value per share for the company when its earnings per share increases or decreases by 10 percent but the P/E multiple does not change

Percentage change in EPS	10%	(10%)
Earnings per share (EPS) [2]	$1.65	$1.35
P/E multiple	12.0x	12.0x
Implied stock price	$19.80	$16.20
Percentage change in stock price from status quo [3]	10%	(10%)

Scenario: Multiple change

Note what happens to the implied value per share for the company when its earnings per share does not change but the P/E multiple increases or decreases by 10 percent

Percentage change in P/E multiple	10%	(10%)
Earnings per share (EPS)	$1.50	$1.50
P/E multiple [4]	13.2x	10.8x
Implied stock price	$19.80	$16.20
Percentage change in stock price from status quo [3]	10%	(10%)

Scenario: Earnings change and multiple change

Note what happens to the implied value per share for the company when its earnings per share and the P/E multiple both increase or decrease by 10 percent

Percentage change in EPS and P/E multiple	10%	(10%)
Earnings per share (EPS)	$1.65	$1.35
P/E multiple	13.2x	10.8x
Implied stock price	$21.78	$14.58
Percentage change in stock price from status quo	21%	(19%)

[1] EPS × P/E multiple = stock price

[2] $1.50 × (1 + percentage change)

[3] (Implied stock price / status quo stock price) - 1

[4] 12 × (1 + percentage change)

Table 4.3 continued

Summary table	Share price	% change from status quo
Status quo	$18.00	0%
EPS change only (+ 10%)	$19.80	10%
EPS change only (- 10%)	$16.20	(10%)
Multiple change only (+10%)	$19.80	10%
Multiple change only (-10%)	$16.20	(10%)
EPS change (+10%) and multiple change (+10%)	$21.78	21%
EPS change (-10%) and multiple change (-10%)	$14.58	(19%)

Synergies

Synergies are either reduced costs or increased revenues created by a merger or other strategic transactions. **Cost synergies** are efficiencies created through improved operating practices, the elimination of redundant functions, and greater economies of scale. For example, if two companies with separate call centers merge and eliminate one of the call centers without affecting productivity or customer service, this is a cost synergy since the two companies can achieve the same level of revenues with reduced costs, thereby improving margins. **Revenue synergies** result from the ability to generate greater revenues through the merger of two companies, such as Acquiror selling its products through Target's distribution network.

Because synergies are subject to uncertainty, it is often informative to analyze synergies as a range of values as opposed to targeting one particular value or estimate for synergies.

Common categories of synergies include:

Cost Synergies

- Consolidated purchasing
- Selling, general and administrative (SG&A) reductions (e.g., back office, marketing, corporate administration)
- Manufacturing and/or plant consolidation
- Distribution benefits
- Better management
- Lower cost of capital
- Synergies from filing consolidated taxes
- Removal of duplicate public company administrative costs

Revenue Synergies

- Access to partner's customer or geographic markets (if different)
- Cross-selling to partner's customers
- Improved market penetration

Synergies are a critical component of the value creation in a strategic transaction because, in theory at least, in an efficient market there is no value creation without synergies. An example may help clarify this concept.

Let us assume that a company is available for sale. Acquiror values Target at $500 million and purchases it for $500 million in cash. Acquiror has paid "fair value" for Target meaning Acquiror purchased an asset worth $500 million by paying $500 million in cash. Has Acquiror created *value* for itself with this transaction? No. Acquiror added a $500 million asset to its business portfolio, it is true, but it *paid* fair market value for it. Acquiror has not created any value since the transaction has a net present value of zero (NPV=0). That is, there is no additional value created after the purchase price of $500 million has been paid to the Sellers.

Let us now change our assumptions slightly. It turns out that this company for which Acquiror paid $500 million has a contiguous distribution area to its own, and Target has underutilized capacity in its sales and distribution system. In addition, Acquiror already has a top-notch management and corporate development team that can assume a number of new responsibilities in addition to their current responsibilities. As a result, Acquiror is able to eliminate the Sales, Distribution, Executive, and Corporate Development functions of Target. All told, those services cost about $20 million annually, which will now flow to Acquiror's bottom line (to earnings). This $20 million of annual cost savings are the pretax synergies created from the transaction. Ultimately, if Acquiror pays "fair value" for Target, then the value creation for Acquiror is the capitalized "value" of all future synergies arising out of the transaction which Acquiror does not give to Target in the form of an increased purchase price.

"Paying away" synergies

If Acquiror paid more than "fair value" for Target on a stand-alone basis, then Acquiror actually paid away to Target some of the value of the transaction synergies rather than keeping the value of those synergies for itself. If there are competing bidders for Target, paying away some of the synergies might be necessary in order to win control of Target. It is important, however, for bidders not to pay Target *more than* fair value plus synergies because, if this is done, the transaction will have a net present value of less than zero (meaning it will be a value-losing

"Paying away" synergies continued

transaction from day one). In Figure 4.4, notice that the maximum price Acquiror should pay for Target is $620 million, which is the sum of the stand-alone value for Target of $500 million plus the value of the synergies of $120 million. If Acquiror pays more than $620 million, Acquiror will pay more than the combined value of (1) Target's value on a stand-alone basis and (2) the capitalized value of the synergies. If Acquiror pays $500 million for Target, Acquiror will keep the $120 million of synergy value for itself. If Acquiror pays Target somewhere between $500 and $620 million, then Acquiror will pay away some of the synergy value and keep some of the synergy value for itself.

Figure 4.4 – Components of Value

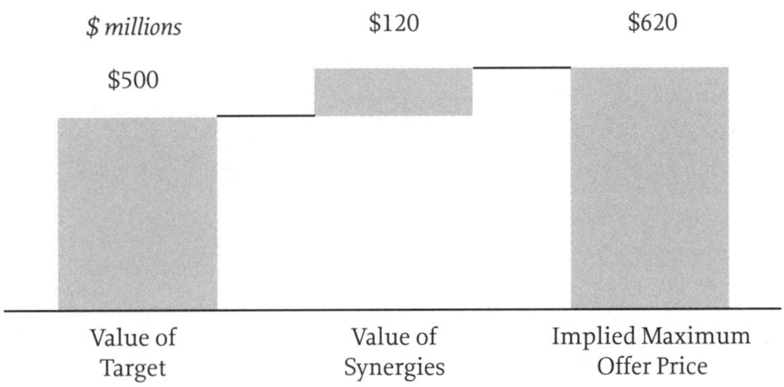

How is the $120 million of synergy value actually calculated? By virtue of Acquiror's ability to absorb this new company without needing to absorb much of its cost structure, it will have $20 million of cost synergies per year that Target does not have on a stand-alone basis. Assuming Acquiror's current P/E multiple is 10x and a 40 percent tax rate, this $20 million of annual savings should generate $120 million of additional value (further assuming P/E is the appropriate method to value this company). The calculation of the $120 million is shown in the following table.

Table 4.5 - Capitalizing Synergies

Savings	=	\$20 million pretax synergies each year
Tax rate	=	40%
After-tax savings	=	\$20 × (1 – 0.4) = \$12 million each year
Incremental earnings	=	\$12 million each year
P/E multiple	=	10x
Capitalized synergies	=	Incremental earnings × P/E multiple
		\$12mm × 10 = \$120 million

Why is P/E such a commonly used metric?

Many people wonder why P/E is such a commonly used valuation metric. Refer to the example above in which a merger generates an additional \$20 million of pretax earnings and, as a result, implies additional value of \$120 million using a P/E multiple method of valuation. Consider this incremental savings of \$20 million per year, or \$12 million after-tax per year, in the context of basic corporate finance. What does this stream of cash flows look like? Since these are incremental earnings that will continue forever (or as long as the company is in existence), we can think of this as a perpetuity in which the annual after-tax cash flow is \$12 million. The way to value a perpetuity is to apply the formula:

$$PV_{perpetuity} = \frac{\text{Cash Flow}}{\text{Discount rate}} = \frac{CF}{r}$$

In this example, CF = \$12 million and the present value = \$120 million. Applying the perpetuity formula, you can calculate an *implied* discount rate of 10 percent.

$$\frac{\text{CF (\$12 million)}}{\text{r (unknown)}} = \text{PV (\$120 million)}$$

To solve for *r*, divide \$12 by \$120

\$12 / \$120 = 0.10, or 10 percent

The implied discount rate in this example is 10 percent, and the inverse of 10 percent is 10 (1 / 0.10 = 10), which is the P/E multiple. Therefore, the inverse of the P/E multiple is the implied discount rate using the perpetuity method of valuation.

Why is P/E such a commonly used metric? continued

Investors use P/E multiples for valuation purposes because it is a proxy for a perpetuity discount rate and therefore is a shortcut cash flow based method of valuation. If the inverse of the P/E multiple represents a perpetuity discount rate, then multiplying earnings per share by a P/E multiple is effectively using the perpetuity method of valuation.

EPS	×	P/E multiple	= Present Value
$12 million	×	10x	= $120 million
Which is the same as			
EPS	/	Discount rate	= Present Value
EPS	/	Inverse of P/E multiple	= Present Value
$12 million	/	10% or 0.10	= $120 million

Since P/E is a method to value the stock or equity of a company, the assumption is that earnings is a proxy for cash flow to equity holders and the inverse of the P/E multiple is equal to the discount rate for an equity holder.

Or, if you consider a growing perpetuity formula in which you divide the cash flow by the result of *(r - g)*, where *r* is the discount rate and *g* is the perpetual growth rate, the inverse of the P/E multiple is equal to the difference between *r* and *g*. In the example above, we might assume that the long-term growth rate (g) is 1 percent or 0.01 and therefore the discount rate (r) is 11 percent or 0.11, so that the implied *(r - g)* is equal to 0.10 (0.11 - 0.01 = 0.10).

Valuation using P/E multiples is often employed by investors due to its simplicity. It is a short cut method of cash flow valuation to equity holders using the perpetuity method or growing perpetuity method of valuation. And it is simple to use because all that is needed to perform the present value calculation is EPS and a P/E multiple.

It is important to remember that while many synergies are positive, there are usually some offsetting costs as well (sometimes referred to as "negative synergies" or "costs to achieve synergies"). Thus, synergies analysis must include the costs to achieve the projected synergies (such as severance expenses for headcount reduction; facility shutdown costs for plant closures, including environmental cleanup; relocation expense; etc.).

Synergies analysis must also include all negative synergies, such as SG&A to replace services formerly provided by a parent company (legal, treasury, audit, etc.), lost sales at either Acquiror or Target due to customer or product cannibalization, transition issues, the potential for disruption to Target's and/or Acquiror's business, and the renegotiation of contracts with change-of-control provisions.

When a transaction is announced, investors will generally give more credit to forecasted cost synergies than to forecasted revenue synergies. The reason is because cost synergies are more easily quantifiable and because they are considered more likely to be achieved.

For example, if a redundant production facility is to be closed as part of a transaction, and that plant has 500 employees with a fully loaded cost per employee (cost of salary plus all benefits) of $67,000 per year, that is $33.5 million of annual pretax cost savings (500 × $67,000 = $33.5 million). This $33.5 million is an identifiable number because the company knows how many employees work at the plant and it also knows what it pays to each of these 500 employees. Because these items are known, there is a high likelihood that the annual pretax cost savings will be close to $33.5 million once the 500 employees are laid off.

A challenging aspect of revenue synergies that is sometimes overlooked is the impact on operating margins from the increased sales. For example, assume a merger of two beverage companies increases output from 75 million bottles to 95 million bottles on a bottling line with a capacity of 100 million bottles. This occurs because Acquiror operates in different markets than Target and therefore has the ability to sell 20 million more bottles than Target did on a stand-alone basis. Because this increase of 20 million bottles is on an existing production line, there is no increase in fixed costs. In the following table notice how the increase from 75 million bottles to 95 million bottles increases the gross margin percentage from 78 percent to 81 percent by reducing the production cost per bottle.

Table 4.6 – Revenue Synergies and Gross Margin Increase

Assumptions		
Fixed operating costs	$9,000,000	
Variable costs (per bottle)	$0.10	
Selling price per bottle	$1.00	
Maximum bottle capacity per plant	100,000,000	
	Existing	**Post-transaction**
Bottles produced	75,000,000	95,000,000
Fixed operating cost	$9,000,000	$9,000,000
Variable cost at 10 cents per bottle	7,500,000	9,500,000
Total costs	$16,500,000	$18,500,000
Cost per bottle (total costs / bottles produced)	$0.22	$0.19
Capacity utilization (bottles produced / maximum capacity)	75%	95%
Selling price per bottle	$1.00	$1.00
Gross margin per bottle (selling price – cost per bottle)	$0.78	$0.81
Gross margin percentage (gross margin / selling price)	**78%**	**81%**

Now assume Acquiror can sell 40 million more bottles (as opposed to 20 million more bottles) so that post-transaction 115,000,000 bottles would be produced. Since the existing production line can only handle 25 million more bottles (because its capacity is 100 million and it currently produces 75 million), changes would be required in order to handle the additional capacity. In order to sell the additional 40 million bottles, let's assume the company adds an additional production line to the factory. The new production line would increase fixed costs by another $9 million but would add another 100 million of bottling capacity, increasing the total capacity to 200 million. Notice in this situation that, even though the number of bottles sold increases by 40 million, the gross margin decreases from 78 percent to 74 percent.

Table 4.7 – Revenue Synergies and Gross Margin Decrease

Assumptions		
Fixed operating costs ($9,000,000 × 2)	$18,000,000	
Variable costs (per bottle)	$0.10	
Selling price per bottle	$1.00	
Maximum bottle capacity per plant	200,000,000	
	Existing	**Post-transaction**
Bottles produced	75,000,000	115,000,000
Fixed cost	$9,000,000	$18,000,000
Variable cost at 10 cents per bottle	7,500,000	11,500,000
Total costs	$16,500,000	$29,500,000
Cost per bottle (total costs / bottles produced)	$0.22	$0.26
Capacity utilization (bottles produced / maximum capacity)	75%	58%
Selling price per bottle	$1.00	$1.00
Gross margin per bottle (selling price – cost per bottle)	$0.78	$0.74
Gross margin percentage (gross margin / selling price)	**78%**	**74%**

This type of change in gross margin is very important to consider and incorporate into a model for valuation analysis or financial impact analysis. Thus when analyzing a potential transaction and considering revenue synergies, be sure to understand the impact of the additional revenues on the Target's operating cost structure and margins.

Introduction to M&A

CHAPTER 5

Caveat Emptor

Latin proverb meaning "Let the buyer beware"

Strategic transactions can range from the formation of a strategic alliance between two local companies to a multi-billion dollar cross-border merger. Because the scope of possible transactions is vast, an M&A banker must be well-versed in a wide range of topics and types of analyses. The world of M&A can be daunting regardless of one's professional background. This chapter is designed as an introduction to many of the basic concepts one would be exposed to while working on an M&A assignment. The chapter begins with an overview of types of strategic transactions, and then goes into some detail on important M&A topics such as buy-side and sell-side processes, types of auction or sales processes, and an overview of a typical deal process. Some of these topics are further described in later chapters.

Types of Strategic Transactions

There are five major types of strategic transactions: (1) joint ventures and strategic alliances; (2) divestitures and acquisitions; (3) sale of a company and mergers; (4) recapitalizations; and (5) restructurings. An overview of each appears below.

Joint Ventures and Strategic Alliances - *A partnership between two companies*

- Joint ventures (JVs) and strategic alliances between two companies can take numerous forms. Both companies are actively involved in negotiating the terms of the agreement.

- Most JVs involve the creation of a new entity (often a partnership or corporation) owned equally by the two companies.

- Each party contributes cash and/or assets to the joint venture to equalize the ownership (meaning money is contributed by a party to increase its pro rata share of the joint venture if the assets it contributes do not equal fifty percent of the value of the JV). Usually, future capital requirements are shared equally between the two owners, or pro rata according to the ownership split.

- JVs often have an independent management committee and/or board of directors, which manages and makes decisions on behalf of the JV.

- JVs are a classic tool to put assets and/or a business to work with another strategic partner where, together, the two parties can create more value from the assets than either partner would on a stand-alone basis *without* either giving up complete operating control or upside (as would be the case in a sale context, which is often the alternative with underutilized assets).

- Terminating a JV can be complex and therefore it is critical that care be used when negotiating the termination provisions, which should be negotiated at the outset.

- Joint ventures are further described in Corporate Restructurings. (Ch.22)

Divestitures – *The disposition or sale of an asset, division, or subsidiary by a parent company*

- A divestiture is the sale of essentially anything on the asset side of the balance sheet, including the sale of individual physical assets, asset bundles, a division, subsidiary stock, a minority interest, real estate, licensing rights, an R&D pipeline, patents or trademarks. A **division** is a functional unit of a company whereas a **subsidiary** is a separate legal entity (a corporation with its own stock) that is wholly owned or majority owned by a parent company. A parent company owns the assets of the division but the division has no stock. A subsidiary is essentially a company within a company whereas a division is an organized set of assets within a company.

- The way in which potential buyers are solicited can take various forms (e.g., public auction, limited auction, negotiated sale, etc.).

- Subsidiary divestitures are further described in Corporate Restructurings. (Ch.22)

Acquisitions – *The purchase of an asset, division, or subsidiary from another company*

- Numerous types of buyers exist, including **strategic buyers** (companies in the same or related industry) and **financial buyers** (including private equity and venture capital firms).

- The form of payment (e.g., cash, stock) by Acquiror in an acquisition is an important consideration. Acquisition Currency is described in Ch.15 and Ch.16.

- Acquisitions are further described in Accretion/Dilution Analysis, Stock Deals, and Deal Mechanics. (Ch.14,15,20)

Sale of Company and Mergers - *The combination of two independent companies*

- A sale of a company can be structured as a merger or a direct acquisition of target stock from target shareholders. Transaction structures are described in Deal Mechanics. (Ch.20)

- A corporate merger usually involves the combination of a target company (Target) with an acquiring company (Acquiror).

- Mergers require a shareholder vote. A combination, however, can also be structured as a tender offer in which a vote is not required if a minimum percentage of Target shares are tendered (i.e., the selling shareholders "vote" by tendering their shares into the tender offer). Tender offers are described in Deal Mechanics. (Ch.20)

- A merger of equals (MOE) occurs when two companies of similar size and value combine in a merger with no clear change of control taking place. In an MOE, there is no real Acquiror or Target and there are meaningful shared roles, governance, and responsibilities in the new company. MOEs are described in Merger of Equals. (Ch.18)

- Legal requirements exist with respect to fiduciary responsibilities of the board in a merger that is in substance a sale of control as compared to a stock merger which is not technically a sale of control. Fiduciary obligations are described in The Deal Team. (Ch.19)

- Form of consideration (cash, stock, cash/stock) has implications on deal and structure. Consideration is described in Acquisition Currency and Stock Deals. (Ch.15,16)

Recapitalizations – *A major change to a company's capital structure*

- Recapitalizations (also called recaps) usually involve a rebalancing or reallocation of the debt and equity accounts, often done in an attempt to maximize shareholder value.

- A recapitalization generally involves a company taking on a significant amount of new debt in order to repurchase a meaningful amount of its stock (either on the open market or from major shareholders) in a single transaction (as compared to ongoing buyback programs).

- Often, assets and business lines are sold in order to generate cash, which is then used to repurchase some equity.

- Recapitalizations are further described in Corporate Restructurings (Ch.22) and leveraged buyouts are described in Leveraged Buyout Analysis. (Ch.12)

Restructurings – *A major change to the structural organization of a company*

- There are two types of restructurings: (1) corporate restructurings and (2) bankruptcy restructurings.

- Corporate restructurings are often done to clarify the strategic focus of a company or to separate a major business line or subsidary.

- Examples of corporate restructuring transactions include: carve-outs, spin-offs, split-offs, tracking stock, and the issuance of an alternative class of stock.

- A large component of any restructuring transaction involves repositioning the restructured company in the public equity and public debt markets.

- Bankruptcy restructurings (also called "workouts" or "workout restructurings") take place when a company is having difficulty servicing its debt obligations and is forced to reorganize its debt and equity to prevent the company from having to liquidate under a bankruptcy proceeding.

- Restructurings are further described in Corporate Restructurings. (Ch.22)

Buy-Side vs. Sell-Side

Except for a true merger of equals, Acquirors are considered to be on the "buy-side" and Sellers or Targets are considered to be on the "sell-side." The sell-side process is very process-oriented, whereas a significant amount of the buy-side process is related to valuation analysis and financing analysis. The key milestones involved in a sell-side process vs. a buy-side process are listed in Table 5.1.

Table 5.1 – Sell-Side Process vs. Buy-Side Process - Major milestones

Sell-Side Process	Buy-Side Process
Review strategic options with management	Review strategic options with management
Decide to sell an asset or a business as part of the company's strategy	Decide to buy an asset or business as part of the company's strategy

Table 5.1 continued

Sell-Side Process	Buy-Side Process
Prepare the business for sale, which would include organizing key documents and preparing financial projections	Screen for assets or businesses to buy; receive word from selling companies that they will be conducting a sale process; approach Targets
Prepare a descriptive memorandum (DM) which is a detailed selling document provided to potential bidders	Register an interest in the business for sale
Send letters and DMs out to potential buyers	Review the descriptive memorandum
Answer questions from potential buyers	Analyze the opportunity and ask questions of Seller
Ask for and receive preliminary bids (called Round I bids or preliminary indications of interest)	Prepare valuation analysis, receive internal approvals, and submit Round I bid
End of Round I, beginning of Round II	
Create a short list of Round II bidders and notify them that they have been selected	If accepted into Round II, prepare for confidential due diligence
Prepare due diligence data room (electronic or physical) and provide access to Round II bidders	Receive due diligence materials and continue to refine valuation analysis; begin developing final bid strategy
Invite buyers for facility tours and management presentations	Attend facility tours and management presentations
Prepare the merger or purchase agreement [1]	Review merger or purchase agreement [1]
Ask for final and binding Round II bids	Submit Round II final bid with desired changes to merger or purchase agreement

[1] This is the sale contract. For a merger it is called a "merger agreement." For the sale of an asset or division it is called a "purchase and sale agreement" or "purchase agreement." See Deal Mechanics. (Ch.20)

Table 5.1 continued

Sell-Side Process	Buy-Side Process
Review final bids	Finalize financing plan for acquisition and begin integration planning
Choose a winner and negotiate the contract	If chosen, negotiate the contract. If not, begin the cycle again
Announce the deal	Announce the deal

Virtual data rooms

In a sale process, seller aggregates all major contracts and other material information in a single place to facilitate buyer review during the due diligence process. The information is located in a "data room" and the process of reviewing the documents is part of due diligence. Due diligence is described in Deal Mechanics. (Ch.20)

Traditionally, data rooms were located in law firm conference rooms or at a seller's corporate office, requiring all buyers to travel to the location of the data room to review its documents.

Increasingly, data rooms are becoming virtual (or electronic) in that all of the documents available for review are scanned and made into digital files. Potential bidders can therefore review these files with secure access to the Internet (or from a CD provided to the bidder) as opposed to having to physically visit a data room. This has obvious benefits, including minimizing the cost of travel for large due diligence teams and providing buyers more time to review documents. In the case of a virtual data room, a small team might still travel to the selling company for the management presentations, to physically visit plants or facilities, or to review documents which are logistically too difficult to scan into a digital file (such as large blueprints).

The Sell-Side Process

Sell-side processes vary based on the industry, the type of asset, and the objectives of management. Seller objectives can include: (1) preferred timing and the need to complete a sale as soon as possible as opposed to having the flexibility to extend the process; (2) the desire for cash versus the flexibility to accept cash, stock, or notes;

(3) minimizing the tax liabilities associated with the sale; (4) minimizing the impact of the sale process on the company's business and employees; and (5) the need to maintain confidentiality during the process. Types of sale options are listed in the following table:

Table 5.2 – Types of Sale Processes

Confidentiality	Sale Options	Description and Comments
Low	Public Auction	• Publicly announce the sale process and invite any interested parties to participate in the process • Best for assets with a wide buyer universe • Significant disruption to business being sold • Public process • Do not need to identify all bidders because they can seek out Seller based on public notice
	Controlled Auction	• Invite selected parties to participate in the process • Best for assets with limited buyer universe • Allows Seller to prescreen participants • No time to deal with "tire kickers"
	Limited Auction	• Invite a small number of parties to participate in the process • Best for assets with limited buyer universe • Desire to keep transaction confidential • Limited business disruption
	Simultaneous negotiations	• Negotiate with only a few potential parties • Best for assets with one to two identifiable partners • Confidentiality is protected
High	Exclusive negotiations	• Directly approach one potential partner • Best for assets with one or two identifiable partners (usually approached serially) • Confidentiality is protected • Onus is on Seller to identify bidders

The goal in running a good auction is to identify the buyer that can deliver:

1. The highest value (taking into account the form of acquisition currency)
2. The best contractual terms
3. Maximum certainty of closing (considering regulatory approvals, financing, etc.)

It is important to note that the highest value is not necessarily the highest price. Sellers consider the "entire package" of these three items, not just the component pieces. A high price is not worth anything to Seller if, for example, Buyer cannot close the transaction. Value can have different components and all sources of value must be considered.

For example, the value of receiving $1 billion in cash from Acquiror is likely to be different than the value of receiving $1 billion in Acquiror stock (which may be worth more or less than $1 billion to Seller at close, depending on whether the stock goes up or down and/or whether there are mechanisms in the deal that protect Seller so that it receives value of $1 billion at close). In addition, receiving stock from a large, highly liquid company is generally safer and therefore more attractive than receiving stock in a smaller, highly illiquid company since stock in a liquid company is easier to convert to cash if Seller wants to after closing. Also, components of the merger agreement or purchase agreement might have positive or negative value, and they must be assessed. For example, if one bidder requires the selling company to fund $100 million in capital expenditures before closing and another bidder does not have the same requirement, then the two contracts have a $100 million value difference before even considering the purchase price.

Most transactions are "friendly", meaning that the two parties come together on their own and are entering into a transaction agreement because they want to. Other transactions begin as "hostile" or more aggressive overtures by one company to another and then become "friendly" when the offer price for Target is acceptable to Target's management and board of directors. Structural defense methods used in hostile transactions are described in Corporate Defense. (Ch.23)

The Deal Process

Rather than try to specify all of the particulars of different types of transactions here, it is more important to describe those aspects of a transaction process that are consistent in most deals. While not all transactions will adhere to this formula – some will take place over the course of two weeks while others might take place over the course of two (or more) years – it is important to understand the general sequencing of events in a transaction. The process described here is a traditional corporate merger or acquisition in which there is a distinct Acquiror and Target.

Respect the company's process

Sometimes, advisors come into a deal environment ready to take control of the process. If the client already has a team in place dedicated to managing the transaction process, this type of attitude from the bankers or lawyers is a recipe for disaster. An M&A banker's role is principally that of an advisor. Sometimes the banking team will be responsible for running the entire M&A process. Other times, the bankers will be less involved in the day-to-day process and negotiation and the banking team's role is principally to provide a fairness opinion to the board of directors. Every situation will be different and it is always best to let the client determine the banker's role.

Phase I: Looking for a Transaction

1. Screening: Using the company's strategic plan as a framework, screening is mainly done by a company's corporate development group. Conclusions will be shared with the company's senior officers, who will then determine whether to move forward to the next phase. Investment bankers may be very helpful with the screening analysis. However, at this stage, there is usually no formal **engagement agreement** (agreement whereby a company hires or engages an outside advisor to do work on its behalf) with an investment bank. Usually, an investment bank meets with a company's executive officers and pitches potential transaction ideas.

2. On the block: Often a company will announce that it has decided to sell assets, a subsidiary, or the entire company (it has put something "on the auction block"). In these situations, Seller's investment bankers will contact a number of potentially interested parties and determine whether those prospective parties are interested in studying the assets or business for sale.

3. Directly approached: In certain circumstances, a company might approach another company directly regarding a potential transaction.

4. White knight: A situation may arise in which a potential target company becomes the subject of a hostile takeover bid. The **white knight** is a friendly partner who attempts to come in and negotiate a deal with Target's management on mutually agreeable terms, thereby avoiding the hostile overture. Target is still sold, but to a preferred partner rather than the hostile Acquiror. See Corporate Defense. (Ch.23)

Phase II: Analyzing a Deal

1. Additional analysis: Regardless of how an opportunity arises, once a company has determined that a potential transaction is of interest, additional analysis will be required to determine whether to proceed to the next stage.

2. Engaging other company participants. At this stage, other business unit specialists (e.g., specialists from information technology, audit, HR, etc.) may be engaged to assist with the analysis. The corporate development group with the assistance of the banking team generally will be responsible for analyzing the financials, preparing the initial valuation model and managing the process. However, specialists from certain business units who have a particular expertise in the asset or company being analyzed might be asked to participate in order to provide a critical point of view. Internal legal and tax counsel also might be brought in at this stage. Depending on the size and materiality of the deal, the board might be informed about the transaction at this stage.

3. Engage outside advisors: The company may choose to engage outside help at this stage, depending on how likely it is that the company will move forward with the transaction and how complex the transaction is. If the transaction is complex, it is important that companies seek outside help earlier rather than later.

If Acquiror decides to move forward ...

Phase III: Planning and Strategizing

1. Plan and strategize: Once the company has decided to move forward with a particular transaction, it must develop a formal plan, strategy, and timeline for the transaction. Depending on the size of the transaction, this is usually done in conjunction with the senior officers, the corporate development team, and financial and legal advisors.

2. Engage advisors: If the company has not already engaged financial and legal advisors, this is the time to do so. Advisors may not be hired if the corporate development and internal legal departments can handle the transaction on their own.

3. Begin due diligence planning: To some degree, this began in Phase II. However, additional specialists in the company might be asked to join the deal team at this time in order to continue preliminary due diligence on the company. As a result of the additional due diligence, the financial analysis will be refined.

4. Discuss with board: Depending on the size and materiality of the contemplated transaction, senior officers may choose to inform the board regarding the transaction.

5. Approach other party: If the company has not yet approached the other party regarding its interest in a potential transaction, this would be the time to do so. Approaching the other party may be as subtle as the CEO or CFO mentioning something over a pre-planned lunch or golf outing or as aggressive as a hostile offer made directly to the public shareholders. In a public auction setting, the approach might include making a non-binding, preliminary indication of interest.

If Acquiror still wants to move forward, and the other party is interested ...

Phase IV: Due Diligence

1. Engage additional advisors: Depending on how much information will be made available to the company during confidential due diligence, how that information will be made available, and what work needs to be done within what time frame, the company may need to enlarge the deal team with additional internal and external advisors.

2. Inform board: If the board has not yet been informed, it would probably occur at this stage (again depending on the materiality of the transaction), prior to beginning confidential due diligence.

3. Sign Confidentiality Agreements: Prior to beginning confidential due diligence, Acquiror will sign a Confidentiality Agreement. If Target is potentially receiving stock as consideration, then Target may also want to perform confidential due diligence on Acquiror. If so, Target would also sign a Confidentiality Agreement in order to receive confidential information on Acquiror. A **Confidentiality Agreement** is a legal agreement which prevents the recipient of confidential information from disclosing that confidential information except under highly defined circumstances, such as to other members of the deal team for them to assist in the due diligence process. A Confidentiality Agreement (CA) is synonymous with a **Non-Disclosure Agreement** (NDA).

4. Exchange information: At this point, confidential information would be exchanged. The type of transaction and consideration will determine whether one side is giving information to the other side (cash deal) or if both parties are exchanging information (stock deal). If Target is running a public sell-side process, it would conduct a formal due diligence process for those bidders who submitted a first round bid and were invited to participate in Round II. Typically, a management presentation is made by Target to prospective Acquirors whereby the selling management team presents its business, operations and strategic plan. This allows Acquiror to meet with various members of the Target management team and ask questions.

5. Perform additional analysis: Based on the new information gathered from the confidential due diligence, the financial analysis will be further refined. Depending on the pace of the transaction, the legal team may decide to begin drafting the Purchase and Sale Agreement or Merger Agreement. Due diligence and legal agreements are described in Deal Mechanics. (Ch.20)

6. Begin integration planning: Integration planning is a major effort and many companies begin the process early on. Integration planning usually begins during the due diligence and negotiation phases.

If Acquiror likes what it sees in due diligence and wants to move forward ...

Phase V: Making an Offer and Negotiating the Deal

1. Make offer: Offers can be made in various ways. In a public auction, Seller requests a formal binding offer letter by a certain date. If negotiating a merger or joint venture, the offer might be communicated by the company's CEO to the other CEO over a meal or other social setting. The context of the transaction will do much to dictate how the offer is communicated.

2. Negotiate the deal: Once an offer has been made, negotiations have begun. Negotiations will continue until both sides have addressed their key issues.

3. Negotiate the contract: Once the key deal terms have been negotiated, it is time to reflect them in a legal document. Officers, lawyers, and bankers will sit together to translate the deal terms into a contract that both parties are satisfied with and willing to execute. The final negotiations of a contract can become extremely contentious. The contract is signed as soon as both sides are satisfied with all of its terms.

4. Review deal terms with board of directors: Special board meetings are generally called to discuss the key terms of the deal and the merger agreement. A few special meetings to update the board are also common before the board votes on the transaction. Legal counsel will regularly advise the board on its fiduciary duties at these meetings. Fiduciary obligations of the board of directors is described in The Deal Team. (Ch.19)

5. Agree on a deal: After major issues have been negotiated and the contract is satisfactory to both sides, the two parties agree to a deal and return to their respective boards to receive final approval to execute the definitive and binding transaction agreement. Even though both sides are in fundamental agreement regarding a transaction, there is no binding agreement until the contract is signed by both parties.

6. Receive board approval: If the transaction requires board approval, senior officers, bankers and attorneys will likely meet with the board for a vote after the terms of the transaction have been negotiated and the parties are in the process of finalizing the contract. Depending on the materiality of the deal, the investment bank(s) may provide a fairness opinion to the board at this time.

7. Sign contract: After the final board meeting to approve the transaction, the two parties sign the merger agreement.

8. Confidential consultation with third parties: With complex or potentially contentious transactions, it is not uncommon for selected professionals to be apprised of the transaction days before an announcement in order to gauge their reaction to the transaction. This is done prior to the public announcement so changes can be made based on the advice provided by the third parties. The third parties might include someone at a credit rating agency, or a jurisdictional regulatory body (if any). Obviously, any third party made privy to the confidential information will be subject to insider trading rules, regulations, and restrictions.

9. Prepare for public announcement: Just before public announcement of the transaction, the company will prepare a formal press release. Also, depending on the size of the transaction, the company might prepare presentations for members of the financial community (e.g., investors, equity analysts, rating agencies, etc.). Depending on the size of the deal, the company might also engage a public relations firm that specializes in preparing deal announcements.

Phase VI: Announcing the Deal

1. Make public announcement: Press releases are generally issued before the market opens on the day of the announcement.

2. Publicly discuss deal: Depending on the size of the transaction, company officials might meet with members of the financial community to discuss the strategic rationale and the financial terms of the transaction. Sometimes a conference call with investors and other members of the financial community takes place the morning of the announcement.

3. "Sell" the deal: During the first few days after a deal announcement, senior officers will actively discuss the merits and terms of the deal with various members of the financial community. Meetings will often be scheduled in groups or as one-on-ones for large and/or influential institutional investors.

4. Make SEC filings: Depending on the materiality of the transaction, SEC filings are required once the transaction is announced.

Phase VII: Receiving Approvals and Closing the Transaction

1. Receive approvals: The approvals required to close the transaction will depend on the materiality or size of the deal and the industry in which it takes place. If a shareholder vote is required to approve the transaction, and the annual shareholder meeting is not imminent, the company might call a special meeting to vote on the transaction. If the business is subject to a regulatory body, such as the Federal Energy Regulatory Commission, the transaction may need regulatory approval prior to closing. A Hart-Scott-Rodino (HSR) filing with the Federal Trade Commission related to antitrust matters also will be required, depending on the size of the transaction.

2. Begin integration process: Integration planning should begin as early as possible so that, at closing, the formal integration will be seamless and further advanced.

3. Continue to sell the deal: This is especially true if the deal was not well received by the market. If the market reaction was weak or negative, private meetings with fund managers and research analysts might be required.

4. Close the transaction: Once all of the requisite approvals have been received, the transaction can close. Closing involves the signing of closing documents, the delivery of cash (or whatever form of payment was agreed to) and handing over the keys (in a manner of speaking).

5. Finalize integration: This may take from a few weeks to several years, depending on the size of the transaction and the process involved.

Analyzing Strategic Transactions

Chapter 6

However beautiful the strategy,
you should occasionally look at the results.

Winston Churchill

As described in Introduction to M&A (Ch.5), there are five basic types of strategic M&A transactions. They are: (1) joint ventures and partnerships; (2) divestitures and acquisitions; (3) sale of a company and mergers; (4) recapitalizations; and (5) restructurings. As an investment banker or a corporate development professional working on any of these transactions, it is important to analyze whether the contemplated transaction satisfies certain important criteria.

Specifically, all M&A related analysis should help answer one or more of the following five questions.

1. *Strategic rationale:* Does the transaction help achieve the strategic plan?
2. *Valuation:* How much is Target worth on a stand-alone basis?
3. *Financial impact:* Does the transaction create value for the shareholders?
4. *Social issues:* How receptive would the other party be to the transaction and can a transaction be executed on terms that are acceptable to both parties?
5. *Constituents:* Would any key constituents oppose the deal?

Focusing on only one of these five questions might mask potential problems with a transaction. As a result, no single analysis should be deemed sufficient to conclude that a contemplated transaction is advisable.

An exhaustive list of M&A analyses is provided in this chapter. Some of these analyses are performed on almost every M&A transaction while others are performed only in specialized circumstances. For example, contribution analysis and natural exchange ratio analysis are more important to consider in fixed exchange ratio stock deals and they are less important to consider in all cash deals. Similarly, social issues related to senior management or the board of directors are very important to consider in corporate mergers, but are less important when considering an asset sale because such high level governance changes are not generally implicated in an asset sale.

The following list of analyses should be used as a reference guide. Where appropriate, the chapter in which a specific type of analysis is further described is noted. Throughout this chapter, the target company is referred to as "Target" and the acquiror company is referred to as "Acquiror."

Strategic Rationale Analysis

The critical questions that should be answered with strategic rationale analysis are:

- Does the transaction allow the company to advance its strategic plan?
- Does the transaction fit into the company's equity and growth story?
- Does Target have an attractive and/or complementary customer base?
- Does Target have something Acquiror needs (e.g., patent, R&D pipeline)?
- Does the transaction expand the company's geographic coverage or footprint?
- Are the product offerings complementary or distribution outlets additive?

Key areas of analysis are provided below.

- ***Business analysis.*** Review of Target's products, services, markets, customers, asset portfolio, distribution, etc. Also includes segment-based, product-based, or geography-based analyses.
- ***Industry trend analysis***. Review of market growth opportunities and profitability of Target's industry as well as Target's market share and market leadership.
- ***Third-party research.*** Review financial community's view of Target's strategic direction by reading equity research reports, fixed income reports, ratings agency reports, and general press commentary about the company.

Valuation Analysis

Assuming a potential transaction is strategically compelling, it is then necessary to evaluate Target's value. Target value should be measured both on a stand-alone basis and on a *relative basis*, meaning compared to industry peers and to Acquiror. It is particularly important to consider the relative valuation levels of Acquiror and Target in stock-for-stock transactions.

The critical questions that should be answered with valuation analysis are:

- What is Target worth on a stand-alone basis, or what is target's intrinsic value?

- Can Target be obtained at that price?

- How is Target valued relative to its industry peers?

- How is Target valued relative to Acquiror?

- What liabilities are associated with Target?

- What is Target's credit profile and stand-alone debt capacity?

- Does Target have any unique tax characteristics which must be considered?

Key areas of analysis are provided below.

Stand-alone valuation analysis

- ***Financial statement analysis***. Valuation analysis should always begin with a reading of Target's financial statements if they are available (e.g., annual report, 10-K, quarterly updates, etc.). The company spends a significant amount of time compiling this information and there is much to be learned about Target's financial situation from reading it. The MD&A in the latest annual report is always a good start. (Ch.3)

- ***Financial performance analysis.*** Includes a more detailed review of Target's financial statements. For example, assess sales growth, profitability, margins, operating and credit ratios, and any other relevant metrics.

- ***Historical stock price analysis.*** The goal is to review the prices at which the stock has traded in the past. Stock price performance should be measured over varying periods of time, such as three months, one year, and three years. Ideally, it is cross-referenced or annotated with major company, industry or economic events to see if there have been any correlations in stock price movement with major events. (Ch.17)

- ***Shares traded analysis.*** Assess the amount of shares traded by volume and at specified price ranges. This can help provide a proxy for the average tax basis of Target shareholders, which is useful information to a potential Acquiror. (Ch.17)

- ***Discounted cash flow (DCF) analysis.*** Determine Target's stand-alone intrinsic valuation, as opposed to relative valuation using methods such as comparable company analysis and comparable transaction analysis. (Ch.8, 11)

- ***Leveraged buyout (LBO) analysis.*** Determine the maximum price a financial sponsor might be willing to pay for Target given Target's cash flows, credit profile, risk profile, and the current state of the debt markets. (Ch.8, 12, 24, 25)

- ***Breakup analysis.*** Determine whether there is value in separating Target's assets or subsidiaries. (Ch.8, 13)

- ***Credit analysis.*** Measure bankruptcy risk, debt capacity, financial risk, and business risk of Target on a stand-alone basis. (Ch.24)

- ***Shareholder total return analysis.*** Assess the return to Target shareholders annually as a percentage of Target's current stock price. Total return comprises share price appreciation and dividends. (Ch.3)

- ***Overall sector and market analysis.*** Determine how current market valuations compare with long-term levels.

Relative Valuation Analysis

- ***Comparable company analysis.*** Determine Target's valuation range based on current trading levels of Target's industry and financial peers. (Ch.8, 9)

- ***Financial and operating peer group analysis.*** This is similar to comparable company analysis, only in more detail. The goal is to review Target's margins, profitability, growth rates, and other important metrics as compared with those of comparable companies.

- ***Relative stock price performance analysis.*** Stock prices are analyzed to assess how Target's stock has performed relative to Acquiror's and other peers in the industry. This is especially useful over a longer time horizon (e.g., one, three, or five years) to see how the companies under analysis react to certain exogenous shocks (as opposed to comparable company analysis, which is current and therefore may not uncover past anomalies). An **indexed stock price** graph includes Target's stock price over a period of time indexed (usually starting at 100) against a weighted average peer group index and/or a market-based index such as the S&P 500. (Ch.17)

- ***Comparable transaction analysis.*** Determine how the contemplated purchase price compares to prices paid and, specifically, multiples paid in comparable transactions. (Ch.8, 10)

- ***Analysis at various prices (AVP) analysis.*** Analyze implied transaction multiples based on a range of potential purchase prices. (Ch.17)

- ***Premiums paid analysis.*** Assess the premiums paid for a controlling interest in past transactions at different time intervals (e.g., transaction price in relation to Target stock price prior to announcement); usually the analysis is performed for various time periods such as 60 days, 30 days, 10 days, 1 day, etc. (Ch.10)

- ***Natural exchange ratio analysis.*** Assess the market-based exchange ratio based on stock prices of both Target and Acquiror at various times in the past. (Ch.18)

- ***Contribution analysis.*** Assess the contribution of each partner to various common metrics such as sales, EBITDA, net income, assets, and cash flow. The contribution percentage of each party is used to determine the fairness of an exchange ratio, usually in a fixed exchange ratio transaction. (Ch.18)

- ***Relative valuation analysis.*** This requires performing stand-alone valuation analysis of both Acquiror and Target -- using traditional methods such as DCF, comparable company analysis and comparable transaction analysis -- and then calculating the implied exchange ratios based on the stand-alone valuation levels. (Ch.18)

Financial Impact Analysis

Many Acquirors will only contemplate transactions that meet certain defined financial impact tests. Some of those financial tests include accretion to earnings per share, achievement of specified returns or hurdle rates, the impact of the transaction on credit ratios or credit ratings, the impact on the company's dividend policy, and the impact of the transaction on long-term earnings.

The critical questions that should be answered with financial impact analysis are:

- Does the transaction increase Acquiror's growth profile at an acceptable risk?

- Does Target diversify Acquiror's revenue stream in a beneficial way?

- Are meaningful revenue synergies available?

- Does Target diversify Acquiror's cash flow stream and risk profile?
- Are meaningful cost synergies available?
- Is the transaction accretive to earnings per share and cash flow per share? If not, when will it become accretive and what synergies does the transaction require in order for it to be accretive?
- What form of consideration (e.g., cash, stock) would Target consider and would Acquiror be willing to offer?
- Does Acquiror have the financial wherewithal to complete the transaction?
- Is it the right time to complete the transaction?
- What are the tax consequences of the transaction?

Key areas of analysis are provided below.

- ***EPS accretion/dilution analysis.*** Compare the profitability per share of the merged entity to the profitability per share of Acquiror on a stand-alone basis. (Ch.14)
- ***Cash flow accretion/dilution analysis.*** Compare the cash flow per share of the merged entity to the cash flow per share of Acquiror on a stand-alone basis. (Ch.14)
- ***Growth rate accretion/dilution analysis.*** Compare the growth rate of the merged entity to the growth rate of Acquiror on a stand-alone basis. (Ch.14)
- ***Value creation analysis.*** Assess the expected valuation of the merged entity relative to Acquiror's valuation on a stand-alone basis; include impact on key metrics including ROE and ROIC. (Ch.14)
- ***Dividend and total return accretion/dilution analysis.*** Measure the effect of the transaction on the company's dividend and total return profile. (Ch. 14)
- ***Ownership impact analysis.*** Assess which shareholders will own what portion of the merged entity going forward. This is only applicable to transactions with stock consideration. (Ch.15,16)
- ***Credit impact or debt capacity analysis.*** Assess the impact of the transaction on Acquiror's balance sheet and credit ratios. (Ch.24)

- ***Ability to pay analysis.*** Assess the maximum price Acquiror can pay based on various financial metrics, including earnings accretion/dilution, credit impact and debt capacity analysis. (Ch.14, 24)

- ***Synergies analysis.*** Assess the cost and revenue structure of Target to estimate potential synergies. Considering the synergies achieved in precedent transactions is also a useful analysis. (Ch.14)

- ***Transaction structure analysis.*** Assess potential structures designed to facilitate a major objective, whether that be tax efficiency, growth, lowest cost of capital, etc.

Social Issues Analysis

Many transactions make great strategic and financial sense, but fail (either before or after announcement) because of "social issues." Examples of social issues include a failure of the parties to agree on management roles and responsibilities, board structure or composition, and/or other factors such as headquarters location. While many of these issues are by definition "soft" and only verified through direct discussions with Target, certain analyses can be helpful in identifying issues important enough to derail a transaction if they are not resolved.

The critical questions that should be answered with social issues analysis are:

- Does Target have a good management team?

- Do the parties share a management philosophy on operational, financial, and personnel related matters?

- Is Target's senior management ready to retire?

- Is Target's management likely to be receptive to a transaction?

- Does Acquiror's management team address succession planning issues for Target, or vice versa?

- Would Target be willing to work with Acquiror on its preferred transaction structure?

- Can the two management teams be combined in a way that would not disrupt business meaningfully?

- Is Target in a situation where it needs Acquiror's help?

- Are both boards likely to approve the transaction (if a vote is required)?
- Is Target closely held by a family?
- How would Target react to an overture?

Key areas of analysis are provided below.

- ***Cultural fit analysis.*** Assess the overall corporate culture of Target and compare it with that of Acquiror.
- ***Review of senior officers and the members of the board of directors.*** Assess various potential trigger points or incentives, including ages, positions, responsibilities, affiliations, stock ownership levels, options and change of control provisions for those options, compensation and golden parachute employment agreements. (Ch.17)
- ***Defense profile analysis.*** Assess Target's structural corporate defenses and susceptibility to a hostile takeover. (Ch.23)
- ***News runs.*** See if any particular insight can be gathered about the company's commitment to and presence in the community. In addition, news runs provide information on Target's plans and goals in the form of articles, management interviews, and company press releases.

Constituents Analysis

Constituents are outside parties that have a stake in the transaction and who may or may not have to approve the transaction. For example, shareholders and regulators are constituents who must vote to approve the transaction. Union leaders and equity research analysts do not vote on the transaction *per se* but they are vocal and their opinions regarding the transaction are meaningful to both Target and Acquiror.

The critical questions that should be answered with constituents analysis are:

- Will the transaction make sense to the financial community?
- Is the transaction simple enough to understand? (Complex deals sometimes get lost on investors and/or regulators.)
- Are both sets of shareholders likely to approve the transaction?
- Does the transaction materially affect either company's credit quality, there-

by affecting the credit risk and price of Acquiror's outstanding debt? Is this transaction a triggering event for any debt?

- Would regulators approve the deal?

- Would unions or any other major constituents oppose the deal?

- Does the transaction create an attractive arbitrage situation thereby putting downward pressure on Acquiror's stock price?

- Does the transaction significantly affect employees and trigger material levels of job losses?

- Does the transaction affect retiree programs?

- Will the loss of corporate presence in the community affect the organization?

Key areas of analysis are provided below.

- ***Shareholder analysis.*** Shareholder analysis is performed to answer questions such as: Is there a majority shareholder? Is the shareholder base largely retail or institutional? What turnover has there been in the shareholder base? At what price(s) did key shareholders buy in? (Ch.17)

- ***Analysis of debt and debt holders.*** As part of credit analysis, and debt capacity analysis, it is important to also review whether any debt has a change-of control provision. Specifically, it is important to determine whether debt or preferred equity holders have any rights associated with a merger or sale of the company. (Ch.24, 25)

- ***Regulatory analysis.*** Determine what regulatory approvals, if any, would be required for the transaction to close. Regulatory analysis should also include an assessment of what the likely regulatory actions might be. Early planning is essential for any transaction which is subject to regulatory oversight. Remember that many larger companies are subject to multiple regulatory jurisdictions and therefore this analysis should be done at the local, regional, national and international levels. (Ch.20)

- ***Constituents analysis.*** Determine whether or not any key constituents (e.g., employees, unions, communities, regulators, etc.) would have reason to oppose the transaction. (Ch.17)

- ***Arbitrage analysis.*** Assess if a risk arbitrageur can profit from the transaction and, if so, what the potential impact on the stock price might be. (Ch.16)

- ***Flowback analysis.*** Assess how many of shares will "flow back" into the home country because Target shareholders who have received Acquiror shares sell them (because they cannot or do not want to own foreign shares), leading to post-transaction downward pressure on Acquiror's stock in its home market. Flowback is an issue in cross-border transactions (e.g., a UK-based company acquires an American company). Analysis should include the potential impact of joining or dropping out of major market indices, such as the S&P 500. (Ch. 20)

- ***Interloper analysis.*** Determine if any other companies might have an interest in the transaction under evaluation such that an interloper might join the battle for Target. Analysis should include review of interlopers' motives and the financial impact of a transaction between the interloper(s) and Target. (Ch.20)

- ***Analysis of major contracts.*** Determine if there are any change-of-control provisions in a major contract with a major supplier or customer which, if terminated, would materially affect the substance or value of Target. (Ch.20)

- ***Integration planning analysis.*** Begin integration planning to determinate what major actions must take place in order to ensure a smooth transition. (Ch.20)

Screening for M&A Transactions

Chapter 7

Search well and be wise,
nor believe that self-willed pride
will ever be better than good counsel.

Aeschylus

The goal of screening is to identify potential M&A transactions that are worthy of more consideration and financial analysis. Very few good transactions just land in a company's lap. Such opportunistic transactions are somewhat akin to a friend offering to sell you her incredible house before putting it on the market. The timing of opportunistic transactions is largely determined by Seller rather than Acquiror (since Acquiror cannot buy until Seller or Target is ready to sell). Therefore, financial flexibility and pre-planning are at a premium - the buyer who can move fastest is likely to be advantaged in an auction or sale process.

Initial Screening

Screening and analyzing potential targets begins with the company's strategic plan. From the strategic plan, a set of criteria emerges for assets, businesses, and/or transactions that could help the company achieve its short-term and long-term goals. For example, does the company's strategic plan call for more diversification in its major product line? Or does it call for the addition of new products in order to reduce dependence on its core business? Prioritizing the issues identified in a company's long-term strategic plan is the important first step.

The next question is one that still falls largely within the purview of the executive suite, and that is whether a company wants to achieve its strategic goals through a "transforming" transaction or by a series of "bolt-on acquisitions" which would complement its organic growth. A bolt-on acquisition, as the name implies, is the addition of a company, division, or line of business that is largely similar or complementary to something that the company does currently, such as a product extension or extending the geographic footprint for a product. From a size perspective, transforming transactions might involve companies of similar or larger size, as compared to bolt-ons which are generally smaller and easier to integrate.

The goal of initial screening is to cast the first net as broadly as possible in order to ensure that all potential acquisition candidates are caught within that net. Initial screening can be broken down into five basic steps.

1. Identify the initial screening criteria that are important to the company, including:

   a. Type of transaction (bolt-on vs. transforming)
   b. Type of assets, technology and/or company sought
   c. Size parameters (could be defined by revenues, assets, market value or other)
   d. Geographic parameters
   e. Business mix
   f. Cultural and management fit

   If working with clients whom you do not know well, you can learn a fair amount about their strategic goals by reading through various sources of information including: SEC filings, the corporate website, equity research reports, credit research reports, fixed income research reports, press releases, speeches given by the company's senior executives, replays of investor calls, and by doing similar research on the company's competitors. In these media, the company's executives are likely to have described corporate strategy and intentions related to M&A activity.

2. Identify which types of companies or industries might contain potential targets that satisfy these initial screening criteria. In addition to public companies, consider which companies might own subsidiaries or assets that are of interest. Also consider private companies.

3. Do searches to identify companies, subsidiaries or assets that might fall into these industry groups. There are a number of ways to begin the company-specific search. These include:

   a. Perform North American Industry Classification System (NAICS) searches using NAICS databases. NAICS has replaced the older Standard Industrial Classification system (SIC).

   b. Review SEC filings in which companies list their industry peers (companies list peers in their annual proxy and sometimes in their 10-K).

   c. Read or scan headlines and perform news article searches on key words in trade journals, business press, magazines, financial dailies (*Wall Street Journal, New York Times business section, Financial Times, Daily Deal, Bloomberg, etc.*), equity research reports, credit research reports, Internet searches, websites, etc. to obtain ideas for potential targets. For example, if working with a pharmaceutical company that is primarily focused on heart-related drugs, you might consider searching major news publications for biotechnology companies working on heart-related projects.

d. Talk and listen to clients, bankers and attorneys, venture capitalists, and industry experts (e.g., doctors and researchers in healthcare, engineers in technology). Go to trade shows and conferences and listen more than talk. Market intelligence is invaluable. Do not, however, speak with anyone about a specific company you may be working with or considering as a potential Target.

e. Review private equity trade journals and review business broker listings.

f. Review patent filings.

g. Review bankruptcy proceedings.

4. From this research, create a list of potential targets that broadly appear to satisfy some of your criteria. This list should be dynamic, meaning you should regularly make changes to it over time as additional information is learned and as the strategic objectives of the company evolve.

5. Whittle that list down by doing more research, learning more about the companies on the list, and performing additional analyses on the short list of companies.

It is important to talk regularly with your team and other industry advisors to challenge ideas and refine screening criteria and findings. Remember that screening for and analyzing companies is not a static exercise – findings will change and grow as knowledge grows, as other companies grow, and as the market changes.

Once the short list of potential transactions has been created, it is time to analyze the potential targets in more detail. The screening criteria should be based on answering the five key questions identified in Ch.6 (which are listed below).

1. *Strategic rationale:* Does the transaction help achieve the strategic plan?
2. *Valuation:* How much is Target worth on a stand-alone basis?
3. *Financial impact:* Does the transaction create value for the shareholders?
4. *Social issues:* How receptive would the other party be to the transaction and can a transaction be executed on terms that are acceptable to both parties?
5. *Constituents:* Would any key constituents oppose the deal?

In general, screening should be performed in the order listed above. The first screening question should always be "Does the transaction help achieve the strategic plan?" A potential Target should not advance to the valuation stage unless the answer to the strategic rationale question is yes. For the short list, valuation and financial analysis should be performed in conjunction with social issues and constituents analysis. As additional analysis is performed, potential targets will be eliminated from the short list and the list will be narrowed down even further. The analyses listed in Analyzing Strategic Transactions (Ch.6) are described in detail in Chapters 8 to 25.

Some potential Targets will fare well given one set of criteria and others might be a better fit given another set of criteria. For example, assume there are three critical screening criteria (A is product mix, B is geographic location and C is credit quality). According to screening criterion A, companies 1 and 2 may be attractive, according to screening criterion B, companies 3 and 4 may be attractive, and according to screening criterion C, companies 5 and 6 may be attractive. The goal of screening is to find the targets that have the *highest overall score* when all important screening criteria are considered rather than the target which is most attractive based on a single criterion.

Common Screening Errors

When screening for Targets and analyzing potential transactions, it is important to identify many potential assets and transactions – not just one. This is important not because Acquiror will acquire multiple companies at once, but because Acquiror may not be able to successfully complete a transaction with its first or even second choice. Therefore a list of desirable Targets should be created and ranked such that, if the first choice is not available, Acquiror can move to the second. Any number of obstacles can derail a transaction, one of the most important of which is the unwillingness of the other side to consider it. Other reasons transactions do not move forward include an inability to raise financing, resistance of either party's board of directors, and issues that come to light during due diligence, to name a few.

Some of the most common screening mistakes are:

1. ***Narrowly defined search criteria:*** One of the biggest mistakes in screening is ruling out companies because they are too "big." It is true that companies often do not want to cede control in a transaction; however, sometimes a transaction with a larger party is the best strategic alternative for a company. It is important to think critically about the screening criteria and not rule out a transaction that could be strategically compelling due to issues such as size or management.

2. ***Eliminating a company from the screening list and never revisiting it:*** It is

good to keep a running list of transactions that have been considered and eliminated. Next to the company name, also list when it was last analyzed and why it was previously eliminated from the short list. Keep this list available and updated so that you can refer back to it in the future. At a later date, that company may grow or change into a partner that is more interesting, desirable, and/or available.

3. ***Not considering private companies or wholly owned subsidiaries:*** Public companies are easier to identify in screening, but there are also a number of companies that might be of strategic interest to an acquiror, including: (1) private companies, (2) divisions or subsidiaries of public companies, and (3) portfolio companies owned by financial sponsors. Therefore it is important to cast the screening net beyond publicly traded companies.

Checklist and Review

Junior bankers sometimes spend too much time trying to answer all of the questions and performing much of the analysis set out in Ch.6 (and staying in the office until 2 a.m. doing so) without first stepping back to think about what the goals are. Often a number of the important screening questions can be answered by doing less than an hour of work. The following checklist might help you develop your own short process for determining whether a company could be a good potential M&A target. After going through these high-level steps, you can address the appropriate analytical questions listed in Ch.6 if a particular transaction or Target continues to be of interest.

- What does the company do?
- What is this company's niche or market specialty?
- Which markets does it serve (by geography, customers, and/or channels)?
- Is it public or private?
- If public, what is its market value and firm value?
- If public, where is it trading (e.g., P/E and EV/EBITDA)?

Part II

Valuation

The Role of Valuation

Chapter 8

Bought a cheap horse, $16 ... he is blind.

Henry John (H.J.) Heinz

Valuation analysis is the act of determining how much an asset, portfolio of assets, stream of cash flows or business is worth. It is performed by corporations, investors, analysts and bankers for a wide range of situations. Examples of when valuation analysis should be performed include: (1) when an investor needs to determine what price should be paid for an investment - the investor could be an individual purchasing securities, or the investor could be a company or group of investors buying another company; (2) as a tool in making strategic decisions; (3) when a company is preparing for an initial public offering, in order to determine a valuation range for its stock; (4) when prospective partners are creating a joint venture, in order to know how to split the partnership fairly; (5) by investment bankers when providing a fairness opinion; (6) by management when issuing stock options, to determine the proper strike price for the options; and (7) in litigation work, in order to determine potential damages. This chapter will provide both a conceptual discussion of valuation and an overview of the most commonly used valuation techniques.

Value is Relative

Value is a *relative* concept, not an *absolute* one. An asset or business may simultaneously be worth a certain price to one buyer and a different price to another buyer, or one price to a buyer at one point in time and a significantly different price to the same buyer at a different point in time. For a seller, that means there is a range of values (not one absolute value) that represents a fair price for the asset or business. In addition, the nominal value of an asset or business can be affected by prevailing macroeconomic conditions, such as the interest rate environment. Specifically, low interest rates lower the cost of capital for a company. A low cost of capital allows buyers to afford higher purchase prices because return thresholds are easier to achieve. The opposite holds true in a high interest rate environment -- with high interest rates, a buyer's cost of capital increases, which drives purchase prices down.

When performing valuation analysis, those new to M&A often try to find one correct answer or one correct number. There is no absolute correct answer or number when it comes to valuation. Instead, a range of values is more appropriate. This is partly because the same asset is worth different amounts to different buyers, and partly because valuation is based on assumptions. Each change in assumptions leads to a different valuation result. It is impossible to know with certainty which assumptions will ultimately prove correct since assumptions relate to the future. Therefore, it is impossible to know with certainty what the "correct" valuation is since it is based on assumptions which have a natural margin of error built into them. As a result, analytically rigorous valuation analysis must recognize that buyer preferences, prevailing conditions and margin of error all play a role in valuation. The only way to capture such disparities is to provide a range of values rather than a specific value when performing valuation analysis.

A business owner or executive might think his business or asset is worth a certain amount -- perhaps someone told him his company was worth a certain value in the past and that particular number has stuck in his mind, or perhaps the company has a team that regularly performs internal valuation analysis. Regardless of how someone has come to believe what his company is *worth*, it is important to remember that no seller can decide independently what her business or asset is *worth*. Nor can a buyer decide independently what an asset or business is *worth*. It takes a willing buyer *and* a willing seller to determine a market value. Also, a buyer cannot buy if the seller is not ready to sell; and a seller cannot sell unless a buyer is ready to buy.

Consider the price you might pay for a home. You cannot go to a "home supermarket," select the home you want with a non-negotiable sticker price on it, and walk to the checkout counter to pay for it. When selling a home, sellers have listing prices that represent the price or value they want for the home. When buying a home, buyers make offers based on (1) what they think the home is worth and (2) what they can afford. Imagine that your friend Steve is a prospective buyer. He has searched and searched and finally found a New York City apartment that he likes which is listed at $800,000. However, given the apartment's size, features, associated liabilities (e.g. plumbing and electrical issues), and the neighborhood, he does not think it is *worth* $800,000. So he makes an offer for $730,000. The seller considers Steve's offer, but decides she would like to hold out for a higher price. A few weeks later, Marc, another buyer, makes an offer for $780,000 and the seller accepts it. They sign a legal agreement binding each other to the sale.

In this example (which is not at all uncommon), two independent buyers came to a different conclusion as to the value of the home. Is one of them right and one of them wrong? No. The same apartment was simply *worth* more to one party than to another. Perhaps Marc works only a few blocks from the building and therefore ascribed a significant amount of value to location. Regardless of the reason, there was $50,000 of value ($780,000 - $730,000 = $50,000) that existed for Marc that did not exist for Steve and, as a result, Marc was willing to pay more for the same apartment.

And the seller who thought her apartment was worth $800,000 realizes that it is only worth $730,000 to $780,000 (which is the range of values offered by interested buyers for the apartment). While more complex, selling a business or a company's asset is not very different in theory from selling a home. Different buyers will come to different conclusions regarding value. Some buyers will be emotional about the company or asset whereas some buyers will make their decision based solely on the financial and strategic merits of the transaction. The goal of a seller is to find the buyer who is willing to offer the highest value and who can deliver the best contractual terms (including, importantly, the greatest certainty to closing).

Valuation tenets

When performing valuation analysis it is important to remember

1. There are no absolute prices, only relative values
2. Different buyers will allocate different values to different components based on how they plan to run the company or use the asset
3. Prevailing factors, such as interest rates, industry growth rates, and consolidation trends, will affect valuation levels

Valuation Methods

The best indicator of value for a public company is the current stock price. The market provides the best leading indicator of fair value because it reflects the price an investor is willing to pay at any given moment for a non-controlling share of the company. However, the current market price must be tested to see if the market price reflects the intrinsic value of the company (i.e., to check if the market is correctly valuing the company). Also, with a private company there is no current stock price to refer to so other valuation methods must be used.

So how do people agree on a value for a non-controlling interest or a controlling interest in a company? Agreed upon valuation methodologies provide a common language for buyers, sellers, advisors, analysts, creditors, lenders and courts. While there are many valuation methods, the five listed below are the most commonly used in M&A and corporate finance analysis:

1. Comparable company analysis
2. Comparable transaction analysis and premiums paid analysis
3. Discounted cash flow analysis (DCF)
4. Leveraged buyout analysis (LBO)
5. Breakup analysis

Some of these methodologies are more appropriate in certain situations than in others. Most often, some combination of these five valuation methodologies is used to triangulate to a valuation range. This means that many or all of these analyses are performed and then a valuation range is determined based on the conclusions from each of the analyses. There are also specialized valuation techniques such as recapitalization analysis and liquidation analysis that are used in specific circumstances. In addition, certain industries, including natural resources, financial institutions, and real estate, have specialized industry-specific valuation methodologies that are regularly used.

Multiples Based Methods

Comparable company analysis and **comparable transaction analysis** are *multiples* based analyses, meaning that the value of a company is calculated as a multiple of a metric, such as earnings per share, cash flow, revenues, or EBITDA. The primary characteristic of comparable *company* analysis is that it is based on current stock prices and generally reflects the value for a **minority interest** (or non-controlling interest). The primary characteristic of comparable *transaction* analysis is that it is based on prices paid in acquisitions for control of the company and therefore includes a **control premium** (or price paid in order to take control of the company, as opposed to a minority share whose owner cannot determine on his or her own how the company is run). Thus, in an efficient market, the only difference in valuation using comparable company analysis and valuation using comparable transaction analysis should be the control premium.

What is a multiple?

If a candy company sold for $100 million and the company had revenues of $50 million for the year ending 2005, then the company sold at a *sales multiple* of 2x 2005 sales.

$$\frac{\$100 \text{ million purchase price}}{\$50 \text{ million in sales in 2005}} = 2\text{x } 2005 \text{ sales}$$

A sales multiple is just one type of multiple; there are many types of multiples that are used in valuation analysis.

Comparable Company Analysis

- The premise behind comparable company analysis is that a non-controlling interest in companies within the same industry or companies exhibiting similar underlying business fundamentals (e.g., growth, profitability, risk, volatility, etc.) should be valued in the equity market on the same relative basis as a multiple of financial and operating metrics.

- Comparable companies (the "trading comp set") are selected and financial multiples are calculated for each of the companies in the trading comp set based on the current stock price of each company in the peer group. Examples of multiples include price to earnings (P/E), enterprise value to EBITDA (EV/EBITDA) and price to book (P/B).

- Multiples from the trading comp set are then applied to the data of the company being valued in order to determine an implied valuation range for the company being valued.

- Comparable company analysis is the best method for valuing a minority interest or for pricing an IPO (initial public offering of a company's stock). It is not as useful of a method in a sale context since comparable company analysis does not include a control premium.

- Comparable company analysis is also referred to as comparable trading analysis. It is described in detail in Comparable Company Analysis. (Ch.9)

Comparable Transaction Analysis

- The premise behind comparable transaction analysis is that a controlling interest in companies within the same industry or companies exhibiting similar underlying business fundamentals (e.g., growth, profitability, risk, volatility, etc.) should be acquired (in a change-of-control transaction) on the same relative basis as a multiple of financial and operating metrics.

- Companies within an industry or peer group that were acquired in a change-of-control transaction are selected (sometimes dating back many years if there has not been much M&A activity in a sector). Financial multiples are calculated for each of the transactions in the comp set based on the sale price of each company in the peer group.

- The types of multiples used in comparable company and comparable transaction analysis are the same – the difference is that comparable company analysis is based on the stock price in the public market and represents a non-controlling share whereas comparable transaction analysis is based on the price an acquiror paid for control of a company and includes a control premium. Examples of multiples include price to earnings (P/E), enterprise value to EBITDA (EV/EBITDA) and price to book (P/B).

- Multiples from the transaction comp set are then applied to the data of the company being valued in order to determine an implied valuation range.

- Premiums paid analysis is often performed in conjunction with comparable transaction analysis. In premiums paid analysis, premiums paid per share of stock in comparable change-of-control transactions are applied to the stock price of the company being valued. For example, assume that in the telecom sector, the average premium paid during the last two years in M&A transactions was 25 percent. Assume you are valuing TelecomWest which is currently trading at $30 per share. You could apply the average 25 percent premium to a share of TelecomWest stock to estimate the implied M&A value per share of TelecomWest.

  $30 per share × (1 + 0.25 average premium) = $37.50 M&A value per share

- Comparable transaction analysis is also referred to as precedent transaction analysis. It is described in detail in Comparable Transaction Analysis. (Ch.10)

What does it mean to "spread comps?"

In finance parlance, the verb "to spread" generally means to prepare a financial analysis using spreadsheet software. Spreading comps means to prepare a set of comps -- the data is literally spread across the columns of a spreadsheet.

Cash Flow Based Methods

Discounted cash flow analysis and **leveraged buyout analysis** are cash flow based methods of valuation which use time value of money fundamentals. With discounted cash flow analysis and leveraged buyout analysis, value is determined based on the projected cash flows that the company or asset generates, discounted by the company's (or asset's) cost of capital. Since DCF and LBO analyses are based on forward looking projections, they are valuation methods which allow a company's operating strategy and growth strategy to be included in the analysis. Valuation using DCF and LBO analysis is determined *intrinsically*, based on what the asset or company generates itself, not based on multiples or metrics from comparable companies or comparable transactions. A derivation of DCF analysis is **discounted equity value analysis** or DEV. The difference between DCF and DEV is that DEV considers only the cash flows to and the value for equity holders, whereas DCF considers cash flows to and the value for both debt and equity holders. LBO analysis goes a step further and makes a determination of value based on how much leverage (or amount of debt) the asset or business can support, thereby maximizing returns to the equity holders.

Discounted Cash Flow Analysis

- The premise behind discounted cash flow analysis is that the firm value or enterprise value (which is the value to both the debt and equity holders of a firm) should equal the present value of the perpetual free cash flows of the company, discounted by the company's weighted average cost of capital. Free cash flow represents all of the cash inflows and outflows of a company excluding any financing related charges such as interest payments to debt holders or dividend payments to equity holders.

- Since DCF analysis is based on projected free cash flows, great care must be taken in developing projections which are reliable, reasonable and which accurately reflect the most likely operating scenario for the company.

- Discounted cash flow analysis is considered the best method for calculating the intrinsic value of a company since value is calculated based on internally generated cash flows of the company, and those cash flows are then discounted based on the inherent risks of those cash flows. There are no "outside" forces in effect such as prices paid for other companies (as is the case with multiples based analysis) or the return required by a private equity investor (as is the case with leveraged buyout analysis).

- DCF is further discussed in Discounted Cash Flow Analysis. (Ch.11)

Leveraged Buyout Analysis

- Leveraged buyout analysis is based on the assumption that a company will be purchased by private investors and the company will become privately held. The buyout will be paid for with debt and private equity.

- Acquiror will raise the highest allowable levels of debt (given the target credit ratings and the market appetite for the company's debt) such that the equity investors contribute the minimum amount of equity practicable, thereby maximizing equity returns.

- The LBO value of the company is the maximum offer price at which the equity investor earns his minimum required equity return. In today's market, most private equity investors require a compound annual return on equity between the high teens and the low thirties, depending on the perceived risk of the investment. Historically, private equity investors would only consider transactions with an annual equity return greater than 25 percent.

- LBO analysis is often used to determine the "floor" value for a company since it represents what a financial buyer would be willing to pay. Since strategic buyers are usually able to generate more synergies than a financial buyer and since strategic buyers tend to have lower return requirements than financial buyers, strategic buyers are generally able to pay more for the same company than a financial buyer.

- LBOs are further discussed in Leveraged Buyout Analysis. (Ch.12)

Breakup Analysis

- The question in breakup analysis is: "What is a company worth if I break it up and sell off the pieces?" It is generally used only if a company operates in more than one major line of business.

- All four of the other methodologies are applied in breakup analysis.

- It is, however, important to consider the tax consequences of breaking up a company and selling off the component pieces, since adverse tax consequences can nullify any additional value that otherwise might have been created in a breakup scenario.

- Breakups are further discussed in Breakup Analysis. (Ch.13)

Valuation Ranges

Once various valuation analyses have been performed, it is important to review the valuation ranges derived from the various methods and use all of that information to determine a valuation range for the company. Investment bankers often create a page called a **football field** to graphically depict the various valuation ranges derived using different valuation methodologies. An example of a valuation football field can be found in Figure 8.1.

In general, a football field will show that the valuation range from comparable company analysis is lower than that of comparable transaction analysis (because comparable transactions include a control premium). This is not always the case, however, especially if there has not been M&A activity in an industry for many years.

Figure 8.1 – Example of a Valuation Football Field

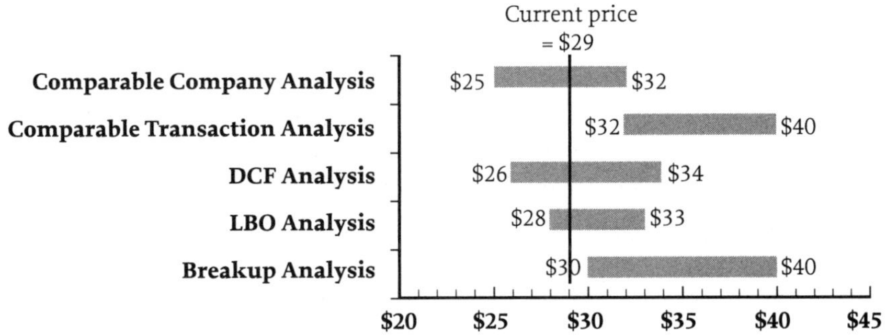

In Figure 8.1, the current stock price of $29 is within the comparable company analysis range of $25 to $32. The comparable company analysis range is less than the comparable transaction analysis range of $32 to $40. This is generally to be expected since comparable transaction multiples include a control premium whereas trading comparables (from comparable company analysis) do not. The comparable company analysis range in Figure 8.1 is generally in line with the DCF analysis range, which means that, currently, investors are properly valuing the company in the public markets relative to its intrinsic value. The breakup analysis range in Figure 8.1 is wider than some of the other methods. This is not uncommon because there is less certainty in the values of several component pieces compared to a single company (because there is execution risk involved with each of the individual sale transactions and also because there may be uncertainty as to the range of values for some of the component pieces).

If the company in Figure 8.1 were for sale and a would-be Acquiror were to offer $38 per share, the offer is likely to be considered "fair" from a financial point of view due to the fact that:

1. $38 represents a $9 per share or 31 percent premium to the current price of $29;

2. $38 is on the high end of the comparable transaction analysis range of $32 to $40 ; and

3. $38 is greater by $4 per share than the high end of the DCF analysis or "intrinsic value" range of $26 to $34.

Although, an offer of $38 per share might be considered fair, other items would need to be weighed before accepting an offer, including the consideration offered (cash vs. stock), and the identity of the bidder, among other things.

Assuming the markets were to properly value this company based on a DCF valuation, the highest value a public investor should be willing to pay for a non-controlling interest is $34 per share. If Acquiror were to offer $38 per share, the offer price would exceed the stand-alone intrinsic value of the company. The only reason a potential acquiror should be willing to pay $38 per share for a company that is, at most, worth $34 on a stand-alone basis is because the potential acquiror can create *more than* $4 per share of synergy value (such that a price of $38 per share is still a value enhancing transaction for Acquiror *even after* paying away $4 in synergy value in order to gain control of Target).

If, in this same example, the DCF analysis range were $35 to $45, as shown in Figure 8.1, as opposed to $26 to $34, as shown in Figure 8.1, Target might not want to accept an offer of $38 per share. If the company believes in the integrity of its strategic plan and its projections, it might want to try and realize its strategic plan and then allow time for the market to reward it with a higher stock price. Assuming the market ultimately does recognize the intrinsic value of the company (assumed here to be the DCF analysis range of $35 to $45), it is possible that this company could be worth more in the public markets than the $38 per share offered by Aquiror.

Figure 8.2 – Example of a Valuation Football Field

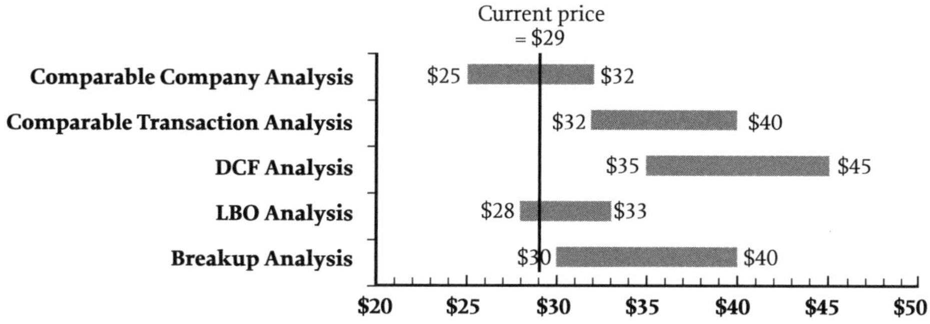

Comparable Company Analysis

CHAPTER 9

Is it not rather what we expect in men,
that they should have numerous strands of experience
lying side by side and never
compare them with each other?

George Eliot

Comparable company analysis (also known as comparable companies, trading comparables, trading comps, or comps) is a very useful valuation tool. Specifically, it is one of the best methods to value a minority interest, or non-controlling share, in a company. The premise behind comparable company analysis is that (1) companies within the same industry or (2) companies with similar business fundamentals (such as earnings and growth prospects) should be valued in the market on the same relative basis as a multiple of financial and operating metrics. To perform comparable company analysis, a comparables group of companies (or comp set) is identified and multiples of financial and operating metrics such as P/E or enterprise value to EBITDA are calculated for each company in the comp set. Based on the comp set's multiples, a range of multiples is applied to the company being valued to determine its implied valuation range. That is, the implied valuation of the company under analysis is determined by taking the multiples of *other companies* and applying them to the company under consideration. This relative valuation method is in contrast to intrinsic (non-relative) methods of valuation such as Discounted Cash Flow Analysis and Leveraged Buyout Analysis. (Ch.11,12)

This chapter begins with a review of the benefits and challenges of comparable company analysis and then describes the steps involved in preparing trading comparables. Numerical examples are provided at the end of the chapter. Key sections of other chapters interrelate with comparable company analysis. As such, to complement this chapter it is important to review The Role of Valuation (Ch.8), Comparable Transaction Analysis (Ch.10), the sections Increasing Shareholder Value and Synergies in Strategic Transactions (Ch.4), Acquisition Currency (Ch.15) and Stock Deals. (Ch.16)

Key Benefits

One of the advantages of comparable company analysis is that it is based on current stock prices which, for publicly traded companies, are quoted every day the stock market is open. Market efficiency means that trading values, in theory, should provide a strong indicator of a company's value, adjusted for any market-specific drivers. Also, a company's current stock price is the most transparent metric for measuring shareholder value.

Since comparable company analysis is based on current stock prices, it is one of the best methodologies for determining the probable value of a company prior to a public offering of its stock (ultimately, the market itself will determine whether that indicative value was correct). In addition, comparable company analysis is the best methodology to determine the value of a *non-control* investment in a company which is publicly traded. Comparable company analysis is also used to determine whether a company is vulnerable as a potential takeover candidate. If the public market value (as reflected in the stock price) is significantly less than the intrinsic value of a company (based on discounted cash flow analysis or leveraged buyout analysis), the company could be vulnerable to a takeover. This is because another company or a private investor might determine that an adequate return could be generated just by buying all of the shares of the undervalued public company at the lower price, plus a control premium, and receiving the company's cash flows over time.

Key Challenges

A major shortcoming of comparable company analysis in M&A is that it represents a minority holding and does not include a control premium. An even bigger shortcoming is the difficulty of finding a truly "comparable" company. Since all companies differ – even within industries – one cannot perfectly extrapolate a value for Company B based on Company A's stock price unless one can also account for, and value, all of the differences between Companies A and B. Another shortcoming is that comparable company analysis works very well if companies in the comp set are large and liquid (such that a meaningful amount of the company's stock trades each day). If, on the other hand, companies in the comp set have poor market fundamentals (such as small capitalization, small public float, and/or low trading volume), it can be difficult to extrapolate good conclusions from the comp set because the fundamental premise of comparable company analysis is that the company's share price is a view held by the market; if, due to various factors, the stock is not changing hands often, it calls into question the validity of the conclusions and whether the stock price is truly reflective of the market's current view. Lastly, the market can sometimes be emotional (in contrast to the common assumption that it is always rational). As a result, if comparable company analysis is performed using stock prices which are substantially higher or lower due to macroeconomic events or news of that day, then the conclusions derived from the analysis could be mistakenly high or low.

When to Use Trading Comparables

As mentioned previously, comparable company analysis is extremely useful for valuing a company for an initial public offering and for valuing minority investments. Comparable company analysis is also used in M&A analysis, more often in measuring relative values when structuring a merger or joint venture and less often in an acquisition (due to the lack of a control premium). In an acquisition, comparable transaction analysis and discounted cash flow analysis are the primary tools.

Preparing Trading Comparables

There are six major steps in calculating trading comps:

1. Screen for and identify comparable companies

2. Separate the pure plays from the diversified companies (based on business mix)

3. Separate liquidity anomalies based on size (based on market value)

4. Identify and categorize ratios and multiples to be evaluated (based on industry)

5. Check all data with source material and prepare comparable multiples

6. Analyze the data and draw conclusions

These six steps are described below. Numerical examples are provided at the end of this chapter.

1. ***Screen for and identify comparable companies:*** The task of identifying comparable companies for valuation purposes is very similar to identifying comparable companies as acquisition targets. Comparable companies are companies which operate in similar business lines or have comparable asset portfolios. For example, if the goal is to value a luxury goods company in the men's clothing sector, then the first screen of comparable companies should include all publicly traded high-end men's retailers. The second screen for comparable companies, however, should encompass any retailer in the luxury goods market, including those that service women and children as well, since all luxury goods retailers (regardless of whether they cater to men or women) are exposed to similar consumer risks and market dynamics. A third screen

might include luxury service providers in the travel, car and boat, real estate and food and beverage sectors since the same consumers of high-end clothing are also likely to purchase luxury vehicles and take expensive vacations.

Look beyond the industry

There are many different ways in which companies can be comparable. Some of the more familiar delineations are similar assets, product lines, size (e.g., market value, assets, and/or revenues), regions of operations, and business models. It is important, however, not to limit the search for comparable companies to those companies solely within the same industry. Companies in other industries might be comparable based on other important metrics such as growth prospects or cyclicality. Examples of characteristics that can be used to determine a comp set include: (1) comparable business lines; (2) comparable business fundamentals such as growth prospects, total return profiles, cyclicality or profitability levels; (3) market value or liquidity; and (4) investor classes (commonality of owners).

Once metrics have been identified, search for companies using the followings methods:

a. Perform a NAICS code search; NAICS is the North American Industry Classification System and has replaced the older U.S. Standard Industry Classification system (SIC codes). The NAICS was developed jointly by the U.S., Canada, and Mexico to provide comparability in statistics about business activity across North America.

b. Review equity, fixed income and credit research reports written about the company, industry and/or sector to see if other comparable companies are mentioned. Also, most analysts cover a particular industry so any other companies covered by the research analyst that covers the company under analysis are likely to be comparable to the company being valued.

c. Review industry and trade journals to search for information about other comparable players.

d. Read SEC filings from the company being valued and other industry players. Specifically, check the annual proxy and the annual report in which many companies list a self-selected peer group, usually for purposes of calculating executive compensation if it is tied to the company's stock price performance.

2. ***Separate pure plays from diversified companies:*** **Pure play** companies are publicly held companies that have one major business line which closely resembles one or more of the business lines, composition, or function of the company under evaluation. **Diversifieds** are companies that operate two or more major business lines. Within the food sector for example, Tootsie Roll is a pure play because it is only in the candy line of business whereas Nestle is a diversified company because it is involved in candy but it also has other business lines including baby foods, cereals, dairy products, beverages, food service and pet care. The purpose of separating the pure plays from the diversifieds is to determine whether there is a difference in valuation levels between pure play companies and diversified companies and to provide a better comp group for the company under evaluation. Pure play companies assist the valuation process greatly since little effort is required to adjust the company to make it "comparable" to the one under analysis (if that company is also a pure play).

3. ***Separate liquidity anomalies based on size:*** This is really a refinement of the description of "comparable" companies. A company is not comparable if it is much larger or much smaller than the company being valued. This does not mean that the much larger or much smaller comparable company cannot provide valuation guidance, but it does mean that the valuation guidance needs to be tempered by a recognition of the size differential and its significance (e.g., much larger companies may have better margins due to bulk purchasing or more advantageous distribution, while much smaller companies may have higher purchasing costs due to size-related risk, resulting in diminished profitability). Larger companies have significantly more market liquidity than smaller companies and that affects how comfortable an investor might be with regard to holding a large position in a particular stock (the more liquidity, the more opportunity there is to sell a position without having to do so at a discount to the current market price). The more liquid the market is, the greater the likelihood that the market price reflects the fair value of a minority share of the company.

4. ***Identify and categorize ratios and multiples to be evaluated:*** It is very important to analyze those multiples that are relevant for a particular industry. In general, more traditional stable earning / stable growth companies will be valued on a P/E or cash flow basis. High growth companies in industries such as technology and biotech often have low or even negative cash flow and/or earnings due to high research and development (R&D) and start-up costs. Such companies tend to be valued on revenue multiples because earnings (P/E) or cash flow (enterprise value to EBITDA) multiples would not be meaningful.

5. ***Check all data with source material and prepare comparable multiples:*** When preparing trading comps for a live transaction or important meeting, it is important to use source data (e.g., data found in the company's most recent SEC filings or its company reports) whenever possible in order to yield the most accurate results. Do not rely on equity research multiples or other third-party published data. Also, check your work. You might find that a company is trading at a significant premium or discount to its peer group. Before drawing conclusions from that "fact," first check the input and make sure that the anomaly is not caused by a typographical error or transposed number. It is critical that all of the market data used for the comparable companies (e.g., closing stock prices) are taken as of the same day (for comparability) and that it is the most current information available.

6. ***Analyze data and draw conclusions:*** As mentioned, use the trading comps to help ask the right questions. Look at the various companies to see whether they tend to trade at a premium (or a discount) to the company under analysis across all metrics. See if there appears to be a reason for this – it might be due to the company's size, its liquidity, or simply its leadership position within its market. However, do not draw too many conclusions from limited data. If the comp group is a limited sample set and none of the companies seems to be trading in line with another, you probably should not use that trading comp information to draw concrete valuation conclusions. Also, remember that while data should be used to draw conclusions, they do not by themselves provide the answers. There is no right or wrong answer to be found in data – they are just indicators that you should use, in conjunction with good judgment, to draw conclusions.

Additional Pointers

The following is a list of pointers to keep in mind when performing comparable company analysis. The following can serve as a checklist when reviewing your or someone else's work.

- Companies are generally referred to as "trading at a premium" or "trading at a discount" relative to industry competitors. "Multiple expansion" is the concept of a company's multiple rising (from 10x to 12x, for example) and "multiple compression" is the concept of a company's multiple falling (from 12x to 10x, for example).

- Trading comps show how a company is performing relative to its industry competitors. Many factors can affect why certain companies trade at a premium or discount to the average or median of the comparables. For example,

a. Leaders within an industry (either based on size, market penetration or reputation, among other things) will generally trade at a premium and poor performers will generally trade at a discount to the industry average.

b. Companies with higher levels of liquidity (meaning more shares are available on the open market for buying and selling at any given moment) tend to trade at a premium to companies with lower levels of liquidity.

c. Companies with higher levels of debt (more leverage) tend to see their equity value and cash flow multiples compress relative to industry peers with less debt since higher levels of debt places additional pressure on earnings and cash flow (in order to service interest payments). This pressure increases risk for the equity holder. See also Credit Analysis and Sources of Capital. (Ch.24,25)

- If a company is trading at a discount to its peer group on numerous ratios but is well-regarded in the industry, it should spur additional study of the company to learn why this is happening. Perhaps a large percentage of the company is held by a major shareholder (therefore there is a small public float or limited liquidity for investors) or perhaps the company is undergoing a major litigation case and, as a result, the market is discounting the stock. Or you might notice that a company trades at a premium to its peers on a P/E basis but in line when comparing cash flow or EBITDA multiples. After doing your homework, you might learn that the company has significant DD&A charges because it is amortizing more modern equipment or R&D and, because of this, you should focus more on the cash flow multiples than on the earnings multiples. The point is that trading comps will not spell out all the answers but they will prompt you to ask the right questions.

- It is important to use the same date for all market data. This means that all stock prices, future earnings and cash flow estimates, and dividend information should be taken from the same day and should be taken at the end of the day, after the market has closed (e.g., market data and all estimates as of July 24, 2006). Remember to note the date of the market data in the footnotes of the comparable company analysis so that the reader of the information knows how current the analysis is.

- If possible, try to use balance sheet and income statement data from the same point in time (e.g., all data as of December 31, 2005). Be sure to note the date of the balance sheet data in the footnotes.

- Calendarize when required to ensure that all data is "apples-to-apples" data (i.e., to ensure that items for one year are from January 1 to December 31 for all companies in the comp set since some companies have a fiscal year which is different from a calendar year); otherwise, seasonality is introduced as a potentially distinguishing factor. Calendarizing is described later in this chapter.

- Exclude nonrecurring items from earnings, cash flow or EBITDA so that one-time items such as restructuring charges and sales of major assets do not skew results. The goal is to iron out nonrecurring items in order to reflect as closely as possible what the company would look like on a run-rate basis going forward.

- Do not include the company you are valuing in the comp group. Inclusion in the comp set will skew the results. Set it off below the comp set for easy comparison.

- Remember that too many adjustments, no matter how well intentioned, can inadvertently distort the data, leading to multiples that are of limited value. Footnote any adjustments.

- Weigh median values of multiples more than mean (or average) values. Mean values are often skewed by outlying data and therefore can be misleading (though often both mean and median multiples are calculated and shown in the analysis).

- It is always best to perform comparable company analysis using source company data such as SEC 10-K and 10-Q filings. Document the source information and keep records of historical trading comp analysis for comparative reference.

- Use other financial data and key operating ratios to more fully inform the conclusions drawn from the trading comps.

- Regularly check for stock splits and other recent events that might affect the valuation of the company under analysis. For example, if a stock split was announced, this will change the shares outstanding in the analysis. In addition, you need to ensure that any future EPS or cash flow per share estimates taken from IBES or First Call are based on the new shares outstanding, adjusted for the stock split.

- When building a financial model, group all assumptions together (e.g., on one page in your model if possible) and color code them so they are readily identifiable as assumptions as opposed to calculations. Never hard-code numbers. Instead, have everything run as a calculation and only hard-code assumptions.

- Create a separate page as an output page and only put items on the output page that are relevant for decision making. Keep the output pages simple and easy to understand.

- Although a large comp set is ideal, there will be circumstances when only one or two companies are truly comparable. It is better to use only a few truly comparable companies than a larger comp set filled with non-comparable companies.

- Do not be afraid to use judgment when appropriate; just be sure to footnote whatever assumptions or adjustments are made in the calculations so that someone can easily trace all steps and adjustments in the analysis.

- Be sure to calculate multiples based on future (often called "forward") earnings, cash flow or EBITDA in addition to "trailing" or historical data. Investors often ascribe more weight to forward year estimates than to historical numbers.

Comparable company analysis involves preparing the comp set and then applying the multiples from the comp set to the company under analysis to determine an implied valuation range. Comparable company analysis will be performed for TradingCo and the results are provided in the following Tables 9.1 to 9.3. In Tables 9.1 and 9.2, a review of the output of the comp set is provided. The multiples are applied to TradingCo to prepare a valuation analysis using comparable companies in Table 9.3.

Developing Trading Comparables

Let's take a look at a comp group for TradingCo. First let's review the calculations and how they are calculated. Notes which describe each of the columns in Figure 9.1 are provided on the following page, with the numbers in parentheses corresponding to the numbered notes.

Table 9.1 – Comparable Company Analysis - TradingCo

$ millions, except for per share data

	(1)	(2)	(3)	(4)	(5)	(6)	(7)	(8)	(9)	(10)	(11)	(12)	(13)	(14)	(15)
Company	**Current price**	**Shares outst.**	**Market value**	**Net debt**	**Enterp. value (EV)**	**Net Debt /EV**	**LTM P/E**	**FY1 P/E**	**FY2 P/E**	**LTM EV/ EBITDA**	**LTM EV/ EBIT**	**LTGR %**	**Price/ book**	**Div. yield**	**FY1 PEG**
Comp A	$65.43	52.0	3,402	1,250	4,652	27%	22.0x	19.1x	17.5x	8.0x	10.3x	10.0%	2.3x	1.5%	1.9x
Comp B	$35.98	75.0	2,699	341	3,040	11%	25.0x	22.3x	19.5x	8.4x	11.0x	12.0%	2.5x	2.2%	1.9x
Comp C	$15.88	125.0	1,985	2,210	4,195	53%	18.0x	17.0x	15.0x	7.6x	9.7x	10.0%	2.3x	3.0%	1.7x
Comp D	$26.98	55.0	1,484	750	2,234	34%	24.0x	22.4x	20.7x	6.0x	8.4x	8.0%	2.2x	1.9%	2.8x
Comp E	$23.54	15.0	353	425	778	55%	12.0x	10.6x	9.7x	8.1x	10.2x	12.0%	2.0x	3.0%	0.9x
Median			1,985		3,040	34%	22.0x	19.1x	17.5x	8.0x	10.2x	10.0%	2.3x	2.2%	1.9x
Mean			1,985		2,980	36%	20.2x	18.3x	16.5x	7.6x	9.9x	10.4%	2.3x	2.3%	1.8x
High			3,402		4,652	55%	25.0x	22.4x	20.7x	8.4x	11.0x	12.0%	2.5x	3.0%	2.8x
Low			353		778	11%	12.0x	10.6x	9.7x	6.0x	8.4x	8.0%	2.0x	1.5%	0.9x
TradingCo	$35.00	50.0	1,750	850	2,600	33%	21.0x	18.0x	16.7x	7.8x	10.0x	10%	2.0x	2.4%	1.8x

Footnotes are provided on the following page

Notes to Table 9.1 are provided below. Many of these items are further described in Financial Statement Basics. (Ch.3)

1. ***Current stock price***: Be sure to use the closing stock price from the same date for all comps and include the date of the stock prices in the footnotes.

2. ***Shares outstanding***: Be consistent in using fully diluted shares for all comps. To calculate fully diluted shares for trading comps, use *exercisable* options as opposed to *outstanding* options since only vested options should be included for trading analysis. In comparable *transaction* analysis, outstanding options are usually used to calculate fully diluted shares for the target company (as opposed to just the vested options) since the assumption is usually made that, in a change-of-control transaction, all of the target company's options will vest immediately. A detailed discussion of exercisable options and outstanding options as well as a description of how to calculate fully diluted shares outstanding can be found in Financial Statement Basics. (Ch.3)

3. ***Market value of equity***: Current stock price × fully diluted shares outstanding = market value of equity. Market value is also referred to as equity value.

4. ***Net debt***: Short-term debt + long-term debt + capitalized leases + preferred stock – cash and cash equivalents (sometimes listed as marketable securities) = net debt. Book value numbers for debt are usually used for debt and preferred stock since the assumption is that the market value of debt is similar to the book value of debt. If, however, the companies in the comp set are in a state of financial distress, then the market value of their debt is not likely to be equal to the book value of debt. In these situations, it is better to use the market value of debt.

5. ***Enterprise value***: Market value of equity + net debt + minority interest = enterprise value. Represents total value of the firm, including both equity and debt holders. A common mistake is to accidentally omit preferred stock from net debt when calculating enterprise value. Enterprise value is also referred to as firm value.

6. ***Net debt to enterprise value***: Net debt / enterprise value. Represents a metric for leverage. Leverage is often calculated based on market value of debt and book value of debt to capture any anomalies arising out of a difference between the book value and the market value of the debt.

7. ***Price to LTM earnings***: Price to earnings (P/E) multiple based on LTM earnings (LTM = Latest Twelve Months). Be sure to make adjustments for irregular charges (e.g., nonrecurring accounting or restructuring charges).

8. ***Price to FY1earnings***: P/E multiple based on estimated year end earnings for the current year. Use the median EPS estimate from IBES, First Call, or a comparable source of estimated earnings. "E" means estimated.

9. ***Price to FY2 earnings***: P/E multiple based on estimated year end earnings for the following year. Use the median EPS estimate from IBES, First Call, or a comparable source of estimated earnings. "E" means estimated.

10. ***Enterprise value to LTM EBITDA***: Enterprise value / LTM EBITDA. EBITDA is Earnings Before Interest, Taxes, and DD&A. Calculate EBITDA using the latest SEC filings (10-Q and 10-K).

11. ***Enterprise value to LTM EBIT***: Enterprise value / LTM EBIT. EBIT is Earnings Before Interest and Taxes. Calculate EBIT using the latest SEC filings (10-Q and 10-K).

12. ***Estimate for long-term earnings growth***: An estimate for EPS CAGR (Compound Annual Growth Rate) for the next three to five years. A 10 percent LTGR on base year earnings of $1.00 would be $1.10 in Year 1 {$1.00 × (1 + 10%)}, $1.21 in Year 2 {$1.10 × (1 + 10%)}, etc. Use IBES, First Call, Bloomberg, or a comparable source for the estimated long-term growth rate.

13. ***Market value to book value of equity***: A multiple of the market value relative to the book value. Book value of equity can be found in the latest balance sheet.

14. ***Dividend yield***: (last quarterly dividend × 4) / current share price = dividend yield. Represents the annual amount of capital returned to shareholders in the form of dividends relative to the current stock price.

15. ***P/E to growth rate (PEG)***: FY1 P/E / (long-term growth rate × 100). The reason it is (long-term growth rate × 100) is a simplifying matter. If you do not multiply the growth rate, which is a percentage, by 100 to yield an integer, then the PEG values will be in the hundreds (i.e., 20x PE / 10% = 200x PEG without adjustment and 2x with adjustment).

For a more comprehensive description of these financial metrics, refer to Financial Statements Basics. (Ch.3)

Calculating LTM numbers

Calculating LTM numbers is very straightforward. Start with the most recent annual value, add the most recent quarterly value (through 1Q, 2Q, or 3Q) and subtract the comparable value from a year ago. For example, assume the following annual and quarterly data.

2005 year end earnings	$150 million
2006 1Q-3Q earnings	$130 million
2005 1Q-3Q earnings	$110 million

The LTM earnings as of the end of 3Q 2006 would be $170 million.

3Q 2006 LTM = $150 million + $130 million - $110 million = $170 million

Calendarizing comparables

When comparing two or more companies (either when preparing comps or when performing merger analysis), one must make adjustments so that all companies are measured over the same twelve-month period (or "on the same fiscal year-end"). This adjustment process is called "calendarizing" comparables. Assume Company A has a 9/30 fiscal year-end and Company B has a 12/31 fiscal year-end. In order to compare their FY1 EBITDA trading multiples, you must first adjust Company A's EBITDA to be measured over the same time frame as B. To estimate Company A's FY1 EBITDA based on Company B's 12/31 fiscal year-end, multiply Company A's FY1 EBITDA by .75 (to approximate EBITDA for 1/06-9/06) and multiply its FY2 EBITDA by .25 (to approximate EBITDA for 10/06-12/06).

			EBITDA			EV / FY1 EBITDA	
$ millions	Fiscal year-end	Enterprise value	FY1	FY2	FY1Adj.	Unadjusted	Adjusted
Company A[1]	9/30/06	$800	$100	$125	$106	8.0x	7.5x
Company B[2]	12/31/06	$500	$65	$75	$65	7.7x	7.7x

[1] FY1 adjusted = ($100 × .75) + ($125 × .25)
[2] No adjustment needs to be made for Company B

Reading Trading Comparables

Now let's try and analyze the data. Numbers are just numbers without knowing how to read them. Look for discrepancies and trends and try to draw conclusions from them. The numbers in parentheses above the columns correspond to the numbered notes on the following pages.

Table 9.2 – Analyzing Comparable Company Analysis - TradingCo

$ millions, except for per share data

			(1)	(2)		(3)	(4)	(5)		(6)		(7)		(8)	
Company	**Current price**	**Shares outst**	**Market value**	**Net debt**	**Enterp value**	**Net Debt /EV**	**LTM P/E**	**FY1 P/E**	**FY2 P/E**	**LTM EV/ EBITDA**	**LTM EV/ EBIT**	**LTGR %**	**Price/ book**	**Divd. yield**	**FY1 PEG**
Comp A	$65.43	52.0	3,402	1,250	4,652	27%	22.0x	19.1x	17.5x	8.0x	10.3x	10.0%	2.3x	1.5%	1.9x
Comp B	$35.98	75.0	2,699	341	3,040	11%	25.0x	22.3x	19.5x	8.4x	11.0x	12.0%	2.5x	2.2%	1.9x
Comp C	$15.88	125.0	1,985	2,210	4,195	53%	18.0x	17.0x	15.0x	7.6x	9.7x	10.0%	2.3x	3.0%	1.7x
Comp D	$26.98	55.0	1,484	750	2,234	34%	24.0x	22.4x	20.7x	6.0x	8.4x	8.0%	2.2x	1.9%	2.8x
Comp E	$23.54	15.0	353	425	778	55%	12.0x	10.6x	9.7x	8.1x	10.2x	12.0%	2.0x	3.0%	0.9x
Median			1,985		3,040	34%	22.0x	19.1x	17.5x	8.0x	10.2x	10.0%	2.3x	2.2%	1.9x
Mean			1,985		2,980	36%	20.2x	18.3x	16.5x	7.6x	9.9x	10.4%	2.3x	2.3%	1.8x
High			3,402		4,652	55%	25.0x	22.4x	20.7x	8.4x	11.0x	12.0%	2.5x	3.0%	2.8x
Low			353		778	11%	12.0x	10.6x	9.7x	6.0x	8.4x	8.0%	2.0x	1.5%	1.3x
TradingCo	$35.00	50.0	1,750	850	2,600	33%	21.0x	18.0x	16.7x	7.8x	10.0x	10%	2.0x	2.4%	0.9x

Footnotes are provided on the following page

Notes to Table 9.2 are provided below.

1. ***Market value***: To facilitate the reading of the trading comps, it is useful to first organize the comps by some important metric (market value of equity and enterprise value are the most common but it can be any important metric). The companies in TradingCo's comp group are ranked according to market value (largest to smallest). Also, notice that Company E is significantly smaller in terms of market value than the other companies (about 1/3 the size of the next smallest company and only 1/10 the size of the largest company). Keep this in mind as you review the comps and use judgment to determine whether you think Company E is truly comparable to the other companies and to the company you are trying to value.

2. ***Net debt***: Notice that Company B has a low level of net debt and corresponding low leverage relative to the other companies in the comp group. This low net debt could be because Company B has significantly lower debt levels than its peers or because it is sitting on a very large cash reserve (remember that net debt = total debt + preferred equity - cash, so the cash amount serves as an offset to the debt and preferred equity amounts). This cash reserve could be due to a recent significant asset sale for cash without an immediate redeployment of the capital or Company B may not operate with as much debt as its competitors (you cannot tell from the multiples alone, but at least you will be prompted to find out *why*).

3. ***Net debt to enterprise value***: Company B has a significantly lower net debt load than its peers while Companies C and E have higher net debt levels. Check to see if these net debt levels have a corresponding effect on the company's multiples. Notice how Company B, with low level of net debt, tends to trade at a premium to its peers on numerous metrics whereas Company E tends to trade at a discount, probably because of its high level of net debt. However Company E is also smaller, so consider whether size might be the difference. In this case, Company C also trades at a discount to the peer group, so the net debt level does appear to be a major factor.

4. ***Price to LTM earnings***: Notice how Company E trades at a significant discount on a P/E basis compared to the other companies. It does not appear to be due to its growth (since Company E's long-term growth rate is in line with the other companies in the comp set). Further analysis of its business, profitability, and operating margins, among other things, is called for.

5. ***Price to FY1 earnings***: Notice how Company B and Company E are trading relative to others in the comp group.

6. ***Enterprise value to LTM EBITDA***: Company D seems to be trading at a discount to its peers on an EBITDA basis, but at a premium on a P/E basis. It is important to always try to figure out anomalies such as this. For example, research on the company might reveal that it has significantly larger depreciation charges than the other companies. If this relationship does not make immediate sense to you, think of the underlying math of multiples: In this case the LTM FV/EBITDA multiple could be low because the firm value is low (smaller numerator leads to smaller quotient) *or* because the EBITDA value is high (larger denominator leads to a smaller quotient). Again, it is impossible to tell from the multiples themselves because they are the result of two different numbers and a mathematical operation, so further analysis of Company D's LTM EV and LTM EBITDA is warranted.

7. ***Long-term growth rate***: Notice how Company C has lower growth prospects than most of its peers and notice that it trades lower relative to the others.

8. ***Dividend yield***: Notice how Company C also compensates for its slower growth by paying a higher dividend relative to its stock price. Total return to a shareholder is measured both by share price appreciation *and* dividend yield since both are forms of value being returned to the shareholders.

Drawing Valuation Conclusions

Now let's use the data and value TradingCo. The numbers in parentheses above the columns correspond to the numbered notes on the following pages.

Table 9.3 – Comparable Company Analysis - TradingCo

$ millions, except for per share data

	(1)		*(2)*	*(2),(3)*		*(3)*	*(2),(3)*		*(4)*	*(4)*	
	Multiple Range		**TradingCo**	**Implied enterprise value**		**Net**	**Implied market value of equity**		**Shares**	**Implied market value of equity per share**	
	Low	**High**	**data**	**Low**	**High**	**debt**	**Low**	**High**	**outst.**	**Low**	**High**
LTM P/E	18.0x	24.0x	$1.67	2,353	2,854	850	1,503	2,004	50	$30.06	$40.08
FY1 P/E	17.0x	22.5x	$1.94	2,499	3,033	850	1,649	2,183	50	$32.98	$43.65
FY2 P/E	15.0x	20.0x	$2.10	2,425	2,950	850	1,575	2,100	50	$31.50	$42.00
LTM EV/EBITDA	7.5x	8.5x	333.3	2,500	2,833	850	1,650	1,983	50	$33.00	$39.66
LTM EV/EBIT	9.5x	10.5x	260.0	2,470	2,730	850	1,620	1,880	50	$32.40	$37.60
Price/book value	2.2x	2.3x	875.0	2,775	2,863	850	1,925	2,013	50	$38.50	$40.25
Dividend yield	2.5%	2.0%	$0.84	2,530	2,950	850	1,680	2,100	50	$33.60	$42.00
							Median			**$32.98**	**$40.25**
							Mean			**$33.15**	**$40.75**
						(5)	**Selected value range**			**$33.00**	**$40.00**
						(6)	**Current price**				**$35.00**
						(7)	**Premium/(discount) to current price**			**(5.7%)**	**14.3%**

Footnotes are provided on the following page

Notes to Table 9.3 are provided below.

1. Identify multiple ranges from the comparable company analysis, as opposed to choosing specific multiples (e.g., for LTM P/E, a *range* of 18x to 24x was chosen as opposed to choosing just the median number from the comp group of 22x). Choosing a single multiple value such as 22x implies a level of precision that does not exist with comparable company analysis (or any other type of valuation analysis); a range of multiples is more realistic. Also, use judgment in choosing the ranges. It should not be a mechanical extrapolation from the data. For example, the actual LTM P/E range was 12x (low) and 25x (high). However, a data range of 12x to 25x would be too wide. If the data range is too wide, the valuation conclusions also will be too wide, which decreases the utility of the data and calls into question the conclusions.

2. Calculate the implied values based on the actual company data and the chosen multiple ranges. The values in this column are the actual TradingCo figures. For example, $2.10 is TradingCo's FY2 EPS and $260 million is TradingCo's LTM EBIT.

3. For each valuation multiple, multiply the selected multiple range by the appropriate TradingCo value to yield an implied TradingCo valuation range for that particular metric. If you are using a market value per share multiple such as P/E or dividend yield, you will calculate the per share market value and then back into the market value and enterprise value numbers (by multiplying by TradingCo's shares outstanding and then adding net debt, respectively). If you are using a market value or enterprise value multiple, you will back into the market value per share number by subtracting net debt from enterprise value and dividing the implied market value by TradingCo's shares outstanding.

   In the following example, all dollars ($) are in millions, except per share data.

   For example, TradingCo's LTM EPS is $1.67 and the multiple range chosen for LTM P/E is 18x to 24x. Multiply the chosen multiples by TradingCo's actual LTM EPS to calculate an implied market value of equity per share.

   18x LTM P/E × $1.67 LTM EPS = $30.06 implied market value per share
   24x LTM P/E × $1.67 LTM EPS = $40.08 implied market value per share

   Next, multiply the implied market value per share by the fully diluted shares outstanding.

$30.06 × 50 shares outstanding = $1,503 implied market value
$40.08 × 50 shares outstanding = $2,004 implied market value

Finally, add net debt to the implied market values to calculate implied enterprise values.

$1,503 market value + $850 of net debt = $2,353 implied enterprise value
$2,004 market value + $850 of net debt = $2,854 implied enterprise value

To illustrate using an enterprise value multiple, let's now consider the LTM EV/EBITDA multiple range of 7.5x to 8.5x and TradingCo's LTM EBITDA of $333.3 million. First calculate an implied enterprise value based on TradingCo's LTM EBITDA and the multiple range.

7.5x × $333.3 TradingCo EBITDA = $2,500 implied enterprise value
8.5x × $333.3 TradingCo EBITDA = $2,833 implied enterprise value

Next, subtract net debt from the implied enterprise value to arrive at an implied market value.

$2,500 implied enterprise value - $850 net debt = $1,650 implied market value
$2,833 implied enterprise value - $850 net debt = $1,983 implied market value

Finally, divide the implied market value by TradingCo's fully diluted shares outstanding to arrive at an implied market value of equity per share.

$1,650 / 50 shares outstanding = $33.00 implied value per share
$1,983 / 50 shares outstanding = $39.66 implied value per share

4. Regardless of the valuation multiple you are using, the goal is to estimate an implied value per share of equity because that is the metric to compare to the current stock price. The results of implied market value per share should be checked by also calculating median and mean values and by considering the upper and lower limits of the range as well.

5. Upon analyzing the implied market values per share, the next step is to determine the valuation range based on all of the results using data and judgment.

6. Lastly, always compare the valuation range to the current market price to see if the current stock price is within the comparable company range, above the range, or below the range.

7. The low end of the value range of \$33 is 5.7 percent less than the current market price of \$35 {(\$33 / \$35) – 1)} = -5.7% and the high-end of the value range of \$40 is 14.3 percent greater than the current market price of \$35 {(\$40 / \$35) – 1)} = 14.3%.

Comparable Transaction Analysis

Chapter 10

Wise men say, and not without reason,
that whosoever wishes to foresee the future
might consult the past.

Nicolo Machiavelli

Comparable transaction analysis (also known as precedent transaction analysis, transaction comps, precedent acquisition analysis and precedent paid analysis) is similar to comparable company analysis in that multiples from comparable transactions are used to draw valuation conclusions. The difference between comparable company analysis and comparable transaction analysis is that in comparable transaction analysis the prices paid in previous transactions are used to calculate the multiples, as opposed to the current stock prices which are used in comparable company analysis. As with comparable company analysis, it is important to note that comparable transaction analysis is *relative* (to other companies and other transactions). This is in contrast to intrinsic value (or non-relative) methods of valuation such as discounted cash flow analysis and leveraged buyout analysis.

This chapter begins with a review of comparable transaction analysis and its benefits and challenges. Also included in this chapter is a review of the key transaction terms normally provided in a deal announcement. Numerical examples of comparable transaction analysis are provided for cash-based and stock-based transactions. Key sections of other chapters interrelate with comparable transaction analysis. As such, to complement this chapter it is important to review The Role of Valuation (Ch.8), Comparable Company Analysis (Ch.9), the sections on Increasing Shareholder Value and Synergies in Strategic Transactions (Ch.4), Acquisition Currency (Ch.15) and Stock Deals. (Ch.16)

The Control Premium

To perform comparable transaction analysis, a comparable group of transactions (or comp set) is identified and multiples of financial and operating metrics such as P/E or enterprise value to EBITDA are calculated for each transaction in the comp set. Based on the comp set's multiples, a range of multiples is applied to the company being valued to determine its implied valuation range. That is, the implied valuation of the company under analysis is determined by taking the multiples paid for comparable companies in *other transactions* and applying them to the company under consideration.

Transaction comparables allow one to analyze the premium paid to gain control of the target company (the control premium), whereas *trading* comparables allow one to value a minority (or non-controlling) share of the company. In theory, the only difference between the trading multiple and transaction multiple values for a company should be the value of the control premium.

Calculating the control premium

When measuring the level of the "control premium" paid in a transaction, it is important to compare the stock price the day before the transaction announcement (or another period of time such as the stock price five days, ten days or twenty days before the announcement) and the offer price per share offered in the transaction. For example, if the offer price for Target is $25 per share and the stock price the day before the announcement were $20, the "control premium" would be $5 per share or 25 percent calculated as follows:

$25 offer price - $20 stock price before announcement =
$5 control premium

($25 offer price / $20 stock price before announcement) - 1 =
25% control premium

If the transaction were rumored in the market before the announcement date, compare the offer price per share to the stock price the day before the rumor was in the market (and therefore likely to have been reflected in the stock price). The rumor date could potentially have been weeks, if not months, prior to the announcement date, so it is important to be particularly careful when determining the latest date at which no merger buzz was priced into the target company's stock price.

Key Benefits

The main premise of comparable transaction analysis is that companies within the same industry should sell in a change-of-control transaction for the same relative value as a multiple of financial and operating metrics. Comparable transaction analysis is one of the key methodologies for estimating a company's M&A sale value. It is an especially good indicator of sales value if a liquid M&A market exists since it represents actual multiples and premia paid by buyers within an industry. Comparable transaction analysis is also a good tool to identify M&A trends within certain industries.

Key Challenges

As with trading comps, one of the biggest shortcomings of using transaction comps is the difficulty of finding a truly "comparable" transaction. For example, let's assume we are considering a transaction between JuiceCo (a potential acquiror) and SodaCo (the target). Two months ago, a transaction took place in the beverage industry between CoffeeCo and TeaCo. Since SodaCo and TeaCo are beverage companies, the multiples from the TeaCo transaction could be used to estimate an M&A value for SodaCo. However, upon further analysis of the CoffeeCo/TeaCo transaction, you notice that CoffeeCo had an exceptionally large amount of synergies with TeaCo (a level of synergies that are much higher than those between JuiceCo and SodaCo). Significant synergies would enable CoffeeCo to offer a higher price for TeaCo and still create value for its shareholders with the transaction. The premium paid by CoffeeCo for TeaCo, therefore, might be high relative to the appropriate premium JuiceCo should pay for SodaCo (and the corresponding transaction multiples in the CoffeeCo/TeaCo transaction also might be high relative to what is appropriate for SodaCo). In essence, because so many factors lead to valuation, it is difficult to know with certainty whether the JuiceCo/SodaCo transaction is directly comparable to the CoffeeCo/TeaCo transaction.

Using transaction comps requires a familiarity with the industry in order to have a good sense for which multiples are truly comparable (e.g., "dog" vs. "crown jewel" assets should command different valuation multiples). And just as with trading comparables, prevailing market conditions--such as the interest rate environment or the state of the credit, lending and/or stock markets-- also can lead to distortions in transaction multiples. Another shortcoming of transaction comps is that there can be periods of transactional *in*activity in an industry, and so transaction comps can become outdated, which diminishes their value to the user. Similarly, limited public data on private companies or subsidiaries can make it exceptionally difficult to prepare a meaningful set of transaction comps for private company or subsidiary-level transactions. In spite of these many challenges, comparable transaction analysis is one of the major pillars of M&A valuation.

Identifying Transaction Comparables

The mechanics of calculating transaction comps are very similar to those of calculating trading comps. In fact, the six major steps taken in calculating trading comps are also taken in calculating transaction comps. The key difference is that instead of using current market data for the stock price, the price paid for the target company is used to calculate multiples (also known as the offer price, the transaction price, or the purchase price). Sometimes this purchase price is straightforward because the company will announce the price paid per share. Sometimes it is not as straightforward because the company will announce an exchange ratio (as opposed to a price) and one would need to calculate the implied purchase price (examples of this are provided later in this chapter).

The most common way to find comparable transactions is to perform a transaction search by industry or by NAICS (North American Industry Classification System) using a database such as Thomson Financial or Dealogic. The most common time frame to check for precedent transactions is within the past five years (although transactions which took place within the last one to two years are more comparable than those that took place within the last three to five years). A longer or shorter time horizon may be required depending on M&A activity for the industry in question. For example, there may have been a flurry of activity in the sector such that comps from two years ago are outdated, or there may have been no activity in the past five years, so a longer time horizon is more appropriate.

Once a comparable transaction has been identified, one must gather information about the transaction to prepare the multiples. A press release issued by the target or acquiror company is the most reliable source of information about the transaction terms (if either of the companies is publicly traded and if the transaction is material to the public company, the press release announcing the transaction should be filed as an 8-K at the time of the announcement by the public company). To calculate multiples, the most recent balance sheet and income statement (of the target company) will be required. For public companies, use the most recent financial statements available at the time of the announcement. For example, for a deal announced February 15, check first to see if the company's December 31 financials have been filed. If not, use the financials filed as of September 30 from the previous year to prepare the multiples and then, when the December 31 financials become available, update the transaction comps with the more current data (since the acquiror would have been using the December 31 financials for a February 15 transaction and the idea of transaction comps is to calculate as closely as possible the multiples paid from the perspective of the acquiror). For public companies, it is likely that the target company will issue a proxy statement describing the proposed transaction which the shareholders will review prior to voting on the deal (the acquiror also will issue a proxy statement if its shareholders need to vote on the transaction). This proxy statement is filled with information about the transaction and, as soon as it is publicly available, should be referenced to update the transaction comps as appropriate. For forward-looking multiples such as FY1 P/E (FY1 meaning "forward year 1" or the most current fiscal year from the date of the transaction announcement), forward-looking EPS estimates as of the date of the announcement will be needed.

If calculating transaction multiples for deals which occurred well in the past, it is important to be careful about making sure forward EPS estimates are used *as of the date of the announcement.* For example, assume it is June 30, 2005 and you need to calculate multiples for a transaction announced August 15, 2004. For a transaction announced August 15, 2004, you will need forward EPS estimates for the target *as of August 15, 2004.* Assuming the target company is on a December 31 fiscal year end, these would be EPS estimates for the fiscal year ending 2004. The 2004 EPS estimates (as of August 15, 2004) would be used to calculate FY1 P/E multiples. The 2005 EPS estimates (as of August 15, 2004) would be used to calculate FY2 P/E multiples. Also, for a transaction announced August 15, 2004, the June 30, 2004 balance sheet should be used because that was the most current balance sheet at the time the transaction was agreed to.

Private company transactions

For private companies, it is often very difficult to find balance sheet and income statement data. The best option is to comb through as many news articles and third-party reports as are available on the company and on the transaction in search of any information regarding implied transaction multiples. Industry-specific journals and magazines are particularly good sources for this.

Databases such as Dealogic and Thomson Financial provide their own calculations for transaction multiples. This is fine for a "quick and dirty" analysis. However, if the transaction comps are being used in a live deal or any other important purpose, you should create your own transaction comps from public filings and company documents in order to ensure the analysis is correct rather than relying on the work of others.

Reading Deal Announcements

The deal announcement is the press release issued by the target company (Target) or the acquiror company (Acquiror) on the day of the announcement. Refer to the company-issued statement (as opposed to news articles written about the transaction) when gathering information to calculate transaction multiples. For public companies, company-issued press releases can be found in 8-K SEC filings, usually on the day of the announcement.

Some of the key information items in a deal announcement are listed on the following page.

Announcement date: This is the date a transaction is publicly announced (usually a day the market is open). The announcement date is not the "rumor date" or the date information about the transaction leaked into the marketplace but rather the date the companies formally announce the transaction.

Closing date: In a transaction announcement, the companies often state the estimated closing date for the transaction (or the expected number of months before closing) based on the requisite approvals the companies will need to obtain. Transactions can close in as little time as a few weeks (for small and/or private deals) or as much time as 12 to 24 months (and sometimes longer in heavily-regulated industries with multiple levels of regulatory approvals required before the transaction can close).

Acquiror: This is the acquiring entity (can be another company, a group of investors, or a single investor). The Acquiror is the entity paying cash, stock or other consideration to the selling shareholder(s). In a stock-for-stock exchange, the Acquiror is generally the company whose stock will survive in the transaction.

Target: This is a description of the assets, division, subsidiary, company or portfolio of companies being purchased by Acquiror. For acquisitions of assets, a division or subsidiary, the transaction announcement usually includes a brief description of what is being sold. If Target is an entire company, the selling shareholders are the shareholders of Target; if Target is a subsidiary, division or assets of a company, the selling shareholder is the parent company. Proceeds from the sale go to the selling shareholder(s).

Offer price: The offer price is the price paid for the equity of Target, usually quoted as a price per share for a publicly traded company and usually quoted as an aggregate amount for a private company. If the transaction is a stock deal, the exchange ratio might be quoted instead of the offer price per share.

Exchange ratio: In stock deals, the exchange ratio is the number of Acquiror shares issued per Target share. It is calculated by dividing the offer price per Target share by the Acquiror's stock price at the time of the announcement (offer price for Target / Acquiror stock price = exchange ratio). Exchange ratios are further described in Stock Deals and Merger of Equals. (Ch.16,18)

Premium: If Target is a public company, the premium paid is the percentage between the offer price and Target's stock price the day before the transaction announcement. Premiums can be calculated for longer time periods (for example, the premium paid over the stock price two weeks before announcement, or one month before announcement).

Percentage acquired: This is the percentage of Target's stock acquired in the transaction. Unless specified, it is a safe assumption that Acquiror is purchasing 100 percent of Target's equity. However, there are many circumstances in which Acquiror purchases less than 100 percent of Target's equity. It is important to differentiate in the transaction comparables between the acquisition of a majority of the voting power of Target (which purchase price should include a control premium) and the acquisition of less than a majority of the voting power of Target (which purchase price would *not* include a control premium, although the purchase price could be at some premium relative to the current stock price to reflect the acquisition of some control but not majority control).

Equity value: This is the price paid by Acquiror for all of Target's equity. It is calculated as the offer price per Target share multiplied by the number of fully diluted shares outstanding of Target. Equity value is also referred to as "deal value." This is in contrast to enterprise or transaction value.

Assumed net debt: This includes all of Target's net debt to be assumed by Acquiror in the transaction, including any of Target's preferred stock to be assumed in the transaction.

Transaction value: This is the price paid by Acquiror for all of Target's assets (equity plus assumed debt). It is calculated as equity value plus assumed net debt. Transaction value is also referred to as enterprise value or firm value. Be careful about differentiating between equity values which exclude assumed debt and transaction values which include assumed debt.

Consideration: This is what is paid (e.g., cash, stock, notes, etc.) by Acquiror to Target shareholders. The percentage of each type of consideration (if some combination of cash, stock and/or notes is offered) should be noted. Consideration is often stated as a percentage, such as 50 percent cash/50 percent stock, or 100 percent stock, etc.

Terms/structure: Any specific terms related to the transaction are usually included in the announcement. Examples include the percentage of Target's equity acquired (if less than 100 percent), if there is stock consideration whether the exchange ratio is fixed or floating, or if the exchange ratio has a cap or collar, etc. Exchange ratios are further described in Stock Deals. (Ch.16)

Social issues: In a merger of equals, or acquisitions in which the Target company will continue to play a meaningful role in the newly combined company, certain social issues might be included in the deal announcement, including who will hold key management positions in the new company, what the post-transaction composition of the board of directors will be, where the company's headquarters will be, and what the new company's name will be, among other things.

Synergies: Often, the companies will announce the synergies they expect to realize in the transaction. Sometimes, cost synergies are separated from revenue synergies. Synergies are further described in Strategic Transactions and Analyzing a Strategic Transaction. (Ch.4,6)

Developing Transaction Comparables

To describe how to develop and use transaction comparables, we will consider an example in the cellular phone market. Assume the goal is to value SouthCellularCo, a regional cellular company in the southern United States. From your research you have determined that two transactions in the cellular phone industry have taken place recently which you believe to be comparable to SouthCellularCo. The first transaction is an all stock merger between TelephoneCo and WestCellularCo. The second transaction is a part stock, part cash acquisition of EastCellularCo by CableCo. To perform comparable transaction analysis of SouthCellularCo, you must first calculate the transaction multiples for WestCellularCo and EastCellularCo.

Let's begin by calculating the transaction multiples for WestCellularCo. The following is an excerpt from TelephoneCo's press release announcing the transaction.

> *February 15, 2006, San Francisco:* TelephoneCo announced today that it has entered into a definitive merger agreement with WestCellularCo. As a result of the merger, each share of WestCellularCo common stock outstanding will be converted into the right to receive 1.5 shares of TelephoneCo common stock.

Upon doing research into the two companies' financial statements and SEC filings, the following facts are determined:

1. On February 14, 2006 WestCellularCo's closing stock price was $40 and TelephoneCo's stock price was $32.

2. From reviewing the year end balance sheets and income statements for both companies, you determine that as of December 31, 2005:
   - WestCellularCo had 110 million fully diluted shares outstanding, $2.25 billion of net debt and book value of equity of $3 billion
   - *WestCellularCo's LTM (latest twelve months) earnings and EBITDA were $250 million and $950 million, respectively*
   - TelephoneCo had 335 million fully diluted shares outstanding

3. *As of February 14, 2006, the median 2006 EPS estimate from the various research analysts who cover WestCellularCo was $2.50 per share.*

There is now enough information to calculate transaction multiples for the TelephoneCo/WestCellularCo transaction.

1. Since the press release stated that each share of WestCellularCo stock would be converted into TelephoneCo stock, you can conclude that TelephoneCo is the Acquiror and WestCellularCo is the Target. In general, the company whose stock survives is the Acquiror. The opposite is true in some reverse mergers (which are transactions in which the Target company's stock survives); reverse mergers, however, are not common and generally are used if Acquiror is a private company and would like to be a public company after the merger is complete and so the private company merges with a publicly held Target. It is determined that this transaction is comparable to an acquisition of SouthCellularCo. Recall that transaction multiples reflect the value that Acquiror ascribes to Target. This transaction would *not* be comparable if it were WestCellularCo buying TelephoneCo because in that case the transaction multiples would be for the purchase of a telephone company and not for the purchase of a cellular company.

2. The companies did not explicitly state the offer price per share in the deal announcement, so it must be calculated. The exchange ratio of 1.5x is the number of TelephoneCo shares that will be issued per WestCellularCo share. The exchange ratio is calculated by dividing the offer price for Target by Acquiror's share price:

   $$\frac{\text{Offer price for Target}}{\text{Acquiror price}} = \text{Exchange ratio}$$

   Since the exchange ratio of 1.5x is stated in the deal announcement, and Acquiror's stock price the day before the announcement was $32, the implied offer price for Target can be calculated by multiplying $32 by 1.5.

   $$\frac{\text{Offer price for Target}}{\$32} = 1.5\text{x}$$

   $$\text{Offer price for Target} = \$32 \times 1.5$$
   $$\text{Offer price for Target} = \$48$$

   This means that each WestCellularCo shareholder will receive $48 per share of value per WestCellularCo share (based on TelephoneCo's share price of $32). This also means that if TelephoneCo's share price moves up or down, the value per WestCellularCo share will move up or down (since the value per WestCellularCo share is equal to the TelephoneCo share price multiplied by the exchange ratio). For example, if TelephoneCo's share price moves from $32 to $30, then the value of the offer for WestCellularCo will fall from $48 to $45 ($30 x 1.5 = $45) per share. Fixed and floating exchange ratios are described in more detail in Stock Deals. (Ch.16)

3. Next we can calculate the premium paid to gain control of WestCellularCo. The premium is usually calculated on a percentage basis by dividing the offer price for Target by Target's stock price the day before the transaction announcement and then subtracting one in order to arrive at a percentage:

$$\frac{\text{Offer price for Target}}{\text{Target price pre-announcement}} - 1 = \text{Premium paid}$$

Based on WestCellularCo's share price of $40 before the transaction announcement, the transaction value of $48 represents an $8 per share or 20 percent premium for each WestCellularCo share.

$$\frac{\text{\$48 offer price}}{\text{\$40 pre-transaction price}} - 1 = \text{Premium paid}$$

($48 offer price / $40 pre-transaction price) - 1 = 0.2 = 20 percent premium paid

4. To calculate the equity value for the transaction, the offer price per share is multiplied by the fully diluted shares outstanding for WestCellularCo. Based on a deal price of $48 per share and WestCellularCo's 110 million fully diluted shares outstanding, the market value of this transaction is $5.28 billion.

$48 per share × 110 million WestCellularCo fully diluted shares = $5.28 billion

5. The transaction value (or enterprise value) of the transaction is the equity value plus the assumed net debt of WestCellularCo. Based on the equity value of $5.28 billion and the net debt as of WestCellularCo's most recent balance sheet of $2.25 billion, the enterprise value of the transaction is $7.53 billion.

$5.28 billion equity value + $2.25 billion of assumed net debt = $7.53 billion

6a.To calculate the LTM P/E multiple, divide the equity value of $5.28 billion by WestCellularCo's LTM earnings of $250 million. The LTM P/E multiple for this transaction is 21.1x.

$5.28 billion equity value / $250 million LTM earnings = 21.1x LTM P/E

6b.We could also calculate the LTM P/E just as we will calculate the FY 1 P/E in (7) below, that is, using an earnings per share value rather than an aggregate earnings value. In order to do this, we first convert the aggregate LTM earnings value into an LTM earnings per share value. To do so, first divide the LTM earnings of $250 million by the fully diluted shares outstanding of 110 million to arrive at LTM EPS of $2.27. Now divide the offer price per share of $48 by the LTM EPS estimate of $2.27. The LTM P/E multiple for this transaction is 21.1x.

$250 million LTM earnings / 110 million fully diluted shares = $2.27 LTM EPS
$48 equity value per share / $2.27 LTM EPS = 21.1x LTM P/E

7. To calculate the P/E multiple based on the expected earnings for 2006, divide the offer price per share of $48 by the 2006 median EPS estimate of $2.50. The FY1 (future year 1) P/E multiple for this transaction is 19.2x.

   $48 equity value per share / $2.50 2006 EPS = 19.2x FY1 P/E (or 2006 P/E)

8. To calculate the price to book multiple, divide the equity value of $5.28 billion by the book value of equity of $3 billion. The price to book multiple for this transaction is 1.8x.

   $5.28 billion equity value / $3 billion book value of equity = 1.8x price/book

9. To calculate the transaction value to EBITDA multiple, divide the transaction value of $7.53 billion by the LTM EBITDA of $950 million. The transaction value to LTM EBITDA multiple for this transaction is 7.9x.

   $7.53 billion transaction value / $950 million LTM EBITDA = 7.9x

10. Now calculate the pro forma ownership of shares between TelephoneCo shareholders and WestCellularCo shareholders. Since WestCellularCo shareholders will receive 1.5 TelephoneCo shares per WestCellularCo share, then TelephoneCo will issue an additional 165 million shares of its stock to WestCellularCo shareholders.

    110 million WestCellularCo shares
    × 1.5 exchange ratio
    = 165 million TelephoneCo shares issued to WestCellularCo shareholders

11. In combination with the original TelephoneCo shares of 335 million, the new company now has 500 million shares outstanding, 67 percent owned by TelephoneCo shareholders and 33 percent owned by WestCellularCo shareholders.

    335 million "old" shares owned by TelephoneCo shareholders
    + 165 million "new" shares issued to WestCellularCo shareholders
    = 500 million pro forma shares

335 million TelephoneCo shareholders / 500 million pro forma shares = 67%
165 million WestCellularCo shareholders / 500 million pro forma shares = 33%

Now that we have calculated multiples from our first comparable transaction, let's turn our attention to the second comparable transaction. Below is the deal announcement for the acquisition of EastCellularCo by CableCo.

March 21, 2006, New York: CableCo announced today that it has agreed to buy EastCellularCo. Under the merger agreement, each share of EastCellularCo common stock outstanding will be converted into the right to receive (i) $8 in cash and (ii) a fractional share of CableCo common stock. The fractional share of CableCo common stock that EastCellularCo shareholders receive will be determined by an exchange ratio calculated by dividing $8 by the closing sale price of CableCo common stock on the trading day immediately before the closing date of the merger.

Upon further analysis of the two company's financial statements and SEC filings, the following facts are determined:

1. *On March 17, 2006 EastCellular's closing stock price was $12 and CableCo's stock price was $40. March 17 market information is used as opposed to March 19 because the transaction was announced on Monday, March 20; therefore Friday, March 17 is the last trading day prior to the announcement of the transaction.*

2. *From reviewing the year end balance sheets and income statements for both companies, it is determined that as of December 31, 2005:*
   - *EastCellularCo had 225 million fully diluted shares outstanding, $1 billion of net debt and book value of equity of $2.5 billion*
   - *EastCellularCo's LTM (latest twelve months) earnings and EBITDA were $200 million and $675 million, respectively*
   - *CableCo had 120 million fully diluted shares outstanding*

3. *As of March 17, 2006, the median 2006 EPS estimate from the various research analysts who cover EastCellularCo was $0.95 per share.*

Now transaction multiples for the CableCo/EastCellularCo transaction can be calculated.

1. It is fair to conclude from the deal announcement that EastCellularCo is the Target and CableCo is the Acquiror.

2. Upon close of the transaction, EastCellularCo shareholders will receive a combination of stock and cash comprising $16 of total value. The cash portion of the offer is $8 per share. The stock portion is based on a floating exchange

ratio, determined at close by dividing $8 by the closing price of CableCo on the trading day immediately before close. Based on CableCo's share price before announcement of $40, this translates into 0.2 shares of CableCo, but that can change between announcement and close.

$8 stock value / $40 CableCo's stock price = 0.2 exchange ratio (for stock)

Unlike the TelephoneCo/WestCellularCo transaction, which was a fixed exchange ratio offer, this transaction is a floating exchange ratio offer. The value of the stock consideration is $8, regardless of whether or not CableCo's stock price goes up or down before the closing. For example, if CableCo's stock price rose to $45, the value of the stock consideration would still be $8, but the number of CableCo shares issued per EastCellularCo share would be 0.178 ($8 stock value / $45 CableCo stock price = 0.178 exchange ratio). Fixed and floating exchange ratios are described in more detail in Stock Deals. (Ch.16)

The offer price per share of EastCellularCo is $16, comprised of the $8 in cash and the $8 in CableCo stock.

$8 of cash + $8 stock value = $16 offer price

3. The offer price of $16 per share represents a 33 percent premium for each EastCellularCo share based on EastCellularCo's closing stock price of $12 just before announcement.

   ($16 offer price / $12 pre-transaction stock price) – 1 = 0.33 = 33% premium

4. Based on a deal price of $16 per share and EastCellularCo's 225 million fully diluted shares outstanding, the market value of this transaction is $3.6 billion.

   $16 offer price × 225 million EastCellularCo fully diluted shares = $3.6 billion

5. Based on EastCellularCo's net debt of $1 billion, the transaction value (or enterprise value) of the transaction is $4.6 billion.

   $3.6 billion equity value + $1 billion of assumed net debt = $4.6 billion

6a.To calculate the LTM P/E multiple, divide the equity value of $3.6 billion by EastCellularCo's LTM earnings of $200 million. The LTM P/E multiple for this transaction is 18.0x.

   $3.6 billion equity value / $200 million LTM earnings = 18.0x LTM P/E

6b. We could also calculate the LTM P/E just as we will calculate the FY 1 P/E in (7) below, that is, using an earnings per share value rather than an aggregate earnings value. In order to do this, we must first convert the aggregate LTM earnings value into an LTM earnings *per share* value. To do so, first divide the LTM earnings of $200 million by the fully diluted shares outstanding of 225 million to arrive at LTM EPS of $0.89. Now divide the offer price per share of $16 by the LTM EPS estimate of $0.89. The LTM P/E multiple for this transaction is 18.0x.

$200 million LTM earnings / 225 million fully diluted shares = $0.89 LTM EPS
$16 equity value per share / $0.89 LTM EPS = 18.0x LTM P/E

7. To calculate the P/E multiple based on the expected earnings for 2006, divide the offer price per share of $16 by the 2006 median EPS estimate of $0.95. The FY1 (future year 1) P/E multiple for this transaction is 16.8x.

$16 offer price / $0.95 2006 EPS = 16.8x FY1 P/E (or 2006 P/E)

8. To calculate the price to book multiple, divide the equity value of $3.6 billion by the book value of equity of $2.5 billion. The price to book multiple for this transaction is 1.4x.

$3.6 billion equity value / $2.5 billion book value of equity = 1.4x price/book

9. To calculate the transaction value to EBITDA multiple, divide the transaction value of $4.6 billion by the LTM EBITDA of $675 million. The transaction value to LTM EBITDA multiple for this transaction is 6.8x.

$4.6 billion transaction value / $675 million LTM EBITDA = 6.8x

10. In terms of pro forma ownership, EastCellularCo shareholders will receive 0.2 CableCo shares per EastCellularCo share (if CableCo's share price the day before closing is $40), meaning they will own 45 million shares of CableCo after the close of the transaction.

$8 stock value / $40 CableCo stock price = 0.2x exchange ratio
0.2 exchange ratio × 225 million EastCellularCo shares = 45 million CableCo shares

11. In combination with the original CableCo shares of 120 million, the new company now has 165 million shares outstanding, 73 percent owned by CableCo shareholders and 27 percent owned by EastCellularCo shareholders.

120 million "old" shares owned by CableCo shareholders
\+ 45 million "new" shares issued to EastCellularCo shareholders
= 165 million pro forma CableCo shares outstanding

120 million CableCo shareholders / 165 million pro forma shares = 73%
45 million EastCellularCo shareholders / 165 million pro forma shares = 27%

12. Because this is a floating exchange ratio deal, the number of shares issued to EastCellularCo shareholders and the pro forma ownership will change if CableCo's share price moves up or down from the current $40. For example, if CableCo's share price moved to $45, CableCo would only issue 0.18 CableCo shares per EastCellularCo share for a total of 40 million CableCo shares.

    $8 stock value / $45 CableCo stock price = 0.18x exchange ratio
    0.18 exchange ratio × 225 million EastCellularCo shares = 40 million CableCo shares

    In combination with the original CableCo shares of 120 million, the new company would have 160 million shares outstanding, 75 percent owned by CableCo shareholders and 25 percent owned by EastCellularCo shareholders.

    120 million "old" shares owned by CableCo shareholders
    \+ 40 million "new" shares issued to EastCellularCo shareholders
    = 160 million pro forma CableCo shares outstanding

    120 million CableCo shareholders / 160 million pro forma shares = 75%
    40 million EastCellularCo shareholders / 160 million pro forma shares = 25%

    Therefore, if CableCo's share price increases from $40 to $45, CableCo's ownership of the new company post merger rises from 70 percent to 75 percent.

Let's now summarize the transaction multiples from the two recent cellular transactions.

Table 10.1 – Comparable Transaction Analysis

$ millions, except per share data

Target	Acquiror	Announcement date	Offer price	Premium	Equity value	Transaction value	LTM P/E	FY1 P/E	Transaction value/LTM EBITDA	Price/ book
WestCellularCo	TelephoneCo	2/15/05	$48.00	20%	$5,280	$7,530	21.1x	19.2x	7.9x	1.8x
EastCellularCo	CableCo	3/21/05	$16.00	33%	$3,600	$4,600	18.0x	16.8x	6.8x	1.4x

One of the first things to notice in this transaction comp set is that the price paid for WestCellularCo is higher on a multiples basis than the price paid for EastCellularCo, but the premium paid over the stock price was higher for EastCellularCo than for WestCellularCo. Upon further analysis you determine that, due to population growth in key cities in California, WestCellularCo is growing faster than EastCellularCo, which could explain why the multiples paid for WestCellularCo were higher than those for EastCellularCo. You further learn that EastCellularCo was trading at a significant discount on several metrics prior to the acquisition, which could help explain why the premium paid over the stock price was higher for EastCellularCo (that is, the EastCellularCo stock price was depressed prior to the transaction and so the $4 control premium per share to the EastCellularCo stock price may have been artificially high as a percentage of the pre-announcement stock price; to check this, it would be a good idea to calculate the premium over the EastCellularCo stock price 30, 60 and 90 days before announcement).

Since this transaction comp set will be used to value SouthCellularCo, it is important to determine whether SouthCellularCo is more similar to WestCellularCo or to EastCellularCo in terms of growth. You also notice that WestCellularCo is larger in equity value and in enterprise value than EastCellularCo but that both companies are fairly large in terms of size. Before using these multiples to value SouthCellularCo, it is important to make sure that SouthCellularCo is comparable to both of these companies in terms of size. Assuming SouthCellularCo is comparable in size, let's now use the transaction multiples above and apply them to SouthCellularCo's data to prepare a valuation analysis. This is similar to the way a valuation range was estimated using trading comparables in Comparable Company Analysis. (Ch.9) First, determine multiple ranges based on the comparables analysis. Then apply the range of multiples to the company being valued. From those implied equity values and firm values, judgment is applied to determine a selected range of values per share and those values are compared to the current stock price of SouthCellularCo.

Table 10.2 – Comparable Transaction Analysis – SouthCellularCo

Footnotes to Table 10.2 correspond to the numbered notes on the following page and describe each of these calculations.

$ millions, except per share data

	Multiple range		South CellularCo	Implied Transaction value		Assumed	Implied equity value		Fully diluted	Implied equity value per share	
Multiple	Low	High	data	Low	High	net debt	Low	High	shares outstanding	Low	High
LTM P/E[1]	18.0x	21.1x	$150	3,450	3,915	750	2,700	3,165	150	$18.00	$21.10
FY1 P/E[2]	16.8x	19.2x	$1.15	3,648	4,062	750	2,898	3,312	150	$19.32	$22.08
LTM FV/EBITDA[3]	6.8x	7.9x	$500	3,400	3,950	750	2,650	3,200	150	$17.67	$21.33
Price/book[4]	1.4x	1.8x	$1,750	3,200	3,900	750	2,450	3,150	150	$16.33	$21.00
Premium[5]	20%	33%	$15.00	3,450	3,743	750	2,700	2,993	150	$18.00	$19.95
								Mean		$17.86	$21.09
								Median		$18.00	$21.10
								High		$19.32	$22.08
								Low		$16.33	$19.95
								Selected range		$17.75	$21.25
								Current stock price[6]		$15.00	$15.00
								Premium to current price[7]		18%	42%

Footnotes are provided on the following page

Notes to Table 10.2 are provided below.

$ millions, except per share data

1. 18x LTM P/E × $150 of LTM earnings = $2,700 equity value
   $2,700 equity value + $750 of net debt = $3,450 transaction value
   $2,700 equity value / 150 diluted shares outstanding = $18.00 per share

2. 16.8x FY1 P/E × $1.15 FY1 EPS = $19.32 equity value per share
   $19.32 per share × 150 diluted shares outstanding = $2,898 equity value
   $2,898 equity value + $750 of net debt = $3,648 transaction value

3. 6.8x LTM FV/EBITDA × $500 LTM EBITDA = $3,400 transaction value
   $3,400 transaction value - $750 of net debt = $2,650 equity value
   $2,650 equity value / 150 diluted shares outstanding = $17.67 per share

4. 1.4x price/book × $1,750 book value of equity = $2,450 equity value
   $2,450 equity value / 150 diluted shares outstanding = $16.33 per share
   $2,450 equity value+ $750 of net debt = $3,200 transaction value

5. (1 + 20% control premium) × $15.00 SouthCellularCo stock price = $18.00 equity value per share
   $18.00 equity value per share × 150 fully diluted shares outstanding = $2,700 equity value
   $2,700 equity value + $750 of net debt = $3,450 transaction value

6. The current stock price for SouthCellularCo is $15 per share

7. ($17.75 equity value per share / $15.00 stock price) -1 = 18% premium

Judgment needs to be applied when determining the selected multiple range. For example, if the range of LTM P/E multiples were 10x to 25x, you might determine that the range is too wide for useful conclusions and, for the valuation analysis, you might use a tighter range of 15x to 19x. It depends on the transactions in the comp set and the company being valued. The selected per share range of $17.75 to $21.25 in Table 10.2 is also based on judgment. You might determine that a wider or narrower spread of values is more appropriate, if SouthCellularCo's stock price were particularly volatile, for example. Determining the multiples to use and the value range to choose is not a science. You must use judgment based on the information you have, as well as industry knowledge and an assessment of prevailing market conditions.

Additional Pointers

The following is a list of pointers to keep in mind when performing comparable transaction analysis. The following can serve as a checklist for reviewing your or someone else's work. This list should be read in conjunction with the Additional Pointers list provided in Comparable Company Analysis. (Ch.9)

- Be on the lookout for unusual adjustments or transaction structures such as deferred payments and earnouts, which should be treated as a component of value.
- Exclude nonrecurring items so that one-time items such as restructuring charges and sales of major assets do not skew results.
- Use schematics (boxes and arrows) to draw complex transactions; sometimes pictures help to visually understand complex transactions.
- Consider both historical based multiples (e.g., LTM P/E) as well as forward-looking multiples (e.g., P/E based on next year's EPS) to ensure that there is not a specific event in the past year (or the current year) which is artificially depressing or inflating values.
- Weigh median values of multiples more than mean (or average) values. Mean values are often skewed by outlying data and therefore can be misleading (though often both mean and median multiples are calculated and shown in the analysis).
- Provide summary recent financial data and key operating ratios on all the transactions in the comp set as backup information to more fully inform the conclusions drawn from the transaction comps.

Discounted Cash Flow Analysis

Chapter 11

There is no such thing as absolute value in this world.
You can only estimate what a thing is worth to you.

Charles Dudley Warner

As set forth in The Role of Valuation (Ch.8), several different valuation methodologies should be used in conjunction to triangulate to a valuation range for a company. However, if a practitioner had to choose a single valuation methodology to use, it would probably be discounted cash flow (DCF) analysis. DCF analysis is well liked by lawyers, bankers, investors, corporations, courts and academics because (a) it can be tailored to value any company, asset, project or investment, and (b) it requires only projected cash flows and an assessment of risk. Many corporations use DCF analysis to value potential acquisition targets as well as to evaluate internal projects. Within an M&A context, DCF analysis is sometimes the only valuation method utilized, particularly if no publicly traded comparable companies or comparable transactions are available.

DCF analysis is based on the fundamental corporate finance premise of risk vs. reward: *the value of a company, project, investment, or asset is equal to the present value of its future cash flows discounted based on the risk of those cash flows* (see Corporate Finance Basics (Ch.2)). DCF is a method for estimating the intrinsic value of a company since it is based on the company's own cash flows and the risk of those cash flows (as opposed to comparables-based analyses, which are based on multiples derived from *other* companies).

The underlying premise of a DCF analysis for purposes of corporate valuation is that the value of a firm (the enterprise value, or value to both debt and equity holders) is equal to the present value of the firm's unlevered free cash flows, discounted at the weighted average cost of capital (WACC) for the firm. Unlevered free cash flows are cash flows generated by the company before financing costs, such as the payment of interest to debt holders or the payment of dividends to equity holders. To determine the implied value to the equity holders only, net debt is subtracted from the enterprise value indicated by the DCF analysis. Also, the value of any assets or liabilities that are not involved in the generation of the cash flows are added or subtracted from the DCF value.

Key Benefits

DCF is considered one of the best proxies for stand-alone or intrinsic valuation because it is less influenced by external factors than other valuation methodologies. DCF analysis also offers the flexibility to value separate units, subsidiaries and assets. It is particularly useful in an M&A context since it is a forward-looking analysis and therefore the projections can incorporate expected changes to a company's long-term strategic plan and to key variables including growth rates and operating margins. Finally, a DCF value may be adjusted for non-operating items such as environmental liabilities or excess assets.

Key Challenges

The biggest challenge in using DCF analysis is that DCF valuations are based on projections and projections are never perfect. Rather, they are merely an educated guess about the future. Also, those who prepare financial projections tend to have an optimistic bias regarding the company's future prospects (for example, company managers tend to have an optimistic view about their company's growth prospects and company managers often prepare internal projections). This optimistic bias may result in DCF valuations that overstate value. Another challenge that can lead to overstated DCF valuations occurs when the calculated WACC used to discount a company's cash flows is derived from larger, less risky peers. That is, if the WACC is artificially low, the resulting DCF value will be overstated.

Another common mistake is to develop projections that do not cover a full operating cycle for the company. If company projections only go out five years, for example, but a major change to the business will occur in year seven, then the DCF analysis based on 5-year projections might overstate or understate value (depending on whether the year seven change is negative or positive, respectively) because that year seven event will not be reflected in the projections. To avoid this risk, it is important to develop projected financial statements over at least one business cycle (usually five to ten years) or until cash flows at the end of the projection period are "normalized." In addition, DCF analysis is often very sensitive to certain assumptions (e.g., sales growth rates, operating margins, capital expenditures, method of calculating terminal value, projection period, etc.) and so particular care must be taken in forecasting those variables.

Depending on practical requirements and the availability of data, DCF analysis can be very simple or extremely elaborate. Ultimately, the quality of the projections used for the analysis will determine the integrity of the DCF analysis. If someone other than yourself prepared the initial set of projections (which commonly occurs in practice), it is important to be critical of the assumptions underlying the projections as well as the assumptions used to calculate the WACC.

Key Components

The three key components of a DCF analysis are: (1) the unlevered free cash flows, (2) the weighted average cost of capital, and (3) the terminal value. Each of these components are described briefly here and in detail later in the chapter.

1. **Unlevered free cash flows (FCF)**: the free cash flows generated by a company for a specified projection period. Most projection periods are for five, seven or ten years. It is important that the end of the projection period represents a steady state period for the company. "Unlevered" means they are cash flows before accounting for financing costs such as interest or dividends. Unlevered free cash flows are discounted using the WACC to determine the present value of the firm during the projection period.

2. **Weighted average cost of capital (WACC)**: the blended cost for both the debt and equity capital of a project or company. The cost of debt and the cost of equity are the rates of return required by debt and equity providers, respectively. The weighted average cost of capital is the blended discount rate (r) applied to the free cash flows and the terminal value to calculate a present value.

3. **Terminal value (TV)**: the estimated value of the business for the period from the end of the projection period into perpetuity. The present value of the terminal value is added to the present value of the unlevered free cash flows to determine the present value of the firm.

Before discussing the three key components in detail, let's review a basic numerical example to show a DCF analysis at work. Notes describing key aspects of the following example are provided after Table 11.1.

Building projection models

A number of good books and tools exist that describe in detail how to build projection models. Therefore, this chapter does not go into detail regarding the development of financial projections. Instead, this chapter describes how to perform DCF analysis using an existing set of financial projections. A list of recommended books and resources on building projection models can be found in the Appendix.

Table 11.1 – Simplified DCF Example

$ millions, except per share data											
Discounting period (n)	**0**	**1**	**2**	**3**	**4**	**5**	**6**	**7**	**8**	**9**	**10**
Year	**2005**	**2006**	**2007**	**2008**	**2009**	**2010**	**2011**	**2012**	**2013**	**2014**	**2015**
Present value of projection period											
Unlevered free cash flow (CF_n)[1]	$150	$165	$182	$300	$330	$360	$400	$440	$485	$535	$590
Weighted average cost of capital (r)[2]	8%										
Present value formula[3]		$= \frac{\$165}{1.08^1}$	$= \frac{\$182}{1.08^2}$	$= \frac{\$300}{1.08^3}$	$= \frac{\$330}{1.08^4}$	$= \frac{\$360}{1.08^5}$	$= \frac{\$400}{1.08^6}$	$= \frac{\$440}{1.08^7}$	$= \frac{\$485}{1.08^8}$	$= \frac{\$535}{1.08^9}$	$= \frac{\$590}{1.08^{10}}$
Present value of free cash flows (PV)[4]		153	156	238	243	245	252	257	262	268	273
Total present value of free cash flows[5]	2,346										
Present value of terminal period											
Unlevered free cash flow in Year 10[6]											590
Long-term growth rate (g)[7]											3%
Unlevered free cash flow in Year 11 (CF_{11})[8]											608
Present value formula: growing perpetuity[9]											$= \frac{\$608}{(.08-.03)}$
Present value of terminal value in Year 10 (CF_{10})[10]											12,154
Present value formula[11]											$= \frac{\$12,154}{1.08^{10}}$
Present value of terminal value[12]	5,630										
Total enterprise value[13]	7,976										
Net debt and preferred equity[14]	(3,500)										
Implied equity value[15]	**4,476**										
Diluted shares outstanding	175										
Implied value per share[16]	**$25.58**										

Footnotes are provided on the following page

Notes to Table 11.1 are provided below.

1. Unlevered free cash flow (CF_n) is operating cash flow before interest payments, before dividends, and after capital expenditures. Numerical examples of how to calculate unlevered free cash flows are provided in the following section.

2. Weighted average cost of capital (WACC) is the discount rate (r) used for the present value calculations. It is the sum of a company's after-tax cost of debt and cost of equity (which is already after-tax) weighted based on the company's optimal capital structure. Numerical examples of how to calculate WACC are provided in the following section.

3. The present value formula for a future cash flow is: $PV = [CF_n / (1 + r)^n]$. Present value is described in Corporate Finance Basics. (Ch.2)

4. The present value of each year's projected unlevered cash flow is calculated based on that year's free cash flow (CF_n) discounted at the 8 percent discount rate (r) or WACC for (n) periods.

5. All of the present values are added together to determine the present value of the unlevered free cash flows during the projection period. $2,346 million represents the sum of the present values of the cash flows in Years 1 through 10.

6. $590 million is the unlevered free cash flow in the last year of the projection period (CF_{10}). The growing perpetuity method will be used to calculate the terminal value in this example. Terminal values, terminal multiples, and growing perpetuities are described in more detail in the following section.

7. 3 percent is an estimate for the long-term growth rate (g) for this company's free cash flows.

8. $608 million is an estimate for the unlevered free cash flow in Year 11 (CF_{11}) calculated by multiplying the Year 10 unlevered free cash flow by one plus the long-term growth rate.

   $$CF_{11} = CF_{10} \times (1 + g)$$
   $$\$608 \text{ million} = \$590 \text{ million} \times (1 + 0.03)$$

9. The present value formula for a growing perpetuity is: $PV = [CF_n / (r - g)]$. In this example CF_{11} is CF_n. Growing perpetuities are described in Corporate Finance Basics. (Ch.2)

$$PV_{10} = CF_{11} / (r - g)$$
$$PV_{10} = \$608 \text{ million} / (.08 - .03)$$
$$PV_{10} = \$12{,}154 \text{ million}$$

10. $12,154 million is the terminal value in Year 10. The terminal value is calculated using the growing perpetuity method and is based on the unlevered free cash flow in Year 11 of $608 million ($CF_{11}$), the 8 percent discount rate (r) and the 3 percent long-term growth rate (g).

11. The terminal value of $12,154 million is a Year 10 number. This must now be discounted back to a Year 0 number in order to add it to the present value of the cash flows during the projection period of $2,346 million (since the cash flows in the projection period have already been discounted back to Year 0 numbers). Recall that only numbers as of the same time can be added together. Thus all numbers are discounted to a Year 0 basis (their present value), at which point they can be added together.

12. $5,630 million represents the present value of the Year 10 terminal value of $12,154 million.

$$\$5{,}630 \text{ million} = \$12{,}154 \text{ million} / (1.08)^{10}$$

13. The present value of the cash flows during the projection period of $2,346 million and the present value of the terminal value of $5,630 million are added together to determine the estimated enterprise value of $7,976 million as of the end of 2005 (or Year 0).

14. The company's net debt and preferred equity of $3,500 million as of the end of 2005 (or Year 0) are subtracted from the enterprise value to determine the estimated equity value.

15. $7,976 million enterprise value - $3,500 million of net debt and preferred equity = $4,476 million of implied equity value.

16. $4,476 million of equity value is divided by fully diluted shares outstanding of 175 million to determine an estimated equity value of $25.58 per share as of 12/31/2005.

Unlevered Free Cash Flow

Unlevered free cash flow is the operating cash flow generated by all assets (both tangible and intangible) used by the company in the provision of goods or services, adjusted for capital expenditures, and unlevered or free from financing considerations including interest expense and dividends. People sometimes refer to this as being "independent of the capital structure." The theory for using unlevered cash flows is as follows: (1) a company's assets are capable of generating a certain level of cash flow, (2) the cost to acquire and maintain the assets is accounted for as capital expenditures, (3) the value of an enterprise should be equal to the productive value of its assets, less any capital expenditures and (4) that value should be independent of how the assets were paid for.

Said another way, the ability to use an asset and generate cash from that asset is separate from how the asset was financed. Perhaps a comparison to a home will help clarify this concept. Assume you buy a home with a 20 percent down payment and an 80 percent mortgage. Alternatively, you might have made a 40 percent down payment and mortgaged 60 percent. The point is that the mortgage amount (or amount of debt) has no impact on the physical home itself nor does it affect the value of the home agreed upon between you and the seller. Similarly, the financing for a company is independent of the asset value in a DCF valuation.

There are a few methods to calculate unlevered free cash flow. The two most common methods are illustrated in Table 11.2 after the income statement and cash flow statement.

Method 1: Starting with cash flow from operations
Begin with cash flow from operations and adjust for after-tax interest expense to convert the cash flows from being "levered" (meaning after subtracting interest expense) to being "unlevered" (meaning before subtracting interest expense).

Method 2: Starting with EBIT
Begin with earnings before interest and taxes (EBIT) and tax effect EBIT to arrive at earnings before interest but after tax (EBIAT), and subtract changes in working capital and other non-cash charges.

Regardless of the method, capital expenditures must be subtracted to arrive at unlevered free cash flow. Also, any method selected should yield the same answer.

Table 11.2 – Calculating Unlevered Free Cash Flow

$ thousands

	2006	2007	2008	2009	2010
Income Statement					
Revenues	$55,000	$65,000	$72,000	$75,000	$80,000
Cost of goods sold	(33,000)	(39,000)	(43,200)	(45,000)	(48,000)
Gross margin	22,000	26,000	28,800	30,000	32,000
Selling, general, administrative	(11,000)	(13,000)	(14,400)	(15,000)	(16,000)
EBITDA	11,000	13,000	14,400	15,000	16,000
DD&A[1]	(2,875)	(3,234)	(3,558)	(3,825)	(4,016)
EBIT	8,125	9,766	10,842	11,175	11,984
Interest expense	(850)	(867)	(884)	(902)	(920)
EBT	7,275	8,899	9,958	10,273	11,064
Income taxes (40% tax rate)	(2,910)	(3,560)	(3,983)	(4,109)	(4,426)
Net income	$4,365	$5,339	$5,975	$6,164	$6,638
Cash Flow Statement					
Net income	$4,365	$5,339	$5,975	$6,164	$6,638
DD&A	2,875	3,234	3,558	3,825	4,016
Inc./(dec.) in deferred tax liability	400	450	500	550	600
(Inc.)/dec. in net working capital	(500)	(510)	(520)	(531)	(541)
Cash flow from operations	7,140	8,514	9,512	10,008	10,713
Capital expenditures	(4,000)	(4,250)	(4,500)	(4,750)	(5,000)
Cash flow from investing	(4,000)	(4,250)	(4,500)	(4,750)	(5,000)
Dividends paid	(1,091)	(1,335)	(1,494)	(1,541)	(1,660)
Net new debt issued	250	300	275	300	290
Net new equity issued	0	0	0	0	0
Cash flow from financing	(841)	(1,035)	(1,219)	(1,241)	(1,370)
Net change in cash	$2,299	$3,229	$3,794	$4,017	$4,344

[1] DD&A is not always listed separately on the income statement. If it is not, you need to refer to the cash flow statement to determine the amount of DD&A during a period.

Table 11.2 continued

$ thousands

	2006	2007	2008	2009	2010
Method 1: Starting with Cash Flow from Operations[1]					
Cash flow from operations	$7,140	$8,514	$9,512	$10,008	$10,713
(1) Add back after-tax interest					
Pretax interest expense	850	867	884	902	920
Tax rate	40%	40%	40%	40%	40%
After-tax interest expense[2]	510	520	531	541	552
(2) Subtract capital expenditures[3]	(4,000)	(4,250)	(4,500)	(4,750)	(5,000)
Unlevered free cash flow	$3,650	$4,784	$5,543	$5,799	$6,265
Method 2: Starting with EBIT					
EBIT	$8,125	$9,766	$10,842	$11,175	$11,984
(1) Subtract taxes on EBIT					
Tax rate	40%	40%	40%	40%	40%
Taxes on EBIT[4]	(3,250)	(3,906)	(4,337)	(4,470)	(4,794)
EBIAT	4,875	5,859	6,505	6,705	7,191
(2) Adjust EBIAT					
Add DD&A	2,875	3,234	3,558	3,825	4,016
Inc./(dec.) in deferred tax liability	400	450	500	550	600
(Inc.)/dec. in working capital	(500)	(510)	(520)	(531)	(541)
(3) Subtract capital expenditures[3]	(4,000)	(4,250)	(4,500)	(4,750)	(5,000)
Unlevered free cash flow	$3,650	$4,784	$5,543	$5,799	$6,265

Different methods but same answer

[1] Cash flow from Operations (CFFO) is also known as Operating Cash Flow (OCF)

[2] Pretax interest expense × (1 - tax rate)

[3] Net of any asset sales

[4] EBIT × tax rate

A shortcut for estimating free cash flow

A shortcut method of "approximating" free cash flow is to (1) start with EBITDA, (2) add or subtract changes to net working capital, (3) subtract capital expenditures, and (4) tax effect the resulting number. This shortcut only works if annual DD&A approximates annual capital expenditures. This is a back-of-the-envelope method and should be used only for estimating free cash flow (not calculating it). Note that in Table 11.2 this method would not result in an accurate estimate of free cash flow because the company in the example is a net investor, which means that it is currently investing more in capital expenditures than it is depreciating (capex > DD&A).

	EBITDA
+/-	(Increase)/decrease in net working capital
=	Levered cash flow
×	(1 - tax rate)
=	Estimate for unlevered cash flow
-	Capital expenditures and investments
=	Estimate for unlevered free cash flow

Common Errors in Calculating Free Cash Flow

There are a number of errors commonly made when calculating unlevered free cash flow. Several of them are listed below to help you avoid these pitfalls.

- Unlevered free cash flow projections are an extension of stand-alone company projections. When building stand-alone company projections for purposes of DCF analysis, it is important that every effort is made to develop a base case that accurately reflects an operating cycle for the company.

- The "base case" valuation should be based on "base case" projections. Base case projections should not be overly aggressive. If aggressive projections are warranted given the company's industry and/or growth prospects, then this scenario should be named the "high case" or "growth case" and should be considered in conjunction with a moderated "base case."

- Sensitivity analysis should be performed to analyze the effects on the projections of changes in basic assumptions (e.g., changes in margins, increases in costs, changes to sales growth rates, loss of a key customer, etc.).

- The end of the projection period should represent a "steady state" or normal business environment.

- If analyzing a cyclical company or industry, ensure that the projection period includes at least one full business cycle and that the projection period does not end in a peak or valley of the cycle. You want to make sure that the final year of the projection period, from which the terminal value is calculated, is not overstated or understated vis-à-vis a normal year.

Need to stress-test numbers

When given a set of financial projections, many people have the tendency to accept them "as is." Whenever you are in the business of drawing conclusions from financial projections, it is your responsibility to first stress-test them. You must look for inconsistencies and/or holes in the assumptions. You should calculate year-over-year changes to see if there are material differences in assumptions from one year to the next. **Hockey sticks** (historical numbers which are flat followed by highly optimistic projections, causing a graph of the numbers to resemble the outline of a hockey stick) are easy to pick out and should be caught with relatively little effort. You should also look for less obvious inconsistencies, such as whether the annual capital expenditure is at least equal to the annual rate of depreciation (since net PP&E should not be a depleting asset for a growing or stable company), or if cash flow growth in the projections is being driven by unrealistic margin improvement. You need to ensure that the projections you use to perform your DCF analysis can withstand scrutiny, and it begins with your own scrutiny.

Weighted Average Cost of Capital

The **weighted average cost of capital** (WACC) is the discount rate used in DCF analysis. The WACC represents the cost of capital for the firm, given the risk of its assets and business, and takes into consideration the optimal capital structure for the business. The cost of capital (like the unlevered free cash flows) is forward-looking and is predicted based on the expectations of the company's future performance.

WACC is a blended discount rate based on a company's cost of debt and cost of equity and the company's optimal capital structure. In a DCF analysis, the WACC (adjusted for the number of periods) is used in the divisor of the company's cash flows. Mathematically, a smaller divisor means a larger quotient, so as the cost of funding a company (the WACC) decreases, the value of the company increases and, vice versa, as the WACC increases, the company value decreases.

For example, assume two WACCs (5 percent and 10 percent) for the same cash flow to be generated in Year 1 of $100 million. The present value using the 5 percent WACC is $95.2 million compared with $90.9 million for the same $100 million cash flow in Year 1 using a 10 percent WACC.

Table 11.3 – Lower vs. Higher WACC Example

$ millions	**r = 5 percent**	**r = 10 percent**
$PV = \frac{CF_n}{(1+r)^n}$	$PV = \frac{\$100}{(1+.05)^1}$	$PV = \frac{\$100}{(1+.10)^1}$
	PV = $95.2	PV = $90.9
	Lower WACC = higher value	Higher WACC = lower value

The WACC calculation is as follows:

$$WACC = (K_e \times \%_e) + [(K_d \times (1 - t)) \times \%_d]$$

where:

Cost of debt	K_d
Cost of equity	K_e
Percent of debt in capital structure	$\%_d$
Percent of equity in capital structure	$\%_e$
Marginal tax rate	t

What is CAPM?

Cost of equity (K_e) is determined using the Capital Asset Pricing Model (CAPM). There are many finance books which describe CAPM in detail so the concept will only be summarized here.

The cost of equity can be estimated based on a company's non-systematic (or company-specific) risk relative to the overall market. This non-systematic risk is represented by the number beta (ß) which measures the degree to which the return on a security (such as a company's stock price) and the market return move together (or are correlated). A company with a beta of 1 moves with the same relative changes as the market. If a company has a beta of 1 and the market increases 10 percent, the company's stock price should also increase 10 percent. On the other hand, if a company has a beta of -2 and the overall stock market increases 10 percent, the company's stock price is expected to decrease 20 percent.

The calculation for the cost of equity (K_e) using CAPM is as follows:

$$K_e = R_f + \beta (R_m - R_f)$$

where:

Risk-free rate	R_f
Beta	β
Market return	R_m
Market risk premium	$R_m - R_f$

The cost of debt is generally the company's cost to borrow new long-term debt in the current market environment. The cost of debt is adjusted by (1 minus the tax rate) since interest expense is tax-deductible (therefore, the after-tax cost of debt is lower than the nominal or pretax cost of debt). The cost of equity is not adjusted because equity is already an after-tax item.

The 10-year U.S. Treasury bond is generally used as a proxy for the risk-free rate since it is effectively default-free. Economic research companies such as Barra calculate both historic and projected betas for publicly traded companies. Many professionals use the return on the S&P 500 or the Dow Jones Index to measure market return. Be sure to check for the standard proxies used by your firm when it comes to estimating the risk-free rate, market return and the market risk premium since many firms have internal policies and procedures with respect to these items.

A basic example showing the calculation of WACC is provided below.

Table 11.4 – Calculation of Weighted Average Cost of Capital (WACC)

Market assumptions		1. Calculate the cost of equity (already after-tax)	
Risk-free rate (R_f)	4%	$K_e = R_f + ß (R_m - R_f)$	
Market return (R_m)	10%	$K_e = 0.04 + 1.5 (0.10 - 0.04)$	
Market risk premium (R_m - R_f)	6%	**K_e =**	**13.0%**
Company-specific assumptions		2. Calculate the after-tax cost of debt	
Cost of debt (K_d)	7%	$K_{d(after\text{-}tax)} = K_d \times (1 - t)$	
Beta (ß)	1.50	$K_{d(after\text{-}tax)} = 0.07 \times (1 - 0.4)$	
Marginal tax rate (t)	40%	**$K_{d(after\text{-}tax)}$ =**	**4.2%**
Capital structure			
Percentage debt ($\%_d$)	55%	3. Calculate the weighted average cost of capital	
Percentage equity ($\%_e$)	45%	$WACC = (K_e \times \%_e) + (K_{d(after\text{-}tax)} \times \%_d)$	
		$WACC = (0.13 \times 0.45) + (0.042 \times 0.55)$	
		WACC =	**8.2%**

A shortcut for estimating WACC

A shortcut method of "approximating" WACC is to multiply the estimated costs of capital by the percent of each type of capital within the capital structure and add those together. This is a back-of-the-envelope way to help stress-test your analysis. See Table 11.5

Table 11.5 – Shortcut Method of Approximating WACC

$ millions Type of capital	Amount	Percent of total	Pretax cost of capital[1]	After-tax cost of capital[2]	Weighted cost of capital[3]
Senior debt	$500	24%	6% - 7%	3.6% - 4.2%	0.88% - 1.02%
Subordinated debt	300	15%	8% - 10%	4.8% - 6.0%	0.70% - 0.88%
Total debt	$800	39%			1.58% - 1.90%
Preferred equity[4]	$250	12%	8% - 12%	8.0% - 12.0%	0.98% - 1.46%
Common equity[5]	1,000	49%	10% - 15%	10.0% - 15.0%	4.88% - 7.32%
Total equity	$1,250	61%			5.85% - 8.78%
Total capital	$2,050	100%			7.43% - 10.68%
				Midpoint	**9.06%**

[1] Expected return for different asset classes based on risk of company's capital

[2] Based on a 40% tax rate. Pretax cost of capital × (1 - tax rate) = after-tax cost of capital

[3] Percent of total capital × after-tax cost of capital = weighted cost of capital

[4] Based on non-tax-deductible preferred equity, which is why pretax = after-tax costs

[5] Cost of equity is already an after-tax value, which is why pretax = after-tax costs

Do not use Acquiror's WACC

When performing DCF analysis in an M&A transaction, many new finance professionals make the mistake of using Acquiror's WACC to value Target (i.e., they use Acquiror's WACC to discount Target's unlevered free cash flows). It is a mistake to use Acquiror's WACC to value Target; rather, Target's WACC should be used to value Target's free cash flows. The reason Acquiror's WACC should not be used is that the discount rate should relate to the risk of the cash flows. Since Target's cash flows are being valued, Target's WACC should be used. Let's consider an example to illustrate the point.

ABC Machine Tools has developed a new technology for deep water oil drilling. Given the risk related to ABC's business, ABC's management determines that a 15 percent WACC is appropriate for purposes of discounting ABC's cash flows. *continued*

Do not use Acquiror's WACC continued

To move its prototype to the next stage, ABC management feels that it must sell equity to a larger player who can provide ABC the growth capital it needs. Two buyers are considering the acquisition of ABC Machine Tools. The first potential buyer is BigOilCo, a global oil and gas company with a diversified portfolio of producing assets around the world. The other potential buyer is SmallOilCo, a startup company interested in making investments in the oil services industry. Given BigOilCo's leadership position, large size and diversified portfolio, BigOilCo's management determines its WACC to be 9 percent. Given SmallOilCo's size and the start-up nature of its portfolio, SmallOilCo management determines its WACC to be 20 percent.

What WACC should BigOilCo and SmallOilCo use to value ABC Machine Tools?

The appropriate WACC to value ABC is ABC's WACC of 15 percent, regardless of BigOilCo's WACC of 9 percent and SmallOilCo's WACC of 20 percent. The 15 percent discount rate is the appropriate one to use because it is the discount rate related to the risk of ABC's cash flows. If BigOilCo were to apply its lower WACC of 9 percent to ABC's cash flows, it would mistakenly *overvalue* ABC. If SmallOilCo were to apply its higher WACC of 20 percent to ABC's cash flows, it would mistakenly *undervalue* ABC.

Terminal Value

The present value of the unlevered cash flows during the projection period represents only a portion of the total value of the firm. The cash flows which occur after the projection period also have value. **Terminal value** represents the value of the cash flows which occur after the projection period.

Figure 11.6 - Timing of Terminal Value

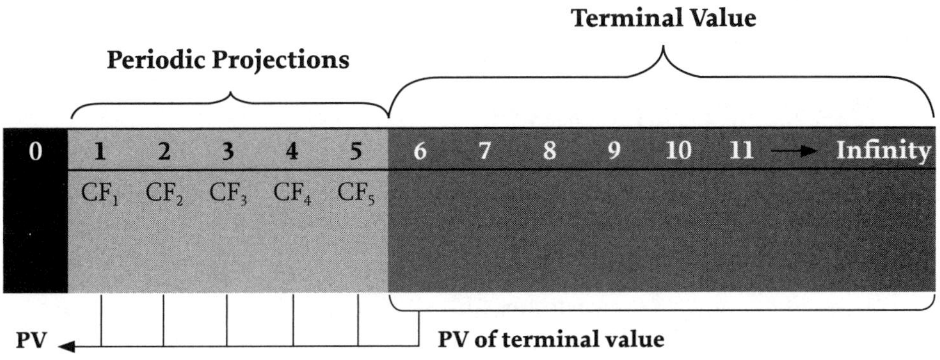

Since terminal value usually accounts for a meaningful percentage of the total value in a typical DCF valuation, the method by which it is calculated is just as important as the cash flow projections themselves. For a company that is cash flow negative during the projection period (sometimes seen with companies operating in new industries or with new technologies), the terminal value calculation is especially important since the terminal value can exceed 100 percent of the valuation.

There are two generally accepted methods for projecting the terminal value. The first is called the **terminal multiple method** (also called the exit multiple method) and the second is called the **perpetuity growth rate method**. Both methodologies are often used in conjunction to provide a sanity check for the chosen method as well as an additional data point.

Terminal multiple method: This uses a comparable company or comparable transaction method of analysis to estimate the terminal value, depending on whether the analysis assumes that ownership of the company is maintained after the projection period (comparable company) or sold after the projection period (comparable transaction). A valuation multiple is applied to the company's financial data in the last year of the projection period such as an enterprise value to EBITDA multiple. Note that for comparability, if an equity value multiple (e.g., P/E) is used as the terminal multiple, net debt must be added back at that period in the future to gross up the equity value to an enterprise value since the perpetuity method already yields an enterprise value. Since the EBITDA value to which the multiple is applied is the EBITDA of the last year in the projection period, the terminal multiple itself should be a trailing or last-twelve-months (LTM) multiple and not a forward-looking multiple (if, however, you choose to use a forward EBITDA to calculate the terminal value, be sure to apply a forward EV/EBITDA multiple to the forward EBITDA).

Exit multiples for terminal value calculations should not be materially different from entry multiples so that an investment decision is not predicated on multiple expansion. For example, the terminal value calculation should not assume that an asset purchased for 6x EBITDA can be sold after Year 5 for 8x EBITDA. If, at the end of the projection period, the market has moved and the company can be sold for 8x EBITDA, all the better. However, if, at the end of the projection period, the market has not moved (i.e., no multiple expansion), an investment decision which required multiple expansion as a prerequisite of profitability has been avoided.

Since the terminal value represents an estimated value as of the last year of the projection period, the terminal value must be discounted back to Time 0 in order to add it to the present value of the cash flows from the projection period. For example, assume a company has EBITDA of $175 million in the fifth year of the projection period. The $175 million is multiplied by an EBITDA multiple (7x in this example). The $1,225 million is a Year 5 value and must be discounted back five years to a present value which can be added to the present values of the cash flows from the projection period. We will assume a WACC of 9 percent.

1. EBITDA in Year 5 = $175 million. Apply a multiple based on comparable companies (assume 7x for this example).

   $$\$175 \text{ million} \times 7 = \$1{,}225 \text{ million}$$

2. $1,225 million is a value in Year 5 (or at Time 5). Discount $1,225 million to Time 0 by dividing it by one plus the discount rate raised to the fifth power.

   $$PV = \frac{\$1{,}225 \text{ million}}{(1 + .09)^5}$$

   $$PV = \$796 \text{ million}$$

3. $796 million is the present value of the terminal value. This can be added to the present value of the unlevered free cash flows during the projection period to arrive at the total estimated enterprise value.

Use a comparable *trading* multiple if the assumption is that the company will not be sold after the projection period. Use a comparable *transaction* multiple if the assumption is that the company will be sold after the projection period.

Perpetuity growth method: This method uses the perpetuity formula to value the company as of the terminal date, based on the assumption that the company will operate forever. A perpetuity that grows over time is called a growing perpetuity.

Most terminal value calculations using the perpetuity formula assume a growing perpetuity and a low perpetuity growth rate (1 to 3 percent annually, for example). For this method, take the unlevered free cash flow in the last year of the projection period, grow it one year to represent the unlevered free cash flow in Year 1 of the terminal value period, and apply the growing perpetuity calculation. As with the terminal multiple method, the growing perpetuity calculation will yield a value as of the end of the projection period (Year 5 in this example). The terminal value must then be discounted back to Time 0 (or Year 0) in order to add it to the present value of the cash flows from the projection period. The formulas for a perpetuity and a growing perpetuity are provided below. Both are described in Corporate Finance Basics. (Ch.2)

Perpetuity (perpetual or infinite term)

$$PV = \frac{CF_n}{r}$$

Growing perpetuity (based on a constant, annual growth rate)

$$PV = \frac{CF_n}{(r - g)}$$

Where CF_n = the unlevered free cash flow in the first year *after* the end of the projection period. To calculate CF_n, multiply the unlevered free cash flow from the last year of the projection period by one plus the growth rate (1 + g).

$$CF_n = CF_{\text{last year in projection period}} \times (1 + g)$$

Assume a company with a 5-year projection period and unlevered free cash flow of $100 million in the fifth year. We will assume a long-term growth rate of 2 percent and a WACC of 9 percent (g = 2 percent and r = 9 percent).

1. Grow the Year 5 unlevered free cash flow for one year using the long-term growth rate (g) of 2 percent.

   $CF_5 \times (1 + g) = CF_6$
   $100 million × (1.02) = $102 million

2. Apply the growing perpetuity formula to the Year 6 unlevered free cash flow of $102 million. The discount rate (r) is 9 percent and the long-term growth rate (g) is 2 percent.

$$TV = \frac{CF_6'}{(r - g)}$$

$$TV = \frac{\$102 \text{ million}}{(.09 - .02)}$$

$$TV = \$1{,}457 \text{ million}$$

3. $1,457 million is the value of all unlevered free cash flows after Year 5 (therefore a Year 5 number). Discount this terminal value by 5 years to yield a Time 0 value for the terminal value so that it can be added to the present values of the cash flows from the projection period.

$$PV = \frac{CF_n}{(1 + r)^n}$$

$$PV = \frac{\$1{,}457 \text{ million}}{(1 + .09)^5}$$

$$PV = \$947 \text{ million}$$

4. $947 million is the present value of the terminal value. This can be added to the present value of the free cash flows from the projection period to arrive at the total implied enterprise value.

Common Errors in Calculating Terminal Value

A few additional pointers on terminal value calculations to help avoid common mistakes:

- When using the growing perpetuity formula, it is a common mistake to forget to grow the final projection year unlevered free cash flow by one year to calculate CF_n (which is then used as the cash flow in the perpetuity or growing perpetuity formula). Remember to first multiply the last year's unlevered free cash flow by $(1 + g)$ to estimate CF_n before applying the growing perpetuity formula.

- The terminal value is not always a mechanical extrapolation of the last projected year's unlevered free cash flow. Make sure that all long-term relationships are evaluated and any necessary changes are made. For example, even if a company has been growing at 10 percent a year during the projection period, it is not going to grow 10 percent a year in perpetuity. If it did, over time the value of the company would be greater than the U.S. or even world economy, which obviously is not realistic. The growth rate for the perpetuity calculation needs to be reduced to a realistic, sustainable level. Most DCF analyses assume a perpetuity growth rate of 1 to 3 percent annually (which approximates the long-term GDP growth rate).

- Review whether the underlying risk of the entity has changed materially over the course of the forecast period. In selected cases, this may necessitate altering the discount rate used for the terminal value (i.e., use a different WACC for the terminal value than the one that was used for the periodic cash flows). For example, if a blockbuster drug is coming off-patent for a pharmaceutical company in seven years and there is no blockbuster product in the R&D pipeline, the discount rate for the terminal value calculation should be recalculated (i.e., raised from that used for the periodic cash flows to account for the higher risk of the terminal value) given the increased risk of market competition after the patent expiration.

- When using the perpetuity method, cross-check the reasonableness of the exit multiples implied by this method. Similarly, when using the exit multiple method, cross-check the reasonableness of the perpetuity growth rate implied by this method. This is shown in Table 11.11. It is common to calculate an enterprise value using both methods.

- Review the proportion of the total value which is represented by the terminal value.

Now that we have reviewed: (1) unlevered free cash flows, (2) WACC, and (3) terminal value, let's summarize the mechanics of performing a DCF analysis.

1. Develop baseline financial projections for the company or asset

2. From those projections, calculate the unlevered free cash flows for the projection period

3. Calculate the terminal value (use both terminal multiple and perpetuity growth methods)

4. Calculate the weighted average cost of capital (WACC) for the company or asset

5. Discount the unlevered free cash flows to their present value

6. Discount the terminal value to its present value

7. Add the present value of the unlevered free cash flows to the present value of the terminal value

8. Adjust the total present value to reflect other assets and liabilities not utilized in the generation of the cash flows, if any

9. Subtract net debt and preferred stock to arrive at a value for common equity

10. Divide equity value by diluted shares outstanding to arrive at an equity value per share

11. Engage in sensitivity analysis to provide a valuation range

12. Review the analysis and draw conclusions

Midyear Convention

Projections are an estimate of the cash flow a company will generate in a given year. That cash flow will likely be earned continuously throughout the year as opposed to coming in a lump sum at the end of the year. Most DCF analysis, however, assumes that a cash flow is received as a lump sum at the end of the year and then discounts that cash flow a full year. To more accurately reflect the ongoing nature of cash generation throughout the year, some practitioners apply a midyear convention to a company's cash flows as opposed to an end-of-year convention. With a midyear convention, a cash flow is assumed to occur in the middle of the year (e.g., on June 30, for a calendar year company) and is then discounted for *half a year.*

For example, assume a projection of $100 million for the calendar year 2006. In a DCF analysis using the end-of-year convention, it is assumed that $100 million is received by the company at the end of December, whereas using midyear convention it is assumed that $100 million is received at the end of June.

Figure 11.7 - End-of-year vs. Midyear Convention for DCF Analysis

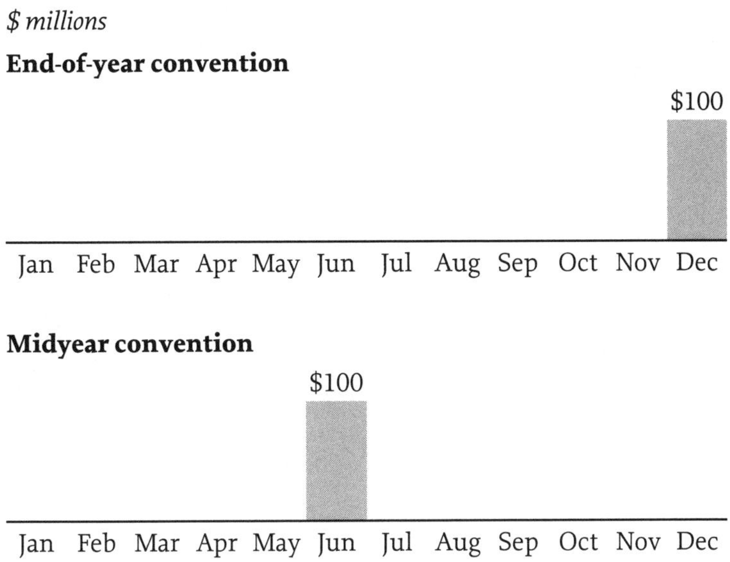

There are two separate ways to apply the midyear convention. The first method uses the same discounting calculations as the end-of-year convention and then makes a single adjustment to the entire present value (including both periodic projections and the terminal value). The second method requires an adjustment to each periodic cash flow as well as the terminal value. Both methods yield the same result.

Method 1: Adjust the entire present value by moving it forward one-half period

To use the midyear convention, calculate the present value as you would using the end-of-year method, then subsequently make an adjustment to the calculated present value by moving it forward by half a period. This adjustment is required because, by assuming that the cash flows occur in the middle of every period (June in our example), the calculated present value will be a value as of the end of June in Year 0 because each cash flow was discounted a full period rather than a half period. For example, the Year 5 cash flow as well as the terminal value are assumed to occur on June 30 of Year 5. By discounting five full years, they are now present values *as of June 30 of Year 0,* or six months too early since the present value calculation should be as of December 31, Year 0. To adjust the present value to be as of the end of Year 0 (December in our example), you must take the value and move it forward by one-half period by multiplying it by one plus the discount rate raised to the power of 0.5 (6 months / 12 months = ½ or 0.5).

Figure 11.8 - Midyear Convention - Method 1

Assume a discount rate of 5 percent and our $100 million example. The present value of $100 million after one year using the end-of-year convention would be $95.2 million whereas the present value using the midyear convention would be $97.6 million.

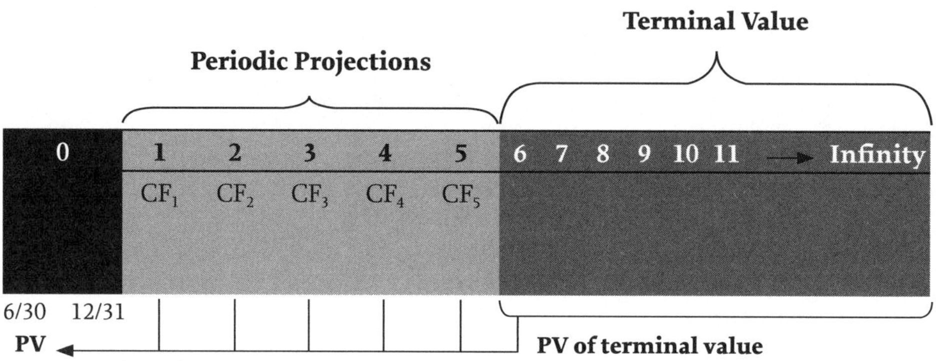

6/30 to 12/31 is the period by which the present value is "over-discounted" in Method 1. This is why the present value must then be multiplied by $(1+r)^{0.5}$ to yield a value as of Dec. 31, Year 0

Table 11.9 - Midyear Convention Yields a Higher Valuation

$ millions

End-of-year convention		Midyear convention	
$CF_1 =$	\$100	$CF_{.5} =$	\$100
$PV_0 =$	$\frac{\$100}{(1+.05)^1}$	$PV_{-.5} =$	$\frac{\$100}{(1+.05)^1}$
$PV_0 =$	**\$95.2**	$PV_{-.5} =$	\$95.2
		$PV_0 =$	$\$95.2 \times (1+.05)^{.5}$
		$PV_0 =$	**\$97.6**

As you can see from this simplified example, valuation using the midyear convention will yield a higher valuation level than using the end-of-year method. This is because cash flows are assumed to occur earlier in the midyear convention and, based on classic corporate finance theory, cash flows that occur earlier have more value. Said differently, the divisor of cash flow 1 (CF_1), the WACC or (r), is raised to the power of 0.5 in the midyear convention while it is raised to the power of 1.0 in the end-of-year convention.

Using the example of a discount rate of 5 percent, the divisor for the midyear convention is $(1.05)^{0.5} = 1.025$ and the divisor for the end-of-year convention is $(1.05)^{1.0} = 1.05$. As noted earlier, a smaller divisor will lead to a larger quotient, in this example $97.6 million for the midyear convention vs. $95.2 million for the end-of-year convention. While this is only a single cash flow example, this principle of a smaller divisor leading to a larger quotient will hold true for all cash flows, as demonstrated in Table 11.10.

Method 2: Adjust each individual cash flow by reducing each discounting period

Under this method, each periodic cash flow and the terminal value are all discounted by one-half period less. Thus CF_1 is discounted not by $(1 + r)^1$ but rather by $(1 + r)^{0.5}$. Similarly, CF_2 is discounted by $(1 + r)^{1.5}$, CF_3 is discounted by $(1 + r)^{2.5}$, CF_4 is discounted by $(1 + r)^{3.5}$, and CF_5 and the terminal value are discounted by $(1 + r)^{4.5}$. Each discounted cash flow using the midyear convention is larger than its corresponding discounted cash flow using the end-of-year convention (for positive cash flows; the opposite is true for negative cash flows). As a result, using the midyear convention (either method 1 or method 2) returns a higher DCF valuation than using the end-of-year convention (again, for positive periodic cash flows and terminal value).

Table 11.10 - Midyear Convention Yields a Higher Valuation

End-of-year convention

$ millions, except per share data

Discounting period (n)	**0**	**1**	**2**	**3**	**4**	**5**
Year	**2005**	**2006**	**2007**	**2008**	**2009**	**2010**
Present value of projection period						
Unlevered free cash flow (CF_n)	$150	$165	$182	$300	$330	$360
Weighted average cost of capital (r)	8%					
Present value formula		$= \frac{\$165}{1.08^1}$	$= \frac{\$182}{1.08^2}$	$= \frac{\$300}{1.08^3}$	$= \frac{\$330}{1.08^4}$	$= \frac{\$360}{1.08^5}$
Present value of free cash flows (PV)		153	156	238	243	245
Total present value of free cash flows	$1,035					

Midyear convention

$ millions, except per share data

Discounting period (n)	**0**	**0.5**	**1.5**	**2.5**	**3.5**	**4.5**
Year	**2005**	**2006**	**2007**	**2008**	**2009**	**2010**
Present value of projection period						
Unlevered free cash flow (CF_n)	$150	$165	$182	$300	$330	$360
Weighted average cost of capital (r)	8%					
Present value formula		$= \frac{\$165}{1.08^{0.5}}$	$= \frac{\$182}{1.08^{1.5}}$	$= \frac{\$300}{1.08^{2.5}}$	$= \frac{\$330}{1.08^{3.5}}$	$= \frac{\$360}{1.08^{4.5}}$
Present value of free cash flows (PV)		159	162	248	252	255
Total present value of free cash flows	$1,075					

Checking a DCF Model

There are a variety of ways to check DCF analyses. As you become more experienced and facile with this type of analysis, you will develop your own methods of checking the reasonableness of a DCF analysis. Below are some suggestions that should help in checking your or someone else's model.

- Change the discount rate in your model to zero and the present value of the cash flows should equal the sum of the nominal cash flows. If this does not make intuitive sense to you, think about the underlying math: a discounted cash flow analysis takes a nominal cash flow and divides it by (1 + discount rate); but if the discount rate is 0, then the discounting factor (i.e., the divisor) = (1 + 0) or 1, and any number divided by 1 equals itself. Moreover, 1 to the power of n equals 1 ($1^n = 1$) and so the number of discounting periods does not matter.

- Any numbers that are inconsistent may be due to an inputting error, so double-check inconsistent numbers to make sure they are not typographical errors.

- Entry and exit multiples should be relatively similar so that a high DCF valuation is not predicated on a higher exit multiple in a few years. Neither multiple expansion nor multiple compression (lower exit multiple in a few years) should be assumed unless a specific reason exists and is clearly footnoted in the analysis.

- Do not adjust the WACC to address your confidence in the projections (or lack thereof). Instead adjust or "haircut" the projections themselves and use the WACC that you believe best represents the cost of capital for the company. Said differently, if you believe the projected cash flows are too aggressive, reduce the nominal cash flows to represent a more realistic base case and maintain the WACC that is most appropriate for the risk of those cash flows. Do not make an adjustment that should be made to the cash flows by adjusting the discount rate up or down.

- The projections should represent the *expected* value of free cash flows and the ranges should take into account the different business scenarios *most likely* to occur during the projection period. Use sensitivity analyses and a range of assumptions to reflect uncertainty.

We will now review a comprehensive DCF example that incorporates all of the concepts discussed in this chapter. Note that the example provided in Table 11.11 is independent of all other examples in Chapter 11.

Table 11.11 - Comprehensive Discounted Cash Flow Analysis (calculate PV of free cash flow)

$ millions

Discount period	0	1	2	3	4	5	6	7	8	9	10
Year	2005	2006	2007	2008	2009	2010	2011	2012	2013	2014	2015
Earnings before interest and taxes (EBIT)	$1,000	$1,100	$1,210	$1,331	$1,464	$1,611	$1,772	$1,949	$2,144	$2,358	$2,594
Taxes on EBIT[1,5]	(400)	(440)	(484)	(532)	(586)	(644)	(709)	(780)	(857)	(943)	(1,038)
Earnings before interest after taxes (EBIAT)	600	660	726	799	879	966	1,063	1,169	1,286	1,415	1,556
Adjustments to EBIAT											
Depreciation and amortization	300	330	363	399	439	483	532	585	643	707	778
Deferred taxes	100	110	121	133	146	161	177	195	214	236	259
Net working capital[5]	(200)	(220)	(242)	(266)	(293)	(322)	(354)	(390)	(429)	(472)	(519)
Other operating accounts[5]	(100)	(110)	(121)	(133)	(146)	(161)	(177)	(195)	(214)	(236)	(259)
Capital expenditures[5,6]	(300)	(330)	(363)	(399)	(439)	(483)	(532)	(585)	(643)	(707)	(778)
Unlevered free cash flows[2]	**$ 400**	**$ 440**	**$ 484**	**$ 532**	**$ 586**	**$ 644**	**$ 709**	**$ 780**	**$ 857**	**$ 943**	**$1,038**
WACC 9.00%											
Present value formula		= $440	= $484	= $532	= $586	= $644	= $709	= $779	= $857	= $943	= $1,037
		1.09^{1}	1.09^{2}	1.09^{3}	1.09^{4}	1.09^{5}	1.09^{6}	1.09^{7}	1.09^{8}	1.09^{9}	1.09^{10}
Present value of free cash flow[3]		$404	$407	$411	$415	$419	$423	$426	$430	$434	$438
Present value of cash flows[4]	**$4,208**										

[1] EBIT × tax rate; excludes taxes on interest expense
[2] EBIAT +/- adjustments for non-cash charges and changes in working capital minus capital expenditures
[3] Present value of unlevered free cash flow, discounted at the weighted average cost of capital (WACC)
[4] Sum of the present value of free cash flows in Years 1 to 10
[5] Negative numbers (values in parentheses) are uses of cash; positive numbers are sources of cash
[6] Capital expenditure matches DD&A so there is no increase or decrease in net PP&E

Table 11.11 continued (calculate PV of the terminal value)

$ millions, except per share data

Perpetuity Growth Rate Method	
WACC	9.00%
Assumed Perpetuity Growth Rate	3.00%
Unlevered free cash flow in 2015	$ 1,038
Unlevered free cash flow in 2016[1,2]	1,069
Terminal enterprise value in 2015[2]	17,810
Present value of terminal value[3]	7,523
Present value of cash flows[4]	4,208
Implied enterprise value in 2005[5]	11,731
Cash as of year-end 2005	250
Total debt as of year-end 2005	(5,000)
Net debt as of year-end 2005	(4,750)
Implied equity value in 2005[6]	6,981
Diluted shares as of year-end 2005	300
Implied equity price per share[7]	**$23.27**
Implied 2015 EBITDA Multiple [8]	5.3x

[1] Free cash flow in 2015 × (1 + growth rate of 3%)
[2] Using perpetuity growth formula: CF_n / (discount rate - growth rate)
[3] Terminal value discounted for 10 years to arrive at 2005 value
[4] Sum of present value of cash flows
[5] Present value of terminal value + present value of cash flows
[6] Implied enterprise value - 2005 net debt
[7] Implied equity value / diluted shares outstanding
[8] Terminal enterprise value in 2015 / EBITDA in 2015

Terminal Multiple Method		
WACC	9.00%	9.00%
Assumed EBITDA Exit Multiple	5.0x	6.0x
EBITDA in 2015[1]	$ 3,372	$ 3,372
Terminal enterprise value in 2015[2]	16,859	20,231
Present value of terminal value [3]	7,122	8,546
Present value of cash flows [4]	4,208	4,208
Implied enterprise value in 2005 [5]	11,329	12,753
Cash as of year-end 2005	250	250
Total debt as of year-end 2005	(5,000)	(5,000)
Net debt as of year-end 2005	(4,750)	(4,750)
Implied equity value in 2005 [6]	6,579	8,003
Diluted shares as of year-end 2005	300	300
Implied equity price per share [7]	**$21.93**	**$26.68**
Implied Perpetuity Growth Rate [8]	2.7%	3.7%

[1] 2015 EBITDA = 2015 EBIT + 2015 DD&A
[2] 2015 EBITDA × assumed EBITDA exit multiple
[3] Terminal value discounted for 10 years to arrive at 2005 value
[4] Sum of present value of cash flows from projection period
[5] Present value of terminal value + present value of cash flows
[6] Implied enterprise value - 2005 net debt
[7] Implied equity value / diluted shares outstanding
[8] Solve for (g) using the growing perpetuity formula (CF_n / (r - g) = PV)

Table 11.11 continued (perform sensitivity analysis)

Implied equity price per share ($) [1]

WACC	Perpetuity Growth Rate (%)				
	2.75%	2.88%	3.00%	3.13%	3.25%
8.50%	$25.89	$26.53	$27.20	$27.90	$28.64
8.75%	$23.97	$24.55	$25.15	$25.78	$26.43
9.00%	$22.21	$22.73	**$23.27**	$23.83	$24.42
9.25%	$20.58	$21.05	$21.54	$22.05	$22.58
9.50%	$19.08	$19.51	$19.95	$20.41	$20.89

Implied equity price per share ($) [3]

WACC	EBITDA Exit Multiple (x)				
	5.00x	5.25x	5.50x	5.75x	6.00x
8.50%	$23.41	$24.66	$25.90	$27.14	$28.38
8.75%	$22.66	$23.88	$25.09	$26.31	$27.52
9.00%	**$21.93**	$23.12	$24.30	$25.49	**$26.68**
9.25%	$21.21	$22.37	$23.53	$24.69	$25.86
9.50%	$20.52	$21.65	$22.78	$23.92	$25.05

Implied equity price per share ($) [2]

WACC	EBIT Growth Rate (%)				
	9.00%	9.50%	10.00%	10.50%	11.00%
8.50%	$23.99	$25.56	$27.20	$28.90	$30.67
8.75%	$22.11	$23.60	$25.15	$26.76	$28.43
9.00%	$20.39	$21.80	**$23.27**	$24.79	$26.38
9.25%	$18.81	$20.15	$21.54	$22.99	$24.49
9.50%	$17.35	$18.63	$19.95	$21.33	$22.75

Implied equity price per share ($) [4]

WACC	EBIT Growth Rate (%)				
	9.00%	9.50%	10.00%	10.50%	11.00%
8.50%	$20.53	$21.94	$23.41	$24.94	$26.52
8.75%	$19.84	$21.22	$22.66	$24.16	$25.71
9.00%	$19.17	$20.52	**$21.93**	$23.39	$24.91
9.25%	$18.51	$19.84	$21.21	$22.65	$24.13
9.50%	$17.87	$19.17	$20.52	$21.92	$23.37

[1] Based on growing perpetuity method; assumes EBIT annual growth rate of 10 percent
[2] Based on growing perpetuity method; assumes perpetuity growth rate of 3 percent
[3] Based on terminal multiple method; assumes EBIT annual growth rate of 10 percent
[4] Based on terminal multiple method; assumes EBITDA exit multiple of 5x

Note: two-variable data tables, as the name suggests, only allow for two variables to change. However, there are multiple variables in nearly every model. As a result, for each sensitivity table, all but two variables must be fixed throughout the table.

Leveraged Buyout Analysis

Chapter 12

If a little money does not go out,
great money will not come in.

Chinese proverb

A **leveraged buyout** (LBO) is a specialized kind of acquisition with four distinguishing characteristics. Generally speaking,

1. The acquiror in a leveraged buyout is a financial sponsor. The financial sponsor pays for the target company with equity (raised through a private investment fund) and debt.

2. Compared to strategic buyers, financial sponsors use higher levels of debt to fund their acquisitions, thereby increasing the return on equity (also called leveraging their equity returns). Given that there are higher levels of debt in an LBO, the more senior debt (bank debt) in an LBO is often secured by the assets of the company and the subordinated debt is usually unsecured and rated below investment grade (also known as high yield).

3. If the target company is publicly held, the financial sponsor acquires all of the publicly traded equity of the target company, thereby taking the company private. As a result, an LBO is sometimes called a "going private" transaction.

4. Management of the target company often participates financially in the transaction, with a meaningful equity stake in the company post-LBO.

Given the high leverage in an LBO, companies with stable and growing cash flows in more mature industries tend to be good candidates since those stable cash flows can be used to make debt payments. The financial sponsor contributes equity to fund the purchase and will generally plan to hold the LBO company for anywhere from three to five years, at which point the financial sponsor will seek to exit the investment either by selling the company to another buyer or by taking the company public via an IPO and selling its stake in the initial and/or subsequent offerings. From the time it makes the investment until the time it exits the investment via a sale or equity market IPO, a financial sponsor generally hopes to earn a compound annual return on its equity of 15 to 35 percent, depending on perceived risk. A financial sponsor might be satisfied with a return in the high teens for a more secure investment which required little sponsor time and attention, whereas the sponsor might require a return in the low 30s for a more risky investment.

Financial sponsors, private equity firms, LBO firms

New finance professionals are sometimes confused by the terms financial sponsor, private equity firm and leveraged buyout firm. In essence, they all refer to the same thing. Financial sponsor is synonymous with private equity firm or leveraged buyout firm. This first term arose from the fact that the private equity firm is the financial "sponsor" of a leveraged buyout transaction because it provides the equity component. That is, the firm champions a proposed transaction and also provides the equity necessary to purchase the target company.

A private equity or leveraged buyout firm is an organization formed to (1) raise a committed pool of capital (called a "fund"); (2) invest the fund's money by buying companies (called "portfolio companies"); (3) work with the portfolio companies to grow the value of the businesses; and (4) sell the portfolio companies to generate substantial gains.

Companies that buy other companies are considered "strategic buyers" since their transactions are generally both strategically and financially motivated. Financial sponsors, on the other hand, are considered to be more financially than strategically motivated. Thus, when selling a company, the buyer pool is often segregated between strategic buyers (industry participants) and financial buyers (financial sponsors).

Financial vs. strategic buyers

In general, sponsors tend to stay away from auctions in which a number of strategic buyers are likely to participate. This is because strategic buyers are likely to have greater synergies with the target than financial sponsors and because the equity returns required by sponsors tend to be higher than those of strategic buyers. Because of these two market dynamics, strategic buyers can typically afford to pay more for the same target company than a financial sponsor.

Sponsors are often thought of as financial engineers because of their "quantitative focus" and comfort designing capital structures to improve equity returns. In the 1980s and 1990s, most sponsors were able to achieve their return thresholds relying largely on financial engineering and restructuring. Today, private equity firms, like strategic players, must be able to add value somehow, either through industry expertise or operating expertise. Many private equity deals today are done as partnerships in which one sponsor brings a fair amount of the capital to the partnership and the other sponsor brings industry or operating expertise (either through the sponsor's senior management or through one of the sponsor's portfolio companies). These transactions in which financial sponsors team up in order to acquire a company are called "club deals."

LBO Analysis

LBO analysis is similar to DCF analysis in that it is a forward-looking methodology that takes into account the company's future cash flows and the risk profile of those cash flows. Despite differences in nomenclature, the same four elements of periodic cash flows, terminal value, discount rate, and present value exist in both DCF and LBO analysis. In each type of analysis, three of the elements are given and you must solve for the fourth. The main difference between the two types of analysis is that DCF analysis solves for the present value (the enterprise value of the firm) whereas LBO analysis solves for the internal rate of return (IRR) to the equity investors (meaning it solves for the equity discount rate) and the profit to those equity investors based on the price paid or enterprise value. LBO analysis helps an investor answer the question "If I want to earn at least a 25 percent compound annual rate of return (or whatever the return threshold is) on an equity investment, and I believe in this set of projections, what is the highest purchase price I can pay?"

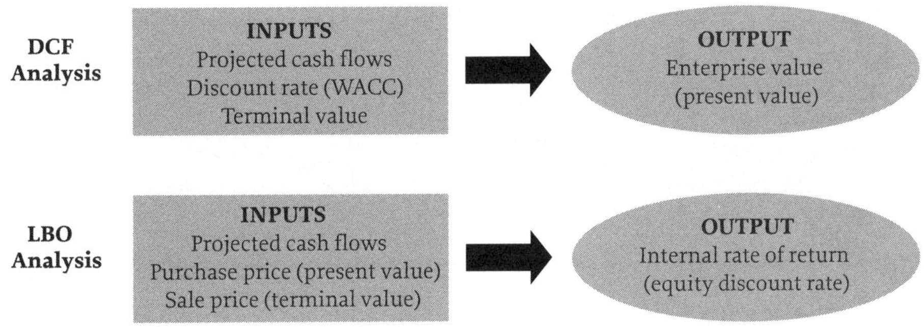

Importance of EBITDA to financial sponsors

Sponsors are particularly interested in a company's ability to generate cash flow from operations (most often measured by EBITDA). For back-of-the-envelope analysis, a sponsor begins with existing EBITDA, thinks about how it might be able to improve or grow EBITDA if it were the owner, and considers what capital expenditures would be required to maintain and grow projected EBITDA. A sponsor also will think about what multiple of EBITDA it might need to pay in order to win control of the target company.

Key Components

In Discounted Cash Flow Analysis (Ch.11), three components were introduced as key to any DCF analysis, the company's: (1) unlevered free cash flows during the projection period, (2) the weighted average cost of capital or WACC (which is the discount rate (r) used in the analysis), and (3) the terminal value at the end of the projection period. In performing LBO analysis, there is a slight variation to these three components. Instead of focusing on unlevered free cash flows, for example, LBO analysis focuses on cash flows available for debt service. Differences in the calculation of cash flows between LBO and DCF analysis are described below.

Cash flow available for debt service (CFADS): Just as with DCF analysis, building a projection model is the first step in LBO analysis. The projection model is used to estimate the company's future cash flows. Whereas DCF analysis focuses on the unlevered free cash flows (before debt and equity holders are paid), LBO analysis focuses on the cash flow available for debt service (before equity holders are paid). Unlevered free cash flows (used in DCF analysis) do not include after-tax interest expense whereas cash flow available for debt service (used in LBO analysis) includes interest expense and taxes, taking into account the tax shield generated by the interest expense. The theory underlying this difference is that DCF analysis is independent of the capital structure. In LBO analysis, on the other hand, the capital structure is an integral part of the transaction and therefore the calculation of cash flow available for debt service does not add back after-tax interest expense. To summarize the key difference between unlevered cash flow (for DCF analysis) and cash flow available for debt service (for LBO analysis) is after-tax interest expense.

DCF ANALYSIS Unlevered free cash flow		LBO ANALYSIS Cash flow available for debt service	
Start with	Net income	Start with	Net income
Increase	Depreciation and amortization	Increase	Depreciation and amortization
Increase/ (decrease)	Changes in deferred taxes	Increase/ (decrease)	Changes in deferred taxes
Increase/ (decrease)	Other non-cash charges	Increase/ (decrease)	Other non-cash charges
(Increase)/ decrease	Changes in net working capital	(Increase)/ decrease	Changes in net working capital
Equals	Cash flow from operations	Equals	Cash flow from operations
Increase	After-tax interest expense	N/A	Do not adjust for interest expense
Decrease	Capital expenditures	Decrease	Capital expenditures
Equals	**Unlevered free cash flow**	Equals	**Cash flow available for debt service**

Note: all values in parentheses are uses of cash; all values not in parentheses are sources of cash

Entry and exit values: In LBO analysis, an internal rate of return (IRR) for the equity holders is calculated based on (1) the equity component of the purchase price of the investment (the present value), (2) dividends paid to equity holders, if any, during the projection period, and (3) the sale price of the equity (the cash flow to equity holders at the end of the projection period). In LBO parlance, the purchase price is considered the entry value and an **entry multiple** is calculated based on the entry value. Most financial sponsors focus on the entry multiple of enterprise value to EBITDA (EV / EBITDA) or simply the "entry EBITDA multiple." The exit value is the value at which the financial sponsor expects to sell LBO company in the future. If the financial sponsor is likely to sell LBO company to another buyer, then the exit value should be compared to M&A transaction multiples. If the financial sponsor is likely to sell LBO company's equity into the public equity market via an IPO, then the exit value should be compared to trading multiples. The **exit multiple** is the enterprise value to EBITDA (or other multiple such as P/E) based on the price at which LBO company is assumed to be sold in the future. The exit value in LBO analysis is similar to the terminal value in DCF analysis. Sponsors typically assume the same exit as entry EBITDA multiple in their analysis, but the value implied by the exit multiple is compared with the value implied by market multiples to benchmark the assumed exit multiple and to provide a sanity check.

Internal rate of return (IRR): In DCF analysis, the weighted average cost of capital (WACC) is the discount rate (r) used to discount the projected free cash flows and the terminal value. In LBO analysis, the internal rate of return (IRR) is the discount rate that yields a present value equal to the equity capital invested. The internal rate of return for the equity holders is calculated based on: (1) the equity component of the purchase price (cash flow at Time 0), (2) dividend payments made during the projection period, if any, and (3) the sale price or market value of the equity in the future (cash flow at Time *n*). Generally, a range of purchase prices is considered and, ultimately, a purchase price and amount of equity capital invested is determined based on an IRR that is acceptable to the financial sponsor given the projected cash flows, the exit value, and the risk of those cash flows and exit value. As with other corporate finance practitioners, sponsors will accept lower IRRs for lower risk investments and will demand higher IRRs for higher risk investments.

Can't take an IRR to the bank

Although IRR is an important first step in LBO analysis, it is the first of many important return metrics considered by the sponsor. It is common to hear the phrase "You can't take an IRR to the bank" or "You can't eat an IRR." This refers to the fact that banks and lenders who provide much of the capital required to execute an LBO do not care about equity returns (the return to the sponsor). Rather, lenders care about getting repaid their capital plus interest. For lenders, cash flow and leverage multiples (which are described later in this chapter and in Credit Analysis (Ch.24)) are as important in LBO analysis as IRR.

Another consideration in focusing on IRR is that, ultimately, sponsors care about "profit," or the multiple of the investment earned relative to the invested capital. This means that sponsors strike a balance between maximizing IRR and maximizing the net dollars returned. For example, assume a $100 million investment over the course of 1 year, 4 years and 7 years with IRRs of 45%, 35% and 25%, respectively. See Table 12.1. Although the 1-year investment has the highest IRR with 45%, sponsors are likely to forsake this higher IRR for greater dollar profits as shown in the 4-year and 7-year scenarios (assuming a comfort with the risk of holding the investment for a longer period).

Table 12.1 – IRR vs. Multiple of Investment

$ millions

Equity capital invested	Term	IRR	Equity value at exit[1]	Profit[2]	Multiple of investment[3]
$100	1 year	45%	$145	$45	1.45x
$100	4 years	35%	$332	$232	3.32x
$100	7 years	25%	$477	$377	4.77x

[1] Capital invested × $(1 + \text{IRR})^{\text{number of years}}$
[2] Equity value at exit - capital invested
[3] Equity value at exit / equity capital invested

Simplified LBO Analysis

Now that we have reviewed the theory and the major concepts underlying an LBO, let's review a simple numerical example to see how LBO analysis works in practice. Consider SportsCo, a company that makes specialty cycling apparel. SportsCo had $50 million in revenues and $4 million in net income in 2005. As of year end 2005, it also had $10 million of outstanding bank debt and $1 million of cash on the balance sheet. On January 1, 2006, Sponsor will acquire the equity of SportsCo for $54 million in cash.

The LBO analysis for SportsCo is also provided in its entirety at the end of this chapter in Table 12.16.

1. Begin with Target's stand-alone financials

SportsCo's stand-alone financial information is provided below.

Table 12.2 – SportsCo Stand-alone

$ thousands

Income Statement	2004	2005	Capitalization	12/31/05
Revenues	$43,000	$50,000	Bank debt	$10,000
Cost of goods sold	(25,370)	(30,000)	Shareholders' equity	35,000
Gross margin	17,630	20,000	Total capitalization	$45,000
Selling, general, administrative	(8,600)	(10,000)		
EBITDA	9,030	10,000	Capitalization (%)	
DD&A	(2,250)	(2,500)	Bank debt	22%
EBIT	6,780	7,500	Shareholders' equity	78%
Interest expense	(700)	(700)	Total capitalization	100%
EBT	6,080	6,800		
Taxes	(2,432)	(2,680)	Cash	$1,000
Net income	$3,648	$4,120		

2. Calculate transaction multiples for Sponsor's acquisition of SportsCo

On January 1, 2006, Sponsor will acquire all of SportsCo's equity for $54 million in cash. The $10 million of existing debt will be refinanced with the new acquisition debt (which is what normally occurs with LBOs). The $1 million of existing cash will not be used to fund in the acquisition.

The transaction value is $63 million ($54 million of equity value + $9 million of existing net debt = $63 million). The "entry multiples" paid by Sponsor include:

- 6.3x 2005 EBITDA
- 8.4x 2005 EBIT
- 13.1x 2005 net income
- 1.5x book value of equity

Table 12.3 – SportsCo Transaction Multiples

$ thousands

Transaction Multiples ("entry" multiples)

Equity value	$54,000		
Existing debt[1]	10,000		
Existing cash[1]	(1,000)		
Enterprise value[2]	$63,000		
Enterprise value multiples		Equity value multiples	
Enterprise value	$63,000	Equity value	$54,000
2005 EBITDA	10,000	2005 net income	4,120
Enterprise value/EBITDA	6.3x	P/E	13.1x
Enterprise value	$63,000	Equity value	$54,000
2005 EBIT	7,500	Book value of equity	35,000
Enterprise value/EBIT	8.4x	Price/book	1.5x

[1] Total debt - cash = net debt
[2] Purchase price for SportsCo equity + existing net debt

3. Calculate the post-transaction capitalization for SportsCo

To fund the acquisition, Sponsor will use $45.5 million from a new bank loan and $19.5 million will be contributed as equity from Sponsor's fund. Sponsor will not use any of SportsCo's $1 million of cash on hand to fund the acquisition (it will remain as cash on Target's balance sheet and will be used to fund working capital). Post-transaction, SportsCo will have capitalization of $45.5 million of outstanding debt and $19.5 million in book equity. Miscellaneous transaction fees amount to $1 million.

Table 12.4 – SportsCo Post-Transaction Capitalization

$ thousands

Sources and Uses

Acquisition debt	$45,500	Purchase of equity	$54,000
Equity from Sponsor	19,500	Repayment of existing debt	10,000
Total sources	$65,000	Transaction fees	1,000
		Total uses	$65,000

Pre- and Post-Transaction Capitalization

	Pre-transaction		Adjustments[1]	Post-transaction	
Pre-transaction debt	$10,000	22%	($10,000)	$0	0%
Acquisition debt	0	0%	45,500	45,500	70%
Total debt	10,000	22%	35,500	45,500	70%
Shareholders' equity[2]	35,000	78%	(15,500)	19,500	30%
Total capitalization	$45,000	100%	$20,000	$65,000	100%

[1] Purchase accounting adjustments for shareholders' equity are described in Accretion / Dilution Analysis. (Ch.14)

[2] $19.5 million is the amount of equity contributed by Sponsor. The net adjustment of -$15.5 million reflects the elimination of old book equity of $35 million and addition of new book equity of $19.5 million (-$35 million + $19.5 million = -$15.5 million).

Pre-transaction, SportsCo was capitalized with 22 percent debt and 78 percent shareholders' equity. After the buyout by Sponsor, SportsCo is capitalized with 70 percent debt and 30 percent shareholders' equity. Essentially, much of the equity capital in SportsCo was removed (from 78 percent of total capitalization pre-transaction to 30 percent of total capitalization post-transaction) and replaced with debt financing (from 22 percent of total capitalization pre-transaction to 70 percent of total capitalization post-transaction).

Tranches of debt

The presentation of SportsCo's post-transaction debt has been simplified. In practice, the $45.5 million of debt taken on in the LBO usually would be comprised of several tranches of debt, each with different risk characteristics, subordination, security requirements, return requirements, and levels of equity participation. In addition, the tranches of debt often would come from different lenders and/or investor pools. In the SportsCo example, the existing debt is refinanced with new acquisition debt (which is what normally occurs in practice). However if, for some reason, existing debt were not refinanced (meaning existing debt would "roll over"), it is likely that the existing debt would be subordinated to the new acquisition debt. See Credit Analysis and Sources of Capital. (Ch.24,25)

How would Sponsor have determined that $54 million was an appropriate offer price for the equity of SportsCo (or $63 million for the net debt and equity)?

Prior to making the offer for SportsCo, Sponsor would have developed an LBO model (also referred to as an equity model) to calculate its equity returns based on a range of potential offer prices and would have chosen a price that yielded an acceptable equity return given SportsCo's inherent risk. In addition to LBO analysis, Sponsor would have cross-referenced the offer price using other valuation methodologies (e.g., comparable transaction analysis).

If working on a live transaction, it would be important to develop a full set of financial projections to perform LBO analysis (the projections should include a full income statement, balance sheet and cash flow statement). Many times in finance, however, a "quick and dirty" analysis is performed to gauge whether or not the transaction is viable prior to beginning the arduous and time-consuming task of creating a full set of financial projections. In fact, most of the models built in investment banking are "quick and dirty" models and only a small percentage of models built are full-blown, three-statement financial projections. While the SportsCo model shown in its entirety in Table 12.16 would be considered a "quick and dirty" model, the same adjustments and calculations would be performed in a full three-statement model.

4. Review the historical financials for SportsCo

Begin with a review of SportsCo's historical financials to determine historical margins and growth rates. For an actual transaction (as opposed to an initial analysis), Sponsor would conduct due diligence in order to develop a good understanding of SportsCo's historical margins and growth rates, which Sponsor would then use to make assumptions about future margins and growth rates for purposes of financial modeling. In the absence of due diligence, simple calculations such as the ones shown in Table 12.5 below would be sufficient.

Table 12.5 – SportsCo Historical Margins and Growth Rates

$ thousands

Income Statement	2004	Margins	2005	Margins	'04-'05 growth
Revenues	$43,000		$50,000		16%
Cost of goods sold	(25,370)	59%	(30,000)	60%	
Gross margin	17,630	41%	20,000	40%	13%
Selling, general, administrative	(8,600)	20%	(10,000)	20%	
EBITDA	9,030	21%	10,000	20%	11%
DD&A	(2,250)	5%	(2,500)	5%	
EBIT	6,780	16%	7,500	15%	11%
Interest expense	(700)	2%	(700)	1%	
EBT	6,080	14%	6,800	14%	12%
Taxes	(2,432)	6%	(2,680)	5%	
Net income	$3,648	9%	$4,120	8%	13%

Note: margins are based on percentage of revenues, e.g., cost of goods sold margin = cost of goods sold / revenues. This is a common way to analyze margins, as a percentage of revenues. It is sometimes referred to as "common size analysis" because it allows for the comparison of operating performance of companies of disparate sizes.

5. Make assumptions for the projection period

Using margins and growth rates from the historical period(s) available, make assumptions for margins and growth rates during the projection period. As with all financial analysis, the quality of the assumptions will dictate the quality of the output of the model. On paper, any transaction can be made to work with assumptions (and therefore financial projections) that are optimistic enough. Therefore, it is important that assumptions be reasonable. Initially, the assumptions should be reflective of the company's past performance. Any improvement from that past performance (e.g., increase in annual sales growth, decrease in raw material costs, decrease in required capital expenditure, etc.) should occur only after that particular item has been studied and Sponsor has determined that the company's historical performance can be improved upon, thus justifying a change in assumptions. As mentioned in Discounted Cash Flow Analysis (Ch.11), this book does not delve into detail regarding how to prepare financial statement projections. Many good books on this topic already exist, some of which are listed in the Appendix.

Projection period: A major assumption is that SportsCo will be sold by Sponsor to another buyer after a 5-year ownership period. Therefore, a 5-year projection model is created and estimates will be made for exit values at the end of the fifth year.

Revenues: Another major assumption for the SportsCo model is that it will be driven primarily by revenue growth. That is, revenues will grow by a certain percentage annually but major aspects of the income statement will remain constant as a percentage of revenues (said another way, margins will generally stay flat during the projection period). Thus cost of goods sold (COGS), selling, general and administrative expenses (SG&A) and depreciation, depletion, and amortization (DD&A) will remain a constant percentage of revenues for each year during the projection period. Revenue growth is projected to be 15 percent in the first year. The rate of revenue growth rate slows each year during the 5-year projection period until it reaches 5 percent annual growth from 2009 to 2010. Sponsor has made this assumption based on industry and market share analysis.

DD&A: DD&A is expected to be 5 percent of revenues each year. This is an overly simplified assumption -- but simplified assumptions are often used in quick and dirty analysis. In practice, the assumption for projected DD&A would be developed after studying SportsCo's assets and creating a depreciation schedule for those assets.

Capital expenditures (capex): The assumption for the projection period is that annual capex is equal to annual depreciation. This is another simplified assumption. Setting capex equal to depreciation is a common financial modeling assumption. The underlying logic is that if capex equals depreciation, those assets that are getting older (through depreciation) are being repaired or replaced (through capex). The assumption is that the asset base should remain constant since the aging of assets (depreciation) is exactly offset by new investment in the asset base (capex). Note that this capex is *maintenance* capex because it is only maintaining the asset base, not improving it. In order to increase/improve the asset base (for example, to move into a new market, create a new product line, or support growing sales), capex would need to exceed depreciation for a period of time (this is called *investment* or *growth* capex). For financial projections that have high rates of revenue growth, it is important to consider an appropriate rate of investment capex in addition to maintenance capex.

Capital expenditures vs. DD&A

In LBO analysis, capital expenditures are extremely important assumptions and significant time is spent during due diligence determining the nature and amount of capex that has been spent in the past as well as how much capex is required to sustain projected growth rates. Less time is spent on approximating DD&A since this is a non-cash charge. What is important is estimating the tax shield benefit generated by any DD&A because this translates into dollars saved through reduced taxes.

Working capital: Calculating working capital as a percentage of sales is another simplifying assumption. In a fully integrated three-statement (income statement, balance sheet, cash flow statement) financial model, projections would be made for individual balance sheet items and changes in working capital would then be calculated based on the projected balance sheets. Working capital is calculated as current assets minus current liabilities, excluding cash and short-term debt.

Tax rate: 40 percent is a common assumption for income taxes for financial modeling purposes. While the actual blended (federal, state and local) tax rate may be lower, 40 percent is generally considered a conservative starting point. Another simplified assumption is that there is no year-over-year change in deferred taxes (if there were, this would be an adjustment when calculating cash flow). Deferred taxes are described in detail in Taxes and M&A. (Ch.21)

Interest rate: Given the significant change in total debt as a result of the LBO and the degradation in SportsCo's credit quality post-transaction as shown in Table 12.10, an assumption is made that the interest rate on debt increases from 7 percent pre-transaction to 10 percent post-transaction to reflect this increased risk. Credit quality and credit analysis are described in detail in Credit Analysis and Sources of Capital. (Ch.24,25)

Purchase accounting: Under purchase accounting, SportsCo's assets and liabilities would be adjusted to fair market value after the acquisition by Sponsor. The fair market value of $54 million paid for SportsCo's equity ($63 million is paid for SportsCo's equity and debt) would be allocated among its assets and liabilities. Any excess of the equity purchase price over the allocated fair market value of identifiable assets less liabilities would be recorded as goodwill. Purchase accounting rules and goodwill are described in Accretion/Dilution Analysis. (Ch.14) In this simplified example, the assumption is made that no write-up of SportsCo's assets takes place for GAAP accounting or tax accounting purposes.

Table 12.6 – SportsCo Key Assumptions for Projection Period

	Historical		Projected				
Key assumptions	**2004A**	**2005A**	**2006**	**2007**	**2008**	**2009**	**2010**
Annual revenue growth	-	16.3%	15.0%	12.5%	10.0%	7.5%	5.0%
Cost of goods sold margin	59.0%	60.0%	60.0%	60.0%	60.0%	60.0%	60.0%
SG&A margin	20.0%	20.0%	20.0%	20.0%	20.0%	20.0%	20.0%
DD&A margin	5.2%	5.0%	5.0%	5.0%	5.0%	5.0%	5.0%
Capex margin	-	5.0%	5.0%	5.0%	5.0%	5.0%	5.0%
Working capital margin	-	2.0%	2.0%	2.0%	2.0%	2.0%	2.0%
Tax rate	40.0%	39.4%	40.0%	40.0%	40.0%	40.0%	40.0%
Interest rate on total debt	-	7.0%	10.0%	10.0%	10.0%	10.0%	10.0%

Choosing the actual values for these key assumptions would be one of the most heavily debated aspects of Sponsor's proposed investment in LBO company. As noted earlier, a financial model is fairly straightforward -- if the inputs prove correct, then the outputs should accurately predict the actual company performance.

6. Develop financial projections for SportsCo

Based on key assumptions, develop a set of financial projections that yield an estimate of cash flow available for debt service. To do this, prepare a projected income statement, then make the adjustments to move from net income to operating cash flow, and finally subtract capital expenditures. Once cash flow available for debt service is calculated, you can assume that the entirety of that cash flow is used to reduce acquisition debt. In financial modeling, it is common to assume that all excess cash (the amount above and beyond the base level of cash required for normal business operations) is used to pay down debt until all acquisition debt is retired, at which point a cash balance may begin to build. In practice, most LBO companies are re-sold, re-leveraged, or sold to the public via an IPO before all acquisition debt is repaid.

Table 12.7 – SportsCo Financial Projections

$ thousands	**Historical**		**Projected**				
Cash flow build up	**2004A**	**2005A**	**2006**	**2007**	**2008**	**2009**	**2010**
Revenues	$43,000	$50,000	$57,500	$64,688	$71,156	$76,493	$80,318
Cost of goods sold	(25,370)	(30,000)	(34,500)	(38,813)	(42,694)	(45,896)	(48,191)
Gross margin	17,630	20,000	23,000	25,875	28,463	30,597	32,127
SG&A	(8,600)	(10,000)	(11,500)	(12,938)	(14,231)	(15,299)	(16,064)
EBITDA	9,030	10,000	11,500	12,938	14,231	15,299	16,064
DD&A	(2,250)	(2,500)	(2,875)	(3,234)	(3,558)	(3,825)	(4,016)
EBIT	6,780	7,500	8,625	9,703	10,673	11,474	12,048
Interest expense[1]	(700)	(700)	(4,432)	(4,154)	(3,795)	(3,357)	(2,847)
EBT	6,080	6,800	4,193	5,549	6,879	8,117	9,201
Taxes	(2,432)	(2,680)	(1,677)	(2,220)	(2,751)	(3,247)	(3,681)
Net income	$3,648	$4,120	$2,516	$3,329	$4,127	$4,870	$5,521
Net working capital		1,000	1,150	1,294	1,423	1,530	1,606
Net income			$2,516	$3,329	$4,127	$4,870	$5,521
DD&A			2,875	3,234	3,558	3,825	4,016
(Increase)/decrease in net working capital			(150)	(144)	(129)	(107)	(77)
Other non-cash charges			0	0	0	0	0
Operating cash flow			5,241	6,420	7,556	8,588	9,460
Capital expenditures			(2,875)	(3,234)	(3,558)	(3,825)	(4,016)
Cash flow available for debt service			$2,366	$3,186	$3,998	$4,764	$5,444

Note: Positive numbers are cash inflows (sources of cash) and negative numbers, which are shown in parentheses, are cash outflows (uses of cash).

[1] See Step 7 for the interest expense calculation (Table 12.8).

7. Retire acquisition debt with excess cash during projection period

Given the large amount of debt post-acquisition, one of the first tasks after an LBO is to reduce acquisition debt. All of SportsCo's cash flow available for debt service will be used to retire transaction debt. After five years, 43 percent of the acquisition debt has been paid off (as shown in Table 12.8). Shareholders' equity increases each year based on SportsCo's net income. An assumption is made that no dividends are paid to Sponsor during the projection period.

Table 12.8 – SportsCo Financial Projections

$ thousands	**Actual**	**Adjusted**	**Projected**				
Capitalization	**2005A**	**2005**	**2006**	**2007**	**2008**	**2009**	**2010**
Cash flow available for debt service			$2,366	$3,186	$3,998	$4,764	$5,444
Acquisition debt to be retired[1]			(2,366)	(3,186)	(3,998)	(4,764)	(5,444)
Adjusted cash flow after debt service			0	0	0	0	0
Acquisition debt (beginning of year)			45,500	43,134	39,948	35,951	31,187
Acquisition debt to be retired			(2,366)	(3,186)	(3,998)	(4,764)	(5,444)
Acquisition debt (end of year)			43,134	39,948	35,951	31,187	25,743
Percentage of acquisition debt remaining			95%	88%	79%	69%	57%
Percentage of acquisition debt retired			5%	12%	21%	32%	43%
Average debt for the year[2]			44,317	41,541	37,950	33,569	28,465
Interest rate on debt			10%	10%	10%	10%	10%
Interest expense on debt[3]			4,432	4,154	3,795	3,357	2,847
Shareholders' equity (beginning of year)			19,500	22,016	25,345	29,473	34,343
Add: net income			2,516	3,329	4,127	4,870	5,521
Less: dividends paid			0	0	0	0	0
Shareholders' equity (end of year)			$22,016	$25,345	$29,473	$34,343	$39,863
Total debt	$10,000	$45,500	43,134	39,948	35,951	31,187	25,743
Shareholders' equity	35,000	19,500	22,016	25,345	29,473	34,343	39,863
Total capitalization	$45,000	$65,000	$65,150	$65,294	$65,423	$65,530	$65,606

[1] Acquisition debt to be retired is equal to cash flow available for debt service as calculated in Table 12.7 since the assumption is that all CFADS will be used to retire debt.

[2] Average debt for the year is [(Acquisition Debt Yr. 1 + Acquisition Debt Yr. 2) / 2] to reflect the fact that acquisition debt is retired over the course of the year. Average debt is used because using the higher beginning of year value would overstate annual interest expense and using the lower end of year value would understate annual interest expense.

[3] Average debt for the year × interest rate on debt.

Cash sweep

In the SportsCo projection model, excess cash is used to pay down debt (for example, 2006 cash flow available for debt service is $2.366 million, which is used to reduce total debt from $45.5 million at the beginning of 2006 to $43.134 million at the end of 2006). This is called a "cash sweep." The logic behind a cash sweep is that any and all cash requirements have already been captured and are reflected in the cash flow available for debt service line. Therefore, any cash available at that point (excess cash) should be "swept" out of the cash account and used to pay down debt. Said differently, there is no better use of that cash than to pay down debt, especially since the company is highly leveraged. Over time that conclusion may change and, over time, compelling investment opportunities may arise (e.g., a new factory, a joint venture, an acquisition, etc.) which would justify using that cash for alternative purposes but, typically, during the early years in an LBO the most important financial priority is to pay down acquisition debt.

8. Calculate credit ratios "out-of-the-box" and during the projection period

Due to the heavy debt loads associated with leveraged buyouts, lenders are justifiably concerned about the risk of default by the LBO company (for non-payment of interest, non-payment of scheduled principal, or breach of financial and other covenants). Lenders and debt investors use credit ratios to help determine credit risk, among other things, when making lending or investment decisions and also to protect and monitor their investments on an ongoing basis. Credit risk analysis is used to determine how much debt LBO company can handle, as well as on what terms and at what rates of interest.

While any number of credit metrics might be used to assess the risk profile of a company, there are two major types of credit ratios which are commonly used: (a) leverage ratios and (b) coverage ratios.

- Leverage ratios measure the *amount* of debt on the company. Debt to EBITDA and debt to total capital, for example, are common leverage ratios. Lower leverage ratios are safer (indicative of less debt relative to cash flow or less debt relative to equity in the capital structure, respectively).

- Coverage ratios measure the ability of the company's cash flows to *cover the interest and principal* or "service the debt." As such, the fixed payment aspect of the debt (such as interest expense) is usually the denominator in coverage ratios, and a cash flow metric is the numerator. The higher the coverage ratios, the more breathing room an LBO has (e.g., EBITDA could decline and the company could still make its fixed interest payments).

SportsCo's credit ratios improve considerably during the projection period due to the retirement of acquisition debt (which reduces total debt for leverage ratios as well as interest expense for coverage ratios) and the increase in cash flows (which increases the numerator for coverage ratios). Note in Table 12.8 that total capitalization actually changes very little over the projection period. However, as shown in Table 12.9, the composition of that capitalization changes significantly (70 percent debt and 30 percent equity post-LBO in 2005 to 39 percent debt and 61 percent equity by the end of 2010).

Table 12.9 – Composition of Total Capitalization

$ thousands	Adjusted	Projected				
	2005	2006	2007	2008	2009	2010
Total debt	$45,500	$43,134	$39,948	$35,951	$31,187	$25,743
Shareholders' equity	19,500	22,016	25,345	29,473	34,343	39,863
Total capitalization	$65,000	$65,150	$65,294	$65,423	$65,530	$65,606
Year over year growth in total capitalization	n/a	0.2%	0.2%	0.2%	0.2%	0.1%

	Adjusted	Projected				
	2005	2006	2007	2008	2009	2010
Total debt	70%	66%	61%	55%	48%	39%
Shareholders' equity	30%	34%	39%	45%	52%	61%
Total capitalization	100%	100%	100%	100%	100%	100%

Table 12.10 – SportsCo Projected Credit Ratios

$ thousands	Pro forma transaction	Projected				
Credit ratios	**2005**	**2006E**	**2007E**	**2008E**	**2009E**	**2010E**
Inputs						
Total debt	$45,500	$43,134	$39,948	$35,951	$31,187	$25,743
Total capital	65,000	65,150	65,294	65,423	65,530	65,606
EBITDA	10,000	11,500	12,938	14,231	15,299	16,064
EBIT	7,500	8,625	9,703	10,673	11,474	12,048
Interest expense	4,432	4,432	4,154	3,795	3,357	2,847
Capital expenditures[1]	2,500	2,875	3,234	3,558	3,825	4,016
Debt amortization	0	2,366	3,186	3,998	4,764	5,444
Leverage ratios (lower is better)						
Total debt / total capital	70%	66%	61%	55%	48%	39%
Total debt / EBITDA[2]	4.6x	3.8x	3.1x	2.5x	2.0x	1.6x
Total debt / (EBITDA - capex)	6.1x	5.0x	4.1x	3.4x	2.7x	2.1x
Coverage ratios (higher is better)						
EBITDA / interest expense	2.3x	2.6x	3.1x	3.8x	4.6x	5.6x
(EBITDA - capex) / interest expense	1.7x	1.9x	2.3x	2.8x	3.4x	4.2x
EBITDA / (interest + amortization)[3]	1.5x	1.7x	1.8x	1.8x	1.9x	1.9x
(EBITDA - capex) / (interest + amortization)[3,4]	1.1x	1.3x	1.3x	1.4x	1.4x	1.5x

[1] Capital expenditures are assumed to be equal to DD&A

[2] It is common to measure total debt to EBITDA as well as senior debt to EBITDA. In our simplified example we do not distinguish between senior debt and subordinated debt and so this second ratio is not shown.

[3] Amortization here refers to scheduled principal amortization (repayment of debt principal), not DD&A. 2005 ratios include Year 1 amortization (2006E amortization of $2,366). For purposes of these two credit ratios, 2006E amortization is counted twice since it is included in both the proforma and the 2006E ratios.

[4] This ratio must be at least 1.0x

Out-of-the-box credit ratios

The term "out-of-the-box" refers to those financial metrics, including credit ratios, immediately upon close of a transaction. If the LBO company has enough cash flow to begin retiring acquisition debt fairly quickly after the transaction closes, credit ratios generally improve considerably from those "out-of-the-box" because both sides of the equation are moving (cash flows are getting stronger and interest expense is getting smaller since transaction debt is being paid down). Therefore, it is important to look at credit ratios over the projection period as well as credit ratios out-of-the-box. An LBO is most vulnerable out-of-the-box since (a) debt is at its highest point (assuming no subsequent financial distress), (b) any planned asset sales still must be executed, and (c) there has been no time yet for management to implement improvements to operations.

9. Calculate the exit value for SportsCo at the end of the projection period

In the last year of the projection period, calculate an exit value based on whatever exit method is most likely for SportsCo. If, for example, Sponsor assumes it will sell SportsCo to another buyer (as opposed to selling equity in the public market via an IPO), M&A transaction multiples would be the more appropriate exit multiples to use (note that if Sponsor assumes that it will take SportsCo public via an IPO, trading multiples would be the more appropriate exit multiples to use). Also, since transaction multiples tend to be higher than trading multiples (because of the control premium), this assumption probably leads to a higher IRR than would have been the case if Sponsor had assumed an exit via a public market IPO. The decision on exit method and valuation would be studied at the outset of the transaction, but the ultimate decision on disposition would be taken opportunistically whenever Sponsor chose to exit the investment.

A general first assumption is that the exit enterprise value to EBITDA multiple (EV/EBITDA) is the same as the entry multiple. To calculate the exit value, multiply EBITDA in the last year of the projection period by the assumed exit multiple to determine the estimated enterprise value in that year (e.g., Year 5 in a 5-year projection model). Subtract estimated net debt (which is total debt less excess cash) in that same year (Year 5 in this example) to determine the estimated value for the equity holders in Year 5. Other potential exit value metrics include trailing (i.e., Year 5) multiples of net income, EBIT, or book value.

Some practitioners focus not on trailing multiples (e.g., multiples of Year 5 EBITDA or Year 5 net income) but rather on forward multiples (e.g., multiples of Year 6 EBITDA or Year 6 net income in this example). The mechanics for the calculation of forward multiples are the same as the calculation of trailing multiples, with the exception that the metrics are taken from the year *after* the assumed sale rather than *before* it. Since projections generally trend upward, the use of forward multiples usually results in lower multiple values than the use of trailing multiples. For example, SportsCo had an entry EV/EBITDA multiple of 6.3x on a trailing basis (EV of $63 million and 2005 EBITDA of $10 million). On a forward basis, this entry EV/EBITDA multiple would have been 5.5x ($63 million / $11.5 million) since 2006 EBITDA was $11.5 million.

Table 12.11 – SportsCo Exit Value

$ thousands			Projected		
Exit value	**2006E**	**2007E**	**2008E**	**2009E**	**2010E**
EBITDA in exit year					$16,064
EBITDA exit multiple[1]					6.3x
Implied enterprise value in exit year					101,200
Less total net debt in exit year (total debt net of cash of $1 million)[2]					(24,743)
Implied equity value in exit year (2010)					$76,457
Net income in exit year (2010)					$5,521
Implied P/E multiple in exit year (2010)[3]					13.8x
Entry P/E multiple (2005)[4]					13.1x

[1] Assumes the exit multiple equals the EBITDA entry multiple, which was $63,000 / $10,000 = 6.3x
[2] From Tables 12.8 and 12.3. Total debt in 2010 of $25,743 less cash in 2010 of $1,000 equals $24,743
[3] $76,457 / $5,521 = 13.8x
[4] $54,000 / $4,120 = 13.1x

10. Calculate equity IRR and multiple of investment (MOI) for Sponsor

Once an equity value has been calculated in the exit year, an internal rate of return (IRR) can be calculated for the equity investment. Based on the projected equity cash flows, IRR is the discount rate that yields the present value of the equity capital invested or, said differently, the discount rate that yields a *net* present value of zero. The equity component of the purchase price of SportsCo was \$19.5 million. The \$19.5 million is, therefore, a negative cash flow at Time 0 (or 12/31/2005 in this example). The equity value in the exit year of \$76.457 million is the value of cash proceeds Sponsor expects to receive if it sells SportsCo for 6.3x 2010 EBITDA, after adjusting for outstanding net debt in 2010 of \$24.743 million. Most financial software has a function that will calculate IRR. However, it is always a good idea to cross-check the calculated IRR to ensure that the calculation was done properly. In addition to calculating the implied IRR, a Sponsor would want to calculate its implied profit and multiple of profit over initial investment.

Table 12.12 – SportsCo Calculation of IRR and MOI

\$ thousands		Projected				
Exit value	**12/31/05**	**2006E**	**2007E**	**2008E**	**2009E**	**2010E**
Equity cash flows	(\$19,500)	-	-	-	-	\$76,457
Internal rate of return	**31.4%**					
Equity cash flows	(19,500)					76,457
Present value formula	$= \frac{\$19,500}{(1+0.314)^0}$					$= \frac{\$76,457}{(1+0.314)^5}$
Present value	(19,500)					19,500
Net present value	0					
Equity profit[1]	\$56,957					
Multiple of investment[2]	**3.92x**					

[1] Value of equity upon exit - initial equity invested
[2] Value of equity upon exit / initial equity invested

11. Perform sensitivity analysis on IRR and MOI for Sponsor

As with all financial analysis, it is a good idea to perform sensitivities on key assumptions once a basic financial model has been created.

Table 12.13 – IRR and MOI Sensitivity to EBITDA Exit Multiple

$ thousands

		IRR Sensitivity				
		EBITDA exit multiple				
		5.5x	6.0x	6.3x	6.5x	7.0x
Sponsor's equity contribution	$18,500	28.0%	31.1%	32.8%	33.9%	36.5%
	$19,000	27.3%	30.4%	32.1%	33.2%	35.8%
	$19,500	26.7%	29.7%	31.4%	32.5%	35.1%
	$20,000	26.0%	29.1%	30.8%	31.8%	34.4%
	$20,500	25.4%	28.4%	30.1%	31.2%	33.7%

		MOI Sensitivity				
		EBITDA exit multiple				
		5.5x	6.0x	6.3x	6.5x	7.0x
Sponsor's equity contribution	$18,500	3.44x	3.87x	4.13x	4.31x	4.74x
	$19,000	3.35x	3.77x	4.02x	4.19x	4.62x
	$19,500	3.26x	3.67x	3.92x	4.09x	4.50x
	$20,000	3.18x	3.58x	3.82x	3.98x	4.39x
	$20,500	3.10x	3.49x	3.73x	3.89x	4.28x

Returns on Private Equity Investments

Both financial sponsors and investors in private equity funds are extremely sensitive to private equity returns. The sponsors are sensitive because IRRs reflect on the financial sponsor's prowess as an investor and the return determines the sponsor's carried interest in the profits (carried interest is described later in this chapter). The investors are sensitive because lower returns mean fewer absolute dollars being returned to them.

Private equity returns have been and continue to be under pressure. There are several reasons for this. First, after sustaining losses on aggressively capitalized LBOs in the late 1980s, lenders now require more equity in transactions, often in the 25 to 35 percent range. With more equity in the transaction, all other things being equal, there is a larger initial investment which results in lower equity returns.

Second, in classic economic theory, the "excess" returns of private equity firms have attracted competition, thereby putting pressure on returns. Said differently, the high returns of early entrants into private equity attracted competition. With so many more market entrants and the low interest rates of the 1990s and 2000s, a significant number of LBOs have been undertaken. In addition to the LBOs undertaken by financial sponsors, many companies have undertaken internal strategic reviews and have sold off assets and reinvested proceeds in higher earning projects, essentially taking the actions that a financial sponsor might have taken.

Traditional LBO Candidates

An LBO succeeds or fails based on the LBO company's ability to generate enough cash to make the interest and principal payments on a timely basis, as well as management's ability to grow the company and create value. What kinds of companies are able to do this? It is not a certain kind of company (since there have been successful LBOs in many different industries), but rather there are certain characteristics of successful LBOs regardless of industry. Specifically, financial sponsors typically look for: (1) asset-rich companies with certain characteristics (undermanaged companies, companies with strong brands, growth or upside potential, and out of favor companies), (2) stable cash flows, (3) low capital expenditure requirements, and (4) excess assets that can be sold off to generate cash.

Asset-rich companies: Asset-rich is a broad term and includes companies with good assets which have been under- or poorly managed. It also includes companies with strong brands, growth or upside potential, and companies that have lost favor for some reason. As the U.S. economy transitions from a manufacturing-based economy to a service-based economy, it becomes increasingly difficult to identify traditional LBO candidates in the U.S. since many service companies are "people-rich" but "asset-poor." Much of a service company's worth is comprised of people as well as intangible assets such as goodwill and intellectual property. As valuable as these are, they do not provide the same collateral value for a loan as hard assets such as inventory, receivables, and machinery.

Stable cash flows: The desire for stable cash flows arises out of the fixed payment nature of the debt taken on in an LBO. Structuring an LBO transaction is an exercise in backing into the capital structure. Financial sponsors assess what they believe the cash flows of a company will be and then utilize as much debt in the capital structure as they deem prudent (given those cash flows and their risk), thereby maximizing the return on equity. Interest payments are required and, if there are amortizing loans, principal payments are required as well. The timing of these interest and principal payments can vary (e.g., quarterly, semiannually, annually), but all of them share the characteristic that if the LBO company fails to make a scheduled interest or principal payment, the company may be in default on its borrowings and a series of punitive measures may come into play.

Low capital expenditure requirements: Capital expenditures are a use of cash and therefore a reduction in cash flow. Even though these capital expenditures may, in the long term, provide an excellent return on investment, any capital expenditure reduces the amount of cash flow available for debt service. Traditionally, private equity firms have tended to shy away from companies with significant capital requirements, including high technology, software, media and bio-technology.

Excess assets: The projected cash flows probably will have utilized the majority of the productive assets of the company (i.e., to produce widgets, one needs a widget-making machine, widget-wrapping machine, etc.). However, it is possible that the projected cash flows do not reflect *all* of the assets of the company. A widget manufacturer, for example, may not need a ski lodge in Vermont acquired under previous management. These so-called excess assets can be sold off to pay down acquisition debt immediately after the close of the transaction. Selling off excess assets to pay down acquisition debt is a classic LBO strategy, but it is much more difficult to find excess assets in today's environment both because there are fewer conglomerates after three decades of LBO activity and because many companies have undertaken restructuring programs (such that excess assets identified by company management have already been sold in a company's regular course of business). In LBO analysis, it is important not only to assess whether the LBO candidate has excess assets that can be used to pay down debt, but also whether the LBO candidate has non-debt liabilities that are not on the balance sheet and/or are not implicated in the production process since these will reduce value. Examples include underfunded pension liabilities, environmental exposure, remediation expenses and copyright or trademark infringement, to name a few.

Screening for LBO Candidates

Below is a list of screening criteria that can be used when searching for LBO candidates.

Corporate orphans: Traditionally, this was the most fertile hunting ground for financial sponsors. In the 1960s, there was a trend in corporate America towards conglomeration, which was the notion that a centralized holding company could provide a series of common services (e.g., treasury, legal, finance) to all of the holding company's subsidiaries in disparate industries. By the end of the 1970s this notion of conglomeration lost favor and over the next two decades the concept of corporate clarity gained adherents. The major thesis of corporate clarity was that all businesses under a holding company should be related. Under this school of thought, ITT, which was a well-known conglomerate, should not have owned Sheraton Hotels, Wonder Bread (Continental Baking Co.), Avis Rent-a-Car, and Hartford Insurance, as it did. In contrast, corporate clarity argued that a frozen food company might have a frozen pea division, a frozen corn division, and a frozen strawberry division, with all of the businesses having similar distribution channels, using similar freezing technology, etc. Any assets, divisions, or subsidiaries which did not fall within that shared characteristic of frozen food would be sold off, and financial sponsors would be likely buyers.

Companies in need of growth capital: Traditionally, companies requiring growth capital took the route of an initial public offering (IPO). However, a sale of equity to the public and a sale of equity to a financial sponsor are both sales of equity, simply to different buyers. As such, a financial sponsor might buy the company, provide the required growth capital to the portfolio company, and then either undertake an IPO of a now-larger company, or simply sell the now-larger company to a strategic player.

Out of favor companies: Just as there are companies whose stock prices rise sharply due to a strong buzz regarding either the company itself or the underlying industry (such as technology stocks from 1998-2001), there are companies whose stock prices fall sharply due to widespread investor retreat from either the company itself or the underlying industry (such as technology stocks from 2001-2003). Such a situation can frustrate management teams who believe, often with good reason, that the company's prospects and value proposition remain strong in spite of the low stock price. When stock prices stay flat for well-run companies with good growth prospects, such companies are good candidates for an LBO. In an interesting twist, in today's market it is sometimes the management team that approaches the financial sponsor rather than the other way around.

Family-owned companies with no succession plan: When a founder of a family-owned business is near retirement age and no clear successor is in place, the founder is often interested in selling the business. Family-owned businesses are commonly sold to financial sponsors.

Divestitures mandated by regulators: The Federal Trade Commission and the Department of Justice, which jointly oversee antitrust activity in the U.S., sometimes require the sale of certain divisions or subsidiaries of combining companies as a condition of approval for a proposed merger. The purpose of the required sale(s) is to encourage competition within the industry in question. These mandated divestitures can provide excellent opportunities for financial sponsors for two reasons: (a) the division or subsidiary may be an excellent company that is being sold only because government regulators forced the sale; and (b) Seller may prefer a financial sponsor as a buyer over another industry player both to avoid potential antitrust concerns (this is particularly relevant in oligopolistic and/or regulated industries) and to prevent an industry competitor from strengthening itself by buying Seller's division or subsidiary.

Companies in need of operating expertise: This describes all companies since every company, at least in theory, can be improved. More practically, many financial sponsors have in-house operating executives (many of whom were previously senior executives in major manufacturing and service companies), which allows the financial sponsors to offer an LBO candidate not only financial engineering assistance but also assistance with sourcing, operations, distribution, strategy, and all of the other areas of execution expertise required of a company in today's competitive global environment.

Companies in need of financial expertise: As companies grow, the challenges of a successful business sometimes outstrip the founder's management abilities. These situations provide good opportunities for financial sponsors as sponsors generally bring significant financial as well as operating expertise to the table.

Participants in an LBO

Private equity firms are the financial sponsors of a leveraged buyout transaction and play numerous roles within each transaction. Among those roles played by the financial sponsor are:

- Finding the LBO target
- Negotiating to buy the company
- Financing and closing the LBO
- Operating the company
- Overseeing and working with the senior executives of the company
- Making major strategic and financial decisions
- Deciding how and when to exit the investment in the company

However, private equity firms cannot undertake their acquisitions without the support of two important constituencies: management of the LBO company and the many lenders and investors who provide the debt (non-equity) capital.

The management team of an LBO company is responsible for running the company on a day-to-day basis. The financial sponsor usually remains actively involved and in regular communication with management, but it is up to the management team to execute on the strategic and financial plan. There are several reasons why a management team would sign up for the challenge of running a highly leveraged company:

- For senior management, an LBO represents an opportunity to earn wealth beyond what is generally possible in a public company. This is done by investing along with the financial sponsor in the new equity. Financial participation by management is often a prerequisite for financial sponsor participation because it aligns management's interests with those of the financial sponsor and reduces agency issues.

- New equity could provide growth capital for business expansion and/or M&A activity, when growth capital might not otherwise be available.

- As a private company, and therefore free of the quarterly earnings focus that public companies are subject to, a management team can focus on a multi-year horizon, even if it resulted in a dip in short-term earnings.

- Being a private company frees management from increasingly onerous public company compliance and regulation (e.g., Sarbanes-Oxley in the U.S., shareholder lawsuits, etc.). Note that a company must file with the SEC if either its equity or its debt is publicly held, so this benefit only exists if the company also has no public debt outstanding.

Who invests with private equity firms?

Investors in private equity firms include institutional investors such as insurance companies, public and private pension funds, foundations, and university endowments, as well as wealthy individuals and families. Insurance companies, for example, take money today in exchange for the promise of protection against the insured risk at some time in the future. In the interim, the insurance companies invest that money so that they will have the money to pay off claims as they occur. Insurance companies follow a portfolio theory approach to their investments (as do most entities that manage large amounts of money). This means that their investments are spread across a spectrum of choices, each of which exhibits different yield, risk, and timing characteristics. For example, some portion of their capital will go into marketable securities (stocks and bonds), some portion into real estate, some portion into non-marketable securities (stocks and bonds that are not registered and therefore not publicly salable), some portion into cash, and some portion into what are often called "alternative investments," which generally consist of hedge funds, venture capital funds, and private equity funds. The institutional investors who make up the preponderance of private equity investors often commit funds to several different firms, and also, over time, may invest in several different funds of the same private equity firm.

Broadly speaking, there are three major levels in a capital structure (senior debt, subordinated debt, and equity (common and preferred)). However, within each of these broad categories there might be any number of permutations. In any given LBO, the debt portion of the capital required to acquire a company can range from 50 percent (50 percent equity) to 90 percent (10 percent equity) of total capitalization. As a result, lenders and debt investors play a critical role in LBOs. In order to fund an LBO, financial sponsors often arrange multiple classes of securities called tranches from which lenders (banks, hedge funds, etc.) and investors (bond investors, insurance companies, hedge funds, etc.) can choose, with each tranche exhibiting different risk/reward characteristics (e.g., different degrees of security, return thresholds, and degrees of equity participation). Historically, different lenders specialized in providing certain specialized types of capital. More recently, some traditional banks have transitioned from offering mostly senior debt to offering capital at multiple levels of the capital structure. Also, hedge funds have moved aggressively into lending money across capital classes. Ultimately, every transaction is different and both the percentage of debt in the capital structure and its pricing will be dependent on the state of the capital markets at the time the LBO is undertaken.

What is a club deal?

"Club deals" in private equity are increasingly popular. A club deal is a transaction in which two or more private equity firms acquire a company together. The idea behind club deals is twofold: first, it allows private equity firms to work together to undertake increasingly larger transactions. Second, it allows firms which are undertaking these increasingly larger transactions to diversify the risk of such a large transaction because there are several "owners" of the LBO company. For example, if each of five private equity firms has a single transaction equity investment limit of $200 million (implying a maximum transaction size of $600 million at a 33 percent equity to total capitalization ratio), their collective transaction equity investment limit is $1 billion once they have banded together (5 × $200 million), which implies a maximum transaction size of $3 billion at a 33 percent equity to total capitalization ratio. During due diligence it is common for sponsors working together to split roles and responsibilities and also to share information.

Structure of a Private Equity Firm

A private equity firm usually raises and manages one fund at a time, although sometimes a new fund is raised and invested at the same time that an older fund is being completed. Within each fund, the private equity firm is the general partner (GP) of the partnership (usually through a separate entity), and each of the investors in the fund is a limited partner (LP). Those who invest in private equity do not invest in the private equity firm itself, but rather into a fund raised by the private equity firm, which the private equity firm then invests on behalf of itself and its limited partners. Thus ABC Financial Sponsor might raise money to undertake leveraged buyouts. Investors would invest in ABC Fund I, which fund would itself be a limited partnership (with the financial sponsor as the general partner and all investors as limited partners) and might consist of $100 million of private equity. If, after several years, ABC had finished investing and/or committing most or all of the equity in ABC Fund I, it might undertake fundraising for ABC Fund II, which might include some, none, or all of the investors from Fund I. If ABC had successfully invested all $100 million from Fund I, it might seek to raise a larger Fund II (e.g., $250 million). If ABC successfully invested all $250 million from Fund II, it might seek to raise $500 million in Fund III.

The $100 million in the Fund I example, $250 million in the Fund II example, and $500 million in Fund III may not seem like very much money with which to purchase several companies, as financial sponsors seek to do with each fund. However, it is important to recall that these fund amounts ($100 million, $250 million, and $500 million in the example above) are for the *equity* portion of the capital structure only. Therefore, if one thinks about a capital structure comprised of 33.3 percent equity to total capitalization (which is toward the conservative end of the spectrum; a 20 percent equity to total capitalization figure would be more aggressive, and in the late 1980s there were equity stakes of as little as 5 percent), that means ABC Fund III could acquire companies worth $1.5 billion in enterprise value once the borrowed funds are layered in, and even more than $1.5 billion assuming a lower equity contribution. This figure of $1.5 billion in purchasing power is calculated as follows:

$500 million in equity = 33.333% of total capitalization of all fund investments

$$500 = 0.33333x$$

$$x = 1{,}500$$

where x = total capitalization (debt and equity)

The total purchase price of all investments could be up to $1.5 billion, comprised of 33 percent equity and 67 percent debt.

Occasionally one might hear that a financial sponsor has a certain amount of "dry powder" or "acquisition firepower." This refers to the purchasing power of the remaining equity on an equity-only basis and the purchasing power of the remaining equity on a leveraged basis (meaning after accounting for accompanying debt), respectively. For example, if ABC firm had invested $350 million of Fund III, it has $150 million of dry powder (pure equity) remaining (of the $500 million in the fund, $350 million has already been invested or committed) but it has $450 million in acquisition firepower ($150 million of equity and $300 million of debt, assuming the same 33 percent equity to total capitalization).

Private equity firms generally take a portfolio approach to their investments for a fund. While the financial sponsor hopes that all of the investments it makes will be successful, it recognizes that a 100 percent success rate is unlikely, if not impossible. From one fund, three investments might be highly profitable, four might be profitable, two might be mildly profitable, and one might be unprofitable. With such a distribution of results, the fund itself might have a highly profitable overall IRR, even if each of the individual company investments was not highly profitable.

The lifetime of a typical private equity fund is approximately ten years (often five to six years to invest and four to five years to "harvest" or exit from the investments) with two- to three-year extensions, if required. It is important to note that while the investment period is typically five years, the ultimate exit period must take place portfolio company by portfolio company, with the sponsor exiting each investment as opportunistically as possible. That is, by definition all LBO companies are available for sale to another buyer or to the equity markets at any time at the right price. A financial sponsor will sell a portfolio company as quickly as it can taking into consideration equity returns and profit.

Generally speaking, the two factors that most greatly affect the length of time a financial sponsor owns a portfolio company are the performance of the company itself (if the company is performing poorly, there are few buyers and certainly none at a premium price) and the performance of the overall capital markets (if financing is inexpensive and plentiful, there may be multiple buyers and therefore the financial sponsor can sell out at a higher price). It is also important to note that the longer an investment is held, the higher the sale price (in dollars) must be to yield the same annualized return or IRR. For example, to achieve a 35 percent IRR on a $500 million equity investment after one year requires an equity sale price of $675 million, whereas a 35 percent IRR on a $500 million equity investment after two years requires an equity sale price of $911 million.

Scenario 1: $500 million × (1 + .35) = $675 million (profit = $175 million)

Scenario 2: $500 million × (1 + .35) × (1 + .35) = $911 million (profit = $411 million)

How Financial Sponsors Are Compensated

Financial sponsors are compensated in three primary ways: (1) management fees paid semiannually out of the fund, (2) advisory fees or "transaction" fees paid on a deal-by-deal basis, and (3) carried interest (more commonly referred to as "carry") paid at the end of the life of a fund.

Management fee: This is a fee paid by a private equity fund's limited partners (the fund's investors) to the general partner of the fund (the financial sponsor). The management fee, which is usually paid semiannually in advance, is typically in the range of 1.5 to 2 percent of the committed value of the fund, although it varies from fund to fund and is negotiated in the initial partnership agreement. Thus, if a fund had raised $100 million, the management fee would likely be $2 million annually. The management fee is used to cover the salaries and other operating expenses of the financial sponsor. All transaction costs (for transactions which close as well as for those which do not close) as well as professional services fees (e.g., legal, accounting, consulting, auditing, etc.) are borne by investors, either indirectly through the portfolio companies or directly based on the amount of capital contributed (i.e., in proportion to their percentage participation in the fund). Management fees are not shared with the fund's limited partners and serve as compensation to the financial sponsor only. There is often a full or partial offset for any fees paid to the financial sponsor for fees such as transaction fees, directors' fees, and portfolio company fees.

Advisory fee: When a financial sponsor buys a portfolio company, its principals work on sourcing the opportunity, valuing the company, and structuring the transaction. As a result, the financial sponsor is often paid an advisory fee for doing this work. This advisory fee, which is paid by the LBO company to the financial sponsor, is similar to the fee that a company might pay to an investment bank for executing a transaction. The advisory fee paid to the financial sponsor essentially treats the financial sponsor as an in-house investment bank that worked on the acquisition of the LBO company. Advisory fees are often split between the general partner (the sponsor) and the limited partners (the investors) based upon the terms of the partnership agreement.

Carry (or carried interest): This refers to the participation of the financial sponsor in the profits of an investment and is typically paid and recalculated upon each return of capital to investors. Carry is calculated by taking the fund's profit, after accounting for the return of management fees and any preferred return owed to the limited partners, and multiplying that amount by the percentage of carry the general partner will retain. While carry is typically 20 percent, all economic terms in private equity --including the percentage of carry-- are subject to negotiation between the specific financial sponsor and its investors and are stated in the partnership agreement.

Table 12.14 - Basic Calculation of Carry in an LBO

$ millions

Basic Carry Calculation (assumes a 5-year equity investment of $100 million)	
Ending equity value for all owners	$500
Percentage owned by Management	10%
Percentage owned by Fund	90%
Ending equity value for Fund[1]	450
Invested equity for Fund	(100)
Equity return for Fund[2]	350
Multiple of investment for Fund[3]	4.5x
Equity internal rate of return for Fund[4]	35.1%
Equity return before adjustments	$350
Decrease by management fees paid to GP[5]	(10)
Decrease by amount of preferred return to LPs on invested equity[6]	(50)
Decrease by preferred return to LPs on management fees to GP[7]	(0.5)
Equity return subject to carry	290
Percentage carry	20%
Value of carry to financial sponsor[8]	$58

[1] Ending equity for all owners × percentage owned by Fund
[2] Ending equity value for Fund - initial invested equity
[3] Ending equity value for Fund / invested equity
[4] $[(\text{Ending equity value for Fund / initial invested equity})^{0.2}] - 1$
[5] Based on 2% annual management fees related to that capital. Invested equity × .02 × 5 years
[6] Based on 8% annual preferred return to LPs compounded semiannually for 5 years.
For period 1, $[(100 \times .04) \times (1+.04)^{10}]$ + for period 2, $[(100 \times .04) \times (1+.04)^{9}]$ + for period 3, $[(100 \times .04) \times (1+.04)^{8}]$ + for period 4, $[(100 \times .04) \times (1+.04)^{7}$ + for period 5, $[(100 \times .04) \times (1+.04)^{6}]$ + for period 6, $[(100 \times .04) \times (1+.04)^{5}]$ + for period 7, $[(100 \times .04) \times (1+.04)^{4}]$ + for period 8, $[(100 \times .04) \times (1+.04)^{3}]$ + for period 9, $[(100 \times .04) \times (1+.04)^{2}]$ + for period 10, $[(100 \times .04) \times (1+.04)^{1}]$
[7] Based on 8% annual preferred return to LPs on management fees paid, compounded semiannually for 5 years. Calculated similarly to Footnote 6 above.
[8] Percentage carry × equity return subject to carry

Clawbacks

One of the major issues regarding financial sponsor compensation relates to how profit or carry on a private equity fund has evolved. In the early days, the financial sponsor received 20 percent of the profit of each individual investment. Now, typically, the sponsor receives 20 percent of the profit of the investments taken as a whole. This issue is often referred to as the concept of "deal-by-deal" economics versus "aggregate" economics.

When carry was calculated on a deal-by-deal basis, this favored financial sponsors at the expense of their limited partners: on bad investments the investors lost their principal while on good investments the financial sponsor took 20 percent of the profit. Over time, as equity returns have decreased and investors have become more aggressive in protecting their positions, compensation mechanisms have changed. It is now common to see "clawbacks," which serve to "charge" the financial sponsor for investments which performed poorly by aggregating the returns of both successful and unsuccessful investments. The financial sponsor is then compensated on the basis of this aggregated performance (i.e., all investments of the entire fund).

Investors prefer this type of compensation structure because it serves as an added incentive for the financial sponsor to work out unsuccessful investments and also aligns interests more purely in that the financial sponsor and the investors both benefit if an investment succeeds and both suffer if an investment does not succeed. There can be many different types of clawbacks, but they all perform the same function of seeking to make financial sponsors more accountable for all of the fund's investments. Ultimately, the goal of a clawback is to encourage overall accountability by the GP for all investments and it functions to ensure that LPs are "repaid" out of GP funds, if needed, in a retrospective accounting.

Table 12.15 - Calculation of Adjusted Carry with Clawback

$ millions

With Clawback	
Equity return from Company A (from Table 12.14)	$290
Equity loss from Company B before adjustments[1]	(60)
Decrease by management fees paid to GP for Company B[1,2]	(10)
Decrease by amount of preferred return to LPs for Company B[1,3]	(50)
Decrease by preferred return to LPs on mgmt. fees to GP for Company B[1,4]	(0.5)
Return subject to carry for A+B (after clawback)[5]	169
Percentage carry	20%
Value of carry to financial sponsor[6]	$34
Initial 20% carry on Company A (pre-clawback)[7]	$58
Adjusted 20% carry on Companies A+B (post-clawback)	34
Reduction in carry due to clawback[8]	(24)

[1] Assume that Company B was also a $100 million equity investment over 5 years which was sold for $40 million.
[2] Based on 2% annual management fees related to that capital. Invested equity × .02 × 5 years
[3] Based on 8% annual preferred return to LPs compounded semiannually. See Table 12.14 footnote 6 for calculation.
[4] Based on 8% annual preferred return to LPs on GP management fees, compounded semiannually. See footnote 6 in Table 12.14 for the form of calculation.
[5] Equity return from Company A + equity loss from Company B and associated Company B costs.
[6] Percentage carry × return subject to carry
[7] From Company A stand-alone (see Table 12.14)
[8] Adjusted carry - initial carry

Table 12.16 – SportsCo LBO Example in its Entirety

$ thousands

Income Statement	2004	2005	Capitalization	12/31/05
Revenues	$43,000	$50,000	Bank debt	$10,000
Cost of goods sold	(25,370)	(30,000)	Shareholders' equity	35,000
Gross margin	17,630	20,000	Total capitalization	$45,000
Selling, general, administrative	(8,600)	(10,000)		
EBITDA	9,030	10,000	Capitalization (%)	
DD&A	(2,250)	(2,500)	Bank debt	22%
EBIT	6,780	7,500	Shareholders' equity	78%
Interest expense	(700)	(700)	Total capitalization	100%
EBT	6,080	6,800		
Taxes	(2,432)	(2,680)	Cash	$1,000
Net income	$3,648	$4,120		

Table 12.16 continued

Transaction Multiples ("entry" multiples)

Equity value	$54,000	Enterprise Value Multiples		Equity Value Multiples	
Existing debt[1]	10,000	Enterprise value	$63,000	Equity value	$54,000
Existing cash[1]	(1,000)	2005 EBITDA	10,000	2005 net income	4,120
Enterprise value[2]	$63,000	Enterprise value/EBITDA	6.3x	P/E	13.1x
		Enterprise value	$63,000	Equity value	$54,000
		2005 EBIT	7,500	Book value of equity	35,000
		Enterprise value/EBIT	8.4x	Price/book	1.5x

[1] Total debt - cash = net debt
[2] Purchase price for SportsCo equity + existing net debt

Table 12.16 continued

$ thousands

Sources and Uses

Acquisition debt	$45,500	Purchase of equity	$54,000
Equity from Sponsor	19,500	Repayment of existing debt	10,000
Total sources	$65,000	Transaction fees	1,000
		Total uses	$65,000

Pre- and Post-Transaction Capitalization

	Pre-transaction		Adjustments[1]	Post-transaction	
Pre-transaction debt	$10,000	22%	($10,000)	$0	0%
Acquisition debt	0	0%	45,500	45,500	70%
Total debt	10,000	22%	35,500	45,500	70%
Shareholders' equity[2]	35,000	78%	(15,500)	19,500	30%
Total capitalization	$45,000	100%	$20,000	$65,000	100%

[1] Purchase accounting adjustments for shareholders' equity are described in Accretion / Dilution Analysis. (Ch.14)

[2] $19.5 million is the amount of equity contributed by Sponsor. The net adjustment of -$15.5 million reflects the elimination of old book equity of $35 million and addition of new book equity of $19.5 million (-$35 million + $19.5 million = -$15.5 million).

Table 12.16 continued

$ thousands

Income Statement	2004	Margins	2005	Margins	'04-'05 growth
Revenues	$43,000		$50,000		16%
Cost of goods sold	(25,370)	59%	(30,000)	60%	
Gross margin	17,630	41%	20,000	40%	13%
Selling, general, administrative	(8,600)	20%	(10,000)	20%	
EBITDA	9,030	21%	10,000	20%	11%
DD&A	(2,250)	5%	(2,500)	5%	
EBIT	6,780	16%	7,500	15%	11%
Interest expense	(700)	2%	(700)	1%	
EBT	6,080	14%	6,800	14%	12%
Taxes	(2,432)	6%	(2,680)	5%	
Net income	$3,648	9%	$4,120	8%	13%

Note: margins are based on percentage of revenues, e.g., cost of goods sold margin = cost of goods sold / revenues. This is a common way to analyze margins, as a percentage of revenues. It is sometimes referred to as "common size analysis" because it allows for the comparison of operating performance of companies of disparate sizes.

Table 12.16 continued

Key assumptions	Historical		Projected				
	2004A	2005A	2006	2007	2008	2009	2010
Annual revenue growth	-	16.3%	15.0%	12.5%	10.0%	7.5%	5.0%
Cost of goods sold margin	59.0%	60.0%	60.0%	60.0%	60.0%	60.0%	60.0%
SG&A margin	20.0%	20.0%	20.0%	20.0%	20.0%	20.0%	20.0%
DD&A margin	5.2%	5.0%	5.0%	5.0%	5.0%	5.0%	5.0%
Capex margin	-	5.0%	5.0%	5.0%	5.0%	5.0%	5.0%
Working capital margin	-	2.0%	2.0%	2.0%	2.0%	2.0%	2.0%
Tax rate	40.0%	39.4%	40.0%	40.0%	40.0%	40.0%	40.0%
Interest rate on total debt	-	7.0%	10.0%	10.0%	10.0%	10.0%	10.0%

Table 12.16 continued

$ thousands	Historical		Projected				
Cash flow build up	**2004A**	**2005A**	**2006**	**2007**	**2008**	**2009**	**2010**
Revenues	$43,000	$50,000	$57,500	$64,688	$71,156	$76,493	$80,318
Cost of goods sold	(25,370)	(30,000)	(34,500)	(38,813)	(42,694)	(45,896)	(48,191)
Gross margin	17,630	20,000	23,000	25,875	28,463	30,597	32,127
SG&A	(8,600)	(10,000)	(11,500)	(12,938)	(14,231)	(15,299)	(16,064)
EBITDA	9,030	10,000	11,500	12,938	14,231	15,299	16,064
DD&A	(2,250)	(2,500)	(2,875)	(3,234)	(3,558)	(3,825)	(4,016)
EBIT	6,780	7,500	8,625	9,703	10,673	11,474	12,048
Interest expense[1]	(700)	(700)	(4,432)	(4,154)	(3,795)	(3,357)	(2,847)
EBT	6,080	6,800	4,193	5,549	6,879	8,117	9,201
Taxes	(2,432)	(2,680)	(1,677)	(2,220)	(2,751)	(3,247)	(3,681)
Net income	$3,648	$4,120	$2,516	$3,329	$4,127	$4,870	$5,521
Net working capital		1,000	1,150	1,294	1,423	1,530	1,606
Net income			$2,516	$3,329	$4,127	$4,870	$5,521
DD&A			2,875	3,234	3,558	3,825	4,016
(Increase)/decrease in net working capital			(150)	(144)	(129)	(107)	(77)
Other non-cash charges			0	0	0	0	0
Operating cash flow			5,241	6,420	7,556	8,588	9,460
Capital expenditures			(2,875)	(3,234)	(3,558)	(3,825)	(4,016)
Cash flow available for debt service			$2,366	$3,186	$3,998	$4,764	$5,444

Note: Positive numbers are cash inflows (sources of cash) and negative numbers, which are shown in parentheses, are cash outflows (uses of cash).

[1] See Step 7 for the interest expense calculation (Table 12.8).

Table 12.16 continued

$ thousands	Adjusted		Projected				
Capitalization	**2005A**	**2005**	**2006**	**2007**	**2008**	**2009**	**2010**
Cash flow available for debt service			$2,366	$3,186	$3,998	$4,764	$5,444
Acquisition debt to be retired[1]			(2,366)	(3,186)	(3,998)	(4,764)	(5,444)
Adjusted cash flow after debt service			0	0	0	0	0
Acquisition debt (beginning of year)			45,500	43,134	39,948	35,951	31,187
Acquisition debt to be retired			(2,366)	(3,186)	(3,998)	(4,764)	(5,444)
Acquisition debt (end of year)			43,134	39,948	35,951	31,187	25,743
Percentage of acquisition debt remaining			95%	88%	79%	69%	57%
Percentage of acquisition debt retired			5%	12%	21%	32%	43%
Average debt for the year[2]			44,317	41,541	37,950	33,569	28,465
Interest rate on debt			10%	10%	10%	10%	10%
Interest expense on debt[3]			4,432	4,154	3,795	3,357	2,847
Shareholders' equity (beginning of year)			19,500	22,016	25,345	29,473	34,343
Add: net income			2,516	3,329	4,127	4,870	5,521
Less: dividends paid			0	0	0	0	0
Shareholders' equity (end of year)			$22,016	$25,345	$29,473	$34,343	$39,863
Total debt	$10,000	$45,500	43,134	39,948	35,951	31,187	25,743
Shareholders' equity	35,000	19,500	22,016	25,345	29,473	34,343	39,863
Total capitalization	$45,000	$65,000	$65,150	$65,294	$65,423	$65,530	$65,606

[1] Acquisition debt to be retired is equal to cash flow available for debt service as calculated in Table 12.7 since the assumption is that all CFADS will be used to retire debt.

[2] Average debt for the year is [(Acquisition Debt Yr. 1 + Acquisition Debt Yr. 2) / 2] to reflect the fact that acquisition debt is retired over the course of the year. Average debt is used because using the higher beginning of year value would overstate annual interest expense and using the lower end of year value would understate annual interest expense.

[3] Average debt for the year × interest rate on debt.

Table 12.16 continued

$ thousands

	Adjusted	Projected				
	2005	2006	2007	2008	2009	2010
Total debt	$45,500	$43,134	$39,948	$35,951	$31,187	$25,743
Shareholders' equity	19,500	22,016	25,345	29,473	34,343	39,863
Total capitalization	$65,000	$65,150	$65,294	$65,423	$65,530	$65,606
Year over year growth in total capitalization	n/a	0.2%	0.2%	0.2%	0.2%	0.1%

	Adjusted	Projected				
	2005	2006	2007	2008	2009	2010
Total debt	70%	66%	61%	55%	48%	39%
Shareholders' equity	30%	34%	39%	45%	52%	61%
Total capitalization	100%	100%	100%	100%	100%	100%

Table 12.16 continued

$ thousands	Pro forma transaction	Projected				
Credit ratios	**2005**	**2006E**	**2007E**	**2008E**	**2009E**	**2010E**
Inputs						
Total debt	$45,500	$43,134	$39,948	$35,951	$31,187	$25,743
Total capital	65,000	65,150	65,294	65,423	65,530	65,606
EBITDA	10,000	11,500	12,938	14,231	15,299	16,064
EBIT	7,500	8,625	9,703	10,673	11,474	12,048
Interest expense	4,432	4,432	4,154	3,795	3,357	2,847
Capital expenditures[1]	2,500	2,875	3,234	3,558	3,825	4,016
Debt amortization	0	2,366	3,186	3,998	4,764	5,444
Leverage ratios (lower is better)						
Total debt / total capital	70%	66%	61%	55%	48%	39%
Total debt / EBITDA[2]	4.6x	3.8x	3.1x	2.5x	2.0x	1.6x
Total debt / (EBITDA - capex)	6.1x	5.0x	4.1x	3.4x	2.7x	2.1x
Coverage ratios (higher is better)						
EBITDA / interest expense	2.3x	2.6x	3.1x	3.8x	4.6x	5.6x
(EBITDA - capex) / interest expense	1.7x	1.9x	2.3x	2.8x	3.4x	4.2x
EBITDA / (interest + amortization)[3]	1.5x	1.7x	1.8x	1.8x	1.9x	1.9x
(EBITDA - capex) / (interest + amortization)[3,4]	1.1x	1.3x	1.3x	1.4x	1.4x	1.5x

[1] Capital expenditures are assumed to be equal to DD&A

[2] It is common to measure total debt to EBITDA as well as senior debt to EBITDA. In our simplified example we do not distinguish between senior debt and subordinated debt and so this second ratio is not shown.

[3] Amortization here refers only to scheduled principal amortization (repayment of debt principal), not DD&A. 2005 ratios include Year 1 amortization (2006E amortization of $2,366). For purposes of these two credit ratios, 2006E amortization is counted twice since it is included in both the proforma and the 2006E ratios.

[4] This ratio must be at least 1.0x

Table 12.16 continued

$ thousands

Exit value	2006E	2007E	2008E	2009E	2010E
			Projected		
EBITDA in exit year					$16,064
EBITDA exit multiple[1]					6.3x
Implied enterprise value in exit year					101,200
Less total net debt in exit year (total debt net of cash of $1 million)[2]					(24,743)
Implied equity value in exit year (2010)					$76,457
Net income in exit year (2010)					$5,521
Implied P/E multiple in exit year (2010)[3]					13.8x
Entry P/E multiple (2005)[4]					13.1x

[1] Assumes the exit multiple equals the EBITDA entry multiple, which was $63,000 / $10,000 = 6.3x
[2] From Tables 12.8 and 12.3. Total debt in 2010 of $25,743 less cash in 2010 of $1,000 equals $24,743
[3] $76,457 / $5,521 = 13.8x
[4] $54,000 / $4,120 = 13.1x

Exit value	12/31/05	2006E	2007E	2008E	2009E	2010E
				Projected		
Equity cash flows	($19,500)	-	-	-	-	$76,457
Internal rate of return	**31.4%**					
Equity cash flows	(19,500)					76,457
Present value formula	$= \frac{\$19,500}{(1+0.314)^0}$					$= \frac{\$76,457}{(1+0.314)^5}$
Present value	(19,500)					19,500
Net present value	0					
Equity profit[1]	$56,957					
Multiple of investment[2]	**3.92x**					

[1] Value of equity upon exit - initial equity invested
[2] Value of equity upon exit / initial equity invested

Table 12.16 continued

$ thousands

		IRR Sensitivity				
		EBITDA exit multiple				
		5.5x	6.0x	6.3x	6.5x	7.0x
Sponsor's equity contribution	$18,500	28.0%	31.1%	32.8%	33.9%	36.5%
	$19,000	27.3%	30.4%	32.1%	33.2%	35.8%
	$19,500	26.7%	29.7%	31.4%	32.5%	35.1%
	$20,000	26.0%	29.1%	30.8%	31.8%	34.4%
	$20,500	25.4%	28.4%	30.1%	31.2%	33.7%

		MOI Sensitivity				
		EBITDA exit multiple				
		5.5x	6.0x	6.3x	6.5x	7.0x
Sponsor's equity contribution	$18,500	3.44x	3.87x	4.13x	4.31x	4.74x
	$19,000	3.35x	3.77x	4.02x	4.19x	4.62x
	$19,500	3.26x	3.67x	3.92x	4.09x	4.50x
	$20,000	3.18x	3.58x	3.82x	3.98x	4.39x
	$20,500	3.10x	3.49x	3.73x	3.89x	4.28x

Breakup Analysis

Chapter 13

The wise man puts all his eggs in one basket
and watches the basket.

Andrew Carnegie

Breakup analysis is a valuation methodology that considers the aggregate value of the component pieces of a company – as compared with analyzing the value of the company taken as a whole. It is intended to answer the question: *is the sum of the parts greater than the value of the whole?* As a result, breakup analysis is sometimes referred to as **sum of the parts analysis**.

Breakup analysis is used in conjunction with other valuation methodologies to analyze companies with *two or more major* and *distinct* business segments. When performing breakup analysis, it is critical to consider (a) the tax consequences and (b) the execution risk of separating or selling an asset or subsidiary.

Breakup analysis is an important valuation exercise to perform when considering the acquisition of a target company that has assets or subsidiaries which the acquiror does not or may not want, or if the target company has assets which might be valued more highly by another private buyer or by the public equity market. The goal in performing breakup analysis is to examine the feasibility of separating those assets which are not desired from those assets to be retained and to see if, upon separation, the transaction still creates value for the acquiror.

Assume for example that ConglomerateCo has two subsidiaries, PaperCo and CableCo. Acquiror would like to acquire PaperCo and believes PaperCo, the subsidiary, is worth \$500 million. Acquiror further believes it can acquire all of ConglomerateCo for \$900 million and subsequently sell CableCo for \$500 million. If Acquiror is successful in selling CableCo at that \$500 million price it is effectively acquiring PaperCo (before accounting for any tax liability arising from the sale of CableCo) for \$400 million (\$900 million purchase price for all of ConglomerateCo less \$500 million sale price for CableCo). Since Acquiror believes PaperCo is worth \$500 million, if the tax ramifications of selling CableCo are less than \$100 million, Acquiror can acquire all of ConglomerateCo, sell CableCo and thereby obtain PaperCo at a price that is less than what Acquiror believes PaperCo is worth on a stand-alone basis. Such a transaction would create value for Acquiror.

Developing Breakup Analysis

There are six major steps to breakup analysis:

1. Value the major business segments individually
2. Identify and allocate liabilities to the major business segments
3. Consider potential tax implications of separating major business segments
4. Assess other assets and liabilities not included in Step 1 (e.g., non-revenue producing real estate, etc.)
5. Add up the tax-adjusted values of the major business segments
6. Compare the breakup valuation to the valuation for the entire company

1. ***Value major business segments individually:*** Each major business segment of Target should be valued independently. The valuation method(s) selected to value each segment will depend largely on the type of asset or subsidiary and the most likely method of disposing of the business. For example, if an IPO or a spin-off is the likely separation method for a major business segment, then comparable company analysis should be the primary valuation method. If the major business segment is likely be sold to another company, then comparable transaction analysis and DCF analysis would be the best valuation methods. If the major business segment is likely to be of interest to private equity buyers, LBO analysis would also be useful. In practice, unless Acquiror is at the transaction stage with a company (and as a result has inside information regarding all of Target's operations), it might be difficult to find detailed financial data at the subsidiary level or asset level, thereby limiting the analysis to comparables based on broadly available financial data -- at least until the confidential due diligence phase when inside information is made available.

2. ***Identify and allocate liabilities to major business segments:*** If financials per business segment are provided or are otherwise publicly available, this step might be relatively straightforward. If they are not, Acquiror will need to make reasonable assumptions regarding the allocation of liabilities, which include debt and non-debt liabilities (e.g., accounts receivable, pension obligations, etc.). These assumptions will be refined as Acquiror performs confidential due diligence and has access to additional information.

3. ***Consider potential tax implications of separating major business segments:*** The tax consequences of separating assets or businesses can be significant. Tax issues are explored in Taxes and M&A and Corporate Restructurings. (Ch.21, 22). The important point for breakup analysis is that the tax consequences of separating a business can be significant and no separation analysis should be undertaken without considering the potential tax liability as it may render a

breakup to be dilutive to value as opposed to value enhancing. The estimated tax costs of separating each business should be allocated to that particular business, serving as an offset to the value of the asset or subsidiary.

4. ***Assess other assets and liabilities not included in Step 1:*** This is the same exercise one would undertake in a DCF analysis. (Ch.11) The idea is to determine whether there are any additional pockets of value or cost whose worth is not captured in the valuation done in Step 1, and to adjust the valuation upward or downward accordingly. Other assets and liabilities might include non-revenue producing real estate, environmental or litigation liability, and overfunded or underfunded pensions, among other things.

5. ***Add up the tax-adjusted values of the major business segments:*** Tax-adjusted enterprise values for the various assets and businesses should be added together. Unallocated company debt should then be subtracted from this total to yield an estimated market value of equity. This number will be divided by the number of shares outstanding to arrive at an estimated breakup value per share.

6. ***Compare this breakup valuation to the valuation of the entire company:*** By comparing the breakup value ranges to values for the entire company, it is possible to analyze whether the sum of the parts is likely to be greater than the whole. It is never possible to say with certainty that the sum of the parts is greater than the whole because there is always execution risk involved in the breakup -- Acquiror might not be able to sell or separate the business at the estimated price. However, breakup analysis will better inform an Acquiror's planning when making a bid for an entire company. Also, after accounting for the sale or separation of the other businesses, Acquiror might find that it can obtain a coveted asset or business at a significantly lower (breakup adjusted) price than if it bought the desired business directly.

To illustrate how a breakup analysis is performed, let's consider DiversifiedCo which has three major business segments: (1) a publishing subsidiary, (2) a telecom subsidiary, and (3) a real estate portfolio. Assume Acquiror only wants to keep the publishing subsidiary. Therefore Acquiror will first acquire all of DiversifiedCo and then Acquiror will sell the telecom subsidiary and the real estate portfolio in subsequent transactions. In Table 13.1 each of these three major business segments is independently valued. DiversifiedCo's debt is allocated among the three business segments and then a range for the estimated market value of equity is determined for each of the three business segments. Assume that the sale of the stock of the telecom subsidiary and the sale of the real estate portfolio will each trigger a tax liability. Therefore the firm value range for these two major business segments is an after-tax range of values. No tax is due on the publishing subsidiary because it is being retained. Notice also that there is a pension surplus which represents value to DiversifiedCo. Since it is not allocated to a major business segment, the pension surplus is added to the sum of the three major business segments as an "other asset" not included in the valuation of the individual business segments. Even after accounting for the estimated tax implications of separating the telecom subsidiary and the real estate portfolio, DiversifiedCo is worth more on a breakup basis ($27.00 - $34.30 per share) than its current market price of $19.00 per share.

Table 13.1 – Breakup Analysis of DiversifiedCo

	Enterprise value range[1]			Allocated	Market value of equity range[2]		
$ millions, except per share data	**Low**	-	**High**	**debt**	**Low**	-	**High**
Business segments - to be retained							
Publishing Subsidiary	$900	-	$1,100	($450)	$450	-	$650
Business segments - to be divested							
Telecom Subsidiary (after tax)	650	-	750	(300)	350	-	450
Real Estate Portfolio (after tax)	100	-	140	0	100	-	140
Total business segments[3]	1,650	-	1,990	(750)	900	-	1,240
Other assets to be retained	100	-	125	0	100	-	125
Pension surplus (after tax)	350	-	350	0	350	-	350
Total values - entire company[4]	2,100	-	2,465	(750)	1,350	-	1,715
Fully diluted shares outstanding					50	-	50
Implied breakup value per share[5]					$27.00	-	$34.30
Current share price					$19.00	-	$19.00
Estimated control premium to buy entire company					20%	-	25%
Implied offer price[6]					$22.80	-	$23.75
Value created in breakup[7]					**$4.20**	-	**$10.55**

[1] Estimated enterprise value range for major subsidiaries; after-tax values are estimated for entities to be divested

[2] Allocated net debt is subtracted from enterprise value ranges to estimate a range for the market value of equity

[3] Represents sum of enterprise value, allocated net debt and market value of equity, respectively, for the three major business segments

[4] Represents sum of enterprise value, allocated net debt and market value of equity, respectively, including other assets and the pension surplus

[5] Total breakup value for the entire company divided by the fully diluted shares outstanding

[6] Current share price multiplied by (1 plus the estimated control premium) to estimate a potential offer price required to obtain the company

[7] Implied breakup value per share minus the implied offer price per share

Part III

M&A Analysis

Accretion/Dilution Analysis

Chapter 14

What lies behind us and what lies before us
are tiny matters compared to what lies within us.

Ralph Waldo Emerson

Various types of analyses are performed to assess the financial impact of a transaction. Taken collectively, these analyses are referred to as **financial impact analyses**. Accretion/dilution analysis and credit impact analysis are considered two of the most important financial impact analyses. Accretion/dilution analysis is described in this chapter and credit impact analysis is described in Credit Analysis. (Ch.24)

Accretion/dilution is a fancy way of asking whether a transaction increases (accretes) or decreases (dilutes) the EPS (or some other metric) of Acquiror on a pro forma basis relative to the same metric on a stand-alone basis. Thus, accretion/dilution analysis is always a relative analysis that compares Acquiror's financial results *before* the acquisition to Acquiror's projected financial results *after* the acquisition.

The most common forms of accretion/dilution analysis are:

1. Earnings per share (EPS) accretion/dilution
2. Cash flow per share (CFPS) accretion/dilution
3. Growth rate accretion/dilution
4. Dividend accretion/dilution
5. Value accretion/dilution

Accretion/dilution nomenclature

While there are multiple forms of accretion/dilution analysis (in fact, it can be done for almost every metric), EPS accretion/dilution is the most common. Therefore, if not specified, it is safe to assume that accretion/dilution refers to EPS accretion/dilution.

Why Perform Accretion/Dilution Analysis?

EPS accretion/dilution analysis is widely used in M&A analysis because it is an indicator of Acquiror's stock price pro forma the transaction (pro forma means assuming the transaction has occurred). Since many publicly traded companies are valued based on P/E multiples, a transaction that is accretive to EPS should be accretive to value and vice versa (assuming the same P/E multiple pre- and post-transaction). Alternatively, a company announcing a transaction which is dilutive to EPS would need an increase in its P/E multiple in order to avoid a negative impact to value.

To illustrate this, let's consider SurfCo, a publicly traded surfboard company. Assume that SurfCo's current stock price is $25. Based on SurfCo's 2006 EPS of $1.25, SurfCo's 2006 P/E multiple is 20x.

$25 share price / $1.25 2006 EPS = 20x 2006 P/E multiple

Assume SurfCo acquires CycleCo and the transaction is accretive to SurfCo's 2006 EPS by $0.05 per share. This means that after accounting for the transaction, SurfCo's 2006 EPS would be $1.30 as opposed to $1.25.

$1.25 2006 EPS + $0.05 in accretion = $1.30 2006 EPS pro forma

The $0.05 of accretion is equal to 4 percent accretion. The 4 percent accretion is calculated by comparing the pro forma EPS of $1.30 to the pre-transaction EPS of $1.25 and measuring the percentage increase or decrease.

($1.30 pro forma EPS / $1.25 pre-transaction EPS) - 1 = 4 percent accretion

Assuming SurfCo maintains its P/E multiple of 20x, the new share price after giving effect to the accretive transaction would be $26, as compared to the current share price of $25.

$1.30 2006 EPS × 20x P/E multiple = $26 share price pro forma

This new share price of $26 is 4 percent greater than the pre-transaction share price of $25.

($26 pro forma share price / $25 pre-transaction share price) - 1 = 4 percent

As shown here, assuming Acquiror's P/E multiple does not change (which for most practitioners is a conservative assumption), EPS accretion/dilution is a proxy for share price accretion/dilution.

The examples provided in this chapter are examples of "bottom-up" accretion/dilution analysis. Bottom-up means that the analysis is driven by the stand-alone EPS estimates for each company, rather than from the "top-down," which means based on full sets of financial statements (e.g., full-blown income statement, balance sheet, cash flow statement). Bottom-up analysis is used by practitioners most of the time. It is used when screening for potential targets, analyzing contemplated transactions, and performing interloper analysis.

The effort involved in building a full-blown merger model usually is merited only if a transaction is at a stage at which confidential information has been exchanged and there is enough data available to build full-blown financial models for both Acquiror and Target. Absent this level of information, building two sets of financial statements and a merger model is not likely to enhance the accretion/dilution analysis due to the number of assumptions which would be required. In fact, given the additional complexity and much greater margin for error, it might actually serve to negatively affect the analysis. Although dynamic merger models are more flexible and allow you to run many more scenarios (e.g., changes in operating margins, changes in capital structure, changes in dividend policy, etc.), they take significant time to prepare and the level of precision they tend to provide is not always necessary. In fact, bottom-up models are often used, even in live transactions. Although the methods and calculations described in this chapter apply to both bottom-up and top-down merger models, it is important to master the bottom-up method (which is described in this chapter) as it is the method used most often.

Basic Principles

EPS accretion/dilution analysis is much simpler to perform than people make it out to be. In fact, a practitioner should be able to perform bottom-up accretion/dilution calculations with a piece of paper and a pencil or simply her calculator. A fancy financial model does not necessarily yield a better answer. As noted above, too many bells and whistles in a model might add complications that dilute the utility of the analysis (or, worse yet, increase the likelihood of error).

Before delving into the details of how to perform accretion/dilution analysis, let's first review the basic principles or tenets of accretion/dilution. Hopefully, this review of basic principles will help simplify this (often misunderstood) M&A analysis. These basic principles should also serve as a running list of things to double-check when building your own model and when checking someone else's model.

Simplify, don't over-engineer

Rule number one is to simplify. Accretion/dilution analysis, even of complex transactions, can be distilled to two essential questions: *(1) what does Acquiror get in the transaction* and *(2) what does the transaction cost Acquiror*? In other words, for every transaction, Acquiror receives something (e.g., an asset, a stream of cash flows, cash flows generated from a business, cash from the sale of an asset, etc.) and must pay something (e.g., the interest rate on debt used to finance the acquisition, Acquiror shares issued to Target shareholders, the lost cash flows of a sold asset, tax liabilities, etc.).

Three simple steps

Accretion/dilution can be simplified to three simple steps: (1) combine Acquiror and Target earnings, (2) make transaction adjustments (based on transaction assumptions and proper accounting methods), and (3) compare Acquiror's pre-transaction and post-transaction EPS. If post-transaction EPS is greater than pre-transaction EPS, the transaction is accretive. If post-transaction EPS is less than pre-transaction EPS, the transaction is dilutive.

As shown in Figure 14.1, the only step that requires care is Step 2 (make transaction adjustments). Step 1 is merely addition and Step 3 is nothing more than determining which number (pre- or post-transaction EPS) is larger.

Figure 14.1 – Simple Steps to Accretion/Dilution

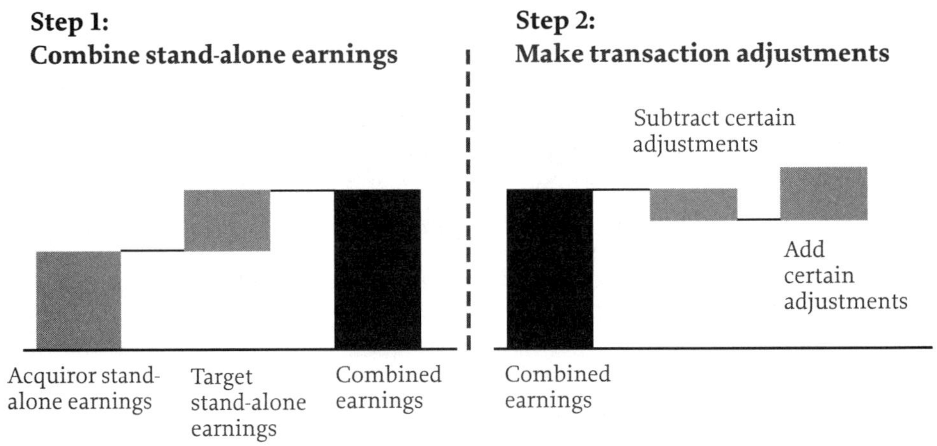

Step 3: Compare pre- and post-transaction EPS

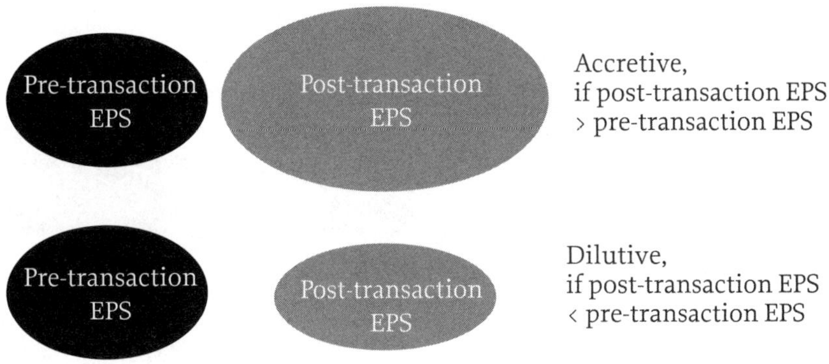

Simplify the adjustments

Transaction adjustments are relatively straightforward to perform once you have some facility with basic accounting concepts (which will be discussed in the following sections). As you get into the details of the accounting methods, think of transaction adjustments as belonging to one of three "buckets." The first bucket includes transaction "costs" including interest expense paid on transaction debt and shares issued to Target shareholders. The second bucket is comprised of transaction "benefits" such as cost or revenue synergies. The third bucket is comprised of accounting adjustments. One common adjustment is the additional depreciation required for the GAAP books triggered by an asset write-up (more on this in the following section).

Figure 14.2 – Transaction Adjustment "Buckets"

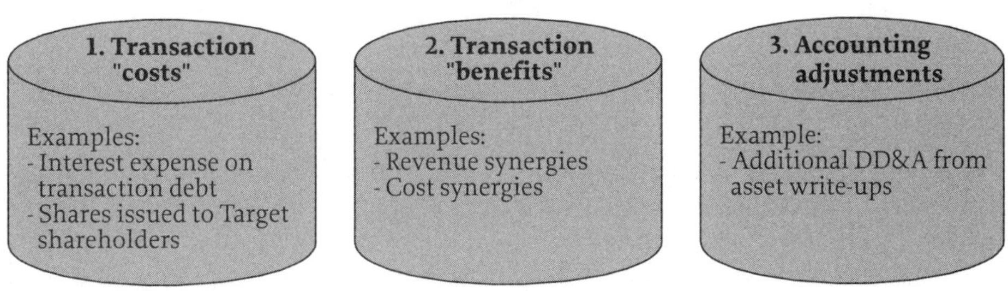

Once adjustments have been categorized into "buckets," all you have to do is add them up to determine the net amount of transaction adjustments. Specific numerical examples of transaction adjustments are described later in this chapter.

Figure 14.3 – Adding Up Transaction Adjustments

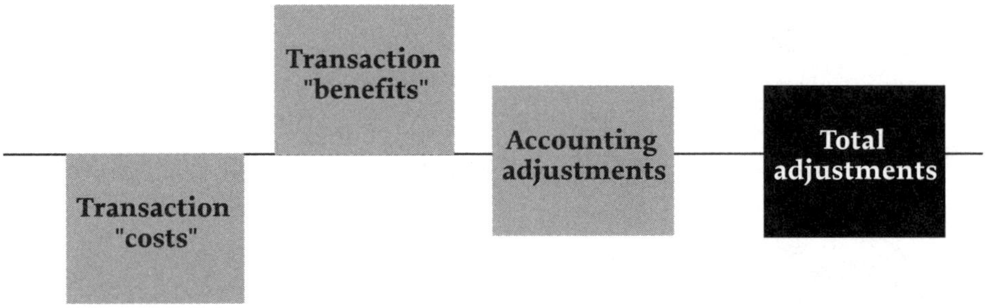

Transaction costs are usually negative numbers	Transaction benefits are usually positive numbers	Accounting adjustments could be negative or positive depending on the adjustment	Total adjustments could be negative or positive depending on the magnitude of various adjustments

Measure incremental change

When performing accretion/dilution analysis, remember to adjust only for *incremental* change. For example, when calculating pro forma EPS, add or subtract only those changes to Acquiror's EPS which result from the transaction such as (a) after-tax interest expense owed on any acquisition debt or (b) synergies triggered by the combination of the two companies. Many new practitioners make the mistake of adding or subtracting absolute changes instead of incremental changes.

The reason that only incremental change is measured is because all other elements of Acquiror's and Target's financial performance are already reflected in their stand-alone EPS values. For example, a common mistake is to add Acquiror's stand-alone interest expense to the transaction-related interest expense in order to calculate pro forma EPS. However, interest expense that is not related to the transaction is already factored into Acquiror's pre-transaction EPS estimates. Therefore, treating all of Acquiror's interest expense as a transaction adjustment would have the effect of counting Acquiror's non-transaction-related interest expense *twice*, which would erroneously decrease pro forma EPS by the amount of Acquiror's pre-transaction interest expense.

A simplified accretion/dilution process is provided in Table 14.4. Recall from earlier that Step 1 in accretion/dilution analysis is to add up Acquiror and Target earnings and Step 2 is to calculate transaction adjustments. The only interest expense that should be included in Step 2 is the "incremental" interest expense triggered by the transaction itself.

Table 14.4 – Stand-Alone Items vs. Transaction Adjustments

Step 1		Step 2	
Acquiror	**+ Target**	**+/- Transaction adjustments**	**= Pro forma**
Revenues	Revenues	+ Revenue synergies	
- Cost of goods sold	- Cost of goods sold	+ Cost benefits	
- SG&A	- SG&A	+ SG&A benefits	
- DD&A	- DD&A	- DD&A from write-ups	
- Interest expense	- Interest expense	- Interest from transaction debt	
- Taxes	- Taxes	-/+ Tax effect all adjustments	
= Earnings	= Earnings	= Total after-tax adjustments	= Pro forma earnings
/ Shares outstanding	/ Shares outstanding	+ New Acquiror shares issued	/ Pro forma shares
= Stand-alone EPS	= Stand-alone EPS		= Pro forma EPS

Compare stand-alone and pro forma EPS to determine accretion or dilution

Relative size matters

When performing accretion/dilution analysis, remember that relative size matters. A large company with a market value of $20 billion can undertake a $100 million acquisition and the acquisition is unlikely to have a discernible impact on its financial statements (e.g., the transaction will not "move the needle"). However, if a smaller company with a market value of $100 million were to make a $100 million acquisition, the acquisition would double the size of the company. Relative size should be reviewed when deciding how much effort to put forth analyzing EPS accretion/dilution.

No absolute answer – perform sensitivities

Assumptions have a natural margin of error built into them and accretion/dilution analysis is based on a number of transaction assumptions. Sensitivity analysis allows one to measure the magnitude of changes to the results due to changes in key variables. It is very important to perform sensitivity analysis when performing accretion/dilution analysis since a transaction that is accretive (to EPS or another metric) based on one set of assumptions can become dilutive based on another set of assumptions. The danger is that most analysis using a financial model is based on one "case" or "scenario" (which, by its very nature, assumes one set of assumptions). Focusing on just one scenario could be misleading and lead to poor decisions.

Unless you are fairly certain about all of the assumptions in your analysis, it is a good idea to perform sensitivity analysis and consider a range of cases, not just one case or scenario. Given the nature of M&A negotiations, you are not likely to know with certainty all of the transaction assumptions until the two parties are close to signing an agreement. Until that point in a negotiation, accretion/dilution analysis should consider sensitivities based on a range of assumptions.

Tax effect income statement adjustments

Whenever calculating EPS accretion/dilution, you must make adjustments for any tax consequences, if so required. It is a common mistake to forget this step. Income statement adjustments must be tax-effected because earnings are *already* an after-tax number and therefore any adjustments that will be added to or subtracted from earnings also must be after-tax values. Any item that is a pretax number must be tax-effected before it can be added to or subtracted from earnings in order to calculate pro forma earnings per share, so that all adjustments made are on a comparable or apples-to-apples basis. This includes interest expense, synergies, and depreciation, among other things. To tax effect a pretax number, multiply the pretax number by one minus the tax rate.

Pretax number × (1 – tax rate) = after-tax number

This assumes no tax loss carry-forwards, tax credits, or other special tax characteristics (which change the calculation of the tax liability) and also that the company has positive earnings (i.e., is profitable). Taxes are described in more detail in Taxes and M&A. (Ch.21)

Tax effecting vs. grossing-up for taxes

When making adjustments for taxes you will hear the terms "tax effecting" and "grossing-up for taxes." One is essentially the inverse of the other. To "tax effect" a pretax item such as depreciation, interest expense, or synergies, *multiply* the pretax number by one minus the tax rate to arrive at an after-tax number. After-tax numbers can be added to or subtracted from earnings because all numbers are now on an equal basis as after-tax numbers.

Tax effect = pretax number (e.g., depreciation or interest) × (1 – tax rate)

To tax effect $100 million of pretax interest expense, for example, multiply $100 million by one minus the tax rate of 40 percent to arrive at $60 million of after-tax interest expense. The $60 million of after-tax interest serves to reduce earnings.

$$\$100 \text{ million pretax interest} \times (1 - 40 \text{ percent tax rate}) = \$60 \text{ million after-tax}$$

Grossing-up for taxes is the inverse of the calculation for tax-effecting. To gross-up a number for taxes, begin with an after-tax number and *divide* it by one minus the tax rate to arrive at a pretax number.

$$\text{Gross-up} = \frac{\text{After-tax number (e.g., earnings, after-tax interest expense)}}{(1 - \text{tax rate})}$$

To gross up $60 million of after-tax interest, for example, divide $60 million by one minus the tax rate of 40 percent to arrive at $100 million of pretax interest expense.

$$\$60 \text{ million} / (1 - 40 \text{ percent tax rate}) = \$100 \text{ million pretax}$$

Partial- year adjustments in year transaction closes

Care must be taken with the EPS accretion/dilution analysis in the year in which the transaction takes place because, in most cases, a transaction will not close exactly at the end of Acquiror's fiscal year. Therefore, the first year of combined operations will only include a partial year of (a) Target's operations and (b) any transaction adjustments. For example, if a transaction closes on September 30 and Acquiror's fiscal year end is December 31, every transaction adjustment for the first year would be multiplied by 25 percent (or 1/4) to account for the fact that the transaction would only be in effect for one quarter of the first year. That is, Acquiror would only own Target for 25 percent of Acquiror's fiscal year and so Acquiror would only reflect in its financial statements 25 percent of the transaction's effects in that first year.

For example, if Target had annual earnings of $100 million and a transaction closed on September 30, Acquiror would only recognize one-quarter of the $100 million, or $25 million ($100 million × 0.25 = $25 million), because Target's previous owners, who owned Target for the other three-quarters of the year, received the other $75 million of Target's annual earnings. Similarly, if annual interest expense on the transaction debt were $100 million, Acquiror would recognize only $15 million in after-tax interest expense in Year 1 ($100 million pretax × (1 – 0.4) × 0.25 = $15 million) due to the fact that the debt was only outstanding for 3 months (25 percent of the year). Under the same principle, if the transaction were to close on March 31, every transaction adjustment for the first year would be multiplied by 75 percent. For all subsequent years, no partial-year adjustment is needed.

Changes in capital structure

It is important to note that accretion/dilution to EPS can be greatly affected (and even manipulated) by a change to a company's capital structure (i.e., by the mix of cash/stock used in the transaction). Because EPS (unlike EBITDA) is post-interest expense and is a metric of equity value (not enterprise value), capitalization cannot be ignored when evaluating a transaction. Theoretically, a more highly leveraged company should trade at a lower P/E multiple. Said another way, there is more risk associated with owning stock in a company that has increased its relative debt load, and consequently investors should apply a lower multiple to that company. Therefore, although an Acquiror can usually make a transaction seem more accretive (or less dilutive) by becoming more highly leveraged pro forma, this should result in downward pressure on a company's multiple (all else being equal). However, it is possible that in spite of increased leverage, Acquiror could see no change to its multiple or even multiple expansion if investors believe the strategic benefits of the transaction outweigh the impact of increased leverage.

Cost of equity vs. cost of debt

In general, financing an acquisition with debt is less expensive than financing it with equity. As a result, as the use of cash increases (a less expensive form of capital), the transaction becomes more accretive. For further discussion on the differences between using cash and stock as acquisition currency, see Acquisition Currency and Stock Deals. (Ch.15,16)

Use diluted shares outstanding for Target

Diluted shares outstanding are calculated by adding basic shares outstanding to (i) additional shares from options using the treasury method and (ii) additional shares from convertible securities using the if-converted method. Recall from Financial Statement Basics (Ch.3) that the formula to calculate options using the treasury method is as follows:

$$\frac{\text{Current stock price} - \text{Strike price}}{\text{Current stock price}} \times \text{Number of options} = \text{Additional shares}$$

To calculate diluted shares in a merger scenario, the "current stock price" in the model is the assumption for the *offer* price per Target share, *not* the current market price for Target (because at the time the transaction closes the "current" price will be the "offer" price).

Many options have a change-of-control trigger such that the options accelerate and become exercisable in the event of a change of control (they still must be in-the-money to actually convert into shares). When performing merger accounting it is best to calculate diluted shares outstanding for Target based on total in-the-money *outstanding* options. This is different from comparable company analysis or discounted cash flow analysis, in which case it is better to use in-the-money *exercisable* options to calculate diluted shares outstanding. Using total outstanding options, as opposed to exercisable options only, is a more conservative assumption since it assumes that all outstanding options will be triggered in the stock merger, not just those which are already exercisable. While working on a live transaction, if you learn during the negotiations that not all options will be triggered and become payable (based on how the transaction is structured from a legal perspective), you can always revert to using only in-the-money exercisable options for purposes of calculating diluted shares outstanding. However, it is usually best to begin with the most conservative assumption (meaning the assumption that would convert the most number of options), which means using outstanding options for Target and not exercisable options. For Acquiror, you should use in-the-money exercisable (*not* outstanding) options to calculate diluted shares outstanding since Acquiror's options will not be triggered in the sale because there is no change of control for Acquiror.

Transaction expenses

The costs of arranging financing, which can range from 1 to 2 percent of the amount of the debt raised, are amortized over the life of the debt. M&A fees, which can range from 0.5 to 1 percent of the transaction value for deals greater than $250 million in transaction value and up to 5 percent for smaller transactions, are expensed but must be funded with cash. Some practitioners add a line for transaction expenses in their models to account for these expenses while some do not, based on the assumption that transaction fees would be written off as non-recurring items in the first year of the transaction and should not be considered in measuring the recurring pro forma EPS for Acquiror.

Accounting Treatments

Since accretion/dilution analysis is a relative analysis, the practitioner needs a company's financial statistics before (pre-transaction) and after (pro forma) the transaction in order to perform any type of accretion/dilution analysis. For publicly traded companies, obtaining the pre-transaction financial statistics is straightforward. Companies such as First Call and IBES publish consensus EPS estimates (gathered from equity research analysts) for most publicly traded companies. Estimating pro forma numbers, however, requires more work. To calculate a pro forma financial statistic, adjustments must be made to account for the transaction. This requires some understanding of the applicable accounting rules.

Accounting concepts in this chapter

A number of accounting terms and concepts are discussed in this chapter. As with other parts of this book, the concepts discussed in this chapter are GAAP financial accounting concepts, unless otherwise noted and except for the tax-specific chapters (Ch.21,22). The disclosure requirements and accounting methods discussed in this chapter pertain to companies that follow GAAP for financial reporting purposes.

Companies in specific industries may not be subject to all of the GAAP rules and concepts described in this section. If working with a company in an industry with specialized accounting or reporting methods (examples include financial institutions, oil and gas, real estate, and municipal or non-profit entities), be sure to reference accounting rules for that specialized industry.

Before analyzing the accretion/dilution effects of a transaction, it is important to consider the accounting treatment used for the transaction. Without understanding the appropriate accounting treatment, you will not know how to "do the math" to make the proper adjustments. There is a GAAP accounting treatment for every type of M&A or financing transaction. This chapter, however, only covers M&A transactions in which an investor company purchases some portion of the common voting stock (i.e., equity) of another company and intends to hold the investment for an unknown period of time. This chapter does not cover investments in debt securities, short-term investments, or investments in trading securities. Accounting methods for these transactions can be found in most financial accounting textbooks.

Under GAAP, the level of "control" acquired in a long-term equity investment is a key factor in determining how to account for the investment. The investor company's intent with respect to disposal of the investment is another key factor. The level of control or influence generally can be inferred from the percentage of Target's common voting stock owned by Acquiror. However, other factors may determine influence or control (many of these distinguishing factors are described in the following sections). Therefore, judgment should be used to test the level of control rather than a strict literal interpretation of the numerical guidelines.

The schematic in Figure 14.5 illustrates four levels of questioning employed to determine the proper accounting method to use for a specific type of long-term, non-trading, equity investment.

1. The first question is: Does the investor company *control* the target company? In general, control is deemed to exist if the investor company owns greater than 50 percent of the common voting stock of the target company. However, this is not always the case. If control exists, the **consolidation method** is used.

2. If the answer to the control question is "no," the next question is: Does the investor company *have significant influence over* the target company's operating and financial policies? In general, significant influence is deemed to exist if the investor company owns between 20 and 50 percent of the common voting stock of the target company, although this is not always the case. If significant influence exists, the **equity method** is used.

3. If the answer to the significant influence question is "no," the next question is: Is the *fair market value of Target's security readily available*? The fair market value of a security can exist if the security trades on an organized trading exchange such as the NYSE or the NASDAQ or in over-the-counter (OTC) trading in which public market values are readily available. If the fair market value for the security is readily available, the **available-for-sale method** is used.

4. Finally, if the fair market value of the security is not readily available, the **cost method** is used.

Figure 14.5 –Accounting for Investments

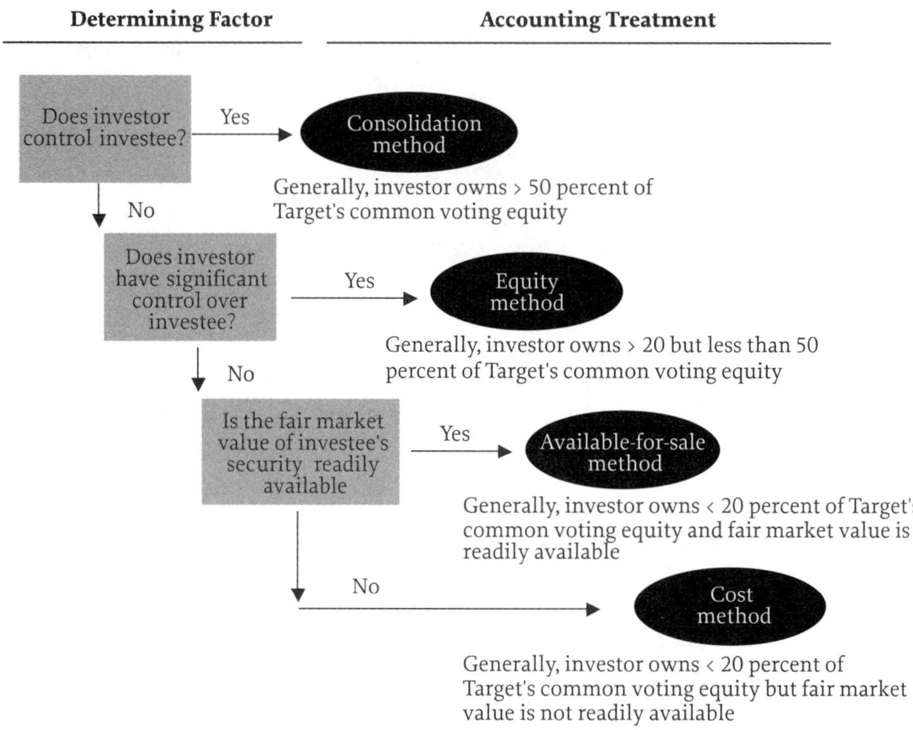

Consolidation Method

As described in Figure 14.5, the **consolidation method** of accounting is used if Acquiror is deemed to have control over Target. Under the consolidation method, Target is treated as a subsidiary of Acquiror and Target's financial statements are consolidated into Acquiror's financial statements. In general, the consolidation method is used if Acquiror owns greater than 50 percent of Target, although "control" is the litmus test and the 50 percent threshold is just a guideline.

In consolidation accounting, **intercompany transactions** (meaning transactions between Parent and Subsidiary) are eliminated and the subsidiary's financial results are then added to (or consolidated into) the parent company's financial statements. **Purchase accounting** is the accounting method used to account for business combinations of unrelated entities. Purchase accounting is required for all business combinations in the U.S. (except for the combination of non-profit entities).

Elimination of pooling accounting

The SEC and FASB eliminated pooling accounting in 2001 with pronouncement of FASB Statements No. 141 and 142 (which also superseded FASB's previous APB 16 on business combinations). Currently, only purchase accounting can be used to account for business combinations. If referencing a text that describes pooling accounting, disregard the discussion on pooling accounting because that method is no longer allowed. FASB Statements No. 141 and 142 also eliminated the amortization of goodwill. Instead of amortizing goodwill, goodwill is now periodically tested for impairment (impairment occurs if the fair market value of goodwill is less than the book value of goodwill). Goodwill is further described in the following section.

Minority interest

If a parent company (Parent) owns more than 50 percent but less than 100 percent of another company (Subsidiary), a **minority interest** account is created to account for the percentage of the consolidated entity not owned by Parent. For example, if Parent owns 70 percent of the voting stock of Subsidiary and public investors own the remaining 30 percent, Parent would consolidate 100 percent of Subsidiary for GAAP accounting purposes but Parent would show a minority interest account equal to the 30 percent of Subsidiary that Parent does not own. Minority interest is a component of equity on Parent's balance sheet to reflect the fact that Parent does not own 100 percent of Subsidiary, in spite of the fact that 100 percent of Subsidiary's financial results are included in Parent's financial results under consolidation accounting. In addition, minority interest in earnings also shows up on Parent's income statement: it represents the amount of Subsidiary's income or loss that does not belong to Parent and instead belongs to the 30 percent public shareholders. Thus in consolidation accounting, Acquiror incorporates all of Target and then reflects the amount of Target it does not own using the minority interest account in its financial statements. This is in contrast to the equity method of accounting in which Acquiror only incorporates the amount of Target it actually owns.

Tax consolidation and DRD rules vs. GAAP rules

If Parent owns 80 percent or greater of Subsidiary and the owned Subsidiary stock represents at least 80 percent of the total value of the Subsidiary, in addition to preparing consolidated GAAP financial statements, Parent also can prepare consolidated taxes, from which 100 percent of the dividends received from Subsidiary by Parent are excluded - this is the so-called dividends-received deduction (DRD).

The 80 percent ownership threshold for consolidated tax accounting is a tax rule, created and implemented by the IRS. If a corporation owns 80 percent or more of another corporation, Parent can file a consolidated tax return for Parent and Subsidiary. This is different from the GAAP rule for consolidation method accounting. GAAP allows consolidation accounting if a corporation owns 50 percent or more of another corporation. Other important differences between GAAP and tax accounting are described in Taxes and M&A. (Ch.21)

- The implications of purchase accounting are described below. A comprehensive numerical example of these accounting implications is provided in the following section using consolidation accounting.

- In purchase accounting, Target's balance sheet is adjusted to fair market value (meaning all of the identifiable assets and liabilities are recorded at their current fair market value), regardless of what the historical cost of those assets and liabilities was. This is also referred to as writing up (if the fair market value is greater than the book value) or writing down (if the fair market value is less than the book value) the balance sheet. Target's adjusted balance sheet, which represents the fair market value of Target's assets and liabilities, is consolidated into Acquiror's balance sheet.

- Acquiror's balance sheet is combined with Target's balance sheet at Acquiror's pre-transaction book value. No write-up or write-down takes place for Acquiror's assets, liabilities, or equity, only for Target's assets, liabilities, and equity.

- The purchase price for Target's equity is allocated to Target's identifiable assets and liabilities (net identifiable assets = identifiable assets – liabilities) based on fair market value. Purchase price in excess of fair value of Target's net identifiable assets is allocated to goodwill. For example, if Target had identifiable assets of $1,000 million and liabilities of $600 million and Acquiror purchased Target's equity for $1,200 million, the goodwill amount would be $800 million.

	$1,000 million of identifiable assets
-	600 million of liabilities
=	$400 million of net identifiable assets

	$1,200 million purchase price
–	400 million in net identifiable assets
=	$800 million in goodwill

- The allocation of purchase price to Target's net identifiable assets is one of the most controversial aspects of purchase accounting, since much judgment goes into determining the fair market value of Target's assets and liabilities. The equity purchase price must be allocated to the fair market value of intangible assets, such as intellectual property, in addition to tangible assets such as net PP&E. FAS 141 and 142 provide some guidance as to how to determine the fair market values of Target's identifiable assets and liabilities. For example, the fair market value of net PP&E should be replacement cost for similar assets with similar capacity. Accounting specialists are often brought in during due diligence to determine the fair market value of Target's net identifiable assets. Refer to a definitive GAAP guide on business combinations for additional guidelines.

- At transaction closing, various balance sheet transaction adjustments are made in purchase accounting.

  a. In adjusting Target's balance sheet to fair market value, write-ups increase the book value of Target's identifiable assets and/or liabilities and write-downs decrease the book value of Target's identifiable assets and/or liabilities. An asset write-up is the difference between the fair market value of an asset and the historical book value (carrying cost on Target's balance sheet). Asset write-ups are also discussed in Taxes and M&A. (Ch.21)

  b. Target's existing goodwill is eliminated and new goodwill is calculated based on the purchase price paid for the equity of Target less the fair market value of Target's net identifiable assets.

  c. Negative goodwill is not created if the purchase price of Target's equity is less than the fair market value of Target's net identifiable assets. Instead, the book value of PP&E is reduced by the amount of negative goodwill on the assumption that the assets are over-valued. If negative goodwill exceeds the amount that can be written down, Acquiror immediately records an extraordinary gain to recognize the difference between purchase price and fair market value. For example, if Target had identifiable assets of $900 million, liabilities of $600 million, and a purchase price of $200 million, the calculated goodwill amount would be -$100 million ($200 million in purchase price – ($900 million in net identifiable asset – $600 million in liabilities) = -$100 million in goodwill). Instead of recording negative goodwill, Target's assets and liabilities would be written down to their lower fair market value. In our example, identifiable assets might be written down from $900 million to $800 million so that the negative goodwill of -$100 million would be recalculated to become 0 ($200 million – ($800 million - $600 million) = 0). Transactions with negative goodwill are not common.

d. In stock acquisitions and mergers, assets and liabilities are written up or down to fair market value for GAAP purposes and not for tax purposes (in asset acquisitions, however, they are written up or down to fair market value for book and tax purposes). In a stock acquisition or merger, a deferred tax liability is created if any depreciable assets are written up during the fair market value exercise for GAAP purposes and not for tax purposes. If depreciable assets are written down during the fair market value exercise, a deferred tax asset is created. This concept is described more fully in Taxes and M&A. (Ch.21)

e. Target's equity account is written up or down to the fair market value amount of the equity consideration paid in the transaction.

- After the transaction has closed, Acquiror's income statement recognizes all of Target's income or loss, less any minority interest in earnings if Acquiror owns less than 100 percent of Target, and adjusted for partial year if required (which is usually the case).

- If a depreciable asset has been written up to a new fair market value, the new written-up value must be depreciated over the life of the asset. Since the asset was already being depreciated at its previous value, accretion/dilution analysis only accounts for the "new" depreciation. For example, if an asset were written up from $20,000 to $30,000 with a useful life of 5 years, the incremental depreciation would be $2,000 per year [($30,000 - $20,000) / 5 = $2,000]. The "existing" depreciation of $4,000 per year is already reflected in the EPS of the asset's owner ($20,000 / 5 = $4,000) and so no adjustment is required for the existing depreciation.

- Goodwill is not amortized. Goodwill is kept on the balance sheet at the acquisition cost. However, goodwill is regularly tested for impairment. If the company believes the carrying value (or balance sheet value) of goodwill is greater than the fair market value of the goodwill, a write-down for the goodwill impairment must be recognized. The goodwill write-down would flow through net income (as a non-recurring charge) and would reduce net income. Except for any potential cash tax benefit, write-downs are non-cash events.

- Although goodwill is no longer amortized, other intangible assets such as patents that have been written up still must be amortized over the estimated useful life of the intangible asset. One area in which the amortization treatment is unclear is in regard to in-process research and development (in-process R&D). Historically, as much purchased in-process R&D as possible would be expensed at the time of the acquisition, the presumption being that one cannot reasonably estimate the useful life of in-process R&D. However, FASB has proposed the capitalization and future amortization of acquired in-process R&D costs.

- From an EPS accretion/dilution standpoint, Acquiror recognizes all of Target's income plus or minus any transaction-related income statement adjustments as described above. If any synergies are assumed in the transaction, the after-tax value of the synergies is included as an adjustment to Acquiror net income for accretion/dilution purposes. Acquiror also will need to account for how the investment was paid for. For example, if Acquiror used debt to pay for the acquisition, the accretion/dilution analysis must include the cost of financing the acquisition debt. If Acquiror issued stock to Target's shareholders in exchange for shares of Target, the newly issued shares must be accounted for in the accretion/dilution analysis. Thus, how the investment was paid for will be reflected either in (a) the earnings portion of the EPS calculation (earnings are reduced because of increased interest expense from the transaction debt) and/or (b) the shares outstanding portion of the EPS calculation (shares outstanding are increased as a result of the new shares issued to Target shareholders).

Step-by-Step Accretion/Dilution

Recall the three steps we discussed at the beginning of the chapter: (Step 1) combine Acquiror and Target earnings, (Step 2) make transaction adjustments (based on transaction assumptions and proper accounting methods), and (Step 3) compare Acquiror's pre-transaction and post-transaction EPS. We will expand upon these three simplified steps (which are primarily related to the income statement) as well as discuss adjustments to the balance sheet (Step 4) and discuss sensitivities (Step 5).

Figure 14.6 – Step-by-Step Accretion/Dilution

Accretion/Dilution Steps	Detailed Steps
1. Combine earnings	a. To combine earnings, you first need to gather stand-alone financial statistics for Acquiror and Target
2. Make transaction adjustments	a. To make transaction adjustments, you first need to determine the transaction assumptions
	b. Calculate transaction values (e.g., equity value and enterprise value paid by Acquiror for Target)
	c. Calculate shares issued (if stock is used) and interest expense (if cash/debt is used) to acquire Target
	d. Determine fair market value of Target's assets and liabilities and calculate whether any write-ups or write-downs are required. Also determine if DD&A adjustments are required
	e. Determine revenue and cost synergies, if any
	f. Identify other adjustments, if any (e.g., transaction-related expenses, partial-year adjustments)
3. Compare stand-alone and pro forma EPS	a. Calculate Acquiror's pro forma EPS
	b. Compare Acquiror's pro forma EPS to stand-alone EPS
	c. Calculate additional synergies to break-even EPS (if any)
4. Make balance sheet adjustments	a. Eliminate Target's old goodwill and calculate new goodwill
	b. Record new transaction debt (if any) and adjust Target's equity to fair market value
	c. Combine Acquiror and Target balance sheets and calculate stand-alone and pro forma capitalization and leverage ratios
5. Perform sensitivities	a. Perform sensitivities on all major transaction assumptions

To illustrate these accretion/dilution steps, let's consider a simple transaction between CoffeeCo and TeaCo. On January 1, 2006, CoffeeCo announces it will purchase 100 percent of the stock of TeaCo for $40 per share. This $40 per share of acquisition consideration is comprised of a combination of 40 percent cash and 60 percent stock. The transaction is expected to close on June 30, 2006.

Figure 14.7 – Diagram of CoffeeCo and TeaCo transaction

Transaction Summary [1]

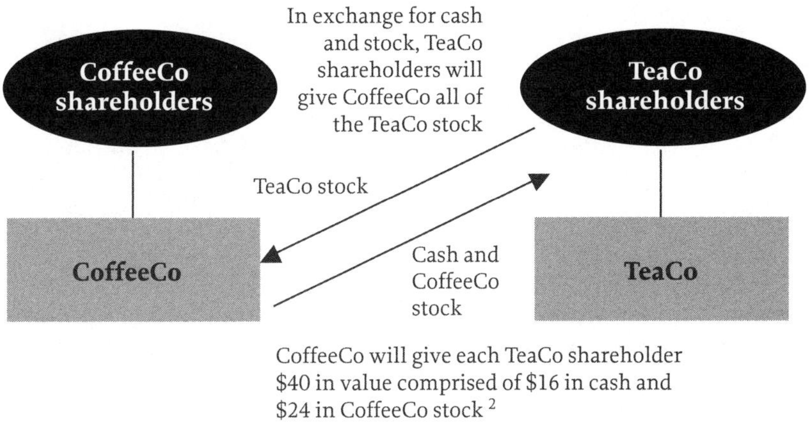

Pro forma the transaction

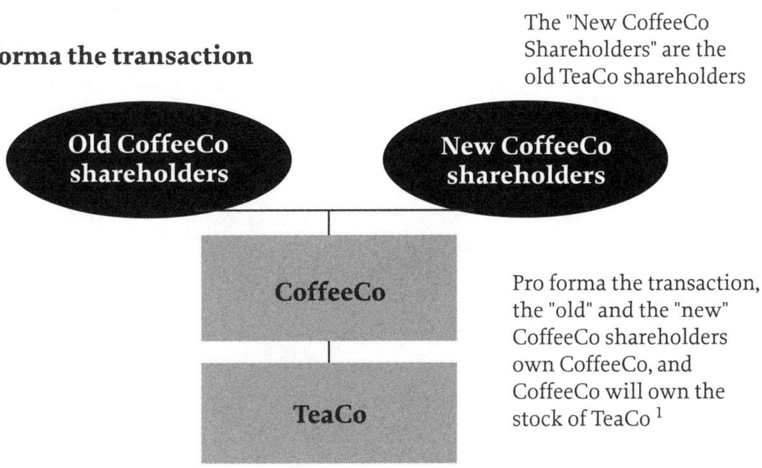

---

[1] Represents a functional description of the merger, not a legal representation
[2] 40% cash × $40 offer value = $16 in cash value (and $24 in stock value)

1a. Gather stand-alone assumptions for CoffeeCo (Acquiror) and TeaCo (Target)

To calculate even a simple accretion/dilution analysis, you need the following assumptions (additional stand-alone information is helpful, but these items are required to perform the analysis) for both companies.

a. Projected EPS for the next one to three years
b. Long-term EPS growth rate for the next three to five years
c. Fully diluted shares outstanding
d. The current stock price (if a public company)
e. Pre-transaction balance sheets, if available

Upon gathering these stand-alone assumptions, it is a good idea to calculate basic metrics such as market value, enterprise value, P/E multiples and price/book multiples for both companies. If you do not have access to internal company projections, First Call or IBES are reputable sources for EPS projections. The most recently available balance sheet is the best source for a pre-transaction balance sheet. At this stage, you can also calculate stand-alone earnings for Acquiror and Target and add them together.

Stand-alone assumptions for CoffeeCo and TeaCo are provided in Table 14.8.

Table 14.8 – Pre-transaction Assumptions for CoffeeCo and TeaCo

$ millions **Pre-transaction balance sheet**	*Acquiror* **CoffeeCo**	*Target* **TeaCo**	*Combined* **Pre-adjustments**
Cash	$300	$75	
Short-term assets	1,700	225	
Net PP&E	12,000	1,000	
Goodwill	0	200	
Total assets	$14,000	$1,500	
Short-term debt	$500	$125	
Short-term liabilities	700	75	
Long-term debt	3,800	350	
Deferred tax liabilities	300	25	
Long-term liabilities	700	125	
Shareholders' equity	8,000	800	
Total liabilities and equity	$14,000	$1,500	
Current stock price	$25	$32	
Diluted shares outstanding	450	75	
Market value[1]	$11,250	$2,400	$13,650
Net debt[2]	$4,000	$400	$4,400
Enterprise value[3]	$15,250	$2,800	$18,050
2006 EPS[4]	$1.75	$2.00	
2007 EPS[4]	$1.85	$2.25	
Long-term growth rate[4]	5%	10%	
2006 P/E[5]	14.3x	16.0x	
2007 P/E[5]	13.5x	14.2x	
Price/book value[6]	1.4x	3.0x	
2006 earnings[7]	$788	$150	$938
2007 earnings[7]	$833	$169	$1,001

[1] Stock price × diluted shares outstanding
[2] Short-term debt + long-term debt + minority interest - cash
[3] Market value of equity + net debt
[4] EPS and long-term growth rate estimates from a reputable source such as First Call
[5] Current stock price / EPS in a given year
[6] Market value / book value of equity (from balance sheet)
[7] Diluted shares outstanding × EPS in a given year; earnings are before transaction adjustments; numbers may not tie due to rounding

2a. Determine transaction assumptions

The next step is to make the transaction assumptions which will be used in the combination analysis. Transaction assumptions include:

a. The percentage of Target's stock that will be acquired
b. The offer price paid per Target share (or, alternatively, you can make an assumption for the premium to the current stock price paid per share of Target)
c. The percentage of cash and/or Acquiror stock to be offered to Target shareholders
d. The interest rate on any acquisition debt Acquiror may undertake
e. Assumptions for the fair market value of Target's assets and liabilities
f. The useful life for any of Target's depreciable assets that will be written up or written down in the analysis
g. Any estimated cost or revenue synergies
h. The tax rate to be used
i. An estimate for when the transaction will close

Your model should be set up so that you can make changes to any of these assumptions and see how the change affects the analysis. At this stage it is also important to note whether or not Acquiror and Target are on the same fiscal year. If they are not on the same fiscal year, Target's EPS projections must be calendarized in order to make them comparable to Acquiror's EPS projections before Target's net income can be added to Acquiror's net income. Calendarizing is described in Comparable Company Analysis. (Ch.9)

Transaction assumptions for the CoffeeCo and TeaCo transaction are provided in Table 14.9.

Table 14.9 – Transaction Assumptions for CoffeeCo and TeaCo

$ millions, except per share data

Transaction assumptions	
Offer price for TeaCo	$40
Current TeaCo stock price	$32
Implied premium paid for TeaCo[1]	25%
Percentage of cash consideration[2]	40%
Percentage of equity consideration	60%
Fair market value of TeaCo's net PP&E[3]	$1,750
Existing book value of TeaCo's net PP&E[4]	$1,000
Useful life of written-up net PP&E (in years)[5]	20
Tax rate[2]	40%
Interest rate on acquisition debt[2]	8%
Date of transaction completion[2]	6/30/06
Pretax transactions synergies[6]	$50

[1] (Offer price for Target / Target current share price) -1: [($40 / $32) -1]
[2] A transaction assumption
[3] An estimate for fair market value of net PP&E
[4] From Target's pre-transaction balance sheet
[5] Estimate of useful life for depreciable assets to be written up
[6] Estimate of cost and revenue synergies

2b. Calculate transaction values

The transaction equity value is equal to the offer price per share of Target multiplied by the diluted shares outstanding of Target. Target's diluted shares outstanding would be calculated based on its outstanding options (as opposed to exercisable options) unless you know with certainty that Target's outstanding options will not be triggered by the transaction.

Transaction equity value = offer price × Target's diluted shares outstanding

Transaction equity value and Target's net debt are added to arrive at transaction enterprise value.

Transaction enterprise value = transaction equity value + Target's net debt

The transaction values for TeaCo are provided in Table 14.10.

Table 14.10 – Transaction Equity and Enterprise Values

$ millions, except per share data

Transaction equity and enterprise values	
Offer price for TeaCo	$40
TeaCo diluted shares outstanding	75
Transaction equity value[1]	$3,000
TeaCo net debt[2]	$400
Transaction enterprise value[3]	$3,400
Cash consideration	40%
Cash consideration[4]	$1,200
Stock consideration	60%
Stock consideration[5]	$1,800

[1] Office price × diluted shares outstanding ($40 × 75)
[2] Short-term debt + long-term debt + minority interest - cash
[3] Transaction equity value + Target net debt ($3,000 + $400)
[4] Transaction equity value × percent of cash ($3,000 × 0.4)
[5] Transaction equity value × percent of stock ($3,000 × 0.6)

2c. Calculate shares issued (if stock is used to acquire Target) and/or interest expense on transaction debt (if cash/debt is used)

In order to determine the number of Acquiror shares issued to Target shareholders, you must first calculate the transaction **exchange ratio**. The exchange ratio is the number of Acquiror shares provided in exchange for one Target share and is calculated by dividing the offer price per share (i.e., the amount paid to Target shareholders) by Acquiror's share price.

Exchange ratio = Offer price for one Target share / Acquiror share price

To calculate the new shares issued to Target shareholders, multiply Target's diluted shares outstanding by the exchange ratio (which will yield the number of Acquiror shares issued if Acquiror offers 100 percent stock consideration) and multiply that product by the percentage of stock consideration offered in the transaction (to account for any cash consideration offered).

Target's diluted shares outstanding

× Exchange ratio

× Percentage of stock consideration in transaction

= Newly issued Acquiror shares

In the CoffeeCo and TeaCo example, the exchange ratio is calculated by dividing the $40 offer price for TeaCo by CoffeeCo's share price of $25.

$40 offer price for TeaCo / $25 CoffeeCo share price = 1.6x exchange ratio

To determine the number of CoffeeCo shares issued to TeaCo shareholders, we must then multiply the exchange ratio by the number of TeaCo diluted shares outstanding *and* by the percentage of stock offered by CoffeeCo.

CoffeeCo will exchange 72 million CoffeeCo shares in exchange for 60 percent of TeaCo's shares. The other 40 percent of the transaction equity value will be paid to TeaCo shareholders in cash. After accounting for these 72 million shares issued to TeaCo shareholders, CoffeeCo will have 522 million diluted shares outstanding.

Table 14.11 – Calculation of Exchange Ratio and Newly Issued Shares

$ millions, except per share data

Exchange ratio and newly issued CoffeeCo shares	
Offer price for TeaCo	$40
CoffeeCo current share price	$25
Exchange ratio[1]	1.6x
TeaCo diluted shares outstanding	75
Percentage of stock consideration	60%
CoffeeCo shares issued to TeaCo[2]	72
CoffeeCo pre-transaction shares outstanding	450
CoffeeCo shares issued to TeaCo	72
CoffeeCo's pro forma shares outstanding[3]	522

[1] Offer price for Target / Acquiror current price ($40 / $25)
[2] Target shares outstanding × exchange ratio × percentage of stock consideration (75 × 1.6 × 0.6)
[3] CoffeeCo pre-transaction shares outstanding + newly issued CoffeeCo shares (450 + 72)

If debt were used to finance any part of the transaction, then the annual cost of the acquisition debt must be calculated and subtracted from Acquiror's pro forma net income in order to calculate EPS accretion/dilution. The annual interest expense is equal to the amount of the acquisition debt multiplied by the interest rate on the acquisition debt. The acquisition debt is equal to the amount of Target's equity purchased with cash consideration.

$$\text{Annual pretax interest expense} = \text{acquisition debt} \times \text{interest rate on debt}$$

$$\text{Annual after-tax interest expense} = \text{pretax interest expense} \times (1 - \text{tax rate})$$

Since CoffeeCo purchases TeaCo using 40 percent cash consideration and 60 percent stock consideration, and the transaction equity value is $3,000 million, CoffeeCo needs to raise $1,200 million in acquisition debt to finance the transaction. With an interest rate on acquisition debt of 8 percent, this translates into $96 million of pretax annual interest and $57.6 million of after-tax annual interest expense.

Table 14.12 – Calculation of Interest Expense on Acquisition Debt

$ millions

Annual interest expense on acquisition debt	
Transaction equity value	$3,000
Cash consideration - percentage	40%
Cash consideration[1]	$1,200
Interest rate on acquisition debt	8%
Annual pretax interest expense[2]	$96.0
Tax rate	40%
Annual after-tax interest expense[3]	$57.6

[1] Transaction equity value × percentage cash consideration ($3,000 × 0.4)
[2] Cash consideration × pretax interest rate on debt ($1,200 × 0.08)
[3] Pretax interest expense × (1 - tax rate) [$96 × (1 - 0.4)]

Using existing cash on the balance sheet

If the assumption is to use existing cash on the balance sheet (as opposed to issuing new debt to fund the acquisition) for some (or all) of the equity purchase price, you still need to "charge" Acquiror's net income for the cash used. That is, this cash on hand was not without value. Thus, if this cash is used to invest in Target, the interest income that the cash would have earned is lost and Acquiror must be "charged" by reducing Acquiror's interest income. If using cash on hand which was presumed to be generating interest income, a general assumption is to charge Acquiror between two and five percent pretax interest on the cash used (or whatever prevailing rates of return are for cash and short-term investments). Said another way, embedded in Acquiror's earnings projections is interest income from that cash on hand, and if any of this cash is used to finance the transaction, an adjustment must be made by reducing Acquiror's after-tax interest income by the amount [cash used × pretax interest rate earned × (1-tax rate)].

Using existing cash on the balance sheet continued

For example, if Acquiror has $100 million cash on its balance sheet and it chooses to use that money to acquire Target for $100 million, that money is not free simply because Acquiror did not have to borrow it from a bank. It has a cost, which is the interest income it would have earned. Assuming Acquiror earns 3 percent on its cash balance, the adjustment that must be made is a reduction in Acquiror's net income of $1.8 million.

	$100 million
×	0.03 cash interest rate
×	0.6 tax adjustment
=	$1.8 million

Target's outstanding debt

When performing EPS accretion/dilution analysis, an assumption is generally made that Target's outstanding debt (its existing debt, not the transaction-related debt) will simply roll over when the transaction closes. This means that all outstanding debt will continue to be outstanding at the existing terms and rates when the transaction closes. If, based on specific characteristics of Acquiror and Target, you have reason to believe that, upon closing the transaction, Target's outstanding debt will need to be refinanced and the refinancing rate would be substantially higher or lower than the existing rate on Target's outstanding debt, you must make an adjustment to Target's earnings to account for the increase or decrease in interest expense, just as was done for Acquiror immediately above. If the debt will roll over, no adjustment needs to be made for purposes of accretion/dilution analysis because the costs of that existing debt are already reflected in Target's stand-alone EPS estimates.

2d. Determine the fair market value of Target's assets and liabilities and calculate whether any write-ups or write-downs are required. Also determine if DD&A adjustments are required.

GAAP requires that all assets and liabilities be adjusted to fair market value in purchase accounting (written up or down, as the case may be). In practice, an accountant will perform this appraisal of assets and liabilities just prior to the closing of a transaction. However, unless you are near that stage in a transaction, or unless the company has recently commissioned an appraisal, you must make an assumption for the fair market value of Target's assets and liabilities for purposes of calculating EPS accretion/dilution.

Making assumptions for Target's balance sheet

Think about Target critically and ask yourself: *Is there anything particular about this company that would lead me to think that the fair market value of its assets and/or liabilities is significantly greater or less than the book value of those assets and/or liabilities?* In practice, most bankers make the general assumption that current assets and liabilities on the balance sheet are already at fair market value (the reasoning is that these assets and liabilities are short-term in nature, and so the values are not likely to change much within one year). Therefore, it is generally (but not always) assumed that no write-up or write-down for short-term items is needed. Another assumption is that outstanding debt is on the balance sheet at fair market value. However, if Target is a distressed company which might not be able to refinance new debt at the same rates as its existing debt, you might consider a write-down to the value of outstanding debt. Or it might be the case that Target has distressed debt (and the balance sheet already reflects that lower value of debt) and Acquiror's credit quality is strong; therefore, after the transaction closes, it might make sense to *write up* the value of Target's debt. When performing EPS accretion/dilution analysis, most times an assumption is made that some write-up will take place for a company's net PP&E because, in general, most things cost more today than similar items in previous years, and so it is especially likely that the fair market value of long-lived assets like PP&E would be higher today than when they were acquired. Real estate holdings is another category in which you might have reason to think that a write-up is required in a purchase if the fair market value of the real estate has risen since it was purchased.

If a depreciable asset is written up to fair market value, the amount of the write-up must be depreciated over the useful life of the asset for GAAP purposes. This additional depreciation must be recognized as an adjustment to pro forma net income for purposes of calculating EPS accretion/dilution.

Since depreciation is a pretax number and net income is an after-tax number, the annual depreciation from the write-up must be tax effected before it can be subtracted from Acquiror's pro forma net income. To tax effect depreciation, multiply the annual depreciation by one minus the tax rate.

After-tax depreciation = pretax depreciation × (1 – tax rate)

Assume the fair market value of TeaCo's net PP&E is $1,750 million, compared with the book value of TeaCo's net PP&E on TeaCo's balance sheet of $1,000 million. This means that the required adjustment to fair market value will be a write-up of $750 million.

$1,750 million fair market value - $1,000 million book value =
$750 million asset write-up

Table 14.13 – Calculation of Write-up and Additional Book Depreciation

$ millions

Asset write-up and additional annual depreciation	
Fair market value of PP&E	$1,750
Book value of PP&E	$1,000
Asset write-up[1]	$750
Useful life of written-up assets (years)	20
Additional annual pretax depreciation from write-up[2]	$37.5
Tax rate	40%
Additional annual after-tax depreciation from write-up[3]	$22.5

[1] Fair market value of PP&E - book value of PP&E ($1,750 - $1,000)
[2] Asset write-up / useful life of written-up assets ($750 / 20)
[3] Additional annual depreciation × (1 - tax rate) [$37.5 × (1 - 0.4)]

2e. Determine revenue and cost synergies, if any

Most synergies estimates are made by a company's operating executives. Most company executives think in terms of the expenditures their groups make, for example $100 million for a new factory. However, that $100 million is a tax-deductible expense (a pretax number), the after-tax cost of which is $100 million × (1-tax rate). Since operating executives usually estimate synergies, these estimates are usually pretax estimates. Therefore, if any synergies are assumed in the transaction, the synergies must be tax-effected prior to adding them as a transaction adjustment for calculating pro forma EPS.

$$\text{Annual after-tax synergies} = \text{annual pretax synergies} \times (1 - \text{tax rate})$$

Assume that a transaction between CoffeeCo and TeaCo generates $50 million of annual pretax synergies. After accounting for taxes, this translates into $30 million of annual after-tax synergies.

Table 14.14 – Calculation of After-Tax Transaction Synergies

$ millions

Transaction synergies	
Annual pretax synergies	$50.0
Tax rate	40%
Annual after-tax synergies[1]	$30.0

[1] Annual pretax synergies × (1 - tax rate) [$50 × (1 - 0.4)]

For a complete discussion of revenue and cost synergies, refer to the section Synergies in Strategic Transactions. (Ch.4)

2f. Identify other adjustments, if any

It is important to ask yourself whether the transaction you are working on has any particular characteristics that require additional adjustments be made prior to completing the accretion/dilution analysis. For example, some practitioners add an adjustment to account for the interest expense owed on cash required to fund transaction-related fees (e.g., fees paid to lenders or investment bankers, costs required to shut down operations or move headquarters, costs required to let go of certain employees post-closing, etc.). All deals are unique so it is important to consider whether there is anything specific that might affect the income statement that should be considered in the accretion/dilution analysis.

3a. Calculate Acquiror's pro forma EPS

Once all of the transaction adjustments have been calculated, the adjustments can be added to the net income of Acquiror and Target to arrive at Acquiror's pro forma net income. Care must be taken with the first year of the EPS accretion/dilution analysis because, in most cases, a transaction will not close exactly at the end of Acquiror's fiscal year. Therefore, the first year of combined operations should only include a partial year of Target's operations and a partial year of any transaction adjustments. In addition, in most cases it is only possible to find EPS projections for one or two years into the future. To project EPS estimates beyond that period, apply the long-term growth rate estimate (from First Call or IBES) to each year's EPS after the last projected EPS estimate. For example, if you have a projected EPS for Acquiror of $1.50 in FY2 and the long-term growth rate estimate for Acquiror is 10 percent, multiply $1.50 by the sum of one plus 10 percent to estimate FY3 EPS.

$$\$1.50 \text{ FY2 EPS} \times (1 + 10 \text{ percent long-term growth rate}) = \$1.65 \text{ FY3 EPS}$$

In Step 2 we made the assumption that the transaction between CoffeeCo and TeaCo would close on June 30, 2006. At the end of 2006, therefore, CoffeeCo only recognizes six months of TeaCo's 2006 earnings and six months of transaction adjustments (from July 1 to December 31). Why is that? Because CoffeeCo only became the owner of TeaCo on June 30 (when the transaction closed) and therefore CoffeeCo only received TeaCo's earnings and recognized transaction adjustments for the six months out of that first year during which CoffeeCo owned TeaCo. In 2007 and beyond, CoffeeCo recognizes a full year of TeaCo's earnings and a full year of transaction adjustments because CoffeeCo will own TeaCo for the entirety of each subsequent year. Because CoffeeCo and TeaCo's fiscal years both end on December 31, no additional adjustments need to be made to calendarize TeaCo's earnings. Since we only have EPS estimates for CoffeeCo and TeaCo for the years 2006 and 2007, apply the long-term growth rate for each company to its respective 2007 EPS to estimate 2008 EPS, then take those 2008 EPS estimates and multiply them by each company's respective long-term growth rate to estimate 2009 EPS. In the following Table 14.15 the "E" after each year means that the numbers are "estimated" results and not "actual" or "historical" results.

Table 14.15 – Calculation of Acquiror's Pro Forma EPS

$ millions, except per share data

Pro forma net income	**2006E**	**2007E**	**2008E**	**2009E**
CoffeeCo pre-transaction EPS[1]	$1.75	$1.85	$1.94	$2.04
CoffeeCo diluted shares outstanding	450	450	450	450
CoffeeCo pre-transaction net income	$787.5	$832.5	$874.1	$917.8
TeaCo pre-transaction EPS[2]	$2.00	$2.25	$2.48	$2.72
TeaCo diluted shares outstanding	75	75	75	75
TeaCo pre-transaction net income	$150.0	$168.8	$ 185.6	$ 204.2
Percent of year included	50%	100%	100%	100%
Partial year adjustments[3]	$75.0	$168.8	$185.6	$204.2
Combined earnings[4]	$862.5	$1,001.2	$1,059.8	$1,122.0
Transaction adjustments[5]				
Transaction interest expense (Table 14.12)	($57.6)	($57.6)	($57.6)	($57.6)
Additional depreciation from write-up (T. 14.13)	($22.5)	($22.5)	($22.5)	($22.5)
Estimated synergies (Table 14.14)	$30.0	$30.0	$30.0	$30.0
Total annual adjustments	($50.1)	($50.1)	($50.1)	($50.1)
Percent of year included[3]	50%	100%	100%	100%
Partial year adjustments[3]	($25.1)	($50.1)	($50.1)	($50.1)
Pro forma CoffeeCo earnings[6]	$837.5	$951.1	$1,009.6	$1,071.9
Pro forma CoffeeCo sh.outst. (annual)(Table 14.11)	522	522	522	522
Pro forma sh.outstanding adjusted for partial year[7]	486	522	522	522
Pro forma EPS[8]	**$1.72**	**$1.82**	**$1.93**	**$2.05**

[1] 2006 and 2007 EPS and long-term growth estimates from a reputable source such as First Call or IBES
2008 EPS = 2007 EPS × (1 + long-term growth rate) [$1.85 × (1 + 5%) = $1.94]
2009 EPS = 2008 EPS × (1 + long-term growth rate) [$1.94 × (1 + 5%) = $2.04]

[2] 2006 and 2007 EPS and long-term growth estimates from a reputable source such as First Call or IBES
2008 EPS = 2007 EPS × (1 + long-term growth rate) [$2.25 × (1 + 10%) = $2.48]
2009 EPS = 2008 EPS × (1 + long-term growth rate) [$2.48 × (1 + 10%) = $2.72]

[3] Only 50% of 2006 is included because the transaction will close on June 30, 2006. For subsequent years, 100% is included

[4] Acquiror net income + Target net income after adjusting for partial year in 2006

[5] All transaction adjustments are after-tax numbers. Recall that negative numbers are costs (shown in parentheses) and positive numbers are benefits.

[6] Combined earnings + total transaction adjustments after adjusting for partial year in 2006

[7] Acquiror shares outstanding + newly issued shares, adjusted for partial year in 2006 [450 + (72 × 0.5)]

[8] Pro forma earnings / pro forma shares outstanding

3b. Compare Acquiror's pro forma EPS to stand-alone EPS

After calculating Acquiror's pro forma EPS, it can be compared to Acquiror's pre-transaction EPS. If the difference between pre-transaction EPS and pro forma EPS (the EPS accretion/dilution) is a positive number (pro forma EPS > stand-alone EPS), then the transaction is accretive. If the difference is a negative number (pro forma EPS < stand-alone EPS), then the transaction is dilutive. It is common to calculate accretion/dilution on a dollar per share basis as well as on a percentage basis.

EPS accretion/dilution (per share) = pro forma EPS – pre-transaction EPS

EPS accretion/dilution (percentage) = (pro forma EPS / pre-transaction EPS) - 1

Notice in Table 14.16 that the transaction is dilutive in the first few years but that the level (or percentage) of dilution decreases each year, so much in fact that it is accretive by 2009. This occurs because TeaCo is growing at a faster rate than CoffeeCo (recall that TeaCo's long-term growth rate was 10 percent compared to CoffeeCo's long-term growth rate of 5 percent). This is why companies sometimes enter into dilutive transactions. If Target is growing faster than Acquiror, Acquiror might be willing to sustain some level of dilution in the early years for the benefit of a higher growth rate (and accompanying accretion) in the future.

Table 14.16 – EPS Accretion/Dilution for Acquiror

EPS accretion/dilution	2006E	2007E	2008E	2009E
CoffeeCo pre-transaction EPS	$1.75	$1.85	$1.94	$2.04
CoffeeCo pro forma EPS	$1.72	$1.82	$1.93	$2.05
Accretion/dilution[1]	($0.03)	($0.03)	($0.01)	$0.01
Accretion/dilution[2]	(1.5%)	(1.5%)	(0.4%)	0.7%

[1] Pro forma EPS - pre-transaction EPS
[2] (Pro forma EPS / pre-transaction EPS) - 1
Note: numbers may not match precisely due to rounding

3c. Calculate additional synergies to break-even EPS (if any)

If a transaction is dilutive, it is helpful to know how much in additional synergies is required so that the transaction is **break-even to EPS** (break-even means the point at which the transaction is neither accretive nor dilutive; that is, the EPS costs of the transaction exactly balance the benefits). For example, Acquiror might balk at the idea of undertaking a transaction with five percent dilution. However, if the synergies to break-even analysis suggest that the additional synergies required to break even are a relatively small number and attainable within a short period of time, Acquiror might reconsider the transaction.

Recall that a synergies analysis undertaken during the course of a transaction is, by its very nature, an exercise in estimation whereas a model assumes a single estimate for synergies. Since your synergies estimate is likely to be a range of values as opposed to one number, it is important to perform sensitivity analysis on synergies assumptions. As Acquiror learns more about Target during due diligence the range of synergies values is likely to narrow; however, it is unlikely to ever be a specific number.

Since synergies are often quoted and thought of as a pretax number, you must calculate the additional synergies to break even on a pretax basis. To do this, multiply the dilution per share by the number of pro forma shares outstanding. This provides the estimate for additional earnings required to break even. However, this is an after-tax number and must be converted to a pretax number. This is done by taking the additional earnings required to break even and dividing it by one minus the tax rate. This is also known as "grossing-up" the number for taxes and was discussed earlier in the chapter. This provides an estimate for *additional* pretax synergies required to break even. The "additional" is stressed since there may already be an estimate for synergies included in the accretion/dilution analysis and therefore this calculation enumerates the additional amount required to reach break-even (recall that the previous synergy estimate, whatever it was, yielded a dilutive transaction and these additional synergies are required to take the proposed transaction from being dilutive to being break-even). If this additional amount is added to the synergies amount that is already included in the analysis, this is the estimate for total pretax synergies to break even.

$$\text{Earnings required to break even} = \text{EPS dilution} \times \text{pro forma diluted shares outstanding}$$
$$\text{Additional pretax synergies to break-even} = \frac{\text{Earnings required to break-even}}{(1 - \text{tax rate})}$$

As shown in Table 14.16, the transaction was dilutive for CoffeeCo in all years except for 2009, at which point the transaction became slightly accretive. Therefore we can calculate the additional pretax synergies to break-even EPS for years 2006, 2007, and 2008. Additional synergies to break even are not required in 2009 because the transaction is already accretive in that year by $0.01 per share.

Table 14.17 – Additional Pretax Synergies to Break Even for CoffeeCo

$ millions, except per share data

Pretax synergies to break-even EPS	**2006E**	**2007E**	**2008E**	**2009E**
Accretion/dilution	($0.03)	($0.03)	($0.01)	$0.01
Pro forma shares outstanding	486	522	522	522
Additional after-tax annual synergies to break-even[1]	$26.1	$14.6	$4.3	n/a
Tax rate	40%	40%	40%	40%
Additional pretax annual synergies to break-even[2]	$43.5	$24.3	$7.2	n/a

[1] Accretion/dilution × pro forma shares outstanding

[2] After-tax annual synergies to break-even / (1 - tax rate)

Note: figures in 2006 column for additional synergies represent annual figures; however, the transaction will close on June 30, 2006, so only one half (50%) of these figures would apply. Thus the calculations for additional synergies to break-even in 2006 would be:

$43 million in pretax synergies × (1-40%) = $26 million in after-tax synergies

$26 million × 50% of the year for the partial year adjustment = $13 million in adjusted after-tax synergies

$13 million / 486 million shares = $0.03 per share

$0.03 per share in additional synergies + ($0.03) per share in dilution = $0.00 per share, which is break-even

4a. Eliminate Target's old goodwill and calculate new goodwill

As discussed, in purchase accounting Target's balance sheet must be recorded at fair market value. If an asset or liability is recorded on Acquiror's balance sheet at a higher amount than it was recorded on Target's balance sheet, a write-up is required as part of the transaction adjustments. If a depreciable asset is written up, the additional amount by which the asset is written up must be depreciated over the asset's useful life for GAAP purposes. However, the asset will only be written up for GAAP book purposes and not for tax purposes. In our example, the purchase of TeaCo by CoffeeCo is a purchase of stock. In a stock purchase, Acquiror adjusts Target's assets and liabilities to fair market value for GAAP purposes *but not for tax purposes.* For tax purposes, Acquiror records Target's assets and liabilities at Target's tax basis. This is called a "carryover" basis in Target's assets and liabilities for tax purposes. For further discussion on basis, see Taxes and M&A. (Ch.21)

To reconcile the GAAP and tax differences related to the additional depreciation on the GAAP books (because Target's balance sheet was adjusted to fair market value for GAAP accounting purposes) that does not take place for the tax accounting books (because Target's balance sheet was not adjusted to fair market value for tax accounting purposes), a deferred tax liability account must be created. The deferred tax liability created from the asset write-up is equal to the amount of the asset write-up multiplied by the tax rate. This concept is described in greater detail in Taxes and M&A. (Ch.21)

$$\text{Deferred tax liability created from write-up} = \text{asset write-up} \times \text{tax rate}$$

The fair market value of TeaCo's net PP&E was assumed to be $1,750 million, while the book value on Target's balance sheet of net PP&E was $1,000 million. An adjustment is required to account for the $750 million write-up ($1,750 million - $1,000 million). A deferred tax liability will be created for $300 million, which is equal to the asset write-up of $750 million multiplied by the tax rate of 40% ($750 × 40 percent).

Table 14.18 – Balance Sheet Adjustments Related to Asset Write-up

$ millions

Balance sheet adjustments related to asset write-up	
Fair market value of PP&E	$1,750
Book value of PP&E	$1,000
Asset write-up[1]	$750
Tax rate	40%
Deferred tax liability created from write-up[2]	$300

Balance sheet	**CoffeeCo**	**TeaCo**	**Adjustments**	**Pro forma[5]**
Cash	$300	$75		
Short-term assets	1,700	225		
Net PP&E[3]	12,000	1,000	$750	$13,750
Goodwill	0	200		
Total assets	$14,000	$1,500	$750	
Short-term debt	$500	$125		
Short-term liabilities	700	75		
Long-term debt	3,800	350		
Deferred tax liabilities[4]	300	25	$300	$625
Long-term liabilities	700	125		
Shareholders' equity	8,000	800		
Total liabilities and equity	$14,000	$1,500	$300	

[1] Fair market value of PP&E - book value of PP&E ($1,750 - $1,000)
[2] Asset write-up × tax rate ($750 × 0.4)
[3] In the adjustments column, net PP&E increases by $750, which is the amount of the asset write-up
[4] In the adjustments column, deferred tax liabilities increase by $300
[5] The pro forma column is the sum of the columns for Acquiror, Target, and Adjustments
Note: all adjustments are provided in Table 14.21 This shows only the first step, which is why the adjustments do not yet balance as they do in Table 14.20

If Target has any existing goodwill, it must be eliminated and new goodwill must be calculated. New goodwill is equal to the cost of Target's equity (purchase price of equity) less the fair market value of Target's assets and liabilities. Another method to calculate new goodwill is: the cost of Target's equity less the identifiable net asset value of Target (based on Target's pre-transaction book value), less any write-ups, plus any write-downs, plus any deferred tax liability created from any asset write-ups. The identifiable net asset value is Target's assets less liabilities less Target's existing (old) goodwill.

Goodwill Adjustment Calculation: Method 1

Purchase price of Target's equity

- Fair market value of Target's identifiable assets and liabilities

= New goodwill

Goodwill Adjustment Calculation: Method 2

Purchase price of Target's equity

- Net asset value of Target (book value of assets - liabilities, excluding Target goodwill)

- Value of asset write-ups and/or value of liability write-downs

+ Value of asset write-downs and/or value of liability write-ups

+ Deferred tax liability created from asset write-ups

- Deferred tax asset created from liability write-ups

= New goodwill

Goodwill is not "cost less book value"

A common mistake is to assume that goodwill is equal to the purchase price of Target's equity minus the net book value. This is incorrect. Goodwill is equal to the purchase price of Target's equity minus the fair market value of Target's identifiable assets and liabilities. Or said another way, new goodwill is the purchase price of Target's equity less the book value of Target's identifiable assets and liabilities *only after accounting for* write-ups and/or write-downs. This is why, in the calculation above, in addition to subtracting the net asset value, the value of any write-ups are subtracted, the value of any write-downs are added, and the value of any deferred tax liabilities created from the asset write-ups are added in order to calculate new goodwill.

Intangible assets and goodwill

Intangible assets (such as copyrights, patents, and customer lists) produce value, even if the asset itself cannot be seen or felt. In spite of the fact that these assets are intangible, they can be identified. Goodwill is also an intangible asset, but it is an *unidentifiable* asset since it is the residual value after all other identifiable assets and liabilities have been identified (and some portion of the purchase price has been allocated to them). Identifiable intangible assets must be amortized over their useful lives. The only caveat to that is the intangible asset of purchased in-process R&D. Any purchase price allocated to purchased in-process R&D must be expensed immediately. This treatment of in-process R&D, however, is under discussion by FASB.

To calculate the new goodwill generated in CoffeeCo's acquisition of TeaCo, begin with the transaction equity value paid to TeaCo shareholders of $3,000 million. In Table 14.19, new goodwill is calculated using both method 1 and method 2 described on the previous page. New goodwill in the transaction is $1,950 million. The adjustment to goodwill of $1,750 million is based on adding new goodwill of $1,950 million and eliminating TeaCo's old goodwill of $200 million.

Table 14.19 – Calculation and Recording of Goodwill Adjustment

$ millions

Calculation of goodwill adjustment

Method 1		
Transaction equity value		$3,000
Fair market value of identifiable assets		
Cash		(75)
Short-term assets		(225)
Net PP&E (based on adjusted fair market value)		(1,750)
Fair market value of liabilities		
Short-term debt		125
Short-term liabilities		75
Long-term debt		350
Deferred tax liabilities		325
Long-term liabilities		125
New goodwill[1]		$1,950
Method 2	Different methods but same answer	
Transaction equity value		$3,000
TeaCo's net asset value[2]		(600)
Asset write-up for PP&E		(750)
Deferred tax liability created by asset write-up		300
New goodwill[3]		$1,950
Eliminate old TeaCo goodwill[4]		(200)
Goodwill adjustment for balance sheet[5]		$1,750

[1]

FMV of Target's identifiable assets	$2,050
FMV of Target's identifiable liabilities	(1,000)
FMV of Target's net identifiable assets	$1,050
Transaction equity value	$3,000
FMV of Target's net identifiable assets	(1,050)
New goodwill	$1,950

[2] Book value of Target assets - liabilities - Target existing goodwill ($1,500 - $700 - $200)

[3] Equity value - net asset value - asset write-up + deferred tax liability ($3,000 - $600 - $750 + $300)

[4] In purchase accounting, Target's existing goodwill is eliminated

[5] New goodwill - Target existing goodwill (to eliminate Target goodwill) ($1,950 - $200)

Table 14.19 continued

$ millions

Balance sheet	CoffeeCo	TeaCo	Adjustments	Pro forma[1]
Cash	$300	$75		
Short-term assets	1,700	225		
Net PP&E[2]	12,000	1,000	$750	$13,750
Goodwill[3]	0	200	1,750	1,950
Total assets	$14,000	$1,500	$2,500	
Short-term debt	$500	$125		
Short-term liabilities	700	75		
Long-term debt	3,800	350		
Deferred tax liabilities[4]	300	25	$300	$625
Long-term liabilities	700	125		
Shareholders' equity	8,000	800		
Total liabilities and equity	$14,000	$1,500	$300	

[1] The pro forma column is the sum of the columns for Acquiror, Target and Adjustments
[2] See Table 14.18
[3] See Table 14.19
[4] Asset write-up × tax rate ($750 × 0.4)
Note: not all adjustments have been made yet

4b. Record new transaction-related debt and adjust Target's equity to fair market value

If debt is used to finance any part of the equity purchase price, this acquisition debt is recorded as an adjustment to the balance sheet as additional long-term debt. In addition, the adjustment to equity is equal to the amount of the Target equity purchase price paid for with equity less the book value of Target's equity. Another way to think of this concept is you will *write up* or *write down* the equity amount to an amount equal to the equity-financed portion of the purchase price.

Adjustment to equity

A common mistake is to write up Target's equity account to the equity purchase price ($3,000 million in our example). Target's equity should be written up to the amount of the equity consideration paid ($1,800 million in the example because only 60 percent of the $3,000 million equity purchase price was stock consideration; the other 40 percent was cash consideration). In a 100 percent stock transaction, the equity consideration paid is equal to the equity purchase price. However, in a 100 percent cash transaction, the equity consideration paid is equal to zero (because no equity was provided to Target's shareholders and therefore the fair market value of Target's equity is now zero). Therefore, the amount of the equity write-up or write-down (i.e., the equity adjustment) is equal to the equity purchase price multiplied by the percentage of equity paid in the transaction less the book value of Target's pre-transaction equity.

Transaction equity value
× Percentage of stock consideration
\- Target's pre-transaction book value of equity
= Transaction adjustment to Target's equity

A good way to test that the financial model is working properly is to enter an assumption of 100 percent cash and 0 percent stock. Then check to see that the adjustment for Target's equity is a negative amount (because Target's existing equity is eliminated in purchase accounting and there is no new equity since Acquiror is paying with 100 percent cash) equal to the book value of Target's pre-transaction shareholders' equity. In this situation, once the negative adjustment is added to Target's pre-transaction equity value, the pro forma value of Target's equity should be zero. If this is not the case, check the model since the equity adjustment is not being calculated properly.

CoffeeCo purchased TeaCo with 40 percent cash and 60 percent stock. With an equity purchase price of \$3,000 million, the value of the cash consideration is \$1,200 million (\$3,000 × 40 percent) and the value of the stock consideration is \$1,800 million (\$3,000 × 60 percent). The cash consideration of \$1,200 million is acquisition debt that must be included in the balance sheet as an adjustment to long-term debt. For equity, since TeaCo has an existing book value of equity of \$800 million and fair market value of the stock consideration paid for TeaCo is \$1,800 million, an adjustment of \$1,000 million to the equity account is required so that the new value of TeaCo's book equity is \$1,800 million.

Table 14.20 – Record Acquisition Debt and Adjust TeaCo's Equity

$ millions

Record acquisition debt and adjust value of TeaCo's equity

Transaction equity value	$3,000
Cash consideration	40%
Cash consideration[1]	$1,200
Equity consideration	60%
Equity consideration[2]	$1,800
TeaCo's existing book value of equity	$800
Write-up required for TeaCo's equity[3]	$1,000

Balance sheet	CoffeeCo	TeaCo	Adjustments	Pro forma[4]
Cash	$300	$75		
Short-term assets	1,700	225		
Net PP&E	12,000	1,000	$750	$13,750
Goodwill	0	200	1,750	1,950
Total assets	$14,000	$1,500	$2,500	
Short-term debt	$500	$125		
Short-term liabilities	700	75		
Long-term debt[5]	3,800	350	$1,200	$5,350
Deferred tax liabilities	300	25	300	625
Long-term liabilities	700	125		
Shareholders' equity[6]	8,000	800	1,000	9,800
Total liabilities and equity	$14,000	$1,500	$2,500	

[1] Equity purchase price × percentage of cash consideration ($3,000 × 0.4)
[2] Equity purchase price × percentage of stock consideration ($3,000 × 0.6)
[3] Equity consideration - Target's existing book value of equity ($1,800 - $800)
[4] The pro forma column is the sum of the columns for Acquiror, Target and Adjustments. Note: this column will only balance when filled in, as shown in the following Table 14.21
[5] Long-term debt increases by $1,200, which is the amount of the acquisition debt (cash consideration)
[6] Equity increases by $1,000, which is the amount of the equity adjustment calculated in Footnote 3

4c. Combine Acquiror and Target balance sheets (as adjusted)

Before adding up other components of Acquiror and Target's assets and liabilities, be sure to check that all balance sheet transaction adjustments balance. If they do not, go back and check the individual adjustments in the model. It is easier to find errors at this stage before actually adding up all the other parts of the balance sheets of Acquiror and Target.

Once all the transaction adjustments have been accounted for and balance, it is time to add up all the other items for Acquiror and Target. Once those have been added across (horizontally) to determine the pro forma value for each line item, the pro forma assets can be summed and the pro forma liabilities and shareholders' equity can be summed (vertically).

The only rows remaining to be added for the pro forma balance sheet are cash, short-term assets, short-term debt, short-term liabilities, and long-term liabilities.

Table 14.21 – Add Up All Other Balance Sheet Values

$ millions

Balance sheet	CoffeeCo	TeaCo	Adjustments	Pro forma[1]
Cash	$300	$75	-	$375
Short-term assets	1,700	225	-	1,925
Net PP&E	12,000	1,000	$750	13,750
Goodwill	0	200	1,750	1,950
Total assets	$14,000	$1,500	$2,500	$18,000
Short-term debt	$500	$125	-	$625
Short-term liabilities	700	75	-	775
Long-term debt	3,800	350	$1,200	5,350
Deferred tax liabilities	300	25	300	625
Long-term liabilities	700	125	-	825
Shareholders' equity	8,000	800	1,000	9,800
Total liabilities and equity	$14,000	$1,500	$2,500	$18,000

[1] The pro forma column is the sum of the columns for Acquiror, Target, and Adjustments

5a. Perform sensitivities on all major transaction assumptions

The last step should always be to perform sensitivity analysis in order to assess the sensitivity of the results to changes in key assumptions. Although we only show one sensitivity analysis here, it is common practice to perform sensitivity analysis on every key transaction assumption.

Let's review the sensitivity of results to changes in two key variables: the purchase price for TeaCo and the percentage of cash/stock consideration offered to TeaCo shareholders. Consider a range of purchase prices per TeaCo share from $36 to $44 in $2 increments. Let's also consider a range of cash consideration ranging from zero percent to 100 percent of the equity purchase price, in 20 percent increments. We will consider the impact of these two assumptions on CoffeeCo's 2007 EPS accretion/dilution. The boxed items in Table 14.22 are results based on the initial transaction assumptions of $40 per TeaCo share and 40 percent cash consideration.

Table 14.22 – Sensitivity Analysis for 2007 EPS accretion/dilution

2007 EPS accretion/dilution for CoffeeCo ($ per share)

		Offer price per TeaCo share				
		$36	$38	$40	$42	$44
Percentage	0%	($0.04)	($0.06)	($0.08)	($0.01)	($0.12)
of cash	20%	($0.02)	($0.04)	($0.06)	($0.07)	($0.09)
consideration	40%	$0.01	($0.00)	($0.03)	($0.05)	($0.06)
	60%	$0.04	$0.02	$0.00	($0.02)	($0.03)
	80%	$0.07	$0.05	$0.04	$0.02	$0.00
	100%	$0.10	$0.09	$0.07	$0.06	$0.04

2007 EPS accretion/dilution for CoffeeCo (% change)

		Offer price per TeaCo share				
		$36	$38	$40	$42	$44
Percentage	0%	(2.3%)	(3.3%)	(4.3%)	(5.3%)	(6.3%)
of cash	20%	(1.0%)	(2.0%)	(3.0%)	(4.0%)	(4.9%)
consideration	40%	0.5%	(0.5%)	(1.5%)	(2.5%)	(3.4%)
	60%	2.0%	1.1%	0.1%	(0.8%)	(1.8%)
	80%	3.7%	2.8%	1.9%	1.0%	0.1%
	100%	5.6%	4.7%	3.9%	3.0%	2.1%

Notice in Table 14.22 that as the amount of cash/debt used to fund the transaction increases, so does EPS accretion. This is because, in general, financing an acquisition with debt is less expensive than financing it with equity. As a result, as the use of cash increases (a less expensive form of capital), the transaction becomes more accretive. However, it is important to remember that at some point this increased leverage (in spite of being a lower-cost form of capital) will become so great that it will actually decrease Acquiror's value by putting downward pressure on Acquiror's P/E multiple as the capital structure becomes overweighted with debt. At that point, the value decrease in Acquiror results from the fact that the risk of bankruptcy is greater than the benefit of lower-cost capital.

Growth Rate Analysis

One of the biggest drivers of a higher P/E multiple is a higher expected growth rate. As a result, a primary reason companies undertake M&A transactions is to increase the company growth rate (given the company's risk appetite), with the expectation of being rewarded with a higher pro forma P/E multiple, and therefore stock price. The metric by which growth rates are often measured is the long-term EPS growth rate (calculated as the CAGR or the compound annual growth rate) for a projected period of three to five years.

$$\text{CAGR} = [(\text{last period value} / \text{first period value})^{[1/(n-1)]}] - 1$$

Where n = number of periods

CoffeeCo's long- term growth rate pre-transaction is 5.2 percent. Pro forma the transaction, Acquiror's compound annual growth rate increases to 6.0 percent. The transaction therefore is accretive to Acquiror's long-term growth rate even though the transaction is dilutive to EPS in the first years.

PEG Ratio

In general, companies with higher growth rates tend to trade at higher P/E multiples. In order to uncover potential disparities between a company's growth rate and its P/E multiple, the PEG ratio, or P/E to growth rate, is calculated.

$$\text{PEG ratio} = (\text{P/E} / \text{growth rate}) \times 100$$

For example, TeaCo, has a 2006 P/E multiple of 16x and a long term growth rate of 10%. As a result, TeaCo would have a PEG ratio of 1.6x [(16 / 0.10) × 100 = 1.6x]. In contrast, CoffeeCo, has a 2006 P/E multiple of 14.3x and a long term growth rate of 5%. As a result, CoffeeCo would have a PEG ratio of 2.9x [(14.3 / 0.05) × 100 = 2.9x].

Table 14.23 – Growth Rate Analysis

	2006E	2007E	2008E	2009E
CoffeeCo pre-transaction EPS	$1.75	$1.85	$1.94	$2.04
CoffeeCo year-on-year growth rate[1]		5.7%	5.0%	5.0%
CoffeeCo pre-transaction EPS CAGR[2]				**5.2%**
TeaCo pre-transaction EPS	$2.00	$2.25	$2.48	$2.72
TeaCo year-on-year growth rate[1]		12.5%	10.0%	10.0%
TeaCo pre-transaction EPS CAGR[2]				10.8%
Pro forma EPS	$1.72	$1.82	$1.93	$2.05
Pro forma year-on-year growth rate[1]		5.7%	6.2%	6.2%
Pro forma EPS CAGR[2]				**6.0%**
Growth rate accretion/dilution: year-on-year[3]		0.0%	1.2%	1.2%
Growth rate accretion/dilution: compound annual growth[4]				0.8%

[1] (Future year EPS / previous year EPS) - 1
[2] (2009E EPS / 2006E EPS) $^{(1/3)}$ - 1
[3] (Pro forma year-on-year growth) - (Acquiror year-on-year growth pre-transaction)
[4] (Pro forma growth rate) - (Acquiror pre-transaction growth rate)
Note: Numbers may not tie due to rounding. All numbers in the tables are from a financial model.

Equity Method

Recall from Figure 14.5 that the **equity method** of accounting for investments is used if the investor has significant influence over Target's operating and financial policies. While the method is usually used when the investor company owns 20 to 50 percent of the target company, the 20 to 50 percent threshold is only a guideline. The equity method of accounting is required if the percentage of voting stock owned by the investor company, *in conjunction with other factors*, gives the investor company the capacity to exercise significant influence (but not control) over the operating and financial policies of the target company. In addition to the percentage of voting stock owned, other indicators that the investor company has significant influence over the target company include:

1. Representation by the investor company on investee's board of directors
2. Involvement by the investor company in any policy making of investee
3. Material reliance by investee on the investor company or vice versa
4. A significant influence by the investor company over investee in comparison to other shareholders

Other factors in addition to these might also be used to prove or disprove the test of significant influence. If evidence exists to disprove significant influence, the investor company must use the available-for-sale method (if a fair market value for the security exists) or the cost method of accounting (if no readily available fair market value for the security exists). If the equity method of accounting is not used and the investor company owns greater than 20 percent of the target company, the reason for not using the equity method must be disclosed in the investor company's financial statements.

The accounting implications of using the equity method of accounting are described below.

- For GAAP accounting, an investment in Target using the equity method is initially recorded on the balance sheet at cost (this is consistent with the GAAP principle that items be recorded on the balance sheet at fair market value). The investment account is usually called "investments in affiliates."

- Acquiror recognizes income each year based on the proportionate share of earnings or loss earned by Target. Target's earnings or loss might be different from any dividends paid to shareholders.

- Under the equity method, an assumption is usually made that all earnings of Target will be distributed to shareholders as dividends. Therefore, the dividend tax liability that flows through the income statement is based on Target's earnings recognized in the period. The dividends-received deduction (DRD) is applied when calculating the GAAP tax liability. For tax purposes, taxes would be due on any dividend income received from Target (after accounting for the DRD deduction). If the tax liability recognized on the GAAP income statement is different from the actual cash tax payment (which is often the case), a deferred tax liability would be created to reconcile the difference. Deferred taxes as well as other differences between GAAP and tax accounting are described in Taxes and M&A. (Ch.21)

DRD rules as of 2005

If a corporation owns stock in another corporation, the IRS currently allows the investor company to exclude a percentage of the dividends received from the target company prior to determining the tax liability owed by the investor company on the dividends received. These are called **dividends-received deduction** (DRD) rules. As of 2005, DRD rules allowed the following:

- If a corporation owns less than 20 percent of the common stock of another corporation, 70 percent of the dividends received can be excluded from the taxable income when calculating the tax liability.

- If a corporation owns more than 20 percent but less than 80 percent of the common stock of another corporation, 80 percent of the dividends received can be excluded from the taxable income when calculating the tax liability.

- If a corporation owns greater than 80 percent of the common stock of another company (vote and value), the corporation can consolidate the subsidiary for tax purposes and therefore exclude 100 percent of any dividends received. This is called tax consolidation and is further described in Taxes and M&A. (Ch.21)

It is important to note that DRD rates can, and do, change so consult with a tax specialist on the current DRD rates when working on a live transaction.

- Acquiror's proportionate share of Target's earnings or loss flow through Acquiror's income statement, into shareholders' equity via retained earnings, and into the investment in affiliates account on the asset side of Acquiror's balance sheet. Acquiror's investment in Target as well as its proportionate share of Target's earnings and losses is usually shown as a one-line item on Acquiror's balance sheet. In accounting parlance, this is referred to as **one-line consolidation**.

- Acquiror does not record its proportionate share of Target's dividends on its income statement. Dividends are treated as a return on capital and reduce the investment in affiliates account on the asset side of Acquiror's balance sheet. Dividends received, less taxes owed on the dividends, also increase Acquiror's cash.

- Unlike the available-for-sale method, there is no periodic fair market value exercise involved in the equity method.

- A sale or a write-down of the investment resulting from a valuation test could reduce the value of the investment on the balance sheet.

- When Acquiror sells its stock in Target, Acquiror realizes capital gain or loss for book purposes based on the selling price and the book value of the investment (which has been updated periodically for Acquiror's share of Target's earnings and losses as well as for dividend distributions). Capital gain and loss are described in Taxes and M&A. (Ch.21)

- From an accretion/dilution standpoint, Acquiror recognizes its proportionate share of Target's earnings or losses as well as the tax liability on dividends received. Acquiror also needs to account for how it paid for the investment. For example, if Acquiror used debt to pay for the acquisition, the accretion/dilution analysis must account for the cost of financing the acquisition debt. If Acquiror issued stock to Target in exchange for shares of Target, the newly issued shares must be added to shares outstanding in the accretion/dilution analysis. As a note, in the U.S. it is not common for Acquiror to issue shares to Target shareholders in exchange for less than 50 percent of Target, although it does happen occasionally. These types of cross-holdings are more common in Europe, Asia, and Latin America.

- The fair market value paid for Target is likely to be different (most likely higher) than the book value of Target on Target's balance sheet. In equity method accounting, Target does not revalue its balance sheet to fair market value the way it does in purchase accounting (when using the consolidation method, which is described in the previous section). However, Acquiror must allocate its purchase of Target's equity to identifiable assets and liabilities of Target (just as it would in purchase accounting). If any of the purchase price is allocated to a write-up of a depreciable asset of Target, Acquiror must recognize **"phantom amortization"** or **"phantom depreciation"** of any phantom write-ups. They are considered "phantom" because they do not flow through Acquiror's income statement nor do they flow through any of Target's financial statements. The amortization or depreciation from any asset write-ups of depreciable assets only flows through Acquiror's balance sheet as a reduction to the investment in affiliates account with a corresponding reduction in the other comprehensive equity account.

Table 14.24 – Effect of Equity Method Accounting

	Income Statement: Net income	Balance Sheet: Assets	Balance Sheet: Liabilities and Equity
Initial investment	No effect	Increase assets, and (1) Decrease cash, and/or[1]	(2) Increase debt or common equity[1]
Adjustment to fair market value	No effect	No effect	No effect
Share of Target's earnings/(losses)	Increase/(decrease) net income	Increase/(decrease) assets	Increase/(decrease) retained earnings (equity)
Share of Target's dividends	No effect	Decrease assets, and Increase cash	No effect
Taxes due on dividends	Decrease net income by book taxes	Decrease cash by cash taxes	Decrease retained earnings (equity) for book taxes and increase or decrease deferred tax liability for the difference between book and cash taxes
Phantom depreciation of write-ups of Target's depreciable assets	No effect	Decrease assets	Decrease other comprehensive income (equity)

[1] Depending on how the initial investment is financed, with cash and/or stock, respectively

Cost and Available-For-Sale Methods

Both the **cost method** and the **available-for-sale method** are used if neither "control" nor "significant influence" can be proved (and if the equity security is not purchased as part of a trading operation). In general, one of these two methods is used if Acquiror owns less than 20 percent of Target's common voting stock and if the stock is not owned as part of a trading operation. The 20-percent rule, however, is a guideline more than a hard rule. The real test is whether "control" or "significant influence" over Target can be proved. Both the cost method and the available-for-sale method recognize that no significant influential relationship exists between Acquiror and Target and that the investment by Acquiror in Target is passive. Since preferred stock owners generally do not exert control in the company, preferred stock investments are generally accounted for using the available-for-sale method (if the fair market value of the security is readily available) or the cost method of accounting (if the fair market value of the security is not readily available).

The principal difference between the cost method and the available-for-sale method is that the available-for-sale method is used if the fair market value of the investment (i.e., the value of Target's equity) is readily available. A security is deemed to have a readily available fair market value if the security trades on an organized trading exchange such as the NYSE or the NASDAQ or in OTC trading in which public market values are readily available.

With the available-for-sale method, Acquiror must adjust the carrying value of the investment in Target to the fair market value in its financial statements. Because of this, the available-for-sale method is also referred to as a form of **marked-to-market accounting**. The difference between the initial cost of the investment and the fair market value is **unrealized gain or loss**.

- If the fair market value is greater than the historical cost, the investor company has an **unrealized gain** related to the investment.

- If the fair market value is less than the historical cost, the investor company has an **unrealized loss** related to the investment.

Unrealized gain or loss bypasses the income statement and flows directly to the shareholders' equity account via "other comprehensive income," which is a component of equity. The gain or loss becomes "realized" when the investment is sold, transferred or disposed of. At that point, the realized gain or loss flows through the income statement. The distinction between trading securities and non-trading securities is an important one because unrealized gains or losses flow through net income for trading securities, but not for available-for-sale securities.

The cost method of accounting is used if the fair market value of the equity security is not readily available. If no public market for the equity security exists and no readily available fair market value exists, then the investor company does not have to record the investment at fair market value or record unrealized gains or losses in shareholders' equity. The cost method investment is recorded at cost and no periodic adjustments need to be made.

SEC Rule 13D

The SEC has a disclosure requirement for investors in equity securities. If an investor (either another company, an individual investor, or an investment company on behalf of investors) beneficially owns five percent or more of a publicly traded company, the investor is subject to SEC Rule 13D and must disclose the investment. **SEC Rule 13D** requires that if an investor beneficially owns greater than five percent of a publicly traded company, the investor must disclose in a public filing the number of shares it owns on a periodic basis, among other things. The company itself also must disclose any 13D investors in an annual proxy statement. The 13D investors can usually be found in the section titled "Beneficial Ownership of Shares" in a company's annual proxy statement. The annual proxy statement is mailed to shareholders prior to the annual shareholder meeting and can be found on the SEC's website (www.sec.gov) under form DEF-14A along with the company's other SEC filings.

The cost method and the available-for-sale method are described together in this chapter because, from an EPS accretion/dilution standpoint, the mechanics are generally the same. Differences do arise, however, with respect to the balance sheet. The accounting implications of using the cost method of accounting and the available-for-sale method of accounting are provided below. Any differences between the two methods are described where appropriate.

- For GAAP accounting, an investment in Target is initially recorded on the balance sheet at cost (this is consistent with the GAAP principle that items be recorded on the balance sheet at fair market value).

- The historical cost is maintained on the balance sheet going forward when using the cost method of accounting.

- With the available-for-sale method, the fair market value of the investment is updated each reporting period with the investor recognizing unrealized gains and losses on its balance sheet. Unrealized gains or losses, however, do not flow through the income statement and therefore do not affect net income. Instead, unrealized gains and losses flow directly into shareholders' equity through the equity account named "other comprehensive income."

- For both methods, Acquiror recognizes income each year based on the proportionate share of dividends received from Target.

- Taxes would be due on any dividend income received from Target according to dividends-received deduction (DRD) rules. Unrealized gains and losses are not recognized for tax purposes until a sale occurs. However, since unrealized gains and losses are recognized for GAAP, a deferred tax benefit or liability would be recognized on the GAAP books based on any unrealized gain or loss.

- Dividends received (less taxes) from Target flow through Acquiror's net income and ultimately into Acquiror's shareholders' equity via retained earnings.

- Acquiror does not record its proportionate share of Target's earnings or losses in either its income statement or in its balance sheet. Only dividends received are recognized.

- A write-down of the investment resulting from a valuation test could reduce the value of the investment on the asset side. Write-downs occur when there has been a permanent reduction in value; write-downs are not taken when there has only been a temporary decline in value.

- When Acquiror sells its stock in Target, Acquiror will "realize" a capital gain or loss for the difference between the selling price and the book value of the investment (which, for investments using the available-for-sale method, has been updated periodically for changes in the fair market value of Target's equity and for cost method investments is equal to the historical cost). At the time of sale, "realized" capital gain or loss would flow through the income statement. Capital gain and loss are described in Taxes and M&A. (Ch.21)

- From an accretion/dilution standpoint, Acquiror recognizes its proportionate share of dividends received less the tax liability from its investment in Target as additional income. Acquiror also needs to account for how it paid for the investment. For example, if Acquiror used debt to pay for the acquisition, the accretion/dilution analysis must account for the cost of financing the acquisition debt. If Acquiror issued stock in exchange for shares of Target, the newly issued shares must be added to shares outstanding in the accretion/dilution analysis. As a note, in the U.S. it is not common (although it does occasionally happen) for Acquiror to issue equity to Target in exchange for less than 20 percent ownership of Target. These types of cross-holdings are more common in Europe, Asia, and Latin America.

Table 14.25 summarizes the effect of an available-for-sale method investment and cost method investment on Acquiror's financial statements.

Table 14.25 – Effect of Available-for-Sale Method and Cost Method

Available-for-sale method	Income Statement: Net income	Balance Sheet: Assets	Balance Sheet: Liabilities and Equity
Initial investment	No effect	Increase assets, and (1) Decrease cash, and/or[1]	(2) Increase debt or equity[1]
Adjustment to fair market value	No adjustment	Increase/ decrease assets based on unrealized gain/loss	Increase/decrease other comprehensive income (equity) based on unrealized gain/loss
Share of Target's earnings	No effect	No effect	No effect
Share of Target's dividends	Increase net income	Increase cash	Increase retained earnings (equity)
Cash taxes due on dividends	Decrease net income	Decrease cash	Decrease retained earnings (equity)

Cost method	Income Statement: Net income	Balance Sheet: Assets	Balance Sheet: Liabilities and Equity
Initial investment	No effect	Increase assets, and (1) Decrease cash, and/or[1]	(2) Increase debt or equity[1]
Adjustment to fair market value	No adjustment	No adjustment	No adjustment
Share of Target's earnings	No effect	No effect	No effect
Share of Target's dividends	Increase net income	Increase cash	Increase retained earnings (equity)
Cash taxes due on dividends	Decrease net income	Decrease cash	Decrease retained earnings (equity)

[1] Depending on how the initial investment is financed, with cash and/or stock. respectively

Acquisition Currency

Chapter 15

The more alternatives,
the more difficult the choice.

Abbe D' Allaniva

Just as with any item that is purchased, when an asset or company is acquired it must be paid for. Sounds simple enough. But how are assets and companies actually *paid* for?

Most individual assets are paid for with cash. When a company is purchased, it can be paid for with cash, Acquiror's stock, notes or some combination of the three. Notes (which are essentially IOUs and are often referred to as "seller's paper") are not as common as cash or stock; and when they are used it is usually for smaller or private deals. Payment (or, to borrow a term from contract law, consideration) can also be tied to future results, such as is the case with an earnout agreement. **Earnout agreements** are payments made to Seller long after the transaction has closed (usually one to three years) and are usually tied to Target's future financial results. However, for now let's keep things simple and discuss cash and stock transactions.

The **consideration** (the cash or stock) with which Acquiror pays for Target is referred to as the **acquisition currency**. If cash is used as acquisition currency, Acquiror will either use cash that it has on hand in its bank accounts or it will borrow cash by taking on debt either from a bank or from debt investors. In M&A parlance, the acquisition currency terms "using cash" (funded by debt) or "using debt" are used interchangeably. If stock is used as acquisition currency, Acquiror will issue Acquiror stock in exchange for Target stock. Acquiror can also pay for Target with cash and then subsequently raise new equity in the capital markets. This second step is used if Target prefers cash over stock but if Acquiror prefers to finance the acquisition with equity over cash.

And to whom does Acquiror pay the acquisition currency? Acquiror pays the owner or owners of whatever is being sold. The owner or owners is considered the Seller.

As shown in Figure 15.1, if Acquiror buys assets or a subsidiary from another company, it will pay the selling company from which it is buying the assets or subsidiary.

Acquiror will not pay the shareholders of the selling company. The selling company owns the assets or subsidiary being sold. Therefore, the selling company is the Seller and Seller is the recipient of the payment (either cash or stock) from Acquiror.

Figure 15.1 – Buying Assets or a Subsidiary from a Company

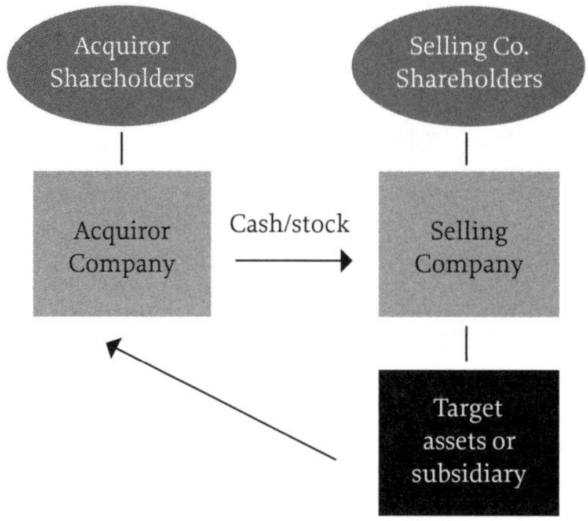

As shown in Figure 15.2, if Acquiror purchases the stock of another company (Target) and/or merges Acquiror with Target, Acquiror either buys the shares of Target directly from or exchanges Acquiror shares with Target shareholders. Cash or stock is paid to Target shareholders. The shareholders are the owners of Target and so the shareholders are the Sellers who receive the payment (either cash or stock) from Acquiror.

Figure 15.2 – Buying Another Company

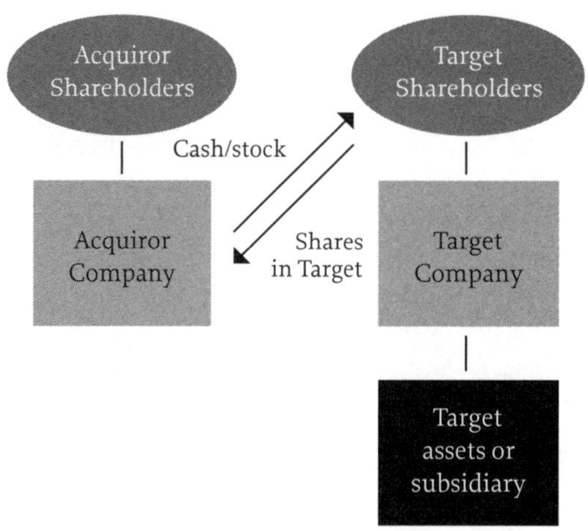

Cash vs. Stock Consideration

Whether Acquiror uses cash or stock has many implications for all the parties involved. These considerations are summarized below and discussed in more detail in the following section.

Key considerations of using cash or stock for Acquiror include:

1. The dilution to ownership for Acquiror shareholders
2. The accretion or dilution impact on earnings per share and earnings per share growth rates for Acquiror shareholders
3. The impact on Acquiror's balance sheet, cash flow, financial flexibility, and credit rating if cash/debt is used
4. Any tax benefits arising out of the transaction
5. Attractiveness of Acquiror's stock to other parties

Key considerations of using cash or stock for Seller include:

1. The value received in the transaction (including any protection of that value if stock is used as acquisition currency)
2. Any tax liabilities triggered by the transaction
3. Seller's desire to hold Acquiror's stock, if stock is received
4. Fiduciary duties of the board of directors related to selling the company for cash or stock

In most (but not all) cases, it will be more expensive for Acquiror to issue stock (or use equity) for Target than to pay with cash (or use debt). The cost/benefit of issuing debt vs. equity is described in Credit Analysis and Sources of Capital. (Ch.24,25) At the end of this chapter, situations in which equity is less expensive than debt are described.

The choice of acquisition currency depends on the goal, since the goal often dictates the answer. Thus the question of acquisition currency partly depends on what a company can "afford" in terms of dilution or balance sheet impact. The tradeoff varies from company to company and it is up to a company's management and board to determine the appropriate acquisition currency based on its own strategic and financial priorities at the time of the transaction.

For Acquiror, the choice of acquisition currency affects both the income statement, namely earnings per share, and the balance sheet, namely leverage.

- In terms of the income statement, namely EPS (which is calculated by dividing net income by fully diluted shares outstanding):

a. An all cash offer increases interest expense but does not affect shares outstanding (all other things being equal, the numerator of the EPS calculation decreases but there is no change to the denominator).

b. The reverse happens with an all stock offer; there is no change to interest expense but shares outstanding increase (the denominator of the EPS calculation increases but there is no change to the numerator).

- In terms of the balance sheet impact, namely leverage,

  a. An all cash offer increases total debt, decreases financial flexibility and degrades credit quality.

  b. Since an all stock offer entails the issuance of equity, an all stock offer reduces total debt as a percentage of total equity, increases financial flexibility and improves credit ratios.

In general, if Acquiror has strong credit, strong cash flow and unused debt capacity on its balance sheet, it will tend toward issuing debt in order to achieve the lowest after-tax cost of funding. By not issuing equity to Target, Acquiror will not dilute the ownership of its shareholders. However if Acquiror has weak credit, weak cash flow or not much debt capacity, it will tend toward issuing stock in order to strengthen its credit ratios and balance sheet.

The confluence of credit, earnings, and valuation is dynamic, not static, so the optimal cash/stock mix in an acquisition depends on the desire to maintain or improve credit vs. the desire to improve earnings growth. In practice, sensitivities should be performed based on various acquisition scenarios. In addition, multiple factors influence the ultimate decision on cash vs. stock consideration, including the sensitivity analyses, Acquiror's priorities, the number of other bidders (if in an auction scenario), tax implications and Target's priorities. In the following section the major considerations of using all cash, all stock, or some combination of cash and stock are described in more detail.

100 Percent Cash Consideration

The principal implications of using all cash as the acquisition currency are listed below.

1. ***Increase in interest expense:*** Every source of capital has a cost. In the case of cash, it is the interest expense that must be paid on the borrowed funds or the loss of interest income from using cash on hand. Since interest expense is tax-deductible, the annual cost of using cash in an acquisition is the *after-tax*

cost of debt based on the interest rate Acquiror would pay on the acquisition debt. The financial impact of using cash as acquisition currency is described in Accretion/Dilution Analysis. (Ch.14)

2. ***Acquisition likely to degrade credit quality:*** In general, a transaction paid for with all cash will degrade Acquiror's credit quality since it usually results in increased leverage and reduced interest coverage ratios. However, this is not always the case and there are additional considerations beside just the credit ratios. If Target has more business risk than Acquiror, a transaction will likely increase the overall credit risk of the newly combined entity, regardless of whether stock or cash is used. Also, if Target is highly leveraged on a stand-alone basis, then adding its existing debt plus the acquisition debt will almost certainly negatively affect Acquiror's credit ratios. However, if Target has better credit quality than Acquiror, a transaction could help diversify and reduce Acquiror's credit risk, even if cash were used. Also, if Target has little or no leverage then it is possible that, even with the additional acquisition debt, Acquiror's credit ratios stay the same or even improve. Issues related to credit risk and credit quality are described in Credit Analysis. (Ch.24)

3. ***No increase in shares outstanding:*** If the purchase is paid for with all cash, no shares of equity are issued. Since shares are representative of ownership and no shares are issued, there is no dilution in ownership for Acquiror shareholders. This should not be confused with dilution in earnings or cash flow; either or both of these still might be diluted even if ownership is not diluted. Calculations to determine EPS and cash flow accretion/dilution are provided in Accretion/Dilution Analysis. (Ch.14)

4. ***Sale for cash is a sale of the company:*** A sale for cash triggers certain fiduciary duties for Target's board of directors with regard to the value received in the transaction. In contrast, in an all stock transaction there is continuity in the shareholders' interest; Target shareholders receive stock in Acquiror and will continue to share in the economic benefits of the new company after the transaction has closed. In a sale for cash, however, Target shareholders have no ongoing interest in the new company. They receive a price per share for their stock and that's the end of their participation in Target. Target shareholders relinquish control of the company and Target management and the board must be able to prove (if contested in court) that Target shareholders received the best value reasonably available for the company (this is normally the highest cash price, but not always). This burden of proof generally requires that Target either undertake a public auction or perform a "market check" with other potential acquirors to see if those other potential acquirors might be willing to offer a higher price for Target. Fiduciary obligations of the board of directors are discussed in The Deal Team. (Ch.19)

5. ***Taxable event to Target shareholders:*** A sale for cash is a taxable event in the eyes of the IRS. If the sale price is greater than Target shareholder's tax basis, the shareholder would owe tax on any capital gain recognized. In an all stock deal (or a deal with consideration comprised of at least 40 percent stock and 60 percent cash[1]), the Target shareholder's basis rolls over into the new stock and the shareholder will not owe tax on the stock consideration received until she sells it, subject to certain limitations and structuring requirements. The cash component of consideration received is always taxable immediately. Tax considerations are discussed in Taxes and M&A. (Ch.21)

6. ***Acquiror captures 100 percent of the upside and downside of the merged entity:*** After the close of the sale, Target's shareholders no longer have any ownership interest in Target. As a result, Acquiror receives 100 percent of Target's performance under all circumstances – good or bad. This can result in increased risk for Acquiror with a commensurate increase in potential returns.

100 Percent Stock Consideration

Just as with an all cash deal, the use of all stock as consideration has certain implications which are listed below.

1. ***Increase in shares outstanding:*** Every source of capital has a cost. In the case of equity, it is the additional shares issued to Target shareholders. Issuing additional shares dilutes the current shareholders' ownership. More important than ownership dilution is whether the company's earnings or cash flow per share are diluted by the transaction. The financial impact of using stock as acquisition currency is described in Accretion/Dilution Analysis. (Ch.14)

2. ***Acquisition may improve credit quality:*** Since issuing equity leads to a larger equity base and therefore a larger denominator in leverage ratio calculations, issuing stock generally improves credit ratios. In most situations, using all stock will improve Acquiror's balance sheet and credit quality. However, if Target has higher credit risk than Acquiror, there is the possibility that even an all stock transaction may degrade Acquiror's credit profile. Ultimately it depends on Target's size relative to Acquiror's. If Target is so small that an acquisition will not affect Acquiror's credit risk or credit quality, the credit

[1] The 40 percent stock/60 percent cash threshold is not part of the IRS tax code. It is guidance based on an IRS ruling on precedent tax-free reorganizations structured as a direct merger or a forward triangular merger. The cash limit is reduced to 20 percent in a reverse triangular merger (also based on guidance). No cash is possible to maintain tax-free treatment in a stock-for-stock exchange. Please review tax-free reorganizations in Taxes and M&A and consult a tax attorney if working on a live transaction. (Ch.21)

impact is less of an issue. However, if Target comprises a meaningful portion of the new company, then Target's credit quality is a very important consideration. Issues related to credit risk and credit quality are described in Credit Analysis. (Ch.24)

3. ***Sharing of the upside and downside with Target:*** Since shares represent an ownership interest in a company, by exchanging their stock for Acquiror stock, Target's shareholders *exchange* their ownership interest in Target for an ownership interest in the newly merged entity (which now includes Acquiror and Target). Thus, after the close of the sale, Target's former shareholders no longer have an ownership interest in Target but they do have an ownership interest in the new company. As a result, Acquiror and Target shareholders both share in the new company's operating and financial performance – good or bad – as well as any value created in the form of synergies.

4. ***Fixed vs. floating exchange ratio and the protection of value:*** In an all stock deal, Acquiror needs to determine whether it wants to offer a floating exchange ratio with fixed value or a fixed exchange ratio with floating value. If the deal is structured with a fixed exchange ratio and floating value, Target might require some level of protection with a cap or collar to ensure that a certain baseline of value is received at closing. Protecting value in a stock transaction is discussed in Stock Deals. (Ch.16)

5. ***Not a sale of the company:*** Relative to the sale of the company for cash (whereby Revlon duties are triggered), a sale for 100 percent stock is not necessarily considered a sale of control of the company since control transfers from one unaffiliated group of public shareholders to another. Fiduciary obligations of the board of directors are discussed in The Deal Team. (Ch.19)

6. ***Not a taxable event for Target shareholders:*** Generally, an all stock transaction can be structured as a tax-free reorganization. Target shareholders roll their tax basis in Target shares into their new Acquiror shares. No capital gains tax will be paid by the shareholders of Target in an all stock transaction (unless they sell their shares in the open market for cash), subject to certain limitations. Tax considerations are discussed in Taxes and M&A. (Ch.21)

7. ***Due diligence is required by Target on Acquiror's stock:*** If Target shareholders agree to receive Acquiror stock in exchange for their own, Target management and board must assess the risks related to accepting Acquiror stock prior to agreeing to a transaction. Although some deal protection measures exist to protect the value of the consideration between the time of announcement to closing, these typically cease when the deal closes. The purpose of Target's due diligence on Acquiror is to investigate and, to the extent possible, ensure

that no major downside scenarios exist such that the value of the stock Target shareholders receive as consideration could fall in value materially relative to Target's current value. The board typically hires one or more investment banks to provide an external fairness opinion related to the consideration received in the transaction. The investment banks would consider the consideration in addition to the liquidity of Acquiror stock and any governance arrangements which may influence future decision making. Due diligence is discussed in Deal Mechanics. (Ch.20)

8. ***Shareholder vote might be required:*** If Acquiror is issuing 20 percent or more of its pre-transaction shares outstanding in the proposed transaction, a shareholder vote by Acquiror shareholders may be required in addition to the vote of Target's shareholders. This is a stock exchange rule for companies listed on either the NASDAQ or the NYSE. Shareholder votes are discussed in Deal Mechanics. (Ch.20)

Cash/Stock Combinations

Instead of using all cash or all stock, many Acquirors use a mixture of cash and stock to tailor the structure to their specific needs. The benefits of using a combination of cash and stock are listed below.

1. ***Can be tailored to the optimal blend of EPS dilution and balance sheet impact:*** The cost of equity and the cost of debt will depend on many factors, including the P/E ratio of Acquiror and the prevailing interest rate environment, respectively. In most cases, however, the cost of debt will be lower than the cost of equity and the lowest acquisition cost will be achieved with the highest percentage of debt. An all cash deal might impact Acquiror's balance sheet too adversely but an all stock deal might be too dilutive to the current shareholders. Therefore, using some stock and some cash allows Acquiror the ability to tailor the cash/stock mix, resulting in an optimal tradeoff between balance sheet impact and EPS dilution.

2. ***Restrictions may exist to obtain tax-free treatment for equity consideration:*** All M&A transactions are either taxable or nontaxable (more properly named as tax-deferred) transactions. Not surprisingly, all other things being equal, tax-deferred transactions are preferred. Many times, making a transaction nontaxable is an important strategic priority, and much effort goes into creating and executing a nontaxable transaction. Over time the IRS has developed strict guidelines on how a transaction must be structured in order for it to be treated as a nontaxable transaction. Using a combination of cash and stock may allow the parties to maintain tax-free treatment on the stock portion of the consideration while still allowing some cash to be paid to

Target shareholders. Tax-free reorganizations are described in more detail in Taxes and M&A. (Ch.21)

Is Equity Ever Cheaper Than Debt?

From an EPS accretion/dilution perspective, are there any circumstances in which the cost of equity is actually lower than the cost of debt? Yes, although it is not common and only occurs when a company has a "supercharged acquisition currency," which means that the company's shares are trading at a very high price-to-earnings (P/E) ratio.

First it may be helpful to review how the price of a share of stock is determined. Shares of a company usually trade as a multiple of that company's earnings per share, or EPS (or whatever valuation metric is relevant for a particular company). The multiple at which companies trade is called the P/E multiple, and the P/E multiple multiplied by EPS equals the company's share price. A company that has EPS of $1 in 2006 and is currently valued at 10x earnings (meaning it has a 10x P/E multiple) will have a stock price of $10 per share ($1 EPS × 10 P/E = $10 share price).

What does this actually mean? This means that a shareholder earns $1 in earnings, or 10 percent, for every $10 of share price paid ($1 in earnings / $10 share price = 10 percent). Recall from Strategic Transactions (Ch.4) that using a P/E multiple method of valuation is a proxy for the perpetuity method of valuation and that the inverse of the P/E multiple is a proxy for the discount rate to an equity holder.

The inverse of the P/E multiple, or 10 percent in the example above, represents many things:

1.The dollar cost of equity; *which is also referred to as*

2.The after-tax cost of equity or earnings yield; *and it also represents*

3.The earnings power of the equity.

Now compare this to the dollar cost of debt. If the cost of debt is 8 percent pretax and the company has a marginal tax rate of 40 percent, then its after-tax cost of debt is 4.8 percent.

8% pretax interest rate × (1 – 40 percent tax rate) = 4.8% after-tax interest rate

In this example, the 10 percent cost of equity is more *expensive* than the 4.8 percent after-tax cost of debt. Note that the cost of equity is already an after-tax cost because earnings per share (the E of the P/E ratio) is an after-tax number whereas the cost of debt must be tax effected because it is a pretax number (and all comparisons must be between similar numbers). If this is not entirely clear, think about what items are pretax and which items are after-tax on an income statement.

Figure 15.3 - Comparision of Pretax and After-tax Line Items

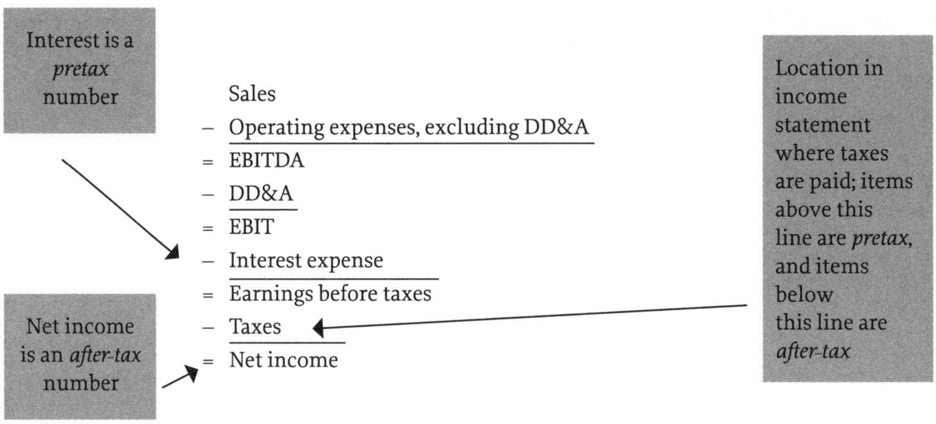

Let's look at a few additional examples of the cost of equity compared to the cost of debt.

Table 15.4 – Cost of Equity vs. Cost of Debt

		Case 1	Case 2	Case 3	Case 4
Acquiror cost of equity					
Share price		$10	$20	$30	$60
Earnings per share		$1	$1	$1	$1
P/E ratio		10x	20x	30x	60x
After-tax cost of equity	=	1/PE	1/PE	1/PE	1/PE
	=	1/10	1/20	1/30	1/60
	=	10.0%	5.0%	3.3%	1.7%
Acquiror cost of debt					
Interest on debt (r)		8%	8%	8%	8%
Target tax rate (t)		40%	40%	40%	40%
After-tax cost of debt	=	r × (1-t)	r × (1-t)	r × (1-t)	r × (1-t)
	=	8% × (1-40%)	8% × (1-40%)	8% × (1-40%)	8% × (1-40%)
	=	4.8%	4.8%	4.8%	4.8%
Least expensive currency		Debt	Debt	Equity	Equity

Notice that for very high P/E companies, the cost of issuing equity is remarkably low. This is generally because there is the expectation by investors that earnings in such companies will grow at a faster rate than earnings of companies with lower P/E ratios. In Case 4, for example, each additional $60 share of stock costs the company only 1.7 percent of earnings. Or said another way, this company only needs to deliver earnings equal to 1.7 percent of the stock price to maintain its $60 stock price ($1 EPS / $60 stock price = 1.7% in equity return in the form of earnings). Earnings is a proxy for equity return because equity holders expect earnings will be distributed to them as dividends or reinvested in the company on their behalf.

This is why companies trading at a high P/E multiple will tend to issue equity instead of debt in M&A transactions. For them, equity is a less expensive form of capital than debt. This is also why, assuming no other transaction costs, if a high P/E company acquires a low P/E company with stock, the transaction should be accretive to Acquiror EPS and, vice versa, if a low P/E company acquires a high P/E company for stock, the transaction should be dilutive to EPS.

Another way to think of it is like this – for every $60 invested by a shareholder in Case 4, the company only has to return $1 in earnings to sustain its $60 share price, assuming it can sustain its growth rate. Compare that to a slower growth company such as the company that is trading at 10x P/E in Case 1; this company must return $1 in earnings per share to sustain its $10 stock price.

The financial impact of using stock versus cash in an acquisition is discussed in Accretion/Dilution Analysis. (Ch.14)

Ownership Dilution

Ownership dilution occurs when Acquiror stock is provided to Target shareholders in exchange for Target stock. The dilution occurs because Acquiror shareholders are giving up some of their ownership in Acquiror in exchange for control of Target. If Target shareholders accept cash in exchange for their stock, there will be no ownership dilution for Acquiror shareholders since they will still own 100 percent of the new Acquiror (which includes Target's business). If, on the other hand, Target's shareholders receive shares of Acquiror in exchange for their shares in Target, then Acquiror's ownership in the newly merged entity will be diluted.

Numerical examples are often the best way to help explain ownership dilution. In Table 15.5, three scenarios are provided; one in which Acquiror buys Target using all cash, one with all stock and one with an equal mix of cash and stock. Notice the ownership dilution to Acquiror shareholders in each of the three scenarios.

Table 15.5 – Ownership Dilution

	100% cash	50% cash/ 50% stock	100% stock
Offer price for Target	$20	$20	$20
Target fully diluted shares outstanding	125	125	125
Target equity value[1]	$2,500	$2,500	$2,500
Acquiror share price	$25	$25	$25
Acquiror fully diluted shares outstanding	200	200	200
Acquiror equity value[1]	$5,000	$5,000	$5,000
Transaction			
Cash consideration - percentage	100%	50%	0%
Cash consideration - dollar value[2]	$2,500	$1,250	$0
Stock consideration - percentage	0%	50%	100%
Stock consideration - dollar value[3]	$0	$1,250	$2,500
Exchange ratio[4]	N/A	0.8x	0.8x
Shares issued to Target[5]	0	50	100
Acquiror shares outstanding	200	200	200
NewCo shares outstanding[6]	200	250	300
Shares issued to Target	0	50	100
Target percentage ownership in NewCo[7]	0%	20%	33%
Acquiror shares in NewCo	200	200	200
Acquiror percentage ownership in NewCo[8]	100%	80%	67%
Dilution of Acquiror ownership[9]	0%	20%	33%

[1] Share price × fully diluted shares outstanding
[2] Target equity value × percentage cash
[3] Target equity value × percentage stock
[4] Target offer price / Acquiror stock price
[5] Target fully diluted shares outstanding × exchange ratio × percentage stock offered
[6] Shares issued to Target + Acquiror fully diluted shares outstanding
[7] Shares issued to Target / NewCo shares outstanding
[8] Acquiror fully diluted shares / NewCo shares outstanding
[9] 100 percent - Acquiror percentage ownership in NewCo

Acquisition Finance

The financing of an acquisition with cash is in many ways similar to financing the purchase of a house. It is best to arrange financing ahead of the technical closing date in order to show credibility to Target and to negotiate from a position of strength. While this seems straightforward – and it can be – there are also many fees involved with arranging financing, so the lowest interest rate offered may not be the lowest overall cost (lowest APR in mortgage parlance). Some of the largest fees in acquisition financing are the arrangement fee (for arranging the loan), the syndication fee (for arranging the bank syndicate), and the commitment fee (so that "committed funds" are available when Acquiror makes its bid). Companies generally begin discussing acquisition finance alternatives with their relationship banks on a confidential basis prior to making a bid so that the bid is not contingent on financing.

In most cases in which cash is the acquisition consideration, a type of interim financing called **bridge financing**, which often lasts between one and four months, is used to close the transaction. It is called bridge financing because it "bridges" Acquiror from the close of the transaction to a time when Acquiror can "take out the bridge" with a permanent financing arrangement in either the bank market or capital market. While this all works well in theory, there is a large caveat that applies: Acquiror (with its lenders) has to make sure it can "take out" or refinance the bridge with long-term or "permanent" financing. If there is a change in Acquiror's financial condition, or if there is a problem with the integration of Target, or simply a major change in financial markets, Acquiror may have difficulty in arranging permanent financing and be stuck with what is called a "hung bridge." This situation is especially dangerous because most bridge financing arrangements have onerous escalator or step-up clauses, which regularly increase the interest rate over time, making continued reliance on the bridge financing extremely expensive. The risks of a hung bridge are avoided entirely in an all stock transaction because there is no cash consideration that must be refinanced. Raising capital and important considerations related to financing are discussed in detail in Sources of Capital. (Ch.25)

Stock Deals

Chapter 16

Friendship is nothing else than an accord in all things,
human and divine, conjoined with mutual goodwill and affection,
and I am inclined to think that, with the exception of wisdom,
no better thing has been given to man by the immortal gods.

Cicero

In an acquisition of or merger with another company, Acquiror can choose to pay for Target with cash, stock, or a combination of both. The challenges and benefits of using cash vs. stock are described in Acquisition Currency. (Ch.15) This chapter describes the technical issues that arise out of using stock as an acquisition currency, including the difference between fixed and floating exchange ratios and the use of collars, caps or floors to protect value in a stock transaction. This chapter should be read in conjunction with Acquisition Currency and Merger of Equals. (Ch.15,17)

Signing and Closing

When two parties agree to a transaction, they sign a legal contract binding them to the transaction. If the contract is material for a party that is a public company, the signing of this agreement is an event which the public company must disclose. Therefore the "signing" of the contract is usually commensurate with the "announcement" of the transaction. As such, throughout this book, the terms "at signing" and "at announcement" refer to the same period in time. For most transactions, a period of time exists between the signing and the "closing" of the transaction. During this time, the parties solicit approval from any constituencies that must approve the deal, including shareholders and regulators. For smaller and less complicated transactions, this period of time can be very short. For other deals, the period of time between signing and closing can be long (longer than a year for certain types of transactions). The "closing" is the period of time when the ownership of Target is legally transferred to Acquiror.

The mechanics of using cash are straightforward. For example, if Acquiror offers $20 per share for 100 percent of Target using cash as the acquisition currency, Target shareholders will receive $20 per share in cash (before the payment of any taxes) when the transaction closes. Having sold their ownership interest in Target for $20 per share, after the transaction closes Target shareholders will have no ownership interest in the newly combined company (NewCo) and Acquiror shareholders will own 100 percent of NewCo. With an all cash transaction, there is no risk that the value offered to Target shareholders will change between signing of the agreement and closing of the transaction nor is there a risk that the ownership split will change: $20 per share offered at announcement will be $20 per share paid at closing, and Acquiror shareholders will own 100 percent of Target after closing.

Table 16.1 - 100 Percent Cash Acquisition

At announcement	Ownership % of Target	Ownership % of Acquiror	Value of Offer to Target
Target	100%	0%	$20
Acquiror	0%	100%	
At closing		**Ownership % of NewCo**	**Value of Offer to Target**
Target		0%	$20
Acquiror		100%	

In contrast to the use of 100 percent cash as acquisition currency, the use of stock as an acquisition currency is more complicated since the ownership of NewCo and/or the value of the offer for Target shareholders might change between announcement and closing (since the value of the currency --Acquiror's stock-- changes every day the stock market is open).

Table 16.2 – Transaction with Stock Consideration

At announcement	Ownership % of Target	Ownership % of Acquiror	Value of Offer to Target
Target	100%	0%	$20
Acquiror	0%	100%	
At closing		**Ownership % of NewCo**	**Value of Offer to Target**
Target		Depends on exchange ratio	Depends on exchange ratio
Acquiror		Depends on exchange ratio	

In a stock-for-stock exchange, Target shareholders exchange their ownership claim in Target for some ownership claim in NewCo based on the deal exchange ratio. And the value of the offer at closing for Target shareholders is also dependent on the deal exchange ratio.

Exchange Ratios

The deal exchange ratio is the number of Acquiror shares to be exchanged for each Target share in a stock-for-stock exchange. The exchange ratio is calculated as:

Offer price for Target / Acquiror's share price = exchange ratio

In a stock deal, the value (or offer price) for Target at announcement is Acquiror's closing price (usually quoted based on the last trading day before the deal is announced) multiplied by the exchange ratio. For example, assume Acquiror purchases Target in an all stock deal and the exchange ratio agreed to at signing was 3x (this means that at closing Acquiror will deliver 3 Acquiror shares for each Target share). If Acquiror's stock price the day before announcement was $20, then the offer price for Target quoted at announcement would be $60 ($20 Acquiror stock price × 3 exchange ratio = $60 offer price for Target shareholders).

As noted above, two of the major concerns when using stock as acquisition currency relate to (a) the *value* received by Target shareholders at closing and (b) the *ownership split* between Acquiror and Target shareholders at closing. Since Acquiror's stock price is a moving object (stock prices fluctuate every day the market is open), and the value received by Target shareholders at closing is equal to the exchange ratio multiplied by Acquiror's stock price, there exists the risk that the value delivered to Target shareholders at closing of the transaction can differ from the value at signing (when the deal was initially agreed to). Alternatively, the two parties might not care about whether the value changes between signing and closing; instead they might care about whether or not the NewCo ownership split is fixed between signing and closing.

Until now, exchange ratios have been discussed generically. However, there are two types of exchange ratios: fixed exchange ratios and floating exchange ratios. The type of exchange ratio used in a transaction depends on whether Acquiror wants to (1) fix the ownership split or (2) to fix the value delivered to Target shareholders at closing.

1. A **fixed exchange ratio** is one that does not move during the period from signing to closing regardless of whether there is movement in Acquiror's share price (hence the word "fixed"). Since the exchange ratio is fixed and the exchange ratio determines the number of Acquiror shares issued per Target share, the ownership split between Acquiror and Target does not change between signing and closing in a fixed exchange ratio transaction. The value delivered to Target shareholders, however, moves up or down depending on changes in Acquiror's stock price.

2. A **floating exchange ratio** is one in which the exchange ratio moves up or down or floats during the period from signing to closing, depending on Acquiror's stock price (hence the word "floating"). However, since the exchange ratio floats, and the exchange ratio determines the number of Acquiror shares issued per Target share, the ownership split between Acquiror and Target also changes each time Acquiror's stock price changes. The value delivered to Target shareholders, however, does not change between signing and closing.

Figure 16.3 on the following page visually shows the differences between fixed and floating exchange ratios. Both fixed and floating exchange ratios are described in detail in the following sections.

Figure 16.3 – Fixed vs. Floating Exchange Ratios

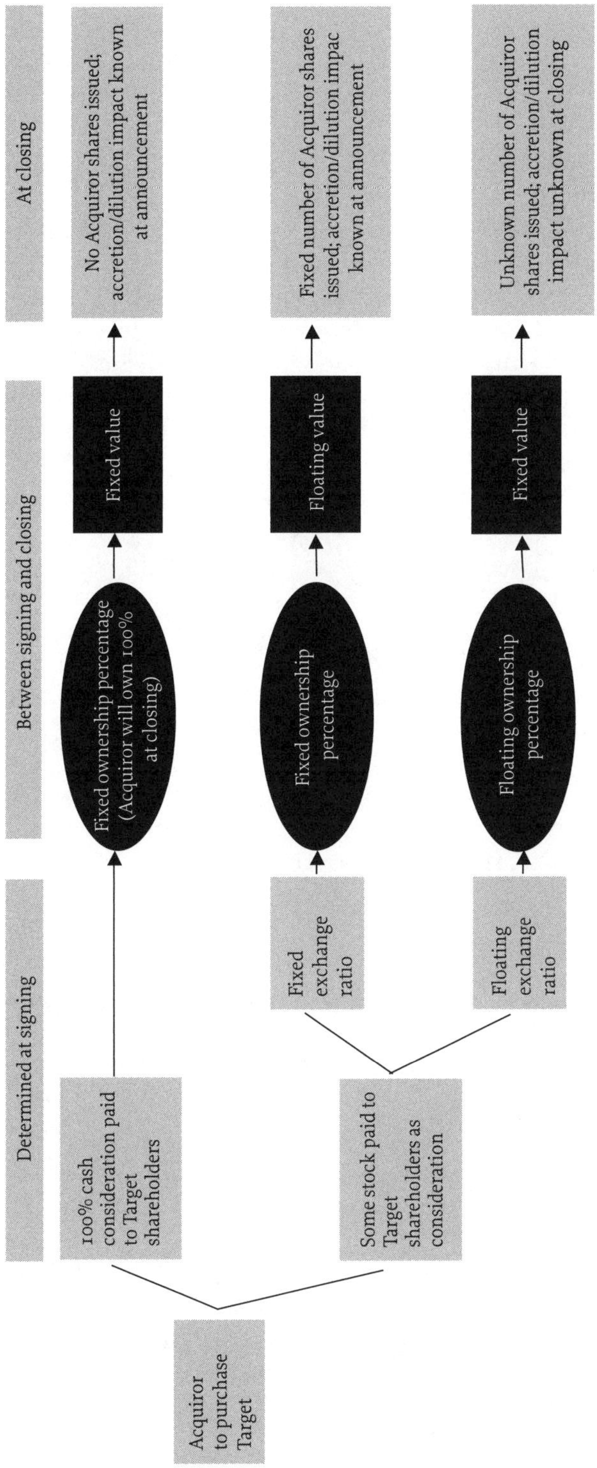

Fixed Exchange Ratio

With a fixed exchange ratio, there is floating value but a fixed ownership split. Given these two features, fixed exchange ratios are preferred in a merger of equals in which the ownership split of the new company is the key negotiating point.

1. ***Floating value:*** A fixed exchange ratio is one in which the exchange ratio does not change from signing to closing. It is fixed at announcement and does not move -- regardless of whether there is movement in Acquiror's share price. Thus if Acquiror's stock price rises during the time from signing to closing, the value delivered to Target shareholders also rises lockstep with the percentage increase in Acquiror's share price. Similarly, if Acquiror's stock price falls in the interim between announcement and closing, the value delivered to Target shareholders also falls. With a fixed exchange ratio, the ultimate value delivered to Target shareholders is directly tied to fluctuation in Acquiror's share price.

2. ***Fixed ownership split:*** Since a fixed exchange ratio provides for a non-alterable number of Acquiror shares to be exchanged for Target shares, the ownership split does not change between signing and closing. Since the ownership split is fixed at announcement, the accretion/dilution impact also is fixed at announcement.

To describe fixed exchange ratios, let's assume a transaction in which Acquiror purchases Target in a stock-for-stock exchange. Acquiror offers Target a fixed exchange ratio of 0.5 Acquiror shares for each Target share outstanding. This fixed exchange ratio of 0.5 represents a 25 percent premium to Target's current stock price of $16.

Assumptions	**Acquiror**	**Target**
Share price	$40	$16
Premium to Target's share price		25%
Offer price for Target[1]		$20
Exchange ratio (fixed)[2]		0.5x

[1] Share price × (1 + premium): {$16 × (1 + 0.25)}

[2] Target offer price / Acquiror share price: ($20 / $40)

Assume that four months (120 days) pass between the time the deal was announced and the closing. Further assume that during those four months Acquiror's share price has fallen from $40 to $30. Let's review what that means in terms of value delivered to Target shareholders at closing.

Table 16.4 – Fixed Exchange Ratio - Acquiror Share Price Falling

	Signing				Closing
Fixed exchange ratio	Time 0	+30 days	+60 days	+90 days	+120 days
Acquiror share price	$40.00	$37.50	$35.00	$32.50	$30.00
Percent change from announcement		(6.3%)	(12.5%)	(18.8%)	(25.0%)
Fixed exchange ratio	0.5x	0.5x	0.5x	0.5x	0.5x
Percent change from announcement		0%	0%	0%	0%
Value to Target[1]	$20.00	$18.75	$17.50	$16.25	$15.00
Percent change from announcement		(6.3%)	(12.5%)	(18.8%)	(25.0%)
Premium to pre-transaction price[2]	25.0%	17.2%	9.4%	1.6%	(6.3%)

[1] Acquiror share price × exchange ratio

[2] (Value to Target / Target's pre-transaction price of $16) - 1

Notice that the value received by Target shareholders at closing is $15. This is based on Acquiror's stock price at closing of $30.

$30 Acquiror share price × 0.5 exchange ratio = $15 value to Target

The value per Target share of $15 represents $5 less than the offer price of $20 four months before. Originally, at signing, the value per Target share of $20 (based on Acquiror's stock price at announcement of $40) implied a $4 per share or 25 percent premium to Target's pre-transaction price of $16. Now, at closing, the value per Target share of $15 (based on Acquiror's stock price at closing of $30) implies a $1 per share or 6.3 percent *negative* premium to Target's pre-transaction price of $16.

Now consider the same transaction but, in this case, Acquiror's share price has risen from $40 to $50. Notice that as Acquiror's share price rises, Target shareholders benefit in lockstep. By the time the transaction closes, Target shareholders receive $25 per share, which represents a premium of $9 per share or 56.3 percent to Target's pre-transaction price of $16 per share.

Table 16.5 – Fixed Exchange Ratio - Acquiror Share Price Rising

	Signing				Closing
Fixed exchange ratio	Time 0	+30 days	+60 days	+90 days	+120 days
Acquiror share price	$40.00	$42.50	$45.00	$47.50	$50.00
Percent change from announcement		6.3%	12.5%	18.8%	25.0%
Fixed exchange ratio	0.5x	0.5x	0.5x	0.5x	0.5x
Percent change from announcement		0%	0%	0%	0%
Value to Target[1]	$20.00	$21.25	$22.50	$23.75	$25.00
Percent change from announcement		6.3%	12.5%	18.8%	25.0%
Premium to pre-transaction price[2]	25.0%	32.8%	40.6%	48.4%	56.3%

[1] Acquiror share price × exchange ratio

[2] (Value to Target / Target's pre-transaction price of $16) - 1

Tables 16.4 and 16.5 demonstrate that, in a fixed exchange ratio deal, Target participates in 100 percent of the downside *and* upside of Acquiror's stock price movement since a fixed exchange ratio is used to convert each Target share into a set number of Acquiror shares at closing, regardless of whether Acquiror's shares fall or rise between announcement and closing. Said differently, the downside and upside risk of Acquiror stock price fluctuation is borne by Target. Now that we have looked at the impact on value, consider the fixed exchange ratio impact on the post-transaction ownership split.

Assumptions	**Acquiror**	**Target**
Share price	$40	$16
Premium to Target's share price		25%
Implied offer price for Target		$20
Exchange ratio (fixed)		0.5x
Pre-transaction fully diluted shares outstanding	100,000	180,000
Acquiror shares issued to Target[1]		90,000
Pro forma shares outstanding[2]	190,000	
Pro forma ownership – shares	100,000	90,000
Pro forma ownership – percentage	52.6%[3]	47.4%[4]

[1] Target shares outstanding × exchange ratio

[2] Acquiror shares + new shares issued to Target

[3] Pro forma shares owned by Acquiror / 190,000 total pro forma shares outstanding

[4] Pro forma shares owned by Target / 190,000 total pro forma shares outstanding

For every Target share outstanding, Acquiror will issue 0.5 Acquiror shares. Since Target has 180,000 fully diluted shares outstanding, at closing Acquiror will issue 90,000 Acquiror shares to Target shareholders and, post transaction, Acquiror will have 190,000 fully diluted shares outstanding. As shown in Table 16.6, the ownership split of 52.6 percent for Acquiror and 47.4 percent for Target will not change between signing and closing, regardless of whether Acquiror's stock price moves down or up.

Table 16.6 – Fixed Exchange Ratio – Effect on Ownership

	Signing				Closing
Fixed exchange ratio - falling price	Time 0	+30 days	+60 days	+90 days	+120 days
Acquiror share price	$40.00	$37.50	$35.00	$32.50	$30.00
Percent change from announcement		(6.3%)	(12.5%)	(18.8%)	(25.0%)
Exchange ratio (fixed)	0.5x	0.5x	0.5x	0.5x	0.5x
Value to Target (floating)	$20.00	$18.75	$17.50	$16.25	$15.00
Target pre-transaction shares	180,000	180,000	180,000	180,000	180,000
Shares issued to Target[1]	90,000	90,000	90,000	90,000	90,000
Acquiror shares	100,000	100,000	100,000	100,000	100,000
Pro forma shares outstanding	190,000	190,000	190,000	190,000	190,000
Target pro forma ownership[2]	47.4%	47.4%	47.4%	47.4%	47.4%
Acquiror pro forma ownership[3]	52.6%	52.6%	52.6%	52.6%	52.6%
Fixed exchange ratio - rising price	Time 0	+30 days	+60 days	+90 days	+120 days
Acquiror share price	$40.00	$42.50	$45.00	$47.50	$50.00
Percent change from announcement		6.3%	12.5%	18.8%	25.0%
Exchange ratio (fixed)	0.5x	0.5x	0.5x	0.5x	0.5x
Value to Target (floating)	$20.00	$21.25	$22.50	$23.75	$25.00
Target pre-transaction shares	180,000	180,000	180,000	180,000	180,000
Shares issued to Target[1]	90,000	90,000	90,000	90,000	90,000
Acquiror shares	100,000	100,000	100,000	100,000	100,000
Pro forma shares outstanding	190,000	190,000	190,000	190,000	190,000
Target pro forma ownership[2]	47.4%	47.4%	47.4%	47.4%	47.4%
Acquiror pro forma ownership[3]	52.6%	52.6%	52.6%	52.6%	52.6%

[1] Target shares outstanding × exchange ratio
[2] Shares owned by Target shareholders / pro forma shares outstanding
[3] Shares owned by Acquiror shareholders / pro forma shares outstanding

Floating Exchange Ratio

The effect on value to Target and the pro forma ownership split of a floating exchange ratio is the opposite of the effect of a fixed exchange ratio. With a floating exchange ratio, there is a fixed value and therefore a floating ownership split. Given these two features, floating exchange ratios are preferred in transactions in which the value delivered to Target shareholders is the key negotiating point such as in outright acquisitions.

1. ***Fixed value:*** A floating exchange ratio is based on a fixed offer price (or value) for each Target share. At closing, each Target share is converted into whatever number of Acquiror shares is required to achieve the predetermined value per Target share. Thus if Acquiror's share price fluctuates, it does not impact the dollar value delivered to Target; instead, the number of Acquiror shares required to deliver that fixed dollar value changes.

2. ***Floating ownership split:*** Since a floating exchange ratio does not provide for a predetermined number of Acquiror shares to be exchanged for Target shares (the ratio is determined at closing), the ownership split fluctuates between signing and closing. Since the ownership split is not set until closing in a floating exchange ratio transaction, the accretion/dilution impact changes between signing and closing based on changes in Acquiror's stock price.

Consider the previous example of Acquiror and Target but, instead of a fixed exchange ratio, Acquiror will offer Target a fixed value of $20 per Target share. Therefore the exchange ratio floats based on changes in Acquiror's stock price. Let's first consider how the exchange ratio moves if Acquiror's share price falls from the original $40 to $30 between signing and closing.

Table 16.7 – Floating Exchange Ratio - Acquiror Share Price Falling

	Signing				**Closing**
Floating exchange ratio	Time 0	+30 days	+60 days	+90 days	+120 days
Acquiror share price	$40.00	$37.50	$35.00	$32.50	$30.00
Percent change from announcement		(6.3%)	(12.5%)	(18.8%)	(25.0%)
Value to Target	$20.00	$20.00	$20.00	$20.00	$20.00
Percent change from announcement		0%	0%	0%	0%
Floating exchange ratio[1]	0.500x	0.533x	0.571x	0.615x	0.667x
Percent change from announcement		6.7%	14.3%	23.1%	33.3%
Premium to pre-transaction price[2]	25.0%	25.0%	25.0%	25.0%	25.0%

[1] Value to Target / Acquiror share price

[2] (Value to Target / Target's pre-transaction price of $16) - 1

Notice that value has been protected for Target shareholders and the upside and downside risk of Acquiror stock price fluctuation is transferred to Acquiror. As Acquiror's share price falls, it must issue more shares to Target shareholders in order to deliver the same $20 in value. At signing, Acquiror only had to issue 0.5 Acquiror shares per Target share in order for Target shareholders to receive value of $20 per share at closing. At closing, with Acquiror's share price having fallen from $40 per share to $30, Acquiror must deliver 0.667 Acquiror shares per Target share in order for Target shareholders to receive value of $20 per share at closing.

Let's now consider how the exchange ratio changes if Acquiror's stock price increases.

Table 16.8 – Floating Exchange Ratio - Acquiror Share Price Rising

	Signing				**Closing**
Floating exchange ratio	Time 0	+30 days	+60 days	+90 days	+120 days
Acquiror share price	$40.00	$42.50	$45.00	$47.50	$50.00
Percent change from announcement		6.3%	12.5%	18.8%	25.0%
Value to Target	$20.00	$20.00	$20.00	$20.00	$20.00
Percent change from announcement		0%	0%	0%	0%
Floating exchange ratio[1]	0.500x	0.471x	0.444x	0.421x	0.400x
Percent change from announcement		(5.9%)	(11.1%)	(15.8%)	(20.0%)
Premium to pre-transaction price[2]	25.0%	25.0%	25.0%	25.0%	25.0%

[1] Value to Target / Acquiror share price
[2] (Value to Target / Target's pre-transaction price of $16) - 1

Notice that as Acquiror's share price increases from $40 to $50, the number of shares Acquiror must issue to Target shareholders falls from 0.5 at signing to 0.4 in order for Target shareholders to receive value of $20 per share at closing.

$40 Acquiror share price × 0.5 exchange ratio = $20 value per Target share

$50 Acquiror share price × 0.4 exchange ratio = $20 value per Target share

Now let's consider the floating exchange ratio impact on the post-transaction ownership split. As shown in Table 16.9, the ownership split changes based on fluctuation in Acquiror's share price and therefore changes in the exchange ratio.

Table 16.9 – Floating Exchange Ratio - Effect on Ownership

	Signing				Closing
Floating exchange ratio - falling price	Time 0	+30 days	+60 days	+90 days	+120 days
Acquiror share price	$40.00	$37.50	$35.00	$32.50	$30.00
Percent change from announcement		(6.3%)	(12.5%)	(18.8%)	(25.0%)
Value to Target (fixed)	$20.00	$20.00	$20.00	$20.00	$20.00
Exchange ratio (floating)	0.500x	0.533x	0.571x	0.615x	0.667x
Target pre-transaction shares	180,000	180,000	180,000	180,000	180,000
Shares issued to Target[1]	90,000	96,000	102,857	110,769	120,000
Acquiror shares	100,000	100,000	100,000	100,000	100,000
Pro forma shares outstanding	190,000	196,000	202,857	210,769	220,000
Target pro forma ownership[2]	47.4%	49.0%	50.7%	52.6%	54.5%
Acquiror pro forma ownership[3]	52.6%	51.0%	49.3%	47.4%	45.5%

Floating exchange ratio - rising price	Time 0	+30 days	+60 days	+90 days	+120 days
Acquiror share price	$40.00	$42.50	$45.00	$47.50	$50.00
Percent change from announcement		6.3%	12.5%	18.8%	25.0%
Value to Target (fixed)	$20.00	$20.00	$20.00	$20.00	$20.00
Exchange ratio (floating)	0.500x	0.471x	0.444x	0.421x	0.400x
Target pre-transaction shares	180,000	180,000	180,000	180,000	180,000
Shares issued to Target[1]	90,000	84,706	80,000	75,790	72,000
Acquiror shares	100,000	100,000	100,000	100,000	100,000
Pro forma shares outstanding	190,000	184,706	180,000	175,790	172,000
Target pro forma ownership[2]	47.4%	45.9%	44.4%	43.1%	41.9%
Acquiror pro forma ownership[3]	52.6%	54.1%	55.6%	56.9%	58.1%

[1] Target shares outstanding × exchange ratio

[2] Shares owned by Target shareholders / pro forma shares outstanding

[3] Shares owned by Acquiror shareholders / pro forma shares outstanding

Recall that with a fixed exchange ratio the ownership split is protected and the value floats. However with a floating exchange ratio, as shown in Table 16.9, the value is protected and the ownership floats (through the mechanism of the floating exchange ratio). As Acquiror's share price falls, the exchange ratio increases (more shares issued to achieve the same dollar value) and therefore Acquiror's pro forma ownership of the combined company decreases. As Acquiror's share price rises, the exchange ratio decreases (fewer shares issued to achieve the same dollar value) and Acquiror's pro forma ownership of the combined company increases.

Collars, Caps and Floors

Collars are mechanisms that serve to bracket or bound the fluctuation in a particular type of exchange ratio (fixed or floating). Recall that the exchange ratio decision was initially portrayed as an either/or decision. Either one chose a fixed exchange ratio (fixed ownership and floating value) or one chose a floating exchange ratio (floating ownership and fixed value). In essence, collars can make an exchange ratio both fixed and floating. They are risk shifting mechanisms. Collars create a hybrid exchange ratio which is fixed within a certain band and floating outside that band or, vice versa, floating within a certain band and fixed outside that band. Collars are a way to share the risk of fluctuation in Acquiror's share price so that all risk is not borne by one party or the other.

In the previous exchange ratio examples, Acquiror's share price varied plus 25 percent and minus 25 percent, causing substantial changes to the value received by Target (in a fixed exchange ratio scenario) and causing substantial changes to the number of shares issued by Acquiror (in a floating exchange ratio scenario). Collars can be included with either a fixed or a floating exchange ratio in order to limit (i) the price change exposure for Target or (ii) the shares delivered exposure for Acquiror, respectively.

To describe how a collar works, let's assume Acquiror and Target agree on an exchange ratio of 0.5 Acquiror shares per Target share, and that ratio is based on a purchase price of $20 per share for Target. Let's also assume that Acquiror wants to bracket the value delivered to Target. Acquiror will agree to deliver 0.5 Acquiror shares per Target share as long as the value delivered to Target is no more than 25 percent greater nor 25 percent less than $20 (ranging up to $25 and down to $15). Beyond the collar (or this band of $15 to $25 of value for Target), the fixed exchange ratio turns into a floating exchange ratio and Target shareholders suffer or benefit depending on which way Acquiror's share price moves. If Acquiror share price appreciated above the upper collar limit, or **cap**, Target shareholders would suffer because they would no longer participate; that is, the number of shares issued to Target would decrease proportionally to limit the value at $25 per share. If Acquiror share price fell below the lower collar limit, or **floor**, Target shareholders would benefit because they would no longer participate; that is, the number of shares issued to Target would increase proportionally to guarantee the value at $15 per share.

Using the previous example of a $20 offer price per Target share, notice what happens when Acquiror's stock price rises above $50 or falls below $30. The exchange ratio is fixed within the collar range and floating outside the range.

Table 16.10 – Fixed Exchange Ratio with Collar

Fixed exchange ratio with collar			**Collar Range**						
			Floor				Cap		
Acquiror share price	$20.00	$25.00	$30.00	$35.00	$40.00	$45.00	$50.00	$55.00	$60.00
Percent change from announcement	(50.0%)	(37.5%)	(25.0%)	(12.5%)	0.0%	12.5%	25.0%	37.5%	50.0%
Exchange ratio	0.750x	0.600x	0.500x	0.500x	0.500x	0.500x	0.500x	0.455x	0.417x
Percent change from announcement	50.0%	20.0%	0.0%	0.0%	0.0%	0.0%	0.0%	(9.1%)	(16.7%)
Value to Target[1]	$15.00	$15.00	$15.00	$17.50	$20.00	$22.50	$25.00	$25.00	$25.00
Percent change from announcement	(25.0%)	(25.0%)	(25.0%)	(12.5%)	0.0%	12.5%	25.0%	25.0%	25.0%
Target pre-transaction shares	180,000	180,000	180,000	180,000	180,000	180,000	180,000	180,000	180,000
Shares issued to Target[2]	135,000	108,000	90,000	90,000	90,000	90,000	90,000	81,818	75,000
Acquiror shares	100,000	100,000	100,000	100,000	100,000	100,000	100,000	100,000	100,000
Pro forma shares outstanding	235,000	208,000	190,000	190,000	190,000	190,000	190,000	181,818	175,000
Target pro forma ownership[3]	57.4%	51.9%	47.4%	47.4%	47.4%	47.4%	47.4%	45.0%	42.9%
Acquiror pro forma ownership[4]	42.6%	48.1%	52.6%	52.6%	52.6%	52.6%	52.6%	55.0%	57.1%
Controlling pro forma owner	Target	Target	Acquiror →						

[1] Acquiror share price × exchange ratio

[2] Target shares outstanding × exchange ratio

[3] Shares owned by Target shareholders / pro forma shares outstanding

[4] Shares owned by Acquiror shareholders / pro forma shares outstanding

Notice how the collar protects both Acquiror (at the top end, or cap) and Target (at the bottom end, or floor). If Acquiror's stock price rises, the cap portion of the collar protects Acquiror from ever having to pay more than $25 per Target share (exchange ratio decreases). Without the cap, Acquiror would issue 90,000 shares to Target, regardless of how high Acquiror's stock price traded, and Target would receive value equal to the exchange ratio of 0.5 multiplied by Acquiror's stock price ($30 per Target share if Acquiror share price were $60). If Acquiror's stock price falls, the floor portion of the collar protects Target in that Target will never receive less than $15 per share (exchange ratio increases). Without the floor, Acquiror would issue 90,000 shares to Target, regardless of how low Acquiror's stock price traded, and Target would receive value equal to the exchange ratio of 0.5 multiplied by Acquiror's stock price ($10 per Target share if Acquiror share price were $20).

In addition to the full collar, a transaction can be structured with only a floor or only a cap. If a transaction were structured with only a floor or only a cap, it would protect only one party to the transaction. As shown in Table 16.10, only a floor would protect Target by guaranteeing a *minimum* value to Target shareholders. Only a cap would protect Acquiror by guaranteeing a *maximum* value to Target shareholders.

Collars also can be structured for transactions with a floating exchange ratio. They work in the opposite way as collars for fixed exchange ratio deals. In floating exchange ratio transactions, the *value* is fixed within the collar range and floating outside the range. In summary:

	Within collar		**Outside collar**	
	Ownership	Value	Ownership	Value
Fixed exchange ratio	Fixed	Floating	Floating	Fixed
Floating exchange ratio	Floating	Fixed	Fixed	Floating

Let's look at how a collar would work with a floating exchange ratio deal.

Table 16.11 – Floating Exchange Ratio with Collar

Floating exchange ratio with collar			Collar Range						
			Floor				Cap		
Acquiror share price	$20.00	$25.00	$30.00	$35.00	$40.00	$45.00	$50.00	$55.00	$60.00
Percent change from announcement	(50.0%)	(37.5%)	(25.0%)	(12.5%)	0.0%	12.5%	25.0%	37.5%	50.0%
Exchange ratio	0.667x	0.667x	0.667x	0.571x	0.500x	0.444x	0.400x	0.400x	0.400x
Percent change from announcement	33.3%	33.3%	33.3%	14.3%	0.0%	(11.1%)	(20.0%)	(20.0%)	(20.0%)
Value to Target[1]	$13.33	$16.67	$20.00	$20.00	$20.00	$20.00	$20.00	$22.00	$24.00
Percent change from announcement	(33.3%)	(16.7%)	0.0%	0.0%	0.0%	0.0%	0.0%	10.0%	20.0%
Target pre-transaction shares	180,000	180,000	180,000	180,000	180,000	180,000	180,000	180,000	180,000
Shares issued to Target[2]	120,000	120,000	120,000	102,857	90,000	80,000	72,000	72,000	72,000
Acquiror shares	100,000	100,000	100,000	100,000	100,000	100,000	100,000	100,000	100,000
Pro forma shares outstanding	220,000	220,000	220,000	202,857	190,000	180,000	172,000	172,000	172,000
Target pro forma ownership[3]	54.5%	54.5%	54.5%	50.7%	47.4%	44.4%	41.9%	41.9%	41.9%
Acquiror pro forma ownership[4]	45.5%	45.5%	45.5%	49.3%	52.6%	55.6%	58.1%	58.1%	58.1%
Controlling pro forma owner	Target	Target	Target	Target	Acquiror	→			

[1] Acquiror share price × exchange ratio

[2] Target shares outstanding × exchange ratio

[3] Shares owned by Target shareholders / pro forma shares outstanding

[4] Shares owned by Acquiror shareholders / pro forma shares outstanding

Risk Arbitrage

An **arbitrageur** is a person or firm who enters into transactions to profit when the same security or product is trading at two different prices in two or more markets. For example, if an investor can buy gold from one seller for $45 and simultaneously sell gold to another buyer across the street for $50, then an arbitrageur could profit $5 from entering into the two transactions. The only risk is that one side of the deal might fall through. If there were some way the arbitrageur could guarantee that both deals would happen simultaneously, the deal would be without risk. In an efficient market, arbitrage opportunities are quickly priced out since, if an arbitrage opportunity does exist, arbitrageurs will simultaneously buy and sell until the forces of supply and demand narrow the spread, or profit, to zero.

Risk arbitrage – as the name implies – involves an arbitrage with risk. Risk arbitrageurs are a specialized kind of trader who attempt to profit from simultaneously buying and selling short stocks in merger transactions (or any other major transactions involving the stock of a company such as a major share repurchase or a restructuring). The position is generally opened the day a transaction is announced (or soon after) and closes out the day the transaction closes. It is called risk arbitrage since the investor bears the risk that the transaction does not close, or does close but does so on different terms or on a different timetable from those originally announced.

The participation of these risk arbitrageurs (commonly referred to as "risk arbs") is an important consideration in stock-for-stock exchanges. These highly specialized arbitrageurs seek to profit from Acquiror and Target share price differentials that exist between signing and closing. Trading activity performed by risk arbitrageurs can put downward pressure on Acquiror's share price. As further described below, risk arbs sell Acquiror short, which means they borrow Acquiror shares and then sell them into the market. This increase in supply (if coupled with static demand) results in a decreased Acquiror share price. If there is an adverse market reaction to a proposed acquisition by Acquiror upon announcement, leading to downward pressure on Acquiror's stock price as some investors sell, this risk arb trading can exacerbate it.

In a stock-for-stock transaction, Target's shares are exchanged for Acquiror's shares at closing at a predetermined exchange ratio or predetermined value, depending on whether the exchange ratio is fixed or floating, respectively. Thus, at closing, shareholders of Target hand in their shares of Target (figuratively) and in exchange receive the appropriate number of Acquiror shares (equaling the number of Target shares owned multiplied by the exchange ratio).

When a stock-for-stock transaction is announced, the share price of Target generally trades up from the previous day's close to a little below the offer price implied by the exchange ratio (but not up to the offer price in order to account for the risk that the transaction may not close). As the date of the expected transaction closing gets nearer, Target's stock price approaches the price implied by the exchange ratio until the day of closing, when the market price equals the price implied by the exchange ratio.

For example, Acquiror offers to purchase Target and the exchange ratio is 2x, which means 2 Acquiror shares per Target share. Assume Acquiror's stock price at announcement is $10 per share (therefore the offer price for Target is $20 per share ($10 × 2 = $20). Let's assume the transaction will take approximately one to three months to close (though the period between signing and closing can extend to one to two years for certain highly regulated companies and/or industries). In this example, one month before expected closing Target's share price might be $19.50, two weeks before expected closing it might be $19.80, one week before expected closing it might be $19.90, and the day before expected closing it might be $19.99. As it becomes progressively more likely that the transaction will close (on which date two Acquiror shares worth $20 will be exchanged for each Target share owned), Target's share price moves progressively closer to $20. If this does not make sense, think of it this way: if Target's stock were trading at $19 per share one day before the expected closing, then investors would buy Target shares, hold them for one day, and receive Acquiror shares worth $20 the next day, making $1 per share in the process. Since such easy money is difficult to come by, many investors would try to buy Target stock, thereby driving up the price of Target shares until the return on investment equals the risk that the transaction does not close. Since the transaction risk is very low given that there is only one day until expected closing, the commensurate return is very low as well (only $0.01 for one day in this example).

The goal in risk arbitrage is to capture the spread between Target's current share price and the offer price for Target. If the position is opened perfectly such that the exact number of Acquiror shares is delivered at closing to cover the short position in Acquiror, there is no financial risk. The only risk involved is the risk that the transaction does not close or that the terms of the transaction change (e.g., a change in the exchange ratio and/or length of time to closing), thereby altering the ratio of how many Target shares to buy in order to create a perfect hedge.

What does it mean to sell short?

When an investor buys a share of stock, he gives money to his broker and, in exchange, receives a share of stock. If the price of the stock rises the investor benefits, and if the price of the stock falls the investor loses. To buy stock in this traditional way is to "buy long" or to "go long" a stock. The buyer buys the stock and actually holds the security.

A short sale is the opposite of a long sale. In a short sale, an investor *borrows* a share of stock and immediately sells that share for cash. At some point in the future, the investor buys a share of stock to replace the share she borrowed. If the price of the stock falls in the interim, the investor benefits because she received cash for selling the share when the price was higher and purchased a share to replace the short position when the price was lower. However, if the price of the stock rises in the interim, the investor loses because she received cash for selling the share when the price was lower and had to purchase a share to replace the short position when the price was higher. In essence, shorting a stock is a bet that the stock price will decline. If it declines, the investor makes money. If it rises, the investor loses money.

To illustrate the difference between long and short positions, consider a share of stock for MusicCo. On January 2, MusicCo is trading at $20 per share. On January 2, Rachel goes long (or buys) one share of MusicCo. On the same day, Jennifer shorts (or borrows and sells) one share of MusicCo. In the following table, notice what happens to the value of Rachel's investment and Jennifer's investment when the price of MusicCo rises or falls.

Table 16.12 – Long vs. Short Sales

	MusicCo stock price	Rachel - long buyer	Jennifer - short seller
January 2	$20	Buy 1 share Pay $20	Borrow 1 share Sell 1 share[1] Get $20
Cash inflow/(outflow)		($20)	$20
If MusicCo's share price rises	$25	Sell share of stock Get $25	Buy share of stock Repay borrowed share Pay $25
Cash inflow/(outflow)		$25	($25)
Profit / (loss)		$5	($5)
If MusicCo's share price falls	$15	Sell share of stock Get $15	Buy share of stock Repay borrowed share Pay $15
Cash inflow/(outflow)		$15	($15)
Profit / (loss)		($5)	$5

[1] When one borrows a share to short sell, there is usually a broker margin to pay on the borrowed share(s)

In a stock-for-stock merger, arbitrageurs typically short sell Acquiror's stock; they borrow shares and then sell those same shares into the market. Simultaneously, arbitrageurs go long (buy) Target's stock by buying shares outright at a ratio equal to the number of Acquiror shares that will be delivered upon closing of the transaction at the announced exchange ratio. By doing this, arbitrageurs have created a perfect hedge: in exchange for the Target shares they own, when the transaction closes they will receive exactly the number of Acquiror shares needed to close out their short position on Acquiror. For assuming this risk as well as the time value of money from the time of investment to the closing of the transaction, arbitrageurs require a rate of return (12 to 18 percent annualized is common in medium risk transactions, or around two to three times the cost of capital).

Why is analyzing risk arbitrage important within the context of M&A? The short selling of Acquiror's shares puts downward pressure on Acquiror's stock. Immediately after a deal is announced, this downward pressure may cause Acquiror's stock price to fall because arbitrageurs are buying Target shares and short selling Acquiror shares. Company management and the board might perceive this fall in Acquiror's stock price as the market's negative reaction to the transaction, when it reality it may be nothing more than arbitrageurs taking advantage of a potential profit situation. It is important to be aware of when a risk arbitrage situation is created in order to prepare senior management and the board for potential short-term drops in Acquiror's post-announcement stock price. In fact, much of the downward pressure often seen in Acquiror's share price immediately after a transaction announcement is related to short selling pressure from risk arbitrageurs as opposed to the market not liking the strategic merits or financial impact of a deal. Most long-term investors will take the time to better understand a transaction before making a buy or sell decision.

The mechanics for risk arbitrage (and thus the analysis undertaken in order to assess whether a proposed transaction is likely to attract arbitrageurs) are as follows. A numerical example follows.

1. Purchase the number of Target shares equal to one Acquiror share (this is equal to the inverse of the exchange ratio).

2. Short (borrow and then sell) one Acquiror share.

3. At the closing of the transaction, arbitrageur will receive one Acquiror share in exchange for Target share(s) owned and the arbitrageur will take that share and use it to close out the short position (return the Acquiror share received at closing to those from whom the arbitrageur borrowed the share in Step 2).

4. The net profit (also called the spread) is the value received from selling the Acquiror share less the cost of buying the appropriate number of Target shares (adjusted for dividends and financing costs).

For transactions in which a control premium is paid to Target, arbitrageurs will set up the hedge as described above. For non-premium or low premium mergers, or when the spread has already narrowed, the spread to be earned on the arbitrage opportunity might equate to an annualized return which is too low to generate significant arbitrageur interest. In situations in which investors are bullish on Acquiror in the long run, investors often buy Target's shares as a cheaper way to obtain Acquiror's shares (since Target shares will be exchanged for Acquiror shares at closing). The result is significantly decreased short selling pressure on Acquiror and greater buying support for Target, which keeps the spread between Acquiror and Target share prices fairly narrow. This is in contrast to a typical transaction in which short selling by the arbitrageurs puts downward pressure on Acquiror's stock price while the purchase of Target's stock puts upward pressure on Target's stock price, which usually has the effect of increasing the spread between Acquiror's and Target's stock prices immediately after announcement of a transaction.

To illustrate how merger arbitrage or risk arbitrage works, let's refer back to the Acquiror and Target used in previous examples in this chapter. Recall the assumptions from the fixed exchange ratio transaction.

Acquiror offers Target a fixed exchange ratio of 0.5 Acquiror shares for every Target share outstanding. This fixed exchange ratio of 0.5 represents a 25 percent premium to Target's current stock price of $16.

Assumptions	Acquiror	Target
Share price	$40	$16
Premium to Target's share price		25%
Offer price for Target[1]		$20
Fixed exchange ratio[2]		0.5x

[1] Share price × (1 + premium): {$16 × (1 + 0.25)}

[2] Target offer price / Acquiror share price: ($20 / $40)

We know from the announced terms of the transaction that a shareholder of Target will receive 0.5 shares of Acquiror upon closing. On the morning the transaction is announced, an arbitrageur can buy two shares of Target and borrow and then sell short one share of Acquiror. Therefore at closing, the arbitrageur will receive one full share of Acquiror (2 Target shares owned × 0.5 exchange ratio = 1 Acquiror share received) and use this full share of Acquiror to close out his short position by returning (paying back) the share which was borrowed. Putting numbers to the example:

1. Purchase the number of Target shares equal to one Acquiror share (this is equal to the inverse of the exchange ratio).

    a. Exchange ratio = 0.5

    b. Inverse of the exchange ratio = 1 / 0.5 = 2

    c. Purchase 2 Target shares

    d. $16 per Target share × 2 Target shares = $32 to acquire 2 Target shares

    e. Pay $32 in cash

2. Short (borrow and sell) one Acquiror share.

    a. Borrow 1 share of Acquiror (worth $40)

    b. Short (or sell) the 1 Acquiror share just borrowed for $40

    c. Receive $40 in cash

3. At the closing of the transaction, arbitrageur will receive one Acquiror share in exchange for the two Target shares owned and then will take that Acquiror share received and use it to close out the short position (return the one Acquiror share received at closing to those from whom the arbitrageur borrowed the share in Step 2).

    a. When the transaction closes, arbitrageur receives 1 Acquiror share

    b. Arbitrageur will use this Acquiror share received to close out its short position on Acquiror by returning an Acquiror share to whomever it was borrowed from (usually a bank or brokerage firm)

4. The net profit (also called the spread) is the value received from selling the Acquiror share less the cost of buying the appropriate number of Target shares (adjusted for dividends and financing costs).

    a. The spread is equal to the value of shorting 1 Acquiror share ($40) less the cost of acquiring 2 Target shares ($32)

    b. $40 inflow from Acquiror share sold short - $32 outflow of 2 Target shares purchased = $8 spread

    c. If we assume the transaction took one year to close and that neither Acquiror nor Target paid dividends during the year, the annualized return would be equal to the spread divided by the cost of the transaction.

    d. $8 spread / $32 cost to acquire 2 Target shares = 25% annual return

Other M&A Analyses

Chapter 17

In the last analysis sound judgment will prevail.

Joseph Cannon

This chapter discusses analytical tools used frequently in M&A analysis but which are not described in detail in other chapters. This chapter includes a discussion of: (1) shareholder analysis, (2) technical market analysis, (3) relative valuation analysis, and (4) social issues analysis.

Shareholder Analysis

A change-of-control transaction for a corporation usually requires a shareholder vote and approval by either a majority (greater than 50 percent) or supermajority (usually 66 2/3 percent, but can be anything greater than 50 percent) of Target shareholders. In addition, an Acquiror shareholder vote is required if Acquiror is a public company on the NYSE or NASDAQ and issues more than 20 percent of its pre-transaction shares to Target in the transaction (see Deal Mechanics (Ch.20) for a discussion of this rule). The shareholder vote can take place at the annual meeting of shareholders or at a "special meeting" called for purposes of voting on the transaction.

A company's charter and/or bylaws should state the voting requirements to approve a transaction. If the company's charter or bylaws are silent on the issue, refer to the corporation laws of the state in which the company is incorporated to see what the default shareholder vote approval level is. The bylaws likely will have some limitations as to how or by whom a special meeting of shareholders can be called. Limits on calling special meetings are described in Corporate Defense. (Ch.23)

Since a change-of-control transaction usually requires Target shareholder approval, it is useful for a potential Acquiror to have an understanding of the composition of Target's shareholder base. This is the case for both friendly and hostile transactions. There have been some friendly transactions which failed to receive shareholder approval in spite of the fact that they were endorsed by Target's board of directors and senior management.

How does one go about estimating whether a deal would be approved by shareholders? While there is no way to know with certainty until the time of the vote, there are some shareholder analyses one can undertake to assess the likelihood of approval. If the transaction requires a vote by Acquiror's shareholders also, the analyses described below should be conducted for both Target and Acquiror shareholders.

The following list of key shareholder-related questions should be considered when analyzing a potential transaction.

1. ***Is there a majority shareholder?*** A majority shareholder has control over the fate of the shareholder vote. The majority shareholder (or a representative of the majority shareholder) is likely to be on the board of directors and may also be part of the management team. Since the majority shareholder is generally an insider (by virtue of board and/or management position), the person or group has access to private information and would/should be involved in the negotiation of a change-of-control transaction. Examples of a majority shareholder include a parent company that owns a majority of the stock of a subsidiary (there may be a minority public float of the subsidiary) or an original owner or family member who took the company public but retained a majority voting interest in the company (either in absolute number of shares or through super-voting shares). Prior to announcing a change-of-control transaction, Acquiror would work to have the majority shareholder sign a voting agreement (at the time the transaction papers are signed) that legally commits the majority shareholder to vote in favor of the deal. These so-called shareholder lockups are further described in Deal Mechanics. (Ch.20) Public companies are required to disclose any beneficial owner(s) owning more than five percent of a class of stock. Therefore, a majority shareholder for a public company would be listed in the company's annual proxy in the section describing beneficial ownership.

2. ***Are there a few shareholders who together comprise a major voting interest or a majority interest in the company?*** This often occurs with families who took a company public but decided to retain a major or majority ownership interest in the company. While no single person may have majority control, analysis may show that two or three people together form the majority. As with a majority shareholder, these small groups of shareholders who together comprise the majority are often approached before the deal is announced and asked to sign a voting agreement requiring them to vote their shares in favor of the transaction.

3. ***Are there major shareholders (e.g., 13D and 13G holders) whose opinions would be weighed heavily by other shareholders?*** The SEC's regulation 13D requires that any shareholder who beneficially owns more than five percent of a class of public securities must file a 13D statement of ownership with the SEC. This statement must be filed at the time the shareholder becomes an owner of more than five per-

cent of a class of securities, and subsequent periodic filings also must be made as long as the 5 percent threshold is met. In addition, a filing must be made any time there is a material change in the shareholder's ownership. A 13G filing (which is less cumbersome than a 13D filing) is allowed for certain institutional shareholders (e.g., insurance companies, broker-dealers, banks, etc.) and "passive investors" who own more than five percent of a class of securities but can certify that they do not intend to effect a change-of-control in the issuer. Information about the SEC Regulations 13D and 13G can be found on the SEC's website (www.sec.gov).

Since 13D holders must file with the SEC, it is easy to find out whether the company under analysis has any shareholders who own greater than five percent of the company. Search through the company's SEC filings for 13D filings or check for disclosure of 13D holders in the company's annual proxy statement in the section describing beneficial ownership. Depending on the investor, a 13D holder can be influential and vocal about a transaction (often called "activist shareholders"). This is especially true in the case of hostile transactions in which the prospective Acquiror does not have the support of the company's management or board of directors.

4. ***Are the shareholders of the company largely retail or institutional?*** Institutional shareholders are experienced in analyzing transactions and will determine for themselves whether they agree with the merits of the financial terms offered by Acquiror. As a result, institutional investors are generally more independent than retail investors, who typically follow the recommendations of the board of directors and management. Also, institutional holders tend to own larger blocks of shares than retail holders and so the aggregate number of decision makers is fewer. Conversely, retail holders tend to own smaller numbers of shares, thereby making the aggregate number of decision makers significantly larger (and thus more time-consuming and costly to reach). There are companies (e.g., Thomson Financial) from which shareholder composition data can be purchased. Also, a company's shareholder services department should have some of this data on hand.

5. ***What is the composition of the institutional investors?*** It is also useful to understand the composition of the institutional investors. Institutional investors generally are classified as momentum, yield, specialty, income value, deep value, core growth, index, core value, GARP (growth at a reasonable price), aggressive growth, or growth, although other designations also exist. In addition, funds are often categorized by industry, market sector, or geographic region. For example, there are telecom funds, semiconductor funds, international funds, and funds that track the S&P 500.

   If the transaction under consideration will fundamentally change the profile of the Target *or* the Acquiror, certain fund managers might decide to sell their holdings not because they do not believe in the merits of the deal but because the company no longer falls within the fund managers' "basket classification" and, as a result, the managers can no longer own the shares according to fund rules. Conversely, fund managers may be motivated to buy the shares if the newly combined company obtains a higher weighting in a stock index the managers follow (such as the S&P 500). The ideal situation would be to have new fund managers buy the stock, thereby replacing one type of investor with another and continuously supporting the share price in the process. However, the sale and purchase are rarely simultaneous. In practice, sellers tend to sell before new investors purchase the stock. This type of movement out of a stock, if done by a number of shareholders, creates downward pressure on a company's stock price. It is important to differentiate between downward pressure due to fund managers moving in and out of a stock (due to classification or basket issues) and downward pressure due to a perception of the combined company's intrinsic value.

Institutional holders must file their holdings with the SEC. Since a majority of all shares in the United States are held by institutions (often holding shares in their own names but on behalf of numerous clients), it is possible to obtain a fair amount of data on the holdings of institutional investors from SEC filings. From this data, it is possible to perform an analysis of the types of investors represented in Target's shareholder base. As mentioned above, there are companies (e.g., Thompson Financial) from which shareholder composition data can be purchased. Also, a company's shareholder services department should have some of this type of data on hand.

6. ***Who are the top 10 to 15 investors?*** When performing shareholder analysis, it is a good idea to identify the top 10 or 15 holders in terms of shares held and percentage owned, both individually and in the aggregate. For example, if the top twelve shareholders owned 53 percent of a company which according to its bylaws, only requires a simple majority for a change-of-control, in theory one could focus energy on selling the merits of the deal to these twelve shareholders only (since they represent more than 50 percent of the outstanding vote).

7. ***What is the average tax basis of the shareholders?*** The tax basis a shareholder has in his stock combined with the proposed transaction structure will determine if the shareholder will owe any capital gains tax as a result of the transaction. For some companies, in which many of the shareholders have held the stock for a long period of time, the average shareholder tax basis is likely to be fairly low. For other companies, such as technology companies, which could be trading at significantly lower levels today than a few years ago, this is less of an issue. Tax basis is discussed in more detail in Taxes and M&A. (Ch.21)

8. ***What percentage of the shares is held by management and the board?*** If one knows how much stock or how many options a senior officer or director has in the company (and, ideally, at what price they acquired the stock, what the exercise price is for the options and whether the options held will be triggered in a transaction), it may be possible to determine how senior management and the board will fare financially from the transaction. Information on stock holdings for senior officers and directors of public companies is disclosed in the company's annual proxy.

Technical Market Analysis

Stock price performance, shares traded analysis, and average daily trading volume can be grouped as analyses of a company's market technical data. A review of a company's market technical data is often one of the first types of analysis performed on a potential target and is also one of the first types of analysis a junior banker or finance professional is required to master.

1. ***Historical stock price performance:*** By looking at Target's historical share price performance, one can determine how the company is performing today compared to how it performed in the past. This is important since it provides information as to what offer price might be acceptable and it helps Acquiror better understand what the overall sentiment of Target's management team and board of directors might be regarding valuation. Historical stock price performance (which is depicted with dates on the x-axis and stock prices on the y-axis) can easily be found in most market-based financial databases. Historical stock price graphs are often annotated with major news events. These annotated stock price graphs usually include events specific to the company such as major earnings announcements, changes in senior management, and the announcement of strategic transactions or agreements, as well as macroeconomic events which affected a broad class of stocks. Not surprisingly, trading volume tends to track major events. As a result, in addition to annotating stock price graphs, it is also common to chart stock price performance in conjunction with the volume of shares traded each day.

   Assume you have performed historical stock price analysis for Target and conclude that Target has traded between $20 and $30 per share for the last five years. Further assume that, from valuation analysis and financial impact analysis, a potential acquiror has determined that a price of $38 per share is a fair price to offer. Since the shares have not traded above $30 in five years, there is a strong likelihood that the management and board of Target will at least consider the offer of $38 since it represents a premium of $8 per share or 27 percent over the stock's 5-year high of $30.

   Compare this to a company that was trading around $60 per share for several years until a recent negative announcement about operating results caused the stock to fall to the low $40s. Assume a potential acquiror determines from valuation and financial impact analysis that a fair offer price is $50 per share. This company might not be psychologically ready to review an offer of $50 since just a few months ago its stock was trading around $60 per share. In a situation like this, Target might desire time to rebuild investor confidence and to see if the lower price range is sustained before entertaining offers to sell the company at the new price level.

2. ***Relative stock price performance***: In addition to reviewing a company's historical stock price performance on an absolute basis, it is common to review a company's historical price performance on a relative basis – either compared to an industry peer, an index of industry peers, or a market index such as the S&P 500. In this way, it is possible to determine whether a stock has underperformed or outperformed its peers over a period of time. Relative stock price performance graphs are often called **indexed stock price graphs.** They are usually indexed to 100, which means the first price for all companies in the index on the first day of the graph serves as the base (represented as 100 percent) and over time the stock price performance is measured as a percentage change from that base.

   For example, assume WestCo's stock prices for the month of February ranged from a low of $33.15 to a high of $35.69 and EastCo's stock prices for the month of February ranged from a low of $44.61 to a high of $46.70 (as shown in Figure 17.1).

Figure 17.1 – WestCo and EastCo Stock Price Performance

	WestCo	EastCo
1-Feb	$34.14	$46.70
2-Feb	$33.15	$46.03
3-Feb	$33.75	$46.02
4-Feb	$33.75	$45.86
5-Feb	$34.23	$46.29
8-Feb	$34.03	$46.32
9-Feb	$33.74	$46.16
10-Feb	$33.66	$45.33
11-Feb	$34.20	$45.52
12-Feb	$34.21	$44.61
15-Feb	$34.00	$44.62
16-Feb	$34.69	$45.22

	WestCo	EastCo
17-Feb	$35.20	$45.57
18-Feb	$35.35	$46.16
19-Feb	$35.07	$45.86
22-Feb	$35.43	$45.36
23-Feb	$35.57	$46.11
24-Feb	$35.62	$45.95
25-Feb	$35.69	$45.62
26-Feb	$35.41	$45.44
Low	$33.15	$44.61
High	$35.69	$46.70

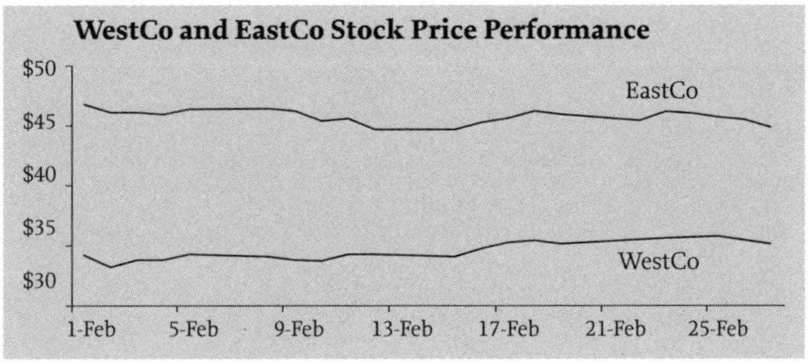

In the stock price graph above, it is difficult to determine whether WestCo performed better or worse than EastCo during the month of February because they have different absolute pricing levels. In order to see how EastCo's stock price performed *relative to* WestCo's stock price, we must index them to the same starting point to be able to compare them. If we index them both to 100 we can see visually which stock has performed better (on a percentage basis) since February 1. To index each company's stock price to 100, divide the day's stock price by the first stock price in the sample set and multiply that by 100. For example, the indexed prices for the first three days of February for WestCo are calculated as follows:

($34.14 WestCo price on Feb. 1 / $34.14 WestCo price on Feb. 1) × 100 = 100.00
($33.15 WestCo price on Feb. 2 / $34.14 WestCo price on Feb. 1) × 100 = 97.10
($33.75 WestCo price on Feb. 3 / $34.14 WestCo price on Feb. 1) × 100 = 98.87

Once all of the prices have been indexed to 100 they can be graphed in the same manner as the graph in Figure 17.1

Figure 17.2 – WestCo and EastCo Indexed Stock Price Performance

	WestCo	EastCo
1-Feb	100.00	100.00
2-Feb	97.10	98.56
3-Feb	98.87	98.53
4-Feb	98.87	98.18
5-Feb	100.26	99.11
8-Feb	99.68	99.18
9-Feb	98.84	98.84
10-Feb	98.60	97.05
11-Feb	100.18	97.46
12-Feb	100.21	95.51
15-Feb	99.60	95.55
16-Feb	101.61	96.81

	WestCo	EastCo
17-Feb	103.11	97.57
18-Feb	103.56	98.84
19-Feb	102.74	98.18
22-Feb	103.80	97.12
23-Feb	104.19	98.73
24-Feb	104.35	98.39
25-Feb	104.56	97.67
26-Feb	103.72	97.29
Low	97.10	95.51
High	104.56	100.00

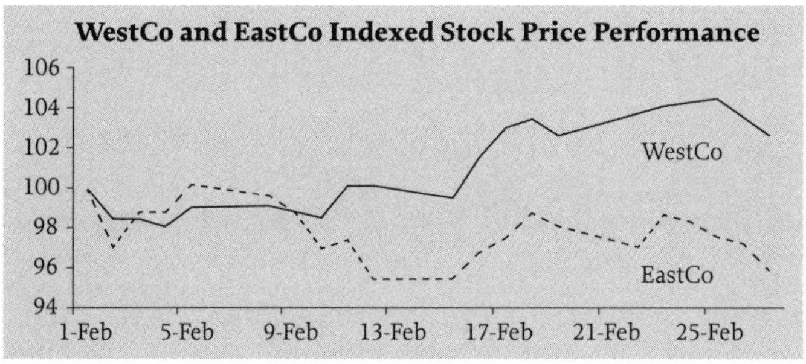

With an indexed stock price graph it is clear that WestCo has outperformed EastCo since February 1. In fact, EastCo did not trade above its February 1 price of $46.70 during the entire month of February. Also, since the two stocks' prices are indexed to 100, it is easy to see that as of February 26, WestCo was trading 3.72 percent above its February 1 price and EastCo was trading 2.71 percent below its February 1 price (100 – 97.29 = 2.71%).

3. ***Shares traded analysis:*** This analysis is an extension of stock price performance analysis as it combines share price performance with the volume of shares traded. It analyzes how often a stock has traded in a certain price range (measured by closing prices) weighted by the volume of shares traded within each price range. The value of knowing the range in which a particular stock has traded (weighted by volume) is twofold. Similar to analyzing the historical share price performance, it allows one to have a better understanding of the price at which shareholders purchased their stock, which is useful in determining an offer price that is likely to be accepted by a majority of the shareholders. Also, the information helps to estimate what the average basis might be for Target shareholders. This is a consideration for taxable deals in which Target shareholders will need to pay taxes on any capital gain, which is measured by the offer price less the investor's basis in the stock. Tax basis is described in Taxes and M&A. (Ch.21)

   To illustrate shares traded analysis, let's consider a company with 155 million shares outstanding. During the last five years the company's stock has traded between $15 and $25. Shares traded analysis considers what volume of shares traded within specified price increments between the $15 and $25 price range, as shown in Table 17.3. During the last five years, in the $15 to $17 price range, 13 million shares have traded; in the $17 to $19 price range, 26 million shares have traded; in the $19 to $21 price range, 55.05 million shares have traded; in the $21 to $23 price range, 24 million shares have traded; and in the $23 to $25 price range, 10 million shares have traded. In total, 128.05 million shares have traded in the last five years. Note that the total shares traded of 128,050,000 in the five years is less than the total shares outstanding of 155,000,000. This is because not every owner of shares has sold her stock in the last five years. On this same point, some of the same shares have been bought and sold more than once in the last five years, although there is no way to know which shares have changed hands (perhaps multiple times) and which have not. The shares traded and the cumulative shares traded are depicted in a graph in Figure 17.4.

Table 17.3 – Shares Traded Analysis

Total shares outstanding	155,000,000					
Price ranges ($2 increments)	$15-$17	$17-$19	$19-$21	$21-$23	$23-$25	Total
Shares traded in each range	13,000,000	26,000,000	55,050,000	24,000,000	10,000,000	128,050,000
Percentage of shares traded in each range[1]	10.2%	20.3%	43.0%	18.7%	7.8%	100.0%
Cumulative shares traded[2]	10.2%	30.5%	73.4%	92.2%	100.0%	-
Percent of float traded in each range[3]	8.4%	16.8%	35.5%	15.5%	6.5%	82.6%

[1] Shares traded in each range / total shares traded of 128.05 million
[2] For example, the cumulative shares traded up to $19 per share is equal to all shares traded from $15 to $19 [(13mm+16mm)/128.05mm = 30.5%]
[3] Shares traded in each range / total shares outstanding of 155 million

Figure 17.4 – Cumulative Shares Traded Analysis

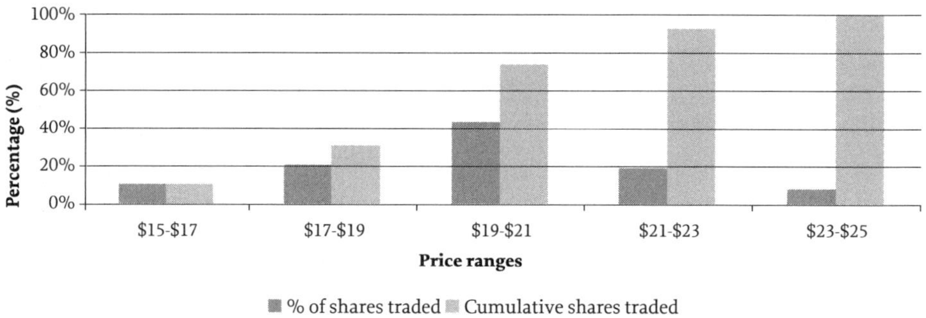

As you can see from the Shares Traded table and the Cumulative Shares Traded graph, even though the 5-year high is $25 per share, over 70 percent of Target's shares traded at a price less than $21 per share during the 5-year period.

Relative Valuation Analysis

As the name suggests, relative valuation analysis is comparative – it compares values of one company to values of another company. Relative stock price performance was described in the previous section on share price performance. Relative share price performance is further described in Merger of Equals (Ch.18) in the discussion of natural historical exchange ratios. Other relative valuation analyses include analysis at various prices and premiums paid analysis, both of which are described here.

Analysis at various prices (AVP) and premiums paid analysis: Both of these analyses are useful when considering the range of potential offer prices for a company. Analysis at various prices allows one to review the implied transaction multiples given a range of offer prices. By doing so, it is possible to compare the implied transaction multiples with multiples paid in comparable transactions. Premiums paid analysis compares the premium under consideration to the premiums paid in previous, comparable transactions. They are both an extension of Comparable Transaction Analysis. (Ch.10)

An example for TargetCo is provided in Table 17.5. First, the premiums paid and transaction multiples from comparable transactions are calculated. (Ch.10) These numbers can be found in the right most column in Table 17.5. Next, a range of potential purchase prices per share of TargetCo is chosen. Currently, TargetCo is trading at $20 per share. The AVP analysis is based on a range of purchase prices between $23 to $27, which represents a range of premiums paid of 15 to 35 percent. In each offer price range, the offer price is multiplied by the company's shares outstanding to arrive at an implied market value of equity. Next, the company's net debt (including preferred stock) of $3 billion is added to the implied values for market value of equity to arrive at a range of values for implied enterprise value. From these two ranges of equity value and enterprise value, the company's EPS, book value of equity, EBITDA and EBIT are applied to calculate various multiples including P/E, price/book, EV/EBITDA and EV/EBIT. The implied transaction multiples are compared to the range of multiples from comparable transactions to see if the implied multiples are in line with comparable multiples.

Table 17.5 – Analysis at Various Prices (AVP)

$ millions, except per share data

TargetCo data		Multiples	$20	Range of offer prices					Comparable Transaction Range
				$23	$24	$25	$26	$27	
$20	Current share price	Implied premium	0.0%	15.0%	20.0%	25.0%	30.0%	35.0%	20%-28%
200	Fully diluted shares outstanding	Market value of equity[1]	$4,000	$4,600	$4,800	$5,000	$5,200	$5,400	
3,000	Net debt including preferred	Enterprise value[2]	7,000	7,600	7,800	8,000	8,200	8,400	
Equity value multiples									
$1.50	FY1 EPS	FY1 P/E[3]	13.3x	15.3x	16.0x	16.7x	17.3x	18.0x	16.0x-19.0x
$1.75	FY2 EPS	FY2 P/E[3]	11.4x	13.1x	13.7x	14.3x	14.9x	15.4x	13.0x-15.0x
2,000	Book value of equity	Price / book value[4]	2.0x	2.3x	2.4x	2.5x	2.6x	2.7x	2.2x-2.6x
Enterprise value multiples									
1,000	LTM EBITDA	LTM EV/EBITDA[5]	7.0x	7.6x	7.8x	8.0x	8.2x	8.4x	7.7x-8.2x
600	LTM EBIT	LTM EV/EBIT[6]	11.7x	12.7x	13.0x	13.3x	13.7x	14.0x	12.5x-13.5x

[1] 200 fully diluted shares outstanding × range of offer prices
[2] Implied equity value + $3,000 of net debt
[3] Range of implied equity values / (EPS × 200 shares outstanding)
[4] Implied market value of equity / $2,000 book value of equity
[5] Implied enterprise value / $1,000 LTM EBITDA
[6] Implied enterprise value / $600 LTM EBIT

Social Issues Analysis

There is a saying that "where you stand depends on where you sit." That is, one's perspective on an issue may be colored by one's relationship to that issue. The management team of Target has a fiduciary and professional obligation to do what it thinks is best for the company's shareholders. However, even though it may be best for shareholders, there is an understandable reluctance by management to pursue options (such as the sale of the company) that may result in the loss of one's job.

Since the ultimate goal of Acquiror in an M&A transaction context is to gain control of Target at a reasonable price, it is wise to understand the motivations of the major players. For example, if most of the members of Target's management team have **golden parachutes** (severance packages payable upon termination), they may be more willing to discuss a transaction with Acquiror than if the transaction were to result in losing their jobs with no other immediate job prospects or compensation. Alternatively, Target's management may be needed by Acquiror in order to better manage the combined company, thereby encouraging Target management to undertake a transaction. Thus, it is a good idea to study the ages, positions, responsibilities, affiliations, and ownership stakes of senior management to determine where their motivations might lie in a potential transaction. In a merger of equals in which there is a more equal sharing of management positions, this becomes an even more important exercise. Information regarding management officers can be found in the company's annual proxy as well as its 10-K filing. Personal knowledge of the key players can be invaluable and this is an important part of the value delivered by advisors such as investment bankers and corporate attorneys.

As with management, it is a good idea to study the ages, positions, responsibilities, affiliations, and ownership stake of Target's board members as well. While board members also have a professional and fiduciary responsibility to act on behalf of the company's shareholders, they tend to have less at stake than a company's senior management since board membership usually is not the board member's primary job. Studying the board composition usually serves one of two major purposes. The first is to determine how to approach a potential Target (many transaction discussions are initiated via discussion with a friendly board member). The second is that, since the board has to approve the deal, knowing the background of the board members as well as their professional affiliations and experiences may help Acquiror to understand how they are likely to respond to a proposed transaction. Information regarding board members can be found in the company's annual proxy as well as its 10-K filing.

Merger of Equals

Chapter 18

Union gives strength.

Aesop

A **merger of equals** (MOE), as the name suggests, is the combination of two companies of roughly equal size and value (usually measured by market value of equity). Some of the distinguishing features of an MOE are summarized below. While parties to a MOE try in a transaction to include these key features, it is important to recognize that a merger of equals -- in the strictest sense -- is rare. A true merger of equals, when it succeeds, can be a powerful value-creation mechanism for both parties. However, MOEs are challenging because they require significant commitment by both parties to fairness in the transaction and a level of corporate selflessness during the integration period. In practice, these are both difficult to achieve.

Key Features of a Merger of Equals

1. An MOE is distinct from a traditional merger in which there is usually a larger Acquiror and a smaller Target. In an MOE, one company's stock survives the transaction (meaning one company's stock will be used for the new company going forward); however, neither party is considered the target company in the literal sense of being smaller and/or "taken over."

2. In a merger of equals, there is no buyer from a "control" or governance standpoint. Shared governance, at both the management and board levels, is a defining characteristic of an MOE.

3. In an MOE, no (or only a limited) control premium is paid to one party (i.e., either A to B or B to A). The theory is that the managements and boards of both companies participate in creating value for the new company going forward and, more importantly, all value created through synergies flows through to the shareholders of both companies, where it is shared according to their respective ownership percentages. As a result, there is no need for a meaningful control premium since both companies are jointly responsible for and will jointly share in the future value creation. In practice, discrepancies in stand-alone valuations often lead to a small premium for one party, but participants try to keep pro forma ownership

as near to 50/50 as possible. Beyond a 60/40 percent ownership split (e.g., 70/30 or 80/20), it becomes more difficult to characterize the transaction as an MOE since Target is not likely to exercise much "control" going forward. If Target shareholders are unlikely to exercise control going forward, they must be compensated for the control they will no longer have by being paid a control premium.

4. MOEs are almost always stock-for-stock exchanges; moreover, they are usually fixed exchange ratio transactions. Negotiations in an MOE center around the fixed exchange ratio since it determines the post-transaction ownership of the new company between the two sets of shareholders. A number of financial and social issues weigh into the negotiation of the exchange ratio. Key social issues that affect exchange ratio negotiations include post-transaction composition of the board and senior management, headquarters, and the company name, among others.

5. In an MOE, value is created for both sets of shareholders through synergies (revenue enhancement and cost savings) and potentially also through the expansion of trading multiples.

Splitting the New Company Equity

One of the key goals in negotiating a merger of equals transaction is to determine how to fairly split ownership of the new company. That is, on a pro forma basis, what percentage of the new company's equity will be owned by Company A and what percentage will be owned by Company B?

Figure 18.1 – Splitting the New Company Equity

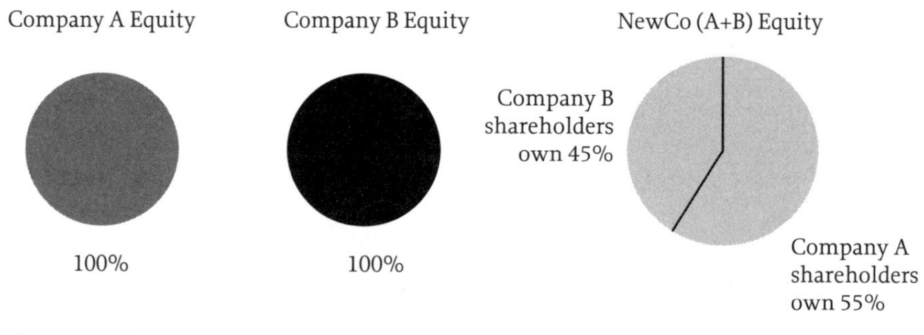

In the example above, how did the two companies determine that Company A shareholders should own 55 percent of NewCo and that Company B shareholders should own 45 percent of NewCo? The split of the pie is negotiated by the two companies based on financial and social contributions to the new company. Social issues play a very important part of the negotiation of an MOE (much more so than in traditional acquisitions) and are described in more detail at the end of this chapter.

Broadly speaking, the three most widely used financial tools to determine financial contribution in a merger of equals are: (1) contribution analysis, (2) historical natural exchange ratio analysis (also referred to as historical market-based exchange ratio analysis), and (3) traditional valuation analysis (which includes comparable company analysis, comparable transaction analysis and discounted cash flow analysis). The goal in all three of these types of analyses is to determine the stand-alone value of each company relative to the other company in order to determine what fixed exchange ratio most fairly allocates ownership of the new company between the two sets of shareholders.

Acquiror and Target terminology in an MOE

In a merger of equals transaction, the participants work very hard to characterize the transaction as two partners coming together for their mutual benefit. As discussed, top management positions are shared, a small or no premium is paid, and expected future synergies are implicitly shared by the two partners because ownership is shared by the two partners. In substance, there is no "Acquiror" and there is no "Target." In spite of this, from a legal and accounting standpoint there must be an "Acquiror" and a "Target."

Assume that in the merger of Company A and Company B, Company A will be the surviving entity (meaning Company A's stock will survive and Company B will receive shares in Company A based upon the agreed to exchange ratio). In such a situation, Company A is considered the Acquiror and Company B is considered the Target - in terms of which stock is used as the Acquiror to calculate the exchange ratio - in spite of the fact that the transaction is structured as a merger of equals.

Another reason why an Acquiror and Target must be designated relates to the accounting treatment of the merger. Under GAAP, one company must be designated the Acquiror and one company must be designated the Target. In purchase accounting, Target's balance sheet would be fair valued and combined with Acquiror's historical balance sheet (meaning Acquiror's balance sheet would not be fair valued). Designation of an Acquiror and Target is necessary in order to account for the transaction properly.

To calculate the split of the new company, an exchange ratio is required. The exchange ratio is the number of Acquiror shares offered in exchange for one share of

Target. Mathematically, the exchange ratio is calculated as: Target offer price / Acquiror share price = exchange ratio.

Most MOEs are structured as fixed exchange ratio transactions with no collar, cap or floor, so that both companies share equally in any increase (or decrease) in the surviving company's stock price. Fixed and floating exchange ratios and caps, floors and collars are described in Stock Deals. (Ch.16)

Consider a simple numerical example with BeerCo and WineCo. BeerCo and WineCo announce that they will combine in a merger of equals to create Beer&WineCo. The transaction will be done "at market," meaning no premium will be paid to BeerCo or WineCo shareholders and the transaction exchange ratio will be based on current market prices. Based on current market values, the pro forma split between the two companies is 51.9 percent for BeerCo and 48.1 percent for WineCo.

Table 18.2 – BeerCo and WineCo – Percent of Combined Equity Value

	BeerCo	WineCo
Current share price	$20	$65
Fully diluted shares outstanding	350,000	100,000
Stand-alone market value of equity[1]	7,000,000	6,500,000
Combined Beer&WineCo equity value[2]	13,500,000	13,500,000
Percent of combined equity value[3]	**51.9%**	**48.1%**

[1] Current share price × fully diluted shares outstanding
[2] BeerCo equity value + WineCo equity value
[3] Stand-alone equity value / combined equity value

Recall that the exchange ratio is calculated by dividing the offer price for Target by the Acquiror share price. If a transaction is done "at market" or at the "natural exchange ratio," then the offer price is equal to the current stock price and the exchange ratio is equal to the current stock price for the company whose stock will not survive (Target) divided by the surviving company's (Aquiror) share price.

The natural or market exchange ratio, assuming BeerCo's stock will survive, is:

For BeerCo shareholders:	$20 / $20 = 1.00x
For WineCo shareholders:	$65 / $20 = 3.25x

This means that for every share of BeerCo, a BeerCo shareholder receives 1 share of Beer&WineCo, and for every share of WineCo, a WineCo shareholder receives 3.25 shares of Beer&WineCo. Notice that the natural exchange ratio of 3.25x is the number that provides a split of the Beer&WineCo shares proportionate to the current market equity values.

Table 18.3 – BeerCo and WineCo – Based on Natural Exchange Ratio

	BeerCo	WineCo	Beer&WineCo[3]
Current share price	$20	$65	
Fully diluted shares outstanding	350,000	100,000	
Natural exchange ratio[1]	1.00x	3.25x	
Post-transaction shares outstanding[2]	350,000	325,000	675,000
Percent of Beer&WineCo[4]	**51.9%**	**48.1%**	**100.0%**

[1] BeerCo's stock will survive; BeerCo exchange ratio ($20/$20); WineCo exchange ratio ($65/$20)
[2] Fully diluted shares outstanding × natural exchange ratio
[3] BeerCo shares + WineCo shares in Beer&WineCo
[4] Shares owned in Beer&WineCo / combined Beer&WineCo shares

Now assume that after performing contribution analysis, historical exchange ratio analysis and valuation analysis, it is determined that a fair ownership split between BeerCo and WineCo should be 55 percent for BeerCo shareholders and 45 percent for WineCo shareholders (as opposed to the ownership percentages of 51.9 percent BeerCo and 48.1 percent WineCo implied by the natural exchange ratio of 3.25x). Thus, instead of the natural exchange ratio of 3.25x, the deal exchange ratio should be the exchange ratio that allocates 55 percent of Beer&WineCo to BeerCo shareholders and 45 percent to WineCo shareholders.

Since the ownership percentage has now been selected, how does one calculate the exchange ratio that yields the selected ownership split? To solve for the proper exchange ratio that splits the new company 55/45, start with the shares outstanding of the company whose stock will survive (BeerCo in our example), and divide BeerCo's fully diluted shares outstanding by the specified ownership percentage post-transaction. The quotient is the number of pro forma shares outstanding for the new company. Subtract BeerCo's shares from that pro forma total and you will get the shares owned by WineCo shareholders. Finally, to calculate the exchange ratio that yields this 55/45 split, divide the number of Beer & WineCo shares owned by WineCo shareholders by the fully diluted WineCo shares outstanding pre-transaction. These calculations are provided in Table 18.4.

Table 18.4 – BeerCo and WineCo – Calculating the Exchange Ratio

BeerCo shares outstanding	350,000
BeerCo's target percentage of Beer&WineCo[1]	55.0%
Implied total Beer&WineCo shares outstanding[2]	636,364
Beer&WineCo shares for WineCo shareholders[3]	286,364
WineCo fully diluted shares outstanding	100,000
Deal exchange ratio[4]	2.864x

[1] The amount of Beer&WineCo that BeerCo shareholders should own after the merger
[2] BeerCo shares outstanding / BeerCo's specified percentage of Beer&WineCo
[3] Implied total Beer&WineCo shares - BeerCo shares outstanding
[4] Beer&WineCo shares for WineCo shareholders / WineCo shares outstanding (pre-transaction)

Once a deal exchange ratio has been calculated (2.864 in this example), check to ensure that upon applying this deal exchange ratio, the pro forma split of the new company is 55 percent owned by BeerCo shareholders and 45 percent owned by WineCo shareholders.

Table 18.5– BeerCo and WineCo – Based on Specified Exchange ratio

	BeerCo	**WineCo**	**Beer&WineCo[3]**
Current share price	$20	$65	
Fully diluted shares outstanding	350,000	100,000	
Deal exchange ratio[1]	1.00x	2.864x	
Post-transaction shares outstanding[2]	350,000	286,364	636,364
Percent of Beer&WineCo[4]	**55.0%**	**45.0%**	**100.0%**

[1] As calculated in Table 18.4
[2] Fully diluted shares outstanding × natural exchange ratio
[3] BeerCo shares + WineCo shares in Beer&WineCo
[4] Shares owned in Beer&WineCo / combined Beer&WineCo shares

Financial Analysis in an MOE

As noted, the three most widely used financial tools to determine the ownership split in a merger of equals are: (1) contribution analysis, (2) historical natural exchange ratio analysis, and (3) traditional valuation analysis (trading comparables, transaction comparables, DCF analysis).

The goal in all three of these analyses is to determine how to split the ownership of the new company fairly. In addition to these analyses, other social issues play into determining the actual deal exchange ratio, such as who will be Chairman or CEO of the new company and how many directors from each company will be part of the new board of directors. For example, assume financial analysis shows that a fair split of Beer&WineCo is 55 percent for BeerCo shareholders and 45 percent for WineCo shareholders. Let's further assume that the Chairman/CEO of BeerCo will become Chairman/CEO of Beer&WineCo and that the company's headquarters will remain at BeerCo's headquarters. BeerCo might be willing to accept a little less than 55 percent of the new company since its Chairman/CEO will be running the new company and since it gets to keep headquarters in its city. In other words, BeerCo might ascribe value to the positions of Chairman and CEO and to the location of headquarters and therefore might be willing to make a financial ownership concession to WineCo shareholders in exchange.

In the following section, contribution analysis, historical natural exchange ratio analysis and valuation analysis are described in terms of how they are applied in merger of equal analysis.

Contribution Analysis

The premise of contribution analysis is that a fair split of the new company pie should be based on what each party brings to the table in terms of key financial or operating metrics. The first step is to determine which metrics should be measured. Then the items brought to the table by each party are added up and calculated to determine what each party contributes as a percentage of the total amount.

In Table 18.6, various financial metrics are considered for BeerCo and WineCo. The actual dollar amount of each company's contribution to each financial metric is listed under the header "Contribution - $ Millions." The percentage of each financial metric that each party brings to the table is calculated in the column entitled "Contribution - Percentage." For example, for the metric "Market Value," BeerCo has a market value of $7 billion and WineCo has a market value of $6.5 billion. Adding the two yields a combined market value of $13.5 billion for Beer&WineCo. Of that $13.5 billion, BeerCo contributed 51.9 percent ($7,000 / $13,500 = 51.9%) and WineCo contributed 48.1 percent ($6,500 / $13,500 = 48.1%).

Table 18.6 - Contribution Analysis

	Contribution - $ millions			Contribution - percentage		
	BeerCo	WineCo	Beer & WineCo	BeerCo	WineCo	Beer & WineCo
Market value	$7,000	$6,500	$13,500	51.9%	48.1%	100%
Enterprise value	11,000	9,000	20,000	55.0%	45.0%	100%
LTM revenues	7,800	7,800	15,600	50.0%	50.0%	100%
LTM EBIT	1,071	808	1,879	57.0%	43.0%	100%
LTM EBITDA	1,446	1,005	2,450	59.0%	41.0%	100%
LTM net income	442	408	850	52.0%	48.0%	100%
Total assets	15,105	11,395	26,500	57.0%	43.0%	100%
Net PP&E	10,941	7,603	18,544	59.0%	41.0%	100%
Customers	3,640	3,360	7,000	52.0%	48.0%	100%
Average				54.8%	45.2%	100.0%

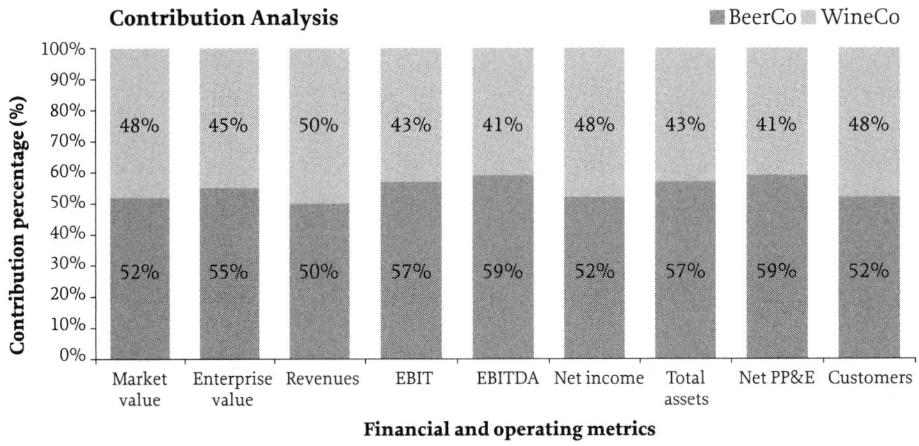

In Table 18.6, the percentages contributed average out to a 54.8 percent contribution by BeerCo and a 45.2 percent contribution by WineCo. However, this does not mean that the ownership split should be 55/45. Contribution analysis is just one indicator; other considerations such as the results from historical natural exchange ratio analysis and valuation analysis must be weighed before an exchange ratio should be chosen. Moreover, social issues can alter whatever ownership split might be implied by the various financial analyses.

> **Different methods of contribution analysis**
>
> It is important to note that practitioners can perform contribution analysis in different ways. As with any type of financial analysis, whenever starting at a new firm, it is important to understand whether a different methodology is used for a particular analysis compared to how you might have learned to do it previously. The old adage "there are many ways to skin a cat" pertains to many things in finance. There is not necessarily a right or wrong way as long as the methodology chosen is analytically correct and applied consistently throughout the analysis.

Historical Natural Exchange Ratios

Evaluating the historical natural exchange ratio is an important analysis with an MOE. The concept is that, even though the two companies are contributing different levels of revenues, assets, earnings, and perhaps even intrinsic value, the only metric that matters is the metric determined by the market – the stock price. This concept is based on the theory that the market is an independent observer and has properly valued each company (so that the fairest natural relationship between Company A and Company B is the "market" exchange ratio).

However, since stock prices change every day the market is open, over time the market exchange ratio changes as either or both companies' stock prices change. Historical natural exchange ratio analysis looks at the implied market-based exchange ratio over time based on closing stock prices. For example, the historical market exchange ratio over a year might imply an ownership split of 55/45 in January, 57/43 in March, 56/44 in June, 51/49 in September, and 47/53 in December. In such a situation, March would have been the most advantageous time for Company A to engage in a transaction (and the most disadvantageous for Company B) and December would have been the most disadvantageous time for Company A to engage in a transaction (and the most advantageous for Company B).

The exchange ratio is calculated as Company B stock price/Company A stock price, where Company A is the surviving stock. Similar to historical stock price performance, historical exchange ratio analysis should be performed for various time periods (e.g., 1 year, 2 years, 5 years, etc.) to see how it has changed over time.

The graph below shows the one-year historical exchange ratio for BeerCo and WineCo. Note the volatility in the ratio over the last year.

1. The current market exchange ratio is 3.25x
2. The exchange ratio went as high as 3.56x in June
3. The exchange ratio went as low as 2.84x in March
4. The average historical exchange ratio for the one year period was 3.15x

Figure 18.7 – One-Year Historical Natural Exchange Ratio

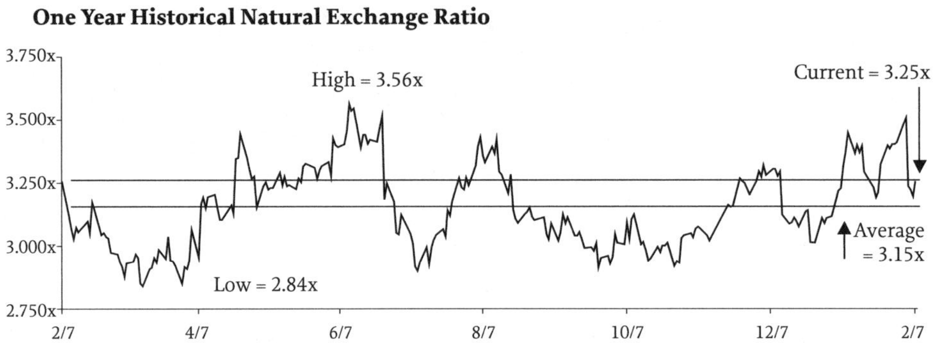

Valuation Analysis and MOEs

In addition to contribution analysis and historical exchange ratio analysis, traditional valuation analysis is performed when analyzing an MOE. For each of the major valuation methods (trading comparables, transaction comparables, discounted cash flow (DCF) analysis), a valuation range is determined for each company on a stand-alone basis. Then, an *implied exchange ratio* is calculated based on the stand-alone valuation ranges for both companies.

For example, after performing DCF analysis for BeerCo and WineCo, assume you have determined that the intrinsic value ranges are $18 to $26 per share for BeerCo and $60 to $70 per share for WineCo. Based on these valuation ranges, you would then conclude that the implied exchange ratio range was 2.692x to 3.333x calculated as follows:

$60 WineCo low price / $18 BeerCo low price = 3.333x
$70 WineCo high price / $26 BeerCo high price = 2.692x

In Figure 18.8, stand-alone valuation ranges are provided for BeerCo and WineCo and implied exchange ratios are calculated for each valuation methodology. These implied exchange ratios are used in conjunction with the information derived from contribution analysis and historical natural exchange ratio analysis to determine the proper exchange ratio based purely on financial considerations. Social issues are then considered in light of these financial conclusions to negotiate a deal exchange ratio that both parties consider fair to their respective sets of shareholders.

Figure 18.8 – BeerCo and WineCo – Stand-Alone Valuation

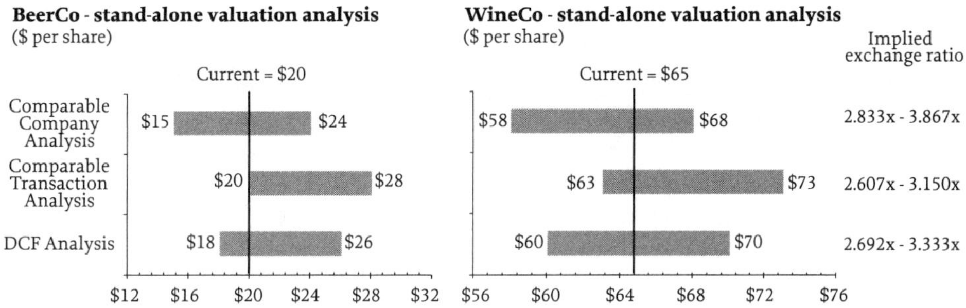

Governance and Other Issues

In negotiating an MOE, a number of social issues must be considered in conjunction with the financial considerations described in the previous section. All of the social issues described in this section are considered metrics of ownership or "control" and therefore play a meaningful part in determining the appropriate deal exchange ratio. Many of these items are negotiated up until the time at which a deal exchange ratio is chosen and a merger agreement is signed.

Composition of board of directors – A 50/50 board split is considered the most equitable treatment for both companies. However, often the board split will be representative of the pro forma ownership split. For example, in a merger of equals that is split in ownership 60 percent for Company A and 40 percent for Company B, the companies might agree to a board comprised of ten directors – six chosen by Company A and four chosen by Company B. In addition to the board split at announcement, initial versus long-term composition of the board also should be considered (e.g., phasing out of board positions over time, which board members are up for re-election first if it is a classified board, and/or replacing retiring Company A directors with new Company B directors, thereby increasing Company B's representation on the board). Also, establishment of board committees (e.g., Audit Committee, Compensation Committee, etc.) with equal representation from the two companies is common.

Senior management – This is a key area of sensitivity since it is difficult to achieve a truly equal balance of power in senior management (the CEO has more power than any other position). In theory it is possible to seek balance using other key jobs (CEO from one company and CFO and Treasurer from the other, for example) or provide the CEO position to one side for a period of time, with the succession going to a senior officer from the other side. The CEO role also can be traded against the Chairman position (CEO to Company A, Chairman to Company B). Arrangements do exist in which two companies in an MOE agree to two CEOs or "co-CEOs," but in practice, these arrangements often do not last long before one of the co-CEOs retires or steps down. Indeed, some practitioners would argue that there is no such thing as a true MOE since one management team usually dominates the newly created company. Employment agreements are often provided for key senior officers at the time a transaction is signed.

Location of headquarters and major facilities – This is especially important for companies with strong ties to the local community. The location of headquarters and/or major facilities affects unions, employees and tax revenues for local communities.

Company name – This is a brand and franchise issue. Market recognition is very important since loss of a brand can translate into lost value. Often, subsidiaries will maintain branded names and only the holding company will use a new name.

Pro forma dividend policy – The companies need to consider the new dividend policy and its impact on dividend yield and total return for both sets of shareholders. In an MOE, the new company often will adopt the dividend policy of the company that paid a higher dividend (either in terms of payout ratio or dividend yield). In this way, neither set of shareholders experiences a reduced dividend and one side benefits from an increased dividend.

Strategy identification – The post-transaction strategy must be communicated to investors at the time the transaction is announced. Since neither side is paid a significant premium in an MOE (recall that an MOE is usually a low-premium or no-premium transaction), it is important that investors understand how the new company will create value for them - since that value was not paid out to them in the form of a control premium at the time of announcement. If the new company's strategy is not well developed or not well communicated, the investors of the Target company might not vote to approve the transaction in light of the low premium and discontent with the strategic direction of the combined company. When most MOEs are announced, the management team communicates how much in synergies they expect to realize from the combination, with such synergies being the source of value creation for both sets of shareholders (and in lieu of a control premium to "Target" shareholders).

Negotiating an MOE

Negotiating an MOE can be very sensitive and its waters should not be entered lightly. Since MOEs are, by definition, pursued by two parties with relative parity, nearly all of the major characteristics of an MOE set forth above are subject to negotiation based on the total package. Also, neither side wants to feel as if it is the *Target*. As a result, posturing and positioning can occur. It is imperative for a successful MOE that both parties approach negotiations with a *positive sum game* approach rather than a *zero sum game* approach. And in MOEs more than in other types of acquisitions, there is a healthy element of quid pro quo such that if Company A's CEO were not chosen for the top job, for example, Company A might name 3 of the top 4 lieutenants to the CEO (although it should be noted that this quid pro quo is partly due to the fact that there is no clearly dominant party who can simply dictate terms).

Another thorny issue in MOEs is the question of transaction risk and deal protection since the absence of a control premium in most cases can serve as an invitation for a competing bidder to make an offer for one or both of the parties. Thus, the parties to an MOE need to have a firm commitment to the transaction and strong deal protection measures written into the contract. Otherwise, the announced transaction might serve as an impetus for an interloper (a competing bidder) to try to break up the transaction with an offer for one of the participants that includes a control premium. The difference, of course, is that the new bidder is proposing an *acquisition* in which the new bidder will clearly be the buyer --with all that entails, including dictating the majority of the governance provisions-- and Target shareholders only owning a minority of NewCo rather than an equal share (or close to it).

Part IV

Transaction Structuring

The Deal Team

CHAPTER 19

Each citizen should play his part in the community according to his individual gifts.

Plato

Executing any transaction requires the involvement of a number of players, and they all are important to its success. Company participants become involved during different stages of a transaction, and their participation may be brief or ongoing. In addition, there are players, unrelated to either party to the transaction, such as advisors and regulators, who play crucial roles. A group of people working on a transaction together is called a **deal team**.

Confidential Information

When bankers, lawyers, consultants, accountants, and others ("advisors") are working for a company on a transaction, their work products are generally privileged (meaning confidential) and seldom made publicly available. One of an investment bank's few work products that is disclosed is a Fairness Opinion provided to public companies that states that a particular transaction is "fair to shareholders from a financial point of view." Since advisors have access to confidential or "inside" information, there are many SEC-governed restrictions on their actions (from insider trading, for example) that are designed to protect shareholders. All inside participants in an M&A or capital raising process for a public company are subject to these SEC rules and regulations. These advisors also may be subject to additional rules and regulations set forth by their own firms, industry oversight boards or other organizations.

Those without access to inside information include investors, traders, arbitrageurs, hedge fund managers, research analysts, the general public, and others who could potentially profit from a transaction. It is a breach of confidentiality if someone with access to inside information shares it with someone without access to inside information (including spouses, relatives and friends). It is illegal if someone with access to inside information makes, participates in, or facilitates investment decisions in public companies based on that confidential information.

What is a CA or an NDA?

Members of a deal team and/or anyone with access to confidential information are required to sign a Confidentiality Agreement prior to gaining access to the confidential information. A **Confidentiality Agreement** ("CA" for short) is essentially synonymous with a **Non-Disclosure Agreement** ("NDA" for short). A CA or NDA is a legal agreement which prevents the recipient of confidential information from sharing that confidential information with anyone except under highly defined circumstances (for example, with members of the deal team). If confidential information is shared with an unauthorized person, the party that shared the information is considered to be in breach of the Confidentiality Agreement and could be legally liable to the other party for the consequences of the breach.

A few third-party participants, such as credit rating agencies and federal or state regulatory commissions, are sometimes provided confidential information before it is made publicly available. These participants are in a position of public trust and are not allowed to profit from that inside information. Outsiders who are provided confidential information are subject to the same insider trading restrictions that apply to other insiders.

The **ethical wall** or **Chinese wall** is an imaginary line drawn between those with access and those without access to confidential information. Within an investment bank, for example, there is an ethical wall between bankers in the Investment Banking Group and others bankers (Sales and Trading, Equity Research and Private Banking). Bankers in the Investment Banking Group are provided confidential information whereas the Sales & Trading, Equity Research and Private Banking bankers utilize public information to conduct their business. Because of the ethical wall, a banker in the M&A Group, for example, is not allowed to have a company-specific conversation with an equity research analyst.

Participants in the Transaction

In the following tables, the major players in an M&A transaction and their roles and responsibilities are described. Whether all of these parties are involved depends on whether a company is on the buy-side or the sell-side and whether due diligence is being performed on the other party. For example, if Target is receiving cash in the transaction and therefore is not performing due diligence on Acquiror, then a due diligence team would not be formed by Target to perform due diligence on Acquiror since it does not have to form an opinion regarding the value of Acquiror stock received in the transaction. However, regardless of whether cash or stock is being used as the acquisition currency, Acquiror would perform due diligence on Target.

Table 19.1 – The Deal Team

Company Participants

Participant	Key responsibilities
Senior Officers	• Make initial decision to pursue a transaction; determine strategy, size, timing, and other parameters • Interview and engage outside advisors; utilize "bake-offs" in which multiple banks and/or law firms are interviewed for a deal • Make decisions on key deal terms (e.g., price, conditions, etc.) and negotiate key transaction terms with the other party • Meet with members of the financial community to discuss strategic rationale and financial impact of the transaction
Board of Directors	• Remain apprised of transaction progress if the transaction is material to the company; advise senior officers • Vote to approve or disapprove the transaction when the vote is put to the board • *See discussion on fiduciary duties at the end of this chapter for additional board responsibilities*
Strategic Development Group	• Oversee all day-to-day aspects of the transaction; act as deal managers • If on buy-side, manage due diligence process; if on sell-side, manage data room, facility tours and management presentations • Work hand in hand with internal and external deal team members to address issues as they arise • Perform internal financial analysis; prepare internal presentations for the board and the financial community
Business Units	• If on buy-side, lead due diligence on operational, accounting, technology and other issues; provide meaningful and specific guidance on potential synergies; if on sell-side, prepare contracts and materials for data room and facilities tours and answer questions as they arise • Lead environmental due diligence (with legal counsel and environmental specialists) • Plan for and manage the integration and implementation of the acquisition, including systems integration

Table 19.1 continued

Company Participants continued

Internal Legal Counsel	• Oversee all legal aspects of the transaction (documents, contracts, environmental liabilities, etc.) • Engage (with senior officers) and oversee external legal counsel • Coordinate with external legal counsel to review all material contracts and agreements of Target during due diligence • Work closely with external counsel in drafting the Purchase and Sale or Merger Agreement and disclosure and closing documents • Participate in deal negotiations (with senior officers, external legal, and financial advisors)
Investor Relations	• Work with public relations advisors to develop how the transaction will be publicly announced • Work with strategic development group to prepare presentations for meetings with the financial community
Human Resources	• Lead due diligence on employee-related issues; provide meaningful guidance on potential synergies • Make recommendations regarding post-closing appointments • Plan and execute severance packages for any company employees let go post-closing

Company Advisors

Participant	Key responsibilities
Investment Bankers	• Provide extensive financial advice and services to the company (financial analysis, deal structuring, deal tactics, financing) • Provide a Fairness Opinion to the board of directors • Work with strategic development group to manage the transaction process • Participate in deal negotiations (with senior officers and legal advisors) • Communicate, on behalf of the company, with the other party and their various advisors

Table 19.1 continued

Company Advisors continued

External Legal Counsel	• Provide extensive legal and strategic advice to the company (deal structuring, deal tactics, legal issues, etc.) • Work with internal legal counsel on legal opinions and review of legal documents related to the transaction • Conduct legal due diligence • Draft Purchase and Sale or Merger Agreement • Participate in deal negotiations (with senior officers and financial advisors) • Participate in preparation of disclosure documents • Prepare closing documents
Local Legal Counsel	• Provide opinions on matters of local and/or state law • Support internal and external legal counsel on various matters
Accountants	• Review and audit (if necessary) financial statements and accounting controls of the Target • Prepare pro forma financials for SEC filings, if required
Public Relations	• In friendly transactions, generally brought in to assist with the deal announcement • In hostile transactions, public relations professionals get involved much earlier in the deal, and are closely involved in the execution of deal strategy, specifically with respect to the "court of public opinion" • Gaining the support of large institutional investors is an important objective in every transaction but is vital in hostile situations so public relations professionals spend a significant amount of their time on this task

External Players and Constituents

Participant	Key responsibilities
Shareholders	• Vote on the transaction, if required • Determine the outcome of a transaction, if vote is required

Table 19.1 continued

External Players and Constituents continued

Debt Holders	• Provide consents and/or waivers to approve a transaction, if outstanding debt agreements require it • Can determine outcome of transaction if key components are dependent upon such consents or waivers
Equity and Debt Research Analysts	• Provide existing and prospective shareholders and bondholders with their perspective on the strategic rationale and the financial impact of the transaction
Rating Agencies	• Provide a credit-oriented perspective on the strategic rationale and the financial impact of the transaction
Governmental Agencies	• Approve the transaction, if required • Examples of governmental agencies include the Federal Trade Commission, State Public Utility Commissions and the Federal Energy Regulatory Commission, banking agencies and other regulatory agencies
SEC	• If the transaction requires a vote, review the disclosure documents (e.g., merger proxy)

Fiduciary Duties of the Board of Directors

Members of a company's board of directors have certain fiduciary duties to the company's shareholders. Fiduciary duties are responsibilities of the board of directors and of management to protect the interests of shareholders. The fiduciary duties described below are: (1) the business judgment rule, (2) Revlon duties, and (3) enhanced scrutiny. While this discussion pertains to Delaware corporate law, most other states have adopted similar statutes. The applicable corporate codes should be referred to when analyzing a specific transaction. Additional issues related to the board of directors in the context of takeovers can be found in Corporate Defense. (Ch.23)

The Business Judgment Rule

- Provides directors with common law protection from liability related to decisions made as a director of a company on behalf of the company as long as the decision satisfies the following characteristics:

a. The decision was informed

b. The decision was made in good faith

c. The director had an honest belief that the actions taken were in the best interests of the company and its stockholders

d. The director discharged his or her duty of loyalty and duty of care

- Under the business judgment rule, directors of a corporation which has received an acquisition proposal are not required to accept any proposal (i.e., they can "just say no" to the proposal) or even to choose the *highest* bid. When presented with an acquisition proposal, the directors may consider other factors, such as:

a. The nature of the consideration offered (e.g., cash or stock)

b. The likelihood that the transaction will close

c. Any financing contingencies

d. Possible delays resulting from regulatory or antitrust issues

e. The bidder's identity and reputation

f. If the applicable law provides, the bidder's plans for the business including the impact of those plans on employees, customers, local communities and the general public (i.e., the company's stakeholders)

Revlon Duties

- Resulted from the 1986 Delaware case of Revlon v. MacAndrews & Forbes Holdings

- Case set forth the duties of directors who have decided to sell or break up the company

- Revlon duties are triggered if any of the following events take place:

a. The board has initiated an active bidding process for a sale of the company

b. The board has decided to effect a business reorganization involving a clear breakup of the company

c. The board has decided to abandon the company's long-term strategy in response to an offer either to break up or sell "control" of the company

- If Revlon Duties are triggered, the directors must obtain the highest value reasonably attainable for the shareholders.
- States that a formal auction is not required, but a market test or equivalent is required
- In the appropriate situation, a market test may be done by having a financial or legal advisor discuss a potential transaction with potential Buyers to determine their interest or lack of interest in a transaction with the selling company.
- Formal auctions represent the most transparent of market tests.
- Revlon duties are not implicated in a transaction which results in Target shareholders becoming part of an undifferentiated group (meaning without a controlling shareholder), even if Target shareholders end up with a relatively small percentage of the combined company. In situations where Target shareholders become part of an undifferentiated group (which is the case if they receive stock from an acquiring company where there is no controlling shareholder) it is not generally deemed to be a "sale of control" of Target.

Enhanced Scrutiny

- Resulted from the 1985 Delaware case of Unocal v. Mesa Petroleum. This was the first hostile transaction in which the Delaware courts imposed a higher fiduciary standard than the business judgment rule on a board of directors.
- Enhanced scrutiny requires a board considering a defensive action to meet an enhanced test before the protections of the business judgment rule are afforded to a board of directors.
- In order to pass enhanced scrutiny, a board of directors must show that (1) it reasonably perceived a significant threat to the company's integrity and (2) the defensive action was reasonable and proportionate to the perceived threat.
- Even if a board meets the requirements of enhanced scrutiny and therefore qualifies for the protections of the business judgment rule, the board still must independently meet the requirements of the Business Judgment Rule before it actually receives the protections of the rule.

Deal Mechanics

Chapter 20

Never breach a covenant,
whether you make it with a false person,
or with a just person of good conscience.
The covenant holds for both the false and the just.

Zoroastrian proverb

While no two M&A transactions are identical, there are certain prescribed steps that occur in nearly every transaction. This chapter will cover these so-called deal mechanics, including: (1) due diligence, (2) the legal contract between the parties, (3) deal protection mechanisms, (4) differences in legal contracts for public and private companies, (5) the methods of acquiring a public company, and (6) issues that arise in cross-border transactions. Members of a deal team are described in The Deal Team (Ch.19), tax issues related to structuring a transaction are covered in Taxes and M&A (Ch.21), and methods used to deter hostile acquisitions are covered in Corporate Defense. (Ch.23)

Due Diligence

Due diligence is the process of investigating and analyzing another company's assets or business. It begins with a review of publicly available information and, if both parties are in agreement, moves into a review of non-public information. A Confidentiality Agreement would be signed by the party receiving the non-public information. Confidentiality Agreements also may contain provisions relating to exclusivity and to non-solicitation. If both parties are disclosing non-public information, in the context of a stock-for-stock merger for example, the parties would sign a mutual Confidentiality Agreement.

What is a Confidentiality Agreement?

A Confidentiality Agreement (CA) is a legal agreement that prevents the recipient of confidential information from disclosing that confidential information except under defined circumstances, such as to other members of a deal team to assist in the due diligence process. A Confidentiality Agreement is also referred to as a Non-Disclosure Agreement (NDA).

Although due diligence can be complex, involving many parties and substantial time and resources, Acquiror has two basic goals during due diligence:

1. Confirm whether it wants to acquire Target
2. If so, determine how much Target is worth to Acquiror

Due diligence is the corporate equivalent of "kicking the tires" and includes actions such as ensuring that a plant that Target says it has in Ohio actually exists (and is owned by Target), assessing the net operating losses (NOLs) that might be available to help Acquiror reduce future tax payments, and reviewing legal and other liabilities associated with Target.

The timing of due diligence

In an auction process in which more than one bidder is potentially interested in Target, formal due diligence usually begins after initial indications of interest have been submitted (i.e., after first round bids). Those bidders chosen to participate in a second round of bidding are invited to conduct more detailed due diligence on Target. In this way, the selling company is able to limit which bidders receive access to a significant amount of Target's confidential information (for a discussion of the sell-side process, see Introduction to M&A (Ch.5)). In a non-auction situation (meaning Target is in exclusive negotiations with one or a small number of potential Acquirors), detailed due diligence usually begins after the Confidentiality Agreement has been executed.

During a transaction process, there is generally limited time available for due diligence. A typical due diligence process therefore includes a fairly standard set of steps:

1. Management presentations in which Target's management describes its business to potential bidders. The management presentation is generally followed by an in-depth question and answer period

2. Tours of major facilities, plants, warehouses or any other major operating sites

3. A review of a physical or electronic "data room" in which major contracts and documents of Target are presented for examination

4. Limited access to selected customers, suppliers, etc.

5. Follow-up to any questions or issues that emerge during the data collection period

Major participants in due diligence include: senior management; business managers from units such as operations, legal, human resources, environmental, R&D, and accounting; outside legal counsel; outside accountants; and investment bankers. Directors of a company do not usually participate in due diligence; instead, the company's senior management, with the help of advisors, shares its due diligence findings with the board and makes recommendations to the board. The board then considers these findings and recommendations and votes on whether to approve the transaction (a board must vote on a transaction if the acquisition is material to the company; this concept will be further discussed later in the chapter).

Due diligence is discussed in this section generally from the viewpoint of Acquiror's due diligence on Target. The comments, however, also apply to Target's due diligence on Acquiror *if Acquiror exchanges its stock for the stock of Target shareholders.* (After an exchange of stock, Target's selling shareholders have an ongoing interest in the merged entity and therefore should have an informed view of their Acquiror partner.) If Acquiror uses cash to purchase Target, Target is not likely to perform due diligence on Acquiror. (Since Target's selling shareholders will exchange their Target stock for cash, not for Acquiror stock, they will *not* have an ongoing interest in the merged entity and therefore are likely to be largely indifferent to Acquiror.) Even in a cash transaction, however, Target could still inquire into Acquiror's plans for Target's business or Target's employees since those issues might be important considerations for Target. Target also will be concerned with Acquiror's ability to deliver on its commitments, including whether Acquiror has sufficient cash or readily available financing to pay the purchase price. For additional information on financing conditions, see closing conditions later in the chapter as well as Sources of Capital. (Ch.25)

Due Diligence Objectives

There are five major objectives in a typical due diligence process:

1. **Verify the financial and business assumptions** underlying the valuation analysis (e.g., how much is Target worth to Acquiror) and financial impact analyses (e.g., how will the transaction affect Acquiror's earnings, cash flow, growth rate, and balance sheet, among other things). Verifying financial and business assumptions includes a detailed review of:

    a. The financial and operating history and outlook for Target's business (to determine Target's intrinsic value), with a particular emphasis on cash flow metrics (e.g., EBITDA) and capital expenditures

b. The liabilities of Target that may be assumed in a purchase (e.g., outstanding debt, environmental liabilities, tax liabilities, etc.), including any liabilities triggered by the transaction itself, such as employee severance costs and/or change-of-control payments to executives

c. The elements of major contracts, such as long-term supply contracts or employment contracts, including whether those contracts would be binding after a sale or change-of-control transaction

d. Target's relationships with major constituencies, including customers, suppliers, unions, and regulatory agencies, as well as an analysis of the transaction's impact on those major relationships

e. The potential opportunities for revenue and cost synergies. (For a discussion of synergies, see Strategic Transactions. (Ch.4))

2. **Assess known liabilities and identify potential liabilities**. Potential liabilities are any items that might become liabilities in the future but cannot be determined and/or quantified at the present time (and, therefore, do not appear as liabilities on the balance sheet). Potential liabilities could include the following:

   a. Pending or threatened litigation (e.g., product liability, discrimination, intellectual property, securities disclosure, etc.)

   b. Product recall or warranty issues

   c. Compliance with laws (e.g., federal laws, state corporation laws, and others)

   d. Environmental liabilities (e.g., cleanup, remediation, and/or decommissioning of old production facilities)

   e. Employee compensation liabilities (e.g., underfunded pensions)

   f. Accounting errors or corporate actions that might require the restatement of previous years' financial statements (e.g., overly aggressive accounting practices, questionable transactions, etc.)

   g. Tax liabilities, including any that might be triggered by the contemplated transaction

Typically, in a private transaction, Acquiror would try to receive **indemnification** from the selling company or the selling shareholders for these potential liabilities. Indemnification is protection against loss or damage (see text box: What is indemnification?). The amount of the indemnification and what it covers is typically negotiated by the two parties in the legal agreement. In a public deal (in which Target is a public company), it is generally not practical to negotiate indemnification because the sellers are a large group of unrelated shareholders. Therefore, instead of negotiating indemnification with the sellers, Acquiror typically would discount the price paid to the selling shareholders by the risk-weighted estimated value of the potential liabilities. In a competitive auction involving a private Target, the negotiation of indemnification with the selling party is generally difficult since another buyer might be willing to undertake the transaction without any indemnification. Any request for indemnification, therefore, could make the requesting bidder's offer less competitive than other bids.

What is indemnification?

Indemnification is protection, often in the form of financial compensation (money paid from one party to another) against loss or damage. Usually, in a private or subsidiary level transaction (public parent selling a subsidiary, so in essence it is like a private transaction), Seller indemnifies Acquiror for specified types of potential liabilities. For example, if Seller agrees to indemnify Acquiror for up to $100 million of *pre-closing* environmental liabilities and an environmental liability becomes known *post-closing* that is related to an event that occurred *pre-closing* (prior to the sale of the company), Seller could be required to pay for the loss up to a maximum amount of $100 million. For a liability greater than $100 million, Seller's exposure is capped at $100 million and Acquiror is responsible for any amount over $100 million.

Anyone or anything can be indemnified as long as it is not prohibited by law, such as indemnification against an illegal act. For example, a company cannot indemnify its officers from liability associated with knowingly breaking the law, but companies can (and many do) indemnify their directors and officers from liability associated with unknowingly and unintentionally breaking the law in the course of their actions on behalf of the company.

Indemnification can also provide protection from the costs of future legal actions, such as the reimbursement of costs and/or provision of legal counsel if sued for an indemnified act. Investment banks, for example, often seek indemnification from future legal liability arising out of advice they provide to their clients.

What is indemnification? continued

Most investment bank engagement agreements have an indemnification provision that states that the client will hold the bank harmless from any action the bank takes on behalf of the client as long as the bank's action does not constitute gross negligence or willful misconduct.

3. **Identify potential "deal killers,"** which are items that, unless addressed, could cause a party to choose not to proceed with the transaction. Deal killers are typically negotiation points about which one party feels strongly, so strongly, in fact, that the party is willing to walk away from the transaction if the situation is not resolved to the party's satisfaction. An example of a deal killer would be a Target CEO only contemplating a transaction if she is provided an ongoing role for a minimum of two years after the transaction closes, and Acquiror refusing to promise a position to the Target CEO. Another example could involve Target only contemplating a transaction if Acquiror agrees to maintain a meaningful presence in Target's home community, and Acquiror intending to shut down Target's local operations. Both of these are examples of positions so far apart that, in general, no amount of negotiation will allow the parties to reach agreement.

4. **Assess the cultural fit** of Acquiror and Target by meeting with Target management and its employees.

5. **Gain enough information to begin preliminary integration planning** and understand important integration issues.

Due diligence undertaken in the potential acquisition of a company is, in many ways, like the due diligence undertaken in assessing a potential home for purchase. Acquiror wants to conduct a thorough inspection of Target so that its senior management and board of directors can make an informed decision regarding the contemplated transaction. For its part, Target also wants to conduct a thorough inspection of Acquiror if Target is planning to accept Acquiror stock as part of the transaction consideration. Failure to conduct due diligence would be the equivalent of buying a home without an inspection. Imagine buying a house without conducting an inspection and realizing immediately after closing the sale that it has a substantial termite problem, and that termite remediation will cost a quarter of the home's value. In this situation, remediation would be Buyer's financial obligation. Had Buyer performed an inspection and the termite problem been discovered, Buyer might have tried to negotiate a reduction in the purchase price to cover the cost of the termite repair work, required termite remediation as a condition to closing, or simply walked away from the entire transaction had Seller not been willing to do the work.

Due Diligence Planning

There are several aspects to successful due diligence:

1. Planning, preparation, and organization by all parties is paramount, including assigning responsibility for key areas of due diligence. The old adage applies: "Failing to plan is planning to fail."

2. Due diligence is project management at its finest. The due diligence manager must be on top of all details. He or she must manage the team, coordinate logistics, work with different business units, and report findings to senior management and the board of directors. Within a company, the due diligence manager is usually a person from the company's corporate development team, and he or she often works closely with the vice president or senior associate on the banking team, the senior associate on the legal team, and the tax and accounting specialists. The project leader from the banking team is usually the main point of contact for the client company with the other party.

3. Communication among all team members on crossover matters is critical (e.g., environmental due diligence involves both operations and legal teams).

4. Given the limited time frame, it is physically impossible to review everything during a due diligence process. In addition, Target will not want to locate and provide diligence materials that are immaterial and/or unimportant. Therefore, it is a good idea to divide all issues into one of three buckets: (1) deal killers, (2) issues that have a material impact on value, and (3) issues that have a minor impact on value. By categorizing every issue into one of these three buckets, the deal team can focus on deal killers and the issues with the greatest value impact. For every item that has a value component, someone on the due diligence team who is qualified to do so should be responsible for estimating that value component.

5. Objectives for each business unit should be identified early on. (Validating the income statement and balance sheet is a responsibility of the accounting team; determining ability to integrate technology systems is a responsibility of the technology and integration teams, etc.).

6. Procedures should be arranged so that if information is needed or a meeting is required, there is one person who coordinates for everyone on the team. Usually the company's due diligence manager does this on the Acquiror side,

and the Target's banker coordinates for the Target due diligence team.

7. There should be an appropriate focus on the social issues (e.g., role of Target management in the new company, Target employee programs to be retained, other potential deal breakers for Target, etc.). Although people tend to focus primarily on the financial issues during due diligence, it is the social issues that often become deal breakers in the heat of negotiations.

8. It is important to communicate key due diligence results promptly to senior management. In this way, diligence findings can be reflected in the valuation and acquisition analyses and also in the negotiation of the acquisition agreement. This is particularly important for provisions related to indemnification and representations and warranties. Indemnification and representations and warranties are described in more detail later in this chapter in the section titled The Legal Agreement.

Areas of Due Diligence

Common areas of due diligence investigation are listed below. When arranging a due diligence team, it is important that someone on the team be responsible for each of these areas of investigation. Keep in mind that, depending on the company or industry, additional areas of investigation could be required.

1. Target's industry and the competitive environment
2. Financial health of Target and integrity of Target's strategic plan
3. Accounting procedures, disclosure, financial controls, and compliance
4. Employment agreements, employee remuneration and benefits (including pensions and healthcare), and issues related to employee termination
5. Insurance and risk management
6. Tax benefits and liabilities that may be inherited with the transaction or may be triggered by the transaction
7. Major contracts and relationships (especially those with change-of-control provisions)
8. Intellectual property, patents, and trademarks
9. Pending or potential litigation
10. Basic legal documents (articles of incorporation/charter, bylaws, board minute books, employee severance agreements, etc.)
11. Debt agreements (especially those with change-of-control-provisions) and the contemplated transaction's impact on credit rating and cost of funding
12. Age and quality of manufacturing equipment and other major assets
13. Analysis of Target's real estate portfolio
14. In-process research and development and the research and development pipeline

15. Sales, marketing, and distribution issues, including cost structure and market penetration
16. Environmental liabilities and remediation programs
17. Computer systems, including age, capability, and compatibility of technology
18. Human resources issues and employee-related costs
19. Integration planning
20. Other issues that may be specific to Target's industry

What is a change-of-control provision?

A **change-of-control provision** is a clause in a contract that allows a change to, or termination of, the contract if one party enters into a change-of-control transaction. A **change-of-control transaction** is one in which —after the transaction—the previous owners are no longer "in control," generally meaning they have sold the majority interest in the company to another company or to a private set of shareholders. Change-of-control provisions can sometimes be triggered by the sale of less than a majority interest in a company. Change-of-control provisions in contracts are important to identify because they may put leverage in the hands of the counterparty to the contract. Essentially, a change-of-control transaction allows the counterparty to renegotiate the terms of the agreement, often to the detriment of Target.

For example, assume that Target has a long-term supply contract with a raw materials company by virtue of which Target receives more than half of its raw materials at a price that is now 40 percent below current market prices. Also, assume that Target's contract with the raw materials company has a change-of-control provision. If Acquiror purchases Target in a change-of-control transaction, the raw materials company would have the ability to renegotiate the supply contract and presumably would do so at market prices. This would increase Target's cost of goods sold, decrease Target's profitability and cash flow, reduce the intrinsic value of Target, and affect the accretion/dilution impact to Acquiror.

Depending on the form of transaction, "assignment" provisions may be as troubling as change-of-control provisions. In an asset sale, in which assets are transferred, an assignment provision would require consent. The law on whether assignment provisions are implicated in a merger is not entirely settled.

What is a change-of-control provision? continued

From a legal perspective, due diligence regarding material facts is required in documents filed with the SEC, including proxy statements and offering documents. This is because shareholders can sue parties for misstatement or omission of a material fact. To establish a due diligence defense in litigation, the party in question must have had reasonable grounds after a reasonable investigation to believe that the statements made in a registration or proxy statement were true at the time they were made and that there were no material omissions or misstatements of material facts.

In the end, the amount of due diligence a particular deal team will undertake depends on the company's appetite for risk, the company's corporate organization, and the company's prior understanding of the assets and industry in which Target operates. While Acquirors in the U.S. have generally become more thorough in their approach to due diligence following the passage of the Sarbanes-Oxley Act, it would not be uncommon to see a five-person due diligence team from one bidder and a fifty-person due diligence team from another bidder for the same Target company.

The Legal Agreement

After Acquiror and Target have agreed upon all of the major deal points, these terms are encapsulated in a legal agreement between Acquiror and Target. If Acquiror directly purchases the stock of Target (e.g., either in a stock-for-stock or cash-for-stock merger), this legal agreement is usually called the **Agreement and Plan of Merger** (often shortened to "Merger Agreement"). A **Stock Purchase Agreement** might be used if Acquiror purchased stock but does not do a merger (for example, if there were very few shareholders and Acquiror wanted to avoid a filing and various rules governing mergers). If assets are sold or a division of a company is sold (as opposed to the stock of a company), this contract is sometimes called the **Purchase and Sale Agreement** or, more commonly, the **Asset Purchase Agreement**. For general discussion purposes in this chapter, all of these different types of contracts will be referred to as an "Agreement." The Agreement is a definitive contract signed by both parties that confirms in writing all of the terms agreed upon by the parties to a transaction.

The first draft of the Agreement is usually provided by whoever has more negotiating leverage, since the first draft is usually slanted in favor of the drafting party. In practice, this often means that the first draft is prepared by Seller in an auction and by Acquiror in a non-auction context (one-on-one negotiation), but this is not always the case. The non-drafting party provides comments on the Agreement and returns its "marked up" contract to the drafting party (marked up meaning the other party has written in its desired changes to the Agreement either by hand or, more commonly, with a black lined electronic version).

> **What is black lining?**
>
> When changes are made to a document, they are usually done using word processing software with tracking features turned on. With tracking features turned on, it is possible to see what has been added and what has been deleted from one draft to the next (including all changes to both language and punctuation). Additions are usually underlined and deletions are usually marked with a straight line through the middle of the text. This process is referred to as "black lining" or "red lining" a document because the changes are usually made with black or red lines.

In an auction, each bidder generally submits its revised version of the Agreement with its final bid, and the marked up contract is considered in conjunction with the bidder's offer price. A heavily marked up contract (many changes from Seller's preferred contract) will likely disadvantage a bidder, unless the offer price is especially attractive. In a non-auction context, the Agreement goes through several rounds of negotiations between the two parties. Once all of the deal points have been negotiated and incorporated into the document and the Agreement is deemed mutually acceptable, the two parties sign the Agreement. Outside legal counsel is generally responsible for making sure that the business agreements between the parties are accurately reflected in the Agreement.

Negotiation of the Agreement is an important and time-consuming task. The Agreement is generally not signed until after the board of directors of Target (and the board of Acquiror if the transaction is material to Acquiror and requires board approval) has approved the transaction. Signing the Agreement is a disclosable event for the SEC (again, if the transaction is material); therefore a public announcement is required promptly after the Agreement is signed. The announcement and a copy of the Agreement would be filed as an 8-K on the day of the announcement.

Following is a summary of the key sections of an Agreement. It is important to note that everything in a contract has a value component. Moreover, the goal of would-be acquirors and would-be sellers is to sign a contract, and each party's approach to each of the following provisions should be viewed through the prism of that goal.

Parties – The Agreement specifically identifies the parties to a transaction (e.g., Acquiror, Target, their subsidiaries if applicable, guarantors, etc.). This is important from a legal standpoint since it identifies who, specifically, is legally responsible for upholding the contract.

Description of assets and liabilities – In a Purchase and Sale Agreement (used for assets), this is a description of the assets to be purchased and any liabilities to be assumed by Acquiror. In a Stock Purchase Agreement (used for stock), there is usually no description of the assets because all of the assets and all of the liabilities of the corporation are conveyed with the sale of stock. In an asset purchase transaction, the **schedule of assets and liabilities** can be substantial since each asset to be sold and each liability to be assumed must be identified in the Agreement. As a simplifying alternative, rather than identifying each asset and liability, the assets being sold might be described as "all assets used primarily in the Business." The definition of Business would then describe the type of business being sold. If this simplifying approach is taken, then specific assets (and perhaps specific liabilities) are often excluded from the assets being sold (for example, the CEO's office furniture, artwork, etc.).

Purchase price – For a publicly held company, this is usually quoted as a price per share (e.g., $30 per share) or an exchange ratio in a stock-for-stock exchange (e.g., 2.5 Acquiror shares per Target share). For a private company, a division, or a subsidiary, the purchase price is usually expressed as an aggregate price (e.g., $500 million). Exchange ratios are described in Acquisition Currency and Stock Deals. (Ch.14,15)

Consideration – This describes the form of consideration (e.g., all cash, all stock, or cash and stock, notes, etc.), which is the currency with which Acquiror actually pays for the purchase. This section will also describe any collars, floors, or caps that are included in the deal (if stock consideration). In an asset deal, any assumed debt and liabilities would be described here. When stock is purchased (e.g., in a merger), the assets and liabilities generally are not described since all assets and all liabilities transfer by operation of law. Collars, floors and caps are described in Stock Deals. (Ch.15)

Additional consideration – This describes any additional payments to Target such as earnouts, contingent payments, or contingent securities (sometimes called contingent value rights or CVRs).

Purchase price adjustments – Adjustments are generally used to ensure that at the time of the closing, Target has a certain level of working capital, net asset value, or some other metric or metrics. Adjustments are used to capture changes between the date of the balance sheet on which Acquiror valued Target and the closing date. Common purchase price adjustments include changes in working capital or changes relative to agreed-to capital expenditures. Purchase price adjustments are seen most often in private transactions and are rarely seen in public company acquisitions.

Representations and warranties (reps and warranties) – Reps and warranties are statements by Acquiror and Target regarding various elements of their respective businesses. A common closing condition is that each party's reps and warranties were true as of the date of the Agreement and are true as of the closing date. Common reps and warranties include valid incorporation, legal authority to enter into the transaction, title to the shares or assets being sold, no material misstatement of fact or omission of material fact in the financial statements, and no known and undisclosed liabilities. Not all reps and warranties will be (or can be) satisfied as of signing or closing, so parties often negotiate exceptions to their reps and warranties, which are included in a separate disclosure schedule that is part of the Agreement.

It is extremely important to renew any exceptions to the reps and warranties so that all desired and agreed-to exceptions are recorded as of the closing date. If the exceptions are not current at closing, the non-current party may be in breach of contract. In addition, parties also negotiate materiality levels (i.e., how significant something must be before it results in a breach of a rep or warranty) and/or material adverse change (MAC) triggers. (The Agreement may be subject to termination if there is a material adverse change in the business; MACs are described below.) Breaching a rep or warranty is considered a breach of contract. If one party is in breach of contract, that party could be financially responsible to the non-breaching party for damages caused by the breach. In public transactions, reps and warranties usually do not survive closing --as with indemnification-- due to the difficulty of trying to enforce them against a disparate set of individual and institutional shareholders.

What is a MAC?

A **MAC** or a **material adverse change** is any event that materially changes the economic substance of the transaction for one, or both, of the parties. A MAC clause protects against events that take place after signing but before closing of a transaction, as well as the discovery of events that occurred pre-signing. This protection usually takes the form of allowing the transaction to be terminated if there is a MAC. The concept of "materiality" has long been a cause of legal wrangling since what one party considers "material" might be considered "immaterial" by the other party. In some contracts, specific metrics are written in to measure materiality (e.g., an event that causes a reduction in ten percent of the assets or net income of one party, etc.).

Pre-closing restrictive covenants – Pre-closing restrictive covenants are restrictions on a party's actions (often the Target) between signing and closing. Examples are provided below. Not every Agreement includes each of these covenants.

Interim operations – Often, the Agreement specifically states that certain actions are not allowed, such as declaring special dividends or divesting or acquiring material assets. This covenant ensures that Target does not pillage the company, thereby leaving a diminished shell in place of the company Acquiror thought it was purchasing, or enlarge it, thereby creating a heavily indebted company.

No shop restrictions – After the Agreement is signed, Target is not allowed to "shop" its deal with Acquiror to other potential bidders. Usually the no shop/no talk provision provides that Target cannot seek out a competing offer, provide information to a third party if that third party is potentially another bidder for Target, or negotiate with a third party regarding a transaction. In the absence of this restriction, Target could take Acquiror's bid and use it to "shop" for another, higher offer using Acquiror's offer as the stalking horse or price to beat. Since Target's board of directors may have a fiduciary obligation in a change-of-control transaction, Target may negotiate a "fiduciary out," or exception, in the Agreement whereby the Target board of directors is able to furnish information and participate in negotiations in response to an unsolicited offer from a third party. Usually the board is able to respond only if the unsolicited offer constitutes, or could be expected to lead to, a "superior proposal" and if, after receiving advice from counsel, the board determines that its fiduciary duties require it to respond. In a sale of a public company, technically, any bid can be topped because Target shareholders can always vote it down, at which point another bidder can buy the company. The purpose of the fiduciary exception in the no shop restriction is to make the process of accepting a better deal less onerous since it enables Target to simply terminate the Agreement (the lower bid) rather than go through the expensive and time-consuming process of holding a shareholder vote on a deal that shareholders would ultimately vote down (because another bidder has publicly announced a better deal). To shortcut this process, the Target board must be able to entertain offers that better serve the shareholders whose interests the board has a fiduciary obligation to protect. To compensate the initial bidder (or highest bidder in a multi-bid scenario) for that risk, the initial (or highest) bidder usually receives a breakup fee if it is topped by another bidder. Once the Agreement is signed, the no shop provision applies until closing. Breakup fees are described in the following section.

Go shop provisions – Increasingly, some companies are putting "go shop" provisions into their Agreements. A go shop provision is the opposite of a no shop restriction. A go shop provision encourages Target to seek other bidders after the Agreement has been signed in order to ensure that Target has maximized value for its shareholders. Breakup fees would still be paid to Acquiror if Target decided to pursue a transaction with another party. Go shop provisions would only be necessary in situations in which Target did not perform a broad-based auction before agreeing to a transaction with Acquiror (e.g., if it entered into exclusive negotiations with Acquiror or only approached a small universe of potential bidders). A go shop provision provides Target's board with more protection from shareholders who might not be satisfied with the deal reached with Acquiror – it essentially says to the shareholders "Yes, we signed this deal, but we can accept other deals if a higher or better one comes in the door."

Post-closing restrictive covenants – Post-closing restrictive covenants are restrictions on a party's actions (often the Target) after the transaction closes. Assuming Target does not have a single large shareholder, post-closing covenants of the type set forth below are not relevant when one public company is bought by another public company because there is no "seller" after the closing who can agree to any covenant (since a public company is owned by many individual and institutional shareholders). Post-closing covenants are most relevant when a company sells a subsidiary to another company (and so Acquiror can seek covenants and other assurances from Seller), which is also when non-compete and non-solicitation provisions are most relevant. Examples include the following:

> ***Non-compete and non-solicitation provisions*** – Many agreements prevent a company selling a division or subsidiary from creating or acquiring a new business to compete with the business being sold to Acquiror (non-compete), and from soliciting employees of the sold business (non-solicitation) for a period of time after the closing of the transaction. This covenant prevents Seller from immediately establishing a competing business and reclaiming customer and supplier relationships, thereby undermining Acquiror's chances for success and also decreasing the value of the business acquired. If Target itself is acquired or merged (rather than a division or subsidiary of Target), Acquiror may seek non-compete agreements from key executives and principal shareholders.

Pre-closing affirmative covenants – Whereas restrictive covenants prevent a party from taking certain actions, affirmative covenants require that a party (often the Target) take certain actions between signing and closing. Examples include the following:

> ***Operation of business in the ordinary course*** – Target must continue to operate its business as it normally would (the language in the Agreement is usually "consistent with past practice" or "in the ordinary course").

> ***Obtaining stockholder approval,*** *if necessary* – Each company must assume this responsibility for itself. There is often a covenant requiring the involved

companies to prepare whatever disclosure documents may be required in connection with the solicitation of shareholder approval. This covenant usually applies only to public company transactions since, in a private company transaction, shareholder approval would normally be obtained prior to signing the Agreement.

Obtaining regulatory approvals – Again, each company must assume this responsibility for itself. However, the lengths to which each company must go to satisfy this requirement is often negotiated and, ultimately, depends on the degree of pain each company is willing to suffer to obtain regulatory approval. For example, Target may not want to close the transaction if it thinks that government-imposed obligations required for approval will significantly reduce the value of the Acquiror stock it is receiving in the deal. Conversely, Acquiror may not want to close if regulators require, as a condition for approval, that Acquiror agree to dispose of specific assets (or assets with a specific dollar value).

"Hell or high water" clause – Each party must do what it can ("come hell or high water") to obtain requisite approvals. This covenant – if the parties choose to include it in the Agreement – ensures that both sides are committed to completing the transaction and are willing to take whatever steps necessary to ensure that the transaction closes. The danger with this clause is that it may require both parties to take actions that are unreasonable to obtain requisite approvals.

Cooperation – Target must allow Acquiror access to the company's books and records. This covenant is partly prospective, so that Acquiror can begin the planning and integration process, and partly protective, so that between the signing and closing of the transaction Acquiror can undertake a detailed examination of the company that it is planning to purchase. Note that there are usually two "cooperation" covenants, though often the pre-closing covenant (this one) is called "Cooperation" and the post-closing covenant is called "Further assurances" (noted below as Cooperation/further assurances).

Post-closing affirmative covenants – Whereas restrictive covenants prevent a party from taking certain actions, affirmative covenants require that a party (often the Target) take certain actions after closing. Examples include the following:

Cooperation/further assurances – This covenant recognizes that the parties may agree to close the transaction even though not all actions that they expected to occur prior to the closing have occurred (e.g., obtaining minor third-party consents) and provides that each party will cooperate with the other to complete those actions post-closing.

Tax filings – Often, there is a post-closing covenant that allocates responsibility for preparing and filing tax returns post-closing that will relate to the "straddle period" – which is a taxable period that includes both the pre-closing and post-closing period.

Taxes – In addition to the covenant on tax filings, there is often a post-closing covenant related to taxes, which can become very complicated. For example, if Acquiror buys a subsidiary out of a consolidated group, that subsidiary is technically liable for the pre-closing taxes of the *entire* company (not just the subsidiary). As a result of the significance of this issue, there is often a separate agreement, called a tax sharing agreement, to deal with the issue.

Books and records – This covenant is common, especially in the sale of a subsidiary or division. In a books and records covenant, Acquiror agrees to give Seller access to the books and records of the sold company, usually for seven years or so. There are usually reasonable limitations on the access (e.g., must be for a valid business purpose, etc.).

Closing conditions – Closing conditions are requirements that must be met before the closing date. If closing conditions are not satisfied by the specified date, then the other party is not contractually obligated to move forward with the transaction. Examples include the following:

Approvals have been obtained – The transaction generally cannot proceed to closing without the appropriate approvals. These can be regulatory, shareholder, or third-party approvals. Third parties who might need to approve a transaction include debt holders (only if required) or major suppliers (if an agreement or contract provides that the suppliers may terminate critical supply agreements upon a change of control). Examples of regulatory agencies that might need to approve a transaction include the Federal Trade Commission (FTC), the Department of Justice (DOJ), the Federal Communications Commission (FCC) and the Federal Energy Regulatory Commission (FERC).

Representations and warranties are materially true – This should be the case as of closing or as of another specified date. In a stock-for-stock exchange, both Acquiror and Seller seek as much protection in the form of reps and warranties as possible (in a cash deal, Acquiror's representations are minimal and Target is mostly interested not in the representations but in receiving its cash). The requirement that the reps and warranties are materially true as of closing is a representation that nothing dramatic has changed between the signing of the Agreement and the closing. This protects Acquiror from having to close if it discovers *after* signing the Agreement that something bad happened to Target *prior to* signing that was not previously disclosed to Acquiror.

No material adverse change – This confirms no material adverse change (MAC) in Seller's business and/or the assets being acquired. The purpose of this condition is to ensure that nothing has occurred between the signing of the Agreement and the closing that would cause Target to be worth materially less than what was bargained for at the time the Agreement was entered into. This requirement protects Acquiror from having to close if it finds out after signing that something had happened that will materially and adversely affect Target.

Financing conditions, if any, have been met – This is particularly important in highly leveraged transactions but can apply in any transaction in which cash is part of the consideration. The reason for this covenant is the same as a mortgage contingency in a home purchase. Acquiror does not want to be contractually obligated to buy Target if it is unable to obtain the financing with which it planned to pay for Target. For this same reason, Target will often resist the inclusion of a financing condition.

Each party has complied with its agreements – This is a catch-all condition and seeks to ensure that each party discharges all of the pre-closing obligations required by the Agreement.

Indemnification – Indemnification is protection to a party for specific types of losses. It usually provides for reimbursement of loss up to a maximum amount (or cap) if a certain event occurs. Indemnification clauses also often provide that no recovery can be made unless a deductible or threshold is first met (a basket). Examples of indemnifiable losses include the following:

Breach of reps and warranties or covenants – The concept here is one of fairness; if one party to the transaction breaches, the other party should be reimbursed for its damages by the breaching party. However, post-closing indemnity clauses are rare in transactions in which Target is publicly held (due to the difficulty of obtaining reimbursement from a large group of ex-shareholders).

Potential liabilities – An example of deal-specific indemnification would be if Target indemnified Acquiror for losses incurred in connection with an ongoing litigation matter (involving Target) that involves Acquiror only by virtue of Acquiror's purchase of the stock of Target (recall that in a stock purchase, *all* assets and *all* liabilities transfer to the Acquiror). This type of indemnification is negotiated and deal-specific. Other examples might include indemnification for environmental liabilities or indemnification for employee-related litigation. Indemnification can be one-sided, in which Seller indemnifies Acquiror, or mutual, in which the parties indemnify each other.

Termination provisions – Termination provisions give rights to each party to cancel the Agreement based on the occurrence of certain events or circumstances. Termination provisions are also referred to as "outs." Examples include the following:

> ***"Drop dead date"*** – Most agreements have a date when either party can terminate the Agreement if the transaction has not closed by then. The purpose of a drop dead date is to allow both parties to move on if, for whatever reason, the transaction gets stalled. Regulatory approvals are often the cause of significant delays.
>
> ***Breach*** – This protects each party from having to comply with the terms of the contract (and go ahead with the transaction) if the other side has not fulfilled its covenants or if the other party's reps and warranties are not true as of the closing date.
>
> ***Material adverse change (MAC)*** – In a stock-for-stock transaction, both parties have the option to terminate the transaction due to a MAC. That is, Acquiror has the option to terminate if there has been a material adverse change in Target, but Target also has the option to terminate if there has been a material adverse change in Acquiror (since Target will receive Acquiror stock, an Acquiror MAC affects Target also). In an all-cash transaction, only Acquiror has the option to terminate for a MAC. Target would not have that right in a cash deal because, from Target's perspective, all that matters is that Acquiror has the cash to pay.
>
> ***Fiduciary out*** – This fiduciary obligation is distinct from, but related to, the so-called Revlon duty, which requires a board of directors to accept the best value reasonably available in a change-of-control transaction in a cash deal (with some exceptions) (for a discussion of Revlon duties see The Deal Team (Ch.19)). Since the board has a legal duty with which it must comply in both cash and stock deals, the provision enables the board to comply with this legal duty by allowing termination in the event that the board's fiduciary obligations to shareholders require the board to accept a superior competing offer.

Deal Protection

Given the high costs of pursuing a transaction, both financial and in terms of time, parties to a transaction are understandably eager to see a deal close (though generally it is Acquiror who seeks deal protection in case its offer is topped; a higher offer actually benefits Target). In order to provide some assurance that their efforts, time, and money were not spent in vain, parties to a transaction generally write **deal protection** mechanisms into the Agreement. These are hurdles or barriers designed to make it unattractive for a third party to break up a transaction. Deal protection mechanisms are also designed to compensate the unsuccessful party for the lost economic and opportunity costs of being "left at the altar." A third party attempting to break up a transaction is called an **interloper**. Deal protection mechanisms cannot prevent all competing offers (without creating a breach of Target board's fiduciary obligations). If an interloper offers more value for Target, even after taking into account the costs involved in breaking up the previous transaction, many times Target's board will recommend the interloper's bid out of fiduciary duty.

Typical deal protection provisions include the following:

Breakup fee – This is a fee that must be paid by one party to the other party if a deal falls apart due to one party walking away from the transaction. Certain events can trigger payment of a breakup fee to the other party:

1. Target's cancellation of the transaction due to the exercise of fiduciary duties

2. Target entering into a transaction with a different party within a certain period of time after the Agreement has been terminated (often 12 to 18 months)

Usually the breakup fee is equal to *2 to 4 percent of Target's equity value.* Breakup fees are generally paid by the party that terminated the deal. If the transaction was terminated by no fault of a party (for example, the drop dead date passed and both parties agreed to cancel the Agreement), then neither party pays a breakup fee. Under Delaware law, company stock options (sometimes called cross options), expenses, and the breakup fee itself are aggregated for purposes of testing the reasonableness of the breakup fee (2 to 4 percent guideline).

No shop/no talk provision – This provision, which is commonly found in public company Agreements, is designed to prevent Target from having discussions with other potential Acquirors after it has signed an Agreement with Acquiror. The "no shop" and "go shop" provisions are discussed in the section on pre-closing restrictive covenants.

Stockholder lockups and irrevocable proxies – These are agreements with major stockholders of Target. If Target has a major stockholder, it is common for Acquiror to ask him or her (or a small group of major stockholders) to agree to certain things and for these agreements to be in writing. Stockholder agreements are usually signed at the time the Agreement is signed. Major stockholder agreements generally require that the stockholder:

1. Not sell his or her stock before the transaction closes
2. Act in support of the transaction. This would include voting in favor of the

transaction, tendering shares (if a tender offer), and not voting in favor of a competing transaction

Usually there is a covenant in the agreement with the major shareholder(s) stating that if the stockholder breaches any of the provisions above, the stockholder grants an **irrevocable proxy** to Acquiror to vote that stockholder's shares. The purpose of the irrevocable proxy is to serve as a form of insurance for Acquiror such that, if the stockholders in question do not vote in favor of the transaction, the voting rights to their shares shift to Acquiror via the irrevocable proxy (a proxy in this context is the written power to vote the shares of the selling shareholders). In this way, once the stockholder lockup and irrevocable proxy agreements have been signed, the selling shareholders' votes will be voted in favor of the transaction either by the selling shareholders (via the voting agreement) or by Acquiror (via the irrevocable proxy since, if the voting agreement is abandoned, the right to vote the shares shifts by proxy to Acquiror).

Crown jewel purchases – This provision gives Acquiror the right to purchase critical assets from Target, the loss of which may make Target unattractive to an interloper. This provision has been prohibited in certain jurisdictions (because it may unduly inhibit alternative bids) and is no longer common.

Company stock options – These are options granted to Acquiror to buy shares of Target that can be exercised if a transaction comes to pass with a different acquiror. For example, if a third party acquires or offers to purchase a certain percentage of Target's stock, or if Target terminates the Agreement, Acquiror can exercise this option and buy a stake in Target. The idea is to make a competing proposal unattractive to a third party since Acquiror would become a new shareholder in Target upon exercise of the option. More practically, if an interloper makes a higher bid for Target and the existing transaction is superseded, then Acquiror's stock options in Target would be triggered, and it would make money on the exercise or sale of its options in Target to the interloper. Company stock options were popular when pooling of interests accounting treatment was available (since the option precluded a competing bidder from obtaining pooling treatment, which was highly desirable). Since pooling treatment no longer exists in the U.S., such options are now used infrequently.

Public vs. Private Agreements

Some key differences in the Agreement exist between private company transactions and public company transactions. Note that "private companies" include subsidiaries of public companies; therefore, if a public company were to divest a subsidiary, that would generally be considered a private deal. Public deals generally refer to transactions in which Acquiror purchases publicly traded stock from a large group of selling shareholders.

Two major issues are responsible for many of the differences between public and private transactions. First, a publicly traded company is already subject to regulated public disclosure requirements, making the business of a public company more transparent than that of a private company. Second, a publicly traded company is usually owned by a large number of individual and institutional shareholders, making certain actions, such as collecting on indemnification provisions post-closing, almost impossible to implement.

Some of the differences between public company and private company transactions are described below:

- The reps and warranties in public company Agreements are generally broadly defined, expire at closing, and are more limited than reps and warranties in a private deal. In a private transaction, for example, it is not unusual to have certain reps and warranties survive for twelve months or longer post-closing. Moreover, in private transactions, the reps and warranties for tax- and environmental-related events typically survive for even longer periods due to the greater amounts of liability associated with them.

- Indemnification for potential liabilities or breach of reps and warranties is rare in public transactions, whereas it is common in private transactions. In public deals, bidders usually account for unknown liabilities with a downward adjustment to the purchase price.

- Purchase price adjustments are rare in public transactions, whereas they are common in private transactions. Purchase price adjustments are commonly tied to changes in working capital or capital expenditures, earnouts based on future performance, or additional payments (called contingent payments) that are contingent on a certain event occurring or not occurring, as the case may be.

- The vast majority of public company transactions are done as mergers, or as tender offers followed by mergers, due to the onerous tax consequences of acquiring the assets of a publicly traded Target and then distributing cash or stock to Target's shareholders. In private company transactions, there is more flexibility with regard to whether the transaction is structured as a merger, a purchase of stock, or a purchase of assets.

- In the context of the sale of a company, exclusive negotiations are rarely allowed in public deals, whereas they are common in private deals. Exclusive negotiations occur when Target is taken "off the market" while Acquiror and Target try to negotiate a transaction.

- Breakup fees in public deals generally range between 2 and 4 percent of Target's equity value. Because it is already difficult to break up a private transaction, breakup fees are unusual in private deals, though non-refundable deposits may be used as "earnest money" or "good faith money" in private transactions.

Corporate Acquisitions

There are three methods of acquiring a publicly traded company: (1) a merger or combination of Acquiror and Target companies; (2) an acquisition of stock directly from Target shareholders using various methods, such as a tender offer followed by a merger to acquire any remaining untendered shares (often called a two-step acquisition); or, more rarely, (3) an acquisition of Target's assets and a distribution of the sale proceeds to Target shareholders. Also, although not technically a method to acquire a company, a proxy contest can be used to gain control of a company's board of directors, which can facilitate a subsequent merger or acquisition.

The methods to acquire a publicly traded company are summarized below and described in more detail in following sections.

1. A **merger** is the most traditional way to acquire a public company and involves the legal combination of two corporations. Mergers are governed by state statutes and require an affirmative vote of either a majority or a supermajority of Target's shareholders for approval. The voting threshold varies from company to company and is laid out either in the company's charter or bylaws or, if the company's charter and bylaws are silent on the matter, is determined by the corporation laws of the state in which Target is incorporated. If Acquiror will issue more than 20 percent of its pre-transaction shares in the merger, then Acquiror shareholders also must vote in favor of the transaction. Merger transactions are further described in the following section.

2. Another method to acquire a publicly traded company is to acquire the stock directly from the shareholders. Acquiror can do this in a privately negotiated transaction with the majority shareholder(s) of Target (more common in private transactions) or, if there is no majority shareholder, Acquiror could use a tender offer process to acquire Target shares directly from minority shareholders (more common in public transactions). A **tender offer** is an offer made directly to Target shareholders and does not require a shareholder vote *if* enough shares are tendered in the process (i.e., shareholders "vote" by choosing to tender or not tender their shares). If less than 100 percent of the shares are tendered, then a second step, a merger, is required in order to gain control of those non-tendered shares. Mergers are

utilized more frequently than tender offers, but tender offers are attractive at times because, under certain circumstances, they can be executed more quickly. Tender offers are further described after the Merger Transactions section.

3. The third method to gain control of a public company is for Acquiror to purchase all of the assets of Target and then for Target to distribute the after-tax sale proceeds to Target shareholders. Generally, this method is highly tax inefficient and therefore is rarely used as a method involving the acquisition of a publicly traded company. The asset purchase method is more common in subsidiary level transactions and sometimes in private transactions. Key tax issues involved in asset purchase transactions and stock purchase transactions are described in Taxes and M&A. (Ch.21) A sale of all or substantially all of the assets of Target requires a shareholder vote just as does a merger. In a subsidiary level transaction, this "shareholder vote" is generally not problematic because the parent corporation usually owns all or a substantial majority of the subsidiary stock and therefore the results of the shareholder vote are a foregone conclusion.

4. Although not a method to acquire the shares of a public company, a **proxy contest** is a method to gain control of a public company's board of directors. It is used in some hostile situations when activist shareholders want to influence the board's actions or put directors on the board who support the dissident shareholders. In a proxy contest, an existing shareholder recommends a new slate of directors (or as many directors as can be nominated at the upcoming annual shareholder meeting). It is important to note that a proxy contest, if successful, only changes the board of directors. The shareholders of Target remain in place. Thus a successful proxy contest is only half the battle. Acquiror would still need to acquire Target by one of the methods described above (merger, acquisition of stock, acquisition of assets). The difference is that, after the successful proxy contest, Acquiror is now dealing with a Target board that is sympathetic to a transaction. Proxy contests are further described after the Tender Offer section.

Merger Transactions

In a **merger**, one corporation is combined with and disappears into another. First, the two parties negotiate and sign a merger agreement. To gain approval for the merger, Target issues a disclosure statement to Target shareholders (called a **merger proxy** if Acquiror offers cash to Target shareholders and called a **merger prospectus** if Acquiror offers all stock or cash-and-stock to Target shareholders) that describes the terms of, reasons for, risks of, and conditions to the proposed merger. The SEC must deem a merger *prospectus* "effective" before shareholders can vote on the transaction because it is a stock issuance, just like any other stock issuance (e.g., an IPO), even though the newly issued stock is being used to pay for Target. While the SEC does not need to deem a merger *proxy* effective if the acquisition consideration is cash (since no stock is being issued), the merger proxy is still subject to the proxy rules and the SEC may provide comments. In the merger proxy or prospectus, Target's management and board will state that they believe the proposed merger is in the shareholders' best interest and that they recommend shareholders vote to approve the deal. In addition, management and the board will describe their reasons for recommending the merger, which would include analyses performed by the company's investment bankers on behalf of management and the board of directors. If a fairness opinion was provided by the company's investment bankers, this would also be referenced in the merger proxy or prospectus.

After a period to review this disclosure statement, Target shareholders vote on the proposed transaction at a shareholder meeting. This can be done at Target's annual shareholder meeting or at a **special meeting** called for the sole purpose of conducting the vote. In a change-of-control transaction, Target shareholders must vote on the deal. If Acquiror is also a public company and will issue more than 20 percent of its pre-transaction shares to Target in the deal, Acquiror's shareholders also must vote to approve the transaction. For example, if Acquiror has 100 shares outstanding and will issue at least twenty-one new shares to Target stockholders in the merger, Acquiror shareholders must vote to approve the transaction. This is a NYSE and NASDAQ exchange rule, not a state law requirement – companies that are not listed on the NYSE or NASDAQ may not be subject to this requirement.

If both Acquiror and Target require a shareholder vote, they will often file a **joint merger proxy** or **joint merger prospectus** instead of each filing its own documents with the SEC.

Mergers are often referred to as **statutory mergers** because mergers are effected by operation of statute or law. Most stock-for-stock mergers are structured as so-called tax-free reorganizations. The most common type of reorganization is a triangular merger in which Target merges into a subsidiary of Acquiror (called a forward triangular merger) or in which a subsidiary of Acquiror merges into Target (called a reverse triangular merger). Tax-free reorganizations are described at the end of Taxes and M&A. (Ch.21)

Mergers require a fair amount of time due to the work involved in preparing the merger proxy or prospectus, notice requirements, and the time and logistics involved in arranging a shareholder vote. In total, a typical merger can take anywhere between twelve and twenty weeks to complete (or more in certain circumstances) from announcement to closing, depending on the scheduled date of the shareholder vote and any required regulatory approvals. The benefit of the merger process, as compared to a potentially shorter process such as the tender offer (described in the following section), is that a merger is an "all or nothing" process. If the company receives a majority of votes in favor of the deal (or a supermajority if such is required by the company's bylaws or state statutes), the transaction is approved and can close (assuming all regulatory approvals are received).

For example, for a Target with a supermajority voting requirement, if 67 percent of shareholders vote to merge Target with Acquiror, Acquiror will own 100 percent of Target's shares upon consummation of the merger. The remaining 33 percent of shares must be sold to Acquiror, even though the shareholders of these 33 percent of shares voted against the transaction.

A merger generally follows the following timeline:

Table 20.1 – Representative Merger Timeline

Weeks	Event(s)
2 – 4	Target and Acquiror (if required) draft the merger proxy (cash consideration) or merger prospectus (all stock or a combination of cash and stock consideration)
2 – 4	SEC reviews disclosures and provides comments
2 – 3	Companies address SEC's concerns, if any
2 – 4	SEC declares merger prospectus effective and companies mail documents to shareholders
3 – 4	Shareholders review documents
1 day	Shareholder vote takes place at the annual meeting or at a special meeting called specifically for the purpose of voting on the proposed transaction
1 – 3	Companies await any other regulatory approvals (could take longer than three weeks)
1 day	Transaction closes and Target merges with Acquiror
Total:	12 – 20 weeks (or longer) depending on SEC issues with the merger proxy/prospectus, the scheduled date of the shareholder vote, and the receipt of any required regulatory approvals

What are appraisal rights?

Most states provide Target shareholders the opportunity to seek appraisal rights for the "fair value" of their shares if (1) they did not vote in favor of the merger and (2) they object to the offer price within a prescribed period of time. In a public stock-for-stock deal, there generally are no appraisal rights under state law. If *appraisal rights* (sometimes called "dissenter's rights") are exercised, an appraisal proceeding is conducted to determine the fair value of the consideration offered. The dissenting shareholders then receive whatever that appraisal proceeding determines is the "fair value" of the Target shares. There are two important considerations related to appraisal rights. First, the price determined in the appraisal proceeding may be higher, lower, or the same as the offer price (i.e., dissenting shareholders may actually end up losing money if the value per Target share determined in the appraisal proceeding is lower than the offer price in the merger). Second, even if appraisal rights are sought and dissenting shareholders contest the price offered for their Target stock, they cannot retain that stock if a majority (or supermajority, if required) of the shares outstanding vote in favor of the transaction. This is true even if the dissenters voted against the merger and decide to contest the price they received for that stock (i.e., the majority has spoken and, since mergers are for 100 percent of the stock, a 67 percent shareholder vote requires the exchange of 100 percent of the stock, regardless of the fact that 33 percent of the shareholders voted against the transaction). Thus the appraisal rights process merely entitles dissenting shareholders to the possibility of additional consideration and, even then, only if the appraisal rights proceeding results in a finding that the merger consideration was less than the fair value of Target shares.

Tender Offers

A **tender offer** is an offer to purchase shares directly from the shareholders of Target *in exchange for cash.* An **exchange offer** is an offer to purchase shares directly from the shareholders of Target *in exchange for all stock or a combination of stock and cash.* With tender offers and exchange offers, each Target shareholder makes an independent decision whether to tender the shares held; thus in a tender offer a shareholder "votes" by choosing to tender shares or not tender shares. If a Target shareholder chooses not to tender her shares to Acquiror, she simply does not do so – no other action is required. The following discussion will refer to both tender offers and exchange offers collectively as "tender offers." Where there is a distinction between a tender offer and an exchange offer, the distinction will be made in the text.

A tender offer can be friendly (meaning Target's management and its board of directors approve of the transaction) or a tender offer can be hostile (meaning Target's management and its board of directors *do not* recommend the transaction).

An acquisition by way of a tender or exchange offer is, by definition, a two-step process; the tender or exchange offer is the first step, and a merger is the second step. This compares with a traditional one-step merger, which requires only the shareholder vote (as described in the previous section). From start to finish a tender offer can take as few as six weeks, making it an attractive method if speed to closing is a goal for the parties since this is much faster than a one-step merger (12–20 weeks). However, as shown in Figure 20.3, a tender or exchange offer *may* be faster than a traditional one-step merger, but it is not necessarily faster (it depends on the results of the tender or exchange offer).

1. ***Step one – tender offer:*** The first step of a tender offer is the offer by Acquiror directly to Target shareholders to purchase their Target shares for the specified offer price. Upon commencing a tender offer, Acquiror must file a Schedule TO (tender offer) with the SEC. If Acquiror offers stock as part of the transaction (i.e., an exchange offer), Acquiror also must file a Registration Statement on Form S-4 to register the Acquiror shares offered in exchange for some or all of Target's shares.

   The document provided to Target shareholders in a tender offer is called an **Offer to Purchase**. The document provided to Target shareholders in an exchange offer is called an **Exchange Offer/Prospectus**, and it is a combination tender offer document plus prospectus since an exchange offer entails the issuance of securities and, therefore, a prospectus is required (unless an exemption can be found in the securities laws). The Offer to Purchase or Exchange Offer/Prospectus, as applicable, is filed as an exhibit to the Schedule TO.

   Within ten business days after Acquiror has filed the Schedule TO, Target must file a Schedule 14D-9 with the SEC pursuant to which Target is required to state whether it (a) recommends the offer to shareholders, (b) does not recommend the offer to shareholders, or (c) makes no recommendation to shareholders.

   In the Schedule TO, Acquiror will state the minimum percentage of shares that must be tendered in order for the tender to close. If Acquiror is unable to obtain this minimum percentage by the time the tender offer period expires (the percentage is usually a majority but can be a supermajority depending on Target's bylaws or the state statute for the state in which Target is incorporated), the offer can be withdrawn or extended. If the offer is withdrawn, no shareholders will receive the consideration offered. (It is as if the offer never existed.) Tender offers also may be extended to increase the likelihood that the specified number of Target shares (the threshold percentage) will be tendered. The minimum threshold chosen in the tender offer is almost always equal to or greater than the voting requirement in a traditional one-step merger. In this way, should a subsequent shareholder vote be required (which will be the case unless 100 percent of Target shares are tendered), approval of the transaction would be guaranteed.

The tender offer must be "open" for at least twenty business days and, during that time, shareholders can elect to tender or exchange their shares. Acquiror cannot "take up" or purchase any shares until the initial tender period has closed. If a change is made to the offer, the tender offer must be kept open for additional time. The length of time that a tender offer must be extended if a change is made depends on the nature of the change. SEC rules require an extension of ten business days for a change in price offered or amount of securities being sought (e.g., 75 percent instead of 67 percent). For other changes, the length of the extension is a judgment call based on previous SEC guidance. After the tender period has run (either the twenty business days or longer, if a change was made to the offer), Acquiror is allowed to purchase the shares tendered to date and to extend the offering period by between three and twenty business days (this is called a **subsequent offer period**).

If the minimum threshold of tendered shares is met, the transaction will move to step two. If the minimum threshold is not met, Acquiror has the option to extend the tender offer or to withdraw it.

2. ***Step two – merger:*** If every share is tendered in step one, there is no need for a second step. However, it is extremely unlikely that every share will be tendered (even a single non-tendered or lost share would prevent 100 percent ownership by Acquiror), so in nearly every instance a second step is required to complete the transaction.

    2a. If 90 percent (or more) of the shares are tendered, Acquiror can effect a **short-form merger** under state law to "squeeze out" the remaining 10 percent (or less) of shares not tendered in the tender offer process. In a short-form merger, there is no shareholder vote -- all remaining shares must be sold. Upon filing of the short-form merger certificate with the Secretary of State, the minority shareholders no longer have any rights to the shares, other than the right to receive the same consideration that was paid to the other shareholders in connection with the tender offer.

    2b. If Acquiror obtains more than the minimum threshold but less than 90 percent, the tender closes but Acquiror must proceed down the traditional merger path in which: (a) disclosures are sent to shareholders, and (b) shareholders must vote in favor of the transaction in order for the transaction to close. This is generally referred to as a **long-form merger**. This merger is exactly the same process described in the previous section on Merger Transactions (also referred to as a "traditional" merger or a "one-step" merger). Since the tender offer in step one closed (and Acquiror therefore already owns a certain number of Target shares), Acquiror will vote those newly acquired shares in favor of the transaction at the shareholder vote. Assuming that the minimum threshold chosen in the tender offer is equal to or greater than the percentage required for approval in a traditional merger (which is usually the case since Acquiror would not want to take up the tendered shares without certainty of completing the transaction), Acquiror already owns enough shares to guarantee a winning shareholder vote.

For example, assume CoffeeCo launches a tender offer for JuiceCo. In JuiceCo's bylaws, a simple majority (greater than 50 percent) is required to approve a merger or change-of-control transaction. CoffeeCo sets as a condition of the tender that at least 60 percent of JuiceCo shares must be tendered (this is the minimum threshold). Further assume that 75 percent of JuiceCo's shares are actually tendered. Since less than 90 percent of the shares were tendered, CoffeeCo cannot use a short-form merger to close the transaction; instead it must go down the traditional merger path and hold a shareholder vote. To approve a merger according to JuiceCo's bylaws, at least a majority of the JuiceCo shares must be voted in favor of the transaction. Since CoffeeCo now owns 75 percent of JuiceCo (as a result of the tender offer, which closed because the 60 percent condition was met), at least 75 percent of the shares will be voted in favor of the transaction, which will then be approved and the merger completed.

Why are shares tendered at the end of the offer period?

Since many shares in corporations are owned by mutual funds and other institutional investors on behalf of individual investors, these professional investors usually wait until the end of the tender offer period before tendering the shares they control in case another, higher offer materializes. Since the tendered shares cannot be purchased by Acquiror until the end of the tender period, and since all shareholders must receive the same consideration (the so-called Equal Treatment Rule), there is little incentive to tender shares early. As a result, most shares are tendered in the last day or two of the offer period.

The following decision tree illustrates the sequencing of a tender offer.

Figure 20.2 – Tender Offer Sequencing

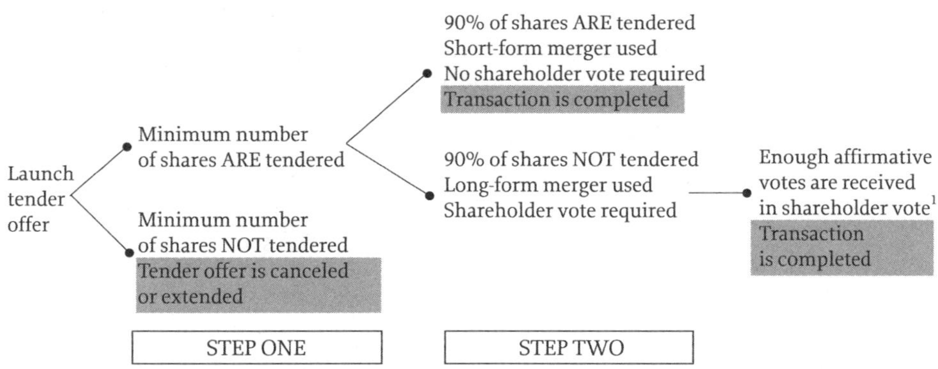

[1] The minimum threshold for the tender to close in Step1 is almost always at least enough shares to win a subsequent shareholder vote, so it would be rare to see a second step merger not win shareholder approval.

A traditional merger vs. a tender offer and merger

The decision between a one-step traditional merger and a two-step tender offer and merger usually depends on a series of factors:

1. ***Regulatory issues*** - If regulatory approval will take two months or longer (i.e., the approximate time required for a traditional one-step merger), the prospective advantage of a speedy tender process is lost.
2. ***Financing*** - Private equity firms must acquire 100 percent of a company before they can leverage it. As a result, these firms usually will not undertake a tender since tender rules require that financing be in place *before* launching a tender. (By comparison, in a merger, the purchased stock does not have to be paid for until *after* the transaction closes.)
3. ***Likelihood of obtaining at least 90 percent*** - If Acquiror believes it can obtain 90 percent (or more) of Target's shares outstanding in a tender, then the tender offer process followed by a short-form merger is a faster transaction to complete than a traditional merger. Recall that once the Schedule TO is filed, the tender offer can close in as few as four weeks (20 business days) if there is no material change to the offer, and if at least 90 percent of the shares are tendered. This can be much faster than a merger in which a merger proxy or prospectus must be filed and a shareholder vote must take place (which can take twelve to twenty weeks or more).

Since a tender offer is made directly to Target's shareholders, it does not require the approval of Target's board of directors or management. Recall, however, that Target must respond with a 14D-9 within ten business days of the tender offer launch with a statement about whether it is in favor of the proposed tender offer. In the case in which Acquiror does not have consent from Target's board or management, such a tender would be considered hostile. Practically speaking, if Target company has a shareholder rights plan in place (more commonly known as a "poison pill" and discussed in Corporate Defense (Ch.23)), it is not economically feasible for Acquiror to undertake a tender offer without Target board approval since a hostile tender would trigger the poison pill. The only way to avoid such a situation would be for Target's board of directors to redeem or otherwise amend the poison pill to allow Acquiror's tender offer to proceed, and the only way Target's board of directors would do so is if the transaction with Acquiror were friendly. It should not be surprising, therefore, to find that many transactions that begin as "hostile" become "friendly" during the course of the transaction.

Note that this general discussion on tender offers assumes that Delaware Corporate Law applies. Statutes of states and other jurisdictions vary and occasionally vary in significant respects. The entire legal situation should always be reviewed with experienced legal counsel when analyzing a transaction, especially given the interplay of federal and state regulation in this area of mergers and acquisitions. (For example, Regulation 14D of the Securities Exchange Act governs tender offers and change-of-control transactions, but state law is relevant with respect to merger provisions, voting requirements, etc.)

The changing legal landscape

A key tender offer rule is that all shareholders must be offered the same consideration (the so-called "best price" rule). Thus, if $20 per share is offered to one shareholder, $20 per share must be offered to all shareholders. However, almost from the adoption of Regulation M-A in October 1999, there was an issue with two-step transactions (cash tender followed by a back-end merger) that created reluctance to use them in spite of their tactical preference over one-step mergers in certain situations (largely related to the potentially faster time to close): there was concern that if management were paid a bonus or received a new employment agreement in a transaction, that bonus or employment agreement could be deemed "additional consideration" for shares held by management such that this "additional consideration" would have to be paid to all shareholders under the "best price" rule. While this particular issue was resolved by the SEC with several amendments to Rule 14-d10[1], Acquiror must be careful in structuring transactions due to the constantly changing nature of applicable laws and regulations.

[1] The major amendments were that (i) "best price" provisions only apply to securities tendered in a tender offer; (ii) any consideration offered and paid for employment compensation, severance, or benefits is not prohibited if it meets certain requirements; and (iii) there is a safe harbor for arrangements approved by certain independent directors of Target or Acquiror, as applicable. CFR Citation: 17 CFR Parts 200 and 240, Release Nos. 34-54684; IC-27542; File No. S7-11-05; Effective Date: December 8, 2006.

In order to further illustrate a merger timeline compared with a tender offer timeline, let's consider various transactions between GroceryCo and OrganicCo – two publicly traded companies listed on the NYSE. The managements and boards of both companies have agreed to a stock-for-stock exchange of GroceryCo shares for OrganicCo shares. Both companies' boards have agreed to the transaction. Assume GroceryCo has 10 million shares outstanding and is trading at $50 per share (therefore the market value of GroceryCo is $500 million). GroceryCo will offer OrganicCo shareholders 1.5 GroceryCo shares per OrganicCo share, which translates into an offer price of \$75 per OrganicCo share (1.5 × \$50 = \$75). OrganicCo has 4 million shares outstanding; therefore, the equity value of the transaction for OrganicCo is \$300 million (4 million shares × \$75 offer price = \$300 million).

GroceryCo and OrganicCo have two options to effect the combination:

1. They can combine in a traditional one-step merger in which both GroceryCo shareholders and OrganicCo shareholders independently hold a shareholder vote to approve or disapprove the transaction. Prior to the shareholder vote, the companies need to prepare and distribute a merger prospectus. If both sets of shareholders approve the transaction in their respective shareholder votes, the transaction can close. This is Example (1) in Figure 20.3. Even though GroceryCo is the Acquiror, note that GroceryCo shareholders also must vote on the proposed transaction because GroceryCo will issue more than 20 percent of its pre-transaction shares to OrganicCo. In fact, GroceryCo will issue 60 percent of its pre-transaction shares to OrganicCo, calculated as follows: 4 million OrganicCo shares × the 1.5 exchange rate = 6 million GroceryCo shares issued to OrganicCo shareholders; 6 million shares issued / 10 million pre-transaction GroceryCo shares = 60 percent, which is greater than the 20 percent threshold.

2. Another option is for GroceryCo to initiate an exchange offer process for OrganicCo's shares. In such a transaction, assume GroceryCo would require that at least 60 percent of OrganicCo's shares be tendered as a condition to the exchange offer closing. Sixty percent is chosen by Acquiror because the voting requirement for OrganicCo in a merger is a simple majority (greater than 50 percent).

   2a. If more than 60 percent but less than 90 percent of OrganicCo's shares are tendered, then the exchange offer will close but GroceryCo and OrganicCo will need to proceed to a second step long-form merger, with a shareholder vote, in order to complete the transaction. This is Example (2) in Figure 20.3.

   2b. If at least 90 percent of OrganicCo's shares are exchanged, then the transaction can close without a traditional (long-form) merger. In this situation, a short-form merger would be used to squeeze out any shares not exchanged. This is Example (3) in Figure 20.3.

Figure 20.3 – GroceryCo and OrganicCo Example

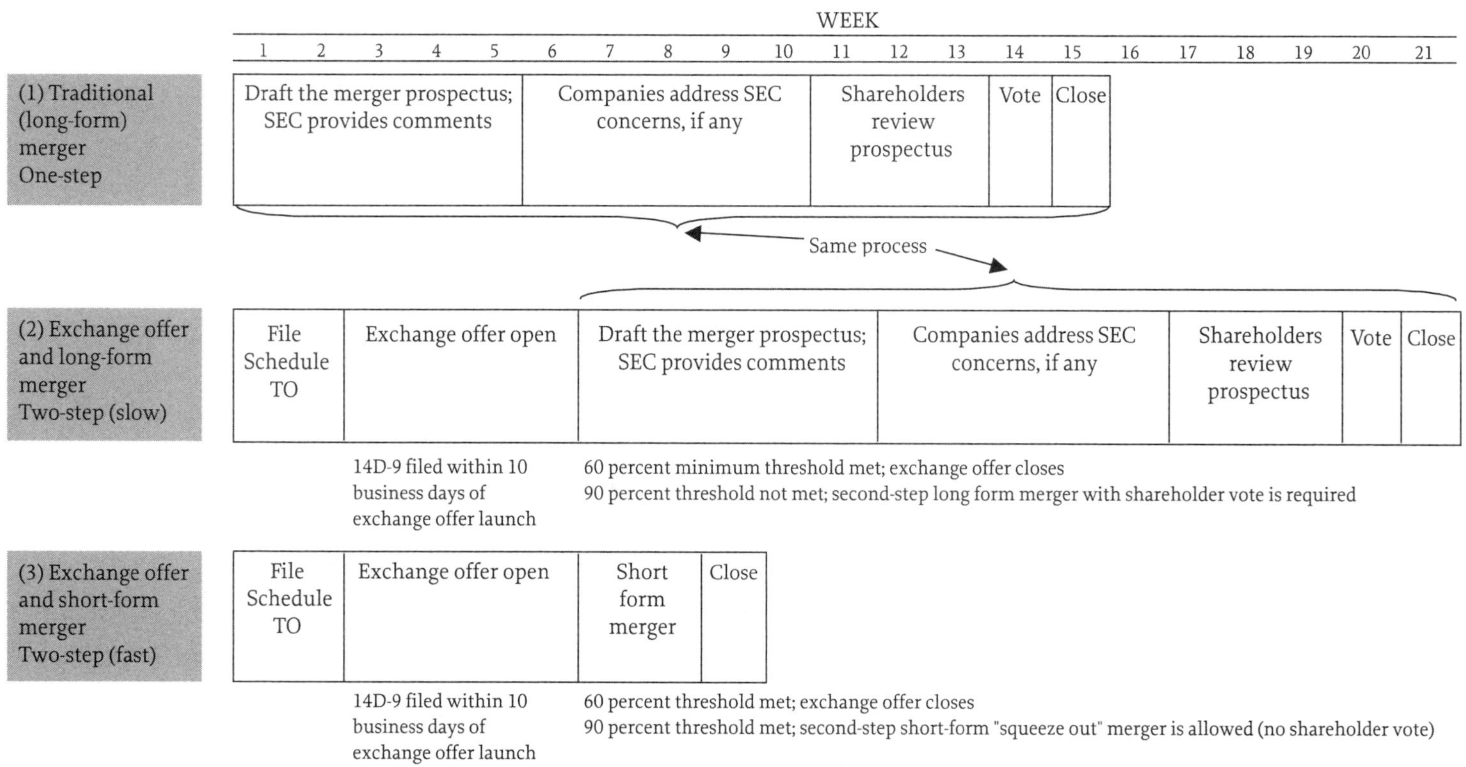

Note: A tender offer is an offer of cash for Target shares; Target shareholders are sent a merger proxy in the case of a tender offer
An exchange offer is an offer of all Acquiror stock or cash and Acquiror stock for Target shares; Target shareholders are sent a merger prospectus in the case of an exchange offer

Proxy Contests

A proxy is a written power of attorney which is given by a shareholder of a corporation and which authorizes a specific vote on the shareholder's behalf at a corporate meeting. It is essentially a mail-in ballot and is used as a facilitating device so that shareholders do not have to show up in person in order to vote at the shareholder meeting of a company in which they own shares. Instead, they can mail in a proxy with their choices marked and those proxies count as if the shareholders had been physically present and had voted at the meeting.

In a proxy contest, Acquiror tries to convince Target shareholders to vote for Acquiror's alternative slate of directors through the medium of a shareholder vote, thereby replacing Target's incumbent board of directors. Proxy contests are used in hostile transactions when a tender offer is not likely to be successful (for instance and most commonly, when a poison pill is in place). Once a new board has been put in place, either the new board can continue to run the company as it sees fit, or the new board can decide to merge itself with another company or sell the company. To actually effect a merger or sale of the company, a merger or tender offer process would still need to take place. The difference is that it would do so with the support of a newly elected board of directors.

In terms of mechanics, the would-be Acquiror purchases shares in Target and then, as a shareholder, proposes a new slate of Target board members. (Any shareholder can do this, usually, unless it is prohibited by the company's bylaws or charter, or by state law.) The purpose of the proxy contest is to obtain enough board seats of Target to control the board and, in effect, control the decisions of the company by ousting the current, transaction-resistant board of directors. Many defense mechanisms, such as a classified board (sometimes called a "staggered" board) or limits on who can call a special meeting, are implemented to make proxy contests more difficult for would-be acquirors. These tactics are described in Corporate Defense. (Ch.23) A more general discussion of directors' duties appears in The Deal Team. (Ch.19)

The proxy contest process can be long, costly, and inefficient. With the proliferation of classified boards (which provide that only a certain number of directors are up for re-election each year, thereby making it impossible to take over a board with only a single annual shareholder vote), proxy contests are seldom used and only in cases in which there is complete refusal by Target to consider a transaction. Although it has shortcomings, a proxy contest can allow Acquiror to obtain control without purchasing a large amount of Target stock, at least in situations in which there is widespread shareholder dissatisfaction with the board. Proxy contests were more common in the 1980s with hostile raiders initiating the proxy contests since, at that time, board members commonly had one-year terms. As a result, often the entire board of directors was up for re-election every year. Although proxy contests never ceased, they have become more common again in the 2000s.

Cross-Border Transactions

In an increasingly global economy, there are more and more cross-border deals. However, there are structural, strategic, and financial impediments to cross-border transactions. For a U.S. acquiror considering cross-border acquisitions, from a structural and strategic point of view there are competition commissions (foreign equivalents of the U.S. Federal Trade Commission and the Antitrust Division of the Department of Justice, which oversee antitrust matters), and differing rules and regulations on merger laws (including, notably, potential restrictions on the ability to lay off employees and to make an offer for only a minority stake). From a financial and technical perspective, there are accounting issues and differences, tax considerations, and flowback issues.

Cross-border transactions using stock as the acquisition currency are particularly complex (e.g., if a foreign acquiror wants to purchase a publicly held U.S. target in a stock-for-stock transaction or vice versa). Companies listed on a U.S. stock exchange must be registered with the SEC. In order to register a security with the SEC, the SEC requires that all disclosures comply with U.S. GAAP or, less stringently, reconcile to U.S. GAAP. It can take three to six months or more for a foreign corporation to prepare financial statements that are in compliance with or reconcile to U.S. GAAP if they are not already compliant.

Many cross-border transactions in which a foreign issuer acquires a U.S. target in a stock-for-stock transaction are done using **American depositary receipts** (ADRs), which are a special type of security that represents shares of foreign companies but is itself a U.S. security. If the foreign acquiror does not have an existing ADR program, one has to be set up, which can be a time-consuming process. Also, depending on the shareholder base, certain investors cannot hold an international security (foreign issuer buying a U.S. company issues foreign stock in exchange for U.S. Target stock) due to the investor's charter. In other cases (U.S. issuer buying a foreign company issues U.S. stock in exchange for foreign Target stock), certain international investors cannot or will not want to hold an American security. As a result there is **flowback.**

For example, assume a merger in which a U.S. stock is issued to foreign Target shareholders in exchange for their Target shares. This newly issued U.S. Acquiror stock is then sold by Target shareholders, resulting in those shares flowing back to Acquiror's home market (the U.S.). This has the net effect of putting downward pressure on Acquiror's share price.

A flowback example

WineCo (based in California) buys ChampagneCo (based in France) in a stock-for-stock merger. The Paris Teachers Fund, a mutual fund representing retired Parisian elementary school teachers, owns 10,000 shares of ChampagneCo. The exchange ratio in the deal is two WineCo shares for every one ChampagneCo share. Therefore, the Paris Teachers Fund receives 20,000 (10,000 x 2) shares of WineCo. However, according to its corporate charter, the Paris Teachers Fund is not allowed to own foreign stocks (either by choice or by charter). Since the Paris Teachers Fund cannot hold foreign stocks, it sells into the market the 20,000 shares of WineCo that it received upon closing of the merger. The sudden supply of WineCo shares on the market puts downward pressure on WineCo's stock price (more supply with static demand equals a lower price) as the Paris Teachers Fund shares "flow back" into the U.S. market (where there is more demand for WineCo's shares).

If Acquiror pays a dividend to its shareholders after the cross-border transaction has closed (either a special dividend or as part of an ongoing dividend plan), there could be substantial tax costs as well as foreign exchange currency risk for shareholders located in the foreign location. This loss of value to taxes can sometimes be partially offset with derivative securities; however, these can be cumbersome and come at a cost to the foreign shareholder. To summarize, cross-border transaction are increasingly common. However, they are more complex to effect than mergers between companies domiciled in the same market.

Taxes and M&A

CHAPTER 21

The trick is to stop thinking of it as "your" money.

An IRS auditor

For most companies, tax is one of the larger expenses paid each year. The importance, therefore, of understanding taxes and how best to manage tax-related matters is an essential skill for a finance professional. The topic of tax is so broad that no chapter of this size could do justice to the subject matter. As such, the scope of tax in this book is limited to tax issues that commonly appear in M&A and corporate finance transactions. Some of these fundamental tax concepts were introduced in Financial Statement Basics (Ch.3), including the difference between GAAP accounting and tax accounting, and deferred taxes (which is the account that reconciles differences between GAAP accounting and tax accounting). This chapter will review and build upon those basic concepts, in addition to introducing other important topics including: (1) taxable income and taxable gain; (2) book value vs. tax basis; (3) inside basis vs. outside basis; (4) operating losses (NOLs) and capital losses; (5) shareholder-level and corporate-level tax; (6) the tax motivations and consequences of selling stock vs. selling assets; (7) asset write-ups and basis step-ups; (8) tax-free reorganizations; and (9) 338(h)(10) elections.

A few prefatory comments are in order. In general, unless otherwise noted, the comments and examples in this chapter relate to:

- C corporations; different rules may (and often do) apply for individuals and pass-through entities such as partnerships, S corporations, and limited liability corporations (LLCs).

- Taxable activities in the United States; if working in a foreign jurisdiction, it is important to review the corporate tax regime of the country in question.

- The tax subject matter as of 2006; tax rules and regulations do change so care should always be taken regarding the applicable tax rules and regulations.

Tax is one of the most difficult topics in finance

A solid grounding in tax differentiates good corporate advisors from great ones. However, do not be discouraged if you have difficulty understanding the tax concepts introduced in this chapter. Even for experienced practitioners, tax is difficult subject matter. For many finance professionals, tax can sometimes seem like a foreign language, so pace yourself, especially on the more advanced topics. The more challenging concepts will be easier to comprehend with additional experience.

Tax advisors

This chapter is not intended as a substitute for a tax textbook or tax counsel but as a primer on important tax concepts. Tax codes are complex and continuously evolving. Tax specialists are able to provide the most current thinking on the subject matter and introduce creative solutions. This chapter should be used to help learn tax concepts, not as a definitive resource on tax matters. It is important that a tax specialist is part of any deal team in order to give advice on that transaction's facts, not the generalizations presented here.

What is Tax?

A tax is a payment levied by and payable to a governmental body such as the U.S. federal government, a state, or a city. In business, there are different types of tax and many different events can trigger a tax payment. A **taxable event** is any action that triggers a potential tax liability. Examples of taxable events for corporations include:

1. The sale of goods or services, which could trigger sales tax
2. The ownership of real property, which could trigger the payment of property tax
3. The operation of a corporation, which could require the payment of corporate income tax
4. The employment of employees, which could trigger various types of employee-related taxes, including Social Security and worker's compensation
5. The sale of an asset, property, or business, which could trigger tax on sale

As a general rule, an event or transaction is taxable:

1. If there has been a change of ownership in an asset, and
2. The new fair market value of the asset can be determined, unless
3. The transaction satisfies an exemption that provides for tax-deferred treatment.

Essentially, any time a transaction occurs in which one party is paying another party for goods, services, assets, property, or stock, the transaction *could* be taxable unless an exemption exists. And, in general, any time cash is received by the selling party, the transaction usually *is* taxable.

Book vs. Tax Accounting

A discussion of tax as it relates to M&A should begin with a discussion of a company's financial accounting records. Public companies and many private companies keep two sets of accounting records -- one set for financial reporting purposes, called the **GAAP books**, and one set for tax purposes, called the **tax books**. Understanding that there are two sets of accounting records, how they interrelate, how they differ, and how they are reconciled is the first step in learning about corporate tax-related issues.

To help differentiate between these two sets of accounting records, throughout this chapter "GAAP" and "TAX" will be capitalized if referring to GAAP accounting or TAX accounting. Tax as a liability or expense, however, will not be capitalized in this chapter. Also, throughout this chapter, the terms GAAP accounting and BOOK accounting, as well as the terms GAAP and BOOK, will be used interchangeably, as they are in practice. In this chapter, TAX accounting is always referred to as TAX accounting.

There are a number of differences between accounting for GAAP and accounting for TAX, so many, in fact, that most accountants are either trained as GAAP specialists or TAX specialists. Some of the most important differences between GAAP accounting and TAX accounting are described below.

1. Generally Accepted Accounting Principles (GAAP) are a set of continuously evolving accounting rules which govern the preparation of reported financial statements. GAAP accounting (also referred to as "book accounting" or "financial accounting") is used to prepare "financial statements *according to GAAP.*" TAX returns are prepared according to TAX accounting rules, which themselves are based on applicable federal, state and local tax codes.

2. While the terms "TAX books" and "GAAP books" are often used in practice to distinguish between the two sets of accounting records which many companies

keep[1], the proper name for the TAX accounting records is "TAX return work papers." Other terms sometimes used for TAX accounting records are TAX books, TAX financial statements, and TAX records (although, strictly speaking, TAX return work papers is the proper term). TAX return work papers are used by corporations to prepare tax returns, and tax returns are submitted to tax authorities.

3. GAAP is created and overseen by the Financial Accounting Standards Board (FASB) and the Securities and Exchange Commission (SEC) whereas U.S. tax code is created and overseen by Congress, the Internal Revenue Service (IRS), the U.S. Treasury, the U.S. judicial system, and state and local taxing authorities. Foreign tax code is overseen by similar governmental entities in foreign countries. Each governmental entity with the power to levy taxes is independent. Thus while tax codes interrelate (a corporation in San Diego, California, USA is subject to federal, state, and local taxes) and payments to other taxing authorities are often recognized in whole or in part (i.e., credit may be given for taxes paid to other taxing authorities), each tax code is distinct. In particular, the U.S. federal tax code is distinct from the various state tax codes, and foreign tax code is distinct from U.S. federal tax code.

4. Tax liabilities appear in both the GAAP financial statements and the TAX return work papers. However, tax liabilities often differ between the GAAP books and the TAX return work papers, most commonly due to differences in accounting treatments between GAAP and TAX. Notably, the tax liabilities as calculated in the TAX return work papers are what must be paid, in cash, to the respective taxing authorities such as the IRS. Tax liabilities calculated from the TAX return work papers are referred to as **cash taxes** because these are the amounts that are actually paid to the government for the reporting period. *This chapter will refer to the tax liability as calculated on the TAX return work papers as "cash taxes."*

5. Companies with publicly held debt or equity registered in the U.S. must file their GAAP financial statements with the SEC (where they are made publicly available). TAX return work papers, in contrast, are generally *not* public information. For private companies, neither the GAAP financial statements nor the TAX return work papers is generally made publicly available.

6. Usually, the Corporate Controller oversees preparation of the GAAP financial statements. Similarly, the Director of Tax oversees preparation of the TAX return work papers and the corporation's tax returns. Internally, a company usually has accountants who specialize in GAAP and tax lawyers and accountants who specialize in TAX. The company's Controller and CFO, however, review both the GAAP books and the TAX return work papers.

[1] Some smaller private companies keep only TAX accounting records since they are private (and thus do not need to keep GAAP books since they do not publicly report their financial results).

7. Fund managers, investment bankers, investors, creditors, rating agencies and other third parties read and review GAAP financial statements to make investment and/or lending decisions. Tax returns, however, are read and reviewed by tax authorities. Tax authorities only review selected TAX return work papers during an audit.

8. Since GAAP are accounting *guidelines*, companies have some latitude in their application. Since members of the financial community use GAAP financial statements to make investment decisions, companies try to *maximize* net income on their GAAP financial statements whenever possible. The reason is that, in general, higher recurring earnings translate into a higher stock price. Companies can *maximize* GAAP earnings by *maximizing* the recognition of revenues and/or *minimizing* tax-deductible expenses in a period, as allowed under GAAP.

9. Conversely, since TAX return work papers are used to determine the cash taxes owed by a company, companies try to *minimize* taxable income (pretax income) on their TAX return work papers in order to *minimize* cash taxes payable (since the tax liability is calculated by multiplying the taxable income by the applicable tax rate). Companies can *minimize* taxable income by *minimizing* the recognition of revenues and/or *maximizing* tax-deductible expenses, as allowed under the applicable tax code. Thus there is a constant tension between trying to maximize reported earnings for GAAP and trying to minimize cash taxes for TAX.

Issues Related to Depreciation

One of the major differences between GAAP accounting and TAX accounting is the treatment of depreciation expense. For TAX accounting, companies generally utilize faster depreciation methods allowed by tax authorities in order to maximize tax-deductible expenses and minimize taxable income, thereby minimizing cash tax payments. Conversely, companies generally try to utilize slower depreciation methods allowed under GAAP in order to minimize tax-deductible expenses, thereby maximizing GAAP reported net income.

To better understand this concept, let's take a look at a simple numerical comparison of BOOK and TAX depreciation methods. Consider a company, PrintingCo, which has just purchased a printer for $1,000.

For illustrative purposes, for both BOOK and TAX let's assume **straight-line depreciation** so that the amount of depreciation each year is equal to the total depreciable amount (purchase price - salvage value) divided by the number of years over which the asset will be depreciated. Although in practice other accelerated depreciation methods often are used for TAX purposes (such as MACRS, double-declining balance and sum-of-the-years' digits), for simplicity this example will use the straight-line method. Let's also assume the printer will have no salvage value at the end of its depreciable life, therefore the depreciable amount is equal to the purchase price.

For BOOK purposes, assume that PrintingCo will depreciate the printer based on a 10-year useful life and so $100 will be depreciated for BOOK purposes each year for 10 years. After 10 years, the asset will be fully depreciated for BOOK purposes (in year 10 book value equals zero).

$1,000 purchase price / 10 years = $100 annual depreciation for BOOK

For TAX purposes, assume that PrintingCo will use accelerated depreciation. (Depreciation on a faster time frame, often for TAX purposes, is called **accelerated depreciation**.) For TAX, PrintingCo will depreciate the printer based on a five-year useful life and thus $200 will be depreciated for TAX purposes each year for five years. After five years, the asset will be fully depreciated for TAX purposes (in year five tax basis equals zero).

$1,000 purchase price / 5 years = $200 annual depreciation for TAX

In Table 21.1, the only difference between the GAAP books and the TAX return work papers is the amount of annual depreciation ($100 for the first year for GAAP and $200 for the first year for TAX). The revenue of $1,250 is the same for both sets of accounting records. In addition, all of the expenses, except for depreciation, are the same. Because the depreciation expense is lower in the GAAP books than the TAX return work papers each year by $100, the GAAP taxable income is higher each year by $100. The composition of that $100 difference is that tax payable is higher in the GAAP books than the TAX return work papers by $40, but GAAP net income is higher than TAX net income by $60 as well.

Table 21.1 - BOOK vs. TAX Income Statement in Years 1 - 5

Income statement - GAAP		**Income statement - TAX**	
Printer cost	$1,000	Printer cost	$1,000
Salvage value	0	Salvage value	0
Useful life (years)	10	Useful life (years)	5
BOOK annual depreciation Yrs. 1-5[1]	100	TAX annual depreciation Yrs. 1-5[1]	200
BOOK annual depreciation Yrs. 6-10[1]	100	TAX annual depreciation Yrs. 6-10[1]	0
Income statement		*Income statement*	
Revenues	1,250	Revenues	1,250
Cost of goods sold	(500)	Cost of goods sold	(500)
Depreciation expense	(100)	Depreciation expense	(200)
SG&A expenses	(200)	SG&A expenses	(200)
Earnings before interest and taxes	450	Earnings before interest and taxes	350
Interest expense	(200)	Interest expense	(200)
Taxable income[2]	250	Taxable income[2]	150
Tax rate	40%	Tax rate	40%
Tax payable[3]	**(100)**	Tax payable[3]	**(60)**
Net income[4]	$150	Net income[4]	$90

[1] Annual depreciation using the straight-line method = (purchase price - salvage value) / useful life
[2] Taxable income = revenues - tax deductible expenses
[3] Tax payable = taxable income × tax rate
[4] Net income = taxable income - tax payable

TAX accounting allows for faster depreciation of the printer than BOOK accounting does; therefore, tax payable to the government in the TAX return work papers (i.e., the cash taxes) shown on the right side of Table 21.1 is $60, which is $40 less than the GAAP taxes of $100 in the GAAP column shown on the left side of the table. But what does that mean? Does PrintingCo actually pay the government $100 or $60? And how does PrintingCo account for this difference of $40 in the cash flow statement?

The TAX return work papers represent the actual amount owed to the government for a period. If, on its TAX return work papers, PrintingCo calculates a tax liability of $60, then it has to pay the government $60 (i.e., cash taxes for the period are $60). But how does PrintingCo account for the fact that the tax payable calculated in its GAAP books is $100? The answer is with an account called deferred taxes.

Deferred Taxes

Deferred taxes are literally the amount of taxes that are not immediately payable (i.e., deferred). Deferred taxes arise when the amount of tax that is owed to the government as calculated on the GAAP books is more (deferred tax liability) or less (deferred tax asset) than what is paid in cash taxes. That is, deferred taxes are taxes that have been recognized on the GAAP books as a liability but have not yet been paid to the taxing authorities (deferred tax *liability* because cash taxes are *not yet* paid) or, vice versa, taxes that have been recognized on the TAX return work papers (and therefore paid as cash taxes) but not yet on the GAAP books (deferred tax *asset* because cash taxes are *already* paid). Deferred taxes usually appear as a line item on a company's balance sheet and can be either an asset or a liability. Also, deferred taxes can be current or long-term.

1. If, for a reporting period, taxes payable in the GAAP financial statements are *greater than* taxes payable in the TAX return work papers, a **deferred tax liability** is created. In other words, a deferred tax liability is created if *cash taxes will need to be paid* in the future. In Table 21.1, PrintingCo calculated a GAAP tax liability of $100 in year one but only calculated a cash tax liability of $60 for TAX accounting. The company has paid $40 *less* in cash taxes than the tax payable as calculated on the GAAP books, and the company must pay that additional $40 as cash taxes at some point in the future. This $40 in taxes is simply *deferred.* Since the company has not yet paid this $40 in taxes but must do so in the future, this $40 is a deferred tax *liability.*

2. If, in a reporting period, taxes payable in the GAAP financial statements are *less than* taxes payable in the TAX return work papers, a **deferred tax asset** is created. In other words, a deferred tax asset is created if *an income tax benefit will be received* in the future. In Table 21.5, PrintingCo calculated a GAAP tax liability of $100 but calculated a cash tax liability of $140 for TAX accounting. The company has paid $40 *more* in cash taxes than the tax payable as calculated on the GAAP books, and the company has a $40 credit for use at some point in the future. This $40 in taxes is essentially prepaid taxes. Since the company has already paid this $40 as cash taxes and need not do so in the future, this $40 is a deferred tax *asset.*

It is important to note that, in practice, companies usually net the two deferred tax accounts (deferred tax liabilities and deferred tax assets) and categorize the resulting net deferred tax account as either a deferred tax *liability* or a deferred tax *asset,* as the case may be. For example, assume a company has a deferred tax liability of $15 million (i.e., the company has recognized a tax liability on the GAAP books of $15 million and will have to pay taxes of $15 million to the tax authorities at some point in the future) and the company also has a deferred tax asset of $10 million in that same period (i.e., the company paid $10 million in cash taxes but will not recognize that payment of $10 million on the GAAP books until some point in the future). The net result would be a deferred tax liability of $5 million (-$15 + $10 = -$5 or a $5 million liability).

In the example in Table 21.1, in which the annual TAX depreciation of $200 is greater than the annual GAAP depreciation of $100 and the annual tax payable in the GAAP financial statements of $100 is greater than the annual tax payable in the TAX return work papers of $60, a deferred tax *liability* account would be created for $40, which is the annual difference between the tax liability calculated on the GAAP books of $100 and the cash taxes paid of $60.

$100 of GAAP taxes - $60 of cash taxes = $40 of deferred tax liability

Some deferred taxes, as in the PrintingCo example in Table 21.1, are temporary timing differences which reverse over time while others are permanent and do not reverse. For example, a difference in depreciation method (and therefore differences in annual depreciation amounts) between GAAP and TAX is a timing difference and therefore a temporary difference. Over time, this difference will reverse out so that any deferred tax liability created reverses and becomes zero (as will be described in Tables 21.5 and 21.6). Other events that can trigger temporary timing differences in taxes payable include differences in valuing inventory, accounting for restructuring charges, and bad debt allowances, among others.

However, not all deferred taxes are temporary and reverse out. Some deferred taxes are caused by permanent differences which are never reversed. If an item is either taxable or tax-deductible for either GAAP or TAX but not for the other (i.e., it is only recognized on one of the two sets of accounting records), then a permanent difference would arise. Interest income received on tax-exempt securities and fines paid to the government are examples of events that would create a permanent difference between BOOK taxes payable and TAX taxes payable because they are only recognized on one of the two sets of accounting records.

To illustrate how a deferred tax liability created by a temporary difference in the recognition of depreciation expense is reversed over time, let's revisit the PrintingCo example from Table 21.1. First let's consider how the deferred tax liability of $40 is created on the balance sheet after the first year. Step one involves the initial purchase of the printer for $1,000. Assume PrintingCo pays for the asset with $500 of debt and $500 of equity. After the purchase, the asset would be recorded on the balance sheet at the fair market value of $1,000.

Now consider the first year of operations with the GAAP and TAX income statements provided in Table 21.1. We know that the GAAP income statement had tax payable of $100 and the TAX return work papers had tax payable of $60. Let's now create the deferred tax liability account with its initial balance of $40 (which is the difference between $100 and $60). In addition, at the end of the accounting period (end of year one), the GAAP balance sheet must account for accumulated depreciation of $100 and net income of $150 (as compared to $200 in depreciation and $90 in net income, respectively, for TAX accounting). The GAAP balance sheet after the first year is provided in Table 21.2.

Is there a deferred taxes account for TAX?

There is not a deferred taxes account for TAX accounting, only for GAAP accounting. For TAX purposes, cash taxes are equal to the tax liability as calculated on the TAX return work papers. However, GAAP accounting must reconcile any difference between the tax liability as calculated on the TAX return work papers (cash taxes) and the tax liability as calculated on the GAAP books, which is why there will usually be a deferred taxes account on the GAAP books.

Table 21.2 – Creation of a Deferred Tax Liability

Calculation of deferred tax liability (BOOK)		
Tax payable on GAAP income statement	$100	
Less: tax payable on TAX income statement	60	
Difference = deferred tax liability (BOOK)	$40	(1) on balance sheets below

Calculation of net PP&E (BOOK)		
Beginning net PP&E	$1,000	
Less: accumulated depreciation (BOOK)	(100)	
Ending net PP&E	$900	(2) on balance sheets below

Calculation of shareholders' equity account (BOOK)		
Beginning shareholders' equity	$500	
Add: net income (BOOK)	150	
Ending shareholders' equity	$650	(3) on balance sheets below

Balance sheets (BOOK)	Year 1		
	Opening	Closing	
Cash[1]	$0	$290	
Net PP&E	1,000	900	(2)
Total assets	$1,000	$1,190	
Deferred tax liability	$0	$40	(1)
Debt	500	500	
Shareholders' equity	500	650	(3)
Total liabilities & equity	$1,000	$1,190	

[1] The cash flow statement is shown in Table 21.3

Let's now consider the impact on the cash flow statement. Notice in Table 21.3 that, since taxes paid in cash to the government were $60 (from the TAX return work papers) and not $100 (from the GAAP financial statements), GAAP cash flow must be adjusted for the difference of $40. Specifically, in order to account for this difference of $40, there is an "add-back" of $40 in the Cash Flow From Operations section for "Change in deferred taxes." That is, the GAAP financial statements show $100 as tax payable, and yet the TAX return work papers show that only $60 was actually paid in cash taxes. As a result, $40 is added back on the GAAP cash flow statement to reflect the fact that there is actually $40 more in cash on hand. Or, thinking of the cash flow statement in terms of sources and uses of cash, the increase of the deferred tax liability is a source of cash of $40 (recall that an increase of a liability and a decrease of an asset are sources of cash; a decrease of a liability and an increase of an asset are uses of cash). Notice how the closing balance sheet in Table 21.2 shows a cash balance of $290. The calculation of the $290 is shown in the cash flow statement below.

Table 21.3 – Cash Flow Statement Reconciliation

Cash flow statement (BOOK)	Year 1
Net income	$150
Add: depreciation	100
Add: change in deferred taxes	40
Cash flow from operations	$290
Beginning cash	$0
Add: cash flow from operations	290
Ending cash	$290

For the sake of simplicity, let's assume that PrintingCo generates the same net income of $150 every year during the 10-year life of the printer. For years one to five, the balance sheet and cash flow statement are as shown in Table 21.4. Notice how the deferred tax liability account increases each year by $40 and shareholders' equity increases each year by $150 (which is the amount of annual net income) during the first five years. In addition, the cash account each year increases by the same $290 as calculated above in Table 21.3.

Table 21.4 – Balance Sheet and Cash Flow Statement Years 1 - 5

Years	**0**	**1**	**2**	**3**	**4**	**5**
Balance sheet (BOOK)						
Cash	$0	$290	$580	$870	$1,160	$1,450
Net PP&E	1,000	900	800	700	600	500
Total assets	1,000	1,190	1,380	1,570	1,760	1,950
Deferred tax liability[1]	0	40	80	120	160	200
Debt	500	500	500	500	500	500
Shareholders' equity	500	650	800	950	1,100	1,250
Total liabilities & equity	$1,000	$1,190	$1,380	$1,570	$1,760	$1,950
Cash flow statement (BOOK)						
Net income		$150	$150	$150	$150	$150
Depreciation		100	100	100	100	100
Change in deferred taxes[1]		40	40	40	40	40
Cash flow from operations		290	290	290	290	290
Beginning cash[2]		0	290	580	870	1,160
Add: cash flow from operations		290	290	290	290	290
Ending cash		$290	$580	$870	$1,160	$1,450

[1] Changes to the deferred tax account only are shown in Table 21.7
[2] Beginning cash in year 2 is equal to ending cash in year 1 and so forth each year

Now let's consider what happens after year five. Table 21.5 is similar to Table 21.1 except that, instead of years one to five, Table 21.5 is for years six to ten. Notice that in years six to ten tax payable for GAAP is *lower* than tax payable for TAX. Also notice that net income for GAAP is *lower* than net income for TAX. Both of these are the opposite of what happened in years one to five because, in years six to ten, the annual depreciation amount for GAAP is still $100 (just as it was in years one to five), but for TAX the asset has been fully depreciated by year five. As a result, there is zero TAX depreciation in years six to ten, resulting in higher taxable income, tax payable (cash taxes), and net income for TAX.

Table 21.5 - BOOK vs. TAX Income Statement in Years 6 - 10

Income statement - GAAP		**Income statement - TAX**	
Printer cost	$1,000	Printer cost	$1,000
Salvage value	0	Salvage value	0
Useful life (years)	10	Useful life (years)	5
BOOK annual depreciation Yrs. 1-5[1]	100	TAX annual depreciation Yrs. 1-5[1]	200
BOOK annual depreciation Yrs. 6-10[1]	100	TAX annual depreciation Yrs. 6-10[1]	0
Income statement		Income statement	
Revenues	1,250	Revenues	1,250
Cost of goods sold	(500)	Cost of goods sold	(500)
Depreciation	(100)	Depreciation	0
SG&A expenses	(200)	SG&A expenses	(200)
Earnings before interest and taxes	450	Earnings before interest and taxes	550
Interest expense	(200)	Interest expense	(200)
Taxable income[2]	250	Taxable income[2]	350
Tax rate	40%	Tax rate	40%
Tax payable[3]	**(100)**	Tax payable[3]	**(140)**
Net income[4]	$150	Net income[4]	$210

[1] Annual depreciation using the straight-line method = (purchase price - salvage value) / useful life
[2] Taxable income = revenues - tax deductible expenses
[3] Tax payable = taxable income × tax rate
[4] Net income = taxable income - tax payable

Now let's consider the balance sheet and cash flow statement in years six to ten. Notice in Table 21.6 that, instead of a deferred tax liability of $40 being created each year as it had done in years one to five, in years six to ten a $40 deferred tax *asset* is created each year (taxes payable for TAX are *greater than* taxes payable for GAAP). This is because, as shown in Table 21.5 above, for years six to ten, in each year GAAP taxes payable are $100 while cash taxes payable are $140. This deferred tax asset nets against the existing deferred tax liability account, resulting in a reduction of $40 in the net deferred tax account each year until the tenth year when the deferred tax liability account reaches zero (that is, as of the end of year ten the net deferred tax account is neither negative (deferred tax liability) nor positive (deferred tax asset)).

Table 21.6 – Balance Sheet and Cash Flow Statement Years 1 to 10

Years	0	1	2	3	4	5	6	7	8	9	10
Balance sheet (BOOK)											
Cash	$0	$290	$580	$870	$1,160	$1,450	$1,660	$1,870	$2,080	$2,290	$2,500
Net PP&E	1,000	900	800	700	600	500	400	300	200	100	0
Total assets	1,000	1,190	1,380	1,570	1,760	1,950	2,060	2,170	2,280	2,390	2,500
Deferred tax liability[1]	0	40	80	120	160	200	160	120	80	40	0
Debt	500	500	500	500	500	500	500	500	500	500	500
Shareholders' equity	500	650	800	950	1,100	1,250	1,400	1,550	1,700	1,850	2,000
Total liabilities & equity	$1,000	$1,190	$1,380	$1,570	$1,760	$1,950	$2,060	$2,170	$2,280	$2,390	$2,500
Cash flow statement (BOOK)											
Net income		$150	$150	$150	$150	$150	$150	$150	$150	$150	$150
Depreciation		100	100	100	100	100	100	100	100	100	100
Change in deferred taxes[1]		40	40	40	40	40	(40)	(40)	(40)	(40)	(40)
Cash flow from operations		290	290	290	290	290	210	210	210	210	210
Beginning cash[2]		0	290	580	870	1,160	1,450	1,660	1,870	2,080	2,290
Add: cash flow from operations[3]		290	290	290	290	290	210	210	210	210	210
Ending cash		$290	$580	$870	$1,160	$1,450	$1,660	$1,870	$2,080	$2,290	$2,500

[1] Changes to the deferred tax account only are shown in Table 21.7

[2] Beginning cash in year 2 is equal to ending cash in year 1 and so forth each year

[3] Cash Flow From Operations (CFFO) is shown in Table 21.3 for years 1-5 ($150 + $100 + $40 = $290), with the deferred tax liability serving as a source of cash (increase of a liability is a source of cash). However, for years 6-10, the change in deferred taxes is reversed to become a deferred tax asset (taxes payable for TAX > taxes payable for BOOK) and so the change in deferred taxes is a negative $40 (increase of an asset is a use of cash) rather than a positive $40. As a result, there is an $80 reduction in annual cash flow beginning in year 6. The calculation of CFFO in years 6-10 is ($150 + $100 - $40 = $210).

Table 21.7 – Components of the Deferred Tax Account

Years	0	1	2	3	4	5	6	7	8	9	10
Deferred tax liability[1]	$0	$40	$40	$40	$40	$40	$0	$0	$0	$0	$0
Deferred tax asset[1]	0	0	0	0	0	0	(40)	(40)	(40)	(40)	(40)
Net deferred tax account	0	$40	$80	$120	$160	$200	$160	$120	$80	$40	$40

[1] Since deferred taxes affect the cash flow statement, positive numbers are sources of cash and negative numbers (in parentheses) are uses of cash; the increase of a liability in each year of years 1-5 is a source of cash and the increase of an asset in each year of years 6-10 is a use of cash.

Let's also consider the difference between the book value of the printer on the GAAP books and the tax basis of the printer on the TAX return work papers. Both book value and tax basis refer to the value of the net PP&E (or, technically, the carrying value on the balance sheet at a given point in time). However "book value" is net PP&E for the GAAP books and "tax basis" is net PP&E for the TAX return work papers (for a detailed discussion, see the section Book Value vs. Tax Basis). For GAAP accounting, one-tenth or $100 of the printer's initial value of $1,000 is depreciated each year for ten years, whereas for TAX accounting, one-fifth or $200 of the printer's initial value of $1,000 is depreciated each year for five years. Thus the printer is fully depreciated for GAAP accounting (book value equal zero) after ten years, but the printer is fully depreciated for TAX accounting (tax basis equal zero) after only five years because of faster depreciation for TAX purposes (accelerated depreciation for TAX).

Table 21.8 – Book Value vs. Tax Basis During Useful Life

Years	0	1	2	3	4	5	6	7	8	9	10
GAAP books											
Gross PP&E	$1,000	$1,000	$1,000	$1,000	$1,000	$1,000	$1,000	$1,000	$1,000	$1,000	$1,000
Annual depreciation	0	(100)	(100)	(100)	(100)	(100)	(100)	(100)	(100)	(100)	(100)
Accumulated depreciation	0	(100)	(200)	(300)	(400)	(500)	(600)	(700)	(800)	(900)	(1,000)
Net PP&E (book value)	$1,000	$900	$800	$700	$600	$500	$400	$300	$200	$100	$0
TAX return work papers											
Gross PP&E	$1,000	$1,000	$1,000	$1,000	$1,000	$1,000	$1,000	$1,000	$1,000	$1,000	$1,000
Annual depreciation	0	(200)	(200)	(200)	(200)	(200)	0	0	0	0	0
Accumulated depreciation	0	(200)	(400)	(600)	(800)	(1,000)	(1,000)	(1,000)	(1,000)	(1,000)	(1,000)
Net PP&E (tax basis)	$1,000	$800	$600	$400	$200	$0	$0	$0	$0	$0	$0
Difference in annual depreciation[1]	$0	$100	$100	$100	$100	$100	($100)	($100)	($100)	($100)	($100)
Deferred tax liability[2]	0	40	40	40	40	40	0	0	0	0	0
Deferred tax asset[2]	0	0	0	0	0	0	(40)	(40)	(40)	(40)	(40)
Net annual deferred tax account[3]	0	40	40	40	40	40	(40)	(40)	(40)	(40)	(40)
Cumulative deferred tax liability acct.[4]	$0	$40	$80	$120	$160	$200	$160	$120	$80	$40	$0

[1] Annual TAX depreciation - annual GAAP depreciation
[2] Difference in annual depreciation × assumed 40% tax rate
[3] Annual deferred tax liability + annual deferred tax asset: ($40 + $0) for years 1-5; ($0 - $40) for years 6-10
[4] Cumulative deferred tax account calculated as year 1 net deferred tax account + year 2 net deferred tax account + year 3 + ... + year 10 net deferred tax account

Deferred tax assets

Deferred tax assets occur when a tax-deductible expense has been recognized on the GAAP books (resulting in lower taxes paid for BOOK) and not yet on the TAX return work papers (resulting in higher taxes paid for TAX). An example of when a deferred tax asset might be created relates to accrued expenses. Tax rules require that for accrued expenses to be categorized as "accrued" at the end of a period, the expenses must have been paid within a reasonable amount of time after period-end. If, however, a company recognized an accrued expense (such as accrued vacation or accrued bonuses for its employees) at the end of a period, but did not pay the expense within a reasonable amount of time after period-end, then a deferred tax asset would be created because, for TAX purposes, the item can no longer be expensed. Therefore, the tax deduction would take place for BOOK purposes, but not for TAX purposes, and the company would pay higher cash taxes (for TAX) than its calculated tax payable (for BOOK).

Deferred tax assets are subject to what is known in accounting parlance as a "realization test." If a company has a deferred tax asset on its balance sheet but events occur such that the company believes it is not likely to recognize the entire benefit of the deferred tax asset in the future, a **valuation allowance** must be created to reserve against the deferred tax asset (thereby reducing the book value of the deferred tax asset to its expected realizable value).

The topic of deferred taxes will be revisited again later in this chapter in the section GAAP Accounting for M&A Transactions.

Effective Tax Rates

Throughout this chapter, a 40 percent corporate tax rate is used in the numerical examples for both GAAP and TAX examples. As of 2006, the federal statutory rate for corporate income tax and corporate capital gain tax is 35 percent.[2] However, state and local taxes can add to the tax burden. State and local taxes paid are deductible for purposes of determining federal income taxes. Broadly speaking, 35 percent is the federal tax rate, state and local taxes add another 5 percent, and about 2 percent to 3 percent of state and local taxes are generally deductible for a net tax rate for cash

[2] This applies to corporations with taxable income greater than $10 million. See IRC §11(b)(1)(D)

taxes of 37 percent to 38 percent. As a result, the 40 percent tax rate assumption is generally considered a conservative assumption.

For both GAAP and TAX, the effective tax rate is calculated by dividing the tax liability in a period by the taxable income for that period. While the federal statutory tax rate is 35 percent, company-specific TAX attributes and characteristics can increase or decrease the effective cash tax rate. Similarly, company-specific GAAP tax attributes and characteristics can increase or decrease the effective GAAP tax rate above or below those statutory rates. The GAAP effective tax rate is often found in the notes to a company's 10-K filing. The GAAP effective tax rate is not necessarily equal to the effective *cash* tax rate. The only way to know the effective cash tax rate, generally, is if a company provides it. A common mistake is to use a company's effective GAAP tax rate and tax-effect TAX items at that GAAP tax rate. When modeling cash tax calculations, one should use 35, 38 or 40 percent as the cash tax rate assumption, not the company's effective BOOK rate (whatever it may be). When modeling GAAP net income, one should use the company's effective GAAP tax rate.

Tax Shields

A **tax shield** is the tax savings generated from taking a tax deduction. A tax shield is calculated by multiplying the amount of the **tax-deductible expense** by the corporate tax rate. Expenses which are tax-deductible provide a tax shield because they "shield" or protect the company from paying higher income tax by reducing taxable income prior to the calculation of income tax payable.

For example, if a company has revenues of $1,000 million, depreciation of $150 million, and a corporate tax rate of 40 percent, the tax shield from the depreciation of $150 million is $60 million, calculated by multiplying the tax-deductible expense of depreciation by the tax rate.

$150 million of depreciation × 40% tax rate = $60 million tax shield

The tax shield of $60 million is money that the company does not have to pay in taxes by virtue of depreciation being a tax-deductible expense.

Let's review another tax shield example. Consider a company that has $1,000 million in revenue. Without any tax-deductible expenses, the company would owe $400 million in corporate income taxes (assuming a 40 percent tax rate). However, after subtracting the $775 million of tax-deductible expenses as shown in Table 21.9, the company's taxable income is reduced from $1,000 million to $225 million and the tax payable is reduced from $400 million to $90 million. The total tax shield of $310 million is equal to the total tax-deductible expenses of $775 million multiplied by the tax rate of 40 percent. By virtue of being able to deduct certain expenses prior to the calculation of taxable income, this company's tax liability is reduced or "shielded" by $310 million.

Table 21.9 – Calculation of a Tax Shield

$ millions

Income Statement		Tax-deductible item	× tax rate →	Value of tax shield
No tax shields				
Revenues	$1,000			
-Tax payable (40% tax rate)	**(400)**			
With tax shields				
Revenues	$1,000			
- Cost of goods sold	(400)	(400)	= 400 × 40%	(160)
= Gross margin	600			
- Selling, general & administrative	(100)	(100)	= 100 × 40%	(40)
= EBITDA	500			
- DD&A	(150)	(150)	= 150 × 40%	(60)
= EBIT	350			
- Interest expense	(125)	(125)	= 125 × 40%	(50)
= Taxable income	225			
- Tax payable (40% tax rate)	**(90)**			
= Net income	$135			
Total		**($775)**	× tax rate →	**($310)**

Taxable Income and Taxable Gain

The type of tax payable by a corporation depends on the underlying taxable event. In general, corporations pay tax on (i) taxable income where "income" is based on ordinary business events (e.g., a company makes and sells widgets) and (ii) taxable gain where "gain" is based on the sale or disposition of company assets, property, or stock of a subsidiary. As of 2006, the same federal tax rate of 35 percent applies to both corporate taxable income and corporate taxable gain. As a result, from a financial modeling perspective, in most cases it is not important to characterize the different types of taxable events since the same 35 percent tax rate applies to corporate taxable income and corporate taxable gain.

Corporate Taxable Income

Corporate income tax is levied on a corporation's **taxable income**, also known as **earnings before tax**.

Taxable income = revenues – tax deductible expenses

Tax payable = taxable income × tax rate

Corporate income tax is paid by corporations on regular operating income. Municipalities and nonprofit organizations do not pay corporate income tax. In addition, limited liability corporations (LLCs), S corporations, master limited partnerships (MLPs), sole proprietorships, partnerships and other pass-through entities do not pay tax at the corporate level. **Personal income tax** is levied on individuals, specifically on household income, dividend income, income from unincorporated businesses, and income from pass-through entities.

Assume CoffeeCo, a corporation and a distributor of fine coffees, sold $10 million of coffee in 2006 and had $7.5 million of tax-deductible expenses in the same year. CoffeeCo would have taxable income of $2.5 million. Assuming a 40 percent corporate tax rate, CoffeeCo would owe $1.0 million of income tax. After accounting for the $1.0 million of tax payable, CoffeeCo would have net income of $1.5 million.

Table 21.10 – Simplified Income Tax Example

$ millions

CoffeeCo	2006
Revenues	$10.0
Tax-deductible expenses	(7.5)
Taxable income	2.5
Tax rate	40%
Tax payable[1]	(1.0)
Net income[2]	$1.5

[1] Taxable income × tax rate ($2.5 × 0.4)
[2] Taxable income - tax payable ($2.5 - $1.0)

Note that this is a simplified example of how a company's tax liability would be calculated since it does not address the differences that arise between the GAAP books and the TAX return work papers when calculating income taxes payable that were discussed in the section Deferred Taxes.

Corporate Taxable Gain

When a corporation sells an asset at a gain (the asset can be a tangible asset, an intangible asset, or stock in another corporation), it must pay tax on the taxable gain. In general, the taxable gain is equal to the selling price minus the tax basis (tax basis is described in detail in the following section).

There are two important considerations to this generalized formula. The first has to do with the type of tax basis used in the calculation of taxable gain (outside basis or inside basis) and the second has to do with the calculation of "selling price." Both considerations are determined by whether the transaction is structured as a sale of stock or a sale of assets.

One of the most important decisions in an M&A transaction is whether the transaction is structured as a sale of stock or as a sale of assets. The reason this decision of stock vs. assets is so important is that the decision has major implications regarding the legal, accounting and tax treatment of the transaction. Most of these implications are discussed later in the chapter in the sections Selling Stock vs. Selling Assets - Tax Issues, and Selling Stock vs. Selling Assets - Non Tax Issues. The point is made here because the calculation of corporate taxable gain is different in a sale of stock than the calculation of corporate taxable gain in a sale of assets.

If selling stock:

> Taxable gain = proceeds from sale - *outside* basis in stock
>
> Tax payable = taxable gain × tax rate

If selling assets:

> Taxable gain = proceeds from sale (including the fair market value of property or services received) + assumed liabilities - *inside* basis in assets
>
> Tax payable = taxable gain × tax rate

Both inside basis and outside basis are discussed in the following section.

For purposes of calculating gain or loss on an *asset* sale, the selling price is not simply the cash received but the total consideration received, *including the cessation of responsibility for a liability.* This distinction is important because, in the context of an asset sale, it generally has the effect of increasing the selling price and therefore increasing the taxable gain which, in turn, increases the tax payable.

> **Basis nomenclature**
>
> In asset sales, accountants and tax lawyers regularly use slightly different terminology when referring to basis. Tax lawyers typically say "cash + liabilities - basis = gain" whereas accountants often say "cash - net basis = gain" where net basis is equal to liabilities minus basis. Note that these calculations are identical, only that the terminology used is different.

According to the Internal Revenue Code, a **capital asset** is generally any property (asset) other than inventory, real property (land) and depreciable property (depreciable assets).[3] The most common capital asset is stock owned of a corporation (whether that shareholder is an individual owning the stock of a stand-alone corporation or whether that shareholder is itself a corporation owning the stock of another corporation). The same federal statutory corporate tax rate of 35 percent applies to (1) taxable income and (2) taxable gain, and the same federal statutory corporate tax rate of 35 percent applies to taxable gain regardless of whether the source of that taxable gain is the sale of (2a) a capital asset or (2b) a non-capital asset.

If the asset sold is a capital asset, then the taxable gain is defined as a "capital gain." **Capital gain tax** is tax due on capital gains. A **capital gain** for TAX accounting purposes is the difference between the selling price of a capital asset and the tax basis of the capital asset. If the selling price of a capital asset is less than its tax basis (meaning the selling price minus the tax basis is a negative number), the transaction will generate a **capital loss**. (For a detailed discussion on capital losses, see the section Net Operating Losses and Capital Losses.)

[3] See IRC §1221(a)

Be careful with "capital asset" terminology

Most corporate finance practitioners define a "capital asset" generically as a major asset purchased for use in the normal course of business that has a useful life of greater than one year and is capitalized (put on the balance sheet and depreciated or amortized), without recognizing that the TAX definition of a capital asset is different than the generic definition. This contradiction between the tax code definition of a capital asset --as basically any asset other than inventory, land, accounts payable, and depreciable assets-- and the use of the term in corporate finance can lead to confusion. Fortunately, this confusion regarding the differing definitions of a capital asset usually has little impact on the calculation of the tax payable upon the sale of an asset because both capital and non-capital asset sales are taxed at the same federal corporate rate of 35 percent as of 2006.

Although the IRS has a specific definition of what constitutes a capital asset, from a financial modeling standpoint the character of the gain is usually unimportant. If a corporation sells an asset (regardless of whether it is a capital asset like stock in another corporation, a depreciable asset, or a non-depreciable non-capital asset such as land), the corporation must pay tax on the gain. And in all scenarios, taxable gain is equal to the selling price minus the tax basis. Thus while differences exist with respect to what constitutes the "selling price" and whether to use inside basis (for a sale of assets) or outside basis (for a sale of stock), only under special circumstances does the type of gain matter (because a separate tax rate and/or tax characteristics may apply). As a result, practitioners usually do not distinguish between the types of gain because "the math" remains the same in most cases. Therefore, unless noted, this chapter will use the term "taxable gain" to refer to both capital gain and non-capital gain (sometimes referred to as "gain on sale").

Let's review two taxable gain examples, one for the sale of a non-capital asset, and one for the sale of a capital asset (in both cases as defined by the IRS). Assume CoffeeCo purchased a coffee roaster in December 2004 for $5 million and in December 2006 decided to purchase a more modern coffee roaster. CoffeeCo has identified a smaller coffee company that would like to buy the old roaster. The smaller coffee company is willing to pay CoffeeCo $3.5 million for the old roaster. Assume the coffee roaster has a five-year useful life, the roaster will have no value at the end of the five years (therefore the salvage value is zero and the depreciable amount is $5 million), and CoffeeCo uses straight-line depreciation. CoffeeCo's annual depreciation for the roaster, therefore, is $1 million.

$5 million depreciable value / 5 years = $1 million of depreciation per year

Assume that CoffeeCo made no capital improvements to the roaster between the time it was bought and sold. Therefore, between 2004 and 2006, CoffeeCo depreciated two years of the roaster's useful life, making CoffeeCo's tax basis in the roaster $3 million as of December 2006.

$5 million - accumulated depreciation of $2 million (2 years) = $3 million

Since CoffeeCo sold the roaster to another company for $3.5 million and the cost of the roaster less the accumulated depreciation (i.e., the basis) was $3 million, the taxable gain on the sale was $0.5 million. Assuming a 40 percent tax rate, CoffeeCo would owe $0.2 million in tax payable and the after-tax cash proceeds would be $3.3 million.

Table 21.11 – Sale of Asset Example

$ millions	
Original purchase price of roaster - 2004	$5.0
Annual depreciation - 2005	(1.0)
Tax basis in 2005[1]	4.0
Annual depreciation - 2006	(1.0)
Tax basis in 2006[2]	3.0
Sale price of roaster in 2006	3.5
Tax basis in 2006	(3.0)
Taxable gain[3]	0.5
Tax rate	40%
Tax payable[4]	0.2
Pretax cash proceeds	3.5
Tax payable	(0.2)
After-tax cash proceeds[5]	$3.3

[1] Purchase price - accumulated depreciation ($5.0 - $1.0)
[2] Purchase price - accumulated depreciation ($5.0 - $2.0)
[3] Sale price - tax basis ($3.5 - $3.0)
[4] Taxable gain × tax rate ($0.5 × 0.4)
[5] Pretax cash proceeds - tax payable ($3.5 - $0.2)

In a separate and independent transaction, assume CoffeeCo sells TeaCo stock in 2006 for $20 million and that CoffeeCo has an outside basis in TeaCo's stock of $12 million. Therefore, the taxable gain in this example would be $8 million and, assuming a 40 percent tax rate, the tax payable would be $3.2 million as set forth in Table 21.12.

Table 21.12 – Sale of Stock Example

$ millions	
Sale price of TeaCo stock in 2006	$20.0
Tax basis in TeaCo stock	(12.0)
Taxable gain[1]	8.0
Tax rate	40%
Tax payable[2]	3.2
Pretax cash proceeds	20.0
Tax payable	(3.2)
After-tax cash proceeds[3]	$16.8

[1] Sale price - tax basis ($20.0 - $12.0)
[2] Taxable gain × tax rate ($8.0 × 0.4)
[3] Pretax cash proceeds - tax payable ($20.0 - $3.2)

Book Value vs. Tax Basis

The previous section noted that taxable gain is calculated by subtracting the tax basis of whatever is being sold from the purchase price. This section will now discuss the concept of tax basis in more detail.

The carrying cost of an asset on a company's GAAP balance sheet is called the asset's **book value** or BOOK carrying cost. The carrying cost of an asset on a company's TAX balance sheet is called the asset's **tax basis**. Every asset on a company's GAAP balance sheet has a book value, and every asset on a company's TAX balance sheet has a tax basis.

Tax nomenclature and tax basis

People often distinguish between the "book basis" and "tax basis" of an asset, especially in the context of the sale of the asset. This is incorrect nomenclature. The term "book basis" does not exist. However, that does not stop bankers and other finance professionals from using it. Basis is purely a TAX concept. "Book value" represents an asset's carrying value for GAAP accounting; "tax basis" represents an asset's carrying value for TAX accounting.

The tax basis of an asset can differ significantly from its book value due to differences in accounting methods between TAX and GAAP (principally due to the timing of recognition of depreciation expense but there are also other causes of differences).

The concept of tax basis is further complicated by the fact that there are two types of tax basis: (1) inside basis and (2) outside basis.

Inside Basis vs. Outside Basis

Inside tax basis (referred to as "**inside basis"**) is the tax basis that a corporation has in its *assets*. **Outside tax basis** (referred to as "**outside basis"**) is the tax basis that a shareholder has in the *stock* of a corporation. If a parent corporation owns stock in a subsidiary corporation, the parent corporation (as the shareholder) has an *outside* basis in the *stock* of the subsidiary corporation, and the subsidiary corporation has an *inside* basis in the *assets* of the subsidiary (so two separate relationships).

In Figure 21.13, notice that Parent Corporation has an inside basis in its assets and an outside basis in any stock it owns in another corporation.

Figure 21.13 – Parent Corporation with Subsidiaries

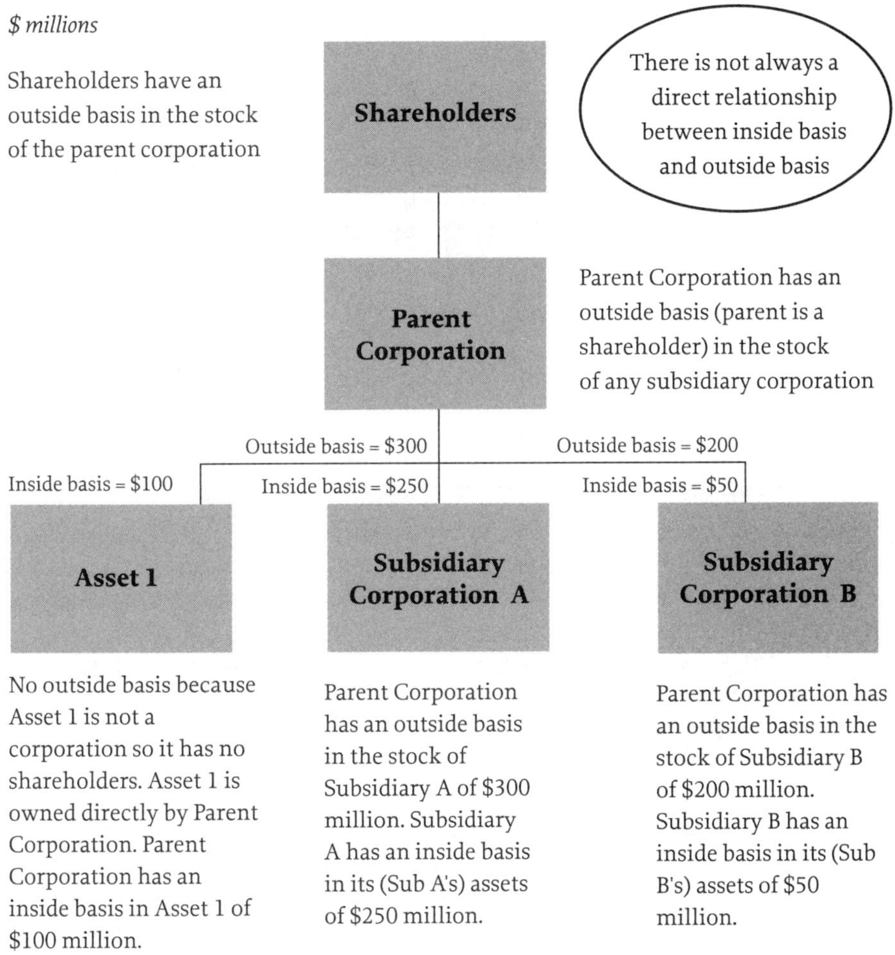

Subsidiaries and divisions

A subsidiary is a corporation (legally formed, incorporated in a state and subject to the corporation laws of that state) owned by a parent corporation. From a GAAP perspective, a corporation is considered a subsidiary if the parent company owns greater than 50 percent of the common voting stock of the subsidiary corporation. A division is not a corporation. A division is an operating unit of a company that uses assets of the company in its business. In the case of a division, the parent company owns the assets of the division directly and the division itself is not a separate legal entity (not a corporation). In the case of a subsidiary, the subsidiary itself --as a stand-alone corporation-- owns its own assets.

What is a consolidated tax return?

If a corporation has a subsidiary (a corporation it owns a majority of or controlling stake in), it is allowed to file a **consolidated tax return** (meaning a combined tax return for the parent corporation as well as the subsidiary corporation) *as long as* the parent corporation is a C corporation and parent owns at least "80 percent of the vote and value" of the subsidiary.[4] If the parent corporation owns less than 80 percent of the voting stock of the subsidiary corporation *or* if the owned subsidiary stock is worth less than 80 percent of the value of subsidiary (e.g., if the subsidiary has two classes of stock with different values and parent owns the lower-valued stock), the subsidiary corporation must file its own tax return and the parent corporation's tax return would not consolidate the subsidiary's financial results.

What Changes Inside Basis?

Depreciation and amortization decrease the inside basis, and capital improvements and additions increase the inside basis. Step-downs due to permanent reductions in value also decrease inside basis. Basis step-ups (an increase in inside basis) occur in an acquisition of assets if the fair market value of the assets is greater than the existing tax basis. (For a detailed discussion, see the sections Selling Stock vs. Selling Assets - Tax Issues, and Basis Step-ups.) Assets with a low inside basis are generally

[4] See IRC §1504(a)(2)

older assets that have been depreciated or amortized over a long period of time.

For example, if a factory initially cost $10 million to build and, for TAX purposes, had a 10-year useful life with straight-line depreciation and no salvage value, after four years the company would have an inside basis of $6 million in the factory.

$10 million purchase price / 10 years = $1 million of depreciation per year

$1 million depreciation × 4 years = $4 million of accumulated depreciation

$10 million - $4 = $6 million inside basis

If the company invested $1 million to build a loading dock, the factory would have an inside basis of $7 million after year four ($10 million – $4 million + $1 million = $7 million).

What Changes Outside Basis?

If a parent corporation owns stock in a subsidiary corporation and that subsidiary corporation is not consolidated for TAX purposes (e.g., parent does not have 80 percent of vote and value), the outside basis is the value that the parent corporation initially paid for the subsidiary stock. At that point the outside basis freezes and does not change.[5] However, if a subsidiary corporation is consolidated for TAX purposes[6], the activities of subsidiary affect parent's outside basis in the stock of subsidiary as follows:

- If a consolidated subsidiary has positive earnings which are used in parent's consolidated tax return, those earnings increase parent's outside basis in subsidiary.
- Contributions of capital by parent to subsidiary also increase parent's outside basis in subsidiary.
- If a consolidated subsidiary has losses which are used in parent's consolidated tax return, those losses decrease parent's outside basis in subsidiary.
- Distributions of cash (dividends) by subsidiary to parent also decrease parent's outside basis in subsidiary.
- If parent's outside basis in a TAX consolidated subsidiary goes negative as

[5] This is generally the case, though it may not always be the case under certain Dividends-Received Deduction (DRD) situations under IRC §1058.

[6] Recall that tax consolidation is allowed if parent owns at least 80 percent of the vote and value of subsidiary. See IRC §1502 consolidated return regulations.

> a result of subsidiary losses sustained, an Excess Loss Account (ELA) is created. Said another way, negative outside basis in the stock of a subsidiary is possible whereas negative inside basis in an asset is not possible (inside basis is simply written down to zero and remains there).

In summary, if a shareholder (which shareholder can be a corporation) owns stock in a corporation which is not a consolidated subsidiary for TAX purposes, shareholder's outside basis in the stock is the purchase price paid for the stock. However, if a parent corporation (a shareholder) owns stock in a subsidiary corporation which is consolidated with parent for TAX purposes, the actions of both parent and subsidiary can affect parent's outside basis in the stock of subsidiary: positive earnings and contributions of capital increase parent's outside basis in subsidiary, and subsidiary losses and dividends/distributions reduce parent's outside basis in subsidiary.

Net Operating Losses and Capital Losses

Net Operating Losses (NOLs)

If a company has taxable income, it pays income tax on that taxable income. If, however, the company has a loss (i.e., tax-deductible expenses are greater than revenues in the period), the company does not pay income taxes for that period since it had no taxable income. Instead of being liable for a tax payment in the loss-making period, the company receives a tax "benefit" which can be used to offset a tax liability, with some limitations. However, the government does not write a check to the company for the amount of that benefit. Instead, these operating losses are "saved," so to speak, and can be applied to other, profitable tax periods. The **net operating losses** (called **NOLs**) created in that period can be used to offset future taxable income or can be applied to previous years' taxable income (subject to limitations). NOLs can also be used to offset future capital gain or can be applied to previous years' capital gain, subject to limitations.

> **NOL carrybacks and carryforwards**
>
> As of 2006, NOLs created in the 1998 tax year or later can be used to offset operating income and capital gain up to two years back (called a **tax loss carryback**) and 20 years forward (called a **tax loss carryforward**.) Generally, taxpayers must carry back the entire amount of the NOL to the two tax years before the NOL year and then carry forward any remaining NOL for up to 20 years after the NOL year. However, it is possible to waive the carry*back* period. If so, then NOLs can only be used in the 20-year carry*forward* period. Once made, this waiver of the carryback period is irrevocable.[7] NOLs created in a tax year prior to 1998 are subject to the older limitations of three years back and 15 years forward.

Capital Losses

Similar to NOLs, if a company has a capital loss (i.e., the sale price of a capital asset is less than the tax basis of the capital asset), the company does not pay capital gain tax (since there was no gain). Instead, the sale generates a capital loss, and the company can utilize the capital loss created in that period to offset future net capital gains or apply it to previous years' net capital gains, subject to limitations. Capital losses can only be used to offset capital gains whereas NOLs can be used to offset (1) income tax and (2) capital gain tax. Because of this and their longer life, NOLs are generally considered more valuable than capital losses.

> **Capital loss carrybacks and carryforwards**
>
> As of 2006, capital losses can be used to offset net capital gains up to three years back (called a **capital loss carryback**) and five years forward (called a **capital loss carryforward**).[8]

To illustrate how a capital loss can be used to offset a capital gain, let's consider ShoeCo, which owns a number of shoe-making subsidiaries. Let's assume that ShoeCo sells the stock of its Athletic Shoe subsidiary for $60 million in 2005 and that ShoeCo has an outside tax basis in the Athletic Shoe Company of $100 million. Therefore, ShoeCo will recognize a capital loss of $40 million on the sale of the Athletic Shoe subsidiary. Let's also assume that in 2007, ShoeCo sells the stock of its

[7] See IRC § 172(b)(1)(A)

[8] See IRC §1212(a)(1)(A)

Leather Shoe subsidiary for $150 million. In 2007, ShoeCo has an outside tax basis of $100 million in the Leather Shoe Company. Therefore, ShoeCo will recognize a capital gain of $50 million on the sale of the Leather Shoe Company.

Table 21.14 – ShoeCo Capital Loss Example

$ millions

Athletic Shoe Company Sale - 2005	
Sale price	$60
Tax basis in stock of Athletic Shoe Company	(100)
Capital gain/(loss)	($40)

Leather Shoe Company Sale - 2007	
Sale price	$150
Tax basis in stock of Leather Shoe Company	(100)
Capital gain/(loss)	$50

If ShoeCo did not have the $40 million capital loss, it would owe $20 million in capital gain tax (assuming a 40 percent tax rate) on the sale of Leather Shoe Company in 2007 and have after-tax cash proceeds of $130 million.

Table 21.15 – ShoeCo Capital Loss Example continued

$ millions

Leather Shoe Company Sale - 2007	
Sale price	$150
Tax basis in stock of Leather Shoe Company	(100)
Capital gain/(loss)[1]	50
Tax rate	40%
Tax payable[2]	20
Pretax cash proceeds	150
Tax payable	(20)
After-tax cash proceeds[3]	$130

[1] Sale price - tax basis ($150 - $100)
[2] Taxable gain × tax rate ($50 × 0.4)
[3] Pretax cash proceeds - tax payable ($150 - $20)

However, since ShoeCo does have a $40 million capital loss from 2005 which it can use to offset the capital gain in 2007, the capital gain tax will only be $4 million instead of $20 million, and the after-tax cash proceeds will be $146 million instead of $130 million. The $40 million capital loss is used to reduce the capital gain from $50 million to $10 million, and the capital gain tax of $4 million is calculated based on the $10 million of adjusted capital gain.

Table 21.16 – ShoeCo Capital Loss Example continued

$ millions

Leather Shoe Company Sale - 2007	
Sale price	$150
Tax basis in stock of Leather Shoe Company	(100)
Capital gain/(loss)[1]	50
Capital loss from sale of stock of Athletic Shoe Co.	(40)
Adjusted capital gain	10
Tax rate	40%
Tax payable[2]	4
Pretax cash proceeds	150
Tax payable	(4)
After-tax cash proceeds[3]	$146

[1] Sale price - tax basis ($150 - $100)
[2] Taxable gain × tax rate ($10 × 0.4)
[3] Pretax cash proceeds - tax payable ($150 - $4)

Essentially, instead of the government giving ShoeCo a cash tax refund of $16 million in 2005 based on the capital loss of $40 million ($40 million × 40% = $16 million) associated with the sale of stock of the Athletic Shoe Company, the government allows ShoeCo to use that $16 million tax benefit in the future as an offset to a capital gain tax liability (which ShoeCo can only use if it has a capital gain within the applicable limitation period). That $16 million benefit is realized in 2007 with the sale of the stock of the Leather Shoe Company. Without the 2005 capital loss from Athletic Shoe Company, the 2007 sale of the Leather Shoe Company would have generated a capital gain tax liability of $20 million. However, with the application of the 2005 capital loss, ShoeCo has an adjusted capital gain of $10 million and only has to pay capital gain tax of $4 million in 2007, the difference being the $16 million of tax benefit from 2005.

Loss disallowance rules

When selling a subsidiary for a loss, certain "loss disallowance rules" must be satisfied in order to ensure that the loss is allowed. A tax specialist must study the consolidated return to ensure that the loss can be used to offset any gain.

Acquired NOLs

NOLs may be "inherited" in an acquisition. That is, if Target has NOLs, Acquiror may be able to use those purchased NOLs after an ownership change (generally whenever more than 50 percent of Target's equity changes hands within a three-year period and it was an acquisition of the stock of LossCo or Acquiror purchased the assets of LossCo in a reorganization). However, there are limitations with respect to how and when Acquiror can utilize acquired NOLs. The most important limitation is called the §382 limitation, after the Internal Revenue Code (IRC) section that governs it. If §382 applies, each year Acquiror can utilize only a percentage of the acquired NOLs: this percentage is calculated by multiplying the long-term tax exempt rate (historically it has been around 5 percent) by the fair market value of Target's equity, which is generally the purchase price of the equity. Limitations on the use of acquired NOLs were put in place to prevent companies from acquiring companies with significant NOLs only so that Acquiror could utilize Target's NOLs (as opposed to acquiring Target for business purposes).

Seek counsel

Net operating losses result in a reduction in taxable income and therefore a reduction in tax payable. Not surprisingly, companies are interested in NOLs because tax is often a significant expense and anything that can legally reduce taxes is of interest to company management. However, since the government depends on taxes for its revenues, the government is equally interested in NOLs, except that in the government's case it is interested in limiting the use of NOLs. As a result of these competing interests, the rules governing NOLs and their use are complex even by tax standards. As a result, tax counsel should be consulted if you are working on a transaction in which Target NOLs are being acquired in order to determine the amount of NOLs that can be utilized by Acquiror annually, especially in light of changes to rules surrounding built-in gain and built-in loss.[9]

To illustrate the §382 limitation, assume Acquiror purchases 100 percent of Target's common equity for $100 million and Target has $20 million of NOLs which will stay with Target after the transaction closes. Further assume that the long-term tax-exempt rate[10] is 5 percent.

To calculate the annual limitation on the use of acquired NOLs under §382, first multiply the equity purchase price (which is indicative of the fair market value of Target's equity) by the long-term tax-exempt rate.

$100 million fair market value of Target's equity
× 0.05 long-term tax exempt rate
= $5 million

This means that a maximum of $5 million of Target's NOLs can be utilized each year. Thus, it would take four years to use up all of Target's $20 million in NOLs, assuming Acquiror had at least $5 million of taxable income to shield in each of those four years.

$20 million in NOLs / $5 million annual limitation = 4 years to use the NOLs

If less than $5 million of NOLs is used by Acquiror in any given year (most commonly if Acquiror did not have enough taxable income to utilize the entirety of the annual allowance of $5 million), the annual limitation is increased to the extent that there is an unused limitation from a prior year. So if Acquiror only used $4 million of NOLs in year 1, it could use $6 million in NOLs in year 2 (assuming Acquiror had taxable income of at least $6 million in year 2).

Prior to the enactment of §382, if Acquiror had $20 million of taxable income in year one, it could have used all of Target's $20 million in NOLs in the first year after close of the transaction. The obvious benefit is the time value of the $20 million recognized in year one as opposed to the $5 million recognized in each of years one, two, three, and four. Thus the purpose of the §382 limitation is to prevent trafficking in NOLs, which might occur if new owners were able to immediately apply 100 percent of Target's NOLs against Acquiror's taxable income.

[9] In the 5-year "recognition period" following an "ownership change" (both as defined in IRC §382), the §382 limitation may be increased by the amount of recognized built-in gain or the recognized built-in loss may be subject to the §382 limitation, depending on whether LossCo has a net unrealized built-in gain or a net unrealized built-in loss, respectively. In 2002 and 2003 the IRS provided guidance regarding computation of recognized built-in gain and recognized built-in loss. See IRC §382(h), Notice 2003-40, and Notice 2003-65 (specifying two acceptable methodologies in identifying recognized built-in gain and recognized built-in loss).

[10] The long-term tax-exempt rate means the highest of the adjusted federal long-term rates in effect for any month in the three-calendar-month period ending with the calendar month in which the ownership change occurs.

Often, one of the benefits for a corporation of filing a consolidated tax return is that the capital losses and operating losses (NOLs) of one subsidiary (Subsidiary A) can be used to offset capital gain or operating income from other parts of the parent company (Subsidiaries B, C and D) filing the consolidated tax return. However, exceptions occur when corporations enter or leave the consolidated group. For example, if Subsidiary A is sold, the NOLs which are allocated to it go with Subsidiary A and those NOLs are no longer available to parent company (i.e., the NOLs are an asset of Subsidiary A and, like other Subsidiary A assets, are sold to new buyer, which is then subject to the §382 limitation with respect to Subsidiary A's NOLs). In addition, if a group member (Subsidiary C) entered the group with NOLs from a pre-consolidation period, those pre-consolidation NOLs cannot be used by the consolidating group. At that point, Subsidiary C's NOLs from the pre-consolidation period are only applicable against Subsidiary C's own taxable income (not the taxable income of the consolidated group). This is the so-called Separate Return Limitation Year (or SRLY). In cases where both the §382 limitation and the SRLY rules apply, the §382 rules prevail.

While the base §382 limitation and the five-year limitation on the recognized built-in gain and recognized built-in loss are the most common of the limitations on the use of acquired NOLs, §269 may apply (and, if so, may prevent Acquiror from succeeding to the use of the NOLs) and so it is important to be aware of these and other potential limitations.

Tax Credits

NOLs serve as an offset to taxable income (pretax income) and therefore reduce taxes by 40 percent of every NOL dollar (or whatever the applicable tax rate is), not 100 percent of every NOL dollar. Many people make the mistake of assuming that NOLs are equal in value to **tax credits**. Tax credits serve as an offset to the actual tax liability owed and therefore reduce tax payable by 100 percent of every tax credit dollar. Said differently, tax credits are a dollar-for-dollar offset to the tax liability while NOLs are an offset to *taxable income* or a 40 percent (or whatever the applicable tax rate is) offset to the *tax liability*.

For example, as shown in Table 21.17, assume that FarmerCo had $100 million in revenue and $60 million in tax-deductible expenses. FarmerCo, therefore, would have taxable income of $40 million.

  $100 million revenue
- $60 million tax-deductible expenses

= $40 million taxable income

Assuming a 40 percent tax rate, FarmerCo would owe $16 million in income tax payable.

$40 million of taxable income × 40% tax rate = $16 million of tax payable

Let's now assume that FarmerCo had NOLs of $10 million that could be applied in 2006. FarmerCo's taxable income (not tax liability) would be reduced from $40 million to $30 million. Assuming a 40 percent tax rate, FarmerCo would owe $12 million in income tax.

$40 million of taxable income - $10 million in NOLs = $30 million adjusted taxable income

$30 million of adjusted taxable income × 40% tax rate = $12 million of tax payable

Thus in the NOL example, FarmerCo's tax payable was reduced from $16 million to $12 million. This $4 million reduction in tax payable is the after-tax value of the $10 million in NOLs.

$10 million in NOLs × 40% tax rate = $4 million of tax savings

If, on the other hand, in 2006 FarmerCo qualifies for $10 million in tax credits from the federal government, FarmerCo's tax liability would be reduced, dollar for dollar, from $16 million to $6 million, which is $16 million of tax payable plus the tax credit of $10 million.

$16 million of tax payable + $10 million in tax credits = $6 million adjusted tax payable

Table 21.17 – Summary of Tax Attributes and Their Effects

$ millions	No tax attributes[1]	NOL example[2]	Tax credit example[3]
FarmerCo			
Revenue	$100	$100	$100
Expenses	(60)	(60)	(60)
Taxable income	40	40	40
NOLs	0	(10)	0
Adjusted taxable income	40	30	40
Tax payable	(16)	(12)	(16)
Tax credits	0	0	10
Adjusted tax payable	(16)	(12)	(6)
Net income	24	28	34
Tax payable with no tax attributes	(16)	(16)	(16)
Tax payable with tax attributes	(16)	(12)	(6)
Cash tax savings	$0	$4	$10
Tax rate	40%	40%	40%
Effective tax rate[4]	40%	30%	15%

[1]40% tax rate; no other tax attributes pro or con
[2]40% tax rate; NOLs of $10 million serves as a reduction to Taxable income
[3]40% tax rate; tax credit of $10 million serves as a reduction to Tax payable
[4]Adjusted tax payable / taxable income

Shareholder-Level and Corporate-Level Tax

There is an important distinction between shareholder-level tax and corporate-level tax. Most discussions of shareholder-level tax and corporate-level tax revolve around the issue of double taxation.

Shareholder-level tax is any tax liability owed by a shareholder of a corporation. When a shareholder receives dividends, if the shareholder is an individual, she pays tax on the dividends received at ordinary income tax rates since dividends are treated as ordinary income for individual income tax purposes.[11] If the shareholder is a corporation, other rules apply on dividends received.

[11] This was the case historically, but is not the case as of 2006. The passage of the Jobs and Growth Tax Relief Reconciliation Act of 2003 (JGTRRA) temporarily reduced the top tax rates on dividends and on long-term capital gains to 15% for individuals. JGTRRA was Amended by the Tax Increase Prevention and Reconciliation Act of 2005 (TIPRA) and now expires in 2010 unless the government extends it.

Corporate-level tax, on the other hand, is tax owed and paid by a corporation. Corporate-level tax can be tax on operating income (taxable income) or tax on gain on sale (taxable gain).

One of the major arguments against the payment of dividends is **double taxation**. The *double* comes from the fact that in certain transactions there is both corporate-level tax and shareholder-level tax. An example of how cash flows through the corporate system illustrates the two levels of tax.

Assume a corporation has taxable income of $100. The corporation has to pay income tax on its taxable income, so that $100 is taxed at 40 percent, leaving the corporation with $60 in net income.

$100 in taxable income × (1 - 40% tax rate) = $60 in net income

Assume the corporation paid all earnings to its one shareholder in the form of a dividend. The shareholder would get taxed on the $60 dividend at 30 percent[12] (or whatever his ordinary income tax rate was), leaving him with $42.

$60 in dividends × (1 - 30% tax rate) = $42 in after-tax proceeds

So the original $100 was taxed twice (corporate-level and shareholder-level tax) and the after-tax proceeds delivered to the shareholder are only 42 percent of the original $100. Said differently, the original $100 in taxable income had an effective tax rate of 58 percent. From a mathematical perspective, we can get to the same place in one calculation by multiplying the percentages of the after-tax corporate proceeds by the after-tax shareholder proceeds:

$60\% \times 70\% = 42\%$ $(0.6 \times 0.7 = 0.42)$.

Not surprisingly, most M&A transactions are structured to try to avoid double taxation. The most common transaction structures are described in more detail later in this chapter and in Corporate Restructurings. (Ch.22)

Selling Stock vs. Selling Assets - Tax Issues

One of the biggest considerations in an M&A transaction --for both buyers and sellers-- is whether the transaction is a sale of stock or a sale of assets. For example, whether the transaction is a sale of stock or a sale of assets determines whether the gain or loss triggered by Seller will be calculated based on the outside basis (basis in

[12] Through 2010, dividends are taxed at a maximum of 15 percent for individuals. However, beginning in 2011 dividend taxation is scheduled to return to its pre-2003 rates of ordinary income. For illustrative purposes, this chapter uses assumptions approximating historical dividend tax rates rather than the 15 percent rate in effect at this writing.

the stock) or the inside basis (basis in the assets). In addition, there are non-tax business considerations (see Selling Stock vs. Selling Assets - Non Tax Issues). A natural tension exists between sellers, who generally prefer to sell stock, and acquirors, who generally prefer to purchase assets. Ultimately, whether the transaction is for stock or for assets --and it is always an either/or decision-- will be determined by the relative amounts of negotiating leverage of Acquiror and Seller, which will differ in every transaction and can even differ markedly over time in the same transaction.

Tax considerations for Seller in choosing whether to sell stock or to sell assets are described below. Non-tax considerations are described in the following section.

1. If stock is sold, the taxable gain or loss for Seller will be determined based on the tax basis Seller has in the stock of the corporation (the outside basis).

2. If assets are sold, the taxable gain or loss for Seller will be determined based on the tax basis Seller has in the assets (the inside basis).

3. In situations in which the ultimate goal is for the cash proceeds to be distributed to shareholders, an asset sale will incur corporate-level tax and shareholder-level tax (i.e., double taxation), whereas a sale of stock (if structured properly) will only trigger shareholder-level tax. In addition, if the transaction is structured as a tax-free reorganization, it is possible that even this shareholder-level tax can be deferred. (Tax-Free Reorganizations are described in detail near the end of this chapter.)

4. Since the outside basis is often higher than the inside basis, Sellers generally prefer to sell stock (outside basis) rather than assets (inside basis) since a higher outside basis results in lower taxable gain and therefore lower tax payable. Lower tax payable results in higher after-tax cash proceeds.

5. Generally (but not always), the inside basis a corporation has in its assets is lower than the outside basis shareholders have in the stock. This occurs because inside basis (basis in assets) is reduced by depreciation and amortization. Outside basis (basis in stock) is not reduced by depreciation or amortization (if not part of a consolidated tax group).

For Acquiror, one of the principal TAX considerations in an acquisition is whether Acquiror will obtain a **basis step-up** in the tax basis of the purchased assets or whether Acquiror will keep ("carry over" is the commonly used TAX term) Seller's tax basis in the assets purchased. A basis step-up occurs when Acquiror is allowed to record purchased assets at their fair market value in Acquiror's TAX return work papers (the fair market value of purchased assets is usually equal to the purchase price). **Carryover basis** occurs when Acquiror must record purchased assets at the

Seller's historical tax basis. That is, the tax basis *Seller* had in the purchased asset is carried over to *Acquiror's* TAX return work papers.

A stepped-up tax basis is preferred by Acquiror for TAX accounting because it results in (1) higher future depreciation expense and therefore lower taxable income and lower cash taxes and (2) the higher the tax basis, the lower the taxable gain and associated tax payable if the asset is subsequently sold. Because a higher tax basis is preferred by Acquiror, and because prices tend to rise in value over time due to inflation, Acquirors typically prefer to have acquired assets recorded in their TAX return work papers at fair market value. It is important to note that while recording assets at fair market value in Acquiror's TAX return work papers usually results in a basis step-up for TAX purposes, it does not guarantee it; basis step-downs do occur, especially in cyclical industries, and in such a case a carryover basis would be preferable for Acquiror. However, Acquiror cannot simply choose whether purchased assets will be recorded on a stepped-up/(down) basis or on a carryover basis; how Seller's assets are recorded on Acquiror's TAX return work papers is determined by whether the transaction is a sale of assets (basis step-up/(step-down) in the purchased assets) or a sale of stock (carryover basis in the purchased assets).

For example, assume CoffeeCo purchased a machine from JuiceCo for $5 million and JuiceCo's tax basis in the machine is $2 million. A basis step-up is allowed for CoffeeCo if CoffeeCo purchased the machine directly (purchased assets); it could record the purchased asset on its TAX return work papers at the fair market value (or the purchase price) of $5 million. However, carryover basis would be required if CoffeeCo purchased the stock of a JuiceCo subsidiary that owned the machine (purchased stock); CoffeeCo would have to record the machine on its TAX return work papers at the JuiceCo subsidiary's historical basis of $2 million.

Tax considerations for Acquiror in choosing whether to buy stock or to buy assets are described below. Non-tax considerations are described in the following section.

1. If Acquiror purchases stock from Seller, Acquiror cannot take a basis step-up in the *assets*; instead, it must carry over Seller's historical basis in the purchased assets. However, Acquiror will have a basis step-up in the *stock* purchased, meaning Acquiror's TAX basis in the purchased stock will be equal to the purchase price (or fair market value) of the stock.

2. If Acquiror purchases assets from Seller, Acquiror can take a basis step-up in the acquired assets. This is valuable to Acquiror because of the tax shield on the additional depreciation which results from writing up the basis of the assets on Acquiror's TAX return work papers.

Selling Stock vs. Selling Assets - Non Tax Issues

In addition to tax-related issues, other non-tax goals and factors often determine whether a transaction is structured as a sale of stock or a sale of assets. That is, tax considerations should influence the transaction structure, not necessarily dictate it. One principal difference between selling stock and selling assets is the concept of what is sold or what goes with the sale. If Assets A, B, and C are purchased from Seller, Asset A, Asset B, and Asset C are transferred to Acquiror, and that is all. The asset purchase agreement can be structured to include certain related liabilities as well, but everything that is to be purchased, asset or liability, has to be identified in the asset purchase agreement. Technically this is referred to as "scheduling assets and liabilities" in the purchase agreement because a list of the assets and liabilities to be sold is literally attached as an exhibit or schedule to the asset purchase agreement.

But what if the item being sold is not a factory or some other specific asset but rather a company or a subsidiary which owns numerous assets and has numerous liabilities associated with those assets? That company also might have working capital or contractual obligations, or environmental remediation obligations. One can begin to see how, in a situation like this, it might be difficult to identify each and every asset and/or liability in a sale. Situations like these are common, which is why business needs often encourage Seller to sell stock rather than assets (notwithstanding Acquiror's TAX-related desire to purchase assets). When the stock of a corporation is sold, everything owned by the corporation transfers to the new owner and no specific assets or liabilities need to be identified in the stock purchase agreement.

In a purchase of stock, Acquiror purchases all of the assets *and* all of the liabilities owned by the company; this is sometimes called "purchasing the balance sheet" because both assets and liabilities are transferred from Seller to Acquiror. Sellers generally want to sell stock in order to "sell the balance sheet." That is, Sellers generally would prefer to sell all of the assets *and* all of the liabilities of the business in question. Sellers usually do not want to sell just the valuable part of the business – the assets – and be left with the liabilities (tax and environmental liabilities, in particular, can turn out to be long-lived and expensive). Imagine what would happen, for example, if a company sold all its assets for $100 million and kept its liabilities, which were on the balance sheet for $80 million. Assume the liabilities ended up costing Seller $125 million. Having sold its operating assets (and therefore unable to earn any more money), the company would not be able to cover its obligations of $125 million.

Asset Write-Ups

Recall that basis is purely a TAX term. As such, basis step-ups and carryover basis are TAX terms, not GAAP terms. For GAAP, the rule is different. For GAAP, a company must record every acquisition at fair market value regardless of whether the transaction is structured as a sale of stock or a sale of assets. For GAAP, this concept is called writing up or writing down assets (short for writing up the book value of assets to fair market value or writing down the book value of assets to fair market value) and is consistent with the fundamental GAAP principle that items should be recorded at fair market value when they are placed on the GAAP balance sheet.

1. An **asset write-up** occurs on Acquiror's GAAP balance sheet if the fair market value of an acquired asset is *greater than* the historical book value at which the asset was recorded on Seller's GAAP balance sheet.

2. An **asset write-down** occurs on Acquiror's GAAP balance sheet if the fair market value of an acquired asset is *less than* the historical book value at which the asset was recorded on Seller's GAAP balance sheet.

Usually, the assumption in an acquisition of assets is that the fair market value of the assets is equal to the purchase price of the assets. However, this assumption does not necessarily hold true in an acquisition of stock. In an acquisition of stock, it is reasonable to believe that there is value paid to the Seller *in excess* of the fair market value of the assets and liabilities. This excess is called **goodwill** (goodwill is discussed in Accretion/Dilution Analysis (Ch.14)). Therefore, while it is generally safe to assume that the purchase price of the asset is equal to the fair market value of the asset, it is *not* safe to assume that the purchase price of stock of a corporation is equal to the fair market value of the purchased assets and liabilities owned by the corporation. In practice, an accounting firm would be hired to determine the fair market value of the assets and liabilities on Target's balance sheet, and then the difference between the amount paid for the equity of Target (the purchase price for the stock) and the fair market value of Target's identifiable assets minus liabilities would be recorded as goodwill. Numerical examples are provided in the section GAAP Accounting for M&A Transactions.

It is common to confuse the TAX term "basis step-up" with the GAAP term "asset write-up." However, they are very different concepts with meaningful accounting differences.

- A **basis step-up** (step-down) occurs when Acquiror recognizes the higher (lower) fair market value of an acquired asset on its TAX return work papers. Seller's lower (higher) tax basis in the sold asset is stepped up (down) to fair market value when ownership is transferred to Acquiror's TAX balance sheet.

- An **asset write-up** (write-down) occurs when Acquiror recognizes the higher (lower) fair market value of an acquired asset on its GAAP books.

Seller's lower (higher) book value in the sold asset is written up (down) to fair market value when ownership is transferred to Acquiror's GAAP balance sheet.

- An asset purchase (which triggers taxable gain/(loss) based on Seller's inside basis, or basis in the assets) allows Acquiror to take an asset write-up (write-down) in the value of the asset on the GAAP books and a basis step-up (step-down) in the value of the asset on its TAX return work papers.

- A stock purchase (which triggers taxable gain/(loss) based on Seller's outside basis, or basis in the stock) allows Acquiror to take an asset write-up (write-down) in the value of the asset on the GAAP books but does not allow Acquiror to take a basis step-up in the value of the asset on its TAX return work papers (carryover basis).

- A stock purchase does allow Acquiror to take a basis step-up in the value of the acquired stock on its TAX return work papers although, as noted earlier, this is generally viewed as less valuable than a basis step-up in the assets since there is no additional depreciation and therefore no cash tax savings associated with a basis step-up in stock.

There is a scenario in which Acquiror can purchase stock and still obtain a basis step-up in the value of the assets on the TAX return work papers (i.e., Acquiror can take a basis step-up in the assets even though it purchased stock, which would normally entail a carryover basis in the assets). This is a highly technical and regulated scenario which is discussed in the section 338(h)(10) Election at the end of the chapter.

In Table 21.18, notice that every transaction triggers an asset write-up or asset write-down for GAAP. Also notice that for TAX, only asset deals trigger a basis step-up/(step-down) while in contrast stock deals provide for a carryover basis in Seller's assets.

Table 21.18 – Accounting for Seller's Assets When Transferred to Acquiror's Balance Sheet

	Acquiror's Accounting for Seller's Assets[3]		
	GAAP books	TAX return work papers	
Type of transaction	Asset write-up/(write-down)[1]	Basis step-up/(down)[2]	Carryover basis[2]
Acquisition of stock	Yes	No	Yes
Acquisition of assets	Yes	Yes	No

[1] Asset write-up if the fair market value of the assets is higher than Seller's book value of the assets; asset write-down if it is lower.
[2] Note the "either/or" aspect of basis for TAX purposes: it is *either* a basis step-up *or* a carryover basis, but never both.
[3] Note also that the form of the acquisition of Seller is an "either / or" proposition in that Acquiror can purchase *either* the stock of Seller or the assets of Seller. The only caveat to this generalization is the existence of special transaction structures such as the 338(h)(10) election discussed at the end of the chapter, which is an acquisition of stock but has characteristics of and is treated for TAX purposes as an asset acquisition.

Basis Step-Ups

In general, the rule is that Acquiror gets to step up to fair market value the basis of whatever is acquired -- if assets are acquired then Acquiror can take a basis step-up in the assets; if stock is acquired then Acquiror can take a basis step-up in the stock.

A basis step-up in assets is generally considered more attractive to Acquiror than a basis step-up in stock because a basis step-up in assets allows Acquiror to depreciate the stepped-up portion of the asset value as additional depreciation for TAX purposes. This additional depreciation provides additional tax shields for Acquiror. Tax shields are valuable because they save the company money which would otherwise be paid out in cash taxes. In the event of a purchase of stock, Acquiror's new, higher basis in the acquired stock provides no immediate TAX benefits (because stock is not depreciated) and may never provide a benefit if Acquiror never sells this acquired stock. For this and other non-tax reasons, in general, acquirors want to purchase assets, not stock.

Let's consider a numerical example between FloristCo and CoffeeCo to illustrate a basis step-up. Assume FloristCo paid $30,000 for a delivery van four years ago and since then has depreciated $20,000 of the van's purchase price. Further assume that the delivery van has a useful life of six years and no salvage value, so annual depreciation is $5,000.

$30,000 purchase price / 6-year useful life = $5,000 in annual depreciation

$5,000 annual depreciation × 4 years = $20,000 of accumulated depreciation

Currently, FloristCo has a tax basis in the van of $10,000.

$30,000 - $20,000 = $10,000 tax basis

Assuming a 40 percent corporate tax rate, FloristCo has received a cumulative tax shield of $8,000 over the four years it has depreciated the van. The tax shield is calculated by multiplying the $20,000 of tax-deductible depreciation expense by the corporate tax rate of 40 percent.

$20,000 of accumulated depreciation × 40% tax rate = $8,000 tax shield

Had FloristCo kept the delivery van for its entire useful life of six years, FloristCo would have received a tax shield of $12,000 from the van, which is based on the $30,000 purchase price, no assumed salvage value, and a 40 percent tax rate.

$30,000 of accumulated depreciation × 40% tax rate = $12,000 in tax shield

Now let's assume FloristCo sells the delivery van to CoffeeCo for $15,000 after owning it for four years. FloristCo will recognize $5,000 of taxable gain and incur tax payable of $2,000.

> $15,000 sale price - $10,000 tax basis = $5,000 taxable gain

> $5,000 taxable gain × 40% tax rate = $2,000 of tax payable

From the IRS' perspective, the IRS provided $8,000 in tax shields to FloristCo ($20,000 × 40 percent = $8,000), but FloristCo is giving the IRS $2,000 back at the time of the sale ($5,000 × 40 percent = $2,000). Therefore the IRS has provided a net $6,000 of tax shields to FloristCo.

> $8,000 in depreciation tax shield - $2,000 tax paid by FloristCo = $6,000 net tax shield

The IRS now will allow CoffeeCo to depreciate the van based on the $15,000 purchase price (which is the fair market value) over the useful life of the van, and CoffeeCo will have $6,000 of tax shield from the $15,000 in depreciation.

> $15,000 in stepped-up basis × 40% tax rate = $6,000 of tax shield

This $6,000 of tax shield is actually comprised of two separate components, (i) depreciation from FloristCo's initial purchase of the van and (ii) depreciation from CoffeeCo's recent purchase.

> $4,000 of initial tax shield "left over" from FloristCo
>
> > ($10,000 of "unused" depreciation × 40% tax rate = $4,000)
>
> + $2,000 of "new" tax shield
>
> > ($5,000 "new" depreciation from basis step-up × 40% tax rate = $2,000)

From the IRS' perspective, it is no coincidence that the $2,000 of "value" to CoffeeCo in the form of an additional depreciation tax shield is equal to the tax paid by FloristCo in the asset sale. The IRS provides a total of $12,000 of income tax benefit (in the form of a depreciation tax shield) to the owner of a delivery van that originally cost $30,000 and has no salvage value. As it turned out, there were two owners of the van during its useful life, and so $6,000 of the tax benefit was provided to FloristCo and $6,000 of the benefit was provided to CoffeeCo. The IRS is indifferent to how many owners of the asset there are, since the IRS is in the same position it would have been had FloristCo owned the van for its entire useful life. The IRS does not win or lose if an asset is sold, transferred or exchanged. Either way, the IRS will only allow a certain amount of tax benefit on one asset in the form of depreciation tax shields; if another buyer wants to take advantage of a tax shield derived from a basis step-up, the IRS will require that the IRS is first repaid any tax benefit it provided to the previous owner in the form of tax payable from Seller's gain on sale.

Table 21.19 – FloristCo and CoffeeCo Basis Step-Up Example

Original depreciable amount of delivery van by FloristCo	$30,000
Tax rate	40%
Tax shield recognized by FloristCo if it keeps van entire useful life[1]	12,000
After four years	
Purchase price	30,000
Accumulated depreciation - TAX	(20,000)
Tax basis of delivery van	10,000
Tax rate	40%
Tax shield recognized by FloristCo[2]	8,000
Sale of van to CoffeeCo	
Sale price to CoffeeCo	15,000
Tax basis of delivery van	(10,000)
Taxable gain[3]	5,000
Tax rate	40%
Tax payable[4]	(2,000)
Net tax shield recognized by FloristCo[5]	6,000
CoffeeCo's tax basis in van[6]	15,000
Tax rate	40%
Tax shield recognized by CoffeeCo[7]	6,000
Total tax benefit provided by IRS[8]	$12,000

[1] Depreciable value × tax rate ($30,000 × 0.4)
[2] Accumulated depreciation × tax rate ($20,000 × 0.4)
[3] Sale price - tax basis ($15,000 - $10,000)
[4] Taxable gain × tax rate ($5,000 × 0.4)
[5] Tax shield recognized on depreciation - tax payable ($8,000 - $2,000); this tax payable is sometimes referred to as "depreciation recapture"
[6] Since it is an asset purchase, CoffeeCo's tax basis in the van is stepped up to the purchase price (from $10,000 to $15,000)
[7] New tax shield is the amount that will be depreciated over the remaining life of the van × tax rate ($15,000 × 0.4)
[8] FloristCo's net tax shield + CoffeeCo's tax shield ($6,000 + $6,000). One could also think of this in its component pieces of: FloristCo's depreciation tax shield - FloristCo's tax paid + CoffeeCo's depreciation tax shield ($8,000 - $2,000 + $6,000 = $12,000).

GAAP Accounting for M&A Transactions

Now that we have discussed the tax ramifications of asset and stock sales, let's review some numerical examples to see how various events are recorded in the GAAP books. The first example "Asset or Stock Sale Example" reviews *Seller's* GAAP accounting for an asset or stock sale. The second example "Stock Acquisition Example" reviews *Acquiror's* GAAP accounting for a stock purchase.

Asset or Stock Sale Example - Seller's Perspective

Previous examples of gain and loss in this chapter calculated the cash tax liability triggered by a sale (the TAX effects). We have not yet considered how the sale is recorded from an accounting perspective on the company's GAAP books. Let's consider the sale of an asset to show how a gain or loss on the sale of an asset is shown on Seller's GAAP books.

We will use the previous PrintingCo example in which the company purchased a printer for $1,000 (Table 21.1). Let's now assume, however, that instead of keeping the printer for ten years as in Table 21.1, PrintingCo sells it after three years at a sale price of $800. Let's look at the difference in gain on sale for BOOK and TAX purposes. Recall that the printer is depreciated based on a ten-year useful life for GAAP purposes and a five-year useful life for TAX purposes. We will assume straight-line depreciation for both BOOK and TAX and zero salvage value. Therefore, the annual depreciation is $100 for BOOK purposes and $200 for TAX purposes in years one through five (and so it encompasses this example). We will assume a 40 percent tax rate. Table 21.8 showed the difference in book value and tax basis for years one to ten and it has been reproduced as Table 21.20 to highlight the sale year. Notice that, at the end of three years, the BOOK net PP&E or book value of the printer is $700 while the TAX net PP&E or tax basis is $400.

Table 21.20 – Printer Book Value vs. Tax Basis

Years	0	1	2	Sale year 3	4	5	6	7	8	9	10
GAAP books											
Gross PP&E	$1,000	$1,000	$1,000	$1,000	$1,000	$1,000	$1,000	$1,000	$1,000	$1,000	$1,000
Accumulated depreciation	0	(100)	(200)	(300)	(400)	(500)	(600)	(700)	(800)	(900)	(1,000)
Net PP&E (book value)	$1,000	$900	$800	**$700**	$600	$500	$400	$300	$200	$100	$0
TAX return work papers											
Gross PP&E	$1,000	$1,000	$1,000	$1,000	$1,000	$1,000	$1,000	$1,000	$1,000	$1,000	$1,000
Accumulated depreciation	0	(200)	(400)	(600)	(800)	(1,000)	(1,000)	(1,000)	(1,000)	(1,000)	(1,000)
Net PP&E (tax basis)	$1,000	$800	$600	**$400**	$200	$0	$0	$0	$0	$0	$0

Now let's calculate the after-tax gain for BOOK and TAX purposes. The book value of the printer after year three is $700 while the tax basis after year three is $400.

GAAP Accounting

Sale price - book value = taxable gain

$800 sale price - $700 book value = $100 BOOK taxable gain

Taxable gain × tax rate = tax payable

$100 BOOK taxable gain × 40% tax rate = $40 BOOK tax payable

Taxable gain - tax payable = BOOK after-tax gain

$100 BOOK taxable gain - $40 BOOK tax payable = $60 BOOK after-tax gain

TAX Accounting

Sale price - tax basis = taxable gain

$800 sale price - $400 tax basis = $400 TAX taxable gain

Taxable gain × tax rate = tax payable

$400 TAX taxable gain × 40% tax rate = $160 cash taxes (TAX tax payable)

Sale price - cash taxes = after-tax cash proceeds

$800 sale price - $160 cash taxes = $640 after-tax cash proceeds

The focus for GAAP accounting is the after-tax *BOOK gain* while the focus for TAX accounting is the after-tax *cash proceeds.* This distinction is important, as will be seen in Table 21.23 when we look at PrintingCo's balance sheet and cash flow statement as adjusted for the sale.

Table 21.21 - Calculating Taxes from Asset Sales

GAAP accounting		TAX accounting	
Purchase price	$1,000	Purchase price	$1,000
Depreciation year 1	(100)	Depreciation year 1	(200)
Book value after year 1[1]	900	Tax basis after year 1[1]	800
Depreciation year 2	(100)	Depreciation year 2	(200)
Book value after year 2[1]	800	Tax basis after year 2[1]	600
Depreciation year 3	(100)	Depreciation year 3	(200)
Book value after year 3[1]	$700	Tax basis after year 3[1]	$400
Taxable gain calculation (GAAP)		**Taxable gain calculation (TAX)**	
Sale price	$800	Sale price	$800
Book value after year 3	(700)	Tax basis after year 3	(400)
Taxable gain for GAAP[2]	$100	Taxable gain for TAX[2]	$400
Tax rate	40%	Tax rate	40%
BOOK tax payable[3]	(40)	Cash taxes (TAX tax payable)[3]	(160)
After-tax BOOK gain[4]	$60	After-tax cash proceeds[5]	$640

[1] Book value = historical cost - accumulated depreciation + capital additions + improvements
Tax basis = historical cost - accumulated depreciation + capital additions + improvements
[2] BOOK taxable gain = sale price - book value; TAX taxable gain = sale price - tax basis
[3] Tax payable = taxable gain × tax rate
[4] After-tax BOOK gain = BOOK taxable gain - BOOK tax payable
[5] After-tax cash proceeds = sale price - cash taxes

After-tax BOOK gain and after-tax cash proceeds

Many people make the mistake of assuming that the after-tax BOOK gain is equal to the after-tax cash proceeds. As Table 21.21 shows, they can be very different. The BOOK after-tax gain is the BOOK *taxable gain* minus the BOOK tax payable. The after-tax cash proceeds is the *sale price* minus the cash taxes. The after-tax cash proceeds represent real cash whereas the BOOK after-tax gain is an accounting gain which will be added to shareholders' equity in the GAAP books after flowing through net income.

And what would happen to the GAAP balance sheet and the deferred tax liability upon sale of the asset? Recall that the printer generated $150 of net income per year. The year three pre-sale GAAP balance sheet and cash flow statement are provided in Table 21.22 (this year three balance sheet and cash flow statement are taken directly from Table 21.6 in which the ten-year balance sheet and cash flow statement for PrintingCo were provided).

Table 21.22 - PrintingCo's Balance Sheet and Cash Flow Statement as of Year 3

PrintingCo	Year 3
Balance sheet (BOOK)	
Cash	$870
Net PP&E	700
Total assets	1,570
Deferred tax liability	120
Debt	500
Shareholders' equity	950
Total liabilities & equity	$1,570
Cash flow statement (BOOK)	
Net income	$150
Depreciation	100
Change in deferred taxes	40
Cash flow from operations	290
Beginning cash[1]	580
Add: cash flow from operations	290
Ending cash	$870

[1] Beginning cash in year 3 is equal to ending cash in year 2 and so forth

Upon sale of the printer for $800, several accounting entries would occur:

1. Cash would increase by the after-tax cash proceeds of $640.

2. Both the net PP&E and deferred tax accounts would be zeroed out. This is because PrintingCo will no longer own the printer and therefore the asset account and its contra accounts (the accumulated depreciation and the deferred tax liability account) also must be eliminated.

3. Shareholders' equity will increase by $60, which is the amount of the BOOK after-tax gain (which flows through net income and from there to shareholders' equity on the balance sheet).

Table 21.23 – Balance Sheet and Cash Flow Statement Adjusted for the Sale

PrintingCo	Year 3	Adjustments	Pro forma
Balance sheet (BOOK)			
Cash	$870	$640 (1)	$1,510
Net PP&E	700	(700) (2)	0
Total assets	1,570	(60)	1,510
Deferred taxes	120	(120) (3)	0
Debt	500	0	500
Shareholders' equity	950	60 (4)	1,010
Total liabilities & equity	$1,570	($60)	$1,510
Cash flow statement (BOOK)			
Net income	$150		$150
Depreciation	100		100
Change in deferred taxes	40		40
Cash flow from operations	290		290
Sale of assets		640 (1)	640
Cash flow from investing		640	640
Beginning cash[5]	580		580
Add: cash flow from operations	290		290
Add: cash flow from investing	0		640
Ending cash	$870		$1,510

[1] Cash increases by the amount of after-tax cash proceeds; see Table 21.21
[2] Net PP&E will be eliminated because the asset has been sold
[3] Deferred taxes associated with the printer are eliminated because the asset is sold; in this example, PrintingCo has a single asset so there are no PP&E and deferred taxes pro forma. Normally, there would still be net PP&E and a deferred taxes account even after adjustment for the sale of an asset.
[4] BOOK equity increases by the BOOK after-tax gain after flowing through net income; see Table 21.21
[5] Beginning cash in year 3 is equal to ending cash in year 2; see Table 21.6

Stock Acquisition Example - Acquiror's Perspective

Assets and liabilities are written up to fair market value on the GAAP books for both stock purchases and asset purchases. In an acquisition of stock, however, Acquiror will have a carryover basis in Target's assets and liabilities in its (Acquiror's) TAX return work papers. To reconcile this difference of an asset write-up for GAAP accounting (resulting in additional depreciation expense in the GAAP books) and a carryover basis of assets for TAX accounting (resulting in no change in depreciation expense in the TAX return work papers), the deferred tax account on Acquiror's GAAP balance sheet will be used.

Recall that the earlier discussion of deferred taxes related to differences in the timing of recognizing depreciation expense. A similar concept applies here when accounting for a stock purchase.[13] For transactions in which there is an asset write-up for BOOK purposes but no corresponding basis step-up in the assets for TAX purposes, a deferred tax account must be created to reconcile the difference between the additional depreciation expense in the GAAP books (from the asset write-up) and the absence of additional depreciation expense in the TAX return work papers (because it is a carryover basis for TAX). The new deferred tax amount is calculated as the amount of the asset write-up or write-down (from the GAAP books) multiplied by the tax rate:

1. In an acquisition of stock, the deferred tax *liability* = asset write-*up* × tax rate, or

2. In an acquisition of stock, the deferred tax *asset* = asset write-*down* × tax rate.

In most cases, the transaction results in an asset write-up and therefore the creation of a deferred tax *liability* (although asset write-downs do occur, and in so doing they would create a deferred tax *asset* account). The deferred tax liability is created at the time of the acquisition and is used as a reserve account each period thereafter until the GAAP asset write-up has been fully depreciated. Each depreciation period after the stock acquisition closes, the deferred tax liability is reduced by the amount of the tax shield recognized on the GAAP books. The reserve created by the deferred tax liability declines each period until it reaches zero at the end of the useful life of the asset (i.e., until the GAAP book value equals the TAX tax basis again). There is no cash effect of the asset write-up because the asset write-up for GAAP purposes was not mirrored by a basis step-up for TAX purposes. The additional depreciation on the GAAP books does not reduce the cash taxes payable (taxes payable as calculated on the TAX return work papers) because there was no corresponding basis step-up for TAX purposes.

[13] Note that in a purchase of assets, there is an asset write-up (for GAAP accounting) and a basis step-up (for TAX accounting) and so no difference exists in the carrying value of the assets between the GAAP books and the TAX return work papers, and so no reconciliation must be made using the deferred tax account.

To illustrate this concept, let's review a numerical example. Assume SmoothieCo pays $600 million to CoffeeCo's shareholders in exchange for 100 percent of CoffeeCo's shares outstanding. SmoothieCo will pay the $600 million to CoffeeCo shareholders in SmoothieCo stock. In other words, SmoothieCo purchases CoffeeCo in a stock-for-stock exchange and the purchase price of CoffeeCo's equity (or stock) is $600 million. Further assume that the fair market value of CoffeeCo's net PP&E is $550 million and that CoffeeCo's other assets and liabilities are already fairly valued (i.e., no adjustment is needed to bring their book values up to fair market value). Also assume a 40 percent tax rate and a useful life of five years for the assets.

Because this is an acquisition of stock and not of assets, SmoothieCo will write up CoffeeCo's assets and liabilities to fair market value for GAAP purposes but not for TAX purposes (that is, the acquired assets will have a carryover basis on SmoothieCo's TAX return work papers).

Notice the asset write-up of $100 million in Table 21.24 (note 1); this is created because the fair market value of Target's net PP&E is $550 million (this fair market value of $550 million is an assumption) but the book value of the net PP&E is only $450 million.

  $550 million of fair market value
\- $450 million of historical book value

= $100 million asset write-up

In the GAAP books, this write-up of $100 million will create an additional depreciation charge each year over the useful life of the assets (because now $550 million must be depreciated over five years, not $450 million).

Also notice the creation of a deferred tax liability account of $40 million (note 2), which will be used to reconcile the different depreciation amounts between GAAP and TAX accounting records since the asset write-up occurs in the GAAP books but there is no corresponding basis step-up in the TAX return work papers. The mismatch of $40 million is equal to the write-up of $100 million multiplied by the tax rate of 40 percent, and is a one-time calculation at the time of the transaction (although the $40 million deferred tax account will be reduced each year until it reaches zero).

$100 million write-up × 40% tax rate = $40 million deferred tax liability

Since the GAAP books get a write-up in assets, they also have a corresponding increase in depreciation (to depreciate the additional $100 million in value by which the assets have been written up in the GAAP accounting records). However, since there is no additional depreciation in the TAX return work papers (there is a carryover basis for TAX purposes), the result is that the GAAP taxes will be *lower* than the cash taxes paid (recall that a higher GAAP depreciation charge results in lower GAAP taxable income and therefore lower tax payable for GAAP). This is where the deferred tax liability account comes in to play. Lower taxes for BOOK accounting from the asset write-up will be offset by a reduction in the deferred tax liability account until the written-up assets have been fully depreciated. Another way to think of it is that a deferred tax liability account is created as a *reserve* which is reduced each year by the amount of the tax shield resulting from the additional GAAP depreciation from the asset write-up.

> \$100 million write-up / 5-year useful life = \$20 million in additional annual depreciation
>
> \$20 million in annual depreciation × 40% tax rate = \$8 million depreciation tax shield

Table 21.24 – Asset Write-Up in a Stock Acquisition

$ millions	(A)	(B)	(C)		(A + B + C)
Balance Sheet	**Acquiror**	**Target**	**Adjustments**	**Notes**	**Pro forma**
Cash	$200	$50	$0		$250
Net PP&E	1,000	450	100	(1)	1,550
Goodwill	0	0	290	(3)	290
Total assets	$1,200	$500	$390		$2,090
Deferred taxes	$100	$50	$40	(2)	$190
Debt	400	200	0		600
Equity	700	250	350	(4)	1,300
Total liabilities & equity	$1,200	$500	$390		$2,090

Notes

(1) Asset write-up = (fair market value of assets) - (book value of assets)

Fair market value of Target's assets (assumption)	$550	
- Book value of Target's assets	450	
= Asset write-up	**$100**	(1)

In practice, all assets and liabilities are fair-valued; however, this example assumes that only the net PP&E needs to be written up (this assumes that all of the other assets and liabilities are already listed on Target's books at fair market value).

(2) Deferred tax liability = (asset write-up) × (effective tax rate)

Asset write-up	$100	
× Tax rate	40%	
= Deferred tax liability	**$40**	(2)

(3) Goodwill = (equity value of transaction) - (net asset value) - (asset write-up) + (defd. tax liability)

Equity value of transaction	$600	
- Net asset value[1]	(250)	
- Asset write-up	(100)	
+ Deferred tax liability	40	
= Goodwill	**$290**	(3)

[1] Net asset value = book value of Target equity - Target's existing goodwill ($250 - $0 = $250)
See discussion of goodwill in Accretion / Dilution Analysis. (Ch.14)

(4) Adjustment to equity = (value of equity consideration) - (book value of Target equity)

Purchase price of equity	$600	
× Purchase price paid in stock	100%	
= Value of equity consideration	600	
- Book value of Target equity	(250)	
= Adjustment to Target equity	**$350**	(4)

Now let's consider the effects of the stock acquisition on the balance sheet and cash flow statement after one year of depreciating the asset write-up for the GAAP books.

Notice in Table 21.25 how the deferred tax liability account is introduced to offset the "new" tax shield that is created for GAAP purposes as a result of the asset write-up. In the TAX return work papers, no basis step-up occurs for the assets since this example is a stock acquisition (carryover basis). Also, the write-up for GAAP purposes has no effect on cash because no more or less cash has been paid to the taxing authorities. In fact, the only things that the additional depreciation from the asset write-up affects are taxable income, taxes payable, and net income for GAAP purposes (which are all reduced). The notation "(GAAP)" after each account below is a reminder that all of these adjustments are for GAAP accounting *only*.

Table 21.25 – Impact of Stock Acquisition[1] on Acquiror's Pro Forma Balance Sheet and Cash Flow Statement

$ millions

Adjustments to Income Statement (GAAP vs. TAX)	GAAP	TAX
Asset write-up	$100	0
Useful life (years)	5	N/A
Incremental depreciation from asset write-up ($100 / 5)	(20)	0
Tax shield on depreciation (for BOOK) based on 40% tax rate	8	0
Net income adjustment (after-tax incremental depreciation (-$20 + $8))	($12)	0

Adjustment to net PP&E (GAAP)	
Beginning balance[2]	$1,550
Less: depreciation	(20)
Ending balance	$1,530

Adjustment to equity account (GAAP)	
Beginning balance[2]	$1,300
Add: net income adjustment	(12)
Ending balance	$1,288

Adjustment to deferred taxes (GAAP)	
Beginning balance[2]	$190
Less: tax shield on depreciation	(8)
Ending balance	$182

Balance Sheet (GAAP)	Opening	Closing
Cash	$250	$250
Net PP&E	1,550	1,530
Goodwill	290	290
Total assets	$2,090	$2,070
Deferred taxes	$190	$182
Debt	600	600
Shareholders' equity	1,300	1,288
Total liab. & equity	$2,090	$2,070

Cash Flow Statement Adjustments (GAAP)	
Net income	($12)
Add: depreciation	20
Less: change in deferred taxes[3]	(8)
Cash flow from operations	0
Beginning cash	250
Add: cash flow from operations	0
Ending cash	$250

[1] Stock acquisitions have an asset write-up for GAAP purposes but an asset carryover basis for TAX purposes.
Asset acquisitions have an asset write-up for GAAP purposes and an asset stepped-up basis for TAX purposes.

[2] From the pro forma column of Table 21.24

[3] Reduction of a liability is a use of cash

Tax-Free Reorganizations

If structured properly, tax-free reorganizations are possible in corporate acquisitions. The Internal Revenue Code (IRC) provides a tax exemption for the exchange of stock or securities in a transaction that has the objective of "reorganizing" corporate structures. In effect, the IRS considers transactions that qualify under the relevant IRC sections to be simply a different way of re-arranging the same parts and therefore does not consider such a re-arrangement to be a taxable event. These are the so-called reorganization provisions of the IRC, and transactions which qualify as tax-deferred under these provisions are known as **tax-free reorganizations**, or "tax-free reorgs." In a qualifying tax-free reorg, generally there is no tax triggered at the *corporate* level and there is a carryover basis in Target's assets (e.g., for TAX purposes, none of Target's assets or liabilities are written up to fair market value). For GAAP purposes, however, as with all acquisitions under GAAP accounting -- stock or assets-- Target's assets and liabilities are written up (or down) to fair market value. Whether there is tax at the *shareholder* level in a tax-free reorg depends on the structure of the transaction and how much cash (if any) is offered as part of the transaction consideration.

Are reorganizations "tax-free" or "tax-deferred"?

There is often confusion between the terms "tax-free" and "tax-deferred" in the context of a reorganization. Strictly speaking, "tax-free" events are actually "tax-deferred" events because taxes will be paid to the IRS on the ultimate disposition of the property received. That is, in a "tax-free" transaction, taxation is merely deferred to a later date.[14]

Tax-free reorganizations are governed by IRC §368, which sets forth the technical requirements in order for a transaction to qualify as a tax-free reorganization. To do so, a transaction must satisfy the structural requirements of the particular form of reorganization and also comply with the following three "judge made" doctrines or tests:

- Business purpose doctrine
- Continuity of shareholder interest doctrine
- Continuity of business enterprise doctrine

[14] The principal exception to this involves the death of an individual shareholder, which provides a step-up in tax basis and avoids income taxes on a subsequent disposition of the stock.

Business purpose doctrine: This doctrine requires that a transaction be motivated by at least one valid business purpose (other than federal tax avoidance, which is not considered a valid business purpose by the IRS). A written "Plan of Reorganization" is advisable but not required by the IRS. From a practical standpoint, buyer would not buy and seller would not sell if no business purpose existed. As a result, in an arm's length transaction between independent parties, the business purpose test is usually satisfied without problem.

Continuity of shareholder interest doctrine: This doctrine requires that, for the transaction to qualify as a tax-free reorganization, a "substantial part" of the consideration paid to Target shareholders must consist of stock of Acquiror (or parent of Acquiror). In past, the IRS would only issue a private letter ruling if stock comprised at least 50 percent of the total transaction consideration, even if under case law lower levels of stock consideration were probably acceptable. Today, "substantial" is generally understood to be satisfied at 40 percent stock consideration, but it depends on the type of reorganization. The rest of the non-stock transaction consideration can be comprised of cash, notes, assets, or other consideration (often referred to collectively as "boot").

The safe harbor works as follows: if a reorganization satisfies all applicable requirements, then the stock portion of the transaction consideration can be tax-deferred until the shareholder's ultimate disposition of that stock (which generally means until it is sold for cash or cash equivalents). Any cash or other consideration is likely to be immediately taxable to the shareholder. Since cash consideration (debt funding) is a less expensive form of capital than equity for most companies, companies like to have the flexibility to limit the amount of equity consideration (preferring to use the less expensive cash consideration) while still preserving the tax-free nature of any equity issued. Shareholders, not surprisingly, also prefer that the equity consideration remain tax-free at the shareholder level since it means they do not have to pay tax immediately on that new equity received.[15]

No one knows how far below 40 percent equity consideration a transaction could go and still have tax-free treatment granted to the shareholders on the equity consideration received. The IRS seems to have indicated that at 30 percent or less stock (at least 70 percent boot), the IRS would not grant tax-free reorganization status to the transaction. If a transaction failed to qualify as a tax-free reorganization, the result would be that all of the transaction consideration, both boot and equity, would

[15] Technically, the IRC provides that the gain recognized equals the lesser of the gain realized and the amount of cash/boot received. For instance, if the shareholder in a "tax-free" reorganization has a basis of $50 in his Target stock, and receives $100 in consideration from Acquiror, the gain realized is $50. If, say, $55 of that $100 in consideration is cash received, the amount recognized as taxable gain is still $50 (the lesser of the cash/boot and the gain realized). On the other hand, if $40 of that $100 in consideration is cash received, the gain recognized is only $40 (the lesser of the cash/boot and the gain realized).

be immediately taxable at the shareholder level (as if the transaction consideration had been 100 percent cash/boot). The test is a simple one of debt vs. equity. In fact, in the Nelson case (U.S. Supreme Court) which arguably originated the safe harbor around 40 percent for the continuity of shareholder interest, the qualifying equity component of the transaction consideration was in the form of redeemable preferred stock.

The 40% safe harbor for equity consideration

Many companies, when structuring a transaction, want a margin of safety with respect to the assumed limit of 40 percent equity consideration since the cost of failing to obtain tax-free reorg status from the IRS is that all 100 percent (both boot and stock) of transaction consideration is immediately taxable at the shareholder level. For example, what happens if Acquiror had a fixed transaction value with 40 percent equity consideration at the date of signing but the stock price subsequently fell such that the transaction consideration migrated to 35 percent equity / 65 percent boot? Such a split of transaction consideration might fail the Continuity of Shareholder Interest Doctrine and, as a result, fail to achieve treatment as a tax-free reorganization. In order to address this issue, the IRS recently promulgated a rule variously referred to as the "Fixed Consideration" or "Date of Signing" rule which holds that the percentages in place at the time of transaction signing are what control, generally.

Continuity of business enterprise doctrine: This doctrine requires that, following the reorganization, Acquiror continues a significant line of Target's business or uses a significant portion of Target's assets. This is intended to ensure that the transaction is a continuation of Target in a different form, the underlying rationale for tax-free treatment. In general, in order to satisfy the continuity of business enterprise doctrine, the test is that Acquiror intends to continue with at least one-third of Target's business or assets.

Table 21.26 lists the most common forms of IRC §368 reorganizations. Which tax-free reorganization structure is selected for any given transaction will be driven by a variety of factors, including the nationality of the companies involved, regulatory considerations, the amount of cash/boot consideration Acquiror will pay Target shareholders, and pre-existing tax considerations. The structure to be used does not need to be decided until the point in a transaction when a draft of the legal agreement is created. At that point it is important to decide what type of structure will be used since the tax structure will dictate the legal form of the acquisition agreement as well as much of the accounting treatment. While Table 21.26 provides a summary of tax-free (or, more technically, tax-deferred) reorganization structures, this list is not all-encompassing; other structures do exist. The structures listed below are among those most commonly used. When structuring an actual transaction, it is important to consult with tax counsel. This information is intended to be informative, not authoritative.

Table 21.26 – Tax-Free Reorganization Forms

Vernacular	Technical name	Common name	Minimum amount of stock consideration for that stock consideration to be tax-free at the shareholder level
Straight A or Straight Merger	368(a)(1)(A)	Statutory merger	40% stock requirement (safe harbor) (see Continuity of Shareholder Interest above)
B	368(a)(1)(B)	Stock for stock	100% voting stock requirement (zero boot)
C	368(a)(1)(C)*	Stock for assets	100% voting stock (in general) (zero boot)
Forward Triangular	368(a)(2)(D)*	Forward triangular merger	40% stock requirement (safe harbor) (see Continuity of Shareholder Interest above)
Reverse Triangular	368(a)(2)(E)*	Reverse triangular merger	80% voting stock requirement (no more than 20% boot)
F	368(a)(1)(F)	Reincorporation or other "mere change" in form	Depends on facts and objectives of the parties; some stock must be issued
G	368(a)(1)(G)*	Bankruptcy reorganization	Depends on the provisions of the bankruptcy plan; some stock must be issued

* These reorganization forms have an additional requirement, i.e., Acquiror must obtain an interest in "substantially all" of Target's assets. For advance private letter ruling purposes, the IRS requires that Acquiror obtain 90% of Target's net assets and 70% of Target's gross assets.

Additional comments related to tax-free reorgs are provided below.

- While, in general, tax-free reorganizations are deemed to be tax-free at the corporate level, whether the transaction is tax-free to shareholders depends on the transaction consideration received. Consideration comprised of cash or other boot is almost always immediately taxable at the shareholder level; stock consideration can generally be tax-deferred, but it depends on how much of the total consideration offered is stock, as discussed above regarding the Continuity of Shareholder Interest Doctrine, and the type of structure utilized.

- With many available legal structures, it is often possible to select a structure that accomplishes the parties' primary goals for the transaction in terms of mix of consideration, nationality of companies involved, ability post-transaction to dispose of assets, ability to select certain assets, etc.

- In general, when practitioners discuss tax structures, they generally do not use the term "merger" but rather focus on whether the transaction is a stock deal or an asset deal. The reason is that, as discussed earlier in the chapter, the decision to purchase stock or to purchase assets has broad ramifications for the transaction structure, taxation, and accounting treatment.

- A "Straight A" (straight merger) is the most flexible structure in terms of qualifying for tax-free treatment. However, 100 percent of the transaction consideration could be immediately taxable if the reorganization structure fails.

- In a Straight A, the equity consideration can be common or preferred stock, and it can be voting or non-voting stock.

- "C" and "forward triangular" reorgs that fail are generally double taxation transactions (taxable at the corporate level and at the shareholder level), and therefore can be risky propositions for the corporations and shareholders involved.

- Benefits of a "C" reorg are that, to some extent, Acquiror can select the assets and, in particular, the liabilities to be included in the transaction, subject to the requirement referred to above that Acquiror must obtain an interest in "substantially all" of Target's assets.

- A triangular merger is often referred to as a subsidiary merger. Triangular mergers use acquisition subsidiaries or "acquisition subs" to effect the merger. There are both forward triangular mergers (Target merges into Acquiror

Acquisition Subsidiary) and reverse triangular mergers (Acquiror Acquisition Subsidiary merges into Target with Target surviving as a subsidiary of Acquiror).

- In a forward triangular merger, Target is merged into an acquisition subsidiary and Target ends up a subsidiary of Acquiror. Usually (but not always), the subsidiary is formed for the purpose of acquiring Target, although Acquiror can (and occasionally does) use an existing subsidiary.

Figure 21.27 – Diagram of a Forward Triangular Merger

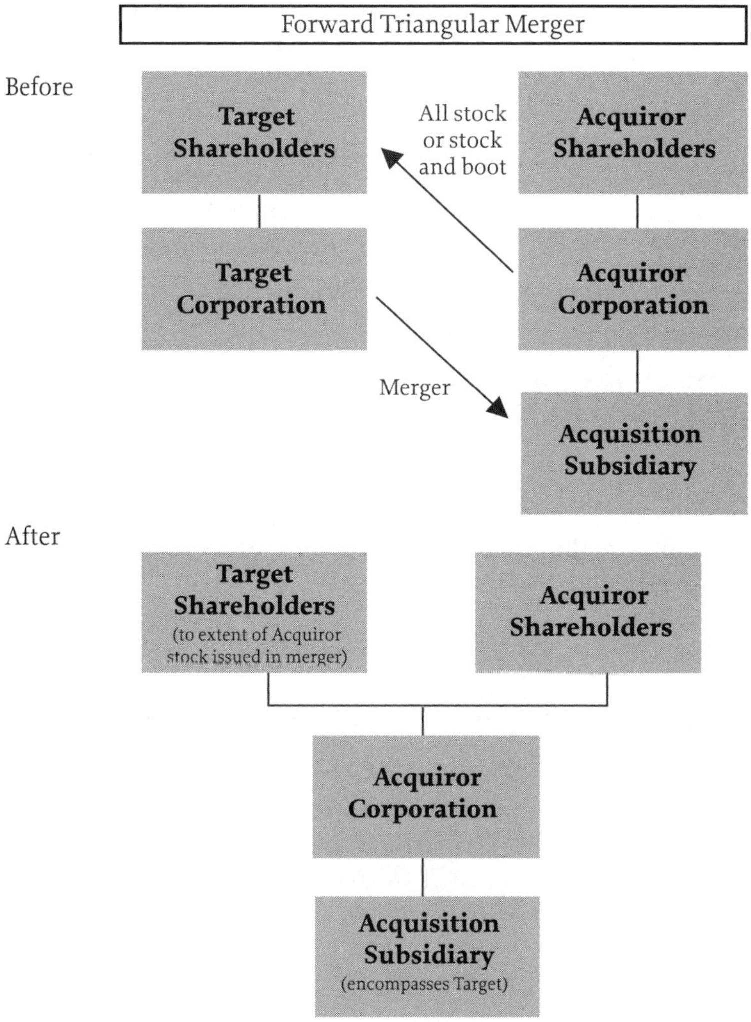

- In a reverse triangular merger, an acquisition subsidiary is merged into Target and Target thereby becomes a subsidiary of Acquiror. Usually (but not always), the subsidiary is formed for the purpose of acquiring Target, although Acquiror can (and occasionally does) use an existing subsidiary.

- A reverse triangular merger is one of the most popular reorganization forms when Acquiror wants to acquire Target but wants to retain Target's legal attributes (i.e., Target continues to exist, but as a subsidiary of Acquiror). Thus, in a reverse triangular merger, Target's assets remain in the same corporate entity and are not transferred.

Figure 21.28 – Diagram of a Reverse Triangular Merger

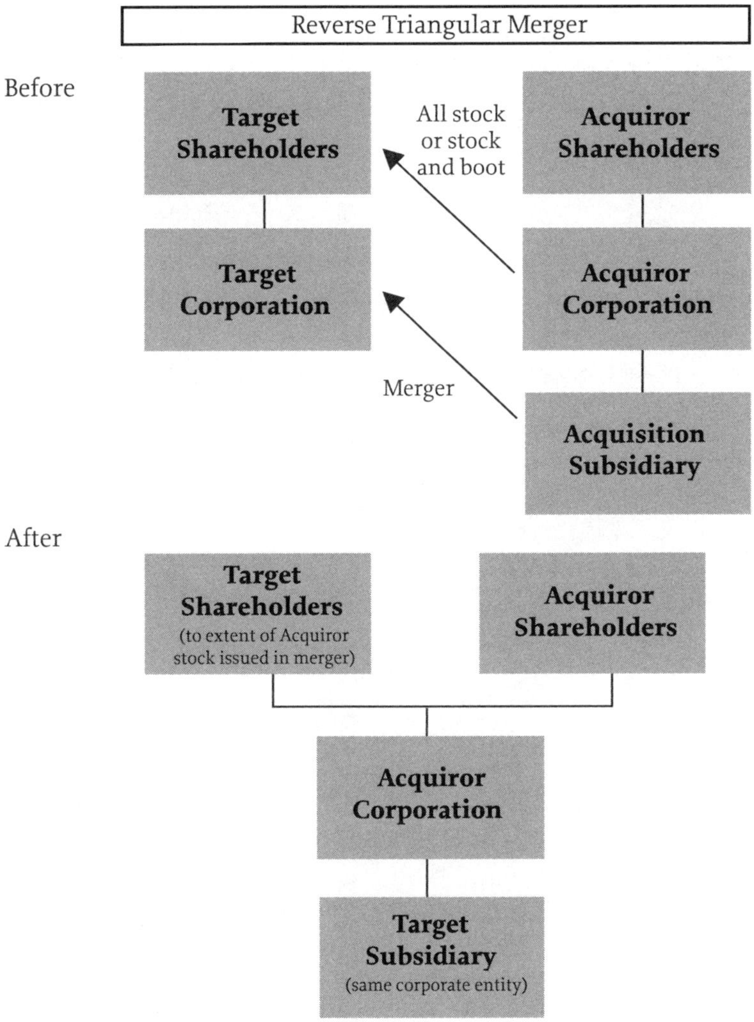

The reverse triangular merger-a popular transaction

Of all tax-free transaction forms, the reverse triangular merger has historically been among the most popular. In a typical reverse triangular merger --§368(a)(2)(E)-- Acquiror Parent creates Acquisition Subsidiary. Acquisition Subsidiary then merges with and into Target, with Target as the surviving corporation. Pro forma, Target is a subsidiary of Acquiror Parent and Acquiror's Acquisition Subsidiary is dissolved into Target.

From a logistical perspective, it is easy to set up a shell company in any state to facilitate a subsidiary merger (for either a forward or reverse triangular merger). Because an Acquisition Subsidiary is merged into Target in a reverse triangular merger, Acquiror Parent is insulated from Target's liabilities (Acquiror Parent is one step removed from Acquisition Subsidiary and therefore one step removed from Target once Acquisition Subsidiary merges into Target).

A more important reason, however, as to why reverse triangular mergers are often used is that they may avoid problems with restrictions on transfer of certain of Target's assets, e.g., leases, licenses, and certain other contracts ("restricted assets"). This is because, in a reverse triangular merger, Acquisition Subsidiary merges into Target with Target surviving. Since all of Target's assets continue to be held by the same legal corporate entity, the restricted assets have not been "transferred" within the normal meaning of that term. This can be an important point because an attempted transfer of restricted assets might render them null and void.[16]

[16] Of course, a reverse merger may not solve the problem if the contractual language imposing the restriction is broad enough to forbid a statutory merger or any other transaction resulting in a change of control of Target. A review of Target's restricted assets will be an important part of Acquiror's due diligence in determining whether and in what form to attempt to acquire Target.

338(h)(10) Election

Normally, in the acquisition of the *stock* of a corporation (Target), Acquiror inherits Target's historical basis in its assets (carryover basis) and therefore does not benefit from a basis step-up in the assets. Normally, in a sale of *assets*, Target retains some or all of its liabilities and therefore Seller (parent company of Target) does not benefit from "selling the balance sheet" by virtue of selling the stock of Target. However, there is a transaction structure called a §338(h)(10) election -- named after the Internal Revenue Code section that governs it -- which is an acquisition of stock (so Seller is able to sell the liabilities of Target along with Target's assets) but which is treated by the IRS as an acquisition of assets (so Acquiror obtains a basis step-up in Target's assets). Thus it can be the best of both worlds since Target sells all its liabilities (since it is a stock sale) but Acquiror also gets the basis step-up and its full depreciation benefits for TAX purposes (because the IRS treats the transaction as an asset sale). In some situations, especially for assets with a very low basis, the additional depreciation from the basis step-up can translate into significant value for Acquiror in terms of a reduction in cash taxes (recall that increased depreciation for TAX purposes results in lower taxable income and therefore lower cash taxes payable). While Target in a 338(h)(10) will transfer all its liabilities (as if it were a stock sale), Seller will recognize taxable gain on the stock sale based on the *inside* basis (since the transaction is a stock sale in form but is treated as an asset sale for TAX purposes). Technically, the first step of the transaction is a deemed asset sale by the acquired corporation followed by a deemed tax-free liquidation under §332.

There are certain requirements that must be met for a 338(h)(10) election. First, it is a joint election, so Acquiror and Seller both must agree to it. Second, it is only available if Target is either an S Corporation or a subsidiary corporation owned 80 percent or more by a parent company, and Acquiror must purchase at least 80 percent of the vote and value of Target within a twelve-month period (i.e., the transaction must be a qualified stock purchase (QSP)). Third, Target must be a domestic corporation. Fourth, the purchase must be for cash or cash equivalent, and it must be a taxable transaction for Seller.

Generally, Seller will only agree to the joint election if Seller is financially indifferent between a sale of stock and a sale of assets. Recall that in an asset sale, which is what a 338(h)(10) election is for TAX purposes, Seller will have to pay income tax based on its inside basis (the basis in the assets), rather than the outside basis Seller has in the stock being sold. Usually the inside basis in the assets is lower than the outside basis in the stock. As a result, making the 338(h)(10) election usually results in a larger taxable gain and larger tax payable for Seller. If Seller has to pay higher taxes if it makes the 338(h)(10) election (which is treated as an asset sale for TAX purposes) than if it sells stock, Seller will choose to sell stock, all other things being equal. In order to induce Seller to make the 338(h)(10) election, Acquiror will have to make Seller financially indifferent between a sale of stock and a sale of assets (the 338(h)(10) election), generally by paying the additional tax Seller would owe under the 338(h)(10) election. Acquiror will choose a 338(h)(10) election (and therefore choose to compensate Seller for this additional tax) only if Acquiror gains an even greater benefit (in the form of the depreciation tax shield as a result of the basis step-up) than the cost of Seller's additional tax.

To illustrate how a 338(h)(10) election works, let's consider ParentCo, a holding company that owns 100 percent of SubsidiaryCo. ParentCo's outside basis in the stock of SubsidiaryCo is \$8 million and SubsidiaryCo's inside basis in the assets of SubsidiaryCo is \$3 million. SubsidiaryCo has no outstanding debt (see Table 21.29 for calculations). Comparing a sale of stock to a sale of assets, both for \$15 million, the stock sale of SubsidiaryCo would trigger tax payable for ParentCo of \$2.8 million and the asset sale (the 338(h)(10) election) would trigger tax payable for ParentCo of \$4.8 million. Therefore, there is a \$2 million benefit to ParentCo if it sells stock as opposed to selling assets, all other things being equal.

Table 21.29 – Comparison of Sale of Stock vs. 338(h)(10) Election

\$ millions

Assumptions	
Sale price for SubsidiaryCo	\$15.0
SubsidiaryCo's inside basis in its assets	3.0
ParentCo's outside basis in SubsidiaryCo stock	8.0
SubsidiaryCo debt	0.0
Tax rate	40%

Tax consequences of a sale of stock of SubsidiaryCo	
Sale price	\$15.0
Outside basis[1]	(8.0)
Taxable gain[2]	7.0
Taxable gain	7.0
Tax rate	40%
Tax payable[3]	2.8
Sale price	15.0
Tax payable	(2.8)
After-tax cash proceeds[4]	\$12.2

Footnotes on next page

[1] Since stock is being sold, the outside basis is used to calculate taxable gain/(loss)
[2] Sale price - tax basis ($15 million - $8 million)
[3] Taxable gain × tax rate ($7 million × 0.4)
[4] Sale price - tax payable ($15 million - $2.8 million)

Tax consequences of a 338(h)(10) election (sale of assets)	
Sale price	$15.0
Inside basis[1]	(3.0)
Taxable gain[2]	12.0
Taxable gain	12.0
Tax rate	40%
Tax payable[3]	4.8
Sale price	15.0
Tax payable	(4.8)
After-tax cash proceeds[4]	$10.2
After-tax cash proceeds if SubsidiaryCo stock is sold	$12.2
After-tax cash proceeds if SubsidiaryCo assets are sold	10.2
Benefit for ParentCo of selling SubsidiaryCo stock	$2.0

[1] Since assets are being sold, the inside basis is used to calculate taxable gain/(loss)
[2] Sale price - tax basis ($15 million - $3 million)
[3] Taxable gain × tax rate ($12 million × 0.4)
[4] Sale price - tax payable ($15 million - $4.8 million)

From ParentCo's perspective as Seller, it would prefer to sell stock since there is a $2 million difference in tax payable based on whether stock ($2.8 million tax payable) or assets ($4.8 million tax payable) are sold. Seller will only agree to the 338(h)(10) election (which is treated as an asset sale for TAX purposes) if Acquiror agrees to reimburse Seller for the additional tax of $2 million to which Seller will be subject by virtue of selling assets rather than stock. Acquiror would only make this additional payment to Seller if the present value of the depreciation tax shield associated with the basis step-up (the ability to step up the basis of SubsidiaryCo's assets to fair market value for TAX purposes) were greater than $2 million. And since this is a joint election that both Acquiror and Seller must make, each must think that making the election is in its best interest.

Let's take a look at the transaction from Acquiror's perspective to see if the depreciation tax shield is sufficient to induce Acquiror to pay Seller an additional $2 million. Assume the assets have a five-year useful life. The purchase price of $15 million is the new fair market value for the assets. Based on the historical inside tax basis of $3 million, the basis step-up associated with a 338(h)(10) election would be $12 million. If the $12 million is depreciated on a straight-line basis for five years, this would generate additional depreciation of $2.4 million per year and a tax shield of $960,000 per year at a 40 percent tax rate ($2.4 million × 40% = $0.96 million). Since these tax shields are cash flows which occur periodically in the future, we can discount these five annual tax shields at a corporate discount rate to determine the present value of the future tax shields. If we assume a 10 percent discount rate, the present value of the additional tax shields from the basis step-up is $3.64 million as shown in Table 21.30. As a side note, some practitioners prefer to discount these types of tax shields at a risk-free rate because they believe the risk of not getting the benefit of the tax shield from a properly executed 338(h)(10) election is essentially non-existent.

Note that, in an asset acquisition (not a 338(h)(10) election), there is the same benefit to Acquiror of a basis step-up in the assets, but there is not the same benefit to Seller who then sells *only* the assets and is still left with the liabilities.

Table 21.30 – Present Value of Additional Tax Shields from Basis Step-Up

$ millions

Assumptions

Fair market value of assets purchased	$15.0
Tax basis in SubsidiaryCo's assets (inside basis)	(3.0)
Basis step-up in SubsidiaryCo's assets	$12.0
Useful life of all assets (in years)	5
Additional annual depreciation from basis step-up (pretax)	$2.4
Tax rate	40%
Annual depreciation tax shield[1] (after-tax)	$0.96
Assumed discount rate	10%

$ millions

Year	1	2	3	4	5
Tax Shield	$0.96	$0.96	$0.96	$0.96	$0.96
Discount rate	10%	10%	10%	10%	10%
Calculation	$= \frac{CF_1}{(1+.10)^1}$	$= \frac{CF_2}{(1+.10)^2}$	$= \frac{CF_3}{(1+.10)^3}$	$= \frac{CF_4}{(1+.10)^4}$	$= \frac{CF_5}{(1+.10)^5}$
Present value	$0.87	$0.79	$0.72	$0.66	$0.60
Sum of present values	$3.64				

[1] This is the amount of the actual reduction in cash taxes each year for five years as a result of the basis step-up on the TAX return work papers, calculated as $2.4 million x 40% = $0.96 million

Since the sum of the present values of the tax shields of $3.64 million is greater than Seller's additional tax liability of $2.0 million triggered by structuring the deal as a 338(h)(10) election (a deemed asset sale) as opposed to a stock sale, Acquiror *should be* willing to pay the additional $2 million of tax to Seller and still come out ahead financially. After paying $2 million (which usually would be in the form of an increased purchase price to compensate Seller for its higher tax bill from the deemed asset sale under the 338(h)(10) election), the net gain or net present value of the 338(h)(10) election for Acquiror would be $1.64 million.

$3.64 million of total present value - $2 million paid to Seller = $1.64 million

If the present value of the incremental tax shields were less than the difference in taxes payable between a stock sale and an asset sale, Acquiror would be unlikely to pay Seller the difference. If so, Seller would be equally unlikely to make the 338(h)(10) election in this situation, and instead would choose to sell stock, with its lower associated tax bill.

Only measure the *incremental* tax shield

When analyzing whether a 338(h)(10) election makes financial sense for Acquiror, a common mistake is calculating the present value of the depreciation tax shields based on the fair market value of *all* of the assets as opposed to calculating the tax shields based only on the *incremental* depreciation which results from the proposed basis step-up. The calculation should be based on the incremental tax shield from the basis step-up since that is the difference between a stock purchase and an asset purchase. In a stock purchase in Table 21.30, Acquiror would already get to depreciate the $3 million of remaining asset tax basis for TAX purposes (that is, Seller's $3 million basis in the assets is carried over to Acquiror, which then depreciates that $3 million just as Seller would have). Therefore, when comparing the benefit of the basis step-up, the comparison should be based on the difference between the stepped-up basis of $15 million and the carryover basis of $3 million, and not the entire fair market value of assets of $15 million.

Corporate Restructurings

CHAPTER 22

So divinely is the world organized
that every one of us, in our place and time,
is in balance with everything else.

Johann Wolfgang von Goethe

A corporate restructuring is a transaction, or set of transactions, which fundamentally changes the structural organization of a business. Generally, restructurings are executed by management as an attempt to maximize shareholder value but they can also be driven by government mandates. The term "restructuring" is also used in the context of workout restructurings, which are driven by bankruptcy or near-bankruptcy situations. This chapter will review corporate restructurings executed for strategic reasons. Corporate restructurings which are the result of bankruptcy or near-bankruptcy situations are the purview of specialized bankers and investors called distressed investors, workout specialists, or turnaround specialists. Bankruptcy-driven restructurings are beyond the scope of this chapter.

Purpose of a Corporate Restructuring

Most restructurings are driven by the desire to optimize the business portfolio and/or the desire to optimize the capital structure. For example, a company might find that its stock is trading at a discount to its peers because investors find its business mix confusing and difficult to value. A solution would be to separate non-core businesses in order to provide more corporate clarity to the market. Or perhaps a company finds that a business unit which participates in a higher growth industry than its parent company is likely to be more highly valued as a stand-alone public company than as part of a larger corporation. In this situation, it could be value enhancing to create two separate publicly traded companies.

Divisions and subsidiaries

There is often confusion between the terms "division" and "subsidiary." A division is an internal unit of a company which is not a separate legal entity. In contrast, a subsidiary is a separate corporation with its own stock, of which greater than 50 percent is owned by the parent company. Subsidiaries generally have higher administrative costs (since they are separate legal entities) but they also offer the benefits of incorporation (limited liability, segregated obligations from parent, a separate stock which can be sold or issued, etc.).

Numerous restructuring alternatives exist, many of which will be discussed in this chapter. Choosing the best method for a given situation requires an understanding of the company's long-term goals and the current business and/or financial constraints preventing the company from achieving those goals. Both strategically motivated restructurings and capital markets-driven restructurings can be beneficial if structured and timed properly.

There are various reasons why a parent company ("Parent") might consider the separation of a major business line and/or subsidiary company ("Subsidiary"). Among the most common are the following:

- Corporate clarity is generally rewarded by the market with higher valuations. The volume of money flowing into funds has created specialty asset managers who seek specific industry, growth, and/or yield characteristics. Moreover, because of disparate risk and return profiles within multi-division (or subsidiary) companies, conglomerate businesses are difficult to value.

- Every company should regularly assess its business portfolio and take steps toward optimizing the asset mix (e.g., sell non-core operations; buy and build core operations). Focusing on a company's core business (in which the company has a leading market share or core competencies) usually provides for greater upside in the equity markets.

- Corporate clarity provides for better use of management's time and experience, as well as company resources. It also facilitates greater management and board accountability. In addition, the removal of potential conflicts of interest between divisions (or subsidiaries) provides for better leverage of management skills.

- Putting non-core or underperforming assets in the hands of owners who might better manage them can provide benefits to all parties involved. Also, underperforming assets might be turned around in the hands of another owner with greater experience, resources and/or complementary businesses.

- Restructuring can improve operating performance by providing a better allocation of resources and capital.
- Separating businesses with different risk profiles and contingent liabilities can provide meaningful changes to credit risk, resulting in a more appropriate cost of capital for all businesses involved.
- It may be more efficient for a subsidiary to access public debt and equity markets on its own, rather than derivatively through the parent company.
- Restructuring allows the company to reposition its equity "story" and/or investor base.

Prior to identifying the best separation technique for a certain situation, it is important to determine and prioritize the goals of the Parent company with respect to the separation since different techniques will satisfy different goals. That is, the order in which goals are ranked may determine which restructuring action is taken, and the restructuring action taken will determine which goals are satisfied. Goals might include the following:

1. Maintain strategic control of Subsidiary
2. Maintain financial control of Subsidiary
3. Create a public market valuation for Subsidiary
4. Create an acquisition currency for Subsidiary
5. Limit the tax consequences of the transaction
6. Raise cash for a specific use of proceeds (e.g., pay down debt, fund an acquisition)
7. Recapitalize Subsidiary and/or Parent (separate into independent credit profiles)
8. Preserve future structural flexibility
9. Preserve jobs for Subsidiary-level employees

10. Preserve rights of or satisfy key constituencies (e.g., minority investors, suppliers, unions)

11. Align management's incentives with company goals

12. Maintain operating synergies

13. Encourage strategic buyers to action

14. Respond to a regulatory mandate

15. Bifurcate the investor base between natural owners of Parent and natural owners of Subsidiary

Public vs. Private Market Separation

Separation techniques can be grouped into two major categories: (1) public market separation and (2) private market separation. As the names suggest, public market separation involves separating Subsidiary to public investors while private market separation involves a sale of Subsidiary to private investors or another company (even if the other company is publicly held, it is considered a private transaction because the subsidiary is not divested directly to public shareholders). Examples of public market separations include IPOs, spin-offs, split-offs and the use of tracking stock. Examples of private market separations include the sale of a subsidiary to a third party for cash or stock, the formation of a joint venture, and a stock or asset swap. These transactions are described in the following sections.

The risks and characteristics of Subsidiary as well as the goals of Parent will help determine whether a public market or private market separation would generate more shareholder value for Parent shareholders. Often, companies will embark upon a dual path and pursue the merits and challenges of both a public market and private market separation. It may not be until well into the pursuit of both types of transactions that a company selects the path it will execute.

The following questions can help determine whether a public or private market separation is better suited to the situation.

Can Subsidiary survive as a stand-alone public company?

Public market separation requires that Subsidiary can survive as a stand-alone public company. This includes having the proper operating infrastructure (e.g., human resources, treasury, legal, accounting, etc.), a credit profile that can support its own debt, and a growth story to support its own equity. Also, it is important that there be a natural investor base for the industry in which Subsidiary operates. In other words, it does Parent no good to issue a public security for a subsidiary for which there is no, or only limited, investor appetite. Public market valuation is dependent on equity market factors such as liquidity, investor appetite, investor base, size, growth prospects, etc. as well as credit-related issues. If Subsidiary is not ready to or willing to undertake the process of preparing itself to be a stand-alone entity, a private market separation is likely to be a better option.

Would Subsidiary be attractive to many buyers?

A private market sale could generate a control premium if Subsidiary is attractive to buyers who can pay for potential synergies. A public market separation, on the other hand, is not likely to generate a control premium and, in some circumstances (based on the state of the markets, liquidity, and investor appetite), may debut at a discount to intrinsic valuation levels.

What is Parent's timing?

Preparing a Subsidiary for an equity market debut (e.g., an IPO, spin-off or split-off) can take nine to twelve months depending on how independently organized, structured, and operated Subsidiary is from Parent prior to the separation. A private sale can be effected rather quickly, depending on the process, since Subsidiary does not necessarily have to be prepared to operate as a fully functioning stand-alone public entity.

Does the transaction need to be confidential?

A public market separation path is highly visible. Due to the reporting regulations of the SEC, employees, investors, competitors and stakeholders all will become aware of the transaction prior to its occurrence. Similarly, if a full auction is used (i.e., widely marketed and publicized), there is more transparency (or lack of confidentiality) to the broader market. In contrast, negotiated private market deals can allow for confidential sales to strategic buyers and/or financial sponsors.

Does Parent want to retain an interest in Subsidiary?

The level of control Parent would like to retain post-separation is an important consideration. Various public and private market separation techniques are described in the following pages. Certain ones, such as the sale of all equity or a spin-off, are complete separations in that, once the transaction is complete, Subsidiary is no longer part of Parent's consolidated group of companies. Other techniques such as an equity carve-out, however, are partial separations such that Parent still maintains some level of control over Subsidiary.

What are the tax ramifications of a separation?

A public market separation may be structured as tax-free or taxable, depending on the separation technique. Private market sales of subsidiaries are generally for cash and, therefore, generally taxable. Tax issues related to subsidiary separations will be discussed in more detail later in this chapter.

Public and Private Market Separation Techniques

The following public and private market separation techniques for subsidiary companies are described on the following pages:

Public Market Separation Techniques

- IPO and/or secondary sale of equity divestiture
- Spin-off
- Split-off
- Tracking stock (also called targeted stock and letter stock)

There are more complex public market separation techniques (e.g., the use of derivative securities, master limited partnerships, etc.) that exist but are beyond the scope of the discussion of corporate restructurings in this book.

Private Market Separation Techniques

- Sale to third party for cash
- Sale to third party for stock
- Joint ventures and partnerships
- Stock or asset swap

In the following section each of these techniques is described in more detail. In all of the examples, Parent is the parent holding corporation, Parent Shareholders are the shareholders who own parent company stock, and Subsidiary A and Subsidiary B are wholly-owned subsidiaries of Parent, each of which is itself a corporation. New Shareholders are equity investors who are not affiliated with existing Parent Shareholders.

It should be noted that there are different tax treatments for different types of separations. As mentioned at the beginning of Taxes and M&A (Ch.21), it is important to consult a tax specialist if working on a specific transaction. This information is intended to be educational and descriptive with respect to tax considerations rather than authoritative.

Figure 22.1 - IPO and/or Public Sale of Equity (public market separation)

1. Parent sells the stock of Subsidiary B to the public market for cash

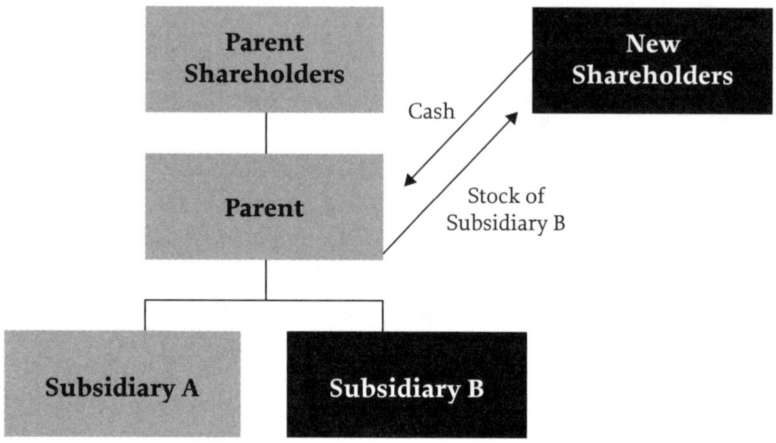

2. If Parent sells all of its interest in Subsidiary B, Parent Shareholders own Subsidiary A through Parent and New Shareholders own Company B (Formerly Subsidiary B)

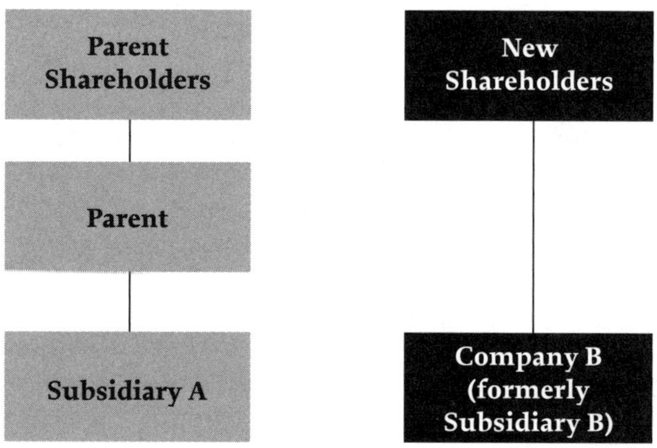

Description: If Subsidiary B is not publicly traded, an IPO is conducted for Subsidiary B whereby Subsidiary B shares are sold to New Shareholders. So as not to flood the market with Subsidiary B shares, in practice an IPO for less than 20 percent usually would occur first; follow-on offerings would be staged over time to match market demand. If Subsidiary B is already publicly traded, secondary offerings are conducted to sell down Parent's interest in Subsidiary B. Cash proceeds from the sale of equity go to

Parent. Subsidiary B might raise debt prior to the IPO. The debt could be contributed to Parent prior to the IPO, effectively allowing Parent to take additional cash out of Subsidiary B (there are tax consequences to this). With a sale of 50 percent or more of Subsidiary B's equity, Parent gives up control of Subsidiary B to New Shareholders.

Best used when: there is strong equity market appetite for Subsidiary B. A 100 percent divestiture is good if a full separation of Subsidiary B is desired and there is sufficient market appetite. Also, Subsidiary B must be a viable stand-alone public company at the time of the IPO.

Divestiture vs. carve-out

A public sale of equity can be effected for virtually any percentage ownership up to and including 100 percent. Generally, if less than 50 percent is sold to the public, the transaction is considered an "IPO carve-out" as opposed to an "IPO divestiture." For tax reasons, most IPO carve-outs are done for less than 20 percent. Most sales of equity for greater than 20 percent are staged over time to manage demand and not flood the market.

Pros: If 100 percent is sold to the public, allows for a complete separation of Subsidiary B from Parent. Also, an IPO provides Subsidiary B with an acquisition currency and a sale of equity provides cash to Parent.

Cons: Cash received by Parent from the sale(s) of equity in excess of Parent's tax basis in Subsidiary B is taxable to Parent. Also, Subsidiary B must be of meaningful size and have an attractive equity growth story in order to create sufficient liquidity and demand in the equity market.

Examples:

- St. Paul Traveler's 2005 sale of its 78 percent interest in Nuveen Investments to public shareholders
- The Limited's 1995 IPO carve-out of 17 percent of Intimate Brands (Victoria's Secret)

Figure 22.2 - Spin-off (public market separation)

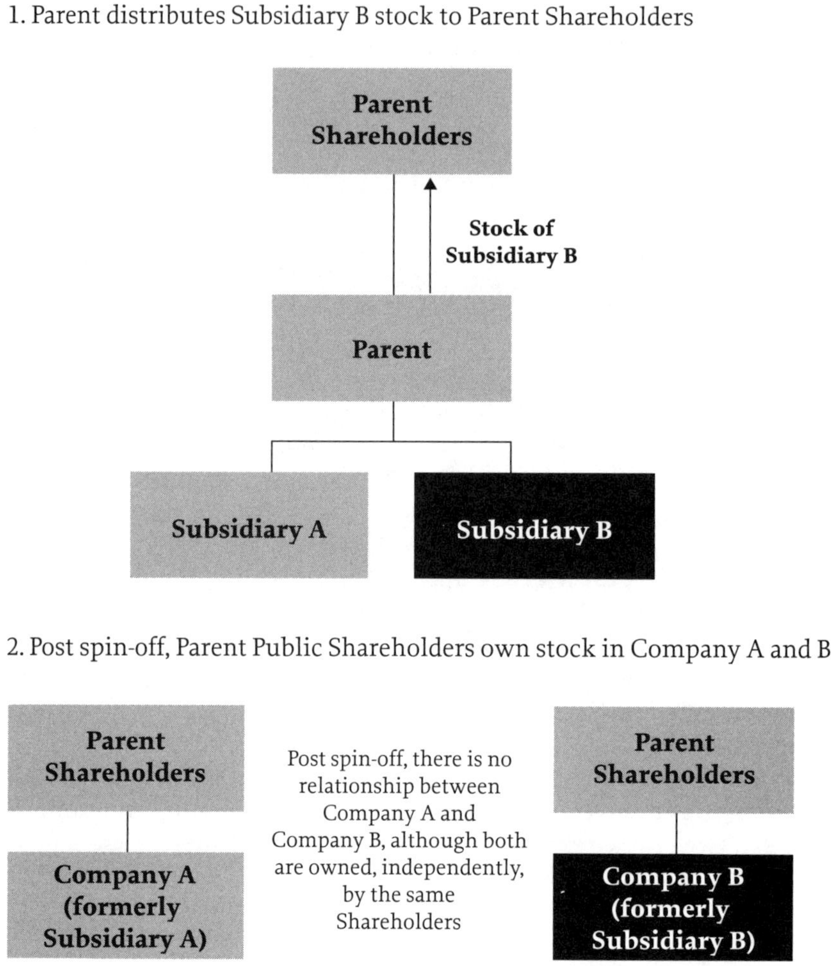

Description: Shares in Subsidiary B are distributed to Parent Shareholders on a pro rata basis (based on the number of Parent shares owned). For example, in a two-for-one distribution, Parent shareholders would get two shares of Company B for each share of Parent owned. In a spin-off every Parent Shareholder receives shares in Subsidiary B. If they do not want those Subsidiary B shares, Parent Shareholders can sell the Subsidiary B shares after the distribution. In a spin-off, Parent gives up control of Subsidiary B and distributes control and value to existing Parent Shareholders. In practice, it is common for Parent to first issue an IPO for less than 20 percent of Subsidiary B in order to establish a public market value and investor base for Subsidiary B before distributing the remaining shares to Parent Shareholders.

Best used when: a full separation of Subsidiary B is desired, there is equity market appetite for Subsidiary B, and/or the tax implications of a separation for cash (e.g., IPO divestiture, sale for cash) make it onerous. Also, Subsidiary B must be a viable stand-alone public company at the time of the spin-off.

Pros: A spin-off can be structured as tax-free (or, more technically, tax-deferred) assuming the applicable IRS requirements are met. To qualify for a tax-free spin-off, among other tests, at least 80 percent of the voting shares of Subsidiary B must be spun-off (hence the IPO carve-out of less than 20 percent), the transaction must be done for a valid business purpose, Parent must have owned (controlled) Subsidiary B for at least five years prior to the spin-off, Subsidiary B must have been involved in an active trade or business for five years, the continuity of interest and device tests must be satisfied, and Subsidiary B cannot be sold within two years of the spin-off in a preplanned sale. If the transaction does not qualify for tax-free treatment (i.e., these or other tests are not met), Parent will be taxed on the separation as if it had sold the stock for cash and Parent Shareholders will be taxed on the proceeds received. (Refer to a tax attorney or tax guidelines for a definitive description of the tax considerations and implications of a spin-off.) Another benefit of a spin-off is that it provides Subsidiary B with its own acquisition currency to pursue M&A transactions. Also, a publicly traded stock can provide management incentives that are directly tied to Subsidiary B's performance.

Cons: The tax-free treatment is not straightforward, and so a spin-off is not always the most efficient alternative. In addition, with two smaller companies in place of one larger company, there is separate borrowing capacity and increased takeover vulnerability for each of the two companies. Lastly, Parent Shareholders may not want to own separate stock in Subsidiary B and they might intend to sell Subsidiary B stock as soon as they receive it in the spin-off, thereby placing downward pressure on the price of Subsidiary B stock. This is similar to what happens in cross-border transactions with flowback. (See Deal Mechanics (Ch.20))

Examples:

- IAC's 2008 spin-off of Ticketmaster, HSN, Interval and Tree.com
- RJR's 1999 spin-off of Nabisco Holdings
- Pepsi's 1997 spin-off of Tricon (now YUM)
- AT&T's 1995 spin-off of Lucent Technologies

Figure 22.3 - Split-off (public market separation)

1. Parent exchanges Subsidiary B stock for Parent stock based on a specified exchange ratio

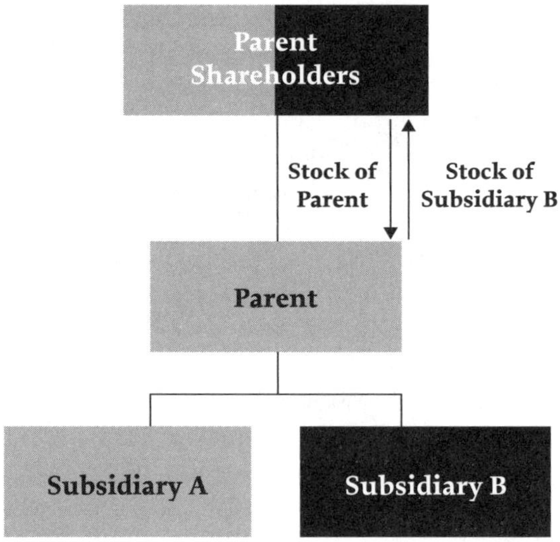

2. Post split-off, some Parent Shareholders own stock in Company A and some Parent Shareholders own stock in Company B

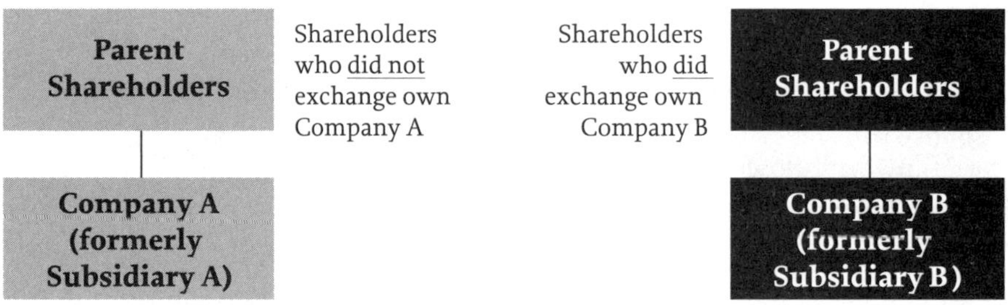

Description: Shares in Subsidiary B are exchanged for Parent stock based on a specified exchange ratio. Unlike a spin-off in which every Parent Shareholder receives stock in Subsidiary B, in a split-off Parent Shareholders choose whether to remain shareholders of Parent or whether to become shareholders of Subsidiary B. In a split-off Parent gives up control of Subsidiary B and exchanges control and value to existing Parent Shareholders who want to own Subsidiary B. In practice, it is common for Parent to first issue an IPO for less than 20 percent of Subsidiary B in order to establish a public market value and investor base for Subsidiary B before the actual split-off.

Best used when: a full separation of Subsidiary B is desired, there is equity market appetite for Subsidiary B, and/or the tax implications of a separation for cash (e.g., IPO divestiture, sale for cash) make it onerous. A split-off is preferred to a spin-off when there is strong reason to believe that certain Parent Shareholders would prefer to own Subsidiary B over Subsidiary A. That is, some Parent Shareholders would prefer to own only Subsidiary A and some only Subsidiary B, but until that choice is available they own Parent in order to own their preferred subsidiary. Also, Subsidiary B must be a viable stand-alone public company at the time of the split-off.

Pros: A split-off can be structured as a tax-free (or, more technically, tax-deferred) event assuming the applicable IRS requirements are met. To qualify for a tax-free split-off, among other tests, at least 80 percent of the voting shares of Subsidiary B must be split off, the transaction must be done for a valid business purpose, Parent must have owned (controlled) Subsidiary B for at least five years prior to the split-off, Subsidiary B must have been involved in an active trade or business for five years, the continuity of interest and device tests must be satisfied, and Subsidiary B cannot be sold within two years of the split-off in a pre-planned sale. If the transaction does not qualify for tax-free treatment, Parent will be taxed on the separation as if it had sold the stock for cash and Parent Shareholders will be taxed on the proceeds received. (Refer to a tax attorney or tax guidelines for a definitive description of the tax considerations and implications of a split-off.) Another benefit of a split-off is that it provides Subsidiary B with its own acquisition currency to pursue M&A transactions. Also, a publicly traded stock can provide management incentives that are directly tied to Subsidiary B's performance.

Cons: Since a split-off requires Parent Shareholders to choose between exchanging for Subsidiary B stock or retaining Parent stock (Subsidiary A), often a premium must be offered to entice Parent Shareholders to exchange Parent stock for Subsidiary B stock. Also, as with a spin-off, the tax-free treatment is not straightforward, so a split-off is not always the most efficient alternative. In addition, with two smaller companies in place of one larger company, there is separate borrowing capacity and increased takeover vulnerability for each of the two companies.

Examples:

- McDonald's 2006 split-off of Chipotle Mexican Grill
- GM's 2000 split-off of Hughes
- Dupont's 1999 split-off of Conoco (now ConocoPhillips)
- The Limited's 1998 split-off of Abercrombie & Fitch (an IPO carve-out in 1996)

Figure 22.4 –Tracking, Targeted or Letter Stock (public market separation)

1. Parent sells Subsidiary B tracking stock to New Shareholders

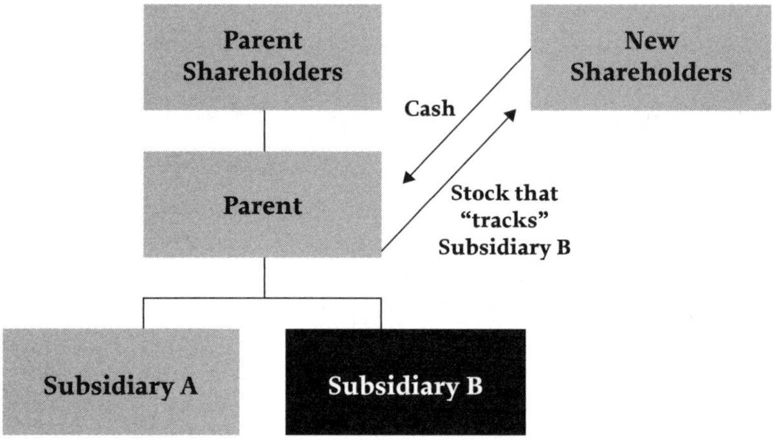

2. Post-sale of tracking stock, Parent has two stocks and two sets of shareholders: Shareholders A and Shareholders B

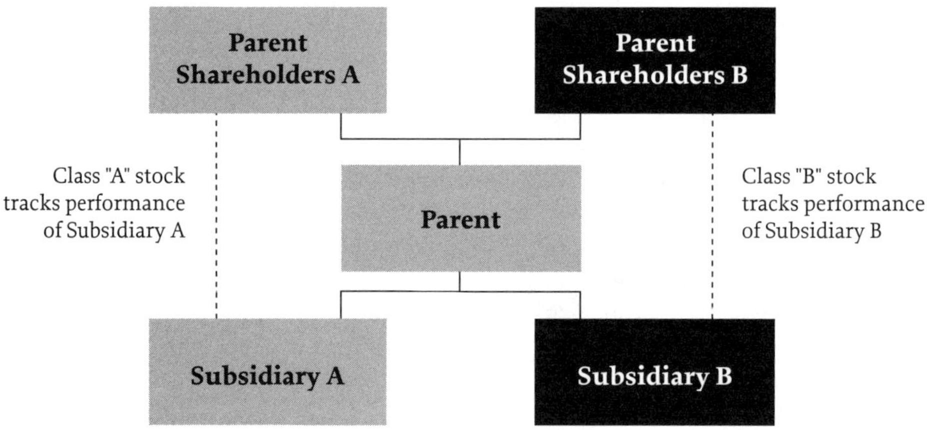

Description: Parent sells a new class of stock that tracks the financial and operating results of Subsidiary B while the original Parent stock continues to reflect the prospects of Subsidiary A. There is no legal separation, however, of Subsidiary B from Parent. Parent retains governance, control, consolidation accounting, etc. of both Subsidiary A and Subsidiary B. Tracking stock is also referred to as targeted stock and letter stock.

Best used when: an economic separation of Subsidiary B is being considered and Parent wants to create a "shadow" public market valuation while still retaining full control of Subsidiary B. Tracking stock is useful if Parent and Subsidiary might want to consolidate from a public market perspective again in the future.

Pros: The separation of financial results for Subsidiary B allows for a separate public equity market valuation for Subsidiary B without a legal separation from Parent. With tracking stock, Parent retains control and financial flexibility for the future. Also, it creates a separate acquisition currency for both Subsidiary A and Subsidiary B. In addition, the issuance of tracking stock can be effected on a tax-free basis, although a number of restrictions exist. (Refer to a tax attorney or tax guidelines for a definitive description of the tax considerations and implications of tracking stock.)

Cons: There is no legal separation with tracking stock. There are several implications of this. First, tracking stock tends to trade at a discount as compared to pure-play peers. Second, unlike traditional equity, the shareholders of tracking stock do not have any claim on the underlying assets after all claims and liabilities have been paid; that residual value would revert to all Parent Shareholders in the example above, not Subsidiary B shareholders as would normally be the case, but Subsidiary A and Subsidiary B shareholders. Third, Parent remains exposed and responsible for all of Subsidiary B's debt and liabilities. Tracking stock is a complex separation structure and is used rarely. Spin-offs, split-offs and subsidiary sales are more common.

Examples:

- Liberty Media's 2006 tracking stocks representing its Interactive group and Capital group
- Dupont's 1998 tracking stock representing its life sciences division
- USX's 1991 tracking stocks representing Marathon Group (oil) and U.S. Steel Group
- GM's 1984 creation of tracking stock to purchase EDS (GM class "E" stock; hence the term letter stock)

Figure 22.5 – Sale of Subsidiary for Cash (private market separation)

1. Parent sells the stock of Subsidiary B to a Private Third Party[1] for cash

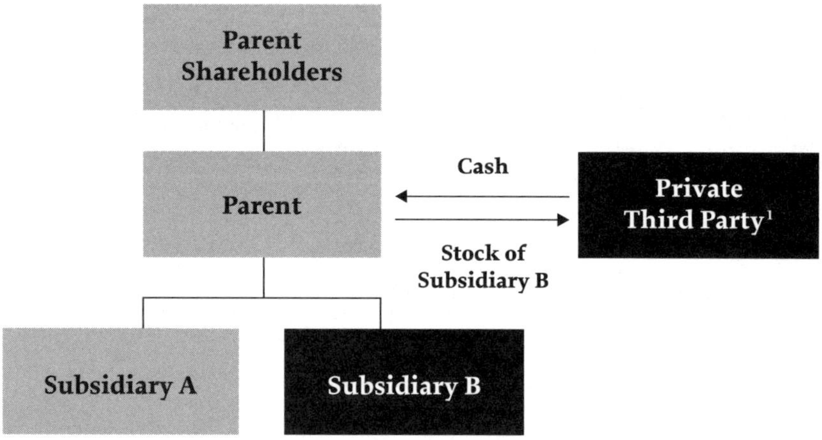

2. Post-sale, Parent Shareholders own Subsidiary A through Parent and the Private Third Party owns Company B (formerly Subsidiary B)

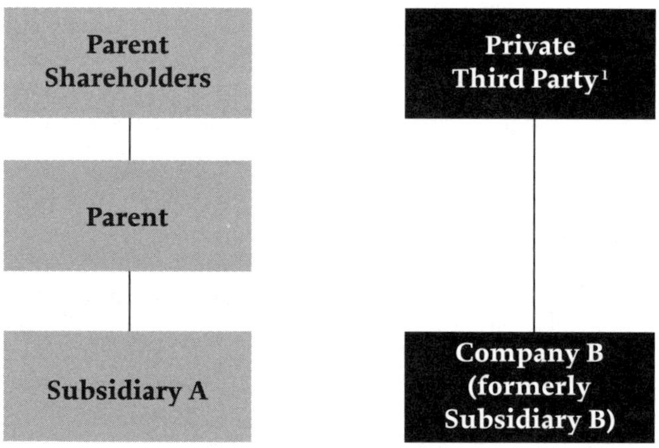

[1] Can be another corporation, a private equity firm or a group of private investors

Description: The stock of Subsidiary B is sold to a private buyer (e.g., another corporation, a private equity firm, a group of private investors or a single investor) for cash. Post-sale, Parent retains no interest in or control of Subsidiary B.

Best used when: a full separation of Subsidiary B from Parent is desired and a universe of strategic and financial buyers exists for Subsidiary B.

Pros: Represents a true economic and legal separation of Subsidiary B from Parent. A private sale is a good option if the private market is likely to generate a strong level of interest and/or if Subsidiary B is not likely to be attractive on its own to the public markets (i.e., as a stand-alone public entity). A sale for cash provides immediate cash to Parent and can be effected quickly, in particular if done as a negotiated sale as opposed to a full-blown auction.

Cons: A sale for cash is a taxable transaction and the tax liability can be significant depending on Parent's tax basis in Subsidiary B. Also, a sale can be disruptive to a business and to management if a full auction process is undertaken.

Examples:

- GM's 2006 sale of 51 percent of GMAC to a consortium led by Cerberus Capital Management
- Ford's 2005 sale of Hertz to a consortium led by Clayton, Dubilier & Rice
- Pernod Ricard's 2005 sale of Dunkin' Brands to a consortium led by Bain Capital

Figure 22.6 – Sale of Subsidiary for Stock (private market separation)

1. Parent exchanges stock of Subsidiary B for stock in a Third Party Corporation[1]

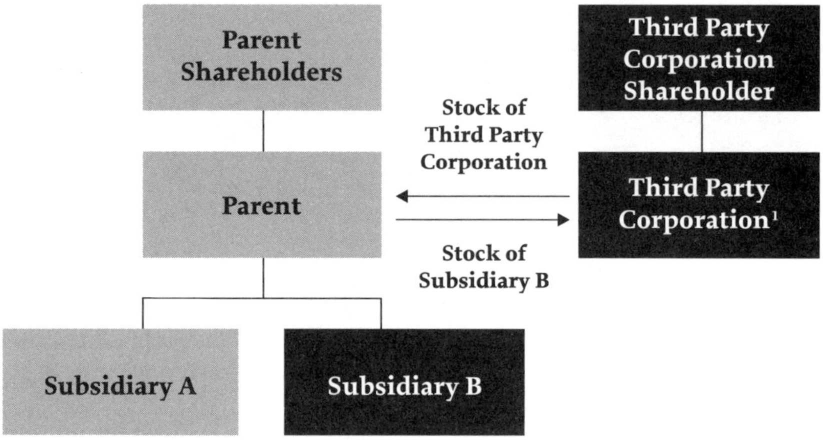

2. Post-sale, Parent owns Subsidiary A and some portion of Third Party Corporation; Third Party Corporation owns Subsidiary B

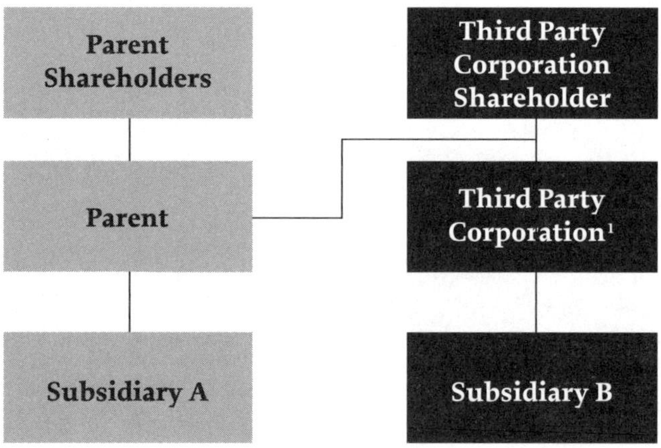

[1] In an exchange of stock, the third party must be a corporation, although it could be a publicly held or privately held corporation

Description: The stock of Subsidiary B is exchanged for stock in another corporation. Post-sale, Parent owns a portion of the Third Party Corporation (the ownership percentage depends on the value of Subsidiary B relative to the value of Third Party Corporation). Subsidiary B is owned and controlled by Third Party Corporation.

Whether Parent has any control over Third Party Corporation depends on its ownership stake and the terms negotiated in the exchange of stock.

Best used when: a full separation of Subsidiary B from Parent is desired but Parent wants to retain some economic exposure to Subsidiary B and Third Party Corporation. Also, while a more complex transaction than a straight sale, a sale for stock can provide an attractive alternative to a situation in which a sale for cash would trigger a meaningful tax liability.

Pros: Like a sale for cash to a third party, a private sale is a good option if the private market is likely to generate strong interest and/or if Subsidiary B is not likely to be attractive on its own to the public markets (i.e., as a stand-alone public entity). An exchange for stock can have some tax benefits (if applicable IRS requirements are met, the transaction can be tax-deferred) as opposed to a sale for cash which would trigger a potential tax liability immediately if the sale price is greater than Parent's tax basis in Subsidiary B. Also, an exchange of stock would allow Parent to retain its stock in Third Party Corporation to sell at some time in the future when the benefits of the combination of Third Party Corporation and Subsidiary B have been realized.

Cons: A sale for stock does not provide Parent with immediate cash to use in other parts of its business (although derivatives could be used to monetize a portion of the equity received). Also, any sale --whether for cash or for stock-- can be disruptive to a business and to management if a full auction process is undertaken. Another challenge with a stock-for-stock exchange is that Parent can only approach corporations whose stock it might be willing to hold (this precludes transactions with financial sponsors and private investors who do not have stock to exchange as well as companies whose stock is unattractive to Parent). As a result, the limitations and challenges of structuring a stock exchange must be weighed against the tax-deferral benefits.

Examples:

- Bank of America's 2006 sale of its Brazil-based BankBoston unit to Itau in exchange for Itau stock
- Bioaccelerate Holdings' 2006 sale of subsidiary Cain Biotech to Accura Pharma PLC in exchange for stock in Accura Pharma
- Citigroup's 2005 sale of its asset management business to Legg Mason in exchange for Legg Mason common and preferred stock, its brokerage and capital markets businesses, and approximately $500 million in cash

Figure 22.7 – Joint Venture and Partnership (private market separation)

1. Parent contributes stock of Subsidiary B to the Joint Venture (JV); Third Party Corporation contributes stock of a subsidiary, assets, and/or cash to the JV; both Parent and Third Party Corporation receive stock in the JV or an interest in the partnership

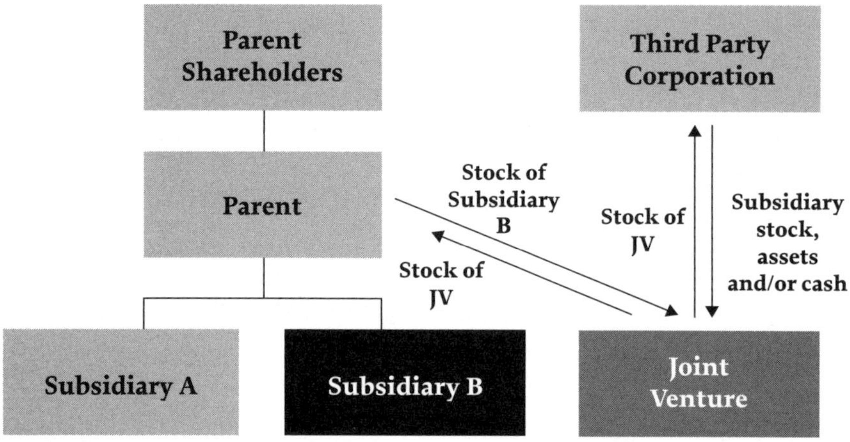

2. Parent and Third Party Corporation each own an interest in the joint venture

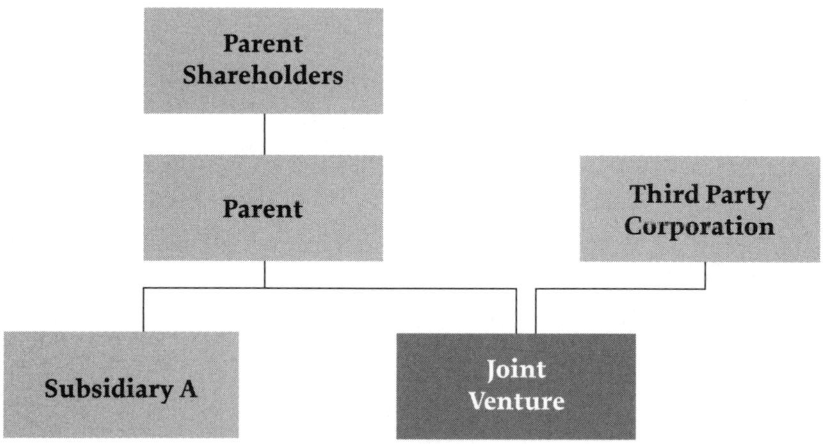

Description: Parent contributes the stock of Subsidiary B to a newly formed joint venture (the joint venture is often structured as a corporation but can be a partnership or limited liability corporation). A Third Party Corporation also contributes the

stock of a subsidiary, and/or assets, and/or cash to the joint venture. Typically, both parties would own the joint venture 50/50, using cash to equalize any difference in the value of contributed assets. A joint venture or partnership agreement would be formed at the outset to specify the terms of the arrangement, in particular separation provisions to spell out how either party can exit from the joint venture in the future.

Best used when: Parent wants to retain economic exposure to and some control over Subsidiary B but believes that it can extract more value from Subsidiary B if it partners with another party, perhaps with certain operating expertise and/or capabilities. A joint venture or partnership agreement is an attractive alternative when an identifiable strategic partner exists with whom Parent would like to enter into a long-term relationship.

Pros: Allows Parent to put Subsidiary B's assets and business to work without giving up economic exposure or full control. A joint venture also allows Parent some flexibility in the future to revert back to full control or ownership, depending on how the terms of the joint venture agreement are drafted. Lastly, contributing Subsidiary B to a joint venture generally would not trigger an immediate tax liability (assuming the transaction is not considered a disguised sale by the IRS). The tax treatment, however, would depend on the specific circumstances of the transaction.

Cons: This type of structure requires Parent to enter into a long-term business relationship with another party. Significant trust and a willingness to work together are required of both parties. It is challenging to (1) find that partner and (2) negotiate terms that are agreeable to both parties. Often, negotiations that begin under the guise of a joint venture or partnership revert to the negotiation of an outright sale because of how complicated it can be to negotiate a joint venture agreement with which both parties are happy.

Examples:

- Yahoo and Telemundo's 2006 joint venture to merge their Hispanic websites
- Sony and Bertelsmann's 2004 joint venture to form Sony BMG
- Time Warner and Liberty Media's joint venture that created Court TV (in 2006 Time Warner purchased Liberty Media's 50 percent interest)

Figure 22.8 – Stock/Asset Swap (private market separation)

1. Parent swaps Subsidiary B for Third Party Corporation's Subsidiary 1

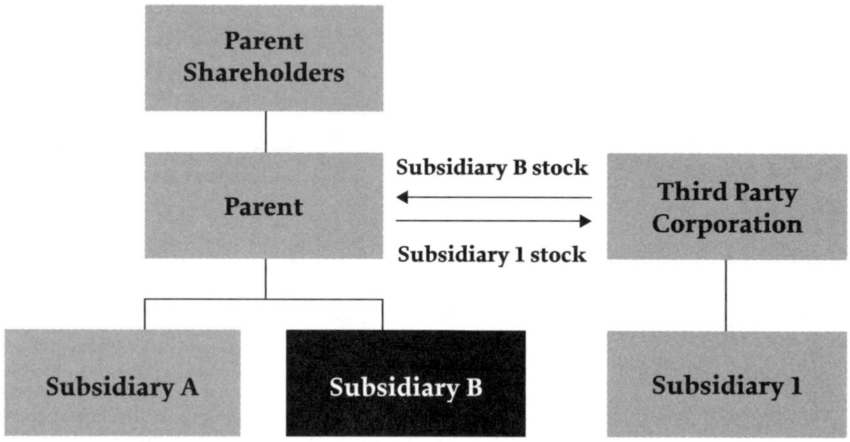

2. After the swap, Parent owns Subsidiary 1 and Third Party Corporation owns Subsidiary B

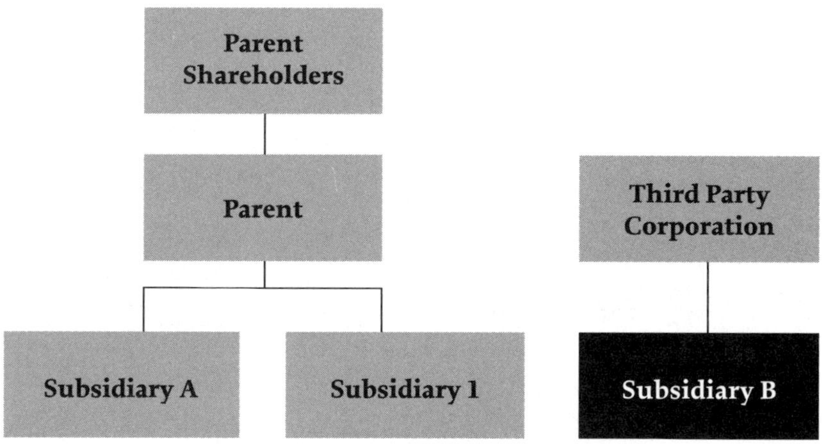

Description: Parent swaps its stock in Subsidiary B or other assets for Third Party Corporation's stock in Subsidiary 1 or other assets. If the values are unequal, one party may add cash to the transaction to equalize values. If applicable IRS requirements are met, the swap may be tax-free (or, more properly, tax-deferred) on the basis of a "like-kind" exchange, though this generally applies to the swap of assets, not stock. After the swap, Parent owns Subsidiary 1 and Third Party Corporation owns Subsidiary B.

Best used when: an identifiable third party exists that (1) owns assets that are similar to Parent's, (2) wants to dispose of those assets, and (3) wants Parent's Subsidiary B.

Pros: Assuming the assets are similar and all the applicable requirements are met, a swap of like-kind assets can be structured as a tax-free exchange. Stock of a subsidiary can be exchanged, as shown in Table 22.8, but it may not qualify as a tax-free transaction.

Cons: Finding the right partner with whom to effect an asset swap is difficult, and ensuring that the swap maintains its tax-free status provides even more challenges. These transactions are difficult to find and execute. However, when they do occur they provide a real benefit for all parties involved.

Example:

- JPMorgan and Bank of New York's 2006 swap of JPMorgan's corporate trust business for Bank of New York's 338 retail branches in the tri-state area.

> **Private letter rulings**
>
> In a transaction such as a spin-off or an IPO carve-out, when the tax ruling from the IRS can alter the economics of a transaction substantially, companies may seek what is called a **private letter ruling** from the IRS. The letter essentially establishes how the IRS will treat the proposed transaction, and the ruling is generally obtained *before* a transaction is executed. In the absence of a private letter ruling, a company may seek a legal opinion from its tax attorneys or some other form of assurance.

Financial Restructuring

A financial restructuring involves making material changes to the company's capital structure as a means of enhancing shareholder value. Financial restructuring or recapitalizations can be limited or extensive depending on the goals of the company. In general, recapitalizations are effected by managing the equity account: either by returning capital to equity owners or by significantly increasing a company's leverage to minimize its cost of capital by minimizing the equity component of that capital.

By minimizing the equity base, a company can increase ROE and potentially EPS. Since the cost of debt is generally lower than the cost of equity, repurchasing equity with borrowed funds can maximize earnings and is generally accretive to EPS and EPS growth rates. Repurchasing stock also tends to send a positive signal to the market, since it implies that management believes the company's current equity valuation levels to be "cheap" relative to the value implied by the company's long-term strategic plan (else it would not repurchase stock; the corollary is that companies prefer to issue or sell equity when they believe their stock is trading at a relative premium). In fact, the bigger the repurchase program and the faster it is executed, the more meaningful the signal. Prior to initiating a major equity-based restructuring program, it is important to assess the short- and long-term cash flow needs of the business to ensure that adequate capital is retained to fund operations and that cash flows are sufficient to service debt (both existing and additional), even in the event of a business downturn. This section should be read in conjunction with Leveraged Buyout Analysis and Credit Analysis. (Ch.12,24)

Examples of financial restructuring transactions are described below.

Special dividend

As the name suggests, a special dividend is a dividend paid to the shareholders of a company that often is more significant in value and less common than the company's normal dividend. A special dividend can be stock or cash but customarily refers to a cash payment, with a stock payment referred to as a "stock dividend." A special dividend allows for a significant restructuring of a company's capital structure. The largest special dividend to date occurred in the summer of 2004 when Microsoft Corporation announced that it would return $32 billion to shareholders. Special dividends generally have an immediate positive effect on share price, although typically the share price will go down after payment of the special dividend.

Large stock repurchase

By significantly increasing demand, a large stock repurchase can provide value to the shareholders of a company by allowing existing shareholders to choose whether to sell out or to remain as shareholders. It can be implemented using various techniques. Large share repurchases generally provide for immediate EPS, ROE, and stock price impact. The size of the proposed repurchase can create execution risk since it may be difficult to get enough shareholders to tender their shares at a reasonable price, especially if the prevailing market sentiment regarding the company is positive. In such cases, a premium may be required to encourage the tendering of shares.

A **Dutch auction** is one method often used in share repurchases. In a Dutch auction, the company announces a maximum price to be paid per share repurchased. The shareholders offer to sell their shares at specific prices up to the maximum price stated by the company, then the company sets a purchase price based on shareholder indications. All shareholders receive the same purchase price in a Dutch auction. **Fixed price tender offers** are another option for a large stock repurchase. In this method, the company announces a fixed price at which it will repurchase shares and any shareholders who want to tender their shares at that price will do so. Major share buyback programs are often initiated in the context of a merger transaction in order to mitigate downward pressure on Acquiror's stock price immediately after announcement of the merger.

For example, ABC Company announces that it will repurchase 7.5 million shares in a Dutch auction at a price range of $14 - $17 per share. The stock is currently trading at $14.25 per share. Each shareholder who is willing to sell his or her shares informs the company (or, more commonly, an agent assigned the task of soliciting shares) of the number of shares shareholder is willing to sell and at what price. This data is then aggregated and ABC Company pays that price per share which yields the number of total shares sought by ABC, in this case 7.5 million shares. All shares tendered at prices up to and including the purchase price per share are repurchased at the purchase price. Thus in Table 22.9, each shareholder who was willing to sell at $15.50 per share or less would receive $15.50 per share sold, even though some were willing to sell as low as $14.25 per share. And those who sought more than $15.50 per share will not sell any of their shares. In total, the Dutch auction share repurchase will cost ABC Company $116.25 million to repurchase 7.5 million shares (7.5 million × $15.50 = $116.25 million).

Table 22.9 - Dutch Auction Example

thousands, except price per share data

Shares tendered	Aggregated total	Aggregated % of total[1]	Tendered price
250	250	3%	$14.25
50	300	4%	$14.50
500	800	11%	$14.75
1,300	2,100	28%	$15.00
2,500	4,600	61%	$15.25
2,900	7,500	100%	$15.50
1,500	9,000	120%	$16.00
1,000	10,000	133%	$16.25
750	10,750	143%	$16.50
		Total cost of repurchase[2]	$116,250

[1] Percent of total 7.5 million shares sought

[2] 7.5 million shares × $15.50 per share

In contrast to a Dutch auction, in a fixed priced auction ABC Company would offer a certain price, say $14.75 per share, and then ABC would repurchase as many shares as were tendered at that price. In a fixed price auction, there is no graduated pricing as there is in a Dutch auction. Rather, there is a single purchase price per share which shareholders either choose to accept or choose to decline. Assuming the same price distribution as in Table 22.9, ABC Company will only repurchase 800,000 shares at a price of $14.75 per share, for a total repurchase price of $11.8 million (0.8 million × $14.75 = $11.8 million).

Table 22.10 - Fixed Price Auction Example

thousands, except price per share data

Shares tendered	Aggregated total	Aggregated % of total[1]	Tendered price
250	250	3%	$14.25
50	300	4%	$14.50
500	800	11%	$14.75
1,300	2,100	na	$15.00
2,500	4,600	na	$15.25
2,900	7,500	na	$15.50
1,500	9,000	na	$16.00
1,000	10,000	na	$16.25
750	10,750	na	$16.50
		Total cost of repurchase[2]	$11,800

[1] Percent of total 7.5 million shares sought

[2] 800,000 shares × $14.75 per share

As this example shows, the benefit of the Dutch auction is that the desired number of shares is repurchased (100 percent of shares sought), but the price per share at which those shares must be repurchased is not known until the tender takes place (the price is the variable). Conversely, the benefit of the fixed price auction is that the desired price per share is paid, but the number of shares which will be repurchased is not known until the tender takes place (the number of shares is the variable).

Ongoing stock repurchase program

An ongoing stock repurchase program is a continuous commitment on the part of a company to enhance shareholder value. Shares are purchased in the open market over a period of time instead of all at once, as is the case with a large stock repurchase. Ongoing stock repurchase programs are used by many companies, often to counterbalance shares issued to employees as compensation or to offset the dilution when options are exercised by employees.

Leveraged recapitalization

A leveraged recapitalization involves increasing the debt level of a company by a significant amount and using the borrowed funds to repurchase a large number of shares, essentially replacing much of the existing equity in the capital structure with debt. The philosophy behind such a transaction is that by leveraging a company and replacing higher-cost equity with lower-cost debt, the value for the equity holders would rise. Leveraged recapitalizations typically are used by financial sponsors when acquiring companies. The would-be new owners raise the maximum amount of debt they can based on the company's assets and cash flow profile and use the funds to purchase the equity of the company from the existing shareholders. The new owner puts new equity into the company and, since the company is now capitalized with higher levels of debt, the value delivered to the equity holder is more significant. Highly leveraged companies, however, are significantly more risky since the additional leverage and higher fixed cost (debt) obligations provide less cushion for the company during business down cycles or broad economic downturns. (See Leveraged Buyout Analysis. (Ch.12))

Corporate Defense

Chapter 23

Do not protect yourself by a fence,
but rather by your friends.

Czech proverb

There are few transactions that attract more attention than hostile takeovers. In a takeover situation, a would-be Acquiror tries to obtain control of a Target that is opposed to the transaction (hence the term "hostile"). Hostile transactions are defined as those that do not have management or board support, as opposed to friendly transactions, which have the support of management and the board. Whereas hostile transactions in the 1980s were typically initiated by financial sponsors who would take over a company and then sell off the pieces or add significant leverage to the company to enhance equity returns, modern day hostile transactions are more often initiated by strategic players interested in companies for strategic and competitive reasons. Corporate defense is the act of helping a publicly traded company (Target) do what it legally can to (1) fight off a hostile overture and try to remain independent or (2) provide Target's management and board with enough time and/or leverage to negotiate a transaction which maximizes value for Target's shareholders.

Legal considerations in corporate defense

This chapter provides an overview of the structural defenses that might help a company facing a hostile takeover. Many legal considerations come into play when discussing corporate defense mechanisms. This chapter is intended as an overview of corporate defense and should not be considered a definitive legal reference. Consult with experienced legal counsel when working on a live transaction.

Purpose of Corporate Defense

There is an intrinsic tension between shareholders, who may benefit from a high bid for Target, and management, who may lose their jobs following a successful takeover. As a result, a kind of truce has developed between managements and the institutional shareholders who have major shareholding positions in many companies: defensive measures that are likely to enhance Target's shareholder value are welcomed, but defensive measures that are truly protective (and thus might prevent shareholders from maximizing value) are discouraged.

Due to a board's fiduciary responsibility to maximize value for its public shareholders, a fully financed, fully priced offer for a publicly held Target is likely to succeed. Thus, structural defenses are designed to maximize value to Target shareholders rather than to guarantee the independence of Target. In general, structural defenses either (1) enhance the powers of the board of directors by enabling them to take certain actions (usually to try to obtain a higher price) or (2) preclude certain actions from being taken (usually to provide the board with enough time to try to obtain a higher price). Put simply, structural defenses provide a board with more negotiating leverage against a company that is aggressively pursuing it.

State Statutes and Delaware

Each U.S. corporation is incorporated in one state, even though it may do business in multiple states and internationally. State statutes regulate key elements of a company's structural defenses. Statutes vary from state to state, and the state of incorporation is important because it determines which state's rules apply to the corporation. Most state statutes regulate the rules for corporate governance by creating laws (state corporation codes) that control or affect a company's articles of incorporation and bylaws. An individual state can pass specific "anti-takeover" laws that prescribe the manner in which a hostile takeover of a company incorporated in that state must take place. In fact, most states have adopted one or more anti-takeover statutes as part of their state corporation laws. These state-specific anti-takeover statutes need to be considered when examining the defensive profile of a company.

Whereas state statutes govern mergers, federal statutes overseen by the SEC govern trading of publicly traded securities. The SEC, for example, has limitations which govern how tender offers can be effected and a would-be Acquiror would need to abide by these limitations if embarking upon a tender offer. Tender offer rules are summarized in Deal Mechanics. (Ch.20)

Finding articles of incorporation and bylaws

A corporation's articles of incorporation (sometimes referred to as its charter) and bylaws must be filed with the Secretary of State in the state of incorporation. For any public company in the U.S., one can locate a company's charter and bylaws by referring to the list of exhibits in the company's latest 10-K filing with the SEC.

> **Do documents include every right?**
>
> No company's charter and bylaws can reflect every possible structural defense. In the event that a company's charter and bylaws do not specifically address a particular issue, the company's documents are said to be "silent" as to that particular matter. In the event that a company's charter and bylaws are silent as to a particular matter, it is important to review the underlying law of the state of incorporation regarding that item. In some states, silence on a matter may mean that the right exists (i.e., a company must actively "opt out") while in other states silence on the matter may mean that the right does not exist (i.e., a company must actively "opt in").

Delaware is particularly well-known as a state of incorporation due to its corporate-friendly policies. From a defense perspective, one of the most important aspects of Delaware incorporation is that Delaware has a separate court system for corporate law called the Delaware Chancery Court, which has long been a leader in the development of corporate law, including defense law. While the state statutes for Delaware are well-known, other states are less well-known. As a result, transactions involving other states may require outside legal assistance (including local counsel of the state of Target incorporation, if necessary). Much of what is included in this chapter relates to Delaware corporations. The state of incorporation for a public company can be found on the cover page of its 10-K, 10-Q and 8-K filings.

When a Hostile Situation Emerges

Although hostile overtures can occur at any time, they are more likely to occur when Target is undergoing some level of internal difficulty or turmoil (e.g., dissent among the board or management regarding the strategic direction of the company, resignation of key executives, shareholder dissatisfaction, poor stock price performance, etc.). The natural corollary is that a hostile overture is less likely to occur when a company's house is in order and the stock price reflects the intrinsic value of the company. In fact, defense professionals often say that the single best defense is a high stock price. When a hostile overture is made, the first thing a company usually does is engage an investment bank and law firm to work as its defense advisors. The bankers and lawyers would then review Target's structural defenses (described later in the chapter) in order to determine what Target's options are. The structural defenses in place prior to the overture will determine how much time Target's management and board have to work with and what types of tools Hostile Acquiror might utilize in its quest to take over Target. Generally, the more structural defenses that Target has in place prior to a hostile overture, the more time and options Target will have.

As part of its fiduciary obligation to maximize shareholder value for Target's shareholders, Target's board and management would have to consider the value of the hostile offer (i.e., the purchase price and the form of consideration) in comparison to the value of its own strategic plan. The investment bank would conduct an internal valuation to opine on the intrinsic value of the strategic plan and to recommend a course of action to Target's board. In addition to an internal valuation, the board (with its advisors) would consider the form of consideration (e.g., stock vs. cash), the likelihood the transaction will close, any financing contingencies, possible delays resulting from antitrust issues, the Hostile Acquiror's identity and reputation, and the Hostile Acquiror's plans for the business. After considering all of these factors, the board would make a decision regarding whether to try to stay independent or whether to pursue negotiations with Hostile Acquiror. If Target's board decided it did not want to negotiate with Hostile Acquiror, according to the **business judgment rule** it can "just say no" to Hostile Acquiror. Directors are entitled to common law protection from any liability arising out of "just saying no" if their decision satisfies the following conditions of the business judgment rule:

a. The decision was informed
b. The decision was made in good faith
c. The directors had an honest belief that the actions taken were in the best interests of the company and its stockholders, and
d. The directors discharged their duties of loyalty and of care

The business judgment rule is further described in The Deal Team. (Ch.19)

If Target's management and board determine that Target's stand-alone intrinsic value is not greater than or equal to the value offered by Hostile Acquiror, and Target still does not want to negotiate with Hostile Acquiror, Target might consider other actions to enhance shareholder value such as a substantial stock buyback or a leveraged recapitalization (these restructuring methods are described in Corporate Restructuring (Ch.22)). Another option would be for Target to consider a friendly transaction with another company with whom Target would be interested in combining. In order to avoid a transaction with Hostile Acquiror, a so-called **white knight** would negotiate a transaction with Target with terms and conditions that are acceptable to Target's board and management. Notably, a white knight transaction is still a transaction, simply with a preferred partner. One of the risks of entering into a combination with a white knight is that if the structure of the deal implies a 'sale of control of the company' (meaning the deal was for cash or substantially for cash and, after the transaction, Target's shareholders will no longer have an ongoing interest in the company), then the combination with the white knight could trigger **Revlon duties**.

What are Revlon duties?

If a board has decided to sell the company, effect a breakup of the company, or abandon its long-term strategy, Revlon duties hold that the board must maximize "the company's value at a sale for the stockholders' benefit." What this has come to mean in subsequent judicial interpretations is that if Revlon duties are triggered, a board has set the company on the course of a sale of corporate control and therefore the board has "to obtain the highest value reasonably attainable for the shareholders," even if that price is offered by Hostile Acquiror, and there is limited (if any) latitude to accept an offer which is not the highest value. Even in the context of Revlon duties, there is still some board discretion, especially with respect to stock consideration or complex transaction structures (since they can be difficult to value), but the basic board requirement of maximizing value for shareholders is unchanged. See The Deal Team (Ch.19) for further discussion.

Because of Revlon duties, a board and management must be careful about entering into a transaction with a white knight or effecting a major corporate restructuring such as the breakup of the company or the sale of a major subsidiary since Target must ensure that whatever it chooses to do does not trigger Revlon duties. If a transaction with a white knight or another restructuring transaction does trigger Revlon duties, Target legally might be forced into accepting a transaction with Hostile Acquiror (assuming Hostile Acquiror ultimately offers 'the highest value reasonably attainable').

Public Relations

The importance of a well-orchestrated public communication strategy in the face of a hostile overture cannot be overstated. It is common for a company that has been approached by a Hostile Acquiror to hire a public relations firm experienced in dealing with hostile situations at the same time it hires an investment bank and law firm to work as defense advisors.

To be effective, the communication strategy during a hostile situation must focus not only on public shareholders but also on other key constituents including employees, unions, suppliers, customers, and regulators. Whereas employees will be most concerned with the loss of jobs, suppliers will be concerned with the potential loss of key contracts, customers will be concerned with the pricing and quality of their products and services, and regulators will be concerned with antitrust issues.

If any of these constituents oppose the transaction with Hostile Acquiror, they may serve as effective ambassadors for Target's desire to remain independent.

Activist shareholders can also be important allies or challenging opponents in a hostile situation. This is a growing issue as hedge funds (who are often, by their nature, considered "activist") become increasingly important players in public securities markets.

Implementing Structural Defenses

Structural defenses should be in place before a hostile overture is made. In fact, if a company decides to implement or enact a defensive measure in response to a hostile overture, a higher fiduciary standard than the business judgment rule comes into play. Under this **enhanced scrutiny**, if a board is considering a defensive action in a hostile situation, the board must meet an enhanced test before the liability protections of the business judgment rule are afforded to the board of directors. Specifically, the board must show that:

a. It reasonably perceived a significant threat to the company's integrity, and
b. The defensive action was reasonable and proportionate to the perceived threat

Due to the requirements of enhanced scrutiny, and also as a matter of sound corporate governance and management, a company should periodically review and make adjustments to its corporate defense profile in light of its long-term strategic plan so that structural defenses are in place before a hostile threat emerges. The origins of enhanced scrutiny are described in The Deal Team. (Ch.19)

Structural Defenses

As discussed in Deal Mechanics (Ch.20), there are three ways an Acquiror can gain control over a public company: (1) a merger, (2) a tender offer, or (3) a proxy contest. Not surprisingly, structural defense methods generally attempt to shift the balance of power from a would-be Acquiror to management or the board of Target in one or more of these three situations.

A company's corporate defenses can be established in one of three ways: by (1) corporate action, meaning the company enacts provisions in its bylaws or charter at the time the company is formed or at some later time in its corporate lifespan; (2) law or statute, unless the company has the ability to, and has decided to, opt out of applicable law; or (3) judicial precedent.

There are three general types of structural defense methods: (1) those that deal with the substance of the shareholder "vote", which generally provide management or the board with greater leverage in merger transactions, (2) those that relate to protecting "value" for all shareholders, which generally are implicated in tender offer situations but are also implicated in mergers, and (3) those that deal with "board-related" defenses, which generally provide the board with greater powers in proxy contests. Some of the most common defense methods are listed in Table 23.1. Each of these methods is described in more detail in the following section.

Figure 23.1 – Structural Defense Methods

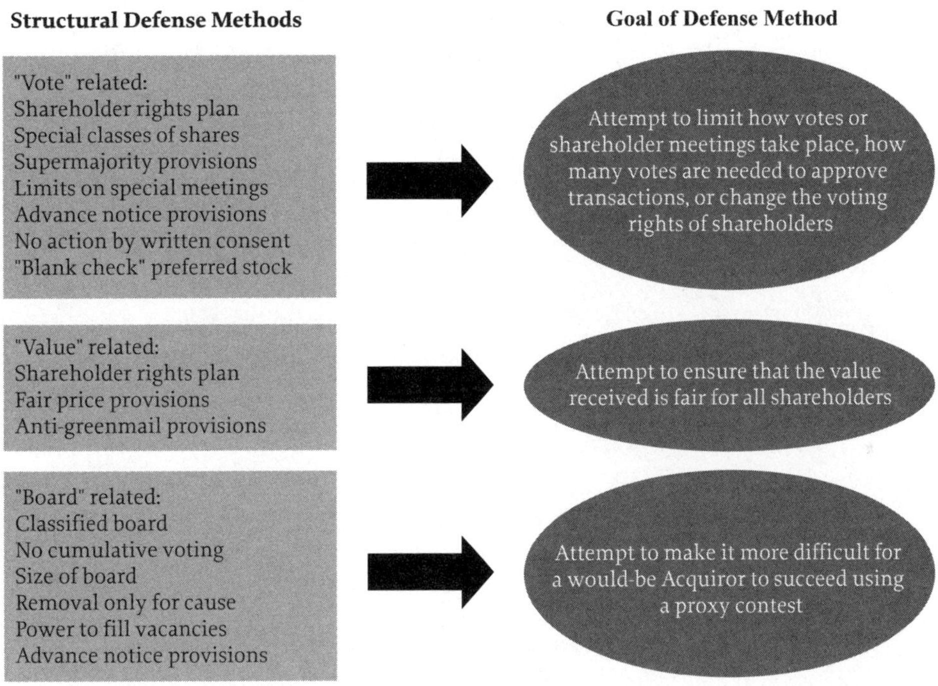

Making changes to structural defenses

A company's articles of incorporation and bylaws can be changed but the difficulty of doing so depends on the nature of the change sought and who has the authority to make that change. Some structural defenses can be put in place or removed only by the board of directors and some require shareholder approval (obviously those that require shareholder approval are more difficult to implement). Refer to a company's charter and bylaws to determine which defenses require shareholder approval and which defenses do not.

Bearhug letters

A bearhug is an unsolicited acquisition proposal sent to Target's management and/or board of directors by a would-be Acquiror. Bearhug letters usually include general terms of the proposed acquisition, including the proposed price. In addition, bearhugs can be "friendly" or "hostile" in that within a bearhug letter there is an implicit or explicit threat to (i) make the letter public (which may have the effect of putting a company "in play" or increasing a company's profile among activist shareholders) and/or (ii) launch a hostile acquisition if there is no response to the offer. Target, the recipient of a bearhug, has some but not unlimited latitude in terms of the responses available to it. Those options are to some degree dependent on the type of corporate planning and defenses the company had in place far in advance of receiving the bearhug letter (legal counsel would need to assess the options available to Target in any given situation). In general, Target must balance its fiduciary responsibilities to shareholders with the legal rules and regulations to which it is subject, all while keeping in mind the fact that it has a business to run.

"Vote" Related Defenses

Shareholder rights plan – One of the best known of all corporate defenses is the shareholder rights plan, or poison pill. It is sufficiently important that it will be treated separately at the end of this chapter. Implementing a shareholder rights plan does not generally require a shareholder vote.

Special classes of shares – It is not uncommon, in particular for companies which initially were owned/controlled by a family or a small group of investors, to have special classes of shares, some of which have super-voting rights. For example, a company might have Class A and Class B shares, both of which have equal economic rights but each Class A share might have one vote per share and each Class B share might have ten votes per share. Often, this group of Class B shareholders might be comprised of a small group of owners. In this situation, a would-be Acquiror might be forced to negotiate a deal with the Class B shareholders (since they control the company in spite of their small number) as opposed to appealing to the broader group of all shareholders. This distinction between the voting rights of two different classes of stock is sometimes referred to as a "low vote / high vote" structure.

Supermajority provision – Requirement that a supermajority (e.g., 67 or 75 percent as opposed to a simple majority of greater than 50 percent) of outstanding shares must approve a change-of-control transaction. In some cases the supermajority requirement applies only if Acquiror is viewed as hostile or if the board does not approve the deal. The reason is that, while supermajority provisions are designed to thwart hostile takeovers, theoretically they can prevent friendly transactions if the supermajority voting percentage is not achieved and if directors are not allowed to waive the supermajority requirement for a friendly transaction.

Limits on calling special meetings – Provides that only certain parties (often directors, chairman, and/or CEO) can call a special meeting of shareholders. Since important corporate actions must be voted on at a shareholder meeting --including, for most companies, the approval of a change-of-control transaction, the removal and replacement of directors, an increase in the number of board seats, and the election of new directors-- the limitation on calling a special meeting of shareholders is an effective way to control which corporate actions are brought to shareholders for a vote.

Advance notice provisions – This provision relates to procedures governing the submission of proposals at shareholder meetings and nominations of directors. The requirement of prior notice regarding proposed shareholder actions is designed to provide management and the board with sufficient time to react to shareholder proposals. For this reason, any matters that a shareholder wants to introduce at the annual shareholder meeting (such as a new slate of directors or a potential merger) must be provided well in advance of the planned shareholder meeting.

No action by written consent – Provides that shareholder action (such as a shareholder vote) is not allowed by written consent (i.e., a written ballot which can be mailed in); instead, an actual shareholder meeting is required. This prevents hostile shareholders from achieving a desired result in an expedited fashion by bypassing the shareholder meeting (and its requirements and restrictions) as the forum for shareholder action. That is, a shareholder meeting must be called in order to vote on important matters and, typically, there are limitations on calling shareholder meetings.

"Blank check" preferred stock – This provision allows the board to issue preferred stock without shareholder approval. It is called "blank check" preferred stock because the board can give the preferred stock virtually any characteristic it chooses, most often super-voting power so as to dilute the holdings of a would-be Acquiror. The ability to issue preferred stock without shareholder action is important because a Hostile Acquiror could vote her shares against the issuance of the preferred stock if a shareholder vote were required. Blank check preferred stock is often used in a shareholder rights plan (poison pill).

Outstanding shares vs. issued shares

To approve a merger, either a majority or supermajority of outstanding shares will be required. "Outstanding" shares are different from "authorized" shares. When a company incorporates, its board of directors generally authorizes some number of shares, say ten million, of which only one million may be issued and outstanding initially. Over time, this number of one million shares outstanding may be increased by subsequent stock sales, the issuance and exercise of employee options, and other corporate actions. This number also may be decreased by corporate actions such as the repurchase of shares by the corporation. These repurchased shares are called treasury shares, which are issued but not outstanding and therefore not counted for voting purposes. See Financial Statement Basics (Ch.3) for a discussion of calculating fully diluted shares outstanding.

"Value" Related Defenses

Fair price provision – Requirement that all shareholders receive equivalent consideration in a bid to acquire the company. This provision was created because Hostile Acquirors were once in the practice of making a bid for, say, 51 percent of a company for $25 per share. Once they had enough shares to control a shareholder vote and therefore ensure a merger (assuming a simple majority was required for a change of control), they might offer only $20 per share for the remaining 49 percent. Fair price provisions were designed to prevent such coercive measures.

Anti-greenmail provisions – In the 1980s some corporate raiders would purchase a block of stock in a company as a form of corporate blackmail and threaten to take over the company. In response, the threatened company repurchased the stock from the raider at a premium, allowing the raider to make a significant amount of money after effectively holding the company hostage (the term "greenmail" is a reference to blackmail and money). In response, anti-greenmail provisions developed. Prior to a target company making a greenmail payment, a specified percentage of non-raider shareholders must approve any purchase of securities from a raider who has held the stock for less than a specified period of time (to exempt long-term shareholders). Another provision might require that the target company offer *all* shareholders the above-market price that is offered to the raider.

"Board" Related Defenses

Classified board or staggered board – In a classified or staggered board, the board of directors is divided into several classes (most director classes are for a three-year term). Each year only one of these classes of directors is up for election. For example, if there were a nine-member board, each year three of the nine board members, representing a class, would come up for re-election. A classified board prevents an Acquiror from replacing the entire board of directors at one annual meeting because only one-third (or fewer if there are more than three classes) of the board members are up for re-election in any given year. Thus, it would take at least two annual meetings (two years) to gain control of the board in this example. The ability to control a board is important because often only the board of directors can remove a poison pill or make alterations to other major structural defenses. In addition, board approval is required before a company can sign a merger agreement.

No cumulative voting – In cumulative voting, a shareholder can cast all of her votes cumulatively for one director as opposed to one vote per director. For example, if there are seven directors and a shareholder holds ten shares of ABC Company, which has cumulative voting, the shareholder has seventy "director votes" (10 shares × 7 directors) and can vote all seventy in favor of a single director as opposed to only ten votes for each of the seven director positions. The idea behind cumulative voting is that minority shareholders can elect at least one director by aggregating their votes.

Size of board – If the size of the board of directors is limited, this is another restriction on an Acquiror who is trying to obtain control of the board. A limit on the size of the board prevents Acquiror from voting to expand the board and placing its own nominees in the newly created openings. Instead, Acquiror must try to obtain existing seats, which is complicated by other defense provisions such as removal of directors only for cause and power to fill vacancies.

Removal of directors only for cause – This provision prohibits the removal of directors other than "for cause" or other than by a supermajority vote. The idea is to prevent Acquiror from removing existing directors without cause and replacing them with Acquiror-friendly directors.

Power to fill vacancies – This provision limits the power to fill board vacancies. Usually, the provision requires that any vacancy in the board of directors may be filled only by a majority vote of continuing directors. The concept here is that any board vacancy that Hostile Acquiror may cause is rendered moot since Hostile Acquiror cannot name new board members without approval of the existing board members. That is, even if Hostile Acquiror manages to create a vacancy on the board, existing board members (rather than Hostile Acquiror) have the right to fill that vacancy.

Delaware-Specific Protections

Delaware has a so-called "interested party" statute designed to protect companies incorporated in Delaware from a hostile acquisition essentially by creating a moratorium on further activity after a potential Acquiror becomes an "interested party" (defined as a party which has purchased 15 percent or more of Target). The statute prohibits the interested party from merging or entering into certain business combinations with Target for three years after the date on which it became an interested party. Interested parties can enter into certain business combinations only if: (1) Target's board approves the combination prior to the transaction in which Acquiror becomes interested; (2) the interested party owns more than 85 percent of Target stock after the transaction in which it became interested; or (3) Target's board and two-thirds of the non-affiliated shareholders approve the combination. These restrictions are significant because of what they imply and the hurdles they put in place for Acquiror. In the case of exception (1), a would-be Acquiror cannot take a stake in Target and then approach Target's board after the initial purchase of 15 percent or more (i.e., as a significant shareholder). Instead, Acquiror would have to approach Target's board prior to taking the 15 percent (or more) stake in Target. In the case of exception (2), the purchase which takes Acquiror past the 15 percent threshold (thereby making Acquiror an "interested party" and therefore subject to restrictions) must also take Acquiror past the 85 percent threshold in order to avoid "interested party" restrictions (i.e., Acquiror must purchase at least 85 percent if it purchases at least 15 percent). In the case of exception (3), Target's board and two-thirds of non-Acquiror shareholders must approve the transaction, which is a difficult level of support to achieve.

Shareholder Rights Plan

The defense mechanism colloquially known as a **"poison pill"** is technically known as a **shareholder rights plan**. The reason is that the mechanism provides existing shareholders with a "right" or "rights" to purchase or receive new shares in the company. For example, one type of shareholder rights plan gives shareholders conversion rights (similar to warrants) for additional shares upon the occurrence of a triggering event, which is usually the purchase of a threshold ownership level by Hostile Acquiror. The purpose of the poison pill is to issue enough shares to existing shareholders that Hostile Acquiror's interests in the company, both voting and economic, are so diluted that it becomes cost prohibitive for Hostile Acquiror to purchase the company. The poison pill is so effective that it has never been directly overcome. As a result of its effectiveness, a poison pill forces Hostile Acquiror to negotiate with Target (if it wants to complete the transaction now) or begin a proxy contest (which could take one to three years, depending on Target's structural defenses).

Upon its introduction in 1984, the utter effectiveness of the poison pill as a corporate defense shifted the goal of hostile acquirors from trying to obtain enough shares for control of the company (often via a tender offer) to trying to gain control of the board of directors (often via a proxy contest). Upon gaining control of the board, the newly elected directors could vote to remove the poison pill. As a result, a number of variations to the poison pill were developed, including the so-called *dead-hand*, or continuing director, provision in which only directors who were in place prior to a proxy contest are allowed to redeem the rights plan. If these "continuing" directors are removed, no other director can redeem the pill. Delaware courts ruled against dead-hand provisions but the legality of dead-hand provisions differs from state to state. A further variation of the dead-hand provision is the *no-hand* or *non-redemption* provision in which no director can redeem the poison pill once the continuing directors (those in place before a proxy contest or consent solicitation, or those voted in by a supermajority of previous directors) are no longer in the majority.

How a poison pill works in theory

Hostile Acquiror believes that Target is worth more than its current market value and initiates a hostile takeover. Target has a poison pill in place with a 10 percent threshold trigger. Hostile Acquiror purchases 11 percent of Target, triggering the poison pill. Shareholders other than Hostile Acquiror are able to buy newly issued Target shares at a substantial discount. Hostile Acquiror is not able to participate in this purchase. As a result of the influx of new Target shares, Hostile Acquiror's ownership percentage is substantially diluted and Hostile Acquiror's economic holding is substantially diluted. Faced with such dilution, Hostile Acquiror has no choice but to cease its hostile overture. If Hostile Acquiror wants to continue, it has only two practical choices: (1) negotiate with Target since only Target's board has the power to redeem the poison pill; or (2) launch a proxy contest to gain control of Target's board of directors because, again, only Target's board has the power to redeem the poison pill.

There are five major elements of a shareholder rights plan.

1. ***Ownership percentage (or "threshold") that activates the pill*** – Poison pills have a threshold ownership level which, when crossed by a hostile acquiror, will activate the poison pill. This threshold was often 20 percent when poison pills were first introduced in the 1980s but has gradually been reduced so that most plans in place now have ownership percentage triggers of 10 percent or 15 percent.

2. ***Discount*** – This is the discount price at which new shares will be offered for sale to existing non-Acquiror shareholders. The purpose of the discount is to financially encourage non-Acquiror shareholders to purchase new shares in Target, thereby diluting the voting and economic value of Hostile Acquiror's existing holdings. In most plans the discount is 50 percent.

3. ***Exercise price*** – The discount is applied to the exercise price to determine the price at which non-Acquiror Target shareholders can purchase new Target stock. The exercise price is not a view of the current value of the company to Acquiror; rather, it represents a potential future trading value. The exercise price is set at the time the rights plan is put in place and most rights plans are valid for ten years (meaning that the exercise price is usually reset every ten years). A company would hire an investment bank to determine the exercise price when a shareholder rights plan is put in place. The investment bank would use the company's internal projections to determine the implied range of future stock prices based on multiples, growth rate analysis, business fundamentals, macroeconomic factors, and exercise price precedents set by other companies. Like trading multiples, exercise price multiples are generally related to earnings growth rates.

4. ***Term*** – Most shareholder rights plans have a duration of ten years. Plans expire and therefore must be renewed at the end of the term; however, at these renewal points there are often battles between shareholders, who believe that the poison pill is simply a protective device designed to entrench management, and management, who believes that without the poison pill a would-be Acquiror would not be forced to pay full value for the company.

5. ***Type of plan*** – There are three major types of poison pill, all of which have the effect of diluting Hostile Acquiror's economic and voting interests in Target. Descriptions and numerical examples of these three plans are provided in the following section.

- ***Flip-in plan***: Target shareholders have the "right" to purchase new shares in Target at a discount to the current Target share price

- ***Flip-in exchange plan***: Target shareholder "rights" are exchanged for new shares in Target with no action taken by Target shareholders

- ***Flip-over plan***: Target shareholders have the "right" to purchase new shares in Hostile Acquiror at a discount to Hostile Acquiror's current share price

Poison pills are becoming harder to renew

In general, poison pills have a set duration, after which they expire and must be renewed by the board of directors. For most companies, implementing a poison pill or renewing an expired poison pill does not require shareholder approval. However, eliminating a poison pill that is already in place before the end of its term generally requires shareholder approval.

As with all things, the board must consider the wishes of shareholders. Since the early 2000s, the number of companies implementing (or renewing) poison pills has declined. This appears to be in response to continued shareholder activism and shareholder desire to support structural defenses that enhance shareholder value but not those which are viewed as entrenching management at the expense of shareholders.

Flip-In Rights Plan

Description: Target shareholders have the right to purchase new Target shares at a discounted price. The creation and subsequent purchase at a discount of these new shares causes substantial dilution to Hostile Acquiror's voting interest in Target. In addition, Hostile Acquiror's economic position is diluted to the extent of the discount and the number of shares purchased.

Assume a company has a **flip-in rights plan** in place with the assumptions set forth below.

Numbers in the example are in millions, except per share data

Step 1: Summarize the key elements of the shareholder rights plan

Hostile Acquiror shares	15
Non-Acquiror shares	85
Total Target shares outstanding	100
Ownership threshold to trigger pill	15%
Current Target stock price	$20
Exercise price	$80
Discount	50%

Step 2: Calculate Hostile Acquiror's pre-dilution voting and economic interest in Target

If Target has only one class of stock, Hostile Acquiror's pre-dilution voting and economic interests will be equal. If Target has more than one class of stock with unequal voting rights, then Hostile Acquiror's pre-dilution voting and economic interests will differ.

	Target shares owned	**Voting ownership of Target[1]**	**Market value[2]**	**Economic ownership of Target[3]**
Hostile Acquiror	15	15%	$300	15%
Non-Acquiror shares	85	85%	1,700	85%
Total	100	100%	$2,000	100%

[1] Shares owned / total shares outstanding
[2] Shares owned × share price of $20
[3] Market value / total market value

Step 3: Calculate the value per share of the new shares issued under the poison pill

Exercise price	$80
Discount	50%
Dollar value of stock purchased at exercise price[1]	$160

[1] Exercise price / discount

Step 4: Calculate the number of new shares issued per each non-Acquiror share

As a result of the poison pill being triggered, new shares are offered to and purchased by non-Acquiror shareholders (Hostile Acquiror cannot purchase new shares). With an exercise price of $80, each non-Acquiror shareholder will receive 8 new Target shares at an effective purchase price of $10 per share.

Dollar value of stock purchased at exercise price	$160
Current stock price	$20
New shares purchased per non-Acquiror share[1]	8
Exercise price	$80
New shares purchased per non-Acquiror share	8
Effective price per share[2]	$10

[1] Dollar value of stock purchased at exercise price / current stock price
[2] Exercise price / number of new shares purchased per non-Acquiror share

Step 5: Calculate the total number of new Target shares issued

As a result of the poison pill, 680 million new shares are issued to non-Acquiror shareholders.

Non-Acquiror shares	85
Shares purchased per non-Acquiror share	8
New shares issued to non-Acquiror shareholders[1]	680

[1] Number of non-Acquiror shares × number of shares purchased per non-Acquiror share

Step 6: Calculate the cash proceeds to the company from selling new stock

Each holder of a non-Acquiror share has the right to buy new stock from the Target company at the exercise price of $80 and the company will receive cash proceeds from these stock sales.

Non-Acquiror shares	85
Exercise price	$80
Proceeds to Target from stock sales[1]	$6,800

[1] Non-Acquiror shares × exercise price per share

Step 7: Calculate the new value per share after the sale of discounted stock to non-Acquiror shareholders

The per share value will be adjusted in the market to reflect the true economic value per share of stock.

Initial capitalization	
Initial stock price	$20
Shares outstanding	100
Initial market value[1]	$2,000
New shares issued under poison pill	
Non-Acquiror shares	85
Exercise price	$80
Cash proceeds to company from stock sale	$6,800

[1] Initial stock price × shares outstanding

Step 7 continued

Post-dilution capitalization[2]	$8,800
Post-dilution shares outstanding[3]	780
New share value[4]	$11.28

[2] Initial market value + cash proceeds to company from sale of stock
[3] Initial shares outstanding + new shares outstanding from sale of stock
[4] Post-dilution capitalization / post-dilution shares outstanding

Step 8: Compare the economic and voting dilution to Hostile Acquiror before and after the poison pill

After triggering the poison pill, Hostile Acquiror's economic and voting interests in Target are reduced by 87 percent and the market value of its interest in Target is reduced by 44 percent. The number of shares owned by Hostile Acquiror does not change, since Hostile Acquiror is affected by, but does not participate in, the dilution caused by the poison pill.

	Number of shares owned	Voting ownership of Target[1]	Market value[2]	Economic ownership of Target[3]	Value per share
Pre-dilution					
Hostile Acquiror	15	15%	$300	15%	
Non-Acquiror shareholders	85	85%	1,700	85%	
Total	100	100%	$2,000	100%	$20.00
Post-dilution					
Hostile Acquiror	15	2%	$169	2%	
Non-Acquiror shareholders	765	98%	8,631	98%	
Total	780	100%	$8,800	100%	$11.28
Dilution for Hostile Acquiror[4]	**0%**	**(87%)**	**(44%)**	**(87%)**	**(44%)**

[1] Shares owned / total shares
[2] Shares owned × market value per share
[3] Market value / total market value
[4] (Hostile Acquiror's post-dilution value / Hostile Acquiror's pre-dilution value) - 1

Flip-In Exchange Rights Plan

Description: Target shareholder rights are exchanged for new Target shares without any action required of Target shareholders. Unlike a flip-in plan in which non-Acquiror shareholders must purchase new shares with cash, in a flip-in exchange plan the exchange provision guarantees dilution, both voting and economic, to Hostile Acquiror's position and does not rely on non-Acquiror shareholders exercising their rights.

As a result of the flip-in exchange of shares, the voting and economic value of Hostile Acquiror's investment is immediately diluted, and that value is redistributed to the company's other non-Acquiror shareholders without any action on their part.

Assume a company has a flip-in exchange rights plan in place with the assumptions set forth below. There is no discount because, in the **flip-in exchange** plan, Target shareholders do not have to purchase new shares. Rather, their shareholder rights are simply exchanged by the company for new shares, which new shares are then distributed to the non-Acquiror shareholders without any action required on their part.

Numbers in the example are in millions, except per share data

Step 1: Summarize the key elements of the shareholder rights plan

Hostile Acquiror shares	15
Non-Acquiror shares	85
Total Target shares outstanding	100
Current Target stock price	$20
Threshold to trigger pill	15%
Shares per right (exchange ratio)	1.0x

Step 2: Calculate Hostile Acquiror's pre-dilution voting and economic interest in Target

	Shares owned	Voting ownership of Target[1]	Market value[2]	Economic ownership of Target[3]
Hostile Acquiror	15	15%	$300	15%
Non-Acquiror shares	85	85%	1,700	85%
Total	100	100%	$2,000	100%

[1] Shares owned / total shares outstanding
[2] Shares owned × share price of $20
[3] Market value / total market value

Step 3: Calculate the total number of new shares issued

85 million new shares are issued to non-Acquiror shareholders under the exchange plan.

Non-Acquiror shares	85
Shares per right (exchange ratio)	1.00
New shares issued to non-Acquiror shareholders[1]	85

[1] Number of non-Acquiror shares × number of shares per right

Step 4: Calculate the new value per share after the issuance of stock to non-Acquiror shareholders

Initial capitalization	
Initial stock price	$20
Shares outstanding	100
Initial market value[1]	$2,000
New shares issued under poison pill	85
Post-dilution capitalization	$2,000
Post-dilution shares outstanding[2]	185
New share value[3]	$10.81

[1] Initial stock price × shares outstanding
[2] Initial shares outstanding + new shares issued under poison pill
[3] Post-dilution capitalization / post-dilution shares outstanding

Step 5: Compare the economic and voting dilution to Hostile Acquiror before and after the poison pill

After triggering the poison pill, Hostile Acquiror's economic and voting interests in Target are reduced by 46 percent, as is the market value of Hostile Acquiror's interest in Target. The number of shares owned by Hostile Acquiror does not change.

	Number of shares owned	Voting ownership of Target[1]	Market value[2]	Economic ownership of Target[3]	Value per share
Pre-dilution					
Hostile Acquiror	15	15%	$300	15%	
Non-Acquiror shareholders	85	85%	1,700	85%	
Total	100	100%	$2,000	100%	$20.00
Post-dilution					
Hostile Acquiror	15	8%	$162	8%	
Non-Acquiror shareholders	170	92%	1,838	92%	
Total	185	100%	$2,000	100%	$10.81
Dilution for Hostile Acquiror[4]	**0%**	**(46%)**	**(46%)**	**(46%)**	**(46%)**

[1] Shares owned / total shares
[2] Shares owned × market value per share
[3] Market value / total market value
[4] (Hostile Acquiror's post-dilution value / Hostile Acquiror's pre-dilution value) - 1

Flip-Over Rights Plan

Description: Target shareholders have the right to purchase new *Hostile Acquiror* shares at a discounted price, serving to dilute Hostile Acquiror's interest in its own company (not Target).

The mechanics of a flip-over plan function the same as a flip-in plan. The only difference, but it is a major difference, is that upon the merger, the plan flips into *Hostile Acquiror* stock, which is the reason the plan is called a *flip-over* plan. Notice that as a result of the flip-over of shares in the merger, the value of Hostile Acquiror's investment in its own company is significantly diluted and that value is redistributed to Target shareholders.

Assume a company has a **flip-over rights plan** in place with the assumptions set forth below.

Numbers in the example are in millions, except per share data

Step 1: Summarize the key elements of the shareholder rights plan

Hostile Acquiror shares in Target	15
Target shares in Target	85
Hostile Acquiror shares in Hostile Acquiror	500
Ownership threshold to trigger pill	15%
Exercise price	$200
Hostile Acquiror stock price	$50
Discount	50%

Step 2: Calculate the value of the new Hostile Acquiror shares to be issued

Upon triggering of the poison pill, each non-Acquiror shareholder of Target has the right to buy newly issued Hostile Acquiror shares at a discount.

Exercise price	$200
Discount	50%
Dollar value of Hostile Acquiror stock purchased[1]	$400

[1] Exercise price / discount

Step 3: Calculate the number of new Hostile Acquiror shares issued per non-Acquiror Target share

With an exercise price of $200 per share, non-Acquiror Target shareholders receive 8 shares of Hostile Acquiror stock at $25 per share.

Dollar value of stock purchased	$400
Current Hostile Acquiror stock price	$50
Hostile Acquiror shares purchased per Target share[1]	8
Exercise price	$200
Shares purchased	8
Effective price per Hostile Acquiror share[2]	$25

[1] Dollar value of stock purchased / current Hostile Acquiror stock price
[2] Exercise price / shares purchased

Step 4: Calculate the total number of new Hostile Acquiror shares issued to non-Acquiror Target shareholders

680 new Hostile Acquiror shares are issued to non-Acquiror Target shareholders.

Target shares	85
Hostile Acquiror shares purchased per Target share	8
Hostile Acquiror shares issued to non-Acquiror Target shareholders[1]	680

[1] Target shares × number of Hostile Acquiror shares purchased per Target share

Step 5: Calculate the proceeds to Hostile Acquiror of selling new stock to Target shareholders

Target shares	85
Exercise price	$200
Proceeds to Hostile Acquiror from stock sale[1]	$17,000

[1] Target shares × exercise price

Step 6: Calculate the new value per share of Hostile Acquiror after the sale of discounted stock to non-Acquiror Target shareholders

After the sale of discounted Hostile Acquiror stock to Target shareholders, the value of Hostile Acquiror stock falls from $50.00 per share to $35.59 per share.

Initial Hostile Acquiror capitalization	
Stock price	$50.00
Shares outstanding	500
Initial Hostile Acquiror market value	$25,000
Proceeds to Hostile Acquiror from stock sale	$17,000
Post-dilution Hostile Acquiror capitalization[1]	$42,000
Initial Hostile Acquiror shares outstanding	500
Hostile Acquiror shares issued to Target shareholders	680
Post-dilution shares outstanding[2]	1,180
Post-dilution Hostile Acquiror capitalization	$42,000
Post-dilution Hostile Acquiror shares outstanding	1,180
New Hostile Acquiror value per share[3]	$35.59

[1] Initial Hostile Acquiror market value + proceeds to Hostile Acquiror from sale of stock
[2] Initial Hostile Acquiror shares outstanding + Hostile Acquiror shares issued to Target shareholders
[3] Post-dilution Hostile Acquiror capitalization / post-dilution Hostile Acquiror shares outstanding

Step 7: Compare the economic and voting dilution before and after poison pill

After triggering the poison pill, Hostile Acquiror's economic and voting interest in itself is reduced by 58 percent and the market value of its interest in itself is reduced by 29 percent. The number of shares owned by Hostile Acquiror in itself does not change.

	Number of Hostile Acquiror shares owned	Voting ownership of Hostile Acquiror[1]	Market value[2]	Economic ownership of Hostile Acquiror[3]	Value per share
Pre-dilution					
Hostile Acquiror	500	100%	$25,000	100%	
Non-Acquiror shareholders	0	0%	0	0%	
Total	500	100%	$25,000	100%	$50.00
Post-dilution					
Hostile Acquiror	500	42%	$17,797	42%	
Non-Acquiror shareholders	680	58%	24,203	58%	
Total	1,180	100%	$42,000	100%	$35.59
Dilution for Hostile Acquiror[4]	0%	(58%)	(29%)	(58%)	(29%)

[1] Shares owned / total shares
[2] Shares owned × market value per share
[3] Market value / total market value
[4] (Hostile Acquiror's post-dilution value / Hostile Acquiror's pre-dilution value) - 1

PART V

CREDIT AND FINANCING

Credit Analysis

Chapter 24

I have known a man to come into my office,
and I have given him a check for a million dollars
when I knew he had not a cent in the world.
The first thing is character.
Before money or property or anything else.
Money cannot buy it, because a man I do not trust
would not get money out of me on all the bonds in Christendom.

J. P. Morgan

Up until now, debt and equity as sources of capital have been discussed in fairly broad, generic terms. The reality, however, is that the sources of capital available to a company are diverse and complex. Credit risk is one of the most important factors in determining what sources of capital are available to a company. Therefore, before a discussion of the capital markets (which can be found in Sources of Capital (Ch.25)), it is important to begin with a discussion of credit. This chapter will review when and why credit analysis is used and then discuss in detail: (1) rating agencies and credit ratings; (2) methods of credit analysis; and (3) credit ratio notching. Credit ratios will be calculated using the financial statements for SampleCo (from Ch.3) and numerical examples for debt capacity analysis will be provided. The chapter begins with a discussion of capital structure and some of the differences between debt investors and equity investors.

Capital Structure

Capital is money a company can use to fund its business. There are two major classifications of capital for a company – debt and equity. Together, the debt and equity of a company is called the **capital structure**. With debt, the company borrows money and promises to return it, with interest, to the lender. With equity, an investor gives the company money and, in exchange, the company gives the investor an ownership share in the company (hence the term "shares" of a company). If the value of the company rises, the equity investor makes money. If the value of the company falls, the equity investor loses money.

What is the capital structure?

Think of a company's balance sheet as two identical bars of equal height with one bar representing the assets and the other bar representing the liabilities and shareholders equity (see Figure 24.1). The **capital structure** represents the mix of debt and equity (the individual slices of the bar on the right hand side) that a company uses to finance its business. It is the capital that, quite literally, paid for the assets of the company.

Figure 24.1 – Capital Structure Diagram

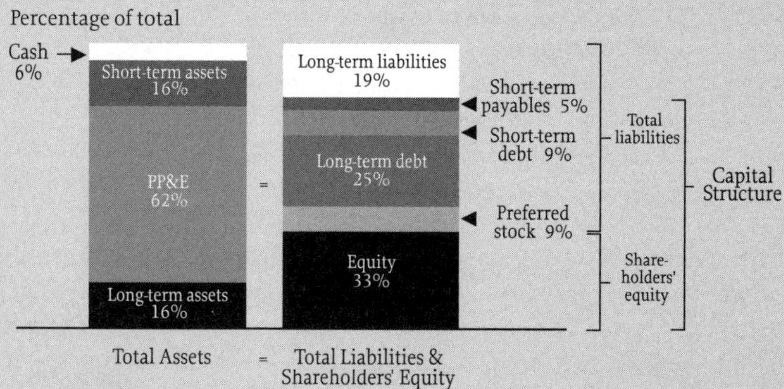

Items that affect a company's debt or equity accounts affect its capital structure. For example, the payment of dividends out of equity, the issuance or repurchase of shares and the issuance or retirement of debt all affect the capital structure.

A company can make changes to its capital structure mix without affecting the asset side of its balance sheet. This process is called **refinancing**. The company in Figure 24.1 can switch from 9 percent preferred stock and 25 percent long-term debt to 5 percent preferred stock and 29 percent long-term debt by issuing new long-term debt and retiring preferred stock with the proceeds. Refinancing the capital structure does not make the bar taller or shorter; it only changes the percentages within the bar.

Debt is generally considered a lower cost source of capital than equity. The reasons for this are described at the beginning of Sources of Capital. (Ch.25)

As described in Corporate Finance Basics (Ch.2), debt and equity investors both require a return on their investment that is commensurate with the risk of the investment. A natural tension exists between companies and investors. A company wants to minimize its financing costs while maintaining financial flexibility, whereas an investor wants to maximize her return on investment while minimizing the risk that she will lose her investment. There is, however, a market clearing price for everything, meaning there is a minimum return that an investor is willing to accept for an investment in a company. The weighted average return to all the debt and equity holders of a company is the company's **cost of capital**. (Ch.2,11) The market clearing price for debt is largely driven by a company's credit risk. **Credit risk** is the likelihood that a company will default on, or fail to pay, its debt obligations. Credit risk is also referred to as bankruptcy risk.

Since a debt holder does not own a stake in the company, he is only focused on whether he will be repaid his investment plus interest. An equity investor, on the other hand, focuses on earnings growth and the value of the total company since she has an ownership stake in the company. Table 24.2 compares the focus of debt investors and equity investors. Notice that much of the debt investor focus is on protection against downside risk, whereas much of the equity investor focus is on growth and upside. A debt holder is exposed to downside risk but does not get any upside value. An equity holder is exposed to both the downside risk and upside value of a company. Said differently, the best case scenario for a debt holder is simply the return of capital with interest. If the company becomes the next Microsoft, the debt holder still receives the return of capital plus interest, while the equity holder's returns grow significantly. Obviously, the opposite holds true as well. If the value of the stock falls dramatically but the company is still able to service its debt obligations, the debt holder receives his return of capital plus interest while the equity holder loses a portion of (or even all of) her initial capital.

Table 24.2 –Debt and Equity Investor Focus

Debt Investor Focus	Equity Investor Focus
• Downside risk	• Upside potential
• Cash flow coverage and earnings sustainability	• Growth in EPS and cash flow
• Conservative financial policies to reduce bankruptcy risk	• Efforts to enhance shareholder value
• Debt levels and coverage ratios	• Return on equity

Continued on next page

Table 24.2 continued

Debt Investor Focus	Equity Investor Focus
• Strong capital structure with conservative use of debt, which provides for liquidity and flexibility (larger percentage of equity in capital structure relative to debt)	• Low cost of capital through efficient use of lower cost debt (smaller percentage of equity in capital structure relative to debt)
• Appropriate strategic actions through bounded risk taking	• Market share enhancement through growth oriented risk taking
• Financially responsible growth plans to sustain cash flows without endangering debt repayment	• Acquisitions to sustain earnings growth and maximize shareholder returns

Credit Analysis

Credit analysis is the act of measuring credit risk. Credit analysis is performed by many different members of the financial community, often for different reasons. Since credit analysis is utilized by so many members of the financial community, it is important for finance professionals to understand what credit risk is and how credit analysis is performed.

Some examples of who performs credit analysis are listed below.

1. A company's managers perform credit analysis to assess the optimal combination of debt and equity which minimizes the company's cost of financing, allows the company to maintain a target credit rating, and maximizes the company's financial flexibility to weather business disruptions and to pursue growth opportunities.

2. Debt investors perform credit analysis to assess the likelihood that a company will default on its debt obligations and thereby to determine the rate of return they require for a debt investment in that company.

3. A rating agency (which is described later in the chapter) performs credit analysis to determine if the credit rating for a company or a particular issue of debt is appropriate and, if it is not, what the appropriate rating should be.

4. An M&A banker performs credit analysis to determine how much new debt a company can issue to fund acquisitions while maintaining a target credit rating.

5. A bank performs credit analysis internally to determine how much regulatory capital it must have in reserves to meet regulations and when making lending decisions for clients.

6. A trader of credit default swaps (also known as credit derivatives) performs credit analysis in order to determine the price for the swap.

Quantifying Credit Risk

Credit risk is measured both for the issuer and for a specific loan or security. Credit risk can be measured in many ways. The most common methods are: (1) a credit rating, (2) a credit spread on debt, and (3) the cost of a credit derivative.

1. A **credit rating** is an opinion provided by a third-party regarding the credit risk or creditworthiness of a company. The credit rating is denominated by a letter or combination of letters and numbers. Credit ratings are described in more detail later in the chapter.

2. A **credit spread** is related to the return required by a debt investor. Most debt is priced based on a reference rate (such as a government bond for bonds or the prime rate for bank debt) plus a credit spread that is specific to the company. The reference rate plus the credit spread is equal to the cost of that particular type of debt for the company or the return to the debt investor. The higher the credit risk, the greater the credit spread. Credit spreads are described in more detail in Sources of Capital. (Ch.25)

3. A **credit derivative** (or **credit default swap** or CDS) is an option that pays the investor if a company defaults on its debt obligations. It is essentially credit insurance for the investor. Therefore the cost of the insurance (measured by the cost of the option) is a measure of the company's perceived credit risk. Just like with insurance, the higher the perceived likelihood that a company will default on its debt (such that the entity which issued the credit default swap has to pay the entity which purchased the credit default swap), the more expensive it is for a party to buy the credit default swap. Derivatives and options are described in more detail in Sources of Capital. (Ch.25)

Credit analysis is used in order to determine all three of these measures of credit risk. Measuring credit risk centers around one critical question: *Do sufficient cash flows exist to service a company's debt obligations?*

To answer this question, the credit analyst and the debt investor must consider two separate risks to which the company is exposed: (1) the business risk of the company or issuing entity and (2) the financial risk of the company or issuing entity. Business risk, which is associated generally with the asset side of the balance sheet, includes things such as the company's strategy with its asset portfolio, the industry in which the company operates, the quality and experience of the management team, and the company's operational processes. For example, companies with a meaningful amount of intangible assets (e.g., intellectual property, patents, etc.) are riskier than companies with a meaningful amount of tangible assets (e.g., manufacturing plants, real estate). This is because tangible assets are easier to sell in a liquidation scenario than intangible assets. Therefore, companies which operate in industries with significant intangible assets (e.g., software) are considered to have high business risk. Financial risk, on the other hand, is related to a company's capital structure. For example, higher levels of debt mean higher financial risk because there are greater financial pressures on the company to service these debt obligations. Lower levels of debt mean lower financial risk for the company.

Credit analysis involves weighing a company's business risk with its financial risk and, from the two, developing a point of view regarding whether the company generates adequate cash flow to service its debt obligations. The lower the level of business risk a company has, the higher the level of financial risk that can be tolerated – and vice versa. For this reason, most leveraged buyouts which use significant levels of debt (and therefore have high financial risk) are in steady, lower business risk industries. (Ch.12) Figure 24.3 lists specific categories of business risk and financial risk. Each business and financial risk is analyzed based on its impact on overall cash flow protection. Together, the assessment of a company's business risk and financial risk is used to determine the credit risk of a particular issuer as well as the credit risk of a particular loan or security.

Given the reliance on business risk indicators, which are highly subjective, credit analysis itself is a highly subjective, opinion-based art. Credit analysis is not scientific; there is no formulaic method to determine the credit risk of an issuer or a specific type of debt. A significant amount of judgment goes into credit analysis.

Credit analysis can be subjective

Like M&A analysis, credit analysis is more an art than a science. Junior professionals will often try to draw credit or debt capacity conclusions solely from an assessment of financial risk (namely from credit and financial ratios). This would be an error. Both qualitative as well as quantitative factors need to be considered when performing credit analysis.

Figure 24.3 – Business Risk vs. Financial Risk

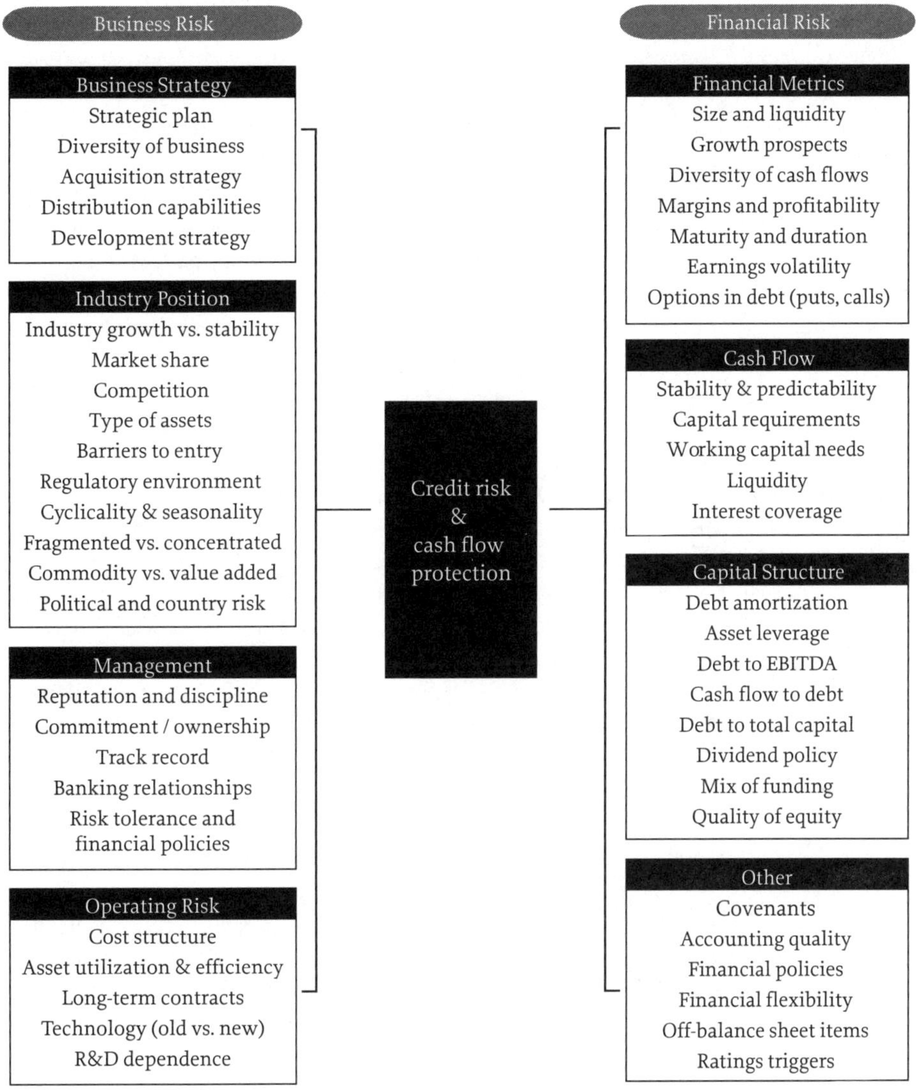

To further describe business and financial risk, let's consider two companies – UtilityCo and TechCo – and compare their credit risk.

> *UtilityCo is a gas utility and operates in a regulated environment, meaning a regulatory body, such as a state public utility commission, determines how much UtilityCo is allowed to earn on its capital. The regulatory environment provides for stable cash flows. Also, because another company cannot build gas pipelines into the homes of UtilityCo's clients, it has a fairly captive customer base. TechCo is a software company*

and develops educational software applications. TechCo has some products that have done well; however, the competition for new software applications is fierce and therefore TechCo commits significant resources to research and development of new software, some of which may never come to market.

Without knowing anything else about these two companies, we can say that the business risk of UtilityCo is lower than that of TechCo. There are many reasons for this, the most important of which is the stability of UtilityCo's cash flows. UtilityCo has a customer base that will continue to use gas day after day. Moreover, the likelihood of a competitor taking away its customers is low. TechCo, on the other hand, operates in a highly competitive business environment and there is no assurance that current customers of TechCo will be customers in the future. This affects cash flow sustainability.

We have determined that UtilityCo has lower business risk than TechCo, but we cannot yet determine whether UtilityCo has lower credit risk than TechCo. We first must layer in an assessment of each company's financial risk, which requires an analysis of the company's capital structure. If we assume that UtilityCo and TechCo have the same capital structure (meaning the same level of debt, the same level of periodic interest obligations, etc.), then we can conclude that UtilityCo has lower credit risk than TechCo. If, however, UtilityCo has high financial risk as a result of extremely high levels of debt, then it *could be* the case that UtilityCo has credit risk equal to or greater than TechCo. What is important to remember is that credit risk is a function of *both* business risk *and* financial risk.

Credit Risk Indicators

Table 24.4 describes some credit risk indicators. Size is a major consideration in credit analysis since larger companies can generally sustain disruption to their business or volatility to their cash flows better than smaller companies. New companies have higher business risk because their asset portfolios are less tested and less diversified, their managements have less experience running the companies, and the industries in which they operate tend to be more competitive. Older, more established companies, on the other hand, have weathered changes to their businesses and have proven they are able to survive cash flow crunches and business disruptions. Also, older, more established companies tend to have larger asset and capital bases than newer companies. Size gives lenders incremental comfort as larger companies have access to multiple financing markets so that, if they cannot access capital from one investor market such as the commercial paper market, for example, they might be able to tap another market, such as the syndicated bank loan market. Smaller companies usually do not have this flexibility. Also, larger companies tend to have assets or divisions which, if faced with a cash crunch, could be sold to reduce debt or used as collateral (or security) for additional debt. Note that these credit indicators, while a good rule of thumb, do not necessarily hold true for every single company. Some large companies and some companies that have been in business for a long time have high business risk, while some smaller and/or newer companies have low business risk. These are generalizations, to help better explain the drivers of credit risk.

Table 24.4 – Credit Risk Indicators

Credit risk	Business characteristics
Highest	Limited resources No track record No assets
Higher	Limited resources Limited track record Limited assets Need for capital New technologies and new market entrants
High	Growing track record Generally cash poor or cash constrained Potential for growth
Medium	Proven track record Cash generating Growing asset portfolio National footprint Branded products
Low	Proven track record Cash flow rich and asset-rich Financial flexibility International footprint Major brands
Lowest	Long-term proven track record World market leaders Cash and asset rich Significant financial flexibility Large market capitalizations

Note: these are generalizations. Credit analysis involves considering all of the business and financial risks of an individual company.

Another good indicator of credit risk is available cash. Recall that credit risk is a measure of how likely it is that a company can repay its debt obligations. Even if a company has extremely high business risk, if it regularly sits on significant cash reserves then creditors feel fairly certain that the company can service its debt obligations. Microsoft is a good example of this. Microsoft operates in an industry with high business risk; however, it is so cash-rich (even after the announcement of its special dividend in 2004) that its credit risk is low relative to its business risk. Also, although Microsoft's industry is high risk, Microsoft's market leadership position and size provides lenders more confidence that they will be repaid as compared with other software companies. Insurance companies are another good example. They generally sit on significant cash balances and therefore tend to have low credit risk, in spite of their high business risk.

Rating Agencies

Rating agencies developed at the beginning of the 20th century as third-party, intellectually independent arbiters of company credit risk. Using its own analytical framework, each rating agency ranks the credit risk of any issuer of debt or specific debt issuance by assigning the issuer and/or the debt a letter rating. Ratings provide a common language or shorthand way for investors to compare and contrast the credit risk of alternative debt investments.

Who is "biased"?

If rating agencies are considered independent *unbiased* arbiters of a company credit risk, *who is biased?* Most other constituents are biased because they have something at stake when it comes to a company's credit risk. For example, a company's management team is biased because it has an interest in raising low cost capital (the lower the risk, the lower the cost of capital). Investors are biased because they want to maximize their own return on their investments but generally do not want to take on excess risk. Investment bankers are biased because they make money when a company undertakes a transaction. Commercial bankers are biased because they have capital at risk when they loan money to a company.

Being biased is not necessarily a bad thing; it just means you have something at stake. A rating agency, on the other hand, should have nothing at stake when it issues a credit rating (other than a bad reputation if a specific credit analysis is wrong). Good credit analysis should be completely unbiased. If it is not, something other than the company's business and financial risk might weigh into the analytical credit conclusions.

Currently, there are four major rating agencies: Moody's Investor Service ("Moody's"), Standard and Poor's Rating Service ("S&P"), and Fitch and Dominion Bond Rating Service. Moody's and S&P are the most widely known. Fitch historically has been well-known within the interbank and structured finance markets, although it has made great strides recently within the U.S. corporate debt market. Although the rating agencies approach their analysis separately, empirical evidence shows fairly consistent rating outcomes from all four companies.

The NRSRO

The real name or designation for a rating agency is a **NRSRO** (Nationally Recognized Statistical Rating Organization). The designation as a NRSRO is provided by the SEC through a no-action letter.[1] In 2003, Dominion Bond Rating Service (DBRS) of Canada was recognized as the fourth NRSRO. Currently, there is some debate regarding the process by which an NRSRO designation is provided to rating agencies.

There are two types of ratings: (1) issuer ratings and (2) debt specific (or issue specific) ratings. Issuer ratings are based on the overall credit risk of the issuing entity and take into consideration the company's entire debt portfolio. Issuers are any entities that issue debt and can include corporations, financial institutions, structured financing entities, municipalities, and sovereign governments. Debt specific credit ratings take into consideration the credit risk of the issuer *and* the debt's specific features, which may provide an investor more or less security. Examples of specific debt features include whether the debt is secured or unsecured and/or whether it is senior or junior in terms of liquidation preference. A difference in ratings provided to a company is called **notching.** Notching is described in detail at the end of this chapter. Liquidation preference is described in Sources of Capital. (Ch.25)

If an entity would like to receive a rating, it would apply for a rating from one or more rating agencies. The process is much more involved for a company that is seeking its very first rating than for those seeking follow-on ratings. Once a rating is received, it is incumbent on the company (and expected by the rating agencies) to keep the rating agencies abreast of any developments. For ratings for new debt, issuers are interested not only in the rating it will receive from the rating agency for the new

[1] A **no-action** letter is a response from the SEC indicating that no civil or criminal action will be taken against an individual (broadly defined, which includes companies) engaging in a particular activity. Companies request a no-action letter from the SEC when the law is unclear or vague regarding something they plan to do. It allows the SEC the ability to review specific action prior to the action taking place. From the company's point of view, it ensures that the SEC will take no action against it since the company has essentially "cleared" the proposed action with the SEC prior to taking it.

debt but also the new debt's impact on any existing credit ratings that the issuer may have outstanding.

Usually, one credit analyst or a team of credit analysts from a rating agency covers a particular company. Credit analysts usually specialize in a particular industry and geographic region. Although a credit analyst covers a company, ratings decisions are usually made by a ratings committee which heavily weighs the opinion of the credit analyst. Because a company's management team is such an important business risk consideration in credit analysis, the management team (which includes the CFO, Treasurer and occasionally the CEO) meets periodically with the credit analyst from each rating agency.

Generally speaking, companies are not required to obtain credit ratings, but many do. Some of the benefits of obtaining a credit rating are listed below. Combined, these benefits are likely to provide for a reduced cost of borrowing.

1. Broadens and deepens the debt investor base
2. Enhances a company's recognition and credit standing in the market by providing an unbiased third-party perspective on the company's creditworthiness
3. Provides greater flexibility with market timing and structuring

Ratings advisory groups

Many investment banks have created an in-house Ratings Advisory Group. Bankers in this group assist clients through any rating agency process and are experts in credit analysis and the ratings process. Bankers from the Ratings Advisory Group work closely with M&A bankers on transactions which involve significant levels of debt. They also work closely with bankers in the Debt Capital Markets groups. Many of the bankers in the Ratings Advisory Group previously worked at one or more of the major ratings agencies and therefore have a deep understanding of how the ratings agencies analyze credit risk.

Ratings and Ratings Scales

Rating agencies provide investors with a third-party view of the overall credit risk or creditworthiness of a company. Ratings are opinions provided by an accredited rating agency. This is done via letter ratings and ratings scales. Ratings are intended to be comparable across industry groups, countries, and financial structuring. This means that an A1 rating from Moody's represents a certain level of credit risk – regardless of the industry or country of the company. Industry risk, country risk, and other specific risks are already factored into the A1 rating. As such, the user of the ratings should not have to make additional adjustments based on industry or country since the rating has already captured those risks as well as, in theory, all others. Ratings are not offers or recommendations to buy, sell, or hold a security. They are opinions on the credit quality or creditworthiness of a particular issuer on a particular loan or debt security.

Industry-specific credit risk

Most companies within a particular industry will naturally fall into the same general ratings classes since the inherent business risks of an industry play an important role in credit analysis. Industry risk, to a large degree, sets the upper limit of a company's credit rating. In highly competitive industries, such as technology, a company's market share or leadership position is extremely important in performing credit analysis. Industries viewed as having above average levels of business risk because of the cyclical or boom/bust nature of the industry include technology, commodity chemicals, integrated steel, airlines, oil and gas production, mining, apparel, and retail. Industries generally viewed as having below average levels of business risk include consumer products, retail food, and regulated utilities due to the ability of these sectors to weather macroeconomic changes without much disruption to their main businesses.

Issuers or specific debt obligations are classified from very low risk (AAA companies for S&P and Aaa for Moody's) to very high risk (before default, C- for S&P and C3 for Moody's). D is the lowest rating and is given when an issuer has failed to make an interest payment (hence it is in default). Companies in the AAA to A range include those that the rating agencies believe have the lowest likelihood of defaulting on their debt. They are generally large and extremely well run companies with low leverage relative to their asset bases, more than adequate liquidity, the ability to meet their cash obligations, and operate in relatively low risk businesses. They are run by reputable managers and are likely to have never defaulted on any debt. In keeping with the risk/reward tradeoff, because the risk of default is very low for companies with higher ratings, their cost of debt is very low.

Look up ratings definitions

Each rating agency has specific definitions for each of its ratings categories. In addition, definitions for ratings can differ between industries and classes of debt. Because of this, it is important to reference each rating agency for a list of its ratings definitions. Many bankers print out each rating agency's definitions and ratings grid and keep them all together for easy reference.

Standard and Poor's	www.standardandpoors.com
Moody's	www.moodys.com
Fitch	www.fitchratings.com
DBRS	www.dbrs.com

The cost of debt increases proportionately as an issuer moves down the ratings scale. This is because as an issuer moves down the ratings scale, the bankruptcy risk increases. If bankruptcy risk is high, then the likelihood that an investor will not receive his investment increases. Investors must be paid a premium (or a higher return) for this increased risk. This concept is further described at the beginning of Sources of Capital. (Ch.25)

Over time, investors have come to view everything lower than Baa3/BBB- as **high yield debt** (also referred to as **non-investment grade** or **junk debt**). Baa3/BBB- and above is considered **investment grade** debt (also referred to as **high grade** debt). Note that there are gradations within each rating. For example, S&P uses a plus (+), flat, and minus (-) demarcation with plus being stronger than flat and flat being stronger then minus. For example, a company might have a rating of BBB+, BBB, or BBB- with BBB+ being stronger than BBB and BBB being stronger the BBB-. Moody's has a similar ranking, but instead of plus, flat and minus, Moody's uses a 1, 2, 3 scale. Split ratings occur when Moody's and S&P are not in agreement on an issuer or a specific loan or security. For example, a split rating might be Baa3/BBB when an identical rating would be Baa3/BBB-. It is more common than not that the major ratings agencies are in agreement on the credit quality of an issuer or a specific debt issue.

Given the enhanced investor focus on liquidity over the past several years, Moody's has implemented a separate ratings grid which is meant to rate a company's liquidity only. Moody's calls this ratings grid **Speculative Grade Liquidity Ratings** (SGLs) and it is intended to measure the chance of default within the next twelve months.

As described at the beginning of the chapter, ratings agencies are only one of many constituents who perform credit analysis. Banks and syndication agents make lending and underwriting decisions on behalf of their clients, and the primary driver of these decisions is credit analysis. Syndication agents are described in Sources of Capital. (Ch.25) Credit due diligence is often as detailed, if not more detailed, than M&A due diligence. Due diligence is described in Deal Mechanics. (Ch.20) As in M&A due diligence, a primary objective in credit due diligence is determining the risk inherent in the projected future cash flows.

Management's role in a company's credit rating

The risk tolerance and track record of a company's managers play a significant role in determining a company's credit rating. Management's outlook on credit may be influenced by the tolerance of public equity investors who may be wary of investing in the shares of a highly leveraged company given the increased risk of default. Or management might be wary of high leverage for competitive reasons since larger and better capitalized competitors can apply pressure through lower pricing or increased promotional or capital spending to improve their position in the industry at the expense of more leveraged competitors. Philip Morris attacking RJR Nabisco via reduced cigarette prices following RJR's 1989 leveraged buyout is a classic example of this.

Recent high profile bankruptcies, such as those of Enron in 2001 and WorldCom in 2002, made investors especially critical of the rating agencies. In order to address these concerns and to provide earlier warning of impending defaults, the rating agencies have implemented stricter guidelines regarding their ratings, many of which are listed below:

1. Shorter time frames for issuers to meet their financial projections
2. Increased focus on earnings volatility
3. Increased focus on liquidity adequacy
4. Increased focus on senior management
5. More attention paid to accounting policies and disclosures
6. More attention paid to technical analysis of stock and bond prices
7. Ratings updated more quickly following a change in risk profile

> **Credit ratings are not static**
>
> A company's credit rating is not a static concept. Where a company falls along the credit spectrum should be evaluated regularly since various factors might affect a company's overall risk profile and/or its tolerance for financial risk. For example, only seven companies in non-financial industries (Johnson & Johnson, Pfizer, General Electric, Merck, United Parcel Service, Exxon Mobil, and Automatic Data Processing) had a AAA rating from S&P in 2004 while twenty non-financial companies had a AAA rating in 1984 (including Procter & Gamble, 3M, Coca-Cola and IBM) and fourteen non-financial companies had a AAA rating in 1994 (including BellSouth and Bristol-Myers Squibb). A lower rating is not necessarily indicative of weakened financial performance. Perhaps the industry risk of these companies changed from 1994 to 2004. Or it could be that management of these companies decided to take on additional debt and take advantage of a lower cost of capital, which subsequently changed their financial risk and credit rating. The important point to take away is that credit ratings change as the economy and businesses change.

Credit Ratios

Credit ratios are financial calculations used to help assess a company's financial risk. As shown in Figure 24.3, financial metrics are only one of many criteria used in performing credit analysis. It is important to remember that all of the criteria in Figure 24.3 should be considered together in assessing credit risk, and that financial credit ratios are not enough on their own to perform sound credit analysis.

Credit ratios are generally divided into four categories:

1. *Coverage ratios:* How much cash is available to service interest obligations?
2. *Leverage ratios:* How much debt does the company have?
3. *Operational ratios:* How profitable and well-managed is the company?
4. *Liquidity ratios:* Can the company service its short-term cash requirements?

The rating agencies provide general guidelines with respect to the credit ratio ranges they will accept for the various ratings categories within specific industries. This means that, for a given business risk, the rating agency will accept a certain level of financial risk for each rating category. A company already in its target rating of BBB+, for example, will try to maintain its debt levels such that its credit ratios fall comfortably within the allowed range required to achieve a BBB+ rating. A company that is trying to move up the ratings scale (such as from BB+ to BBB-) will manage its debt levels down to improve its credit ratios and strengthen its financial risk (for example by issuing equity and/or paying off debt).

Some adjustments may be required when calculating credit ratios to ensure comparability among companies under analysis. Off-balance sheet financing, securitized financing, leases, and underfunded pensions are examples of potential adjustments since these are areas in which companies have some latitude in terms of how this information is (or is not) disclosed.

Some of the most commonly used credit ratios are listed in Table 24.5. Coverage ratios are considered more indicative of credit risk than leverage ratios and operational ratios because they are directly representative of a company's ability to service its debt obligations. Liquidity ratios are also extremely important since, without adequate liquidity, a company cannot survive. Liquidity is cash to service day-to-day needs such as accounts payable, salaries, taxes when they come due, and vendor receivables. The vast majority of bankruptcies occur not as a result of lack of assets but due to a lack of liquidity and an inability to pay obligations as they come due.

Having assets does not mean having liquidity

It is important to understand that bankruptcy is not necessarily caused by a lack of assets but rather an inability to pay debt obligations (meaning interest and/or principal if principal is due) on a timely basis. Thus a company with $25 million of interest payments and no liquidity (or cash) to make those payments can go bankrupt even if it has $500 million in assets. Perhaps the company can sell some of its assets to pay the $25 million of interest payments, but if those assets are used in the production of goods or services, the company may not have the ability to sell the assets just to cover interest expense.

When performing credit analysis for a particular company, it is important to reference (from the rating agencies) the commonly used credit ratios for the industry in which the company operates. Certain credit ratios are used often in some industries and not at all in other industries.

Next to each credit ratio provide in Table 24.5, an (x) means the number is quoted as a multiple, a ($) means the number is quoted as an absolute dollar amount, and a (%) means the number is quoted as a percentage. Each of these credit ratios will be calculated in Table 24.7.

Table 24.5 – Commonly Used Credit Ratios

Coverage ratios [1]	
a. EBIT interest coverage (x)	EBIT / interest expense
b. EBITDA interest coverage (x)	EBITDA / interest expense
c. Cash flow coverage (x)	(Operating cash flow + interest expense) / interest expense
Leverage ratios [2]	
a. Debt to total capital (%)	Debt / (debt + preferred equity + common equity)
b. Debt to EBITDA (x)	Debt / EBITDA
c. Cash flow to debt (%)	Cash flow / debt
d. Absolute levels of debt ($)	Change in debt from period to period
Operational ratios	
a. Return on sales (%)	Earnings / sales
b. Return on capital (%)	Earnings / (debt + preferred equity + common equity)
c. Return on equity (%)	Earnings / common equity
d. EBIT margin (%)	EBIT / sales
e. EBITDA margin (%)	EBITDA / sales
Liquidity ratios	
a. Accounts receivable turnover (x)	Sales / accounts receivable
b. Accounts payable turnover (x)	Cost of goods sold / accounts payable
c. Working capital ($)	Current assets – current liabilities
d. Net working capital ($)	Working capital, excluding cash and short-term debt

[1] Both gross and net interest should be considered when performing credit analysis. Net interest expense is interest expense minus interest income. Net interest is more commonly used in Europe where companies tend to sit on larger cash balances (and thus have more interest income) than in the United States where companies generally have smaller cash balances.

[2] If the company has capital leases outstanding, these are generally included as debt in any credit ratio calculation. Similarly, minority interest should also be treated as a liability.

EBITDA is not equal to cash flow

EBITDA is a proxy for cash flow but it is not identical to cash flow. EBITDA is used because of its ease of calculation since it can be calculated using only the income statement. Cash flow, on the other hand, requires additional information from the income statement and the balance sheet (which together can be used to calculate the cash flow statement).

EBITDA is earnings before interest, taxes, and DD&A. Cash flow is earnings plus non-cash charges and further adjusted by changes in working capital. Although both EBITDA and cash flow adjust for DD&A, EBITDA is *before* interest and taxes, whereas cash flow is *after* interest and *after* taxes. Table 24.6 shows the difference between EBITDA and cash flow. For further clarification, refer to Financial Statement Basics. (Ch.3)

Table 24.6 – Calculation of EBITDA vs. Calculation of Cash Flow

	Calculation of EBITDA		**Calculation of cash flow**
	Sales		Sales
-	Non DD&A operating expenses	-	Non DD&A operating expenses
=	EBITDA	=	EBITDA
		-	DD&A
		=	EBIT
		-	Interest expense
		-	Taxes
		=	Net income (or earnings)
		+	DD&A
		+/-	Changes in deferred taxes [1]
		+/-	Changes in working capital [1]
		+/-	Other operating non-cash charges [1]
		=	Operating cash flow

[1] Deferred taxes, changes in working capital and other operating non-cash charges have a +/- sign in front of them because the amount is added or subtracted depending on whether those changes reflect a cash outflow or inflow. Recall from Financial Statements Basics (Ch.3) that increases in liabilities are a source of cash and increases in assets are a use of cash. Therefore, if the deferred tax liability in the balance sheet increased from $100 in 2005 to $150 in 2006, that would be a $50 source of cash and, on the cash flow statement, there would be an add-back of $50 for changes in deferred taxes.

[2] Includes cost of goods sold, SG&A and other operating expenses; excludes DD&A, interest and taxes.

Calculation of Credit Ratios

Recall SampleCo from Financial Statement Basics. (Ch.3) SampleCo's financial statements will be used to calculate the selected credit ratios in Table 24.5. Although credit ratios for SampleCo are calculated from 2005 financial statements, in practice a credit analyst would calculate these ratios for a historical period and for a three- to five-year projection period as well. Also, if liquidity is of concern for the company, then quarterly credit analysis should be performed, meaning debt levels and credit ratios should be reviewed quarter-to-quarter in addition to year-over-year. A person performing credit analysis would look at trends in the ratios, noting whether the ratios improve or worsen over the projection period. The trends over time are just as important as the ratios on day one and should be factored into the overall assessment of a company's credit quality.

Table 24.7 – SampleCo Credit Ratio Calculations

Balance Sheet	**2004**	**2005**
Assets		
Cash	$200	$165
Accounts receivable	125	150
Inventory	150	125
Other current assets	45	50
Total current assets	520	490
Gross PP&E	1,500	1,900
Less: Accumulated DD&A	(300)	(450)
Net PP&E	1,200	1,450
Other long-term assets	300	300
Goodwill	250	250
Total assets	**$2,270**	**$2,490**
Liabilities & Shareholders' Equity		
Short-term debt	$125	$100
Accounts payable	100	150
Salaries payable	75	65
Taxes payable	45	40
Total current liabilities	345	355
Deferred tax liabilities	200	225
Other long-term liabilities	120	120
Long-term debt	600	700
Common shareholders' equity	1,005	1,090
Total liabilities & equity	**$2,270**	**$2,490**

The footnotes to the financial statements should be reviewed when performing credit analysis in order to search for off-balance sheet liabilities, and also to better understand the nature of the company's debt. For example, if, after reading through SampleCo's notes to financial statements, you notice that all of its $700 of long-term debt is due in 13 months, this would dramatically affect your assessment of the company's credit risk. The maturity schedule of the $700 is not included in the balance sheet but generally would be listed in the notes to the financial statements.

Table 24.7 continued

Income Statement - for the year ending	2005
Revenues	$1,000
Cost of goods sold	(400)
Gross margin	600
Selling, general and administrative	(100)
Earnings before interest, taxes, DD&A (EBITDA)	500
Depreciation, depletion & amortization (DD&A)	(150)
Earnings before interest and taxes (EBIT)	350
Interest expense	(125)
Earnings before taxes	225
Income taxes	(90)
Net income	$135
Shares outstanding-basic	100
Earnings per share (EPS)-basic	$1.35
Dividends	$50
Dividends per share (DPS)	$0.50
Earnings to common	$85

Table 24.7 continued

Cash Flow Statement	2005
Operating	
Net income	$135
DD&A	150
Changes in deferred taxes	25
Changes in working capital	30
Cash flow from operations	340
Investing	
Capital expenditures	(400)
Other changes in assets/liabilities	0
Cash flow from investments	(400)
Financing	
Common dividends paid	(50)
Changes in short-term debt	(25)
Changes in long-term debt	100
Changes in equity	0
Cash flow from financing	25
Beginning cash	200
Total change in cash	(35)
Ending cash	$165

Inputs for credit calculations	2005
Short-term debt	$100
Long-term debt	700
Total debt	800
Common stockholder's equity	1,090
EBIT	350
EBITDA	500
Interest expense	125
Cash flow (also called operating cash flow or OCF)	$340

Table 24.7 continued

Coverage ratios	
EBIT interest coverage: EBIT / interest expense	
EBIT	$350
/ Interest expense	125
= EBIT interest coverage	2.8x
EBITDA interest coverage: EBITDA / interest expense	
EBITDA	$500
/ Interest expense	125
= EBITDA interest coverage	4.0x
Cash flow coverage: (cash flow + interest) / interest	
Cash flow + interest expense	$465
/ Interest expense	125
= Cash flow coverage	3.7x

Leverage ratios	
Debt to total capital: debt / (debt + equity)	
Debt	$800
/ (debt + equity)	1,890
= Debt to total capital	42%
Debt to EBITDA: debt / EBITDA	
Debt	$800
/ EBITDA	500
= Debt to EBITDA	1.6x
Cash flow to debt: cash flow / debt	
Cash flow	$340
/ Debt	800
= Cash flow to debt	43%

Table 24.7 continued

Operational ratios	
Return on sales: earnings / sales	
Earnings	$135
/ Sales	1,000
= Return on sales	14%
Return on capital: earnings / (debt + equity)	
Earnings	$135
/ Debt + equity	1,890
= Return on capital	7%
Return on equity: earnings / equity	
Earnings	$135
/ equity	1,090
= Return on equity	12%
EBIT margin: EBIT / sales	
EBIT	$350
/ Sales	1,000
= EBIT margin	35%
EBITDA margin: EBITDA / sales	
EBITDA	$500
/ Sales	1,000
= EBITDA margin	50%

Table 24.7 continued

Liquidity ratios	
A/R turnover: sales / accounts receivable	
Sales	$1,000
/ Accounts receivable	150
= A/R turnover	6.7x
A/P turnover: cost of goods sold / accounts payable	
Cost of goods sold	$400
/ Accounts payable	150
= A/R turnover	2.7x
Working capital	
Current assets	$490
- Current liabilities	355
= Working capital	$135
Net working capital	
Current assets (excluding cash)	$325
- Current liabilities (exlcuding short-term debt)	255
= Net working capital	$70

Credit Rating Notching

A rating differential for different debt issuances from the same issuer is referred to as notching. Notching is generally caused by (1) contractual subordination, (2) structural subordination, or (3) secured lending.

1. **Contractual subordination** results when debt is subordinated based on features written into the bank loan agreement or bond indenture (the contract between lender and borrower or between investor and issuer, respectively) which names it as "junior" or "subordinated" debt. Junior or subordinated debt gets paid in a bankruptcy situation only after senior debt has been repaid. Contractual subordination is discussed in more detail in Sources of Capital. (Ch.25)

2. **Structural subordination** results when the legal corporate structure of the issuer of the debt protects certain debt holders. For example, debt holders of

an operating subsidiary (Subsidiary) are generally better protected than debt holders of the parent holding company (Parent). This is because, in general, lenders to Subsidiary would put restrictions on the debt that prevent Subsidiary from dividending (or paying out) cash to Parent until Subsidiary's debt obligations were paid. Subsidiary could receive credit support as well from Parent in the form of a guarantee.

Figure 24.8 – Structural Subordination

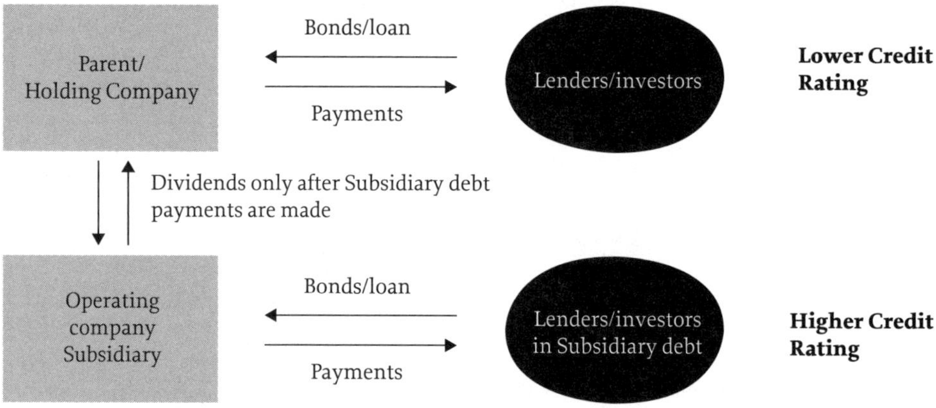

Notice in Figure 24.8 that Subsidiary lenders/investors are paid *before* any dividends are paid to the Parent (and therefore before Parent lenders/investors are paid). After the Subsidiary lenders/investors are paid, then Subsidiary can dividend cash to Parent. Parent can then use that cash to make payments to Parent lenders/investors. The debt of Parent is subordinated *structurally* (by the legal structure of the company) since Parent's lenders/investors get paid only after Subsidiary's lenders/investors are paid. In the event of bankruptcy, the assets of Subsidiary would likely be used to pay Subsidiary lenders/investors in full before any distribution of cash would be provided to Parent. In this example, Parent debt would have a lower credit rating than Subsidiary debt to reflect that structural subordination. In general, debt that is structurally subordinated like this will have a rating that is one or two notches lower than the subsidiary level debt (e.g., BBB+ for the senior Subsidiary's debt and BBB for the Parent's subordinated debt).

However, the credit rating notching is particularly dependent on what economic limitations exist between Parent and Subsidiary. If, for example, Parent can (through legal agreements) use Subsidiary's assets or cash when Parent is in financial distress, Subsidiary is not afforded much bankruptcy protection and its credit rating might be equal to that of Parent. If, however, Subsidiary's cash flows and assets are legally protected, even if Parent were in financial distress, and Subsidiary is a healthy stand-alone credit, Subsidiary is likely to have a stronger credit rating than Parent. Regulatory mandates on operating subsidiaries in regulated industries such as telecom, gas and electricity are considered favorably by the rating agencies since the limitations on distributing cash and assets to Parent are enforced by a third-party regulatory agency, not just enforced via legal contracts negotiated between Parent and Subsidiary on an arm's length basis.

3. In **secured lending**, debt is secured by certain assets, and if the company defaults on its debt, the lenders have claims to those assets.

Figure 24.9 – Secured Lending

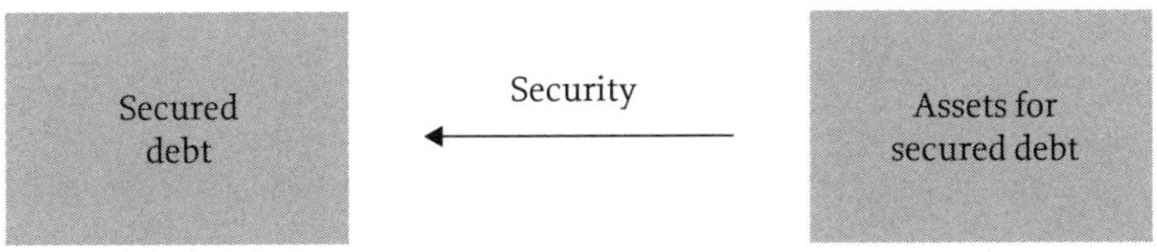

If debt is secured by an asset (shown by the straight line in the figure above), the secured lenders have a first claim to the secured asset(s) in the event of bankruptcy. Unsecured creditors do not have specific claims to any specific assets and would only be paid with cash from assets not used as security. Unsecured debt is therefore considered more risky than secured debt. As a result, secured debt will have a higher credit rating than unsecured debt, because it is more likely to be repaid, either from the earnings of the company or from the forced sale of the asset to repay the secured lender. A home mortgage is an example of a secured loan, and a foreclosure and subsequent sale of the foreclosed home by the bank is an example of what happens with a secured asset in a bankruptcy or liquidation scenario.

To further describe notching, refer to Figure 24.10. Notice the differences among the various issues of debt and the differences between the corporate credit rating and the issues of debt. This degree of notching is not uncommon for a company that issued debt both at the parent level and at the subsidiary level.

Figure 24.10 – Credit Rating Notching

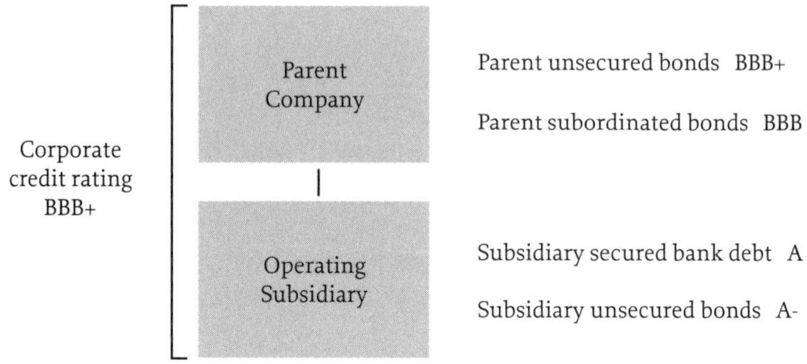

Calculating Debt Capacity

Debt capacity is a function of the prevailing market environment, a company's target capital structure, and/or the company's current or target credit rating. Once a target rating has been identified, the rating agencies will often provide a company's management with target ratios that are acceptable for that target rating. Debt capacity analysis involves solving for the amounts of debt that are allowed, given the target rating and the target credit ratios, and then factoring those numerical conclusions into a broader analysis of the company's business and financial risk. Refer to the business risk and financial risk factors listed in Table 24.3.

Let's consider a basic example to calculate debt capacity based on credit ratios only, while recognizing that other qualitative factors would play into the analysis, including the prevailing market enviroment. In Table 24.11 we have a company that generates $1,700 million per year of earnings before interest and taxes (EBIT). Currently, it has debt outstanding of $5,000 million and book value of equity of $7,000 million. The debt of $5,000 million has annual pretax interest expense of $400 million. The rating agencies have told the company that it must maintain an EBITDA interest coverage ratio of at least 3.0x or a debt to total capital ratio of 50 percent; otherwise it might be at risk for a credit downgrade.

To calculate debt capacity, first determine the target credit ratios. Basic algebra is then used to solve for total debt capacity. The unused debt capacity is the amount of total debt capacity less the existing debt.

Table 24.11 – Debt Capacity Analysis

$ millions

Pre-transaction assumptions		**Implied debt capacity from coverage limit**	
EBITDA	$1,700	EBITDA interest coverage minimum [1]	3x
Interest expense	400	EBITDA	$1,700
Debt	5,000	Implied interest expense [3]	567
Equity	7,000	Assumed interest rate on debt	8%
		= Debt capacity [3]	7,083
Credit ratios		- Existing debt	5,000
Current EBITDA interest coverage[1]	4.25x	= Available debt capacity	$2,083
Current debt to total capital[2]	41.7%		
		Implied debt capacity from leverage limit	
Target ratios to maintain rating		Debt to total capital limit [2]	50.0%
EBITDA interest coverage[1]	3x	Current equity	7,000
Debt to total capital[2]	50%	= Debt capacity [4]	7,000
		- Existing debt	5,000
		= Available debt capacity	$2,000

[1] EBITDA interest coverage = EBITDA / interest expense

[2] Debt to total capital = debt / (debt + equity)

[3] EBITDA interest coverage limit = 3x

x = interest expense	y = total debt capacity
3.0 = $1,700 / x	Interest expense = total debt × interest rate
3x = $1,700	$567 = y × 8%
x = ($1,700/3)	y = $567 / 0.08
x = $567	y = $7,083

With an EBITDA interest coverage limit of 3x this company can raise $2,083 of additional debt if that new debt had an interest rate of 8% ($7,083 - $5,000 = $2,083). If the company raised more than $2,083 of additional debt, the EBITDA interest coverage ratio would be less than 3x. (Recall that in coverage ratios, higher is better.)

[4] Debt to total capital limit = 50%

x = total debt or debt capacity

0.50 = x / (x + $7,000)

0.50 (x + $7,000) = x

0.50x + (0.50 x $7,000) = x

0.50x = $3,500

x = $7,000

With a debt to total capital limit of 50% this company can raise $2,000 of additional debt ($7,000 - $5,000 = $2,000). If the company raised more than $2,000 of additional debt, the debt to total capital ratio would be greater than 50%

Debt capacity vs. acquisition firepower

It is important to differentiate between the debt capacity of a stand-alone entity (of which an example was provided in Table 24.11) and the acquisition firepower in the context of an acquisition. When considering debt capacity in the context of an acquisition, it is important to remember that you need to consider the acquired cash flow and the acquired credit risk of Target *in conjunction* with the cash flow and credit risk of Acquiror.

Changes in Credit Risk

What happens if a company moves outside of its acceptable credit ratio ranges? This might happen due to a large debt-financed acquisition, the beginning of a major construction project, or just a degradation of credit quality. There are three levels of rating agency action that can take place if there has been a change to a company's credit risk. They are: (1) credit outlooks; (2) credit watch; and (3) confirmation of a credit upgrade or downgrade. General descriptions of these three metrics are provided below but you should refer to each individual rating agency for its specific definitions of credit outlook, credit watch, and confirmation.

Every rating has a **credit outlook** that is an assessment of the *potential* direction of a longer term rating. It is not necessarily indicative of a credit watch action or an impending credit upgrade or downgrade. For S&P the credit outlooks are positive, negative, stable, developing, and not meaningful.

Being on **credit watch** means that the rating agency is paying particularly close attention to the issuer with a special focus on shorter term events such as mergers, acquisitions, or restructurings. For S&P, a negative credit watch means that the rating *may* be lowered (but it has not yet been lowered). A positive credit watch means that the rating *may* be raised (but it has not yet been raised). A developing credit watch means that the rating *may* be raised, lowered, or remain the same.

A **confirmation** of a credit upgrade or downgrade is an actual change in rating. Sometimes confirmations in upgrades or downgrades are preceded by a credit watch; however, this is not always the case, especially if the event which causes the credit upgrade or downgrade occurred with little notice (for example, a major oil discovery or an explosion at a primary factory, respectively).

When determining whether a company should be on credit watch or whether a confirmation should be made to upgrade or downgrade the issuer, the rating agencies will perform the same fundamental credit analysis they perform when the rating is first provided. They will weigh both business risk and financial risk and make a determination given the most current information. A credit downgrade or a negative credit watch has many implications, the most important of which are higher borrowing costs and more restrictive covenants for the company. The opposite is true for a credit upgrade or a positive credit watch; lower borrowing costs and fewer and/or less restrictive covenants for a company.

Private Companies

Although companies that do not have public debt outstanding are not as likely to seek credit ratings, the mechanics to perform credit analysis and debt capacity analysis for private companies are the same as they are for public companies. For private companies without public debt, their borrowed funds will likely come from a bank or private investors. The bank or investors will assess credit risk and determine the return they require for a private company's debt. Like public debt investors, private investors may put certain restrictions, or covenants, on the company with respect to coverage ratios and amounts of leverage. In general, these restrictions will limit how much leverage a private company can assume. When new capital is required, lenders will re-assess the credit risk of the company (in the same way that the rating agencies perform credit analysis) pro forma for the new asset or transaction and will make a credit decision for the new project. One key difference between private companies and public companies is liquidity and access to capital. However, it is also the case that some private companies have a financial sponsor (such as a private equity fund or a leveraged buyout fund), which is often seen as a positive characteristic from a credit perspective since it can serve in the same role as a parent company guarantee -- that of an additional source of capital or cash flow protection in the event of financial distress.

Sources of Capital

Chapter 25

The truth is, there is money buried everywhere,
and you have only to go to work to find it.

Henry David Thoreau

Most companies have a wide range of financing options available to them. Determining the optimal combination of debt and equity a company should use to fund its operations requires an understanding of the company's credit risk, its cash requirements, the sources of capital available to it, and the market for those sources of capital (meaning investors' appetite and the available supply of money). This chapter will discuss (1) financing, (2) the various sources of capital available to companies, and (3) the differences between these various markets for capital.

The Capital Markets Group

Within an investment bank, bankers in the Capital Markets Group help companies raise money in the private and public markets. The Capital Markets Group is generally separated into two main divisions: Equity Capital Markets and Debt Capital Markets. Within both Equity Capital Markets and Debt Capital Markets there are sub-groups. For example, within Debt Capital Markets there is (1) the Fixed Income Group, which issues bonds and preferred stock for companies (called fixed income because the investors receive a fixed stream of periodic payments), (2) the High Yield Group, which raises capital for high yield issuers, and (3) the Syndicated Finance Group, which provides large bank loans to clients and then sells off (syndicates) participation in the loans to other banks and broker-dealers.

The Capital Markets Group works directly for clients and therefore has access to confidential inside information. The bankers in the Capital Markets Group work with relationship bankers from the industry-specific Corporate Finance Group as well as with execution bankers from product groups such as M&A and leveraged finance.

Liquidation Preference

Until now, debt has been discussed as a broad category of capital. However, there are numerous forms of debt that a company can issue, each with a different risk/reward profile. In order to describe the risk/return trade-off for a debt holder, let's revisit the concept of bankruptcy risk.

In a bankruptcy, the obligations of a company are subject to a **liquidation preference**, which is the order in which capital providers are repaid with the liquidation value of the assets. Liquidation preference is also called **priority of claim. Liquidation value** is the cash value received from selling off assets; this is different from the book value of assets.

The reason liquidation value is different from, and often lower than, book value is because a liquidation is, in common parlance, a "fire sale" whereas book value is an accounting value based on historical cost and accumulated depreciation. Liquidations are seldom voluntary and potential buyers know this. This gives buyers negotiating leverage which translates into low fire sale prices relative to sale prices in a non-financial distress situation. In a fire sale, the goal is simply to find the buyer who will pay the highest price in cash to the bankrupt company.

Any cash generated from the liquidation (or the sale of assets) is used to pay liabilities and debt first, and the equity holders are paid last. In most liquidation scenarios, little is left over for the equity holders. That is, the company's liabilities and debt often exceed the liquidation value of the company's assets, leaving nothing for the equity holders. From an investor's perspective, the lower the liquidation preference of a given investment, the less likely the investment would be paid in a bankruptcy and therefore the greater the risk borne by the investor. Since investors require a higher return for capital that is lower in liquidation preference, the cost of financing increases for a company as it issues capital that is farther down the capital structure. Thus equity is traditionally the most expensive form of capital.

In addition to credit and bankruptcy risk, interest payments are generally tax-deductible whereas dividend payments to equity holders are not tax-deductible. This is another reason why debt is considered cheaper than equity -- for every dollar paid in interest to a debt holder, the issuing company is allowed to deduct it for tax purposes. Therefore, the cost of debt is reduced by the company's effective tax rate. For example, if the interest required for new debt is 8 percent and the company's effective tax rate is 40 percent, the after-tax cost of debt is only 4.8 percent.

$$8\% \text{ pretax cost of debt} \times (1 - 40\% \text{ tax rate}) = 4.8\% \text{ after-tax cost of debt}$$

Why don't companies issue only debt?

If debt is cheaper than equity, new students of finance often ask "Why doesn't a company fund itself entirely with debt?" There is an optimal amount of debt a company can issue at which point additional debt would make the company too risky (the bankruptcy risk would be too high) and the cost of debt would increase correspondingly. Almost any basic corporate finance textbook will cover this theoretical concept in detail. See the Appendix for a list of recommended corporate finance textbooks.

Liquidation preference means some types of debt are paid before other types of debt. Since the return an investor requires for debt is closely linked to the liquidation preference, features written into the debt that protect the debt investor reduce the cost of debt to the issuer. For example, subordinated debt has a lower liquidation preference than senior debt. In a liquidation scenario, *all* senior debt must be repaid before *any* subordinated debt can be repaid. The return required by subordinated debt investors is higher than the return required by senior debt investors because the likelihood that the subordinated debt would be paid back in full in a default scenario is lower than for the senior debt. The higher return for the subordinated debt holder is matched by the higher risk that the investor undertakes by virtue of the lower liquidation preference of the subordinated debt.

Liquidation vs. reorganization

It should be noted that although there is a liquidation preference, rarely do companies actually *liquidate*. Instead, companies that default on their debt obligations will file for Chapter 11 Reorganization Protection under the Bankruptcy Reform Act before actually liquidating. While in Chapter 11, the company would try to "work out" its debt obligations before actually liquidating. In fact, most Chapter 11 filings result in negotiated debt agreements, not liquidations. Liquidation occurs once a company files for Chapter 7 protection.

Short-term vs. long-term debt

From a legal perspective, short-term debt and short-term payables (often called trade debt) are generally *pari passu* (on equal footing) with long-term debt. However, in a restructuring, certain short-term creditors or vendors whose relationships are critical to the company's operations during the restructuring period are designated as "critical vendors" and are paid before other creditors in order to engender goodwill and to allow the company to continue to operate during the restructuring.

In the following liquidation example, notice that, in a bankruptcy situation, a subordinated debt holder is in the least advantageous repayment position of all debt holders. In this example, the subordinated debt investors only receive $0.47 on each dollar invested, whereas all other debt holders recoup their entire investment. Said differently, the subordinated debt investors in this example lose 53 percent of their investment. Note also that the preferred equity and common equity holders lose their entire investment.

Table 25.1 – Liquidation Example

$ millions, except per dollar value

Assets	Liquidation value [1]	Debt holders	Book value	Amount received	% Paid	Per $
Cash	$30	Short-term debt	$100	$100	100%	$1.00
Accounts receivable	40	Senior secured debt	200	200	100%	$1.00
Inventory	50	Trade payables	90	90	100%	$1.00
Buildings	240	Senior unsecured debt	220	220	100%	$1.00
Other machinery	200	Subordinated debt	275	130	47%	$0.47
Long-term assets	130	Preferred equity	125	0	0%	$0.00
Real estate	50	Common equity	1,000	0	0%	$0.00
	$740	Total	$2,010	$740	37%	$0.37

[1] Liquidation value is not equal to accounting book value

If a company issues debt, it must pay its lenders or debt investors periodic interest payments (unless it is a zero coupon bond, which is described later in the chapter). Interest payments are paid out of a company's operating cash flows. If a company is doing well and cash flows are strong, it can sustain a higher level of fixed interest payments.

However, what if the company is not doing well (either because of macroeconomic factors or company-specific factors)? If the company does not have enough **liquidity** (or assets which can quickly convert to cash to service its fixed interest obligations), it will default on its obligations and may be forced to refinance its debt obligations at higher rates or file for bankruptcy protection. In some forms of debt, if a company misses an interest payment on that debt, there is an **acceleration clause** in the debt agreement that renders the total debt due earlier than originally contracted. In fact, most loans and some bonds have **cross-default provisions** (also called **cross-acceleration rights)** whereby all of the company's outstanding debt comes due if the company misses an interest payment on any of its debt.

Payment default vs. technical default

There is a difference between default due to missing an interest or principal payment and "technical default," which is caused by failing to meet a specified covenant. Covenants are restrictions on the borrower put in place by the lender, such as a limit on future borrowing or maintaining specific credit ratios, while the debt is outstanding. Covenants will be described in more detail later in the chapter. Payment default is more serious than technical default.

It is important to note that any debt or equity issued by a company to investors can be given special features. A company can make any deal it wants with investors and the investors can then price that investment accordingly. The capital markets are efficient, meaning that features put into securities to either increase or decrease risk will be reflected by the price investors are willing to pay for certain investments. The spectrum of sources of capital available to a company is limited only by the limits of financial creativity. New securities are created regularly as investment banks try to develop additional tools to match their clients' needs. All securities, however, fall somewhere within the financing spectrum described in this chapter.

Financing Glossary Terms

Before discussing various sources of capital, let's review some basic financing terms.

Debt: Debt is capital that is borrowed and must be repaid by the company. Often (but not always) the borrower must pay periodic interest on the borrowed funds. Debt investors have claims to their invested capital only (including any interest and underlying assets if the debt is secured). Debt investors are not owners of the company. Debt is higher in liquidation preference than equity. Some debt can be bought and sold in secondary markets for prices that are below or above the face value of the debt, depending on whether the likelihood of debt repayment decreased or increased, respectively, from the time the debt was issued. In most cases, interest payments on debt are tax-deductible. Therefore, issuing debt has tax advantages that issuing equity does not.

Equity: Equity is capital that is provided to a company in exchange for an ownership stake in the company. In liquidation, equity holders get paid after all other providers of capital. Individual units of equity are called stock or shares. Some equity can be bought and sold in a secondary market. Equity holders are entitled to any dividends the company decides to pay; however, unlike interest payments, dividends are not a fixed obligation, meaning that the company can choose whether or not to pay them. Dividends on common stock are not tax-deductible. In most cases, dividends on preferred stock are not tax-deductible (although dividends on certain preferred securities, which have features that are more like debt than equity, can be tax-deductible).

Borrower or issuer: "Borrower" is the entity borrowing money from a bank whereas "issuer" usually refers to an entity issuing securities (e.g., bonds, stock) directly to investors. Entities can be corporations, partnerships, municipalities, governments, agencies, non-profit organizations, schools and universities, trusts, estates and individuals. Agencies are government-sponsored, but not government guaranteed, entities such as the U.S. Postal System, Freddie Mac and Fannie Mae.

Lender or investor: Both lenders and investors are entities that provide money to borrowers or issuers. Banks and finance companies are considered lenders whereas individuals, institutions, and other non-banking entities are considered investors. There are both debt investors and equity investors.

Guarantor: A guarantor is an entity (can be a company or an individual) that provides credit support to a borrower. For example, if an operating subsidiary is issuing debt, the parent company might choose to serve as the guarantor such that if the operating subsidiary defaults on its debt, the lenders or investors can look to the parent company for repayment. It is the corporate equivalent of someone co-signing on an individual loan.

Short-term debt vs. long-term debt: Short-term debt is repaid within one year. Long-term debt is repaid in a period of time greater than one year.

Maturity or term: The amount of time (generally quoted in days for short-term debt and years for long-term debt) during which debt is outstanding, or until the security principal is due.

Par value: The nominal value or face value of debt or equity. Most bonds are sold in par value units of $1,000. This means that if a company issues $250 million in bonds, it will issue 250,000 actual bonds ($250,000,000 / $1,000 = 250,000). Most equity is sold in par value units of $0.01 or with no par value per share. Par value is not equal to market value. The market value of a security can be below, above, or at par.

Liquidity: Liquidity is the nominal amount outstanding of any particular issue not held by insiders. For example, a $500 million bond issue sold in the public market has $500 million of liquidity. Or, consider a company with an equity value of $1 billion but 70 percent is held by insiders. This company would only have 30 percent or $300 million of liquidity (or float).

Liquidity is important since the size of an issue will determine the supply of that issue in the secondary market or the number of potential buyers and sellers at any given time. The greater the liquidity, the easier for an investor to sell her position if she needs to without affecting the price upon selling the investment. Liquidity is valued by investors since it provides them greater flexibility if they need to sell their securities in the open market. Because of this, the market generally favors larger issues over smaller ones. Do not be confused by "liquidity" related to the nominal amount of any particular issue and "liquidity" (or ability to convert assets to cash) available to service short-term debt and vendor obligations. The first is related to how much in securities are available in the public market; the second is related to how much available cash a company has to service its debt obligations and other liabilities.

Interest rate: The annual rate owed on a loan. The interest rate can be a floating rate or a fixed rate. Floating rates are often tied to LIBOR or the prime rate. LIBOR is the London Interbank Offer Rate which is the rate of interest at which banks borrow money from one another in the London Interbank Market.

Coupon rate: The rate used to calculate an annual payment to bond investors. Coupon interest payments are generally paid semiannually, although the rate quoted is an annual number. A bond coupon rate is generally fixed (but not always) and is set at the offering date. The coupon rate is not necessarily equal to the return (or yield) on the debt to an investor. See "yield" for a description of a debt holder's return.

Pricing: Pricing is the way in which banks or investors determine how much an investment is worth (to them). A bank or investor will consider the structure and terms of the proposed debt issue, in addition to the credit risk of the debt, and pay a price based on those factors and the availability of alternative investment opportunities. Pricing for bonds is quoted as a percentage or factor of 100. For example, if a bond prices at 99.875, it means that for every $1,000 it will owe in principal in the future, the company raised $998.75. If a bond prices below 100, it sold at a "discount;" if it prices above 100, it sold at a "premium;" and if it prices at 100, it sold at "par." Regardless of whether the bond is sold at a discount, at a premium, or at par, the issuer must pay 100 percent of the face value at maturity to the bondholders.

Credit spreads: Most debt securities are quoted and priced based on a credit spread (quoted in basis points) over an index. The credit spread measures the amount of credit risk an investor will assume for investing in a particular company or issuance (as opposed to investing in a "risk-free" investment such as a U.S. Treasury bond) based on a given maturity. Since U.S. Government Treasury issued securities are considered "risk-free", U.S. Government Treasury bonds, notes and bills are considered the **benchmark** rate. The credit spread is the numerical measure of the credit risk of the debt and is quoted as a number above the reference rate or benchmark rate. For example, the credit spread on ABC Company's bond might be 120 basis points over the 10-year U.S. Treasury bond. If the 10-year U.S. Treasury Bond is trading at a yield of 4.7 percent, that would mean that ABC Company's 10-year bond would yield 5.9 percent (4.7% + 1.2% = 5.9%). One basis point or 1 bps is equal to one hundredth of a percentage point or 0.01 percent or 0.0001. In the U.S., the index for bank debt is generally LIBOR or the prime rate. The index for bonds and other capital securities is the U.S. Treasury bond with the same maturity as the debt (e.g., a five-year bond would be priced based on a credit spread over the the benchmark rate which is the current yield on a five-year U.S. Treasury bond). If a credit spread over the corresponding treasury bond is small relative to other credit spreads, it is referred to as "tight" or "narrow." If a credit spread is large, it is referred to as "wide." If a credit spread for Company A is smaller than for Company B, Company A's credit spread is referred to as being "inside" Company B and Company B's credit spread is considered "outside" Company A.

Yield: Yield represents the rate of return on a bond based on the coupon and the price at which the investor bought the bond. Mathematically, yield is the discount rate or rate of return required by the debt investor, or the annual coupon rate received on a bond divided by the purchase price. Given a certain purchase price, the yield is the internal rate of return (the IRR) on the investment. The **yield to maturity** is the rate of return an investor earns on the bond based on the remaining life of the bond. The **yield to call** is the return on the bond based on the earliest call date. Calls are options that allow the company to repurchase the debt at an earlier date than the maturity date, usually at a premium. Price and yield have an inverted relationship, which means if the price of a bond rises, its yield falls, and if the price of a bond falls, its yield rises. While this may sound confusing, looking at it from a mathematical perspective should make it clearer. Since yield is equal to the coupon divided by the price (yield = coupon / price), if the purchase price rises (divisor gets larger), mathematically, the yield (quotient) falls. Similarly, if the price falls (divisor gets smaller), mathematically, the yield (quotient) increases. Recall that in most bonds, the bond coupon rate is fixed. However, since prices change daily, the bond's yield also changes daily even though the coupon rate is fixed.

***Yield curve*:** A graph depicting the rate of return for bonds of varying maturities is called a yield curve. Although a yield curve can be drawn for any issuer, it generally refers to the yield curve for U.S. Treasury bonds. The yield on U.S. Government Treasury debt is considered the proxy for risk-free debt. In general, short-term U.S. government bonds have a lower interest rate than medium to long-term bonds. This is because the shorter the period of time until maturity, the smaller the risk that the government will default. In other words, investors have a better sense for the state of the economy in the near term than they do in the long-term. A yield curve is generally drawn with the number of years to maturity on the X-axis and the interest rate on the Y-axis. Occasionally, the yield curve is inverted, which means that long-term debt has a lower interest rate than medium-term debt. An inverted yield curve is not common, but does occur from time to time.

***Amortizing debt vs. a bullet payment*:** Amortizing debt is debt in which the principal is gradually repaid over the life of the loan. In comparison, debt with a bullet payment has a one-time repayment of the entire principal at the end of the term. Loans are generally amortizing whereas bonds generally have bullet payments. Some bonds, however, have **sinking funds** which the issuer pays into that mimic amortization. A sinking fund is managed by a trustee and the issuer makes periodic payments to the fund which represent the repayment of some of the outstanding debt. With every payment by the issuer into the sinking fund, the repayment risk to the investor is reduced.

Bid offer spread: The offer price is the price a seller wants for a security. The bid price is the price an investor is willing to pay. The bid offer spread is the difference between the offer price and the bid price.

Building the book: In a securities offering, investors submit indications of the amount of securities they want to purchase and at what price. The book is the list of committed indications (or commitments) received by the underwriter from all the potential investors. The underwriter builds the book by collecting commitments.

***Syndicate group or syndication group*:** A syndicate group is a group of banks or investors who together provide capital to a borrower. In addition to banks, prime funds, and insurance companies, more recently other institutional investors and hedge funds also participate in syndicate groups. A syndicated loan is a loan arranged by a syndicate group, and a syndicated line of credit is a revolving line of credit arranged by a syndicate group. Although numerous banks and lenders might participate in a syndicated loan, one or two **lead arrangers** or agents are generally chosen to manage the process. The agent bank writes an offering memorandum and circulates it with a term sheet. A loan term sheet is a list of the most important information related to the loan, including the name of the borrower, the size of the issue, important financial and credit statistics of the issuer, the interest rate of the debt, and important features related to the debt such as the term, whether it is fixed or floating, and the major covenants that will be required of the borrower. The agent bank then takes commitments from members of the syndicate group. Each member has a certain percentage it commits to holding (this is called its **hold level**). When the syndicated deal closes, the agent allocates the credit exposure among the participating lenders. Lenders are often allowed to sell down their hold positions to other banks or investors after the deal has closed, thereby creating a secondary market for the syndicated loan. Syndicated loans evolved during the late 1980s and early 1990s to allow for liquidity in the bank market as banks took more active steps to manage risk by minimizing the percentage of any particular loan kept on the agent's own books and thus reducing the lender's credit exposure to any particular borrower or industry.

Underwritten deals vs. best efforts deals: Traditionally, banks would **underwrite** security offerings for companies, which meant the investment banks provided the total amount of capital to the issuer and then syndicated the securities out to a group of investors. In such an arrangement, the bank puts its own capital at risk and assumes the **execution risk** (or the risk that the deal would not be completed). Underwritten deals are also called committed deals. Today, banks sell deals both on an underwritten basis and on a best efforts basis. **Best efforts** basis means that the bank will try its best to raise the desired funds. However, if the desired amount of capital cannot be raised (based on the agreed-to terms), the bank does not have to provide the total amount requested by the company, thereby transferring the execution risk to the issuer. Since a bank assumes more risk in an underwritten deal, the fees on underwritten deals are higher than the fees on best efforts deals. As a result, companies will only *pay* for an underwritten deal when they need the committed funds from the bank.

In a securities offering, an investment bank (or two) will be named to manage the issuance process. This lead bank is called the **bookrunner** or the **joint bookrunner** (if there is more than one lead bank). In addition, there are a number of other syndicate banks (other banks added to the selling team in exchange for a share of the fees). Each of the banks involved is allotted a certain number of securities for sale, and each is then responsible for selling those securities to investors. The number of shares allotted to an investment bank is largest for the lead underwriters with smaller quantities given to the non-lead banks.

Covenants: Covenants are promises and restrictions in the bank loan agreement or **bond indenture** (legal documents governing the agreement between the borrower and the investor). The purpose of a covenant is to protect the lender or investor by ensuring that the borrower does or does not do certain things so as not to jeopardize the investment. Borrowers can default on debt by either not making an interest or principal payment (payment default) or by breaching a covenant (technical default). If an issuer breaches an affirmative covenant, there is usually a grace period for the issuer to address the breach. If, however, an issuer breaches a negative covenant, this usually results in immediate default without a grace period.

> ***Affirmative covenants***: Affirmative covenants are requirements which the borrower must *affirmatively* do. Examples include the payment of interest and the requirement to pay taxes and fees. Other examples include maintaining its corporate existence in good standing and filing relevant documents in a timely manner with the SEC, if required.
>
> ***Negative covenants***: Negative covenants are restrictions or things that the company *cannot* do. Examples include limits on future borrowing, limits on capital spending, and limits on asset sales.
>
> ***Financial covenants***: Financial covenants, such as requirements to maintain certain credit ratios, limits on capital expenditures, net worth requirements, and cash flow or interest coverage requirements, are often included in a loan agreement or bond indenture.

Initial public offering *(IPO)*: An IPO is the first public issuance (sale) of a company's common equity.

Follow-on offering: A follow-on offering is any equity offering (sale) done by a company after its IPO. It may also be called an "add-on offering".

Primary offering: An offering (sale) by a company of new shares to the public, as opposed to a secondary offering of existing shares.

Secondary offering: A secondary offering refers to the public offering (sale) of equity owned by selling shareholders (as opposed to a primary offering, which is the sale of shares by a company). With a primary offering, the company gets the money. With a secondary offering, the selling shareholders get the money. In recent years the terminology has blurred and "secondary" and "follow-on" are sometimes used synonymously.

Block trade: A block trade is a negotiated sale of a large block of securities to one or a few investors. It is also called an **overnight transaction**. Generally, a bank offers to buy a set number of securities at a set price and assumes the risk of subsequently placing the shares in the public market (just as in an underwritten offering).

Fully marketed vs. accelerated marketing: They both refer to the amount of time a company spends meeting with investors prior to selling securities to the public. With a fully marketed transaction, the company (with its bankers) meets with various investors to discuss the upcoming offering. An accelerated transaction involves fewer investor meetings than a fully marketed transaction. Accelerated marketing generally allows for faster execution but it may also lead to lower pricing for the offering (lower price means fewer proceeds to the seller). A fully marketed transaction may take longer than an accelerated transaction, but it also provides for the greatest demand since the issuing company communicates its story to a greater number of investors.

Distribution: The act of selling securities to investors (both institutional and retail investors) is called **distribution**. For an investment bank to be successful in any securities offering, it must have a solid distribution capability. In fact, many of the investment banking mergers and acquisitions which take place are driven by a desire for investment banks to gain access to a wider distribution base for their securities offerings. Distribution capabilities are important both at the time of the offering as well as in the **after market** or **secondary market**, which is the period of time after the initial security offering when securities are bought and sold.

Let's review the various terms in the following press release issued by FinanceCo.

San Francisco, Aug 25, 2006 – FinanceCo Inc. sold $1.5 billion of debt in two parts, a spokesperson from joint lead manager BankEast said on Tuesday. BankWest was the other joint lead manager for the ten-year notes. BankNorth was the lead agent for the 20-year notes.

Borrower – FinanceCo.

First Tranche

Amount $750 million	Coupon 4.125 percent	Maturity 8/15/2016
Type bonds	Issue price 99.687	1st pay date 2/15/2007
Moody's/S&P A3/A	Spread 75 bps over treasuries	

Second Tranche

Amount $750 million	Coupon 5.375 percent	Maturity 8/15/2026
Type bonds	Issue price 99.594	1st pay date 2/15/2007
Moody's/S&P A3/A	Spread 58 bps over treasuries	

This issue has two separate **tranches** (sub-groups) of debt, each of which is being led by a different bank. Both tranches are being issued and priced at the same time.

Amount: par value or face value of $750 million per tranche or $1.5 billion in total.

Coupon: annual interest payment on the notes. Although the coupon is quoted as an annual rate, investors are usually paid semiannually. For example, investors in the second tranche will receive 2.688 percent (5.375 / 2) of their principal amount every six months as an interest payment.

Maturity: date that the notes must be paid in full – 8/15/2016 for tranche one and 8/15/2026 for tranche two. Correspondingly, the notes in tranche one are 10-year notes and the notes in tranche two are 20-year notes.

Issue price: pricing based on investor demand for the notes. FinanceCo raised $747.65 million ($750 × 0.99687) in tranche one and $746.96 million ($750 × 0.99594) in tranche two. Note that even though both tranches priced at a discount, at maturity FinanceCo will have to pay $750 million to the investors of tranche one and $750 million to the investors of tranche two in addition to semiannual interest payments.

1st pay date: the date investors will receive their first coupon payment. For example, on 2/15/2007, the investors in tranche two will receive 2.688 percent multiplied by the dollar amount of notes they purchased in the offering.

Moody's/S&P: most recent credit ratings for this debt.

Spread: credit spread, for the bonds, over treasuries. This means that ten-year U.S. Treasury bonds were trading at 3.375 percent (4.125 - 0.750 percent) and twenty-year U.S. Treasury bonds were trading at 4.795 percent (5.375 - 0.58 percent) the day these notes were sold.

Sources of Capital

Capital can be grouped into five general categories: (1) short-term debt; (2) senior long-term debt; (3) subordinated debt; (4) preferred equity; and (5) common equity. The classes of capital are described briefly here and then described in more detail on the following pages.

1. ***Short-term debt:*** Short-term debt is used to fund working capital or seasonal financing needs and is generally due within one year. Examples of short-term debt are bank lines of credit and commercial paper.

2. ***Senior long-term debt:*** Senior long-term debt is generally used to fund capital expenditures or other long-term needs and is generally payable in more than one year. Senior debt is higher in liquidation preference than subordinated debt. Although debt holders are legally entitled to a periodic stream of interest payments and the repayment of their principal, debt holders do not own a stake

of the company. Long-term debt can be bank loans, bonds, or notes. Convertible debt, which can be senior debt or subordinated debt, is a security that converts into equity at some time in the future based on a predetermined conversion ratio or based on some agreed upon triggering event. The calculation to convert debt to shares of stock can be found in Financial Statement Basics. (Ch.3)

3. ***Subordinated debt***: Subordinated debt is subordinated to senior debt in terms of liquidation preference. Due to the lower liquidation preference, the rate of return required by subordinated debt holders is higher than for senior debt holders. Otherwise, subordinated debt features are generally similar to senior debt.

4. ***Preferred equity:*** Preferred equity is lower in liquidation preference than subordinated debt but higher than common equity. Depending on the preferred stock's features, it can be considered more like equity or more like debt. Preferred equity holders receive a dividend based on a preset rate of return. Preferred dividends are usually **cumulative**, meaning that the company must pay any dividends in arrears (dividends which have accumulated but which have not yet been paid) before it can begin to pay any new preferred dividends or common dividends. Preferred equity can also have convertible features like convertible debt. Since preferred equity receives a fixed, preset rate of return, it is classified as a fixed income product like debt. Preferred equity can be perpetual (meaning it does not have a set maturity date) or it can have a set maturity date, at which point it is redeemed as if it were debt. Deeply subordinated debt and preferred stock with convertible and/or equity-like features are referred to as **mezzanine capital** or **mezzanine financing**. In addition to conversion rights, equity-like features include non-cash pay in kind (PIK) features and warrants.

5. ***Common equity***: Common equity is capital that represents an ownership stake in the corporation and has a perpetual life. Common equity holders receive all of the residual value of a company, meaning all of the value after all of the liabilities and preferred equity holders have been paid. Equity interests can usually be sold to other investors. The manner in which equity can be sold is dependent on whether the equity is public or private. Ownership interests in private companies are generally more difficult to sell than ownership interests in public companies because the market is less liquid.

Although every company is financed with some portion of equity capital, the type and amount of debt or preferred equity issued by a company depends on numerous factors, including the credit risk of the company, the class of investors interested in the company, the amount of leverage the company has, and the risk appetite of senior management.

> **What does fixed income mean?**
>
> In general, any security that pays a periodic coupon or interest payment is considered a fixed income security because the coupon or interest payment is paid regularly (as opposed to equity which may or may not pay dividends). This includes bonds, notes, commercial paper, asset-backed securities and preferred stock. Preferred stock is considered a fixed income security, like bonds and notes, because preferred stock dividends are set upon issuance and generally do not change. Therefore there is a "fixed" payment by the issuer and a "fixed income" for the investor. Even though some bonds and preferred stock have floating rate coupons or dividends, they are still considered to be fixed income. Within an investment bank, fixed income securities are generally handled by one group of bankers whereas equity-linked and equity securities are handled by another group of bankers.

Before discussing debt in detail, let's revisit the differences between investment grade and non-investment grade (or high yield) debt. Recall the discussion in Credit Analysis (Ch.24) on investment grade vs. high yield credit ratings. Investment grade issuers have credit ratings of BBB- or above, and any company with a credit rating below BBB- is a high yield credit. High yield debt is synonymous with non-investment grade debt and junk debt. Because high yield issuers are more risky, high yield debt issues are more costly to the issuer (e.g., higher coupon) and also contain more restrictive covenants.

Non-investment grade companies can issue the same type of senior long-term debt described in this section, but high yield senior debt is issued with many more covenants than investment grade senior debt. Since most institutional investment funds are chartered to invest either in investment grade or non-investment grade debt, the investor pools are different. However, since some high yield issuers are near to investment grade status (e.g., BB+), they can sometimes attract interest from investment grade investors as well as high yield investors. These issuers are called **crossover** issuers.

Short-Term Debt

There are fives types of short-term debt: (1) trade payables; (2) lines of credit; (3) short-term loans; (4) secured short-term financing; and (5) commercial paper.

1. ***Trade credit or payables***: Although not technically considered short-term debt, trade credit is sometimes called "spontaneous financing" and is provid-

ed by *de facto* counter-parties, including vendors, suppliers, employees, and tax authorities. For example, if CarCo buys $100 million in steel from SteelCo and must remit payment in 30 days, SteelCo has effectively "loaned" CarCo that $100 million for 30 days since CarCo benefits from the use of the steel without having to pay for it upfront. Trade credit is used for working capital financing in the same way that a line of credit or commercial paper might be. Companies expend great effort trying to negotiate favorable trade credit terms. Trade credit is found in the balance sheet in short-term liabilities. Most accounts payable are a form of trade credit.

2. ***Revolving lines of credit***: Also referred to as a "revolver," revolving lines of credit are provided to a company by a single bank or a syndicate of banks. A revolver works like a credit card in that a company is given a set credit limit and the company can draw from it up to the credit limit, repay it and re-borrow from it without having to renegotiate terms with the bank. Revolvers usually have a bullet payment requirement before the revolver can be renewed for another 364 days.

   Lines of credit are generally for one year or less but many of them renew automatically, subject to review. A major reason why the maturity of revolvers is less than one year is to limit the regulatory capital a bank must keep in reserve. If a loan will be outstanding for greater than one year, the regulatory capital requirements for a bank are greater. Lines of credit that renew automatically are called **evergreen lines of credit** or **evergreen facilities**. They are usually at a variable interest rate based on a floating index (such as LIBOR or the prime rate) plus a credit spread. Lines of credit can be unsecured or secured (by assets such as accounts receivable or inventory), and committed (meaning the funds are readily available at any time) or uncommitted. Uncommitted means the funds may or may not be available when they are sought and the borrower assumes the risk that funds may not be available. For assuming this risk, the borrower pays a lower fee. In other words, committed funding is more expensive for a borrower than uncommitted funding. **Drawing down** a line of credit means to use up available credit on the revolver. "Sweeping" the revolver means to pay down the outstanding balance so that the balance after the sweep is zero. When a borrower uses funds on a revolver, banks often require a written statement from the borrower that affirms the company is in full compliance with the terms of the revolver agreement and that the company is not in default on other debt.

3. ***Short-term loan***: A short-term loan is similar to a revolving line of credit except that instead of having an open line that can be drawn, repaid, and redrawn, the entire loan amount is provided to the borrower at the beginning of the term and is due within one year. Short-term loans are not particularly common.

4. ***Secured short-term financing***: There are different forms of secured short-term financing. **Factoring** is one form of secured financing utilized commonly by smaller companies which do not have access to lines of credit. Factoring is a process by which a company sells its accounts receivable to a factoring company at a discount in exchange for cash. The factoring company then has claim to the cash received from the company's clients (the factoring company has purchased the company's accounts receivable so that the factoring company receives the cash as the receivables are paid). Asset-based lending is another form of secured financing. Short-term asset-based or securitized lending might include the securitization of a company's accounts receivable, meaning the accounts receivable are used as collateral for some short-term debt. Some companies have ongoing securitization programs in place.

5. ***Commercial paper*** *or CP*: Commercial paper is short-term public debt issued directly to public investors for maturities between two and 270 days. CP can be unsecured but is almost always backstopped by a line of credit (meaning the line of credit from the bank provides a form of guarantee to the CP investors). Commercial paper can also be asset-backed or secured by short-term assets such as accounts receivable. Only high quality issuers (generally companies with a BBB credit rating or higher) can issue CP. It is usually issued at a discount and redeemed at maturity for full face value (therefore the return to the investor is the difference between the purchase price and the face value). It is usually quoted as a basis point spread over LIBOR or the Federal Reserve AA Composite (AA). Since most CP has a maturity date of less than 270 days, CP is exempt from SEC registration. The CP market is extremely liquid and efficient. Money market funds and investment companies are the largest buyers of CP. A CP program can be put in place in four to six weeks and investors almost always require that a revolver be in put place to backstop the CP program. In case the company has financial distress, the revolver backstop can be drawn down to pay the CP investors when the CP comes due. The backstop facility reduces default risk for the CP investors by transferring the risk from the CP investors to the banks. The banks in turn charge the company for this added risk. Given the short-term nature of CP and the reliance on liquidity, separate credit rating grids are used for CP.

Senior Long-Term Debt

Senior long-term debt can be grouped into five major classifications: (1) senior secured loans; (2) senior unsecured loans; (3) senior unsecured bonds, (4) medium-term notes and (5) convertible debt. Senior secured bonds do exist but are not as common. The term senior implies that it comes before subordinated (or junior) debt in liquidation preference.

1. ***Senior secured loan***: Loans and lines of credit can be unsecured or secured by assets of the company. Secured loans can be amortizing or bullet payment. In practice, most loans are amortizing and most lines of credit (revolvers) are bullet payment. Subsidiaries usually pledge physical assets as collateral or security whereas parent holding companies usually pledge stock owned in operating subsidiaries as collateral or security. A large loan is often syndicated to a group of banks or lenders, in which case it is called a syndicated secured loan. With a term loan, all funds are drawn and provided to the borrower immediately when the loan documents are signed. The borrower then repays the borrowed funds during the term of the loan based on an agreed upon amortization schedule. Senior secured loans are common for high yield issuers. Most secured loans are floating rate.

   Term loans can be split into tranches of varying maturity. Term loans are generally callable at par at any time (the company can pay off the loan in its entirety) and therefore provide a level of flexibility that issuing companies find appealing. Term loans are generally used by companies that wish to repay the loan in five to seven years. Since term loans are generally amortizing, they require strong cash flow. Loan pricing is determined by a company's credit risk, the size of the loan, the market conditions at the time the loan is structured, and the relationship between the borrowing company and its commercial banks.

2. ***Senior unsecured loan***: A senior unsecured loan is similar to the secured loan described previously but is not guaranteed by assets. It is often used as part of an acquisition finance program to fund the acquisition of an asset or a company. Senior unsecured loans can also be syndicated. Senior unsecured loans are generally issued by investment grade companies whereas senior secured loans are generally issued by high yield companies. Recall that investment grade debt is debt with a credit rating of BBB- or higher whereas non-investment grade (or high yield) debt is debt with a credit rating of BB+ or lower.

The syndicated loan market

The syndicated loan market now competes directly with the bond market as an alternative source of debt capital for companies. The syndicated loan market is extremely liquid (it is easy to buy and sell an interest in a loan because the bank market is well capitalized and extremely competitive). In addition, SEC registration is not required for syndicated bank loans whereas SEC registration is required for bonds (unless an exemption exists for the bonds). Syndicated loans are especially useful in acquisitions, large refinancings, and for working capital revolvers and back-up commercial paper facilities. Syndicated loans are avail-

The syndicated loan market continued

able to all issuers across the entire credit spectrum. Given their ease and lower cost, syndicated loans exploded during the merger boom of the 1990s as a source of capital for companies. Traditionally only commercial banks invested in syndicated loans; today, a wide range of investors participate in the syndicated loan market, including commercial banks, investment banks, prime rate funds, structured funds, insurance companies and hedge funds.

The syndicated loan market is divided into three general categories:

Syndicated loan category	Characteristics
Investment grade market	BBB- or higher credit rating Minimal covenants/restrictions Unsecured loans Pricing driven by credit rating
Near investment grade (also called crossover market)	BB+ / BB Secured loans Diverse pricing Expanded covenants
Leveraged loan market	BB- or lower credit rating Fully secured borrowing Full financial covenants

Within the unsecured syndicated loan market, there are revolving credit facilities and term loans. Revolving credit facilities are used to fund working capital or as a "backstop" to a commercial paper program. Term loans are used often by borrowers to fund particular projects. Term debt tends to be six to eight years in duration with covenants. As mentioned previously, revolvers tend to have bullet maturities and loans tend to be amortizing.

Just as with public securities, banks raise capital in the syndicated loan market in different ways:

1. Underwritten deal: a firm commitment to raise the funds
2. Best efforts: no guarantee; lower fees (less risk to the bank)
3. Club deal: pre-marketed to a group or "club" of relationship banks

3. ***Bonds***: Bonds are debt securities sold directly to investors. Unlike most loans, in which borrowers repay principal gradually over a period of time according to an amortization schedule, bond principal is repaid at maturity and periodic coupon payments (representing the interest portion of the investment) are paid during the life of the bond. Most bond coupon payments are paid semiannually. Even though bonds are not amortizing, some issuers must make payments to a sinking fund that mimics amortization. The sinking fund reduces default risk and therefore bonds with a sinking fund require a lower premium or return to the bondholders (in other words, bonds with a sinking fund are cheaper for companies to issue than bonds without a sinking fund) because there is less risk borne by the investors.

   Bonds can have almost any maturity, but they are usually issued in terms of 2, 3, 5, 7, 10, 20, 30 or even 100 years (100-year bonds are called Century Bonds). The greatest amount of liquidity, however, exists for bonds with maturities of five, ten and thirty years. Finance companies tend to issue in the short- and medium-term whereas industrial companies (or companies funding long-lived assets) tend to issue in the medium- to long-term. Most high yield issues are in the seven to ten year range whereas investment grade issues are for short, medium and long-term maturities. Bonds can be issued to public or private investors and can have a fixed or floating rate. Bond pricing is driven by the issuer's credit risk, the coupon payment, the term of the issuance, the size of the issuance, and the yield curve at the time of issuance. Prices are quoted as a credit spread over the same dated U.S. Treasury bond.

   Bonds can be secured (such as with first mortgage bonds which are secured by assets) or unsecured. Although most bonds are issued with a set coupon rate that is paid semiannually, some bonds are issued with a floating rate coupon. These are called **floating rate notes** or **floaters**. And some bonds can be issued with no coupon payable at all during the life of the bond. These are called **zero coupon bonds** or **zeroes**. Zeroes are issued at a deep discount and the investor's return is embedded in the deeply discounted price. For example, consider $5,000 in 15-year zero coupon bonds purchased by an investor for $2,500. The investor will not receive coupon payments during the 15-year life of the bond, however, the investor will receive $5,000 at the end of 15 years. The interest therefore is embedded in the principal received at the end of the term as opposed to the interest being paid during the life of the bond. To calculate the implied return for the investor, we use a simple present value calculation.

   $$\text{Present value} = \text{future value} / (1 + \text{discount rate})^{\text{number of years}}$$

   $$\$2{,}500 \text{ present value} = \$5{,}000 \text{ future value} / (1 + r)^{15}$$

Use algebra or a financial calculator to solve for r.

You should calculate a discount rate (r) of 4.729 percent

To test this, insert 4.729 percent into the present value calculation above and test to see if you come up with a present value of $2,500.

$5,000 future value / $(1 + 0.04729)^{15}$ = $2,500 present value

Bonds can be "plain vanilla" or have embedded options. The most common embedded options are puts and calls. A **put option** allows the investor the right to force the issuer to repurchase the bonds, generally at par (or face value). Since this is an option that is advantageous to an investor, bonds with put options are usually priced at a tighter credit spread (they are cheaper for the company to issue compared to a plain vanilla bond because the put option has value to the investor, so the investor is willing to accept a lower yield). A **call option** provides an issuer the right to redeem the outstanding bonds at a predetermined price or percentage (e.g., at 102 percent of face value) and begining on a predetermined date (which is prior to the final maturity date of the bond). The period during which the bond cannot be called (the time before the first call date) is called the **non-call period**. The purpose of the non-call period is to ensure that investors receive their interest payments for some minimum period of time. Investors want to be sure that they will receive their coupon or return for some period of time and therefore investors generally require that there be some non-call period with callable or putable bonds. Bonds with call options usually price at a wider credit spread (e.g., they are more expensive to the issuer compared to a plain vanilla bond). Most high yield bonds have a call option after a certain date and a put option in a change-of-control situation.

Bonds are priced based on a credit spread over the same dated U.S. Government Treasury security. The most important drivers of bond pricing are the bond's credit ratings, the industry in which the issuer operates, the issuer's size, the issuer's overall credit quality, and the liquidity (or absolute size in dollar terms) of the issuance. Another important factor in bond pricing that is not directly related to the issuer is the supply of other issues in the market with the same credit quality as the bond (i.e., other bond issuers competing for the same investors). Bonds can be executed quickly; usually in three to six weeks for investment grade companies, and even shorter if the company has a shelf registration in place with the SEC. Due to the greater need for credit due diligence, high yield executions usually take eight to twelve weeks.

The **gross spread** is the fee an issuer will pay its investment bank to underwrite a bond offering and is amortized over the term of the bond. It is allocated to the manager of the offering, the dealer (if the dealer is different from the manager), and the syndicate. The **re-offer yield** is the rate of return offered to investors by the underwriters after the gross spread has been allocated to the underwriters.

The U.S. bond market is exceptionally large and sophisticated. Publicly issued bonds are regulated by the SEC and issuers must be SEC registrants, unless an exemption exists for the issuer (such as qualifying as a Rule 144A issuer). Rule 144A and private placements are described later in this chapter.

4. **Medium-term notes (MTNs)**: MTNs are bonds sold in tranches according to maturity. The difference between an MTN and a bond is that the tranches of an MTN program can be sold over time as opposed to a bond issue, which is sold all at once. MTNs allow a company to access the fixed income market for small amounts based on market demand by prearranging their SEC documentation. This is called a **shelf registration** since the documentation sits "on the shelf" until the company is ready to issue a tranche from the MTN program, at which point the registration is quickly updated and the securities are sold.

   MTNs provide a significant amount of financial flexibility for a company and have become increasingly popular. If a company implements an MTN program, it files a shelf registration for an aggregate amount that represents the amount of securities it expects to issue over the next few years (say $1 billion), but it only issues a tranche of the MTN program if and when it needs to. For example, a company might issue $250 million of 10-year notes today and then two years from now it might issue another $400 million of 5-year notes. The tranches within an MTN program can have varying terms.

   Other than the way in which they are issued and the varying tranches within a program, MTNs are similar to bonds in that they can have embedded options and other features. They are favored by companies that might not need to raise all the capital at once since market timing risk is reduced. Also, since an MTN program allows companies to issue debt with varying durations, it provides companies with access to a wider distribution network of investors (i.e., different classes of investors) and also allows the issuer to issue debt in the lowest priced maturity (depending on the shape of the yield curve). Thus, if the yield curve is inverted (long-dated securities are less expensive than short-dated securities) the issuer can issue more long-dated notes. If the market for 2-year notes is particularly hot due to strong investor demand at a point in time, an issuer with an MTN program in place can take advantage of this demand and issue a tranche of 2-year notes. Financial institutions such as banks and insurance companies are the largest issuers within the MTN market, although corporate issuers with ongoing capital requirements such as utilities also issue them regularly. Although called "medium-term" notes, MTNs can be issued for practically any maturity. Most MTNs, however, vary in duration from nine months to thirty years.

5. ***Convertible debt***: Convertible debt (usually bonds, but not always) can be converted into equity at some point in the future. Convertible securities are commonly referred to as equity-linked securities. Since the equity component of a convertible bond has value to an investor, the coupon that a company is required to pay on convertible debt is generally lower than on senior unsecured debt, all other things being equal. The lower coupon payment makes convertible bonds attractive securities for a company to issue since they require a lower periodic cash flow requirement.

   Growth companies that need to raise significant amounts of capital to fund R&D and that have meaningful volatility in their stock prices tend to favor convertible bonds since they allow for a debt-like security in the early years with a lower interest payment, and then convert into equity based on a ratio determined at the time the convertible debt is issued. Assuming the stock price rises in the future above the conversion price, the investor essentially bought equity today at a discount. For the company issuing the convertible, they are essentially selling equity forward. They get the proceeds today but do not have to deliver the shares of equity until sometime in the future when the convertible debt converts into equity. Preferred equity also can have convertible features. Convertible debt calculations can be found in Financial Statement Basics. (Ch.3)

Debt vs. equity

As securities become more complex and as debt products have more and more embedded features that are more equity-like than debt-like, the distinction between fixed income and equity-linked securities becomes more gray. In practice, securities that entitle the investor to some degree of ownership are considered equity-linked whereas securities which offer no ownership rights (today or in the future) are considered to be fixed income.

Subordinated Debt

Subordinated debt is located in the capital structure between traditional senior long-term debt and equity. Subordinated debt includes securities which have debt-like characteristics but are junior to senior debt in terms of liquidation preference. Many types of subordinated debt are convertible into equity at some point in the future; however, not all convertible debt is subordinated debt. Convertible debt can also be senior. High yield companies are active issuers of subordinated debt.

Subordinated debt can be either a bank loan or bonds. Junior subordinated debt is debt that is junior to senior subordinated debt, which means that in a liquidation scenario it cannot be paid until all senior subordinated debt has been paid.

Deeply discounted subordinated debt is called mezzanine financing. Most mezzanine financing has equity-linked features.

Preferred Equity

Preferred equity (or preferred stock) is a hybrid instrument that contains various features that may be more or less equity-like. Like common equity, preferred equity pays a dividend. Most preferred dividends are preset (generally at a rate well above the common dividend rate). There is adjustable rate preferred stock in which the dividend rate is tied to an index. Adjustable preferred stock usually has a collar to limit the upper and lower dividend rates. Preferred equity is senior in liquidation preference to common equity. Preferred equity can be perpetual in duration like common equity, or it can have a maturity date like debt. In a liquidation scenario, preferred stockholders are not paid until after all debt obligations have been paid.

Preferred equity dividends can be cumulative or non-cumulative, although cumulative is more common. Cumulative means the preferred dividend must be paid in full prior to the payment of any common stock dividend, but that preferred dividend can generally be deferred at the company's option, which is a useful feature if the company experiences cash problems or financial distress. Therefore, if a company halts the payment of its preferred dividends due to financial distress, any preferred dividends in arrears must be paid before common dividends can be paid once the financial distress has passed. Given the higher risk of not receiving dividends (because with non-cumulative preferred, if the preferred dividend payments are suspended, the issuer does not need to pay missed dividends), non-cumulative preferred stock is more expensive to issue than cumulative preferred stock. This means that non-cumulative preferred stock requires a higher dividend rate than cumulative stock; alternatively, if the dividend rates were equal, investors would price the non-cumulative preferred stock at a discount.

Preferred securities are similar to preferred stock in form but structured in a way that allows companies to deduct the dividend payments for tax purposes – as if the dividend payments were interest payments. This is noteworthy since dividends from straight preferred stock are not generally tax-deductible. Preferred securities with tax-deductible dividends are also called capital securities or trust-preferred securities.

The rating agencies generally view preferred securities as being debt-like instruments and then moderate that view (i.e., move toward treating it as equity) depending on the securities' features. For example, a money market preferred is viewed as being like commercial paper. On the other end of the scale is mandatorily convertible three-year preferred stock, which might get substantial equity credit from the rating agencies because of its equity-like features.

Be careful when using percentage of equity credit

When calculating credit ratios, be careful about allocating a percentage of equity credit for preferred or equity-linked securities. While both Moody's and S&P have published articles about the percentage equity credit they provide to various types of preferred or convertible securities, it is not a purely mathematical calculation. The rating agencies look at each situation individually and do not necessarily crunch every single number according to a stated equity percentage.

Common Equity

Common equity investors are the owners of the company and have claims to the assets of a corporation after all liabilities and debt obligations have been paid. Dividends paid to equity investors are elective, meaning the corporation is not obligated to pay dividends to shareholders. A corporation can pay dividends or suspend the payment of dividends at any time. Those dividends may be cumulative, but noncumulative is more usual. In a corporation, the equity owners have limited liability to the company, which means that an investor is only financially responsible for a company's debts or liabilities up to the amount of the investor's invested capital. In contrast, in a partnership or sole proprietorship, legal liability flows to the owners and might not be limited in amount (meaning the owners could be liable for an amount above their invested capital).

Some companies have different classes of common equity. For example, one class of common equity might have a disproportionately higher share of voting rights than another class; the high vote shares are called super-voting shares. Owner's equity is the common equity of a corporation contributed by the original operating owners of the company. The term owner's equity refers to the founding capital and is generally used when the company is still privately owned. Shareholders' equity is the more common term for the common equity of a publicly traded company.

Public vs. Private Capital

There are benefits to both public and private capital. Liquidity, verifiable market value, and lowest cost of financing are best achieved within a public market. However, the restrictions and regulations around public debt and equity can make it onerous and time consuming. Raising private capital has numerous benefits, including speed of execution and limited disclosure requirements. Due to the limited liquidity, however, private capital is more expensive for a company.

Private debt is raised through private placements and public debt is raised through public markets. For equity, private equity can be raised through private placements or through direct sales to financial sponsors. Public equity is raised through public markets.

Private Placements

Unlike a public sale of securities, a private placement is the direct sale of securities to a limited group of investors, subject to certain limitations. Since qualifying private placements are not regulated by the SEC, restrictions exist to ensure that only investors who are capable of analyzing the risks of the investment without the oversight of the SEC are allowed to invest in them. The private placement market represents a meaningful portion of the total corporate debt and equity markets. Unlike public securities, securities sold in private placements are not registered with the SEC. They are considered restricted securities.

There are two types of limits on private placements. The first relates to that actual issuance of the private placement securities by the company. These limitations are governed by the SEC's Regulation D. The second limit relates to the resale (in a secondary market) of private placement securities. These limitations are governed by the SEC's Rule 144A.

Limitations on investors qualified to participate in private placements are tiered between private placements less than and more than $1 million, according to Regulation D.

- If the private placement is for less than $1 million during a twelve-month period, there are no limits on the number of investors and no restrictions on the manner in which the securities are offered for sale.

- If the offering is for more than $1 million, only accredited investors and no more than 35 non-accredited investors can participate in the private placement. An "accredited investor" is defined in Rule 501(A) of the SEC's Regulation D. In summary, accredited investors include executive officers of the company, purchasers whose net worth exceeds $1 million, persons who have income greater than $200,000 for each of the past two years and who expect to earn at least $200,000 in the current year, and a business entity in as long as the business entity was not created solely for the purpose of investing in the private placement.

Limitations on the resale of private placement securities are governed by Rule 144A.

- Rule 144A allows qualified institutional buyers (QIBs) the right to offer for resale and to purchase private placement securities.

- Essentially, Rule 144A legally allows for a secondary market of private placement securities where qualified buyers can buy and sell the securities. Only resellers of the securities, not the issuer, can rely on Rule 144A.

- Qualifications for QIBs include owning or managing $100 million or more of qualifying securities of issuers not affiliated with the entity. If the institution is a broker-dealer, then the minimum is $10 million. Banks and savings and loans must have a net worth of $25 million.

Private placements are favored by some issuers since they provide for significantly more flexibility and ease with regard to market timing. Private placements are done for almost any type of capital product, including senior and subordinated debt, project finance and leveraged lease debt, real estate and asset-backed debt, and convertible debt. Private placement investors invest in debt across the entire credit spectrum. 144A private placement issues almost always have credit ratings. Non-144A private placements do not require credit ratings and are sold to a smaller universe of investors. Because of their ease and lack of SEC registration, private placements are particularly favored by private companies and foreign issuers. Private placements generally have covenants that are similar to those in high yield or bank debt. Many high yield offerings are done as 144A private placements, with registration rights attached to allow for subsequent trading in the public markets once registration with the SEC becomes effective.

The private placement investor market has grown tremendously in the last several years. Traditionally, the private placement market was used by private companies who had not yet accessed public debt or equity markets. However, a trend has emerged in the private placement market in which public companies (companies that are publicly traded) issue private placement debt or equity. These so-called Private Investments in Public Equity (or PIPE) have most recently been used by public companies that have seen their public market valuations drop considerably and find themselves in need of a meaningful cash infusion or investment from an outside party to allow them to grow or continue to fund their operations. PIPE investments allow public companies to seek capital from a specialized and sophisticated investor pool. Most PIPE investors expect to use the public markets as their exit vehicle for their investment.

Financial Sponsors

Financial sponsors raise money from investors and invest the fund's money in businesses. Private equity firms and leveraged buyout firms (which are essentially synonymous) invest in existing businesses which have a track record of cash flow producing operations. Venture capital firms, on the other hand, invest in new businesses and new technologies, many of which are not yet cash flow positive. A venture capital firm will invest money in exchange for equity or convertible debt in the hope that it will sell or IPO its equity stake within five to seven years at a substantial premium to its original investment. Private equity firms acquire existing companies financed with a large portion of debt (60 to 80 percent) and a smaller portion of equity (20 to 40 percent). They generate their equity returns by increasing efficiency – both in the way a portfolio company runs its operations and in the way it manages its capital structure. There is some crossover between late-stage venture capital and private equity. Financial sponsors are described in detail in Leveraged Buyout Analysis. (Ch.12)

Registration of Public Securities

Companies that issue securities sold in public markets in the U.S. must comply with SEC regulations and are subject to numerous disclosure and filing requirements. These filings and disclosures were put in place to protect the rights of investors. The 1933 Securities Act and 1934 Securities Exchange Act created the SEC and govern the public issuance of debt and equity securities. They were enacted during the Depression, when many investors lost significant amounts of money following the stock market crash of 1929. The 1933 Act requires that any securities "sold" in the U.S. must be registered in the U.S. with the SEC, unless the securities qualify for exemption.

Companies that seek to issue securities to the public market must publicly disclose the following:

1. The terms of the offering (securities issued, use of proceeds, etc.)
2. The potential risks involved with investing in the company or the offering

3. Audited financial data and information about the company. Usually, SEC registrants must have two years of audited balance sheets and three years of audited income statements and cash flow statements
4. Information about the management team and the directors, such as shareholdings in the company and compensation
5. Other material facts relevant to the company and the offering

SEC filings for registered companies and SEC rules and regulations can be found on the SEC's website (www.sec.gov).

Pricing information is not provided in initial securities offering documents. SEC Rule 430A allows for "red herrings" (registration statements filed with the SEC without pricing information) to be deemed "effective" even without the pricing information. Price should not be discussed until the offer order-taking period, which is why it is not included in the red herring. The SEC can choose to review any registration statement it wants. After a review, the SEC submits "comments" to the issuer and the issuer must respond to the SEC comments before the registration statements can be deemed effective by the SEC. An "effective" designation means the SEC no longer has comments on the registration statement. Pricing is determined when the securities are actually offered to the public. The final offer price must be filed within five days of the effective date of the registration statement.

The timeframe between when a company decides that it will raise new public debt or equity and when the securities are actually sold can range from a few days for commercial paper from a well-known issuer to six to nine months for an initial public offering (IPO) of a company's stock. Timing depends on the complexity of the contemplated transaction and the amount of existing information in the market regarding the issuer and the securities. Similarly, registered high yield deals can take ten to twelve weeks as compared with non-registered (not sold to the general public but to accredited investors) 144A placements, which can take around eight weeks.

Underwriters are required to perform due diligence before offering securities for sale to the public. The underwriter must do what is reasonably possible to verify information provided in the registration statements, given a level of materiality. Technically, they must confirm that the registration statements do not contain any material misstatement of fact nor do they omit any material fact. The SEC considers "material" to be anything an investor would consider important in making an investment decision. Due diligence is further described in Deal Mechanics. (Ch.20)

Investors

There are many different types of investors. Most people tend to think of investors as those who buy the stock of a company. However, just as there are many types of securities and different types of capital (debt and equity and everything in between), there are many types of investors besides those who invest solely in public equity markets. There are investors who buy only bonds, buy only derivatives, or only enter into short positions on stock, among other things.

Investors can be classified in one of four general categories: (1) retail investors; (2) institutional investors; (3) banks and finance companies; and (4) private investors.

1. Retail investors are individuals who make investments in companies, just like you, your parents, or your neighbor who purchases shares in Microsoft or Intel through a broker-dealer such as Merrill Lynch or Charles Schwab. Retail investors tend to purchase shares in mutual funds, public equity, and public bonds (government and corporate bonds).

2. The institutional investor market is significantly larger than the retail market. Institutional investors include mutual funds, pension funds, money managers, hedge funds, insurance companies, bank trust companies, state and local governments, and endowments (such as university endowments). Institutional investors are generally investing money *on behalf of* a large pool of investors. They invest in almost every type of investment. The major institutional investor centers in the U.S. are New York, Boston, Chicago and San Francisco.

3. Banks and finance companies are in the business of lending, meaning they have a pool of capital that they can lend to borrowers and they charge the borrowers interest on the borrowed money. Banks are highly regulated and have reserve requirements related to the amount of capital they must keep in house (meaning capital they cannot lend out).

4. Private investors include financial sponsors and individual private investors. Also, many large companies have an in-house private equity or investment subsidiary which uses the company's money to invest in other companies.

In general, government investors and pension funds are the most conservative investors, insurance companies are the most diversified (across credits and markets), banks, finance companies, mutual funds, hedge funds, private equity funds and leveraged buyout funds are the most opportunistic, and investment advisors to the retail market and retail investors are the most focused on yield and well-known company names.

Private equity investors, leveraged buyout investors, asset managers, insurance companies and pension funds are generally considered "buy and hold investors" as opposed to hedge funds who are not necessarily interested in holding the investment for a long period of time. Buy and hold investors are coveted, although opportunistic investors such as hedge funds do provide more market liquidity. Since private equity, leveraged buyout, and corporate buyers tend to purchase "control" positions, they are usually provided access to confidential information prior to making their investment decision. In contract, since most other types of investors purchase minority (non-controlling) positions, these other investors usually do not have access to inside, confidential information.

One of the most important considerations for investors is liquidity because they want to be able to sell their position whenever they might want to or need to, without their sale putting downward pressure on the security's price.

Managing Risk with Derivatives

Managing risk involves identifying potential risks and implementing tools or solutions to minimize the financial or operating impact if the risk event comes to pass. It is akin to purchasing insurance on a car or a home; insurance is purchased in order to help defray the costs of liability or loss if the risk event occurs. The derivatives market evolved as a solution to managing financial risk. Trillions of dollars of derivatives are traded globally with the goal of minimizing risk for an investor or for a company. In fact, the derivatives market is larger than the equity market and the debt market.

A **derivative** is a financial contract whose value is determined by an underlying asset, item or commodity such as an interest rate, the cost of oil per barrel, or a credit rating. A derivative contract is entered into between two parties, called **counter-parties**. The goal of a derivative is to minimize or transfer risk for one party. The other party assumes that risk for a fee. **Hedging** is the act of minimizing risk – any type of risk – by entering into a financial contract with a counter-party who will assume the risk for a fee.

Numerous types of derivatives exist. Examples include forward interest rate swaps, interest rate caps and collars (which put bands around the interest rate on variable rate debt), treasury rate locks, credit derivatives (which provide a hedge against the deterioration of a counter-party's credit risk), and foreign exchange forwards (which hedge foreign currency risk). Essentially, there is a structured product to eliminate almost any type of risk, for a price.

Numerous types of derivatives are used in the equity market, the most widely known of which is an option. Other equity derivatives include swaps, futures, forward distributions of equity, stock buybacks, and synthetic securitizations.

In order to describe how a derivative works, let's consider a "plain vanilla" interest rate swap. An interest rate swap is simply a derivative which allows a company to convert floating rate debt to fixed rate debt (or vice versa). An interest rate swap allows a company with long-term debt the ability to transform the character (fixed vs. floating) of some portion of the debt without having to redeem the debt itself. For example, assume a company has $100 million of 30-year bonds issued and outstanding and these bonds have a fixed rate coupon of 7 percent. If, based on prevailing market conditions, the company decides it would like to transform this fixed rate debt into floating rate debt, it can do so by entering into an interest rate swap with a bank. The company would enter into a $100 million swap whereby the company pays a floating rate to the bank (based on the $100 million principal amount) and the bank in turn pays a fixed rate to the company. By swapping with the bank, the company is able to transform its 30-year fixed rate bond into a 30-year floating rate bond without involving its investors, who would still receive their 7 percent fixed coupon, although the cash flows to pay the 7 percent fixed coupon would come from the bank for the duration of the swap.

An interest rate swap, like most derivatives, is simply a "bet" that a price of something will go up or down. In this example, the company is betting that interest rates will stay below the 7 percent it pays on its bonds. With floating rate interest exposure, the company will pay less than 7 percent thereby reducing its overall interest expense (and ultimately increasing earnings and return on equity). The bank will take this "bet" for a fee, just like a gambling house will take any side of a bet for a fee. If interest rates rise above 7 percent, the company will lose because it will have to pay the higher floating rate interest (as opposed to the fixed rate of 7 percent).

Liability Management

Liability management is the act of managing a company's debt mix to minimize the overall risk and cost of debt for a company (thereby minimizing the company's WACC and increasing the company's return on equity and return on capital). The optimal debt mix needs to be driven by corporate strategic objectives as well as financial objectives.

Examples of liability management include:

Reduce cost of borrowing: Refinance when rates are low, incorporate some lower cost variable debt into the capital structure, negotiate terms and covenants instead of "accepting" terms in order to limit actual and potential costs to the company (if covenants are triggered and in the form of future borrowing rates). Companies with predominately fixed rate debt have taken advantage of historically low interest rates by entering into swaps to convert fixed rate debt to floating, effectively reducing interest expense and adjusting fixed/floating debt ratios. This increases risk, however, since the cost of the debt (which after a swap into floating is now variable rate) will also increase in the future if interest rates rise over time.

Revise maturity schedule: Match assets and liabilities in order to hedge term-related risk, which is the risk that future debt payment obligations will not be matched by future cash flow streams.

Rebalance capital structure: Replace expensive subordinated debt and preferred stock with less expensive senior unsecured debt whenever possible (e.g., when credit profile strengthens).

Employ financial tools: Judiciously use tender offers, swaps, exchange offers, consent solicitations, redemptions, covered calls, factoring, securitization, and hedging to minimize risks and costs.

Eliminate restrictive covenants and contingent liabilities: Do this if the credit profile is stronger than it was when the debt was originally put in place. In other words, renegotiate terms from a stronger bargaining position.

Certain tools manage the asset side of the balance sheet. They are listed below.

FX contracts protect values earned by assets in foreign countries by locking in a certain foreign exchange rate.

Long-term purchase contracts hedge commodity risk if the commodity is required to produce the company's goods or services. In other words, minimize the risk that the cost of important inputs rises.

Credit derivatives protect from changes in the credit profile of counter-parties. See Credit Analysis. (Ch.24)

Factoring allows companies to sell receivables for cash to minimize the carried counter-party risk on trade credit.

Product liability insurance limits future financial exposure based on faulty products.

General business interruption insurance can limit financial exposure from extraordinary events such as hurricanes, earthquakes or strikes.

ACKNOWLEDGMENTS

The Practitioner's Guide to Investment Banking and The Recruiting Guide to Investment Banking were conceived of and written at the same time. As a result, it would be extremely difficult to distinguish between contributions to one book, the other or, in some cases, both. Out of necessity, the following full set of acknowledgments appears in both books.

We are grateful to many people for their unflagging editorial, strategic, and emotional support in bringing these books to fruition. If these books are useful it is only because so many extraordinary friends, colleagues, mentors, and family members helped make them so. Collaborating with all of you on this multi-year project has been a remarkable experience for us both professionally and personally. We are humbled by your knowledge, experience, insights, and willingness to help. On behalf of those whom we hope to help with these books, thank you.

A few individuals, in particular, were instrumental in this project. It is difficult to capture in words the appreciation we have for Jimmy Elliott, Ted McAniff, Bert Valdman, and Roger Wood. Their imprimatur is felt throughout this work. These books are as much theirs as they are ours.

> Jimmy Elliott, head of JPMorgan's Global M&A Group and one of the finest practitioners we know, instilled in us a love for banking and taught us the importance of building the tool chest, step by step. Jimmy never asks anyone to work harder than he himself works. From him we have learned a tremendous amount about winning, the business of investment banking, being an advisor, and that being a teacher is an important element of being a leader. The most important lesson he imparted to us is that there is absolutely nothing to fear if you know what you're doing.
>
> Edward (Ted) McAniff of O'Melveny & Myers LLP, law professor and counsel to us on all things personal and professional, contributed immense time and energy toward this project, not to mention all of our other endeavors. Ted significantly improved a number of sections, provided us thoughtful direction along the way, and field tested material with his students. Ted's commitment to teaching served as inspiration for this project in the same way that his commitment to excellence inspires us every day.
>
> Bert Valdman, chief operating officer of Puget Energy, played a major role in bringing these books to completion. Were it not for Bert, these books might not have been finished. For almost ten years Bert has been a mentor and friend, encouraging us to challenge ourselves and to stay focused on the end-goal while

reminding us to enjoy the journey. Bert was always willing to review sections of the books and many times gave us invaluable advice on both direction and tone.

Roger Wood, head of Power Investment Banking at Rothschild North America and longtime mentor, was tireless in his support of and help in reviewing and editing major sections of the books. Roger taught us the importance of keeping one's eye on the details as well the need to keep true to oneself in spite of what can be immense outside pressures. An outstanding banker, Roger provided comprehensive feedback and detailed comments on how to improve multiple sections of the books.

The M&A, corporate finance, and valuation sections benefited greatly from the wisdom and expertise of some of the most competent finance professionals we know. We hope we have faithfully reflected their knowledge and insights. For reading countless review packages, answering repeated phone calls and e-mails, and for greatly improving this work, we are deeply grateful.

Greg Annick, founder and managing director of Pasadena Capital Partners and former partner at Leonard Green & Partners, was instrumental in editing the leveraged buyout and financial sponsor sections. Greg's exceptional integrity and steadfast commitment to doing what is right inspire us more than he will ever know.

Souren Ouzounian, managing director at Bank of America Merrill Lynch, provided comments, criticism and suggestions on the capital markets, financing and credit sections. A constant source of strength and a trusted confidante, Souren serves as role model to us in many ways.

Steve Raftopoulos, former managing director and head of middle market M&A at Banc of America Securities, provided meaningful comments to the M&A and valuation sections. Steve's sense of humor and down-to-earth manner keep us grounded and focused on what is most important.

Marc Castellani, former principal at Banc of America Securities, was especially helpful in reviewing and editing the valuation sections. In addition, Marc's commitment to training junior colleagues serves as a model for what we want these books to accomplish.

Richard Wong, former vice president at Banc of America Securities and director at Yahoo!, probably responded to more "left field" questions than anyone. One of Richard's greatest virtues, as a friend as well as a banker, is his ability to make anyone comfortable in his presence. His friendship has long been a source of support.

Gavin Wolfe, vice chairman of investment banking at Credit Suisse, provided valuable contributions to various M&A sections. Gavin and his wife Hope helped support this project in many ways over the years.

Peter Cimmet at Olympus Capital provided suggestions which greatly improved the M&A sections. He regularly reminds us that laughter is an important component of success in banking and in life.

Richard Ford, managing director at Bank of America Merrill Lynch, devoted significant time to the accretion/dilution chapter and also shared some of his own writings on the subject, which proved to be very useful as we grappled with simplifying this important and often confusing topic.

James Lind at Berkshire Bridge Capital offered valuable suggestions on the leveraged buyout and financial sponsor sections. Always available for a quick phone call, Jim served as an important sounding board on our many private equity questions.

Julie Bell, director at JH Partners, graciously and tirelessly responded to a deluge of e-mails asking her opinion on numerous topics. Julie was deeply involved in helping shape the glossary and also contributed to the corporate finance and recruiting sections.

Jonathan Adler, partner at Fried Frank, committed an enormous amount of time to review and substantially improve the deal mechanics section. Clients and colleagues alike benefit from his gentle good humor and sheer competence.

Craig Adas, managing partner of the Menlo Park office of Weil, Gotshal & Manges, was unfailing in his willingness to help us improve the legal sections. He has clarified concepts and answered legal questions for nearly ten years now and we are grateful to him for it.

Samuel Thompson, Jr., professor of law and director of the UCLA School of Law Center for the Study of Mergers and Acquisitions, helped us considerably improve the tax sections. He also provided insight and advice on the writing process arising out of his many published articles and books.

Phillip D. Irwin, of O'Melveny & Myers, has been a stellar tax attorney for some five decades and used this deep understanding of tax to clarify complex topics and answer our most difficult questions.

Richard Casavechia, managing director at Bank of America Merrill Lynch and head of M&A Tax Strategies, spent significant time reviewing and clarifying the chapter on Taxes and M&A. He has taught us a great deal about tax over the years.

Ben Benjamin, retired partner from O'Melveny & Myers, reviewed the tax section and clarified a number of concepts.

Derek Whang of The Carlyle Group made valuable contributions to the valuation, leveraged buyout, interviewing, recruiting, and life for a junior banker sections. Derek's signature laugh is priceless as is his friendship.

Ram Seethepalli, former director of business development in Asia for Cendant, has offered help in many ways and on many levels. While his work on the books consisted of reviewing M&A sections, his influence is felt far more broadly.

Maya Tichio, vice president at Deutsche Bank and one of the most detail-oriented and thoughtful people we know, was particularly helpful in developing the glossary as well as the financial statement and corporate finance sections.

Kaoru Ogihara, associate at Spencer Stuart and always gracious and good hearted, provided feedback on the valuation, corporate finance, interviewing and recruiting sections.

Todd McKenzie, executive vice president at Bank of America, was particularly helpful in reviewing the due diligence and deal mechanics sections, sharing anecdotes and clarifying concepts to greatly improve these sections.

John Morris, managing director and co-head of ratings advisory at Lehman Brothers, was tremendously helpful as we developed the credit and sources of capital sections. A thoughtful and pragmatic advisor, John has helped many clients and colleagues learn the intricacies of credit analysis.

Charles Freeman, vice president at JPMorgan, significantly improved the credit sections and clarified a number of challenging concepts. One of the most conscientious and candid professionals we know, Charlie is extremely effective as a credit analyst and as a mentor.

Thomas Musante, managing director at AIG SunAmerica, read through numerous sections and provided characteristically helpful feedback at every turn, including on the covers and introduction.

John Whelan, former vice president at JPMorgan, provided sage advice and feedback on the sources of capital and credit sections. Financial sponsors and industrial clients are fortunate to have John work on their behalf, as are we.

Todd Guenther, managing director at Citigroup, asked difficult questions which served to improve the M&A and valuation sections. Todd has served as a confidante and sounding board on multiple matters over the years.

Marc Junkunc, Ph.D. and assistant professor of management at the University of Miami, was integral in the development of the corporate finance sections. Marc's sensitivity as a teacher and experience as an analyst helped improve these sections tremendously.

Alex Panos, managing director at TSG Consumer Partners, contributed to the leveraged buyout, private equity, and discounted cash flow sections and we appreciate his advice on how to market these books.

Lottie Chi, former director at Primus Asset Management, reviewed the financial statement and corporate finance sections and provided meaningful feedback on a number of items along the way including illustrations and charts.

Will Morris, managing director at Stonehouse Partners, reviewed and improved the leveraged buyout and private equity sections and also serves as a role model for successfully balancing a professional career with a love for the outdoors.

John Tjia, senior manager at Ernst & Young, spent considerable time reviewing the accretion/dilution chapter. John also provided encouragement and advice on the process of writing and publishing which helped us tremendously.

Jim Morris, managing partner of TMG & Associates, was integral in improving the merger accounting and accretion/dilution sections. Jim also shared insights and advice arising from his own experience as an author.

Dan Collin, principal at Monomoy Capital Partners, read through the M&A sections and provided helpful suggestions based on his experience as an analyst and associate.

Philip Arra, president of Hunt Special Situations Group, considerably improved the corporate finance sections.

Joseph Brant was helpful in ensuring that the corporate finance sections were clear, accessible, and written in layman's terms.

Jon Rezneck, associate at Greenhill, provided a number of useful suggestions which served to greatly improve the valuation and financial statement sections.

Robert Tichio, vice president at Riverstone Holdings, provided helpful feedback on the corporate finance sections and served as a sounding board as we developed the investment banking sections.

Tina Chan, former analyst at JPMorgan and associate marketing manager at Clorox, reviewed the accretion/dilution chapter in detail and always reminded us of the virtues of returning home to California.

Patrick Walravens, managing director at JMP Securities, was helpful in improving various M&A sections.

Catharina Min, partner at Reed Smith, reviewed and improved the merger agreement and deal mechanics sections.

Marc Jones, partner at Goodwin Procter, provided constructive comments and suggestions on a number of legal sections.

Don Weil, longtime entrepreneur, provided advice and perspective at multiple points along the way.

Steve Kopff was helpful in improving the tax and accounting sections.

Henry Gosebruch, managing director at JPMorgan, sets the standard and we are all better for it.

Lance Bylow, senior vice president at Barclays, has long been a thoughtful and selfless friend. His encouragement during difficult periods is particularly appreciated.

A number of colleagues made meaningful improvements to the recruiting, interviewing and life on the job sections. As any experienced banker will tell you, interviewing for and landing the job are as difficult and frightening as any M&A or capital raising transaction. We gratefully acknowledge those who played a seminal role in the development of these important sections.

Martin Atkin, former head of recruiting and junior resources at JPMorgan and now senior portfolio manager at Sanford Bernstein, was instrumental in developing the voice and tone of the recruiting and interviewing sections. His additions to the recruiting section improved the work well beyond where it might have been without his input. British by origin, a world citizen by choice and a class act in every respect, Martin has been a role model for us for many years.

Nelson Shing, senior vice president at Nicholas-Applegate and trusted friend, whose counsel has led us on the right path many times. He has long been an extension of the family and also prepared Jerilyn for her very first banking interview many years ago.

Jon Menor, investment analyst at Brandes Investment Partners, reviewed various sections of the book and also served as Jerilyn's better half on many complicated transactions at JPMorgan. He may be the only surfing Hawaiian who can build an Excel model that would make Bill Gates proud.

Lex Miron, executive director at CIBC, introduced us to his colleagues at Savvian, which enabled us to field test material from the book. Lex also provided anecdotal additions to the life on the job sections with the perspective of an older sibling or trusted friend.

Steve Matloff, former associate at Morgan Stanley, made suggestions which caused us to significantly rewrite various sections and we thank him for the encouragement to take this entire process slowly and steadily.

Matthew Rho, vice president at SV Investment Partners, was extremely helpful in editing the recruiting and life on the job sections and enthusiastically supported the project early in the process when we needed encouragement the most.

Christian Charnaux, at Hilton and one of the best at having fun but never letting it get in the way of being competent, provided terrific comments to the life on the job and interviewing sections.

Chris Bell, at Games that Give, and characterized by his love of finance, was helpful in reviewing and editing the recruiting and interviewing sections as well as the corporate finance sections.

Peter Lee, at Blackstone Kailix and a classic American success story, helped us as we first crafted the recruiting and life on the job sections.

Anshuman Vohra, former analyst and now president of Bulldog Gin Company, provided substantial comments for the life on the job sections. Anshuman's extraordinarily positive attitude has always distinguished him personally and professionally.

Kerry Dolan, senior editor at Forbes Magazine and lifelong friend, served as a helpful sounding board throughout the project, assisted with the introduction and covers and responded to our many questions regarding editing and writing.

A heartfelt thank you to those people who touched the book in more ways than they will ever know. For their help, support, and commitment to this project, we are deeply grateful.

Rachel Castillo, sister, friend, and superb at the vastly underrated skill of simply getting things done. From helping edit, to fact-checking, to navigating the publishing world, to helping create the glossary and bibliography, Rachel's contributions to this project and to our lives are immense. If it weren't for her talent in production, we would steer her toward a career in banking.

Mary and Edward Kresky often served the role of counselors and surrogate parents. The quintessential New York couple, whose entertaining stories about New York politics and business provide us with immense pleasure, we greatly appreciate the many pep talks, invitations and home-cooked meals.

Our outstanding interns, Allen Kogan, Marcello Pantuliano, Ross Fox, Yvonne Lin, Candace Jackman, and Maria Pablo, were tireless in their reading, editing, and fact-finding missions. We never would have been able to handle all of this without them.

Sonny and Gloria Kamm gave us countless ideas about the books and always assured us that a little irreverence is a good thing.

Jeanne Leinhardt and Leslie Gardner, managing directors at JPMorgan and, more importantly, colleagues and friends, have long been supportive and willing to go the extra mile on behalf of clients and colleagues.

Julia Min Hwang, executive director, MBA Program at the Haas School of Business at UC Berkeley, was enthusiastically supportive of the books and provided excellent marketing ideas borne of her experience working at Haas and NYU's Stern School of Business.

We are deeply indebted to our employers, JPMorgan, Lehman Brothers, Banc of America Securities, and the Office of Ronald Reagan for giving us an opportunity. We are proud to have been involved with such outstanding institutions and impressive people.

Much of our desire to pursue careers in investment banking started in the classrooms of two influential finance professors. We thank William Cockrum, professor at the Anderson School at UCLA and former vice chairman of A.G. Becker & Co., and Stephen Etter, longtime finance lecturer at the Haas School of Business at UC Berkeley and partner at Greyrock Capital Group, for bringing their love of finance and banking into their respective classrooms. We hope these books do for others what Professors Cockrum and Etter did for us years ago.

The production of these books is a major undertaking, especially for investment bankers who were newcomers to the world of publishing. These books would not have been possible without the creative expertise of a number of specialists who were generous and patient as we came up the curve. In particular, we would like to thank Alejandro Paul, our fantastic and talented graphic designer who probably suffered with us more than anyone else on the actual creation of these books. Gracias por toda su ayuda, su paciencia y su amistad. Thank you to our editors Meghan Ward and Suzanne Young for improving our work literally one page at a time. Our illustrator Jeffrey Bean was terrific at taking our scribbled ideas and translating them into art. Catharyn Martz provided expert indexing, a formidable task in books like these. Candace Hinkle and Laurie Houghton of Sheridan Books were helpful in sharing their book production expertise. And Tracey and Nat Bolton of Bolton Designs and Sarah Sloboda were wonderful to work with as we developed electronic media for this project.

We are grateful to those colleagues who, though they may not have contributed specifically to these pages, were nonetheless instrumental in our professional development and therefore a *sine qua non* for these books. From them we learned a tremendous amount about investment banking and without their mentorship we would not have had the capability or confidence to embark on a project like this. Thank you to the following current or former managing directors at JPMorgan: Laurence Whittemore, Paul Dabbar, Jamie Grant, Sarah Nash, Jacques Aigrain, Avi Lewittes, Rick Escherich, Jim Bold, Hernan Cristerna, Todd Marin, David Jeffries, and Walter Hulse. Also, for being role models and for leading by example, thank you to Bill Williams, senior partner at Sullivan & Cromwell, Judge Alfred T. Goodwin, Senior Judge, Ninth Circuit Court of Appeals, Jose de la Torre, dean of the business school at Florida International University, and Tom Labrecque, former chairman of Chase Manhattan Bank.

To those friends and colleagues with whom we have shared memorable and often comical experiences in and out of the office, thank you for ensuring that the real benefit of banking is our lasting friendships. In addition to the colleagues who helped with the book, thank you to Paul Ward, Nathan Craig, Dave Blechman, Hala Ataya, Martin Kurtz, James Baker, Eddy Allegaert, Howard Rhee, Jamey Spencer, Ladell Robbins, Edouard Metrailler, Sylvia Son, Jay Koval, Helen Shan, Kristin Williams, R.A. McDonough, Greta Kessel, Hank Romaine, James Tashjian, Ian McAllister, Torrey Browder, Steve McKenna, Norm Gretzinger, Brett Pickett, Brad Nii, Derek Idemoto,

Rich Lark, Yancey Spruill, Christiana Voskarides, Chris Martell, Peter Kuhn, Lowell Strug, David Kramer, Luis Galeano, Eileen Smith, Luis Castro, Jon Secor, Chris Reale, Doug Gonsalves, Lori Lancaster, Megan Taylor, Redic Thomas, Thomas Donnelly, James Smith, Ed Hikmet, David Brakoniecki, Alison Dolan, Anu Aiyengar, Sheru Chowdhry, Kelly Hampaul, Karen Wong, Raymond Junior, Fifi Chan, Vera Tzenova, Carl Vevle, Jakeym Hubert, Vielcka Mansukhani, Diana Chen, Sakura Takano, Rohit Mohindra, Tom Miles, Yezan Haddadin, Alejandro Vicente, John Bates, Alex Allgood, Jay Ferguson, Caleb Hsieh, Randal Klein, Stephanie Ng, John Overbay, Tim Panos, Danielle Cheriff, J.D. Moore, David Stonberg, Lachlan Hughson and Chris Winchenbaugh.

Ted Craver, Peter Lersey, Russ Harding, Sandra Seville-Jones, and the rest of the Edison International team, thank you for teaching us that being an advisor is as much about being a good friend as it is being a good banker.

Thank you to the many other clients with whom we were fortunate to work so closely, in particular, Gerald Luterman and Ann Jordan and the rest of the KeySpan Energy team, the Strategic Planning team at Puget Energy, in particular Jim Sant and Don Gaines, and Mark Greenbaum, Emily McNeal and the analysts and associates at Savvian.

We would not have survived New York without the aid, assistance, humor, and occasional ministrations of Lorraine Friedman, Tammy LoCascio, and Jeanne Meehan. We have been and always will be their biggest fans.

Jared Kieling, editorial director at Bloomberg Press, offered encouragement at a critical time in the development process of these books.

Lou Paget, best-selling author and longtime friend, helped us navigate the perils of writing and publishing and offered advice and words of experience along the way.

A heartfelt and sincere thank you to those who have been a pillar of strength for us these last few years, including Ross and Cynthia Peet, Elaine and Mike Darer, Dan Zohar, Amyra Rand, Nicole Smelzer, Carlos Madrazo, Andy Wilcox, Meredith Kenny, Chaco Clotfelter, Greg Warnick, Roxanne Castillo, Sid Wales, John Fish, Matt Tysler, Kacie Stratton, James Scott, Greg Zimmer, Steve and Tami Holsten, John and Kathy Savarese, Neils Bergquist, Bill Thomas, Roger Minami, the Franks, Joan Liechty, Chip and Sarah Blaufuss, Ross Higuchi, Gary Waldron and Sunny Foster, Ann Longyear, the Ryan family, Chip Cushman, Carla de Cervantes, David Rauch, Tom Goepel, Alejandro Ogarrio, Thomas Kelly, Lisa Brant, y nuestros amigos en Buenos Aires: Fernando y Paula Lopez, Gabriel y Florencia Lopez, y Frank y Fabiana Almeida. Their friendship helped us reach the finish line.

We thank our wonderful and supportive families who, in spite of sometimes not knowing exactly what it is we do, always provided assurances that these books would be worth it.

Our parents never ceased to believe in us, offering an unlimited supply of encouragement with a regular and much appreciated sprinkling of optimism.

For years our siblings have been a source of strength, friendship, pride and, occasionally, comic relief. We are indebted to them for keeping us honest and reminding us never to take ourselves too seriously.

To all involved in this journey, thank you for waiting patiently for the conclusion of a process which occasionally seemed interminable. Your good humor, vast reserves of patience, and unwavering support buoyed us on many occasions when the proverbial light at the end of the tunnel seemed far, far away. We hope you are as proud of your contribution as we are grateful for it.

JC and PJM

Appendices

Investment Banks and Advisory Firms

Firms are listed alphabetically. For firms with headquarters outside of the U.S., the New York headquarters are provided.

ABN Amro
Park Avenue Plaza, 55 East 52nd Street, New York, NY 10055
(212) 409-1000, www.abnamro.com

Babcock & Brown
885 Second Avenue, New York, NY 10017
(212) 935-7800, www.babcockbrown.com

Bank of America Merrill Lynch
One Bryant Park, New York, NY 10036
(212) 449-1000, www.ml.com

Bank of Nova Scotia
1 Liberty Plaza, New York, NY 10006
(212) 225-5000, www.scotiabank.com

Barclays
745 Seventh Avenue, New York, NY 10019
(212) 412-4000, www.barclays.com

Blackstone Group
345 Park Avenue, New York, NY 10154
(212) 583-5000, www.blackstone.com

BNP Paribas
787 Seventh Avenue, New York, NY 10019
(212) 841-2000, www.bnpparibas.com.us

BMO Capital Markets
3 Times Square, New York, NY 10036
(212) 758-6300, www.bmocm.com

Brown Brothers Harriman & Co.
140 Broadway, New York, NY 10005-1101
(212) 483-1818, www.bbh.com

Calyon
95 Wall Street, New York, NY 10005
(212) 607-7000, www.calyon.com

Cantor Fitzgerald
499 Park Avenue, New York, NY 10022
(212) 938-5000, www.cantor.com

Capstone Partners
One Boston Place, Boston, MA 02108
(617) 619-3300, www.capstonellc.com

Chanin Capital Partners
11150 Santa Monica Boulevard, 6th Floor, Los Angeles, CA 90025
(310) 445-4010, www.chanin.com

CIBC World Markets
245 Park Avenue, New York, NY 10017
(212) 856-4000, www.cibcwm.com

Citigroup Global Corporate & Investment Banking
388 Greenwich Street, New York, NY 10013
(800) 285-3000, www.citigroupgcib.com

Commerzbank
1251 Avenue of the Americas, New York, NY 10020
(212) 703-4000, www.commerzbank.com

Credit Suisse
11 Madison Avenue, New York, NY 10010
(212) 325-2000, www.credit-suisse.com

Dahlman Rose & Co.
142 West 57th Street, New York, NY 10019
(212) 920-2940, www.dahlmanrose.com

Deloitte & Touche Corporate Finance
1633 Broadway, New York, NY 10019
(212) 489-1600, www.deloitte.com

Deutsche Bank
60 Wall Street, New York, NY 10005
(212) 250-2500, www.db.com

Duff & Phelps
55 East 52nd Street, New York, NY 10055
(212) 871-2000, www.duffandphelps.com

Edgeview Partners
301 South College Street, Suite 3700, Charlotte, NC 28202
(704) 602-3900, www.edgeviewpartners.com

Evercore Partners
55 East 52nd Street, New York, NY 10055
(212) 857-3100, www.evercore.com

Fortis
520 Madison Avenue, New York, NY 10022
(212) 418-8714, www.fortis.com

Friedman Billings Ramsey
1001 Nineteenth Street, Arlington, VA 22209
(703) 312-9500, www.fbr.com

GCA Savvian
150 California Street, San Francisco, CA 94111
(415) 318-3600, www.gcasavvian.com

Goldman Sachs
85 Broad Street, New York, NY 10004
(212) 902-1000, www.goldmansachs.com

Green, Manning & Bunch
3600 Republic Plaza, 370 17th Street, Denver, CO 80202
(303) 240-4800, www.gmbltd.com

Greenhill & Co.
300 Park Avenue, New York, NY 10022
(212) 389-1500, www.greenhill-co.com

Greif & Co
633 West Fifth Street, Los Angeles, CA 90071
(213) 346-9250, www.greifco.com

Harris Williams & Co.
1001 Haxall Point, 9th Floor, Richmond, VA 23219
(804) 648-0072, www.harriswilliams.com

Houlihan Lokey Howard & Zukin
1930 Century Park West, Los Angeles, CA 90067
(310) 553-8871, www.hlhz.com

HSBC Corporate, Investment Banking and Markets
8 Canada Square, Level 35, London E14 5HQ
+44-80-0093-9813, www.hsbc.com

Imperial Capital
2000 Avenue of the Stars, Los Angeles, CA 90067
(310) 246-3700, www.imperialcapital.com

ING Group
230 Park Avenue, New York, NY 10169
(212) 883-1206, www.ing.com

Innovation Advisors
One Penn Plaza, Suite 4115, New York, NY 10119
(212) 268-1501, www.innovationadvisors.com

Jefferies & Company
520 Madison Avenue, 12th Floor, New York, NY, 10022
(212) 284-2300, www.jefco.com

JMP Securities
600 Montgomery Street, Suite 1100, San Francisco, CA 94111
(415) 835-8900, www.jmpsecurities.com

J. P. Morgan
277 Park Avenue, New York, NY 10172
(212) 270-6000, www.jpmorgan.com

Keefe, Bruyette & Woods
787 Seventh Avenue, New York, NY 10019
(212) 887-7777, www.kbw.com

KeyBanc Capital Markets
127 Public Square, Cleveland, OH 44114
(216) 443-2300, www.key.com

Lazard Frères & Co.
30 Rockefeller Plaza, New York, NY 10020
(212) 632-6000, www.lazard.com

Legg Mason
100 Light Street, Baltimore, MD 21202
(877) 534-4627, www.leggmason.com

Macquarie Bank
125 West 55th Street, New York, NY 10019
(212) 231-1000, www.macquarie.com

Moelis & Company
10877 Wilshire Boulevard, Los Angeles, CA 90024
(310) 443-2300, www.moelis.com

Montgomery & Co.
100 Wilshire Boulevard, Santa Monica, CA 90401
(310) 260-6006, www.monty.com

Morgan Keegan
50 North Front Street, Memphis, TN 38103
(901) 579-4539, www.morgankeegan.com

Morgan Stanley
1585 Broadway, New York, NY 10036
(212) 761-4000, www.morganstanley.com

Needham & Co.
445 Park Avenue, New York, NY 10022
(212) 371-8300, www.needhamco.com

Nomura Securities
2 World Financial Center, New York, NY 10281
(212) 608-9120, www.nomura.com

Oppenheimer & Co.
125 Broad Street, New York, NY 10004
(212) 668-8000, www.oppenheimer.com

Pacific Crest Securities
111 SW Fifth Avenue, 42nd Floor, Portland, OR 97204
(503) 248-0721, www.pacific-crest.com

Park Lane Investment Banking
1875 Century Park East, Los Angeles, CA 90067
(310) 201-8496, www.parklaneservices.com

Perella Weinberg Partners
767 Fifth Avenue, New York, NY 10153
(212) 287-3200, www.pwpartners.com

Peter J. Solomon Company
520 Madison Avenue, New York, NY 10022
(212) 508-1600, www.pjsolomon.com

Piper Jaffray
800 Nicollet Mall, Suite 800, Minneapolis, MN 55402
(612) 303-6000, www.piperjaffray.com

Raymond James
880 Carillon Parkway, St. Petersburg, FL 33716
(727) 567-1000, www.raymondjames.com

Revolution Partners
75 Park Plaza, Boston, MA 02116
(617) 375-4200, www.revolutionpartners.com

Robert W. Baird & Co.
777 East Wisconsin Avenue, Milwaukee, WI 53201
(800) 792-2473, www.rwbaird.com

Rothschild
1251 Avenue of the Americas, New York, NY 10020
(212) 403-3500, www.rothschild.com

Royal Bank of Canada
200 Bay Street, Toronto, ON, Canada M5J 2W7
(416) 842-2000, www.rbc.com

Royal Bank of Scotland
101 Park Avenue, New York, NY 10178
(212) 269-1700, www.rbs.com

RSM EquiCo
575 Anton Boulevard, 11th Floor, Costa Mesa, CA 92626
(714) 327-8800, www.rsmequico.com

Sagent Advisors
299 Park Avenue, New York, NY 10171
(212) 904-9400, www.sagentadvisors.com

Sandler O'Neill + Partners
919 Third Avenue, 6th floor, New York, NY 10022
(212) 466-7800, www.sandleroneill.com

SG Cowen & Co.
1221 Avenue of the Americas, New York, NY 10020
(212) 278-6000, www.cowen.com

Societe Generale Securities
1221 Avenue of the Americas, New York, NY 10020
(212) 278-5000, www.sgcib.com

St. Charles Capital
1400 Sixteenth Street, Suite 300, Denver, CO 80202
(303) 339-9099, www.stcharlescapital.com

Stephens
111 Center Street, Little Rock, AK 72201
(501) 377-2000, www.stephens.com

SunTrust Robinson Humphrey Capital Markets
3333 Peachtree Road Northeast, 10th Floor, Atlanta, GA 30326
(404) 926-5217, www.suntrustrh.com

SVB Alliant
181 Lytton Avenue, Palo Alto, CA 94301
(650) 330-3000, www.svballiant.com

ThinkEquity Partners
600 Montgomery Street, 8th Floor, San Francisco, CA 94111
(415) 249-2900, www.thinkequity.com

Thomas Weisel Partners
One Montgomery Tower, San Francisco, CA 94104
(415) 364-2500, www.tweisel.com

Toronto Dominion
66 Wellington Street West, Toronto, Ontario, Canada M5K 1A2
(416) 982-6160, www.tdsecurities.com

UBS Securities
299 Park Avenue, New York, NY 10171
(212) 821-3000, www.ubs.com

UniCredit Group (HVB Capital Markets)
150 East 42nd Street, New York, NY 10017
(212) 672-6000, www.unicreditgroup.com

Wells Fargo Securities
600 California Street, Suite 1600, San Francisco, CA 94108
(415) 645-0800, www.wellsfargosecurities.com

West LB
1211 Avenue of the Americas, New York, NY 10036
(212) 852-6000, www.westlb.com

William Blair & Company
222 West Adams Street, Chicago, IL 60606
(312) 236-1600, www.williamblair.com

WR Hambrecht & Co.
539 Bryant Street, Suite 100, San Francisco, CA 94107
(415) 551-8600, www.wrhambrecht.com

Investment Banks

Glossary of Terms

Throughout the glossary, the terms Acquiror, Target, and Seller are capitalized and refer to the acquiring company, the target company, and the selling shareholder(s), respectively, in an M&A transaction. The term Issuer refers to the company selling securities (equity or debt) to investors.

A

ability-to-pay analysis: M&A analysis used to assess the maximum price Acquiror can pay for Target based on various financial metrics, including EPS accretion/dilution, balance sheet impact, and credit impact.

accelerated depreciation: Any depreciation method that provides for more depreciation in earlier years than the comparable amount of depreciation during that time using the straight-line method of depreciation. Modified Accelerated Cost Recovery System (MACRS), sum of the years' digits, and double-declining balance are accelerated depreciation methods and are often used for tax accounting purposes whereas straight-line depreciation, which is not an accelerated depreciation method, is often used for GAAP accounting purposes. See also **straight-line**.

accelerated marketing transaction: When marketing a securities offering, the Issuer meets only with selected investors. This is in comparison with, and in contrast to, a fully marketed transaction in which the Issuer meets with a broader group of investors. An accelerated marketing transaction is executed on a faster time frame than a fully marketed transaction, usually in recognition of strong investor demand. See also **fully marketed transaction**.

acceleration clause: A covenant found in loan agreements and bond indentures. The clause usually states that the entirety of the obligation is due immediately if the borrower fails to make a scheduled interest or principal payment on the specific debt. Most loans and some bonds also have cross-default provisions (also referred to as cross-acceleration rights) whereby all of the company's outstanding debt comes due if the issuer or borrower misses a scheduled interest or principal payment on any outstanding debt.

accretion/dilution analysis: A financial impact analysis that compares a company's financial results before a proposed transaction to the company's financial results after the proposed transaction. Accretion/dilution is most commonly performed for earnings per share (EPS), but it can also be performed for other financial metrics including cash flow per share and dividends per share (DPS).

accumulated depreciation: The aggregate amount of depreciation recognized to date on a depreciable asset. This is a contra-account to the PP&E account and serves to reduce it. PP&E is property, plant and equipment. PP&E is often quoted both on a gross basis (before accounting for accumulated depreciation) and on a net basis (after accounting for accumulated depreciation). See also **depreciation**.

acquisition: The purchase of a division, subsidiary, or stock of a company or the purchase of individual assets.

acquisition currency: The consideration (e.g., cash, stock, notes, or some combination thereof) paid by Acquiror to Seller(s) in an M&A transaction. See also **consideration**.

additional consideration: Additional payment offered to Seller in an M&A transaction, in addition to cash, stock, and/or notes. Examples include earnouts, contingent payments, and contingent securities.

advance notice provision: A corporate defense mechanism which requires that notice be given to management regarding proposed shareholder initiatives in advance of a shareholder meeting (typically stated as a number of days) in order to provide management and the board of directors with sufficient time to react to the proposed initiative(s). If it exists, this provision is found in a company's bylaws or corporate charter. Companies choose whether or not to have an advance notice provision.

affirmative covenant: Covenant in a legal agreement that requires a party to take a certain action. See also **negative covenant**.

aftermarket: The period of time after the initial offering of a security when the securities are bought and sold. Also referred to as the **secondary market**. See also **distribution**.

agreement and plan of reorganization: Legal agreement used in a merger, if the merger is structured as a tax-free reorganization under the Internal Revenue Code (IRC).

American depositary receipt (ADR): A negotiable certificate that represents ownership of non-U.S. securities but is itself registered on a U.S. exchange. The actual security which is traded on U.S. exchanges is called an American depositary share (ADS).

amortization: The principle of allocating the cost of an intangible asset over its useful life, and then charging off a portion of that cost as an expense each period as the asset is used. Examples of intangible assets include patents and other intellectual property. Amortization for intangible assets is similar to depreciation for tangible assets and depletion for natural resources. As of 2001, goodwill is no longer amortized but is periodically tested for impairment. See also **depletion, depreciation, goodwill**.

amortizing debt: Debt in which the principal is gradually repaid over the life of the debt. In comparison, debt with a bullet payment has a one-time repayment of the entire principal at the end of the term. Most loans are amortizing whereas bonds are generally bullet payments. Bullet payments may also be called balloon payments. See also **bullet payment, sinking fund**.

analysis at various prices (AVP): An M&A analysis used to calculate implied transaction multiples and premia over a range of offer prices.

annuity: A financial instrument whereby an investor pays something today in exchange for the receipt of equal payments paid periodically in the future for a predetermined period of time. The financial instrument will have no value at the end of the period (future value will be zero).

anti-dilutive: If options or other potentially dilutive securities (e.g., convertible debt, warrants) are out of the money (the strike price is greater than the current price), these securities are said to be anti-dilutive, meaning that no rational investor would convert them into equity and therefore there is no potential dilution to existing shareholders. If securities are anti-dilutive, no adjustment would be made to the number of shares outstanding for purposes of calculating diluted shares outstanding.

anti-greenmail provision: A corporate defense method that requires that before a would-be Target can make a greenmail payment to a Raider, a specified percentage of non-Raider shareholders must approve the payment. A greenmail payment is money paid to a Raider in exchange for Raider's shares in Target and is essentially money paid to make Raider go away. If it exists, this provision is found in a company's bylaws or corporate charter. Companies choose whether or not to have an anti-greenmail provision.

arbitrageur: A person or firm who enters into and seeks to profit from transactions when the same security or commodity is trading at different prices in two or more markets at the same time. See also **risk arbitrage**.

asset: Generically, any item which has or may have economic value. From an accounting perspective, assets are listed on one side of the balance sheet, representing the productive capabilities of the firm, and liabilities and shareholders' equity are listed on the other side of the balance sheet, representing obligations and ownership of the firm, respectively. See also **liability**.

asset-based lending: A form of secured financing in which assets are used as collateral for bank loans or other debt such as bonds. Examples include the securitization of a company's accounts receivable, mortgages secured by underlying real estate, and loans secured by a company's assets. See also **secured lending**.

asset purchase agreement: See **purchase and sale agreement**.

asset swap: The exchange of assets between two parties. If structured in accordance with applicable IRS provisions and limitations, an asset swap of "like-kind assets" can be a tax-deferred transaction.

asset write-down: A GAAP accounting concept. A reduction in an asset's book value (for GAAP purposes) to fair market value. Occurs when an asset's fair market value is less than its book value and the lower fair market value is deemed to be a permanent change. In the absence of an acquisition, assets can be written down to fair market value, but they cannot be written up to fair market value (though in the context of an acquisition, assets can be written up or written down to whatever their fair market value is). Except for any potential tax ramifications, an asset write-down is a non-cash event. See also **basis step-down.**

asset write-up: A GAAP accounting event related to purchase accounting. In an acquisition, if the fair market value of an acquired asset or liability is greater than the book value, the asset or liability is written up from the book value to the greater fair market value. Except for certain trading securities, asset write-ups only occur in the context of an acquisition whereas write-downs can occur in an acquisition as well as in the normal course of business if there has been a permanent reduction in the value of the asset.

available-for-sale method: A GAAP accounting method used to account for investments in other companies when the investor corporation does not exert significant control over the investee corporation (typically, but not always, measured as less than 20 percent of investee's equity), and when the fair value of the investee's security is readily available. See also **consolidation method, cost method, equity method.**

B

balance sheet: One of the three financial statements, along with the cash flow statement and the income statement. Represents what a company owns (its assets) and any claims on those assets (its liabilities and shareholders' equity). A balance sheet is a point in time measurement, meaning it measures the balance of accounts on one particular day. Most companies prepare annual and quarterly balance sheets. See also **cash flow statement, income statement**.

bank debt: Money borrowed from banks. In form, most bank debt is either a loan or a line of credit.

basic shares outstanding: Total number of shares issued and outstanding by a company. Basic shares outstanding does not include the dilutive effects of options, warrants, and other convertible securities as well as any treasury shares. Earnings per share (EPS) is generally quoted for both basic shares outstanding and diluted shares outstanding. See also **diluted shares**.

basis points: One basis point is equal to one one-hundredth of one percent. For example, 0.05 percent is equal to five basis points or 0.0005 and 1.0 percent is equal to 100 basis points or 0.01. Most debt securities are quoted in basis points over a same-dated U.S. Treasury security, LIBOR or the prime rate. See also **benchmark rate, credit spread, LIBOR**.

basis step-down: A tax accounting concept. A basis step-down occurs when Acquiror recognizes the lower fair market value of an acquired asset in its tax return work papers. Seller's higher tax basis in the sold asset is stepped down to fair market value when ownership is transferred to Acquiror's tax balance sheet. A basis step-down is undesirable because it decreases the asset's annual depreciation in the tax return work papers, thereby resulting in higher taxable income and, in turn, higher cash taxes. See also **asset write-down, carryover basis**.

basis step-up: A tax accounting concept. In asset purchases, Acquiror is allowed to record purchased assets in its tax return work papers at their fair market value, which is generally (but not always) higher than the tax basis of those assets in Seller's tax return work papers (therefore the term basis step-up; there can be a basis step-down if the fair market value of the asset acquired is less than the tax basis of that asset in Seller's tax return work papers). A basis step-up is desirable because it increases the asset's annual depreciation in the tax return work papers, thereby resulting in lower taxable income and, in turn, lower cash taxes. See also **asset write-up, carryover basis**.

benchmark rate: Since U.S. Government Treasury bonds, notes, and bills are considered a proxy for "risk-free" or "default-free" securities, they are often considered the benchmark rate or reference rate for bonds in the U.S. Most debt securities are quoted and priced based on a credit spread (in basis points) over the benchmark rate for the same-dated security (e.g., 100 basis points over the 10-year Treasury for a 10-year corporate bond). See also **basis points, credit spread**.

best efforts deal: Traditionally, an investment bank underwrote a securities offering for a company under a firm commitment agreement, which meant the investment bank purchased all of the securities Issuer wished to sell and then re-sold those securities to investors. The investment bank put its own capital at risk, owned the securities, and thereby assumed the execution risk (risk that the deal would not be completed). A firm commitment deal is also called an underwritten deal and a committed deal. Today, banks sell deals both on an underwritten basis and on a "best efforts" basis. Best efforts basis means that the bank will put forth its best effort to raise the desired funds on the proposed terms, but as an agent for Issuer, not as an owner of the securities. However, if the desired amount of capital cannot be raised on the proposed terms, the bank is not obligated to provide the total offering amount to the company, thereby transferring the execution risk to Issuer. Club deals are also becoming increasingly popular. A club deal occurs when a small group of Issuer's relationship banks underwrites the transaction together, as a club. See also **syndicate group, underwritten deals**.

bid/offer spread: The bid price is the price an investor is willing to pay for (i.e., bid for) a security. The offer price is the price a seller wants for a security (i.e., the price at which Seller offers the security for sale). The bid/offer spread is the difference between the bid price at which Buyer would like to buy and the offer price at which Seller would like to sell. It is sometimes referred to as the "bid/ask" spread to reflect the price that Seller asks for the security.

blank check preferred stock: Authorization for a company to issue a certain amount of preferred stock, usually found in a company's governing documents (i.e., its bylaws or corporate charter). Blank check preferred stock is generally considered a corporate defense tool since it provides a board of directors the authority to issue up to a predetermined amount of preferred stock on an accelerated time frame, which might be useful in the event of a hostile overture.

block trade: A negotiated sale of a large block of securities to one or a few investors. In a block trade, generally, a bank offers to buy a set number of securities at a set price and assumes the risk of subsequently placing the securities in the public market (just as in an underwritten offering). Also referred to as an overnight transaction.

bond: Debt security that is sold directly to investors. A bond pays periodic interest payments (usually semiannually) during the life of the bond or pays all accrued interest at maturity (as is the case for a zero coupon bond). The interest rate, or coupon rate, is usually fixed over the life of the bond (for this reason, bonds are also called fixed income securities). Bond pricing is directly correlated with prevailing interest rates and the issuer's credit risk. Principal repayment is generally due at maturity but some bonds have sinking funds which provide amortization features. See also **amortizing debt, sinking fund**.

bond indenture: A legal document (a contract) governing the agreement between the Issuer and the investor in a bond financing. The similar governing agreement for a loan (as opposed to a bond) is a loan agreement. See also **loan agreement**.

bookrunner: An investment bank that manages the offering process for a sale of securities. There can be joint bookrunners if more than one bank is managing the securities offering for the Issuer.

book value: The carrying value of an asset, liability or equity on the GAAP accounting records. The carrying value of an item on the tax accounting records is called the tax basis. Book value and tax basis refer to the same concept -- the carrying value of an item on the company's balance sheet, but book value is a GAAP accounting term and tax basis is a tax accounting term. See also **tax basis**.

book value of equity: The value of shareholders' equity on the GAAP accounting records.

boot: A tax accounting term. Non-equity transaction consideration which can include cash, notes, assets, or other consideration. Boot is generally immediately taxable while equity consideration can often qualify for tax-deferred treatment.

borrower: A borrower usually refers to an entity (e.g., an individual, corporation, government, or agency) which borrows money from a bank under a loan agreement. This is in contrast to an Issuer, which usually refers to an entity that issues securities (e.g., bonds) directly to investors under an indenture. See also **issuer**.

breakeven to EPS: For any transaction (i.e., M&A or financing), the point at which there is neither accretion nor dilution to earnings per share as a result of the transaction. See also **accretion/dilution analysis**.

breakup analysis: See **sum of the parts analysis**.

breakup fee: A fee that must be paid by one party to the other party if a transaction falls apart after signing of the agreement and before closing of the transaction due to one party breaching the contract and/or walking away from the deal. Breakup fees are usually two to four percent of the equity value of a transaction, but are subject to negotiation. See also **interloper**.

bridge financing: A type of interim financing often used to close an M&A transaction when cash is the acquisition consideration. Bridge financing is usually replaced by more permanent "take-out" financing soon after the M&A transaction has closed. Bridge financing provides companies the ability to fund an acquisition quickly and the flexibility to replace the bridge financing with permanent financing at a lower cost and/or on more attractive terms and conditions once the exigency of the transaction has passed. Bridge financing is generally more expensive for borrowers than permanent financing, which is why borrowers want to replace any bridge financing with permanent financing as soon as practicable. A "hung bridge" occurs if the company cannot "take out the bridge" due to a change in company conditions, market conditions and/or investor appetite. In the case of a hung bridge, the issuer has no choice but to retain the higher cost bridge financing until circumstances change.

bullet payment: Payment structure for debt in which the principal is due at maturity. This is in contrast to amortizing debt, in which the principal is repaid over the life of the debt. Most bonds have a bullet payment feature (also known as a balloon payment) whereas most loans have an amortizing feature. See also **amortizing debt**.

business judgment rule: Provides directors with common law protection from liability related to decisions made as a director of a corporation as long as the decision satisfies certain criteria including the decision was informed; the decision was made in good faith; the director had an honest belief that the actions taken were in the best interests of the company and its stockholders; and the director discharged her duty of loyalty and duty of care. See also **enhanced scrutiny**.

business purpose doctrine: One of many IRS requirements for a transaction to qualify as a tax-free reorganization. The doctrine requires that a transaction be motivated by at least one valid business purpose. See also **continuity of business enterprise doctrine, continuity of shareholder interest doctrine**.

buy-side process: The process undertaken by Acquiror when acquiring an asset, business or company from Seller. See also **sell-side process**.

bylaws: Corporate provisions which, along with the company's articles of incorporation (sometimes referred to as its charter), serve as the governing documents for a corporation. A corporation's articles of incorporation and bylaws must be filed with the Secretary of State in the state of incorporation. For any public company in the U.S., one can locate a company's charter and bylaws by referring to the list of exhibits in the company's most recent 10-K filing with the SEC.

C

CAGR: See **compound annual growth rate**.

calendar year: January 1 to December 31, which may be different from the company's fiscal year, which can be any 12-month period chosen by the company. See also **fiscal year**.

call option: Provides an issuer of debt or preferred securities the right to redeem the outstanding securities at a predetermined price and beginning on a predetermined date. The most common reason for a company to exercise a call option is that the company can refinance the securities at a lower cost. Many debt and preferred securities have "non-call" periods during which the security cannot be called. Call option also describes an equity derivative which enables the holder to purchase an equity security at a predetermined price known as the strike price. See also **put option**.

cap: The upper limit of a collar used in stock-for-stock transactions. See also **collar, floor**.

capital asset: There are two uses of the term capital asset: a commonly used corporate finance/GAAP accounting term, and a specific, tax accounting term of art. In its most common usage, a capital asset is generically defined as an asset purchased for use in the normal course of business that has a useful life of greater than one year and is capitalized (put on the balance sheet and depreciated or amortized). There is also a specific, tax accounting definition of a capital asset as, generally, any property (asset) other than inventory, real property (land) and depreciable property (depreciable assets). The most common capital asset is stock owned of a corporation. Any gain on sale of a capital asset, as defined for tax purposes only, is subject to capital gain tax. See also **capital gain/loss, capital gain tax, capital loss carryback, capital loss carryforward, capitalized.**

capital expenditures (capex): Capital spent on long-term assets or investments which assets are put on the balance sheet and depreciated or amortized, as opposed to expenses which flow directly through the income statement. Capital assets (using the common, non-tax definition) are placed on the balance sheet and depreciated (for tangible assets) or amortized (for intangible assets) to reflect their multi-year lives. A distinction is sometimes made between maintenance capex (expenditures on general upkeep of an asset) and investment capex (expenditures to improve an asset).

capital gain/(loss): A tax accounting concept. The difference between the selling price of a capital asset and the capital the asset's tax basis. The related GAAP accounting concept is book gain/(loss) on sale.

capital gain tax: A tax accounting concept. Tax due on any capital gain. If the capital asset were sold at a loss (selling price is less than the asset's tax basis), Seller would have a capital loss, which provides a tax benefit. See also **income tax**.

capital loss carryback: A tax accounting concept. When current capital losses are used to offset capital gains which occurred in the past. Carrybacks are subject to IRS limitations. See also **tax loss carryback** (for non-capital losses).

capital loss carryforward: A tax accounting concept. When current capital losses are carried forward to offset capital gains triggered at some point in the future. Carryforwards are subject to IRS limitations. See also **tax loss carryforwards** (for non-capital losses).

capital structure: The debt and equity obligations of a company. Also referred to as the company's capitalization. Components of the capital structure can include long-term debt, short-term debt, high yield debt, preferred stock, and common stock.

capitalization: The debt and equity obligations of a company constitute the company's capitalization. Also referred to as the company's capital structure. See also **capital structure**.

capitalized: If a purchased asset has a useful life longer than one year, it should be put on the balance sheet as a long-term asset, or capitalized. This means that the total cost of the asset is put on the balance sheet when it is initially purchased, and each period over the useful life of the asset a portion of the capitalized asset's value is depreciated (for tangible assets) or amortized (for intangible assets).

carry: Participation of a financial sponsor in the profits of a private equity investment. Carry, which is shortened from "carried interest," is usually 20 percent of the profits of the transaction after certain specified costs have been subtracted, such as after limited partners are paid any preferred return owed, after subtraction of the management fee, and after expenses are subtracted.

carryover tax basis: A tax accounting concept in which Seller's historical tax basis in the sold assets is transferred to the new owner after the sale closes. For example, assume Smith Corporation has a single asset with a tax basis of $10 million in that asset. Jones Corporation buys the stock of Smith Corporation. Since Jones Corporation purchased the stock of Smith Corporation, GAAP accounting rules dictate that when Jones records Smith's assets on Jones's tax return work papers, it does so at Smith's tax basis of $10 million (carryover basis). There is no change in the tax basis of the asset from Smith's tax basis to Jones' tax basis. Rather, Smith's tax basis in the asset is carried over to Jones. See also **basis step-down**, **basis step-up**.

cash flow: Amount of cash received or paid over time. This is separate from accounting profit or loss but can be reconciled to accounting profit or loss via the cash flow statement.

cash flow accretion/dilution analysis: A financial impact analysis that compares the cash flow per share of Acquiror pre-transaction to the cash flow per share of Acquiror post-transaction. See also **accretion/dilution analysis**.

cash flow from financing: One of the three parts of the cash flow statement. Cash flow from financing represents the total cash flow payments and receipts related to financing activities, including the issuance and repayment of debt, the issuance and repurchase of equity, and the payment of dividends.

cash flow from investing: One of the three parts of the cash flow statement. Cash flow from investing represents the total cash payments and receipts related to capital assets, such as capital expenditures, investments, or the sale of an asset or business.

cash flow from operations: One of the three parts of the cash flow statement. Cash flow from operations represents the total cash payments and receipts related to the day-to-day operations of a company, beginning with net income and adjusted for non-cash items such as depreciation and amortization, as well as cash items such as changes in working capital and changes in deferred taxes.

cash flow statement: One of the three financial statements, along with the balance sheet and the income statement. Reconciles the income statement and the balance sheet at the end of a period to determine the actual cash flow generated by a company. Also referred to as the statement of sources and uses. The cash flow statement does not reflect to whom the cash belongs; the balance sheet reflects that; nor does the cash flow statement reflect profitability, which is reflected on the income statement. The cash flow statement simply measures flows of cash received by or paid out by the company. See also **balance sheet, income statement**.

cash taxes: The tax liabilities for the reporting period as calculated in the tax return work papers. These tax liabilities are referred to as "cash taxes" because they are the amounts that are actually paid for the reporting period, in cash, to the respective taxing authorities such as the IRS.

change-of-control provision: A clause in a legal contract that allows a change to or termination of (depending on the language) the contract if one party to the contract enters into a change-of-control transaction.

change-of-control transaction: Any transaction in which the previous owners are no longer "in control" of the company after the transaction is completed, meaning they have sold the majority and/or controlling interest in the company to another company or set of shareholders.

Chinese Wall: See **ethical wall**.

classified board: A corporate defense mechanism in which the board of directors is divided into more than one class (usually three classes, each with a three-year term), with one class of directors up for re-election at each annual meeting. With a classified board, the entire slate of directors cannot be voted off in one annual meeting. If it exists, this provision is found in a company's bylaws or corporate charter. Companies choose whether or not to have a classified board. Also referred to as a staggered board.

closing balance sheet: The balance sheet at the end of the reporting period. For purposes of financial statement analysis, one needs an opening balance sheet (to see the status of all balance sheet accounts at the beginning of the reporting period) and a closing balance sheet (to see the status of all balance sheet accounts at the end of the reporting period) in order to determine how the accounts have changed over the course of the reporting period. See also **balance sheet, opening balance sheet**.

closing conditions: Requirements written into a legal contract that must be met by a party before the transaction can close. There are usually closing conditions which apply to Acquiror and closing conditions which apply to Target. See also **contingencies**.

collar: A contract or derivative which caps or limits the high or low value of a security, respectively. Collars are used in M&A transactions to bracket or bound the amount of fluctuation in an exchange ratio when stock is part of the acquisition currency. See also **cap, floor**.

collateral: An asset or assets pledged by a borrower to secure an obligation. In the event of default on the obligation, this collateral may be taken by the security-holder in partial or total satisfaction of the obligation. See also **asset-based lending, secured lending**.

commercial paper (CP): Short-term public debt with maturities between two and 270 days which is issued through brokers or directly to investors. Commercial paper is issued only by investment grade companies and is often used by the Issuer to fund working capital needs. It is usually one of the least expensive forms of capital due to its short duration and therefore low risk. At maturity, most CP is simply rolled over (extended) rather than redeemed. Issuers are required to maintain a traditional line of credit as an alternative if the market to refinance the CP is unavailable for any reason. This line of credit is called a "CP backstop."

common equity: Capital that represents an ownership stake in the corporation and has a perpetual life. Common equity is lower in liquidation preference than preferred equity. See also **equity, liquidation preference, preferred equity**.

comparable companies: Companies within the same peer or industry group and/or companies with similar operating, business, and/or growth profiles.

comparable company analysis: A multiples-based valuation method used to determine a company's valuation range based on current stock prices of the company's peers. Also referred to as trading comps analysis. Comparable company analysis is a relative valuation method (as opposed to an intrinsic valuation method) in that it derives or implies a value for Company X based on how Company X's peers are trading. Valuation using comparable company analysis does not include a control premium. See also **control premium**.

comparable transaction analysis: A multiples-based valuation method used to determine a company's valuation range based on prices paid and, specifically, multiples paid in comparable M&A transactions. Also referred to as precedent transaction analysis. Comparable transaction analysis is a relative valuation method (as opposed to an intrinsic valuation method) in that it derives or implies a value for Company X based on transactions involving Company X's peers. Valuation using comparable transaction analysis includes a control premium. See also **control premium**.

compounding: The mathematical act of bringing one or more present values forward to a future value using future value formulas. The concept of earning interest on interest is also called compounding interest. Discounting is the mathematical action of bringing one or more future values back to a present value using present value formulas. Both compounding and discounting recognize the time value of money. See also **discounting**.

compound annual growth rate (CAGR): The implied annualized growth rate based on a beginning value and an ending value. CAGR is a theoretical concept since it assumes that the growth rate each year for the entire period is the same.

Most commonly, the formula to calculate CAGR is calculated as:

> $[\,(\text{Last number / first number})^{1/n\text{-}1}\,] - 1$
>
> where n = number of *periods* in the sample set (and so the divisor of the exponent is the number of *compounding* periods)

However, occasionally the calculation of CAGR is seen with the number of *compounding periods*:

> $[\,(\text{Last number / first number})^{1/n}\,] - 1$
>
> where n = number of *compounding periods* in the sample set (and so the divisor of the exponent is the number of *compounding* periods)

compound interest: The process of earning interest each period on the principal as well as on the accumulated interest. See also **compounding, simple interest**.

confidentiality agreement (CA): A legal agreement that prevents the recipient of confidential information from disclosing that confidential information except under defined circumstances, such as to other members of the deal team to assist in the due diligence process. Also referred to as a non-disclosure agreement (NDA).

consideration: Within an M&A context, the form of payment used in an acquisition (e.g., stock, cash, and/or notes). Also referred to as acquisition currency. In a legal contract, consideration is anything of value which is exchanged for a good or service.

consolidated tax return: When two (or more) related corporations file a single tax return. Currently, the IRS allows corporations that own greater than 80 percent of the vote and value of another corporation to file a consolidated tax return (i.e., one tax return for the two corporations as opposed to two separate tax returns). Consolidation for GAAP purposes (generally greater than 50 percent) is defined differently than consolidation for tax purposes.

consolidation method: A GAAP accounting method used to account for investments in other companies when the investor corporation is deemed to have control over the investee corporation (typically, but not always, measured as greater than 50 percent of investee's equity). The investee is treated as a subsidiary of the investor and the investee's financial statements are consolidated into (included in) the investor's financial statements. See also **available-for-sale method**, **cost method, equity method**.

contingencies: Within an M&A context, components of a merger or acquisition agreement which must affirmatively take place for the transaction to close. Also referred to as **closing conditions.**

continuity of business enterprise doctrine: One of many IRS requirements for a transaction to qualify as a tax-free reorganization. The doctrine requires that, following the reorganization, Acquiror continues a significant line of Target's business or uses a significant portion of Target's assets. See also **business purpose doctrine, continuity of shareholder interest doctrine**.

continuity of shareholder interest doctrine: One of many IRS requirements for a transaction to qualify as a tax-free reorganization. The doctrine requires that a material part of the consideration received by Target shareholders consist of stock of Acquiror (i.e., that Target shareholders continue to have an ownership interest in Acquiror by virtue of their receipt of Acquiror stock in exchange for their Target stock). See also **business purpose doctrine, continuity of business enterprise doctrine**.

contractual subordination: Results when debt is subordinated based on features written into the bank loan agreement or bond indenture (the contract between lender and borrower or between investor and issuer, respectively) which in substance or form names the debt as "junior" or "subordinated" to senior debt. Subordinated debt is lower in liquidation preference than senior debt, meaning it does not get repaid until all senior debt is repaid. Contractual subordination is a common cause of credit rating notching. See also **notching, structural subordination**.

contribution analysis: A type of M&A analysis often used in a merger of equals (MOE). The premise is that a fair exchange ratio should be determined based on the contributions of each party to common operating metrics such as sales, EBIT, EBITDA, net income, assets, and equity value.

control premium: Price paid by Acquiror over Target's current trading level in order to obtain voting control of Target, as opposed to the price for a minority share of Target, the ownership of which does not carry with it the ability to control the company. The control premium is typically quoted as a percentage over the current stock price.

convertible securities: Debt, preferred stock, or other securities that can be converted into a specific number of shares of common stock at some point in the future based on specified triggering events.

corporate defense: The act of helping a potential Target do what it legally can in order to remain independent in anticipation of or in the face of a hostile overture from a corporate raider. See also **raider**.

corporate development group: See **strategic planning group**.

corporate income tax: Tax levied on a corporation's taxable income.

corporate-level tax: Tax owed and paid by a corporation. See also **double taxation, shareholder-level tax**.

corporate merger: The combination of two corporations. Mergers are governed by state corporation law. See also **merger, statutory merger**.

cost method: A GAAP accounting method to account for investments in other companies when the investor corporation does not exert significant control over the investee corporation (typically, but not always, measured as less than 20 percent of investee's equity), and when the fair value of the investee's security is not readily available (e.g., if investee corporation is private). See also **available-for-sale method, consolidation method, equity method.**

cost of capital: The return required by providers of capital. See also **weighted average cost of capital (WACC)**.

cost synergies: Cost efficiencies created through improved operating practices and the elimination of redundant functions. See also **revenue synergies, synergies**.

counter-parties: Two parties that enter into either side of a contract.

coupon rate: The interest rate on a bond. Most bond coupons are paid semiannually, but the coupon rate is quoted annually, usually based on a par value of $1,000 per bond. Thus a bond with an 8 percent coupon rate would pay $80 in annual interest, payable in two semiannual installments of $40, based on a par value of $1,000.

coverage bankers: Investment bankers who focus their efforts on building relationships with clients (and are able to discuss numerous products and services with them) and winning business for the investment bank. Also referred to as relationship bankers. Coverage bankers often specialize in an industry (though sometimes in a geographic region) and are different from product bankers, who specialize in the execution of a particular type of financial product (such as M&A, equity capital markets or leveraged finance). See also **product bankers**.

coverage ratio: A type of credit ratio which is used to measure cash flow available to service interest and other fixed obligations such as debt amortization requirements. Therefore, a higher coverage ratio is better since it indicates a larger safety margin of cash flow relative to fixed obligations. Common coverage ratios are EBITDA / interest expense and EBITDA / (interest + amortization). See also **EBIT, EDITDA, leverage ratio**.

credit analysis: Any of a number of analyses used to assess the bankruptcy risk, debt capacity, financial risk, and business risk of a company. A number of factors are considered when performing credit analysis, including credit and financial ratios, the management team, the industry in which the company operates, and legal contracts or regulations in place which govern the receipt of cash flows that can be used to service debt. A common mistake is to assume that credit analysis is entirely dependent on credit ratios. Credit analysis is dependent on a wide range of factors; many are quantitative but some are qualitative. See also **credit risk**.

credit default swap (CDS): A credit derivative that pays the investor if the underlying company defaults on its debt obligations. It is essentially credit insurance for the investor. The cost of the insurance (measured by the cost of the option) is a measure of the company's perceived credit risk. The higher the perceived likelihood that a company will default on its debt (such that the entity which issued the credit default swap has to pay the entity which purchased the credit default swap), the more expensive it is for a party to buy the credit default swap. Also referred to as a credit derivative.

credit impact analysis: Analysis that considers the impact of a proposed transaction (which could be a strategic action or a financing action) on an Acquiror's balance sheet, credit risk, and credit ratios.

credit outlook: An assessment of the potential direction of a longer term credit rating. Every credit rating has an existing rating as well as a credit outlook, although this outlook is not necessarily indicative of a credit watch action or an impending credit upgrade or downgrade. See also **confirmation, credit rating, credit watch**.

credit rating: An opinion provided by a third party regarding the credit risk of a company, which opinion is denominated by a letter or combination of letters and numbers. Moody's, Standard & Poor's (S&P) and Fitch are the three largest rating agencies. Dominion Bond Rating Service of Canada was recognized as a rating agency by the SEC in 2003. The proper name for a rating agency is an NRSRO (Nationally Recognized Statistical Rating Organization). The designation as an NRSRO is provided by the SEC through a no-action letter. See also **no-action letter**.

credit ratios: Financial calculations used to help assess a company's credit risk.

credit risk: The likelihood that a company will default or fail to pay its debt obligations. See also **credit analysis**.

credit spread: Measure of the additional return above the risk-free rate which a debt investor or lender demands for investing in a specific debt security or loan. Credit spreads are typically quoted based on a given maturity and in basis points over an index, such as LIBOR or the benchmark Treasury rate for the same maturity, which are considered proxies for the risk-free rate. For example, if Company X issues 10-year bonds yielding 7 percent and the current 10-year U.S. Treasury bond yields 5 percent, investors would say that this company's 10-year bond has a credit spread of 200 basis points (or 2 percent) over the same-dated U.S. Treasury bond. See also **basis points, credit analysis, credit risk**.

credit watch: Being on credit watch means that the rating agency which issued the credit watch is paying particularly close attention to the issuer with a special focus on shorter term events such as mergers, acquisitions, or restructurings. A negative credit watch means that the rating may be lowered (but it has not yet been lowered). A positive credit watch means that the rating may be raised (but it has not yet been raised). A developing credit watch means that the rating may be raised, lowered, or remain the same. See also **credit outlook.**

cross-acceleration rights: See **acceleration clause**.

cross-default provisions: See **acceleration clause**.

crossover issuers: High yield issuers that are close to investment grade status and therefore can attract both investment grade and non-investment grade (or high yield) investors. In general, fixed income investors invest in either investment grade debt or high yield debt. See also **high yield debt, investment grade debt**.

crown jewel defense: A corporate defense mechanism in which Target sells critical assets, the loss of which is designed to make Target less attractive to a potential Acquiror.

cumulative dividend: A common feature of preferred securities in which the preferred dividend, which can be deferred in times of financial need, must be paid in full prior to the payment of any common stock dividend, regardless of the reason why the dividend was not paid (and therefore accumulated).

cumulative voting: A shareholder's ability to cast all of his or her votes cumulatively for one director as opposed to one vote per director. A provision preventing cumulative voting is a common corporate defense mechanism. If it exists, this provision is found in a company's bylaws or corporate charter. Companies choose whether or not to have cumulative voting.

current assets: Assets that are expected to be converted to cash within one operating cycle or one year. Examples include accounts receivable and inventory. See also **long-term assets**.

current liabilities: Liabilities that are due to a third party in cash within one operating cycle or one year. Examples include accounts payable, short-term debt and taxes payable. See also **long-term liabilities**.

D

DD&A: Depreciation, depletion and amortization. See also **depreciation, depletion, amortization**.

dead hand provision: An optional feature in a poison pill. Provides that only directors who were in place prior to a proxy contest, or consent solicitation, are allowed to redeem the shareholder rights plan. Thus new directors, even if they won a seat on the board, would be unable to redeem the poison pill unless they were approved by the continuing directors. As such, this provision is also called a continuing director provision. See also **no hand provision, poison pill, shareholder rights plan**.

deal protection: Mechanisms written into an agreement to protect a transaction from attack by making it difficult and/or unattractive for a third party to break up a transaction. Examples include no shop / no talk provisions and breakup fees.

deal team: A group of people working together on a transaction. Since any transaction requires the involvement of a number of players, participants on a deal team include company executives as well as professionals unrelated to either party to the transaction such as bankers, lawyers, accountants, and consultants, and may include other professionals. Different deal team members become involved during different stages of a transaction, and their participation may be brief or ongoing.

debt: Capital that is borrowed and must be repaid by the borrower. Usually (but not always) the borrower must pay periodic interest on the borrowed funds (there are times when the interest is embedded into the original cost of the debt instrument). Debt investors have claims to their invested capital only (including any interest and potentially underlying assets if the debt is secured). Debt investors are not owners of the company. Debt is higher in liquidation preference than equity. See also **equity, liquidation preference**.

debt capacity analysis: An analysis used to assess the impact of a prospective transaction on a company's balance sheet, credit risk, and credit ratios. Debt capacity analysis is often done by Acquiror prior to a potential M&A transaction but is also done for other contemplated corporate actions such as a recapitalization or refinancing.

deferred taxes: Deferred taxes arise when taxes payable in a period in the GAAP financial statements differ from taxes payable as calculated in the tax return work papers. That is, deferred taxes arise when the amount that is owed to the government as calculated on the GAAP books is more (deferred tax liability) or less (deferred tax asset) than what is paid as calculated in the tax return work papers (i.e., what is actually paid to taxing authorities as cash taxes). See also **cash taxes**.

deferred tax asset: A GAAP balance sheet account that is created when taxes payable as calculated in the GAAP financial statements are less than taxes payable as calculated in the tax return work papers. A deferred tax asset exists when a tax *benefit* is expected in the future and has been recognized in the GAAP books, but has not yet been recognized in the tax return work papers. Also referred to as a deferred tax benefit.

deferred tax liability: A GAAP balance sheet account that is created when taxes payable as calculated in the GAAP financial statements are greater than taxes payable as calculated in the tax return work papers. A deferred tax liability exists when a tax *liability* is expected in the future and has been recognized in the GAAP books, but has not yet been recognized in the tax return work papers.

depreciation: The principle of allocating the cost of a tangible asset over its useful life, and then charging off a portion of that cost as an expense each period as the asset is used. Examples of tangible assets include factories, cars, and equipment. Depreciation for tangible assets is similar to amortization for intangible assets and depletion for natural resources. See also **amortization, depletion**.

depletion: Conceptually similar to depreciation, but for natural assets that are depleted such as oil and gas reserves and other natural resources. See also **amortization, depreciation**.

derivative: Any type of financial contract the value of which is determined in reference to or by an underlying asset, item or commodity such as an interest rate, the value of a stock, the cost of oil per barrel, or a credit rating.

diluted shares: The number of a company's shares outstanding, adjusted for any stock options and/or potentially dilutive securities such as the equity component of convertible debt or convertible preferred stock. Diluted shares outstanding may be equal to basic shares outstanding (if the company has no options or potentially dilutive securities) but it will never be less than basic shares outstanding. Most EPS estimates are quoted using diluted shares outstanding, not basic shares outstanding. See also **basic shares outstanding**.

discounted cash flow analysis (DCF): A valuation method that determines the value of a project, investment, or company based on the cash flows generated by the project, investment, or company, which cash flows are then discounted by the project, investment, or company's weighted average cost of capital to reflect the risk of those cash flows. As a result, DCF yields a stand-alone or intrinsic valuation, as opposed to relative valuation using methods such as comparable company analysis and comparable transaction analysis, which use data from other companies to imply a valuation of the company under analysis. DCF analysis is comprised of periodic cash flows and a terminal value calculation, both of which must be discounted to the valuation date. It measures the value of a firm to both debt and equity holders. Net debt must be subtracted from the enterprise value to measure the value of a firm to only the equity holders. See also **weighted average cost of capital**.

discounted equity value analysis (DEV): A valuation method that determines the value to the equity holders based on the cash flows generated by the company or asset which flow only to equity holders, discounted by the equity holders' cost of capital.
discounting: The mathematical act of bringing one or more future values backward to a present value. Compounding is the mathematical act of bringing one or more present values forward to a future value. See also **compounding**.

discount rate: The rate of return (r) used as the divisor in present value calculations and which is supposed to represent the risk associated with the cash flow of a particular investment, asset, or business. See also **cost of capital, discounted cash flow analysis, weighted average cost of capital.**

distribution: The act of selling securities to investors (both institutional and retail investors). For an investment bank to be successful in any securities offering, it must have an effective distribution capability. Distribution capabilities are important both at the time of the offering as well as in the aftermarket or secondary market, which is the period of time after the initial security offering when securities are bought and sold.

diversifieds: Companies that operate two or more major business lines. In contrast, companies with only one major business line are pure plays. See also **pure play**.

divestiture: The sale, separation, or disposition of an asset, division, or subsidiary by a parent corporation.

dividend accretion/dilution analysis: Financial impact analysis used to measure the effect of a transaction on the dividend per share of Acquiror and/or Target. See also **accretion/dilution**.

dividend per share (DPS): The dollar amount of dividends paid out per share, usually quoted quarterly or annually. The indicated annual dividend is the latest quarterly dividend per share multiplied by four. Not all companies pay dividends. Smaller and/or cash flow negative companies tend not to pay dividends while larger, cash flow positive companies tend to pay dividends. See also **double taxation**.

dividend yield: The annual dividend received per share of stock divided by the current stock price. Dividend yield and share price appreciation are the two components of total return. See also **total return**.

division: A functional unit of a company that is not organized as a separate legal entity. The difference between a division and a subsidiary is that a subsidiary is itself a corporation majority owned by a parent corporation. See also **subsidiary**.

double taxation: Occurs when both corporate-level tax and shareholder-level tax are triggered. For example, corporate dividends are subject to double taxation: the first level of tax occurs when the corporation must pay taxes on its taxable income (corporate-level tax) prior to calculating net income, and the second level of tax occurs when the shareholder must pay tax on the dividends received (shareholder-level tax). See also **corporate income tax, corporate-level tax, shareholder-level tax**.

DRD rules: Dividends-received deduction rules. The DRD is an IRS deduction which allows eligible U.S. corporations that receive dividends from other U.S. corporations to deduct from their federal taxable income some percentage of the dividends received (i.e., the deducted dividends are tax-free).

dual path: Occurs when a company pursues two strategic paths simultaneously. A company on a dual (or multiple) path prepares to execute two (or more) strategic options and, depending on market conditions, can decide between the options just prior to execution.

due diligence: The process of investigating and analyzing a company's assets or business.

duration of an investment: Length of time an investment is held.

Dutch auction: One method used in share repurchases. In a Dutch auction, the company announces a maximum price to be paid per share repurchased. The shareholders offer to sell their shares at specific prices up to the maximum price stated by the company, after which the company sets a purchase price based on shareholder indications. All shareholders receive the same purchase price in a Dutch auction. See also **fixed price tender offer**.

E

earnings before interest and taxes (EBIT): Earnings before interest and taxes. Income statement metric which represents earnings prior to the payment of interest expense and taxes.

earnings before interest, taxes and DD&A (EBITDA): Earnings before interest taxes, depreciation and amortization. Income statement metric which represents earnings prior to the payment of interest expense, taxes, depreciation, depletion, and amortization.

earnings before taxes (EBT): Earnings before taxes. Line item on an income statement which represents earnings prior to the payment of taxes; also referred to as pretax profit, pretax operating income, pretax earnings, and taxable income.

earnings per share (EPS): Net income divided by diluted shares outstanding (for diluted EPS; basic EPS is calculated as net income divided by basic shares outstanding).

earnings to common: Net income after the payment of dividends. Earnings to common are the earnings which accrue to the common equity account (shareholders' equity) on the balance sheet.

earnout agreement: Potential additional payment from Acquiror to Seller tied to the future results of the acquired entity. If they are triggered, earnout payments are made to Seller after the transaction has closed (usually one to three years) and are usually tied to Target's financial results. Earnout agreements and similar types of consideration which are tied to future results are referred to as contingent consideration since the additional payments are tied to the Target company hitting certain agreed upon metrics (often, but not always, financial in nature).

engagement agreement: A legal agreement signed by a company when it hires or engages an outside advisor to do work on its behalf. The engagement agreement outlines the terms of the engagement. In the context of an investment banking engagement agreement, advisors can arrange an hourly or monthly retainer fee in addition to a "success fee" payable upon the successful culmination of a transaction. The success fee for an investment bank is usually tied to the size and type of the transaction. If the transaction does not close, the success fee is not paid. In an engagement agreement, it is common to request that the bank be reimbursed for reasonable out-of-pocket expenses.

enhanced scrutiny: Level of judicial review applied if a board of directors is considering a defensive action in a hostile situation. Under enhanced scrutiny, the board must meet an enhanced test before the liability protections of the business judgment rule are afforded to it. Specifically, the board must show that (a) it reasonably perceived a significant threat to the company's integrity, and (b) the defensive action proposed (or taken, if after the fact) was reasonable and proportionate to the perceived threat. See also **business judgment rule.**

enterprise value: Represents the value of both the equity (common equity and preferred equity) and the net debt of a company, based on the current market value of common equity. Also referred to as firm value. See also **equity value**.

entry multiple: The valuation multiple (e.g., enterprise value to EBITDA, price to earnings) paid when an investor buys a company. See also **exit multiple**.

EPS accretion/dilution analysis: Financial impact analysis used to compare the earnings per share for a company before and after a transaction. See also **accretion/dilution**.

equity: Equity is capital provided by investors to a company in exchange for an ownership stake in the company. In liquidation, equity holders get paid last, after all other providers of capital. An individual unit of equity is called a stock or a share. See also **common equity, debt, preferred equity**.

equity method: A GAAP accounting method used to account for investments in other companies when the investor corporation has significant influence over the investee corporation (typically, but not always, measured as between 20 percent and 50 percent of investee's equity), but does not control the investee. See also **available-for-sale method, consolidation method, cost method**.

equity value: Represents the aggregate value of shareholders' equity based on the current market stock price. This is separate and apart from the book value of equity. Equity value is also referred to as market value and market value of equity (in contrast to book value of equity). See also **book value of equity, enterprise value, firm value**.

ethical wall: An internal firewall created within an investment bank between those groups with access to confidential client company information and those without access to confidential information. Also referred to as a Chinese Wall.

evergreen facility: A revolving line of credit which renews automatically. Also called an evergreen line of credit. See also **revolving line of credit**.

exchange offer: An offer by Acquiror to purchase shares directly from the shareholders of Target in exchange for Acquiror stock or a mix of cash and Acquiror stock. The difference between an exchange offer (payment in all stock or stock and cash) and a tender offer (payment in cash) is the type of consideration offered by Acquiror to Target shareholders. See also **tender offer**.

exchange offer prospectus: The combination of the exchange offer and prospectus documents provided to Target shareholders in an exchange offer.

exchange ratio: The number of Acquiror shares offered for one share of Target in a stock-for-stock exchange. Calculated as offer price per share for Target divided by Acquiror share price.

execution risk: The risk that a transaction will not close.

exercise price: The price at which an option can be exercised. This is also referred to as the strike price. See also **in the money, out of the money, strike price**.

exit multiple: The valuation multiple (e.g., enterprise value to EBITDA, price to earnings) when an investor sells a company. See also **entry multiple**.

F

face value: The nominal value of a security, often printed on the security itself.

While the term also applies to stocks, it most commonly refers to the "par" value of a bond, which is the amount paid at maturity to the owner of the bond.

fair market value (FMV): The current value of an asset or security, often as determined by the price in an arm's length sale of the asset or security. See also **asset write-down, asset write-up**.

fair price provision: A corporate defense mechanism which requires that all shareholders receive equivalent consideration in a tender offer. The fair price provision developed as a countermeasure to two-tier bids. If it exists, this provision is found in a company's bylaws or corporate charter. Companies choose whether or not to have a fair price provision. In addition, many states have enacted fair price laws which apply to all companies incorporated in those states, whether or not the companies themselves have adopted a fair price provision.

fairness opinion: An opinion provided by an investment bank to a client that states that a proposed transaction is "fair from a financial point of view." The investment bank would perform a number of financial analyses and consider the specific characteristics of the transaction to determine whether the transaction were fair from a financial point of view. A fairness opinion is not tantamount to saying that the proposed price is the best available price or even a good price. The fairness opinion is generally delivered to a company's board of directors at the time the board of directors votes on a proposed transaction.

Financial Accounting Standards Board (FASB): Independent body of accounting professionals responsible for Generally Accepted Accounting Principles (GAAP). Considered by the SEC and others as the authoritative body on GAAP. See also **Generally Accepted Accounting Principles**.

financial buyers: Private equity and venture capital firms. See also **financial sponsors**.

financial covenants: Requirements included in legal agreements (including bank loan agreements, bond indentures, and merger agreements). Examples of financial covenants in a bond indenture include requirements to maintain certain credit ratios or limits on capital expenditures. Financial covenants are designed to protect the lender/investor by alerting them to adverse changes in the borrower's financial profile.

financial impact analyses: Various types of analyses performed to assess the financial impact of a proposed transaction, including credit analysis, accretion/dilution analysis, and debt capacity analysis, among many others.

financial restructuring: Making material changes to a company's capital structure as a means of enhancing value. Examples of financial restructuring transactions include the payment of a special dividend and a recapitalization, among others.

financial sponsors: Private equity and venture capital firms that raise money for an investment fund from outside investors and invest the fund's money by acquiring or investing in businesses, respectively.

firm value: Represents the value of both the equity (common equity and preferred equity) and the net debt of a company, based on the current market value of common equity. Also referred to as enterprise value. See also **equity value**.

fiscal year: The annual period for a company's financial reporting. A company can choose its own fiscal year. For example, a company could have a fiscal year of June 1 to May 31, or December 1 to November 30. Many companies choose a fiscal year based on the calendar year (January 1 to December 31). See also **calendar year**.

fixed exchange ratio: An exchange ratio that does not change between the signing and closing of a transaction, regardless of whether there is movement in Acquiror's share price, resulting in floating value delivered to Target shareholders. This is in contrast to a floating exchange ratio. See also **exchange ratio, floating exchange ratio**.

fixed price tender offer: One method used in share repurchases. In a fixed price tender offer, the company announces a fixed price at which it will repurchase shares. Any shareholders who want to tender their shares at that fixed price will do so. See also **Dutch auction**.

flip-in exchange plan: A shareholder rights plan (poison pill) in which shareholder rights are exchanged by Target for new shares, which are then distributed to Target's non-Raider shareholders without any action required on their part. The creation and subsequent exchange at a discount of these new shares causes substantial dilution to Raider's voting and economic interests in Target. See also **poison pill**.

flip-in rights plan: A shareholder rights plan (poison pill) in which Target shareholders have the right to purchase new Target shares at a discounted price. The creation and subsequent purchase at a discount of these new shares causes substantial dilution to Raider's voting and economic interests in Target. See also **poison pill**.

flip-over plan: A shareholder rights plan (poison pill) that allows Target shareholders to buy Raider shares at a discount. The creation and subsequent purchase at a discount of these new shares causes substantial dilution to Raider's voting and economic interests in Raider. See also **poison pill**.

floating exchange ratio: An exchange ratio that moves up or down between the signing and closing of a transaction, depending on movement in Acquiror's share price, resulting in the delivery of a fixed value to Target shareholders. This is in contrast to a fixed exchange ratio. See also **exchange ratio, fixed exchange ratio**.

floor: The lower limit of a collar used in stock-for-stock transactions. See also **cap, collar**.

flowback: Issue that arises in cross-border M&A transactions. Occurs when Acquiror purchases a foreign company using stock as the acquisition currency, issuing Acquiror shares to Target shareholders in another country. The foreign shareholders might decide to sell Acquiror shares since they do not want to or cannot own shares of a foreign entity, thereby putting downward pressure on Acquiror's stock price as the shares issued to foreign Target shareholders flow back to Acquiror's home market. See also **acquisition currency, flowback analysis**.

flowback analysis: An analysis used to assess how many Acquiror shares will "flow back" into the home country as investors in Target, who have received Acquiror shares, sell them (because they cannot or do not want to own foreign shares), leading to post-transaction downward pressure on Acquiror's stock in its home market.

follow-on offering: An equity offering of new shares done by a company after its initial public offering. See also **IPO, primary offering, secondary offering**.

football field: A summary page created by investment bankers that graphically depicts the various valuation ranges calculated for an asset or company using different valuation methodologies.

forward EPS: Earnings per share for the current year or future years. FY1 (forward year 1) is often used to designate EPS for the current year, FY2 for the EPS of the next fiscal year, and FY3 for the EPS in two fiscal years. See also **trailing EPS**.

free cash flow: Cash flow generated by all assets (both tangible and intangible) used by the company in the provision of goods or services, minus the cost of acquiring and maintaining those assets (e.g., capital expenditures). In a DCF analysis, free cash flow does not account for the cash inflows or outflows related to financing the business and therefore is said to be unlevered or independent of the capital structure. See also **discounted cash flow analysis**.

fully marketed transaction: When marketing a securities offering, the company meets with multiple investors to discuss the upcoming securities offering. A fully marketed transaction takes longer than an accelerated marketing transaction and is designed to elicit the maximum amount of interest in the transaction. See also **ac-**

celerated marketing transaction.

future value: Nominal amount to be received in the future.

G

GAAP books: Financial accounting records prepared according to GAAP rules and regulations. This is in contrast to the tax return work papers, which are accounting records prepared according to the rules and regulations of the IRS and other taxing authorities. See also **tax books**.

gain/(loss) on sale: The difference between the selling price of an asset and the asset's book value (for GAAP accounting). See also **capital gain/(loss)** (a tax accounting concept), **taxable gain/(loss) on sale** (a tax accounting concept).

Generally Accepted Accounting Principles (GAAP): A set of financial reporting guidelines. The Financial Accounting Standards Board (FASB) is considered by the Securities and Exchange Commission (SEC) and the American Institute of Certified Public Accountants (AICPA) to be the authoritative governing body of GAAP. Public companies listed on a U.S. stock exchange must file their financial statements prepared according to GAAP with the SEC, where they become public record.

golden parachute: Severance package for senior executives payable upon termination, takeover, or some other trigger such as "substantial reduction in title and/or responsibilities."

goodwill: In purchase accounting, the value paid for the equity of Target less the fair market value of the net identifiable assets of Target. Net identifiable assets is equal to the fair market value of Target's assets (excluding goodwill) less the fair market value of Target's liabilities. Goodwill is an intangible and unidentifiable asset and represents the portion of consideration paid in an acquisition that is not allocated to an identifiable asset or liability. Goodwill is no longer amortized but must be tested periodically for impairment (at least annually).

greenfield: To grow or develop a business internally. It is the opposite of (and generally the alternative to) purchasing an existing entity or business as a way to enter a new geographic or product market.

gross spread: The fee an issuer pays an investment bank to underwrite a securities offering. It is allocated to the manager of the offering, the dealer (if the dealer is different from the manager), and the syndicate. See also **re-offer yield, syndicate group**.

growing perpetuity: See **perpetuity.**

growth rate accretion/dilution analysis: An analysis used to compare the EPS growth rate of a company before and after a contemplated transaction. See also **accretion/dilution analysis**.

guarantor: An entity (a company or individual) that provides credit support to a borrower.

H

Hart-Scott-Rodino Act (HSR Act): In the U.S., a company seeking to acquire or merge with another company must file advance notice of its intentions with the Federal Trade Commission (FTC) and Assistant Attorney General at least 30 days before closing of the transaction in order to determine if the transaction conforms to antitrust laws. Similar antitrust or competition requirements exist in other regions, especially in European and Asian countries.

hedging: The act of minimizing risk -- any type of risk -- by entering into a financial contract with a third party who will assume some or all of the risk for a fee.

hell-or-high-water clause: In a legal contract, provides that both companies must use their best efforts ("come hell or high water") to obtain all regulatory approvals required for the transaction to close. This provision, if the parties to a contract choose to include it, can require extraordinary measures on the part of either or both companies, depending on the specific circumstances of the transaction.

high grade debt: See **investment grade debt.**

high yield debt: Debt that has a credit rating of BB+ (or equivalent) or lower. Investment grade debt is debt that has a credit rating of BBB- (or equivalent) or higher. Given the greater credit risk associated with a lower credit rating, high yield debt is considered to be riskier than investment grade debt and therefore must provide investors with a higher return to compensate for this greater risk. High yield debt is also referred to as junk debt and non-investment grade debt. See also **crossover issuer, investment grade debt**.

historical stock price analysis: Analysis of the prices at which a stock has traded in the past. See also **indexed stock price graph.**

hockey stick: Graphical depiction of consistent historical financial results followed by highly optimistic projections, causing a graph of the numbers to resemble the outline of a hockey stick.

hold level: In a financing transaction, the percentage level each member of a syndicate group commits to holding or owning; the rest of each syndicate member's allocation can be sold off to reduce the syndicate member's exposure to the transaction in question. See also **syndicate group.**

I

if-converted method: The if-converted method of accounting is used to calculate diluted shares outstanding for convertible debt or preferred stock. The if-converted method assumes that potentially dilutive securities are converted to equity. Therefore, the number of shares outstanding increases, but the amount of debt or preferred equity on the balance sheet decreases, as does interest expense (in the case of convertible bonds) or dividends paid (in the case of preferred equity), reflecting the fact these securities no longer "exist" since they are assumed to have been converted into common equity. See also **diluted shares.**

impairment test (for goodwill): Goodwill is periodically measured for impairment. If the impairment test concludes that (a) the fair market value of goodwill is less than the book value (value on the balance sheet) and (b) the lower fair market value is permanent, a company must write down the book value of the goodwill by the amount of the impairment. Goodwill impairment flows through the income statement as a charge and ultimately into shareholders' equity. A goodwill impairment charge is a non-cash event. See also **asset write-down, goodwill**.

in the money: When the exercise price of an option or the conversion price of a convertible security is less than the current price, indicating that the option or convertible security has immediate value if the option were exercised. See also **out of the money**.

income statement: One of the three financial statements, along with the balance sheet and the cash flow statement. Measures a company's profitability during a period of time (e.g., quarterly, annually). See also **balance sheet, cash flow statement**.

indemnification: Provides that a party will be reimbursed for losses incurred in connection with certain events. Indemnification is protection, often in the form of financial compensation, against loss or damage.

indexed stock price graph: Analysis commonly used to assess a company's stock price performance on a relative basis – either compared to an industry peer, an index of industry peers, or a market index such as the S&P 500. In this way, it is possible to determine whether a stock has underperformed or outperformed its peers over a period of time. Also referred to as relative stock price performance. See also **historical stock price analysis.**

initial public offering (IPO): The first public sale of a company's common equity. An IPO can be either a primary offering of shares (the sale of new shares, with sale proceeds going to the company) or a secondary offering of shares (the sale of shares owned by investors and/or insiders, with sale proceeds going to the sellers and not the company). See also **follow-on offering, primary offering, secondary offering**.

inside basis: A tax accounting concept. The tax basis that a corporation has in its assets. See also **outside basis**.

intercompany transactions: When preparing consolidated financial statements, GAAP requires companies to eliminate intercompany transactions such as transactions between the parent corporation and subsidiary corporation. For example, the payment of a dividend from subsidiary to parent is an intercompany transaction. Most intercompany transactions are eliminated in consolidation.

interim operations: A key section of a merger or acquisition agreement which states that, during the period from signing of the agreement to closing of the transaction, Target must continue to operate its business as it normally would.

interloper: A third party who attempts to break up a transaction. If there is a breakup fee provision in the transaction which interloper attempts to break up, the cost of that breakup fee is usually passed through to the interloper. See also **corporate defense**.

interloper analysis: An analysis used to determine which companies and/or financial sponsors might have an interest in Target and/or the transaction being contemplated. Interloper analysis must take into account the financial effect of any breakup fee.

internal rate of return (IRR): For a stream of cash flows, the specific discount rate which yields a net present value (NPV) of zero. IRR must be calculated iteratively, usually by a financial calculator or financial software. Thus IRR is the discount rate which is calculated to cause the NPV of an investment to equal zero or, said differently, the discount rate which causes the present value (PV) of the future cash flows to exactly equal the value paid for the investment at time zero. See also **net present value**.

intrinsic valuation: The valuation of an asset or company on a stand-alone basis, based only on what the asset or company generates itself and not based on multiples or metrics from comparable companies or comparable transactions. Discounted cash flow analysis (DCF) and leveraged buyout analysis (LBO) are two of the most common intrinsic valuation methodologies. See also **relative valuation.**

investment: The purchase of any asset (physical investment) or security (paper investment) for valuable consideration (cash or stock) in exchange for a claim or right to the asset or a stream of cash payments from the asset and/or security in the future.

investment grade debt: Debt with a credit rating of Baa3/BBB- and above. Also referred to as high grade debt. This is in contrast to high yield debt (also referred to as non-investment grade or junk debt), which is debt with a credit rating lower than Baa3/BBB-. See also **high yield debt**.

investment period: The period of time over which an investment is outstanding. For example, if an investment is made on January 1, Year 1 and the investor liquidates the investment on December 31, Year 5, the investment period is five years.

investment horizon: See **investment period**.

investment duration: See **investment period**.

IRS: Internal Revenue Service. The federal taxing authority in the U.S., which is responsible for ensuring individuals and corporations pay taxes in accordance with the Internal Revenue Code (IRC).

irrevocable proxy: A covenant in a stock purchase agreement with a major stockholder stating that if the stockholder breaches any provisions of the stockholder lockup (which is a contract), the stockholder grants an irrevocable proxy to Acquiror to vote that stockholder's shares. The purpose of the irrevocable proxy is to serve as a form of insurance for Acquiror such that, if the stockholder in question does not vote in favor of the transaction, the voting rights to her shares shift to Acquiror via the irrevocable proxy (a proxy in this context is the written power to vote the shares of the selling shareholders). See also **stockholder lockup**.

issuer: An issuer usually refers to an entity issuing securities (e.g., bonds, stock) di rectly to investors. A borrower usually refers to an entity borrowing money from a bank. Thus in a security issuance, the company seeking the money is the issuer and the providers of the money are the investors who purchase the securities. This is similar to, but with different terminology from, a bank loan in which the company seeking the money is the borrower and the provider of the money is the lender.

J

joint bookrunner: In a securities offering, an investment bank (or two) will be named to manage the issuance process. This lead bank is called the bookrunner or the joint bookrunner (if there is more than one lead bank). Each of the banks involved is allotted a certain number of securities for sale, and each is then responsible for selling those securities to investors. The number of shares allotted to an investment bank is largest for the lead underwriter(s), with smaller quantities given to the non-lead (or syndicate) banks. See also **syndicate group**.

joint merger prospectus/proxy: When Target and Acquiror together issue a merger prospectus or proxy, usually in the context of a friendly transaction. To gain approval for the merger, Target issues a disclosure statement to Target shareholders (called a "merger proxy" if Acquiror offers all cash to Target shareholders and called a "merger prospectus" if Acquiror offers all stock or cash-and-stock to Target shareholders) that describes the terms of, reasons for, risks of, and conditions to the proposed merger. The SEC must deem a merger prospectus "effective" before shareholders can vote on the transaction because it is a stock issuance, just like any other stock issuance (e.g., an IPO), even though the newly issued stock is being used to pay for Target. While the SEC does not need to deem a merger proxy effective if the acquisition consideration is cash (since no stock is being issued), the merger proxy is still subject to the proxy rules and the SEC may provide comments.

joint venture: When two or more companies contribute assets, businesses, and/or cash to a partnership. Most joint ventures are owned 50/50 by the owner companies. In addition, most joint ventures have an independent management team and board of directors, with shared representation by both owner companies.

junk debt: See **high yield debt.**

L

lead arranger(s): In a loan syndicate, the one or two agent banks chosen to manage the syndication process (although numerous banks and lenders might participate in a syndicated loan). The agent bank writes an offering memorandum and circulates it with a term sheet. A loan term sheet is a list of the most important information related to the loan, including the name of the borrower, the size of the issue, important financial and credit statistics of the issuer, the interest rate of the debt, and important features related to the debt such as the term, whether it is fixed or floating, and the major covenants that will be required of the borrower. See also **syndicate group.**

league tables: Investment banking rankings based on selected criteria, such as: volume of equity offerings, volume of M&A deals, and volume of syndicated loans. League tables exist for nearly every product offered by an investment bank, and in every region of the world they are used as a form of marketing by banks to show the bank's strength in a respective product area relative to other providers of that product (other banks).

leverage ratio: A type of credit ratio which is used to measure the absolute levels of debt a company has outstanding at a given point in time. Common leverage ratios include the ratio of debt to total capital (sometimes called the capitalization ratio) and debt to equity. Total capital is all of the debt, preferred equity and common equity issued and outstanding by a company. See also **coverage ratio**.

leveraged buyout (LBO): A transaction in which a financial sponsor (usually a private equity fund or a leveraged buyout fund) acquires Target using a combination of private equity and debt. In leveraged buyouts, the purchase price is usually financed with 60 to 75 percent debt and 25 to 40 percent equity. Once a leveraged buyout has taken place, Target is a private company owned by the financial sponsor.

leveraged buyout analysis: A valuation method whereby the value for a company is determined based on (a) how much debt can be placed on Target and (b) the equity returns required by the financial sponsor for the equity portion of the transaction consideration.

leveraged loan market: Syndicated loan market for non-investment grade credits. The syndicated loan market competes directly with the bond market as an alternative source of debt capital for companies. Most leveraged loans are secured with full financial covenants, befitting their higher risk as non-investment grade issues. See also **high yield debt.**

liability: Generically, any obligation or risk of a firm. From an accounting perspective, liabilities are listed on one side of the balance sheet, representing obligations of the firm, and assets are listed on the other side of the balance sheet, representing the productive capabilities of the firm. Common liabilities include long-term debt, short-term debt, accounts payable, deferred taxes, and accrued expenses. See also **asset**.

liability management: The act of managing the mix of debt instruments in a company's capital structure to minimize the overall cost of debt as well as the overall risk to the company. The primary goal of liability management is to minimize the company's weighted average cost of capital and thereby increase the company's return on equity and return on capital.

LIBOR (London Interbank Offer Rate): The interest rate at which banks borrow money from one another in the London Interbank Market. Floating interest rates on bank loans in the U.S. are often tied to LIBOR as the loans' reference rate.

liquidation preference: In a bankruptcy scenario, the order in which capital providers are repaid with the proceeds of a liquidation of assets. Also referred to as priority of claim.

liquidation value: The cash value received from selling off assets in a bankruptcy or liquidation scenario. This is different from the book value of assets, which is the accounting value based on historical cost. Liquidation value is sometimes referred to as the "fire sale" price.

liquidity: The nominal amount outstanding of any particular issue of a security not held by insiders. In general, investors prefer liquid issues compared to non-liquid issues because it is easier to buy and sell in a larger, more fluid market without affecting the price of the security. In a separate use of the same term, liquidity also refers to the amount of cash a company has on hand.

liquidity ratio: Financial ratio used to determine how easily a company can service its short-term cash requirements.

loan agreement: A legal document (a contract) governing the agreement between the borrower and the bank in a bank financing. The similar governing agreement for a bond (as opposed to a loan) is a bond indenture. See also **bond indenture**.

long-form merger: Traditional merger path in which disclosures are sent to shareholders prior to a shareholder vote, and shareholders must vote affirmatively in favor of the transaction in order for the transaction to close. See also **short-form merger**.

long-term assets: Assets that have lives longer than one operating cycle or one year. Long-term assets can either be tangible such as a factory or intangible such as a patent or goodwill. See also **current assets**.

long-term debt (LTD): Debt that is due in more than one operating cycle or one year. See also **short-term debt**.

long-term liabilities: Liabilities that have lives longer than one operating cycle or one year.

loss on sale: The difference between the selling price of an asset and the asset's book value (for GAAP accounting) when the sale price of the asset is less than the book value.

LTM: Last twelve months. Sometimes referred to as latest twelve months.

LTM EPS: Earnings per share for the last twelve months.

M

management's discussion and analysis (MD&A): Section of the financial statements in which management describes key issues and changes related to the company's business and financial performance during a specified period. Financial statements should always be read in conjunction with the MD&A.

mark to market: Accounting method (typically used to account for trading securities) in which the carrying value of certain items on the balance sheet are adjusted up or down to reflect their current market value.

market value: Represents the aggregate value of shareholders' equity based on the current stock price multiplied by the diluted shares outstanding. Also referred to as equity value. See also **enterprise value**.

material adverse change (MAC): Any event which materially changes the form and/or economic substance of a transaction for one, or both, of the parties. Most legal agreements have a MAC clause that allows the parties to walk away from a transaction if a MAC occurs. See also **no material adverse change condition**.

maturity: The amount of time (generally quoted in days for short-term debt and years for long-term debt) during which debt is outstanding, or until the security principal is due. Common equity (stock) does not have a maturity because it is perpetual. Preferred stock may have a maturity or may be perpetual.

medium-term notes (MTNs): Bonds sold in tranches according to maturity (e.g., 2 years, 5 years, etc.). The difference between an MTN and a bond is that the tranches of an MTN program can be sold over time, as opposed to a bond issue which is generally sold in its entirety at one time. MTNs allow a company to access the fixed income market for smaller amounts based on market demand by prearranging their SEC documentation (a so-called shelf registration). Financial institutions are common issuers in the MTN market. See also **tranches**.

merger: The legal combination of two corporations as governed by state corporation laws. See also **corporate merger, statutory merger**.

merger agreement: The legal contract which represents the agreement between Acquiror and Target in a merger.

merger of equals (MOE): The combination of two companies of roughly equal size and value, generally characterized by a low premium or even no premium. In a merger of equals, there is no traditional Acquiror or Target. Both companies share in the management of the new company going forward.

merger prospectus/proxy: For public companies in the U.S., information and disclosure statement issued to Target shareholders by Target management prior to the shareholder vote to approve or disapprove a proposed merger. A merger prospectus is used if Acquiror is offering some or all stock in exchange for Target's stock. A merger proxy is used if the transaction consideration is all cash. See also **joint merger proxy/prospectus.**

mezzanine capital: Subordinated debt and preferred stock, usually with convertible features. Also referred to as mezzanine financing.

midyear convention: Assumption used in discounted cash flow (DCF) analysis in which a cash flow is assumed to occur in the middle of the year (e.g., on June 30 for a calendar year company) and is discounted for only half a year. This is in contrast to the full-year convention, in which a cash flow is assumed to occur at the end of the year (e.g., on December 31 for a calendar year company) and is discounted for a full year. Use of the midyear convention generally results in higher valuations compared with valuations of the same company using the full-year convention.

minority interest: The portion of a consolidated subsidiary corporation that the parent corporation does not own. See also **consolidation method**.

multiple compression: A decrease in a valuation multiple.

multiple expansion: An increase in a valuation multiple.

N

NASD: National Association of Securities Dealers. A private-sector regulator of the U.S. securities industry. The SEC is a public-sector regulator of the U.S. securities industry.

NASDAQ: National Association of Securities Dealers Automatic Quotation system, an alternative stock exchange to the New York Stock Exchange and other traditional exchanges. See also **NYSE**.

NRSRO: Nationally Recognized Statistical Rating Organization. This is the formal designation for a credit rating agency. The designation as an NRSRO is provided by the SEC through a no-action letter. In 2003, Dominion Bond Rating Service (DBRS) of Canada was recognized as the fourth NRSRO, joining Moody's, S&P, and Fitch. See also **credit rating**.

NYSE: New York Stock Exchange. One of many stock exchanges in the United States, but referred to as the Big Board due to its role as the stock exchange upon which many of the largest companies in the world are listed. With the increasing importance of technology, the NASDAQ exchange has gained prominence. See also **NASDAQ.**

natural historical exchange ratio analysis: An analysis that looks at the implied market-based exchange ratio over time based on closing stock prices of Target and Acquiror. Often used when analyzing a merger of equals.

negative covenant: Covenant in a legal agreement that limits or otherwise puts restrictions on which actions a party can take, or enumerates actions which a party cannot take. See also **affirmative covenant**.

net assets: Assets minus liabilities. The book value of net assets is referred to as net asset value. Net identifiable assets are assets minus liabilities but excluding goodwill (assets - liabilities - goodwill).

net debt: Short-term debt plus long-term debt plus minority interest (if any) plus preferred stock minus cash and cash equivalents. Net debt is added to market value to arrive at enterprise value. See also **enterprise value, equity value**.

net operating losses (NOLs): A tax accounting concept. Operating losses of a company which can be used to offset future income tax (operating profits) or can be applied to previous years' income tax, subject to IRS or other limitations. NOLs can also be used to offset future capital gain or can be applied to previous years' capital gain, subject to limitations. NOLs can offset operating profits or capital gains while capital losses can only be used to offset capital gains. See also **capital gain/(loss)**.

net present value: The future cash flows of an investment discounted to a present value less the value paid for the investment at time zero. The specific discount rate that yields a net present value of zero is called the internal rate of return (IRR). See also **discount rate, internal rate of return**.

no action by written consent provision: A corporate defense mechanism. When there is a no action by written consent provision, a written vote (i.e., action by written consent) is insufficient to take shareholder action. Instead, a physical shareholder meeting must take place before shareholder action can be taken. If it exists, this provision is found in a company's bylaws or corporate charter. Companies choose whether or not to allow action by written consent.

no-action letter: A letter response from the SEC indicating that no civil or criminal action will be taken against an individual (broadly defined, which includes corporations) engaging in a specified activity. Companies request a no-action letter from the SEC when the law is unclear or vague regarding something the company plans to do. It allows the SEC the ability to review an action prior to the action taking place.

no hand (non-redemption) provision: Provides that no director can redeem a poison pill once the continuing directors are no longer in the majority. See also **dead hand provision, poison pill, shareholder rights plan**.

no material adverse change condition: Condition in a legal contract that no material adverse change in Target's business or assets has occurred between the signing of the Agreement and the closing which would cause a material decrease in Target's value. If such change has occurred, various remedies generally are available to Acquiror. See also **material adverse change**.

no shop / no talk restrictions: A provision in a merger or acquisition agreement that prevents Target, subject to Target board of directors' fiduciary duties, from negotiating a transaction with a third party. The provision protects Acquiror since Target could take Acquiror's bid and use it to "shop" for another, higher offer in the absence of these restrictions.

non-call period: A call option provides an issuer the right to redeem outstanding bonds at a predetermined price or percentage (e.g., at 102 percent of face value) and beginning on a predetermined date (which is prior to the final maturity date of the bond). The period during which the bond cannot be called (the time before the first call date) is the non-call period. The purpose of the non-call period is to ensure that investors receive their interest payments for some minimum period of time. Investors want to be sure that they will receive their coupon or return for some period of time and therefore investors generally require that there be some non-call period with callable or putable bonds.

non-compete provisions: A provision in a legal contract that prevents Seller from creating a business to compete with the business just sold. Often required following a merger or acquisition. Also may apply when a senior executive or other person deemed important to a business leaves the business.

non-disclosure agreement (NDA): See **confidentiality agreement**.

non-investment grade debt: See **high yield debt**.

non-recurring items: Income statement charges that are one-time occurrences and are not part of the company's regular course of business. Non-recurring items are usually excluded during financial analysis, which generally seeks to show the business performance on a regular (run-rate) basis.

non-solicitation provision: A provision in a legal contract that prevents prospective buyers from soliciting employees of Target for a specified period of time after a transaction closes, subject to certain exceptions.

notching: Credit rating differentials for the same issuer. For example, if a company has a subsidiary with a credit rating of BBB+ from S&P and the parent company itself has a credit rating of BBB, this is referred to as notching. Notching is often the result of subordination. See also **contractual subordination, structural subordination.**

O

offer to purchase: The document provided to Target shareholders in a tender offer. See also **tender offer.**

one-line consolidation: In GAAP, consolidation of Acquiror's investment in Target as well as its proportionate share of Target's earnings and losses into one line on the income statement and balance sheet. Used for investments classified using the equity method. See also **equity method**.

on the block: A company or set of assets that is for sale is said to be "on the block," which is short for on the auction block.

opening balance sheet: The balance sheet at the beginning of the reporting period. For purposes of financial statement analysis, one needs an opening balance sheet (to see the status of all accounts at the beginning of the reporting period) and a closing balance sheet (to see the status of all accounts at the end of the reporting period). See also **balance sheet, closing balance sheet**.

operating ratio: Any of a series of ratios that show how profitable a company is and/or how efficiently a company is managed.

opportunity cost: Cost of foregoing an investment.

option: A security that allows the owner to buy (call option) or sell (put option) an underlying asset at some predetermined price in the future.

out of the money: When the exercise price of an option or the conversion price of a convertible security is greater than the current price, indicating that the option or convertible security has no immediate value if the option were exercised. See also **in the money**.

outside basis: A tax accounting concept. The tax basis that a shareholder of a corporation has in the stock of the corporation. That shareholder can, itself, be a corporation (Parent) owning the stock of another corporation (Subsidiary). See also **inside basis**.

overnight transaction: See **block trade**.

P

perpetuity: A special type of annuity which has an infinite duration (or, said differently, with a perpetual term). An example of a perpetuity is a royalty with no expiration date.

perpetuity growth rate method: One of two methods to calculate the terminal value of an asset or company in a discounted cash flow valuation. The other method to calculate terminal value is the terminal multiple method. In the perpetuity growth method, the perpetuity formula is used to value the company as of the terminal date, based on the assumption that the company will operate forever. Most terminal value calculations which use the perpetuity formula assume a growing perpetuity and a low perpetuity growth rate (1 to 3 percent annually, for example). As with the terminal multiple method, the growing perpetuity calculation yields a value as of Year *n* (the end of the projection period), which value is then discounted back to the present using the company's weighted average cost of capital. See also **discounted cash flow, perpetuity, terminal multiple method, terminal value**.

personal income tax: Tax levied on individuals, specifically on household income, dividend income, income from unincorporated businesses, and income from pass-through entities such as sole proprietorships or partnerships.

phantom amortization/depreciation: Concept in the equity method of accounting for investments in which Acquiror must recognize "phantom amortization" or "phantom depreciation" of any phantom write-ups if part of the purchase price is allocated to a write-up of a depreciable/amortizable asset of Target. They are considered "phantom" because they do not flow through Acquiror's income statement nor do they flow through any of Target's financial statements.

PIPE: Private investment in public equity. Type of investment made by some private equity firms in public companies. This is not a "going private" transaction since the company remains publicly held.

poison pill: A corporate defense mechanism which provides existing shareholders with a "right" or "rights" to purchase or receive new shares in the company, thereby dramatically diluting the would-be Raider's voting and economic interest. See also **shareholder rights plan**.

power to fill vacancies provision: A corporate defense mechanism which usually requires that any vacancy on the board of directors may only be filled by a majority vote of the continuing directors. If it exists, this provision is found in a company's bylaws or corporate charter. Companies choose whether or not to have a power to fill vacancies provision.

PP&E: Plant, property and equipment. PP&E is usually quoted both on a gross basis (which is before accounting for accumulated depreciation) and on a net basis (which is after accounting for accumulated depreciation). See also **accumulated depreciation, depreciation, depletion, amortization**.

precedent transaction analysis: See **comparable transaction analysis**.

preferred equity: Equity typically with a dividend which has preference to any common equity dividend, and which is ahead of common equity in liquidation preference. See also **common equity, equity, liquidation preference**.

premium paid analysis: An M&A analysis that compares the acquisition premium under consideration for a particular transaction to the premia paid in previous and comparable transactions. See also **comparable transaction analysis**.

pretax earnings: See **earnings before taxes (EBT)**.

pretax operating income: See **earnings before taxes (EBT).**

pretax profit: See **earnings before taxes (EBT).**

present value: The value of an investment stated in today's money.

price to book ratio: Ratio which represents the market value of equity as a multiple of the book value of equity. The price to book ratio formula is: market value of equity / book value of equity.

price to earnings (P/E): Ratio which represents the price of a share relative to its earnings (EPS) in a given period. P/E is usually calculated based on EPS for the last twelve months as well as the projected EPS for the next one, two, or three fiscal years. The price to earnings formula is: stock price / earnings per share (quoted annually).

primary offering: An offering of new shares to the public by a company (with sale proceeds going to the company), as opposed to a secondary offering of existing shares (sale of shares by investors and/or executives, with sale proceeds going to the sellers and not the company). See also **follow-on offering, IPO, secondary offering**.

principal: Within the context of an investment, the principal is the original amount of the investment or loan.

priority of claim: The order in which capital providers are repaid with the liquidation value of the assets. See also **liquidation preference**.

private equity firm: A private fund that acquires existing businesses using significant debt, as well as equity raised from private investors. Also referred to as a financial sponsor or leveraged buyout firm. See also **financial sponsor**.

private letter ruling: Ruling that companies may seek from the Internal Revenue Service (IRS) when contemplating a transaction for which the tax treatment is unclear. The ruling essentially establishes how the IRS will treat the proposed transaction, and it is generally obtained before a transaction is executed. It is often sought when the tax ruling can alter the economics of a transaction substantially. In the absence of a private letter ruling, a company may seek a legal opinion from tax attorneys or some other form of assurance.

private placement: The direct sale of securities to a limited group of investors, subject to certain limitations. Qualified private placements (which can be debt or equity securities) are exempt from registration with the SEC.

pro forma: Pro forma financials are financial statements after giving effect to a proposed transaction (can be a strategic or a financing transaction). Thus pro forma financials for an acquisition would show the financial statements for Acquiror as if the acquisition had taken place.

product bankers: Bankers who specialize in the execution of a particular type of financial product (such as M&A, equity capital markets, or leveraged finance). Product bankers are different from relationship bankers, who cover clients in a specified industry or region and do not specialize in a particular financial product but rather are able to discuss numerous products and services. See also **coverage bankers**.

proxy contest: A method to gain control of a public company's board of directors. Shareholders use proxies to vote on a new slate of directors. If a company has a classified board, it might take two years or more to gain control of a board using a proxy contest.

purchase accounting: The accounting method used to account for business combinations of unrelated entities in which, pro forma the transaction, Acquiror has control over Target.

purchase and sale agreement: Legal agreement used for the sale of an asset or division of a company. A stock purchase agreement is used in the sale of a corporation. See also **stock purchase agreement**.

purchase price: For a publicly traded company, this is usually quoted as a price per share or an exchange ratio if the transaction is a stock-for-stock exchange. For a private company, a division, or subsidiary, the purchase price is usually quoted as an aggregate price for the equity.

purchase price adjustment: In a merger or acquisition agreement, a purchase price adjustment is used to capture changes in value between signing and closing of the transaction.

pure play: Companies with one major business line. Diversified or conglomerate companies, on the other hand, have more than one major business line. See also **diversifieds**.

put option: In a bond context, allows an investor the right to force the issuer to repurchase the securities, generally at par (or face value). In an equity context, enables the buyer of the put option to force a sale of the security to the seller of the put at a specified price (the exercise price). See also **call option**.

Q

quality of earnings: Term used to describe whether the earnings per share of a company is sustainable (high quality of earnings) or is based on non-recurring or one-time items (low quality of earnings). Investors take special care to determine whether earnings include non-recurring items (items that are special and are not part of the company's regular course of business), which will not or cannot be replicated in future years.

R

raider: An individual or company who seeks out companies (Targets) with undervalued assets and then tries to take over Target. Typically, the term "raider" is used if Target is not interested in the overture (and the overture is considered "hostile"). See also **corporate defense, poison pill**.

recapitalization: A major change to a company's capital structure. A recapitalization can be any major change but often refers to the issuance of a significant level of new debt, which may be used either to repurchase equity or to pay a special dividend to equity holders.

refinancing: A change to a company's capital structure, including common actions such as renewing a line of credit with another line of credit (which may or may not have a different interest rate). Refinancing does not affect the asset side of the balance sheet, only the liability and shareholders' equity side. See also **recapitalization**.

regulatory analysis: An analysis used to determine what regulatory approvals, if any, would be required for a transaction to close.

relationship bankers: Bankers who focus their efforts on building relationships with clients (and are able to discuss numerous products and services with them). See also **coverage bankers, product bankers**.

relative stock price performance analysis: A technical analysis that assesses the performance of Target's stock compared to the stock of another company or an index over varying periods of time such as six months, one year, and three years.

relative valuation: Determination of a valuation for an asset or company based on multiples or other comparative metrics. Comparable company analysis and comparable transaction analysis are two of the most common relative valuation methodologies. See also **intrinsic valuation**.

relative valuation analysis: An analysis that requires performing stand-alone valuation analysis of both Acquiror and Target -- using traditional methods such as discounted cash flow analysis, comparable company analysis, and comparable transaction analysis -- and then calculating the implied exchange ratios based on the stand-alone valuation levels. This can be used in any stock-for-stock transaction but is most commonly used in mergers of equals. See also **merger of equals**.

removal of directors "for cause" provision: A corporate defense mechanism which prohibits the removal of directors other than "for cause" or other than by a supermajority vote. If it exists, this provision is found in a company's bylaws or corporate charter. Companies choose whether or not to have a removal for cause provision.

re-offer yield: The rate of return offered to investors by the underwriters after the gross spread has been allocated to the underwriters. See also **gross spread**.

reporting period: Period over which a company's financial performance is measured, such as quarterly, semiannually, or annually.

representations and warranties: In a legal contract, statements by Acquiror and Target about various elements of their respective businesses. Also referred to as reps and warranties.

restrictive covenant: Restriction on a party from taking certain a certain action. See also **affirmative covenant, negative covenant**.

restructuring: A major change to the structural organization of a company. A spin-off is an example of a restructuring transaction.

retained earnings: Line item in the shareholders' equity section of a balance sheet which represents historical earnings which have not been paid out to shareholders as dividends. At the end of every period, net income (from the income statement) flows through to the retained earnings account on the balance sheet. Thus net income increases retained earnings and dividend payments and net losses reduce retained earnings.

return on assets (ROA): Represents the earnings power of the total asset base and is calculated by dividing earnings in a given year by the average total assets for that year.

return on equity (ROE): Represents the earnings power of the shareholders' equity and is calculated by dividing earnings in a given year by the average shareholders' equity for that year.

return on invested capital (ROIC): Represents the earnings power of the total capitalization and is calculated by dividing earnings in a given year by the average total capitalization (debt plus equity) for that year.

revenue synergies: Generating greater revenues through the combination of two companies. For example, revenue synergies occur if Acquiror is able to sell its products through Target's distribution network. See also **cost synergies, synergies**.

reverse split: A stock split which occurs in reverse. Occurs when a company decides to exchange one new share for two (1-for-2), three (1-for-3), four (1-for-4) or more old shares (or whatever ratio the company determines) such that the owner of two, three, four or more old shares, respectively, becomes the owner of one new share. This usually occurs when the stock price has dropped sharply and the company wishes to increase the price per share by simply reducing the number of shares outstanding by exchanging new, higher-valued shares in place of old shares at some pre-determined ratio. Reverse splits do not affect the overall market value of equity but increase share price, earnings per share, dividends per share, and all other per share metrics by the exchange ratio chosen (e.g., multiply all metrics by two for a 1-for-2 split, by three for a 1-for-3 split, etc.). See also **stock split**.

Revlon duties: Fiduciary obligations which apply to a board of directors if the board has decided to sell the company, effect a breakup of the company, or abandon its long-term strategy. If Revlon duties are triggered, a board has set the company on the course of a sale of corporate control and therefore the board has an obligation "to obtain the highest value reasonably attainable for the shareholders," even if that value is offered by a hostile acquiror. If Revlon duties are triggered, there is limited (if any) latitude to accept an offer which is not the highest value. However, there is still some board discretion, especially with respect to stock consideration or complex transaction structures (since they can be difficult to value), but the basic board requirement of maximizing value for shareholders is unchanged.

revolving line of credit (revolver): A set credit limit given to a company by a bank, or a syndicate of banks, whereby the borrower can draw from it up to the credit limit, repay it and re-borrow from it without having to renegotiate terms with the bank. Most revolvers have a term of 364 days, although some are written as "evergreen facilities" which automatically renew every year for a period of three to seven years.

risk arbitrage: Investors who try to profit from simultaneously buying and short-selling stocks of companies in mergers or other stock-based transactions.

risk vs. reward: A basic concept in corporate finance. An investor will lend money in exchange for a return on that money in the future. That return must compensate the investor for the risks involved with the investment. Also referred to as the risk/reward trade-off.

S

Sarbanes-Oxley Act of 2002 (SOX): Created the Public Company Accounting Oversight Board (PCAOB). The Act also requires that any accounting firm that audits an SEC-registered company must be registered with the PCAOB. Other requirements of the Act include greater auditor independence, certifications from a company's CEO and CFO regarding financial reports, stricter regulations on equity analysts, and greater accountability for corporations in the event of corporate fraud and criminal action, among other things. A detailed summary of Sarbanes-Oxley can be found in most comprehensive GAAP accounting books.

schedule of assets and liabilities: Schedule used in an asset purchase transaction which identifies each asset to be sold and each liability to be assumed. As a simplifying alternative, rather than identifying each asset and liability, the assets being sold might be described as "all assets used primarily in the Business," where "Business" is a defined term within the purchase contract.

secondary market: The period of time after the initial security offering when securities are bought and sold. Also referred to as the **aftermarket**. See also **distribution**.

secondary offering: An offering of existing shares to the public by existing investors and/or executives, with the sale proceeds going to the selling shareholders and not the company. While the term "secondary" originated such that the distinction between whether it is a primary offering (new shares issued by the company) or secondary offering (shares issued before and resold by the holders) has to do with the identity of the seller and therefore who receives the proceeds, in more recent years the terminology has blurred somewhat and "secondary" is now sometimes used to describe any follow-on offering. In that same vein, more recently the term "add-on" or "add-on offering" has also been used to describe a follow-on offering. See also **follow-on offering, IPO, primary offering**.

secured lending: Holders of secured or asset-backed debt have claim to the underlying collateral (assets) in the event of default. Secured lending is a common cause of credit rating notching. See also **asset-based lending, credit rating, notching**.

Securities and Exchange Commission (SEC): U.S. federal agency that regulates securities registered in the U.S. with the intent of protecting investors in public securities.

SEC Rule 13D: A Securities and Exchange Commission rule requiring that an investor beneficially owning more than five percent of a publicly traded company must disclose, on a periodic basis in a public filing, the number of shares it owns and its intentions.

security: A paper investment sold directly to an investor, which represents an interest in or claim to something. Stocks and bonds are types of securities.

sell-side process: The process undertaken by Seller when selling an asset, business or company.

senior long-term debt: Debt generally used to fund capital expenditures or other long-term needs. Senior long-term debt is higher in liquidation preference than subordinated debt and is generally payable in more than one year. See also **liquidation preference**.

senior secured loan: A bank loan that is secured by assets of the company or other collateral. See also **asset-based lending, collateral, secured lending**.

senior unsecured loan: A bank loan that is not secured by assets of the company or other collateral.

Series 7: An NYSE-developed and NASD-administered test required in order to sell securities to the public.

shareholder-level tax: Tax liability owed by a shareholder of a corporation. Double taxation is the term that describes transactions that incur both corporate-level and shareholder-level tax. See also **corporate-level tax, double taxation**.

shareholder rights plan: A corporate defense mechanism which provides existing, non-Raider shareholders with conversion rights for additional shares upon the occurrence of a triggering event, usually the purchase of a threshold ownership level by a Raider. Also referred to as a poison pill. See also **poison pill**.

shareholders' equity: See **equity**.

shares traded analysis: A technical analysis that combines the share price at which an investor purchased his shares with the volume of shares traded at each price point. Often used to help determine the offer price in an acquisition.

shelf registration: Type of SEC registration arranged in advance of actually selling the securities to investors. A shelf registration allows a company to access the public market for the sale of securities based on market demand by pre-arranging its SEC documentation. Called a shelf registration since the documentation sits "on the shelf" until the company is ready to issue the securities, at which point the registration is quickly updated and the securities are sold.

short-form merger: Used after a tender offer or exchange offer to purchase any additional shares that were not tendered, assuming a threshold number of shares were tendered (often 90 percent). A short-form merger does not require shareholder approval but must comply with the law of the state in which Target is incorporated. See also **long-form merger**.

short-term debt (STD): Debt used to fund working capital or seasonal financing, and which is generally due within one year. See also **long-term debt**.

short-term liabilities: See **current liabilities**.

short-term loan: Similar to a revolving line of credit except that instead of having an open line that can be drawn, repaid, and redrawn, the entire loan amount is provided to the borrower at the beginning of the term and is due within a specified period, often one year. See also **revolving line of credit**.

simple interest: Process of earning interest each period only on the principal. See also **compound interest**.

sinking fund: Fund managed by a trustee whereby the issuer of bonds makes periodic payments to the fund which represents the repayment of some of the outstanding debt. Allows for debt with a bullet payment effectively to have amortization features. See also **amortizing debt**.

source document: Any document used to determine assumptions when performing financial analysis. Examples include financial statements, loan agreements, company bylaws and articles of incorporation.

special dividend: Dividend paid to shareholders which is not part of a company's ongoing dividend program. See also **recapitalization**.

special meeting: A shareholders' meeting called outside of the regularly scheduled annual meeting.

special meeting provision: A corporate defense mechanism which provides that only certain parties (often directors, chairman, and/or CEO) can call a special meeting of shareholders. If it exists, this provision is found in a company's bylaws or corporate charter. Companies choose whether or not to have a special meeting provision.

speculative grade liquidity ratings (SGLs): A ratings grid that is meant to rate a company's liquidity only. See also **liquidity**.

spin-off: A public market separation technique in which shares of a subsidiary corporation are distributed to shareholders of parent corporation on a pro rata basis. In a spin-off, the parent corporation distributes control of the subsidiary to existing parent shareholders. After the spin-off, subsidiary is a publicly traded company that is no longer affiliated with parent, although it is still owned by the same shareholders as parent. See also **split-off**.

split-off: Similar to a spin-off, however, subsidiary stock is exchanged for parent stock based on a specified exchange ratio. Therefore, in a split-off, parent shareholders choose between owning parent stock or subsidiary stock, whereas in a spin-off, all parent shareholders receive subsidiary stock on a pro rata basis and maintain their parent stock. See also **spin-off**.

staggered board: See **classified board**.

stalking horse: In an M&A transaction, the term used to refer to the bidder with the highest price. A stalking horse's bid is often used to try to encourage higher prices among other bidders in the process. See also **no shop / no talk restrictions**.

statutory merger: Mergers are effected by operation of statute or state law, therefore mergers are sometimes referred to as statutory mergers. See also **corporate merger, merger**.

stock purchase agreement: Legal agreement used for the purchase of the stock of a company. A purchase and sale agreement is used for the sale of an asset or division of a company. See also **purchase and sale agreement**.

stock split: Occurs when a company decides to exchange two (2-for-1), three (3-for-1), four (4-for-1) or more new shares (or whatever ratio it determines) for one old share such that the owner of one old share becomes the owner of two, three, four, or more new shares, respectively. This usually occurs when the stock price has risen sharply and the company wishes to decrease the price per share by simply increasing the number of shares outstanding by exchanging new, lower-valued shares in place of old shares at some pre-determined ratio. Stock splits do not affect the overall market value of equity but reduce share price, earnings per share, dividends per share, and all other per share metrics by the exchange ratio chosen (e.g., divide all metrics by two for a 2-for-1 split, by three for a 3-for-1 split, etc.). See also **reverse split**.

stockholder lockup: If Target has a major stockholder, it is common for Acquiror to ask him or her (or a small group of major stockholders) to agree to certain things and for the agreement(s) to be in writing. Stockholder agreements are usually signed at the time the transaction agreement is signed. Agreements with major stockholders generally require that the stockholder: (a) not sell his or her stock before the transaction closes; and (b) act in support of the transaction, including voting in favor of the transaction, tendering shares (if a tender offer), and not voting in favor of a competing transaction. See also **irrevocable proxy**.

straight-line: Form of depreciation or amortization in which the acquisition cost of an asset is allocated as an expense uniformly over the useful life of the asset. Thus under the straight-line method, an asset with a 10-year useful life and an acquisition cost of $10,000 would have an annual expense of $1,000 ($10,000 / 10 years). Other forms of depreciation in addition to straight-line include sum-of-the-years'-digits, double-declining balance, and MACRS (modified accelerated cost recovery system). See also **amortization, depletion, depreciation.**

strategic buyers: Companies which buy other companies primarily for strategic reasons, as opposed to financial buyers, which buy other companies primarily for prospective financial gain.

strategic planning group: Group within a company which handles strategic and/or financial planning, including preparing forward-looking financial statements and projections, and analyzing potential strategic (i.e., non-financing) transactions. Also referred to as the corporate development group. A Director of Strategic Planning usually heads the strategic planning group and reports directly to the CFO.

strategic transaction: Any action that helps implement a company's strategic plan.

strike price: The price at which an option can be exercised. This is also referred to as the exercise price. See also **exercise price, in the money, out of the money**.

structural subordination: Results when the legal structure of an issuer of debt protects certain debt holders. The most common example is debt issued at a holding company level, which is usually subordinate to debt issued at the operating level. Structural subordination is a common cause of credit rating notching. See also **contractual subordination, notching**.

subordinated debt: Debt that is subordinated to senior debt in terms of liquidation preference. Due to this greater risk, holders of subordinated debt require a higher rate of return than holders of senior debt. See also **liquidation preference, senior debt**.

subsequent offer period: In an exchange offer or tender offer, the time period following the expiration of the initial offer period. During the subsequent offer period, an Acquiror is allowed to purchase the shares tendered up to that time, and also to extend the offering period for an additional period from three to twenty days.

subsidiary: A corporation that is wholly owned or majority-owned by a parent corporation. See also **division**.

sum of the parts analysis: A valuation methodology which considers the value of the component pieces of a company, not the whole. This analysis is used to value conglomerates or diversified companies. Also referred to as breakup analysis.

supermajority provision: A corporate defense mechanism which requires that a supermajority of outstanding shares must approve certain types of transactions, including change-of-control transactions. If it exists, this provision is found in a company's bylaws or corporate charter. Companies choose whether or not to have a supermajority provision.

swap: An option in which one counter-party assumes exposure to some event (such as exposure to interest rates or foreign exchange rates) in exchange for a fee. Interest rate swaps are among the most common type of swap.

syndicate group: A group of banks or lenders who together provide a loan or line of credit to a borrower. In addition to banks, other participants in syndicate groups include prime funds, insurance companies and, more recently, hedge funds. In the context of an offering of securities (debt or equity), a syndicate group is the group of banks other than the bookrunner (or joint bookrunners if there is more than one) added to the selling team in exchange for a share of the fees. Each of the banks involved is allotted a certain number of securities for sale, and each is then responsible for selling those securities to investors. The number of shares allotted to each bank is largest for the lead underwriters with smaller quantities given to the non-lead (or syndicate) banks.

synergies: A catch-all term to describe any manner of increasing earnings and/or cash flow associated with a merger or acquisition, either through increased revenues (revenue synergies) or decreased costs (cost synergies). See also **cost synergies, revenue synergies**.

synergies analysis: An analysis to assess the revenue and cost structure of Target to estimate potential synergies. Can also refer to analysis to determine what level of synergies is required for a transaction to be breakeven to EPS.

T

tax basis: The carrying value of an asset, liability or equity on the tax return work papers. The carrying value of an item on the GAAP accounting books is called the book value. Tax basis and book value refer to the same concept -- the carrying value of an item on the company's balance sheet, but tax basis is a tax accounting term and book value is a GAAP accounting term. See also **book value.**

tax books: Tax accounting records prepared according to the rules and regulations of the IRS and other taxing authorities and used to prepare the corporate tax returns. Properly referred to as tax return work papers. Due to differences in rules and regulations between GAAP and tax accounting, a company's tax liability as calculated on the tax return work papers (cash taxes) is often different from a company's tax liability as calculated on the GAAP books. See also **cash taxes, GAAP books**.

tax credits: Credits provided by a taxing authority that serve as an offset to the actual tax owed. Tax credits are similar to net operating losses in that they serve to reduce taxes, but tax credits reduce the actual tax liability while net operating losses only reduce taxable income (upon which the tax liability is calculated) by the amount of the net operating losses. For example, in a 40 percent tax bracket, $1 in NOLs would reduce tax payable by $0.40 while $1 in tax credits would reduce tax payable by $1. Thus tax credits are comparatively more valuable than net operating losses.

tax-deductible expense: Expense that a company can subtract from its revenues prior to calculating its taxable income. Tax-deductible expenses provide a tax shield. See also **tax shield**.

tax-free reorganizations: Transactions that qualify as tax-free events under the reorganization provisions of the Internal Revenue Code (IRC). See also **business purpose doctrine, continuity of business enterprise doctrine, continuity of shareholder interest doctrine**.

tax leakage: In a transaction, the value lost to taxes.

tax loss carryback: A tax accounting concept. The application of NOLs created in the 1998 tax year or later to offset operating income or capital gain up to two years prior to the loss-making year. See also **capital loss carryback, net operating losses (NOLs)**.

tax loss carryforward: A tax accounting concept. The application of NOLs created in the 1998 tax year or later to offset operating income or capital gain up to twenty years forward after the loss-making year. See also **net operating losses (NOLs)**.

tax return work papers: See **tax books.**

tax shield: The reduction in income taxes provided by virtue of an expense being tax-deductible. The value of the tax shield is calculated as (tax-deductible expense × tax rate).

taxable event: Any action that triggers a potential tax liability.

taxable gain/(loss): A tax accounting concept. The difference between the selling price of an asset and the asset's tax basis. See also **capital gain/(loss), gain/(loss) on sale**.

taxable income: Term for the amount on which corporate income tax is levied for purposes of calculating tax liability. Several terms are used for the equivalent concept, including pretax income, financial pretax earnings, and earnings before taxes. See also **earnings before taxes**.

tender offer: An offer by Acquiror to purchase shares directly from the shareholders of Target for cash. An exchange offer is an offer by Acquiror to purchase shares directly from the shareholders of Target in exchange for Acquiror stock or a combination of Acquiror stock and cash. The difference between a tender offer (payment in cash) and an exchange offer (payment in stock only or stock and cash) is the consideration offered by Acquiror to Target shareholders. See also **exchange offer**.

term sheet: Generic term for any offer to purchase or invest. In general, a term sheet will contain the salient details for the proposed transaction, whether it is an acquisition of a company, an investment in a company, or a financing. For example, a loan term sheet is a list of the most important information related to the loan, including the name of the borrower, the size of the issue, important financial and credit statistics of the issuer, the interest rate of the debt, and important features related to the debt such as the term, whether it is fixed or floating, and the major covenants that will be required of the borrower. Unlike contracts, term sheets are non-binding.

terminal multiple method: This method uses a comparable company or comparable transaction method of analysis to estimate the terminal value in a DCF analysis. A valuation multiple is applied to the company's financial data, such as an enterprise value to EBITDA multiple, in the last year of the projection period. This yields a value as of Year *n*, which value is then discounted back to the present at the company's weighted average cost of capital. The type of terminal multiple used depends on whether the analysis assumes that ownership of the company is maintained after the projection period (comparable company) or sold after the projection period (comparable transaction). See also **discounted cash flow analysis, perpetuity growth method, terminal value**.

terminal value: In a discounted cash flow analysis, terminal value represents the estimated value of the business for the period from the end of the projection period into perpetuity. There are two generally accepted methods for projecting the terminal value. The first is called the terminal multiple method (also called the exit multiple method) and the second is called the perpetuity growth rate method. The present value of the terminal value is added to the present value of the unlevered free cash flows to determine the present value of the firm. See also **discounted cash flow analysis, perpetuity growth method, terminal multiple method**.

termination provisions: In a legal contract, rights of each party to cancel the agreement based on certain prescribed events or circumstances. Also referred to as "outs."

time value of money: A basic corporate finance concept. The value of $1 today is worth more than the value of $1 tomorrow because that $1 today can be invested to yield more than $1 tomorrow.

total debt: Represents the aggregate amount of debt that a company has outstanding at any given point in time. See also **debt, enterprise value, net debt**.

total return: The combination of stock price appreciation and dividends returned to a shareholder. In percentage terms, total return can also refer to the combination of the EPS growth rate plus the dividend yield. See also **dividend yield**.

total return accretion/dilution analysis: An analysis used to measure the effect of a transaction on Acquiror's (or Target's) total return profile.

tracking stock: A separate class of stock designed to "track" the financial and operating results of a subsidiary corporation or division within a larger company. With tracking stock, the parent corporation continues to retain governance, control, and consolidation accounting. Tracking stock is also referred to as letter stock since the first tracking stocks were issued by General Motors and were named for the businesses they represented (e.g., "GM-H" for the Hughes subsidiary, "GM-E" for EDS, etc.).

trailing EPS: Earnings per share for the last twelve months. See also **forward EPS**.

tranches: Sub-groups of debt.

treasury group: A group within a corporation that handles functions related to financial and cash management. See also **liability management**.

treasury shares: Shares that have been repurchased by a company in the open market. They are considered issued but not outstanding and therefore are not eligible to vote or to receive dividends.

treasury stock method: Method used to calculate diluted shares outstanding for options and dilutive securities. Assumes that in-the-money options are exercised and that the company uses the proceeds from the sale of that stock (or security) to repurchase shares in the open market, thereby offsetting the dilutive effect of the exercise of the options or, in the case of convertible bonds, the dilutive effect of the conversion of the securities. See also **convertible securities, if-converted method, options**.

trust preferred equity: A form of capital that is lower in liquidation preference than subordinated debt, but higher than common equity. Holders receive a dividend, which is usually cumulative, based on a predetermined rate of return. This dividend is often tax-deductible, as if it were an interest payment on debt. See also **debt, equity**.

U

underwrite: See **underwritten deals.**

underwritten deals: Traditionally, a bank fully underwrote a security offering for a company, which meant that the investment bank purchased all of the issuer's securities and then re-sold those securities to investors. The bank put its own capital at risk and also assumed the execution risk, which is the risk that the deal would not be completed (and the bank would be left holding a significant percentage of the securities which it was unable to re-sell on the expected terms). An underwritten deal is also called a committed deal. Today, banks sell deals both on an underwritten basis, on a best efforts basis, and in club deals. See also **best efforts deals, syndicate group**.

unlevered free cash flow: The operating cash flow generated by all assets (both tangible and intangible) used by the company in the provision of goods or services, minus capital expenditures, and unlevered or free from financing considerations including interest expense and dividends. These are the cash flows which are discounted for purposes of calculating enterprise value in a discounted cash flow analysis. See also **discounted cash flow analysis**.

unrealized gain/(loss): If the fair market value of an investment is greater (less) than the historical cost, and the investor still holds the investment (i.e., has not sold the investment), the investor has an unrealized gain (loss) related to the investment. Sale of the investment would result in a realized gain (loss).

unwinding: Exiting from a contract, such as a joint venture (JV).

V

value creation analysis: An analysis used to estimate the increase or decrease in the expected valuation of the merged entity relative to Acquiror's valuation on a stand-alone basis.

venture capital firms: Private funds that invest in new businesses and new technologies, many of which are not yet cash flow positive. These firms tend to invest much earlier in a company's life cycle than private equity firms, which tend to invest in companies already generating cash flow. See also **private equity firm**.

W

warrants: Options to purchase equity that are issued with debt securities to increase the marketability of the debt securities by providing an element of equity participation. Also known as a sweetener or an equity kicker.

weighted average cost of capital (WACC): The discount rate used in a discounted cash flow analysis. WACC represents the return required by a company's debt and equity investors, weighted to reflect the proportion of the total capital contributed by each. See also **discounted cash flow analysis**.

weighted average shares outstanding: Shares outstanding calculation used for purposes of calculating earnings per share (EPS). Weighted average shares outstanding for the period accounts for any shares that were issued or repurchased during the period.

white knight: In the face of a hostile situation, a friendly partner who negotiates a deal with Target's management on mutually agreeable terms, thereby helping Target avoid a hostile takeover.

working capital: Current assets less current liabilities. The calculation of working capital usually excludes cash and short-term debt since they are considered financing-related items.

Y

yield: For a bond, yield represents the rate of return based on the bond's interest rate (coupon) and the price at which the investor bought the bond. Mathematically, yield is the discount rate or rate of return required by the debt investor.

yield curve: Graph depicting the rate of return for bonds of varying maturities. Although a yield curve can be drawn for any issuer, it generally refers to the yield curve for U.S. Treasury bonds.

yield to call: The return on a bond based on the earliest call date. Calls are options that allow the company to repurchase the debt at an earlier date than the maturity date, usually at a premium. See also **call option**.

yield to maturity (YTM): The rate of return an investor earns on a bond based on the remaining life of the bond.

Z

zero coupon bonds: Bonds which do not pay a coupon during the life of the bond. Instead, zero coupon bonds (also referred to as zeroes) are issued at a deep discount and the investor's return is embedded within the deeply discounted price.

Suggested Reading and Other Resources

Bibliography and Suggested Reading

Anders, George. *Merchants of Debt: KKR and the Mortgaging of American Business.* New York: Beard Books, 2002.

Argenti, Paul A., ed. *The Portable MBA Desk Reference: An Essential Business Companion.* New York: John Wiley and Sons, 1994.

Bandler, James. *How to Use Financial Statements: A Guide to Understanding the Numbers.* New York: McGraw-Hill, 1994.

Benninga, Simon Z. *Financial Modeling.* Cambridge, MA: MIT Press, 1997.

Benninga, Simon Z., and Oded H. Sarig. *Corporate Finance: A Valuation Approach.* New York: McGraw-Hill, 1997.

Brealey, Richard A., and Stewart C. Myers. *Principles of Corporate Finance.* 5th ed. New York: McGraw-Hill, 1996.

Carey, Omer L., and Musa M. H. Essayyad. *The Esssentials of Financial Management.* Piscataway, NJ: Research and Education Association, 1990.

Comiskey, Eugene E., and Charles W. Mulford. *Guide to Financial Reporting and Analysis.* New York: John Wiley and Sons, 2000.

Crerend, William J. *Fundamentals of Hedge Fund Investing: A Professional Investor's Guide.* New York: McGraw-Hill, 1998.

Damodaran, Aswath. *Investment Valuation: Tools and Techniques for Determining the Value of Any Asset.* 2nd ed. New York: John Wiley and Sons, 2002.

Downes, John, and Jordan Elliot Goodman. *Dictionary of Finance and Investment Terms.* 4th ed. Hauppauge, NY: Barron's, 1995.

Elton, Edwin J., and Martin J. Gruber. *Modern Portfolio Theory and Investment Analysis.* 5th ed. New York: John Wiley and Sons, 1995.

Epstein, Barry J., Ralph Nach, Ervin L. Black, and Patrick R. Delaney. *Wiley GAAP 2005: Interpretation and Application of Generally Accepted Accounting Principles.* Hoboken, NJ: John Wiley and Sons, 2004.

Fabozzi, Frank, and Franco Modigliani. *Capital Markets: Institutions and Instruments.* 2nd ed. Upper Saddle River, NJ: Prentice Hall, 1996.

Fridson, Martin. *Financial Statement Analysis: A Practitioner's Guide.* 3rd ed. New York: John Wiley and Sons, 2002.

Ginsburg, Martin D., and Jack S. Levin. *Mergers, Acquisitions, and Buyouts: A Transactional Analysis of the Governing Tax, Legal, and Accounting Considerations.* 3 vols. New York: Aspen Law and Business, 1997.

Henderson, Schuyler K., and John A. M. Price. *Currency and Interest Rate Swaps.* London: Butterworths, 1984.

Horngren, Charles T., Gary L. Sundem, and John A. Elliott. *Introduction to Financial Accounting.* 6th ed. Saddle River, NJ: Prentice Hall, 1996.

Hull, John C. *Options, Futures, and Other Derivatives.* 3rd ed. Upper Saddle River, NJ: Prentice Hall, 1997.

Ji, Lin and Fiona Wang. *Leveraged Buyouts: Inception, Evolution, and Future Trends.* Perspectives, Vol. 3, No. 6. Rockville, MD: Overseas Young Chinese Forum, 2002.

Koller, Tim, Marc Goedhart and David Wessels. *Valuation: Measuring and Managing the Value of Companies.* 4th ed. New York: John Wiley and Sons, 2005.

Lander, Guy P. *What is Sarbanes-Oxley?* New York: McGraw-Hill, 2004.

Morris, James E. *Accounting for M&A, Equity, and Credit Analysts.* New York: McGraw-Hill, 2004.

Reed, Stanley Foster, and Alexandra Reed Lajoux. *The Art of M&A: A Merger Acquisition Buyout Guide.* 3rd ed. New York: McGraw-Hill, 1999.

Rickertsen, Rick, and Robert E. Gunther. *Buyout: The Insider's Guide to Buying Your Own Company.* New York: Amacom, 2001.

Slifer, Stephen D., and W. Stansbury Carnes. *By the Numbers: A Survival Guide to Economic Indicators.* Cincinnati: International Financial Press, 1995.

Stickney, Clyde P., Roman L. Weil, and Sidney Davidson. *Financial Accounting: An Introduction to Concepts, Methods, and Uses.* 6th ed. San Diego, CA: Harcourt Trade Publishers, 1991.

Tjia, John S. *Building Financial Models: A Guide to Creating and Interpreting Financial Statements.* New York: McGraw-Hill, 2004.

Tracy, John A. *How to Read a Financial Report: Wringing Vital Signs Out of the Numbers.* 6th ed. New York: John Wiley and Sons, 2004.

Wasserstein, Bruce. *Big Deal: 2000 and Beyond.* New York: Warner Books, 2000.

Weaver, Samuel C., and J. Fred Weston. *Finance and Accounting for Nonfinancial Managers.* New York: McGraw-Hill, 2001.

Wert, James E., and Glenn V. Henderson, Jr. *Financing Business Firms.* 6th ed. Homewood, IL: Richard D. Irwin, 1979.

White, Gerald I., Ashwinpaul C. Sondhi, and Dov Fried. *The Analysis and Use of Financial Statements.* 2nd ed. New York: John Wiley and Sons, 1998.

Williams, Jan R., and Joseph V. Carcello. *2005 Miller GAAP Guide Level A: Restatement and Analysis of Current FASB Standards.* New York: Aspen Law and Business, 2004.

Other Resources

Securities and Exchange Commission
Search for SEC filings of public companies and review U.S. securities laws
www.sec.gov

Financial Accounting Standards Board
Review GAAP standards – current and proposed
www.fasb.org

American Institute of Certified Public Accountants
Learn about the AICPA and its role in the U.S. securities industry
www.aicpa.org

The Robert Toigo Foundation
Sponsor of diversity programs, internships, and scholarships in the financial services industry
www.toigofoundation.org

Sponsors for Educational Opportunity
Sponsor of diversity programs, internships, and scholarships in the financial services industry
www.seo-ny.org

TMG & Associates
Training seminars in financial modeling
www.tmga.com

Deal Maven
Online training in financial modeling
www.dealmaven.com

Index

A page number with an *f* or *t* indicates a figure or table on that page; a page number with an *n* indicates a footnote.

A page number with an *f* or *t* indicates a figure or table on that page; a page number with an *n* indicates a footnote.

A page number with an *f* or *t* indicates a figure or table on that page; a page number with an *n* indicates a footnote.

B

A page number with an *f* or *t* indicates a figure or table on that page; a page number with an *n* indicates a footnote.

A page number with an *f* or *t* indicates a figure or table on that page; a page number with an *n* indicates a footnote.

A page number with an *f* or *t* indicates a figure or table on that page; a page number with an *n* indicates a footnote.

A page number with an *f* or *t* indicates a figure or table on that page; a page number with an *n* indicates a footnote.

A page number with an *f* or *t* indicates a figure or table on that page; a page number with an *n* indicates a footnote.

A page number with an *f* or *t* indicates a figure or table on that page; a page number with an *n* indicates a footnote.

A page number with an *f* or *t* indicates a figure or table on that page; a page number with an *n* indicates a footnote.

A page number with an *f* or *t* indicates a figure or table on that page; a page number with an *n* indicates a footnote.

F

A page number with an *f* or *t* indicates a figure or table on that page; a page number with an *n* indicates a footnote.

A page number with an *f* or *t* indicates a figure or table on that page; a page number with an *n* indicates a footnote.

G

A page number with an *f* or *t* indicates a figure or table on that page; a page number with an *n* indicates a footnote.

H

I

A page number with an *f* or *t* indicates a figure or table on that page; a page number with an *n* indicates a footnote.

A page number with an *f* or *t* indicates a figure or table on that page; a page number with an *n* indicates a footnote.

J

L

A page number with an *f* or *t* indicates a figure or table on that page; a page number with an *n* indicates a footnote.

A page number with an *f* or *t* indicates a figure or table on that page; a page number with an *n* indicates a footnote.

N

A page number with an *f* or *t* indicates a figure or table on that page; a page number with an *n* indicates a footnote.

A page number with an *f* or *t* indicates a figure or table on that page; a page number with an *n* indicates a footnote.

A page number with an *f* or *t* indicates a figure or table on that page; a page number with an *n* indicates a footnote.

Q

R

A page number with an *f* or *t* indicates a figure or table on that page; a page number with an *n* indicates a footnote.

S

A page number with an *f* or *t* indicates a figure or table on that page; a page number with an *n* indicates a footnote.

A page number with an *f* or *t* indicates a figure or table on that page; a page number with an *n* indicates a footnote.

A page number with an *f* or *t* indicates a figure or table on that page; a page number with an *n* indicates a footnote.

A page number with an *f* or *t* indicates a figure or table on that page; a page number with an *n* indicates a footnote.

A page number with an *f* or *t* indicates a figure or table on that page; a page number with an *n* indicates a footnote.

A page number with an *f* or *t* indicates a figure or table on that page; a page number with an *n* indicates a footnote.

A page number with an *f* or *t* indicates a figure or table on that page; a page number with an *n* indicates a footnote.

A page number with an *f* or *t* indicates a figure or table on that page; a page number with an *n* indicates a footnote.

Notes

NOTES

NOTES

Notes